THE ROUTLEDGE COMPANION TO INCLUSIVE LEADERSHIP

An important reference work on a practice that is needed more than ever in a VUCA world, this book helps readers understand the importance of responsible and constructive practices and behavior in leadership.

The broad approach to inclusive leadership presented in this volume highlights correlations between inclusive leadership and myriad issues, qualities, and circumstances that serve as foundations or impact factors on it. Some contributors review contemporary concepts and challenges such as change, innovation, the bottom line, sustainability, and performance excellence against inclusive leadership. Other contributors reflect on critical practices and qualities, such as trust, passion, ethics, spirituality, and empathy, and their relationships with inclusive leadership. A range of religious and spiritual influences are also evaluated in the context of inclusive leadership, such as (but not limited to) Buddhism, Taoism, Hinduism, Jainism, and Christianity.

Postgraduate students, instructors, and coaches will appreciate this comprehensive look at inclusive leadership, which has become an urgent concept to be internalized and practiced by all, regardless of positions, possessions, locations, or generations.

Joan Marques is Professor of Management and Dean of the School of Business, Woodbury University, USA. Her research focuses on workplace spirituality, ethics, and leadership. She has published extensively, including the books *Business and Buddhism*, *Leadership*, and *Ethical Leadership*, all published by Routledge.

ROUTLEDGE COMPANIONS IN BUSINESS, MANAGEMENT AND ACCOUNTING

Routledge Companions in Business, Management and Accounting are prestige reference works providing an overview of a whole subject area or sub-discipline. These books survey the state of the discipline including emerging and cutting-edge areas. Providing a comprehensive, up to date, definitive work of reference, Routledge Companions can be cited as an authoritative source on the subject.

A key aspect of these Routledge Companions is their international scope and relevance. Edited by an array of highly regarded scholars, these volumes also benefit from teams of contributors which reflect an international range of perspectives.

Individually, Routledge Companions in Business, Management and Accounting provide an impactful one-stop-shop resource for each theme covered. Collectively, they represent a comprehensive learning and research resource for researchers, postgraduate students and practitioners.

Published titles in this series include:

THE ROUTLEDGE COMPANION TO INNOVATION MANAGEMENT
Edited by Jin Chen, Alexander Brem, Eric Viardot and Poh Kam Wong

THE ROUTLEDGE COMPANION TO THE MAKERS OF GLOBAL BUSINESS
Edited by Teresa da Silva Lopes, Christina Lubinski and Heidi J.S. Tworek

THE ROUTLEDGE COMPANION TO ACCOUNTING IN EMERGING ECONOMIES
Edited by Pauline Weetman and Ioannis Tsalavoutas

THE ROUTLEDGE COMPANION TO CAREER STUDIES
Edited by Hugh Gunz, Mila Lazarova and Wolfgang Mayrhofer

THE ROUTLEDGE COMPANION TO NONPROFIT MANAGEMENT
Edited by Stefan Toepler and Helmut Anheier

THE ROUTLEDGE COMPANION TO INCLUSIVE LEADERSHIP
Edited by Joan Marques

For more information about this series, please visit: www.routledge.com/Routledge-Companions-in-Business-Management-and-Accounting/book-series/RCBMA

THE ROUTLEDGE COMPANION TO INCLUSIVE LEADERSHIP

Edited by Joan Marques

LONDON AND NEW YORK

First published 2020 by Routledge

2 Park Square, Milton Park, Abingdon, Oxon OX14 4RN
605 Third Avenue, New York, NY 10017

Routledge is an imprint of the Taylor & Francis Group, an informa business

First issued in paperback 2021

Copyright © 2020 Taylor & Francis

The right of Joan Marques to be identified as the author of the editorial material, and of the authors for their individual chapters, has been asserted in accordance with sections 77 and 78 of the Copyright, Designs and Patents Act 1988.

All rights reserved. No part of this book may be reprinted or reproduced or utilised in any form or by any electronic, mechanical, or other means, now known or hereafter invented, including photocopying and recording, or in any information storage or retrieval system, without permission in writing from the publishers.

Notice:
Product or corporate names may be trademarks or registered trademarks, and are used only for identification and explanation without intent to infringe.

Publisher's Note
The publisher has gone to great lengths to ensure the quality of this reprint but points out that some imperfections in the original copies may be apparent.

Library of Congress Cataloging-in-Publication Data
A catalog record for this book has been requested

ISBN: 978-0-367-26567-0 (hbk)
ISBN: 978-1-03-217280-4 (pbk)
DOI: 10.4324/9780429294396

Typeset in Bembo
by Apex CoVantage, LLC

Printed in the United Kingdom
by Henry Ling Limited

*This Companion Is Dedicated to
Leaders From All Walks of Life
All Those Who Continue to Strive
Toward Doing Right, With the Infusion
of Understanding, Compassion, and Inclusion
Knowing That Leading Is a Transforming Art
Requiring Insight From Both Mind and Heart*

CONTENTS

About the Editor   *xi*
Notes on Contributors   *xiii*

PART I
Stakeholder Considerations   1

1. Inclusive Leadership, Diversity, and Wakefulness   3
   Joan Marques

2. What Pepper Can't Do (And Why We Should Care)   13
   Ginger Grant and Cheryl De Ciantis

3. Leading as One: Inclusive Leadership Through Unity Consciousness and the Act of Oneness   26
   Duysal Aşkun

4. Inclusive Leadership: People, Engagement, and Performance   42
   William A. Guillory

5. Stakeholder Engagement as an Inclusive Practice   53
   Robert S. Fleming

6. Being Mindful of Change   63
   Kennedy Muema Musyoka, Susan K. Lewa, Catherine W. Maingi, and Sarah M. Mutuku

7. Fostering Inclusive Organizations Through Virtuous Leadership   78
   Aikaterini Grimani and George Gotsis

8 Inclusive Leadership and Emotional Intelligence 99
   Juanita Coleman-Merritt

9 Inclusive Leadership and Responsible Innovation: Toward a
   Contingency Perspective of Leader-Follower Dynamics in Work
   Integration Social Enterprises 109
   Susanna L. M. Chui

PART II
Inclusive Intersections 119

10 Including Everyone With Respectful Pluralism 121
   Debra J. Dean

11 Everyday Leadership: How Can Anyone Be a Leader Every Day?
   Examples of Amish Leadership and Japanese Corporation
   Leadership Training 131
   Sunny Jeong

12 Inclusive Leadership and Religion 143
   *Sarah M. Mutuku, Faith Mutuku Muna, Rachel Mwende M. Murigi,
   and Miriam M. Mutuku-Kioko*

13 Vedantic Leadership 154
   Glen Callahan and Subhasis Chakrabarti

14 Inclusive Leadership and Work-Life Balance 168
   Wanda Krause

15 An American Kaleidoscope: Rethinking Diversity and Inclusion
   Leadership Through the Prism of Gender and Race 177
   Seth N. Asumah and Mechthild Nagel

16 Diversity and Well-being: An Interactive Qualitative Perspective
   From India 190
   Akanksha Jaiswal and Lata Dyaram

17 Transition from Diversity to Inclusion: Auditing the Pulse From an Indian
   Perspective 203
   Aneesya Panicker and Rakesh Kumar Agrawal

18	Cross-Cultural Differences in Inclusive Leadership Perception and Application *Mike Szymanski, Komal Kalra, Evodio Kaltenecker, and Anna Olszewska*	215

PART III
Inclusive Leadership Practices — 223

19	Awakened Leadership: A Roadmap to Inclusion and Morality *Joan Marques*	225
20	Spiritual Leadership: Leading While Spiritual *Sylvia W. Burgess and Karen Martin-Jones*	238
21	Inclusive Servant Leadership in the Context of the Christian Religion *Peter Mutuku Lewa, Susan K. Lewa, and Paul S. Kioko*	250
22	Inclusive Leadership and Soft Skills *Birute Regine*	264
23	Creating Space for Transformation: Cultivating Containers for Inclusive Leadership Development *Trevor Cox*	273
24	From "I" to "We" Through "Female" Leadership: Bringing Inclusion and Inclusiveness to the Next Level *Eleftheria Egel*	288
25	Mahatma Gandhi's Legacy of Values-Based Inclusive Leadership: Lessons to Transcend Religion, Caste, Gender, and Class in Today's Workplace *R. Ray Gehani and Anil K. Maheshwari*	299
26	Are You Joking? Humor and Inclusive Leadership *Laura E. Mercer Traavik*	313
27	Humility, Compassion, and Inclusive Leadership *Elliott Tyler Kruse*	323
28	Am I included? Lessons from Leadership Research in Africa and the African Diaspora *Thomas Anyanje Senaji, Nicole S. Knight, Lemayon L. Melyoki, Bella L. Galperin, Terri R. Lituchy, and Betty Jane Punnett*	333

29 Pathways to Inclusive Leadership and Flourishing Organizations: Creating
    Shared Ventures That Nurture Individual and Team Excellence   346
    Satinder Dhiman

30 Inclusive Leadership Development Through Participatory Inquiry:
    Cultivating Cultural Humility   356
    Ester R. Shapiro and Tariana V. Little

Index   *372*

ABOUT THE EDITOR

Joan Marques has reinvented herself from a successful media and social entrepreneur in Suriname, South America, to an innovative "edupreneur" (educational entrepreneur) in California, USA. Her entrepreneurial career spans over four decades and includes the creation and successful management of companies in public relations and advertising, import and export, real estate, and media productions and a nonprofit focused on women's advancement. In the US, she was the cofounder of the Business Renaissance Institute and the Academy of Spirituality and Professional Excellence (ASPEX).

Based on her impressive career and ongoing influence, Joan was awarded the highest state decoration of her home country, Suriname: Commander (Commandeur) in the Honorary Order of the Yellow Star, in 2015. That same year, she was also awarded the Dr. Nelle Becker-Slaton Pathfinder Award from the Association of Pan-African Doctoral Scholars in Los Angeles, for her exemplary and groundbreaking professional performance. In 2016, she won the Woodbury Faculty Scholarly-Creative Award as well as the Woodbury Faculty Ambassador Award, both awarded by Woodbury University's Faculty Association.

Joan earned a PhD in social sciences (focus: Buddhist psychology in management) from Tilburg University's Oldendorff Graduate School and an EdD in organizational leadership (focus: Workplace Spirituality) from Pepperdine University's Graduate School of Education and Psychology. She also holds an MBA from Woodbury University and a BSc in business economics from MOC, Suriname. Additionally, she has completed post-doctoral work at Tulane University's Freeman School of Business.

Joan is a frequent speaker and presenter at academic and professional venues. In 2016, she gave a TEDx talk at College of the Canyons in California, titled "An Ancient Path Towards a Better Future," in which she analyzed the Noble Eightfold Path, one of the foundational Buddhist practices, within the realm of contemporary business performance. She also presented at the Kravis Leadership Institute at Claremont McKenna College, as a female leader during the annual Women and Leadership Alliance (WLA) conference, resulting in the collective work, "Women's Leadership Journeys: Stories, Research and Novel Perspectives" (Routledge, 2019) in which she contributed the chapter, "Courage: Mapping the Leadership Journey." She annually conducts presentations at the Academy of Management and at business venues in Los Angeles, as well as for professional audiences in Miami and Suriname, South America.

Joan's research interests pertain to awakened leadership, Buddhist psychology in management, and workplace spirituality. Her works have been widely published and cited in both academic and popular venues. She has written more than 150 scholarly articles, which were published in prestigious scholarly journals such as *The Journal of Business Ethics, Business and Society, International Journal of Organizational Analysis, Leadership & Organization Development Journal, Journal of Communication Management, Journal of Management Development,* and *Human Resource Development Quarterly*. Joan has (co)authored and (co)edited more than 20 books, including "*Lead With Heart in Mind*" (Springer, 2019), "*The Routledge Companion to Management and Workplace Spirituality,*" "*Engaged Leadership: Transforming Through Future-Oriented Design*" (with Satinder Dhiman—Springer, 2018), "*Ethical Leadership, Progress With a Moral Compass*" (Routledge, 2017), "*Leadership, Finding Balance Between Acceptance and Ambition*" (Routledge, 2016), "*Leadership Today: Practices for Personal and Professional Performance*" (with Satinder Dhiman—Springer, 2016), "*Business and Buddhism*" (Routledge, 2015), and "*Leadership and Mindful Behavior: Action, Wakefulness, and Business*" (Palgrave MacMillan, 2014).

Joan currently serves as Dean at Woodbury University's School of Business, in Burbank, California, where she works on infusing and nurturing the concept of "Business with a Conscience" in internal and external stakeholders. She is also Full Professor of Management and teaches business courses related to leadership, ethics, creativity, social entrepreneurship, and organizational behavior in graduate and undergraduate programs.

Joan is a member of the executive committee of the Management, Spirituality, and Religion interest group of the Academy of Management, where she serves as the officer for membership and community building. As such, she conducted workshops on qualitative research methods to global cohorts of doctoral students in 2018 and 2019.

NOTES ON CONTRIBUTORS

Dr. Rakesh Kumar Agrawal holds a PhD in behavioral sciences (Department of Humanities and Social Sciences) from the Indian Institute of Technology, Roorkee, besides being a BTech from IIT Bombay and MTech in behavioural and social sciences from IIT Delhi. He has over 16 years of experience in teaching and research. Rakesh has presented papers in reputed international conferences in India and abroad and has published in the *Journal of Human Values* (Sage), *Social Psychology of Education* (Springer), *Benchmarking, An International Journal* (Emerald), *Energy Conversion and Management* (Elsevier), etc. He also has two book chapters on ethics, humanism, and spiritual integrity to his credit (Palgrave). Currently, Rakesh is Chairperson (MDP) and Associate Professor (OB&HRM) at IIM Kashipur. He has also conducted many training programs for organizations such as Bharat Electronics Ltd., Bangalore, LIC of India, NTPC, Moser Baer, TVS, and TATA Motors, among others. He is a professionally trained executive coach and is certified to administer a number of psychometric instruments such as Hogan Assessments, OPQ, MBTI, FIRO-B, and the Saville suite of instruments.

Dr. Duysal Aşkun frequently conducts research in the areas of organizational behavior and spirituality. Her articles were published in highly reputable journals such as *Management Research Review*, *European Management Review*, and *Journal of Business Ethics*. She has been a coeditor of two books on spirituality and has authored two books in the areas of I/O psychology and spiritual psychology. Pursuing the idea and the application of Oneness has been Duysal's passion and spiritual quest for several years. She is the author of the self-help book *Your First Step to Re-Create Your Life in Oneness: Awareness*, using the pen name "Kayla Wholey." Currently, Duysal serves as an adjunct faculty member at Fordham University-Gabelli School of Business, Baruch College, and New York City College of Technology-CUNY while also running workshops on "Spiritual and Personal Development" at the Wellness Center of Teacher's College, Columbia University.

Dr. Seth N. Asumah is State University of New York (SUNY) Distinguished Teaching Professor, Chair, and Professor of Africana Studies and Professor of Political Science at the State University of New York at Cortland. Seth earned his doctorate in government and international relations and master of public administration degrees from Lehigh University, Bethlehem, PA. He is author, coauthor, and coeditor of 10 books and over 100 book chapters, articles, and essays. Seth is a recipient of many international and national awards and honors, including the National Role Model Faculty Award, Minority INC. 2018, State University of New York Distinguished Alumni Award (2016), the Professor Ali A. Mazrui Outstanding Publication and Educational Activities Award (2014), the

American Political Science Association Outstanding Teaching in Political Science Award (2008), and the Rozanne Brooks Dedicated and Excellence in Teaching Award (1999). His honors include the Honor Society of Phi Kappa Phi, the Political Science Honor Society of Pi Sigma Alpha, and the International Honor Society of Phi Beta Delta. He is a Fulbright national screening committee member and a Boren Fellowship national screening committee member.

Dr. Sylvia W. Burgess is a senior partner with One Step at a Time Consulting, LLC, providing services for leadership training and development. Sylvia has over 18 years of experience in teaching, facilitation, curriculum design, leadership development, community engagement, cultural competency, diversity and inclusion, team building, and conflict resolution. She is a published author in the areas of spiritual capital and community engagement. She received her BA in speech and language pathology and MPA from the University of North Carolina Greensboro. She earned a PhD in leadership studies from North Carolina A&T State University. She has proven leadership and senior management experience in business, operational management, and training and with the Center for Creative Leadership. Sylvia has served as an adjunct professor at North Carolina A&T State University in the Leadership Studies doctoral program. She is an ordained minister of the gospel. Her greatest desire is to see women empowered in every area of their lives. She accomplishes this through ministry with Sisters of Joy Ministries. Sylvia is a native North Carolinian and resides in Greensboro, North Carolina, with her daughter Avigayil.

Glen Callahan has been a student, teacher, and practitioner of Vedanta philosophy for 15 years. He spent eight years studying at the Vedanta Academy, India, before cofounding the Vedanta Institute Los Angeles with his wife. He facilitates the discussion and practical integration of Vedanta philosophy for both groups and individuals. He also holds an MTech from Massey University (NZ).

Subhasis Chakrabarti is a Vedanta philosophy teacher at the Vedanta Institute Kolkata, India. He graduated from the Vedanta Academy, Malavli, India, with a diploma in Vedanta philosophy. His diverse research interests range from Western and Indian philosophy to neurobiology and consciousness studies. He holds an MBBS from the University of Kolkata, India.

Dr. Susanna L. M. Chui is Assistant Professor at the Hang Seng University of Hong Kong. Her research interests include leadership and identity, social entrepreneurship, and social impact measurement. She has published in the *Journal of Organizational Behavior and Human Decision Processes* and the Organizational Frontiers Series on research related to leadership identity. Moreover, she has coauthored for a publication under review on employee silence. She has also contributed a book chapter on inclusive leadership. Currently, Susanna is working on a number of publications related to team leadership, impact of inclusive leadership on followers, and ethical leadership. Susanna has over 10 years of experience lecturing on management-related subjects, which include leadership, corporate social responsibility, social entrepreneurship, organizational behavior, and business communication. While pursuing scholarly research, her research experience also extends to examining social impact measurement, CSR, stakeholder management, and human resources issues in organizational contexts.

Dr. Juanita Coleman-Merritt is an educator who has contributed to the field of education as an instructor, program coordinator, and administrator. She has written a number of articles based on her work in education. Her articles include "Effective Parent Outreach: Meeting Parents on Their Own Turf," pp. 12–13, *The Ladder*, Fall 2009, and "The Parent Center Institute," *Promising Partnership Practices*, p. 99 2007, Johns Hopkins University. As an educational administrator, she developed an interest in human resources, inclusive leadership practices, and team-building. She contributed to "A Closer

Look at a Business Renaissance Executive," *The Business Renaissance Quarterly*, Vol. 2 Issue 4, Winter, 2007. Juanita earned a BA at Barnard College, Columbia University, an MS at Bank Street College of Education, an MA in educational administration at Cal State Dominguez Hills, and an EdD in organizational leadership at Pepperdine University.

Dr. Trevor Cox is an assistant professor and the program coordinator for the organizational leadership degree at the University of Central Oklahoma. Trevor teaches classes on leadership, organizations, and adult learning and is heavily involved with faculty development in conjunction with the transformative learning initiatives at UCO. His main areas of research are transformative learning, inclusive leadership, and leadership development. Trevor has presented these topics at many conferences, such as those of the International Leadership Association and the Academy of Management and at the International Transformative Learning Conference. He is currently writing several articles in all three areas. In addition to his teaching and service roles, Trevor also has worked in a variety of leadership and consulting positions helping diverse groups reach their full potential and think more inclusively about their work.

Dr. Debra J. Dean has decades of experience in corporate America as well as years of teaching experience at the university level. She was nominated as one of three top operational excellence leaders at the OPEX Week Business Transformation World Summit 2019. She received the 2018 Outstanding Reviewer award for the management, spirituality, and religion (MSR) community. She was nominated as a top female leader with her previous global workplace. She has also been included in Biltmore's Who's Who of Women Business Leaders, Continental Who's Who of National Business Leaders, and Who's Who Among University Students. Debra was born and raised in Kentucky, spent nine years in Iowa, and currently resides in Colorado.

Dr. Cheryl De Ciantis is cofounder of Kairios, an independent human development research and practice group. She is coauthor of the Kairios Values Perspectives theory and survey and of *What's Important: Understanding and Working With Values Perspectives* (2014). Cheryl served as Senior Faculty and Director of the European Campus of the Center for Creative Leadership in Brussels, and has consulted extensively in public, private, and educational institutions and across business sectors as a coach and designer/facilitator of in-depth experiential creative/reflective development methodologies. An artist and writer, Cheryl obtained her doctorate in mythological studies and depth psychology from Pacifica Graduate Institute. Cheryl's most recent book, *The Return of Hephaistos: Reconstructing the Fragmented Mythos of the Makers* (2019), explores the mythic intersection of art and technology, and the powerful archetype that emanates from the core of current societal attitudes toward both. Cheryl lives with her work and life partner, Dr. Kenton Hyatt, in Tucson, Arizona.

Dr. Satinder Dhiman has delivered pioneer contributions to the field of transformational leadership, workplace spirituality, workplace well-being, sustainability, and fulfillment in personal and professional arena. In 2013, he gave a talk at the TEDx Conference at the College of the Canyons in Santa Clarita, California. Satinder holds a PhD in social sciences from Tilburg University, Netherlands, an EdD in organizational leadership from Pepperdine University, Los Angeles, an MBA from West Coast University, Los Angeles, and a master's degree in commerce from Panjab University, Chandigarh, India, having earned the Gold Medal. He has also completed advanced executive leadership programs at Harvard, Stanford, and Wharton, and has done over 50 conference presentations and more than 50 invited keynotes, plenary sessions, distinguished key guest lectures, and creative workshops—nationally and internationally; published over 60 peer-reviewed journal articles and book chapters; authored, coauthored, coedited, and translated over 25 management, leadership, spirituality, and accounting related books and research monographs. He currently serves as Associate Dean,

Chair, and Director of the MBA program; and as Professor of Management at Woodbury University, Burbank, California.

Dr. Lata Dyaram received her PhD from the Indian Institute of Technology Madras (IIT Madras). She has held various roles in industry and academics. She specializes in industrial/organizational psychology, is currently Associate Professor at Department of Management Studies, IIT Madras, and teaches organizational theory, leadership, and organization development. She has been a valued business partner for customized learning interventions in various industry sectors. Her research and publication interests include employee voice, diversity, cognition, emotions, and behavior in organizations. Her articles on these and other topics have appeared in journals such as *Learning and Individual Differences*, *International Journal of Productivity and Performance Management*, *Employee Relations*, and *International Journal of Organizational Analysis*.

Dr. Eleftheria Egel is an agent of transformation. Her work—as scholar, consultant, and entrepreneur—focuses on unraveling gender imbalances and deeply held limiting beliefs that do not allow for the full emergence of each individual's inner essence and limit organizational well-being and flourishing. The main areas of her research are spiritual, female, global, Islamic leadership, and sustainability. Eleftheria is a prior board member of the Management Spirituality & Religion (MSR) Interest Group of the Academy of Management (aom.org). She is also a mentor for women entrepreneurs with the Cherie Blair Foundation for Women (www.cherieblairfoundation.org/). She wholeheartedly supports the organization AKAWI (www.akawi.org) in Nigeria in their mission to empower women and children as well as various global initiatives that focus on educating girls in developing countries.

Dr. Robert S. Fleming is a professor of management and past dean of the Rohrer College of Business at Rowan University, where he teaches undergraduate and graduate strategic management courses. The focus of his teaching, research, and consulting has been on strategic management and enhancing organizational effectiveness. In addition to a doctorate in higher education administration from Temple University, he has five earned master's degrees including Master of Governmental Administration from the University of Pennsylvania. Robert is a nationally recognized authority on crisis management and fire and emergency service administration, and he is frequently called upon as a subject matter expert on business and emergency management topics by print, radio, and television media sources. His recent professional activities include participating in the Senior Executives in National and International Security Program at the Harvard Kennedy School. Robert is a prolific author. His four most recent books are *Effective Fire and Emergency Services Administration*, *Survival Skills for the Fire Chief*, *Emergency Incident Media Coverage*, and *Achieving Instructional Excellence: A Collection of Essays for Fire and Emergency Service Instructors*.

Dr. Bella L. Galperin is the Dana Professor of Management and Senior Associate Director of the TECO Energy Center for Leadership at the Sykes College of Business at the University of Tampa. Her interests include leadership (in Africa and the African diaspora), ethics, and workplace deviance—both destructive and constructive. She has published in the *Journal of Business Ethics*, *International Journal of Human Resource Management*, *Journal of Applied Social Psychology*, *Leadership Quarterly*, and *International Business Review*, *Journal of African Business*, and other journals. She coauthored a book entitled *LEAD: Leadership Effectiveness in Africa and the African Diaspora* (New York: Palgrave Macmillan, 2017) with Terri R. Lituchy and Betty Jane Punnett. She is a former associate editor of *Cross Cultural Management: An International Journal*. She is also past president of the International Society for the Study of Work and Organizational Values (ISSWOV), an international academic organization. She has worked as a consultant to firms in the telecommunications, pharmaceutical, and clothing industries.

Notes on Contributors

Dr. R. Ray Gehani has earned two doctorate degrees in biopolymer science and engineering from Tokyo Institute of Technology and in technology innovation strategy from the City University of New York. On a Japanese National (Monbusho) Fellowship, he lived, studied, and researched on high-performance polymeric materials in Tokyo, Osaka, and near Kyoto for seven years. Ray has taught a variety of undergraduate, graduate, and executive level courses at Baruch College in New York City, Rochester Institute of Technology in upstate New York, and the University of Akron in Ohio (since 1997). He was elected chair of the College of Innovation Management & Entrepreneurship and Technology Management Section of INFORMS. Ray's research studies on innovation, mindful leadership, strategy, and spirituality have been published in *Long Range Planning*, *Academy of Management Executive*, *Public Administration Review*, *Integral Leadership Review*, and more. He has authored *Management of Technology & Operations* (John Wiley, 1998), *Turning Leaves: An Anthology of Prose and Poetry*, and six other books. He leads the Summit Writers Roundtable of poets and storytellers, speaks Japanese, and gives art tours at the Akron Art Museum.

Dr. George Gotsis is Professor of Philosophy and History of Economics at the Department of History and Philosophy of Science, National and Kapodistrian University of Athens, Greece. His main research interests comprise, among others, diversity management ethics, emerging leadership theories, workplace spirituality, religion in business, and organizational politics.

Dr. Ginger Grant is Associate Dean, Applied Research at Humber College Institute of Technology and Advanced Learning. As an innovation researcher and academic entrepreneur and activist, Ginger's passion is creativity in business—the design, development, and implementation of narrative game plans that transform corporate culture and drive employee engagement and high performance teams for competitive advantage. She has held senior leadership positions and consulted in a variety of fields including engineering, telecommunications, education, transportation, government, law, software development, gaming, and the creative industries. She is a sought after international speaker on corporate culture, high-performance teams, and creativity/innovation and has given several TED talks. Ginger holds a PhD from Pacifica Graduate Institute and certificates in social work and family violence from the University of Waterloo. A recipient of several teaching awards, Ginger is also certified in multiple assessments, including Creative Problem Solving (CPS), Values Perspectives, Cultural Transformation Tools Practitioner (Barrett system), Foursight, MBTI, FIRO-B, EQi, EQ-360, and 4Mat Instructional Design.

Dr. Aikaterini Grimani is a research fellow at the Behavioral Science Group (Policy Research Unit) of Warwick Business School, University of Warwick, UK. She holds a PhD from the Department of History and Philosophy of Science, National and Kapodistrian University of Athens. She has obtained a BA in sociology, an MSc in healthcare management, and an MSc in cognitive science. Her main research interests include employee relations, health and safety at the workplace, worker well-being, inclusive workplaces, and leadership. She has 10 scientific publications in refereed journals, two book chapters, and one book.

Dr. William A. Guillory is President of Innovations International, Inc., and Executive Director of the Center for Creativity and Inquiry. William is an authority on personal and organizational transformation. He has published more than 12 books on this subject including *Realizations*, *How to Become a Total Failure*, *Spirituality in the Workplace*, *Living Without Fear*, and *The Guides*. His most recent series is the Pleiadian Trilogy: *The Pleiadians*, *The Hunt for the Billionaire Club*, *The Consortium*, and *The Aftermath* (of the Pleiadian series). Prior to founding the consulting firm Innovations International Inc., William was a chemical physicist of international renown, publishing more than 100 papers on the application of lasers in chemistry. He has facilitated leadership seminars for more than 400 organizations throughout the world. In addition, he has led retreats globally in personal and spiritual transformation through the Center for Creativity and Inquiry and thewayoftheheart.org; of which he is executive director.

Dr. Akanksha Jaiswal received her PhD from the Indian Institute of Technology Madras (IIT Madras). Her PhD work on workforce diversity and employee well-being was much appreciated and awarded as the best PhD thesis at IIT-Madras. She specializes in human resource management and organizational behavior. She is currently Research Associate at Loyola Institute of Business Administration (LIBA), Chennai, and teaches human resource management. She is a key resource person for application of advanced quantitative statistical tools such as structural equation modeling (SEM) and PROCESS. Her research interests include employee well-being, politics, and diversity and inclusion in organizations. She has published research papers in peer-reviewed international journals such as *Employee Relations* and *International Journal of Organizational Analysis*.

Dr. Sunny Jeong is a compassionate scholar and dedicated educator with five years' experience teaching social entrepreneurship and international business, previously as a visiting assistant professor at the University of Illinois at Urbana-Champaign. Her research interests lie at the confluence of third-person spirituality, religion and business practices, social and cultural capital (religion and belief in fate), and gender. Her teaching areas include international business, global leadership, and social entrepreneurship. She has advised students in international business plan competitions concerning sustainability in Seoul, Korea (2009), London, UK (2010), Sao Paolo, Brazil (2011), and in an upcoming one in Osaka, Japan (2014). Sunny's professional experiences include private consulting services in the area of international expansion strategy and business development planning for small to large companies, new social venture development, and incorporation of L3C and 501(C)3 corporations.

Komal Kalra is a PhD candidate at the Peter B. Gustavson School of Business, the University of Victoria, Canada. She holds a master's in international management from the IE Business School in Spain. Prior to starting the PhD program, Komal was a research fellow at the Institute of Rural Management Anand, India, and at the Centre for Social Entrepreneurship & Enterprises, and she was involved in helping set up entrepreneurship incubation hubs in different industrial sectors. Before that, she worked at Deloitte Touche Tohmatsu. Komal's research revolves around the issues of diversity in teams and organizations. She is currently researching the role of within-subsidiary linguistic diversity on knowledge transfer in multinational corporations.

Dr. Evodio Kalteneckers is an assistant professor at Tecnologico de Monterrey, Mexico. Evodio holds a PhD in strategy completed at Universidade de São Paulo, Brazil. He also holds an MBA from the Harvard Business School and an MSc in industrial engineering from the Federal University of Rio de Janeiro. In his research, Evodio focuses on strategy, Latin America, emerging market multinationals, and international business. He has extensive experience in executive education in international business schools such the Samuel C. Johnson Graduate School of Management at Cornell University (US), The Management Center Innsbruck (Austria), and Fundação Dom Cabral (FDC, Brazil). He is currently a professor-in-residence at the Austral Education Group.

Paul S. Kioko is a Chief Operations Specialist in the United States Navy stationed in San Diego, CA. He has over eighteen years of experience in the U.S. Department of Defense, Training, Management, Military Operations, and Leadership. He holds a Master's of Strategic Leadership degree from the University of Charleston—West Virginia. Mr. Kioko lives in San Diego, CA with his wife, Miriam, and two-year-old son Zion. In his spare time, Paul enjoys road biking, traveling, and spending time with loved ones.

Nicole S. Knight is a lecturer in management studies at the University of the West-Indies. She also serves as the program coordinator, MSc International Management and MSc Management with International Management Specialization. She holds an MBA from London South Bank University

Dr. Wanda Krause is Program Head of the Global Leadership Program and Assistant Professor in the School of Leadership. Her PhD is in politics with a focus on organizational development, where she evaluated the impacts of women's participation in their initiatives on civil society development in international settings. She has lived in six countries and taught and consulted in several as well. She has contributed to the development or the founding of two centers and two MA programs. Wanda has contributed to, written, and edited four books as an award-winning and international bestselling author, namely *Civil Society and Women Activists in the Middle East*; *Women in Civil Society: The State, Islamism, and Networks in the UAE*; *Spiritual Activism: Keys for Personal and Political Success*, and *Citizenship, Security and Democracy: Muslim Engagement With the West*. She has also contributed several journal papers and book chapters. Her work can be found at www.wandakrause.com.

Dr. Elliot Tyler Kruse is a research professor at the EGADE Business School, Tec de Monterrey. He is the head of the leadership research group. He received his doctorate in psychology (social) at UC Riverside. He then completed postdoctoral training at Princeton University, in psychology, and at Vanderbilt University, in management. His research focuses on the relationship between leadership, values, and well-being.

Dr. Peter Mutuku Lewa has extensive working experience in both the public and private sectors. He has been in research, teaching, and consultancy for more than 30 years. He has substantial experience in public sector finance, monitoring, and evaluation of projects in both the public sector and the private sector; strategic planning; global strategy, trading blocks, international trade, curriculum development, and evaluation; evaluation of new university applications with CUE (CHE); transformational leadership development; establishment of new universities; performance contracting in the public sector; performance management in the private sector; and related issues. Peter has worked as a consultant for international agencies and overseas universities and institutions. He has assisted organizations within and outside Kenya to develop their strategic plans, business plans, and action plans geared towards building their capacities. He has traveled widely and has been to such countries as the UK, Germany, the US, South Africa, Indonesia, Malaysia, Austria, Tanzania, Uganda, Zimbabwe, Ethiopia, and Somalia. He holds an MS in development finance and a PhD in development administration from the University of Birmingham. Peter has also supervised several doctoral students.

Dr. Susan K. Lewa holds a PhD in business administration from the Dedan Kimathi University of Technology (DeKUT) in Kenya with a specialization in HRM. She holds an MA in counseling psychology from the United States International University-Africa (USIU-A) and a BEd (Hons.) degree from Kenyatta University in Kenya. She has research interests in leadership, HRM, management, social enterprise, and strategic management. Susan is a lecturer at the Jomo Kenyatta University of Agriculture and Technology (JKUAT) Karen campus in Nairobi, Kenya. She has various publications in the areas of leadership, HRM, management, and psychology.

Tariana V. Little's work embodies what she calls "intentional creativity for social change." It is driven by science, storytelling, and social justice. A research scientist-turned-social entrepreneur, Tariana cofounded and leads EmVision Productions, a media boutique that helps progressive organizations convey how they are changing the world. She coproduced the mini-doc *Stories of Black Motherhood* (2018, 8 min) and served in the *American Journal of Public Health*'s inaugural Student Media Think Tank to help rebrand itself for future generations. Additionally, she is a doctor of public health candidate

(DrPH, 2020) at the Harvard Chan School of Public Health, focusing on innovation in food security. As a queer, multicultural, first-generation scholar from a working-class Dominican-German-Mexican immigrant family in Boston, Tariana serves on several boards of nonprofits benefitting underrepresented youth and communities, and has been named by *El Mundo* and *El Planeta* (New England's largest Spanish-language newspapers) as among the most influential young Latino leaders in Massachusetts.

Dr. Terri R. Lituchy earned her PhD in international organizational behavior from the University of Arizona. She has taught around the world, including in the US, Mexico, Canada, Trinidad, Barbados, Argentina, France, the UK, Czech Republic, Japan, China, Thailand, and Malaysia. She teaches courses on organizational behavior, cross-cultural management, international negotiations, and women in international business, to name a few. Her research interests are in cross-cultural management and international organizational behavior. Terri's current project, LEAD, Leadership Effectiveness and Motivation in Africa, the Caribbean, and the Diaspora has received many awards as well as grants from the SHRM Foundation, Emerald Publishing, McMaster University, University of the West Indies, Concordia University, and SSHRC. She has published books titled *Successful Professional Women of the Americas* (Elgar Publishing, 2006), *Gender and the Dysfunctional Workplace* (Elgar, 2012), *Management in Africa* (Routledge, 2014), and *LEAD: Leadership Effectiveness in Africa and the African Diaspora* (Palgrave, 2017). Terri has over 35 published journal articles. In her spare time, she enjoys traveling, photography, bird watching, and learning about other cultures.

Dr. Anil K. Maheshwari is Professor of Management and Director of MBA in Information Systems at Maharishi University of Management, in Fairfield, Iowa. He teaches courses in data analytics, strategic management, leadership, marketing, and others. His research has been published in *Creativity Research Journal*, *Family Business Review*, and other scholarly journals. He has also presented at the Academy of Management, International Conference on Information Systems, National Teachers Congress, and other major conferences.

Anil has 20 years of IT industry experience, including nine years in leadership roles at IBM in Austin, TX. He has been a professor at the University of Cincinnati, City University of New York, University of Illinois, and others. After completing a bachelor of tech. degree in electrical engineering from the Indian Institute of Technology in Delhi, he earned an MBA from the Indian Institute of Management in Ahmedabad and a PhD in management from Case Western Reserve University, Cleveland, Ohio. As a regular practitioner of Transcendental Meditation™ and TM-Sidhi techniques, he was also awarded the coveted Maharishi Award. He has run a marathon, and he blogs on blissful living at anilmah.com. He is the author of a dozen books on technology, management, and spirituality. His book *Data Analytics Made Accessible* is a #1 global bestseller, published by McGraw-Hill, and translated into other languages.

Catherine W. Maingi is a doctoral candidate and teaching assistant at the United States International University-Africa (USIU-A). Her doctoral research paper is on the effects of integrated financial information systems (IFMIS) on public procurement in Kenyan ministries. Her research interests also include strategic finance and accounting. She holds a master's degree in finance and a bachelor of science in accounting-finance and accounting information systems (AIS) from the USIU-A. She is also a certified public account (CPA). Her teaching assistant courses include Introduction to Finance, Money, and Capital Markets, Investments, Corporate Finance, and Financial Management.

Dr. Joan Marques has reinvented herself from a radio and television producer/host in Suriname, South America, to an academic entrepreneur in California, USA. She currently serves as Dean and Professor of Management at Woodbury University's School of Business. She teaches courses related to leadership, ethics, and organizational behavior in the MBA and BBA programs and presents regularly at academic and professional workshops. Joan holds a PhD from Tilburg University (2011); an EdD from Pepperdine University's Graduate School of Education and Psychology (2004); an MBA from Woodbury University (2000), and a BSc-equivalent degree (HEAO) in economics from MOC, Suriname (1987). She has also completed post-doctoral work at Tulane University's Freeman School of Business (2010). Joan has authored/coauthored/coedited 20 books so far, many with globally renowned publishers such as Springer, Palgrave-MacMillan, and Routledge. She has also been widely published in a variety of scholarly and professional journals worldwide. Her research interests pertain to awakened leadership, Buddhist psychology, and workplace spirituality.

Dr. Karen Martin-Jones is an assistant professor at Bennett College in Greensboro/Winston-Salem, North Carolina. She holds a PhD in educational leadership and administration from North Carolina A&T State University and an MS in computer science from Bennett College for Women. She is also a science teacher and department chair at Guilford County Schools and the founder and CEO of Leaders Emerging Around a Purpose (LEAP), LLC., in High Point, NC.

Dr. Lemayon L. Melyoki is a senior lecturer at the University of Dar es Salaam Business School and a member of the Institute of Directors of Tanzania (IoDT). He obtained a PhD and MBA from the University of Twente, the Netherlands. He has researched and published in peer-reviewed journals and research volumes on the topics of leadership and management, entrepreneurship, and governance. He is currently coordinating and researching an action-oriented entrepreneurship program at the University of Dar es Salaam in collaboration with researchers from the University of Leuphana (Germany). Lemayon is a member of an international research consortium, which is researching leadership and management issues in Africa and diaspora under the Leadership Effectiveness in Africa and Diaspora (LEAD) project. He is also closely involved in the development and governance of the extractive sector in Tanzania and has recently published in the *Journal of Extractives and Society*. He has presented at a number of conferences in Tanzania, the United States, Germany, the United Kingdom, and South Africa.

Dr. Laura E. Mercer Traavik is an associate professor in the department of Leadership and Organizational Behavior and the Associate Dean for the Master of Science Program in Leadership and Organizational Psychology. She teaches graduate courses in managing workplace diversity, economic psychology, and negotiation. Laura often holds workshops and presentations on negotiation and diversity and inclusion for companies and public organizations across Norway. Her research investigates gender, diversity, and well-being in organizations and negotiations. Laura's current projects focus on inclusion and belonging of women and minorities in specific organizational contexts, artifacts and inclusion, and diversity leadership and norm setting.

Kennedy Muema Musyoka is a doctoral candidate and a teaching assistant at the United States International University-Africa (USIU-A). His doctoral research is on the influence of dynamic capabilities on the performance of Kenyan non-governmental organizations. His research interests also include social enterprises and entrepreneurship and CSR. He holds a master's degree in strategic management from the USIU-A and a bachelor of economics degree from Kenyatta University in Kenya. He is a recent beneficiary of a scholarship from the Global School in Empirical Research Methods (GSERM) training offered by the University of St. Gallen in Switzerland. His teaching subjects include supply chain management, strategic management, and entrepreneurship.

Faith Mutuku Muna is a global health professional working as a program manager at the Clinton Health Access Initiative. She works in the vaccines program supporting the Ministry of Health in Kenya on immunization management, new vaccine introduction, service delivery, and immunization financing. She has over nine years of experience in program management and business management consulting.

Faith holds a master's of business in strategic management and a bachelor's degree in international business administration (finance) from the United States International University (Kenya).

Rachel Mwende M. Murigi is a marketing and communications specialist working with Population Services Kenya (PS Kenya) as Director for the Reproductive Health Program. She has a bachelor's in marketing and communication and a master's in strategic management from United States International University (Africa). Rachel has worked in the field of marketing and communication for over 10 years, including five years of ensuring scale-up of social marketing and communication strategies to improve reproductive health and maternal health outcomes of populations in different contexts. Her skills include the development and execution of demand creation strategies at various levels, creative media and communication campaigns, public private sector coordination, and service delivery innovations.

Sarah M. Mutuku is a strategic account analyst at HD Supply. She has over 15 years of experience in sales and national account management. She holds a bachelor's degree in business administration from United States International University in San Diego, CA. She also has a master's of science degree in international business administration from Alliant International University in San Diego, CA.

Sarah provides strategic and financial analyses in an effort to bridge the gap between goals and operational efficiency. In her current role, she develops strategies that ensure compliance, analyzes sales data to study buying habits and patterns, and recommends corrective action.

Miriam M. Mutuku-Kioko is a senior operations management analyst at Rady Children's Hospital–San Diego. She has over 10 years' experience in health care decision support, operations, and financial systems. She holds a master's of healthcare administration from the University of North Carolina at Chapel Hill. She also has a master's of science in business administration from Alliant International University in San Diego, CA. Miriam has expertise in conducting cost-benefit and financial analyses and feasibility studies for healthcare organizations and applying advanced knowledge of clinical, financial, and systems analysis to translate data into solutions for population health. In her current role, she researches, reviews, interprets, and illustrates population health data for presentation and decision-making as well as provides analytic, planning, and coordination support on projects as assigned. Miriam is passionate about equality and fairness, serving the underserved and marginalized communities, giving back, and serving others.

Dr. Mechthild Nagel is Professor of Philosophy and Africana Studies at the State University of New York, College at Cortland, and a visiting professor at Fulda University of Applied Sciences, Germany. Her most recent coedited books are *Diversity, Social Justice, and Inclusive Excellence: Transdisciplinary and Global Perspectives* (with S.N. Asumah, SUNY Press, 2014), which received the 2016 Book Award from the New York African Studies Association, and *The End of Prisons: Reflections From the Decarceration Movement* (with A. Nocella, Rodopi Press, 2013). Mechthild is Founder and Editor-in-Chief of the online feminist journal *Wagadu: A Journal of Transnational Women's and Gender Studies* (wagadu.org).

Dr. Anna Olszewska is an assistant professor at the Department of Management, Kozminski University (KU). She also holds the academic coordinator of bachelor and master programs in management position and is responsible for international cooperation. Anna received her academic training in Poland (KU, European Academy of Diplomacy), Singapore (Singapore Management University), France (Audencia Business School, ISC Paris), Spain (EADA), and the United Arab Emirates (The

Emirates Academy of Hospitality Management). She acquired her professional experience from institutions such as Chancellery of the President of the Republic of Poland, Encore Event Agency, and The Embassy of the Republic of Poland in Singapore. Her research interests include top management teams, leadership, and communication issues.

Dr. Aneesya Panicker holds a PhD degree in management in the area of diversity and inclusion from the Institute of Business Management, GLA University, Mathura, Uttar Pradesh, India, and a master's in business administration from UP Technical University, Lucknow, Uttar Pradesh. She has over 14 years of experience in teaching and research. She presently works as an associate professor and program coordinator in the Institute of Business Management, GLA University, Mathura. She has completed many certification courses from IIT Delhi and IIT Kharagpur. Aneesya is an avid researcher and has various international and national research publications of repute in her name and has also won many best paper awards. She is a certified professional trainer from The American TESOL Institute and is coordinating an employability program in her current organization. She has conducted many Faculty Development Programs for newly recruited faculties and multiple training programs for middle management level employees of Mathura Refinery and NPCC, New Delhi, on building team and enhancing leadership skills. She has reviewed books on business communication for Tata McGraw-Hill Education Private Limited.

Dr. Betty Jane Punnett holds a PhD in international business from New York University (1984) and is Professor Emerita at the University of the West Indies (Cave Hill) and an academic fellow of the International Council of Certified Management Consultants. She has published widely in international journals and contributed to several books, focusing on cross-cultural issues in international management. Her most recent books are the fourth edition of *International Dimensions of Organizational Behavior* (2019), *Managing in Developing Countries* (2018), and *LEAD: Leadership Effectiveness in Africa and the African Diaspora* (2017). Betty has also recently edited special issues of *International Journal of Cross Cultural Management* (2012), *Canadian Journal of Administrative Sciences* (2014), and *AIB Insights* (2017), as well as presented numerous papers at academic venues around the world. Her recent research has focused on African countries and the Caribbean. She was born in St. Vincent and the Grenadines and now lives there with her husband Donald Wood.

Dr. Birute Regine earned her masters and doctorate degrees in human development at Harvard University, where she was a project manager at the Harvard Project of Development of Girls and Psychology of Women. She collaborated with the psychologist Carol Gilligan and was a teaching assistant for Erik Erikson. She spent 25 years as a psychologist in private practice, was a visiting scholar for two years at the Center for Research on Women at Wellesley College, and an affiliate of the Stone Center. She now works as an executive/life coach, facilitator, international speaker, and consultant. An award-winning author, she coauthored the critically acclaimed *The Soul at Work: Embracing Complexity Science for Business Success*. Her book, *Iron Butterflies: Women Transforming Themselves and the World* won the Nautilus Silver book award in both social change and women's interest categories. She has written for numerous anthologies and periodicals.

Dr. Thomas Anyanje Senaji has wide experience in telecommunications and information and communications technologies (ICTs). He is a consultant on broadband strategy and related areas such as standardization, conformance and interoperability, quality of service/experience, regulation, and human capacity building. Working with the International Telecommunication Union and the Universal Postal Union (UPU), his current consultancy engagements are the development of a model broadband plan and the electrification and connectivity of post offices in the Southern African Development Community (SADC) and the rest of Africa, respectively. He is also worked with

Communications Regulators' Association of Southern Africa, regional CT experts, and the ITU on guidelines for broadband plan deployment in SADC having earlier prepared the SADC conformance and interoperability assessment report (under the ITU) in collaboration with Joshua Peprah (consultant), CRASA, and the SADC secretariat. He has consulted and completed the development of guidelines for the development of broadband master plans for the SADC region and elaborated national broadband strategies for the Republic of Namibia and for the Kingdom of Swaziland. He has developed the national ePost strategy and the Malawi Posts Corporate strategy for Malawi as the lead consultant in collaboration with Chris Schaeke. He is also a specialist in knowledge management and in organizational development and change.

Dr. Ester R. Shapiro is Associate Professor of Psychology, University of Massachusetts Boston; Research Associate, Mauricio Gaston Institute for Latino Research and Public Policy; and Core Faculty in the clinical psychology PhD program focused on culturally meaningful, social justice oriented research, practice, and advocacy and in the Critical Ethnic and Community Studies (CECS) MS program, dedicated to transdisciplinary community partnered research building knowledge for solidarity and social change. A Cuban Jewish Eastern European immigrant, she is committed to helping all families make the most of their opportunities for improving life chances by mobilizing cultural strengths and ecosystemic resources, even when facing societal barriers multiplying burdens of adversity, death, and loss. She wrote *Grief as a Family Process: A Developmental Approach to Clinical Practice* (Guilford, 1994) and is finishing a new book, *Culture, Grief and Family Resilience*. She was Coordinating Editor of *Nuestros Cuerpos Nuestras Vidas* (Seven Stories 2000), the Spanish transcultural adaptation of *Our Bodies, Ourselves*. Ester has also published personal narratives about the impact of multiple immigrations on development in her own Cuban Jewish family, and she is writing an intergenerational immigrant family memoir with recipes.

Dr. Mike Szymanski is a research professor of international business at EGADE Business School Guadalajara. Mike holds a PhD in international management and organizations completed at the Gustavson School of Business, the University of Victoria (Canada). He also holds a master's degree in strategic management from the Warsaw School of Economics and a master's degree in American culture from the University of Warsaw (Poland). Before starting his PhD training, he worked in strategic management consulting (PWC and Deloitte). Mike's research is at the confluence of international business, global leadership, and human resource management. The ultimate goal of his research is to understand how organizations can take full advantage of biculturals (i.e., people who have internalized two distinct cultures, such as Polish-British or Mexican-American individuals) and how these individuals can leverage their strengths in an organizational setting.

PART I
Stakeholder Considerations

1
INCLUSIVE LEADERSHIP, DIVERSITY, AND WAKEFULNESS

Joan Marques

Introduction

This chapter will review three phenomena that are of critical importance in workplace performance: inclusive leadership, diversity, and wakefulness. The foundational purpose of bringing these three phenomena together is to reveal their interdependency and help readers understand why they should be applied in congruence. In the first section, the trend of leadership will be discussed with special emphasis on inclusive leadership. In the second section, an elaboration of diversity is presented, with emphasis on workplace tendencies. This section will particularly highlight several wrong implementations of diversity that lead to less favorable outcomes. The section will subsequently explain the right reason for implementing diversity and link this to inclusive leadership. In the third section, wakefulness will be evaluated, with a special emphasis on its role in inclusive leadership. Two roadmaps for wakeful performance will thereby be shared: AWAKENED, an acronym that brings together the behaviors of authenticity, wakefulness, agility, kindness, evenness (equilibrium), neuroticism, eagerness, and deliberation, and the Noble Eightfold Path, an interrelated system of eight continuous efforts, which are right understanding, right view, right intention, right speech, right action, right livelihood, right effort, right mindfulness, and right concentration. The chapter will conclude by bringing the three phenomena together through a visual impression.

Inclusive Leadership

The practice of inclusive leadership is not a luxury, and in fact not even an option anymore: it is a requirement for any leader who wants to succeed in taking his or her organization to greater heights than before. There is enormous competition in our world, and excelling has never been more challenging than it is today. After all, we can easily learn about the strategies, directions, performances, and leadership of practically any organization on their corporate websites and in their widely available annual reports. The world has become a transparent place, and in many regards, this is a great thing, even though it has its downsides.

One of the main upsides of today's global organizational transparency is the fact that learning from best practices—benchmarking—has never been easier. This means that some common mistakes from the past no longer have to be made if leaders keep their eyes wide open. In organizational performance, transparency is touted as a sign of ethical responsibility and inclusion. Parris, Dapko, Arnold, and Arnold (2016) perceive transparency in organizations as a sign of openness and ethical awareness that reduces skepticism, increases trust and confidence, empowers internal and external stakeholders, and therefore nurtures healthy relationships.

On the downside, transparency places a severe time constraint on the uniqueness of anyone's special services or products compared to pre-internet days, because competitors can quickly find out what is happening in the market. In a study on transparency in China's public healthcare, Yang (2018) acknowledges the earlier mentioned advantages of transparency, but also warns that it can provide stakeholders with a sense of involvement to an extent that their expectations exceed the service or quality received, thus leading to dissatisfaction. Bianchi (2015) adds that there is also room for caution in the fact that the trust relationship created by being transparent can lead to abuse and exploitation of privileges and power. Haesevoets et al. (2019) further caution us in regards to the perceived transparency in workplace communication, where excessive copying of supervisors in email correspondence may be seen as a sign of increased control and consequently invoke a sense of mistrust and unethical behavior rather than trust and ethical performance.

When it comes to leading people, history has taught us that there is a wide range of styles that can be implemented, from highly people-oriented to highly process-oriented and from highly interactive to highly authoritative. While leadership styles can be learned and adopted, individual leaders also have character-based elements that make the application of certain leadership behaviors easier or harder. In recent years, several soft-skill focused leadership styles have gained popularity: awakened, prosocial, servant, authentic, transformational, and situational are just a handful of those. Each of the just mentioned leadership styles carries the common factor of inclusion: leadership is not practiced as a one-way street but as an interactive process, in which all stakeholders have decent input in expressing opinions, proposing ideas, and taking ownership.

Inclusive leadership specifically refers to leaders who are open, accessible, and available when it comes to interacting with their workforce (Nembhard & Edmondson, 2006). The process of including colleagues contributes to an uplifted atmosphere in the workplace (Hollander, 2009). Taking these behavioral patterns into consideration, Ye, Wang, and Li (2018) aver that the general mood created through inclusive leadership leads to better relationships between employees and their leaders, resulting in greater inspiration among employees to learn from their errors and seek continuous improvement. Javed, Mehdi, Abdul, Arjoon, and Hafiz (2019) include the aspect of innovation as a clear outcome of implementing inclusive leadership. They affirm that "inclusive leadership is positively related with innovative work behavior, and psychological safety mediates the effect of inclusive leadership on innovative work behavior" (p. 117). Javed et al. explain this trend as a result of inclusive leaders making important information available to employees and including them in discussions and decision processes, thus granting them a sense of ownership and co-responsibility.

It should be noted that highly interactive leadership styles may not work as well in primarily mechanized workplaces as in organic ones, where production processes are not repetitive, preparedness of employees is higher, and turnover is lower. Because employees usually don't have an intention to stay too long in several mechanistic work environments, it is not easy or ideal for a leader to make collaborative decisions, simply because there might be little input from these employees, due to little interest in the organization's strategic growth. Of course, there may be highly mechanized work environments where employees don't intend to leave any time soon and see their job as something of a steadier nature, so every situation has to be carefully assessed before deciding on the appropriate leadership style.

Inclusion could also be interpreted in multiple ways. Some leaders may decide to implement inclusive leadership by way of making all decisions as a team, while others may be selective in which types of decisions should be made in which team echelon. Yet others may place the inclusive emphasis on a different area, such as providing stakeholders a voice in regards to flexible work hours or job sharing. It is important, however, for leaders to understand that what they consider inclusive may not be perceived as such by others. Especially in diverse work environments, there is a major chance that some groups may feel left out due to a subconsciously displayed bias from the leader. Inclusive leadership systematically tries to avoid such pitfalls. It could be defined as a relational construct that emerges from a process of mutual influence and collective adaptation to fluid environments. Beyond care and compassion, it cultivates deeper and authentic relationships, modeling courage and embracing humane ideals as components of inclusive organizations (Gallegos, 2014). Inclusive leader behaviors involve accountability for creating an inclusive culture, engagement and dialogue, bringing one's true self to work, fostering transparent decision-making, understanding and engaging with resistance, and communicating how inclusion relates to mission and vision (Ferdman, 2014, p. 42).

Inclusive leaders encourage followers to nurture their individual strengths. They make sure there are resources for employee development, and they support their followers in pursuing opportunities for growth and collective progress (Gotsis & Grimani, 2016).

Diversity

Diversity is another topic that has demanded increased attention and awareness in recent decades. Diversity in organizational contexts refers to situations that germinate when employees differ in terms of age, gender, ethnicity, education, etc. (Panicker, Agrawal, & Utkal, 2018). As workplaces become more diverse in regards to generations, ethnicities, genders, and a number of preferences, it has become evident that leaders can no longer apply one-size-fits-all approaches in treating, rewarding, and advocating for employees.

Diversity should be implemented with caution and for the right reasons. There are many organizational leaders who only engage in an effort toward a more diverse workplace when they realize that they are losing customers by remaining too homogeneous. Such reactive diversity is oftentimes detected rather quickly by customers and may lead to alienation anyway.

Just like inclusive leadership, diversity can be interpreted and implemented in numerous ways. The unfortunate reality is, however, that these ways of implementing diversity are oftentimes mere means toward an end (which is mostly profit-focused), and not an end unto themselves.

Some organizations claim to be diverse when the overall picture of their workforce reveals the presence of multiple ethnicities, abilities, and ages. And while this is true in the plain sense of the word, these organizations fail to consider the positioning of many of their members. An in-depth examination of such organizations reveals that the higher echelons are rather uniform, and that diversity only trickles in at the lower levels, where there is no decision power and no solicitation of opinions toward decision-making processes. By implementing this strategy, these organizations keep the controlling mechanisms in the hands of a homogeneous group that is unable to make decisions with the depth that a diverse team would display (Marques, 2008).

Some organizations limit their diversity to location: they tailor their workforce to their local customer base, which usually entails that only the service level of their workforce is diverse, preferably based on designated environmental segments. When operating on a global scale, these organizations apply diversity to accommodate customers in the countries where they operate, but refrain from enabling their employees from various geographic areas to learn from one another. They do not shift workers throughout the organization, so the knowledge of properly accommodating certain groups of customers remains confined within local borders. The outcome of the story is that the deeper advantages of diversity—mutual learning, mindset expansion, greater acceptance, and enhanced insights—remain uncultivated.

Then there are organizations that support diversity in appearance of their workforce overall but insist on uniform, set, and dated perspectives and procedures, thus silencing parts of their workforce, who may know of great alternative options for implementing processes more effectively, based on their difference in background and insights. Some organizations reach out to their customers in their diversity strategy, but do not necessarily believe in diversity as the morally proper thing to do. Their main concern is that customers feel at ease in the store by recognizing salespeople on the floor who come from the same background or racial group as theirs.

Engaging in the right reasons for diversity would entail granting all members of the diverse workforce the same opportunities to advance. Variety in race, gender, education, age, or cultural background will then result in greater insights and creativity at all levels. Engaging in the right reasons would also entail that globally operating organizations ensure optimal internal, integrated, and external learning for all employees. Employee exchange programs should be created and interorganizational travel across geographically dispersed locations should be highly encouraged, so that multi-applicability and rich learning can occur (Marques, 2008). Engaging in the right reasons would thus entail applying diversity in the first place because it is morally correct. The world consists of human beings that are equal to one another, even if they differ in color, shape, size, age, ability, preferences, or gender. If this mindset can become part of the nature of the organization, performance as a whole will be augmented and profits will consequently increase.

Of course, there are advantages and disadvantages to diversity. The most common advantage is that a diverse workforce can be a source of wealth in implementing inventive ways of doing things. Originality can become the winning proposition for such an organization if optimally utilized. Besides, with a world as diverse as ours, diversity in the workplace is just the most natural thing to maintain. The reason, then, why so many organizations still have a problem with implementing diversity is that it requires more caution, warrants greater by slower progress, and requires conflict preparedness. Even though the long-term advantage of a diverse workforce, with its broader base of knowledge and insights, can be rationalized, so too can the fact that a homogeneous workforce may reach faster consensus (due to similarities in backgrounds, insights, and beliefs) and can therefore move more rapidly to decisions.

Additionally, diverse workforces will result in more conflict management, as there is a greater chance of misunderstanding and aversion for the unknown amongst the workforce members. There will therefore be a need for more professional guidance of human resources, which is oftentimes an unwelcome source of expense, especially for smaller organizations.

Arguably the most appealing aspect of the inclusive leadership style is the fact that it considers the inequality of status amongst coworkers and applies diversity as a value ("Diversity as a contributor to leadership effectiveness," 2016). Analyzing data from a sample containing 415,696 respondents, Jin, Lee, and Lee (2017) corroborate that there is a positive correlation between inclusive leadership and diversity. These authors found that, especially for minority workers, diversity policies only become strong when leadership is also inclusive. Frost (2018) adds that having diverse teams is an effective way to improve the quality of decision-making, reduce groupthink, and allow assumptions to be challenged more effectively. Yet, he also points out that those organizations that find that diversity doesn't work for them should take a hard look at their leaders. In line with Jin, Lee, and Lee, Frost underscores that diversity needs to be managed to convert its negatives into positives, which means that inclusive leadership is required. This opinion is shared by Panicker et al. (2018), who affirm,

> [I]nclusion implies removal of obstacles and creating an environment in which every individual is treated respectfully and fairly in terms of equitable opportunities for participation and advancement leading to organizational success. But the unfortunate part is many well-intentioned organizations often neglect the inclusion part by mere giving importance to diversity of workforce which results into disappointing organizational outcomes. Thus, it's vital for the organization not to underestimate the synergy of diversity and inclusion efforts.
> *(p. 531)*

The previous section of the chapter brought the following insights to the surface: when diversity is a phenomenon unto itself, it will not automatically succeed. There are prerequisites that need adhering to, as with all other important strategies:

- The organization's leaders need to be aware of the reasons for implementing diversity and be willing to choose the proper implementation.
- Employees need to be guided in the process of learning how to work together.
- The human resource department needs to be an active and vocal advocate of this trend, and top management needs to be involved and believe in the merit of this phenomenon, not just as another passing fad but as the lasting and most constructive, multi-beneficial response to an increasingly interdependent world (Marques, 2007).

Wakefulness

When considering the phenomena of inclusive leadership and diversity in one's work process, the importance of wakefulness arises. Wakefulness, in this perspective, means maintaining a mindful approach and continuously considering the well-being of all stakeholders. This is not an easy task, as it often happens that multiple stakeholder groups get overlooked in decision-making processes. Wakefulness requires a leader's ability to take a hard look at his or her own values and beliefs and finding out whether they align with the collective. If not, such a leader should be willing to either change his or her paradigms—which is very difficult to do—or enable another individual to take the reins and do the right thing.

It may be useful to first consider some of the challenges that are causing recurring pressure in today's leadership performance:

- Lack of reflection, which can drive us into self-centeredness and failure to consider the effects our decisions have on others.
- Mindless performance, which is the immediate manifestation of a lack of reflection.
- Change aversion, which is a problem many people struggle with, because we are creatures of habit, even when those habits have lost their constructive use.
- Blindly adhering to traditions, which is one of the most common drivers behind mindless behavior: We often get stuck in doing things that were traditionally done this way without reflecting or questioning whether they still make sense today.
- Lack of broad view, which lies at the foundation of many a disastrous decision. Till today, when deforestation practices are implemented, they are done with a deliberate blind eye to the massive damage this practice does, not only to wildlife, which is robbed of its habitat, but also to humanity, which is systematically stripped of its oxygen.
- Too much detail focus, which is a more focused approach to the issue mentioned earlier. We can get so lost in details—a problem that is visible in many workplaces—that we waste precious time on nitpicking, at the expense of the bigger picture and its impact (Marques, 2015).

An easily comprehensible way of considering wakefulness is to think of the acronym AWAKENED, consisting of the following elements: authenticity, wakefulness, agility, kindness, equilibrium, neuroticism, eagerness, and deliberation (Marques, 2018). A brief summary of the aforementioned acronym depict the following:

- *Authenticity* touches on genuine self-knowledge, deeper than the outer layer of behaving. Authenticity is related to our spiritual core and needs to be explored regularly, as we, human beings, are just as much subject to change as anything else that lives. While remaining authentic,

there are still different behavioral cues we have to adhere to in different settings, which makes the quality of being true to ourselves an ongoing effort and a continuous practice of remaining in tune with our core.
- *Wakefulness*, within this scope, should be seen as the opposite of "sleepwalking," which should not be considered in its literal sense but in the realm of mindful versus mindless behavior. Many people sleepwalk through the day, meaning that they behave as if on auto-pilot without thinking deeply on their actions. Once we become aware of this easy snare, however, we can start working on increased mindfulness by paying more attention to our relationships with others as well as with ourselves.
- *Agility* is an absolute must if we want to engage in mindful performance in this fast-paced professional world of ours. Inclusive leaders know that they will fulfill different roles in their interactions with others, some of those will be of a leading nature, while others will be on a more equal basis or in a subordinate role.
- *Kindness* will always be appreciated in any type of interaction with internal and external stakeholders. Making a deliberate effort to be kind to others means that we're making deposits to our emotional bank account, and will reap the benefits when we least expect them.
- *Equilibrium* refers to the critical need to reflect frequently on our actions and thoughts, so that we can remain in touch with our authentic core, and detect early on when negative influences appear on the mental horizon. Inclusive leaders are well aware that regular reflection can bring the need for actions to light that might have otherwise been overlooked.
- *Neuroticism* may initially sound like a quality we want to avoid, but when considering it more deeply, there is a reason why it is considered an intrinsic part of the big five personality traits, along with openness to experience, conscientiousness, extraversion, and agreeableness. While too much neuroticism can lead to emotional instability, it is also critical to keep us on our toes in quick thinking, responsiveness, and dynamic performance, all of which are inevitable qualities of today's leaders.
- Eagerness is also important for leaders to nurture as a wakeful skill, as it triggers enthusiasm to want to do the right thing, to set new trends, to assist others in getting ahead, and to understand the larger scope of any decision to be made.
- Deliberation is a quality that oftentimes delineates the end of a cycle of actions and sets the tone for a new one. Through deliberation we learn important lessons from the people and things we encounter. Deliberation is a powerful tool in helping us to change our lives.

Inclusive leaders need to be and stay awakened if they want to do well, which means they will have to be authentic, wakeful, agile, kind, even (equilibrium), neurotic, eager, and deliberate (Marques, 2018).

Wakefulness could be explained in a variety of ways, and the one used in this chapter is the Noble Eightfold Path, which entails an amalgamation of eight simultaneous considerations toward living and working in the most spiritually sound way. The Noble Eightfold Path is, in fact, a segment of a larger concept, "the Four Noble Truths," which is considered one of the foundational tenets in Buddhist psychology. The Four Noble Truths consist of the following insights:

1. Suffering exists (the First Noble Truth). Bercholz and Kohn (1993) clarify that birth, aging, sickness, death, sorrow and lamentation, pain, grief and despair, association with the loathed, disassociation from the loved, and not getting what one wants are all manifestations of suffering.
2. Suffering has a cause (the Second Noble Truth). Rahula (1959) explains that it is the thirst, desire, greed, or craving that manifests itself in various ways and gives rise to all forms of suffering and the continuity of beings.

3. Suffering can be ended (the Third Noble Truth). Rahula (1959) clarifies that we can only eliminate suffering completely when we eliminate its main root, which is the thirst that was described in the Second Noble Truth.
4. The ending of suffering happens through the Noble Eightfold Path (the Fourth Noble Truth).

The Noble Eightfold Path brings together the efforts of right understanding, right view, right intention, right speech, right action, right livelihood, right effort, right mindfulness, and right concentration (see Figure 1.1).

Thich Nhat Hanh (1998), one of the most revered Buddhist monks in the world, explains the elements on the Noble Eightfold Path in a very illuminating way. He perceives right view as a deep understanding of the Four Noble Truths; right thought as a means to improve right view; right speech as a manifestation of right thought; and right action as a consequence of right view, right thought, and right speech, as well as the path toward right livelihood. Thich further evaluates right effort to be the energy that helps us walk on the Noble Eightfold Path. He states, "Our practice should be intelligent, based on Right Understanding of the teaching. It is not because we practice hard that we can say we are practicing Right Diligence" (p. 99). Thich considers right mindfulness to be the heart of the Buddha's teachings. He clarifies, "When we are mindful, our thinking is Right Thinking, our speech is Right Speech, and so on. Right Mindfulness is the energy that brings us back to the present moment" (p. 64). Finally explaining step eight on the Eightfold Path, right concentration, Thich

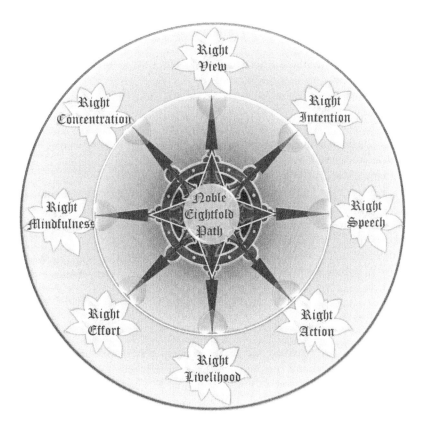

Figure 1.1 The Noble Eightfold Path

affirms, "The practice of Right Concentration is to cultivate a mind that is one-pointed" (p. 105). The earlier brief explanation may have also underscored the interdependency of all the elements of the Noble Eightfold Path: there is no right intention without right view; there is no right speech without right intention; there is no right action without right speech, etc. Furthering Thich's review of the eight elements on the path, we could add the following:

- Maintaining a right view of anything means to do away with negativity, mean-spiritedness, spitefulness, and prejudice. It basically means that we have to strive for a broader view, void of historically instilled blinders. This is not as easy as one would think, since we all carry certain prejudices in us, instilled by our upbringing, our culture, our friends, our beliefs, or other sources.
- Right intention, which is sometimes also referred to as "right thinking" or "right thought," entails that we have to focus consciously on our actions and the thoughts that lead to them. Thus, we have to refrain from making decisions that are based on questionable motives. Right intention can be challenging, because there will always be factors that steer us in different ways, causing us to overlook or forget our real motives.
- Engaging in right speech means that we should deliberately refrain from saying things that have negative effects on others. It also means that we should remain cautious with spreading news of which we are unsure, or of which the contents can be devastating to some. Right speech therefore also means refraining from lying, harshness, backbiting, and useless talk.
- Right action requires a careful examination of our behavior. It encompasses the protection of life and the preservation of the well-being of all living creatures in the broadest sense possible. In Buddhist circles, right action consists of three main considerations: no killing, no stealing, and no sexual misconduct.
- Right livelihood is about the way in which we earn our living. It requires us to ask ourselves a number of reflective questions, such as, Is my job constructive and not harmful to others? Because there are so many facets involved, it can be difficult to be completely sure that you don't engage in wrong livelihood.
- Right effort, sometimes also listed as "right diligence," is a commendable practice, but requires a point of caution: we can direct it to constructive or destructive activities. Therefore, right effort requires that we carefully distinguish our actions, thoughts, and intentions, so that our effort remains constructive.
- When we practice right mindfulness, we also engage in right view, right intention, right speech, right action, right livelihood, right effort, and right concentration. We can achieve mindfulness in several ways. A frequently practiced way is meditation. One of the most well-known forms of meditation is Vipassana, or insight meditation.
- Right concentration has everything to do with focusing on what is important. We have to concentrate in order to be mentally present, and when we do that, we experience each moment to the fullest (Marques, 2019).

Conclusion

This chapter attempted to demonstrate the interdependency between inclusive leadership, diversity, and wakefulness. The foundational premise here is that inclusive leaders are aware of the need to apply diversity for the most important reason, which is that it's simply the morally right thing to do. They have arrived at this awareness through their wakefulness, which they have acquired through life experiences, and a set of reflective approaches that help them maintain a balanced view, and compel them to continue treading a path of value-driven actions.

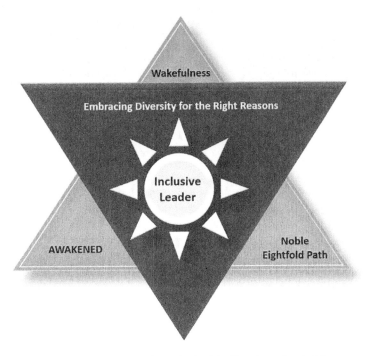

Figure 1.2 The interdependency between inclusive leadership, diversity, and wakefulness

Figure 1.2 depicts the interdependency between the three phenomena discussed in this chapter: an inclusive leader embraces all stakeholders—internal and external, thanks to his or her ongoing practice of wakefulness.

The foundational purpose of bringing these three phenomena together was to reveal their interdependency and help readers understand why they should be applied in congruence. Figure 1.2 aims to clarify this purpose. Leaders are encouraged to consider the three practices explained in this chapter on their path toward leading themselves and others.

References

Bercholz, S., & Kohn, S. C. (1993). *An introduction to the Buddha and his teachings*. New York, NY.: Barnes & Noble, Inc.

Bianchi, M. (2015). Willingness to believe and betrayal aversion: The special role of trust in art exchanges. *Journal of Cultural Economics, 39*(2), 133–151.

Diversity as a contributor to leadership effectiveness: Leadership styles to optimize employee skills and group outcomes (2016). *Strategic Direction, 32*(7), 26–28.

Ferdman, B. M. (2014). *The practice of inclusion in diverse organizations: Toward a systemic and inclusive framework*. In B. M. Ferdman & B. R. Deane (Eds.), *Diversity at work: The practice of inclusion* (pp. 3–54). Oxford: Wiley-Blackwell.

Frost, S. (2018). How diversity (that is included) can fuel innovation and engagement—and how sameness can be lethal. *Strategic HR Review, 17*(3), 119–125.

Gallegos, P.V. (2014). The work of inclusive leadership: Fostering authentic relationships, modeling courage and humility. In B. M. Ferdman & B. R. Deane (Eds.), *Diversity at work: The practice of inclusion* (pp. 177–202). Oxford: Wiley-Blackwell.

Gotsis, G., & Grimani, K. (2016). Diversity as an aspect of effective leadership: Integrating and moving forward. *Leadership & Organization Development Journal, 37*(2), 241–264.

Haesevoets, T., De Cremer, D., Schutter, L. D., McGuire, J., Yang, Y., Jian, X., & Alain, V. H. (2019). Transparency and control in email communication: The more the supervisor is put in cc the less trust is felt. *Journal of Business Ethics, [TBA]*, 1–21.

Hollander, E. P. (2009). *Inclusive leadership: The essential leader-follower relationship*. New York, NY: Routledge.

Javed, B., Sayyed Muhammad Mehdi, R. N., Abdul, K. K., Arjoon, S., & Hafiz, H. T. (2019). Impact of inclusive leadership on innovative work behavior: The role of psychological safety. *Journal of Management and Organization*, 25(1), 117–136.

Jin, M., Lee, J., & Lee, M. (2017). Does leadership matter in diversity management? Assessing the relative impact of diversity policy and inclusive leadership in the public sector. *Leadership & Organization Development Journal*, 38(2), 303–319.

Marques, J. (2008). Workplace diversity: Developing a win-win-win strategy. *Development and Learning in Organizations*, 22(5), 5–8.

Marques, J. (2018). What's new in leadership? *Human Resource Management International Digest*, 26(4), 15–18.

Marques, J. (2019). *Lead with heart in mind: Treading the noble eightfold path for mindful and sustainable practice*. New York, NY: Copernicus-Springer.

Marques, J. F. (2007). Implementing workplace diversity and values: What it means, what it brings. *Performance Improvement*, 46(9), 5–7.

Marques, J. F. (2015). Why wakeful leadership is more important now than ever. *Development and Learning in Organizations*, 29(3), 18–20.

Nembhard, I. M., & Edmondson, A. C. (2006). Making it safe: The effects of leader inclusiveness and professional status on psychological safety and improvement efforts in health care teams. *Journal of Organizational Behavior*, 27(7), 941–966.

Panicker, A., Agrawal, R. K., & Utkal, K. (2018). Inclusive workplace and organizational citizenship behavior. *Equality, Diversity and Inclusion: An International Journal*, 37(6), 530–550.

Parris, D. L., Dapko, J. L., Arnold, R. W., & Arnold, D. (2016). Exploring transparency: A new framework for responsible business management. *Management Decision*, 54(1), 222–247.

Rahula, W. (1959). *What the Buddha taught*. New York, NY: Grove Press.

Thich Nhat Hanh. (1998). *The heart of the Buddha's teaching: Transforming suffering into peace, joy, and liberation*. New York, NY: Broadway Books.

Yang, Y. (2018). Is transparency a double-edged sword in citizen satisfaction with public service? Evidence from China's public healthcare. *Journal of Service Theory and Practice*, 28(4), 484–506.

Ye, Q., Wang, D., & Li, X. (2018). Promoting employees' learning from errors by inclusive leadership: Do positive mood and gender matter? *Baltic Journal of Management*, 13(1), 125–142.

2

WHAT PEPPER CAN'T DO (AND WHY WE SHOULD CARE)

Ginger Grant and Cheryl De Ciantis

Introduction

Imagine this: you are on your daily run, equipped with the minute insertable device you have chosen to wear under your skin that monitors your vital signs moment to moment. It detects that your system is low on potassium. In response, it transmits an order to a 3D printer that loads a small package with a sufficient quantity of gummy bears—cherry flavored, which is your favorite—and it is delivered to you via a drone. You can eat them to return your system to chemical balance. This likely does not sound to most like something that will happen too far into the future, but some of you will know that in Singapore, this is a reality, right now (Mezher, 2018).

Digital technologies have fundamentally changed the game. AI will change everything. The changes in economies, work and employment are already producing a radically different landscape, one that challenges every aspect of society at large and daily life for every one of us. We have already experienced the massive shrinkage of blue-collar jobs replaced by robotics. High-investment careers such as medicine have grown as an employment field. However, consider that experts in robotics in service industries surveyed for a 2015 report by the World Economic Forum (2015) defined one among many specific tipping points expected by 2021: the first robotic pharmacist in the US (p. 23). Another significant expected shift: "The first Artificial Intelligence (AI) machine on a corporate board of directors," as soon as 2026 (p. 21).

In the face of massive change, what is the role of leadership, in real terms? How do we educate and train students, teachers, managers and decision makers to be leaders in a technological environment that changes with each day's news cycle? What is the role of policy and governance, both corporately and politically? What are the implications for species survival given the pressures of rapid climate change? We have to think differently, expand our mindsets and keep expanding them. What have been dismissed as "soft" skills are in fact core skills and have been since we've been human, and before. Primates are social animals, and a combination of recognized hierarchies and modes of cooperation have been key to resource finding and distribution which promote species survival and flourishing (Small, 2008). We are a 'successful' species, but have been so only up to a point in time. We now find ourselves in radical danger of having created the conditions for our own effacement from the planet, causing the imminent extinction of over a million species that support our mutual existence in a critically vital web of vital interconnections (UN Report, 2019).

Both the dire probabilities and the hopeful possibilities require of us adaptability, critical thinking and initiative. They require education in basic literacies (verbal as well as numerate), clear communication, willingness and ability to collaborate and openness to cultural diversities of all kinds (Wagner, 2010). Organizations are increasingly asking for inclusivity, being all of these things in the new employment generation. And they have been asking for a while. In a 2003 TED talk, creativity expert Ken Robinson shocked many by saying that schools kill creativity, that we educate creativity out of our children. Almost 17 years later, we still are making the same mistakes. Too many schools are still focused on cramming information into kids' brains (Harari, 2018, p. 264) that is rendered potentially meaningless by the fact that "Pepper" (a popular robot developed by SoftBank Robotics) is much better at storing and retrieving information than any human will ever be. Further, once you have trained one "Pepper," you have trained thousands or more through advanced networking capability and cloud computing.

The last thing our students need is more information. Instead, they need the ability to make sense of the information being presented, to tell the difference between what is fact and what is opinion, fiction or outright disinformation and manipulation and above all, to combine raw information into insights that are actionable. In order to prepare for the world that is rapidly approaching and which we cannot predict, our current students and future leaders need to learn to 'pivot'—the ability to adapt to change and quickly. But there is more: open-minded leaders need to reprioritize ethics to the top of the list.

On July 23, 2019, the US Federal Trade Commission (FTC) announced a settlement with Facebook that imposed a 5 billion dollar fine, charging that Facebook "deceived its users and 'undermined' choices they made to protect their data." The settlement also "grants federal regulators unparalleled access to the social-networking giant's business decisions for the next two decades—allowing regulators to scrutinize the actions of Facebook's leaders, including chief executive Mark Zuckerberg, and its efforts to launch new products and services" (Romm, 2019). Facebook cofounder Chris Hughes published an op-ed in *The New York Times* in May 2019 laying out the reasons he believes Facebook's aggressive business practices have created a monopoly that should be broken up. The logic might easily apply not only to Facebook but likely to others as well and to aspects of the business practices of all four of the companies whose success has earned them their own collective acronym, FAGA—Facebook, Amazon, Google and Apple. Amazon's aim is to be the world's marketplace, and it pursues this goal relentlessly. "In Q4 of 2016, Apple registered twice the net profits" of Amazon and its cash on hand was "nearly the GDP of Denmark." "In 2016 Google earned 20 billion in profits, increased revenues 23% and lowered costs to advertisers 11% (basically killing the competition)." "The insights into consumer behavior Google gleans from over a billion queries per day makes Google the executioner of traditional brands and media" (Galloway, 2017, p. 5). And all by FAGA selling your data for a large profit, data you provided for free.

Public trouble is not new for many companies, and Facebook is by no means alone in receiving negative scrutiny from vigilant users and would-be regulators alike. Yet even in the global arena created by the internet, where everything everyone does leaves tracks, massive profit has still too often been accompanied by detachment from consequences, dissimulation and denial of responsibility for harms to consumers and constituents. Intriguingly, in the face of unpleasant and public scrutiny from US and EU legislators and regulators, amounting to outright scandal, Facebook's user engagement, counted in likes, comments and clicks on ads, grew through the first half of 2019, and the trend is expected to continue as algorithms improve the user experience (Rodriguez, 2019). Similarly, the trust we place in Google is unrivaled. When was the last time you moved off the first page and continued your search? We automatically assume that the answer we receive from our query is correct. A key question every COO strives to answer every day is, "Is it worth it?" for the dollars spent. In the 21st century, many people, notably younger ones on the cusp of making life choices, are asking, "Is it worth it?" meaning the cost to their souls.

21st-Century Competencies

In a policy document, the province of Ontario (in Canada) identifies the four most prominent competency areas taken from research that "make a measurable contribution to educational attainment,

What Pepper Can't Do

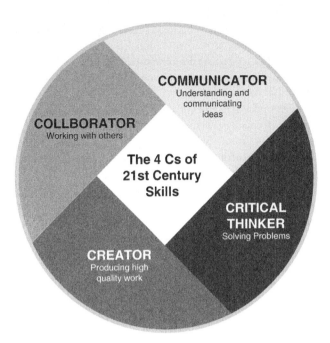

Figure 2.1 Model based on "21st Century Competencies" from The Ontario Public Service discussion document, 2016

relationships, employment, and health and well-being outcomes, and do so for all individuals, not only those in a specific trade, occupation, or walk of life" (Rychen, 2003, pp. 66–67).

The first of these competencies is Critical Thinking, which represents the ability to think logically, evaluate and redefine problem definitions, analyze data from myriad sources, frame and test hypotheses, and formulate solutions that are actionable. Second, Communication is defined not only as the ability to "communicate effectively, orally, in writing and with a variety of digital skills" but also to listen effectively. To the degree that each communication tool "has its own rhetoric," the Communication competence includes "mastering many forms of rhetoric." Third, Collaboration refers to working in teams and learning from as well as contributing to others' learning through participation, and collective sense making through co-constructing meaning. Fourth, Creativity and Innovation includes giving students "experiences with situations in which there is no known answer, where there are multiple solutions, where the tension of ambiguity is appreciated as fertile ground, and where imagination is honoured over rote knowledge" (Uptis, 2014, as cited in The Ontario Public Service, 2016, p. 13). All of these competencies have a fundamental digital literacy component which includes differing forms of digital content as well as being able to take advantage of the opportunities arising from extended reach into nonlocal spaces (The Ontario Public Service, 2016, pp. 12–13).

A first principle for developing 21st-century skills is in fact to recognize the limitations of the language researchers are using, often interchangeably: there is a critical difference between the concepts of skill and competency. They are not in fact interchangeable. Competency is a larger and more encompassing concept, involving, among other aspects, practical application of skills. "It involves the ability to meet complex demands, by drawing on and mobilizing psychosocial resources (including skills and attitudes) in a particular context" (p. 9).

Some pedagogical experts argue that schools should downplay technical skills and emphasize general-purpose life skills (Harari, 2018, p. 266). In his book *Shop Class as Soulcraft* (2010), philosopher and mechanic Matthew B. Crawford notes that fixing things the mechanic has not made requires a distancing from any and all assumptions that would blind him or her to the myriad possible causes for, say, a vintage motorcycle not to start. At the same time, the will to spend the actual time required to find the cause requires passionate drive, a very personal and intimate commitment to excellence in her or his craft—the opposite of cool-headed judgmental distance. By contrast, in a mercantile world reduced to choices between optional features of a new motorcycle, "the consumer is disburdened not only of the fabrication, but of a basic evaluative activity." "The consumer is left with a mere decision, which "takes place in a playground-safe field of options [and] the only concern it elicits is personal preference. The watchword here is easiness, as opposed to heedfulness" (p. 70). What is missing, insists Crawford, is the "handiness" described by Heidegger: "the nearest kind of association is not mere perceptual cognition, but, rather, a handling, using and taking care of things which has its own kind of knowledge" (p. 69). Google, for example, "harnesses the power of 2 billion people 24 hours per day connected by their intentions (what you want) and decisions (what you choose)" (Galloway, 2017, p. 5). But, the problem with technological advance is in actuality contrary to how we usually conceptualize it as engaging by necessity our "instrumental rationality." Rather, we have come to live in a world "that precisely does not elicit our instrumentality, the embodied kind that is original to us" (Crawford, 2010, p. 69) as sentient human beings. Instrumental decisions are increasingly withdrawn, for example, when a new owner lifts the hood of a Mercedes and sees no dipstick, because the oil flow is monitored electronically and the engine light directs the owner to a service agent.

> The effect is to preempt cultivation of embodied agency.... Children so preempted will be more well-adjusted to emerging patterns of work and consumption.... It will not strike them that there is anything amiss in the absence of a dipstick in the Mercedes.
> *(Crawford, 2010, p. 69)*

Under such conditions, can 21st-century competencies achieve more than maintenance of the status quo?

The Automated Future of Work

Two researchers from the Oxford Martin School, economist Carl Benedikt Frey and machine-learning expert Michael Osborne, have quantified the potential effect of technological innovation on unemployment, concluding in 2016 that 47% of total employment in the United States is at risk. Employment will grow in high-income cognitive and creative jobs and low-income manual occupations, but will diminish for middle-income routine and repetitive jobs (Schwab, 2016, p. 38). As companies have worked diligently to simplify jobs, that simplification makes automation more likely. Most businesses want the digital advances that automation brings, but are stuck in their old processes and systems. Our institutions, both public and private, will struggle with the advance of technology. Regulations, labor unions and slow adopters all will battle with the changes to come. As science fiction writer William Gibson once said, "The future is already here—it's just not evenly distributed." Our focus needs to shift to better preparing our workforce to work alongside intelligent machines. Low-risk jobs of the future will be those that require 21st-centurycompetencies as well as an ability to adapt continuously and learn new skills. Industry leaders need to align future workforce strategy with their innovation strategy in order to meet the needs of a rapidly evolving work environment.

Educators and to some degree employers already recognize the fundamental importance of STEM (science, technology, engineering and math) in educating for the future; "STEAM" juices up the complex by adding fundamental emphasis on the arts—humanities, language arts, dance, drama, music, visual arts, design and new media. Artist-activist and educator Sheila Pinkel points out that there is still a component missing from this formulation and that is society. "*Society* needs to be added to create a complete educational model (STEAMS) in which the social implications of science, social science and art are considered as well" (Pinkel, 2015).

We are moving in the more inclusive direction of STEAMS, albeit slowly. Human-centered design (HCD) is a process that exemplifies this kind of integrated model. While rapid advances in technology have increasingly disrupted all sectors of the economy over the last two decades, companies incorporating its principles into corporate strategy have clearly proven that HCD can increase the value of an organization over time (Grant, 2018). The concept of design is not limited to making a product aesthetically pleasing—consider that everything ever made by humans incorporates design. HCD is a creative methodology that emphasizes and celebrates the human factor (the end user, whether client or employee), in all steps of the iterative design process, involving problem identification, user experience (UX) challenges, collaboration, design research, ideation, computer-aided design, fast learning, visualization of ideas, rapid concept prototyping, scaled construction and presentation techniques and concurrent business analysis geared towards the design of new and potentially disruptive solutions. It is a triple-bottom line (social, environmental and economic) methodology to imagine future states and to bring products, services and experiences to market. With regard to the bottom line, the comparison index between HCD/design-driven companies and the S&P index from 2005 to 2014 showed that HCD/design-driven companies (including Google, IBM, Apple, Coca-Cola, Ford, Herman-Miller, IBM, Intuit, Nike and Starbucks, among others) outperformed the S&P by an astonishing 228% (Design Management Institute, 2014). Additionally, the findings of research conducted over a five-year period tracked over 300 publicly listed companies, collected over 2 million pieces of financial data and analyzed over 100,000 design activities. The results were clear. The top quarter results indicated that companies actively engaged in 'design' increased their revenues and total returns to shareholders substantially faster than their industry counterparts—32 percentage points higher revenue growth and 56 percentage points higher returns to shareholders. Companies with top-quarter index scores outperformed industry-benchmark growth by as much as two to one (Sheppard, Sarrazin, Kouyoumjian, & Dore, 2018). When done well, approaches like HCD can spark the creation of products or services that resonate more deeply with the audience, ultimately driving engagement and growth. It leads to better products that solve real-world problems, and when applied as a business-wide framework creates more sustainable businesses that are in touch with their customers and with their employees. As machines can take on more repeatable tasks, the demand for human touch will grow.

The numbers cited previously are deeply seductive. Let's *pivot* here and take a different view for a moment. Critics who have raised questions about HCD point out that generations of highly successful technologies such as automobiles have required that people adapt to technology in life-changing ways, not the other way around. Further, what is the limit to the human touch factor? Author Don Norman reminds us that the more something is tailored for the particular likes, dislikes, skills and needs of a particular target population, the less likely it will be appropriate for others. In the case of medical uses, where intimate 'human touch' in design can target unique pathologies and save lives, this factor is eminently desirable (and managing its costs in itself has promise as a growth industry). By contrast, for example, software has generally become "more complex and less understandable with each revision" (Norman, 2005, p. 17). HCD, when focused on specific end-user desiderata, does not necessarily guarantee systemic thinking with regard to activity sets as holistic and deeply interrelated, which needs to be the mindset of design teams at every stage of the process. It can also be argued that very successful and game-changing technologies in the past have ignored the preferences of the individual user and instead required that users adopt and adapt to gain its indisputable benefits. Further, how is human touch data generated and collected for design purposes? Companies rely increasingly on remote data gathering and are able to profile end-user preferences without resorting to 'human touch' at all, in the sense of putting people together in a space where real-time dialogue can occur, and reoccur. Incorporating the principles of methods like HCD into corporate strategy has proven to increase the value of an organization over time, but is the financial metric measure enough?

And, what about when self-teaching machines, such as that near-future non-human corporate board member, edge into the far more complex domains of decision-making enabled by deep machine learning? The late Stephen Hawking said in 2017, "Success in creating effective AI could be the biggest event in the history of our civilization. Or the worst" (Kharpal, 2017).

The Need for Ethics

The Western idea that science and technology are 'objective,' standing by definition outside the subjective frame of human ethics, is a very long-standing one. David Roochnik, professor of philosophy at Boston University, infers its origin in the writings of Solon (c. 600 BCE), who argued that though we can decide how we will dispose of the products of our *technê*, the ancient Greek word from which we derive 'technology,' it is *moira*, 'fate,' not human will or instrumentality, that determines the outcome. Our intentions may be for good or ill, but the outcome, intended or otherwise, lies in the hands of the gods and not in ours (Roochnik, 1996, p. 28). By the time of the dialogues of Plato (428–348 BCE) and the writings of Aristotle (384–322 BCE), objective value—the measurable quality of a thing—resides in the domain of *technê*, but ethical value, the worth of a thing in the context of what is good for human communities, resides exclusively in the disposition or intent of the possessor of technical knowledge, rather than in the technology itself or its manifested products. In other words, "guns don't kill people, people kill people." Perhaps the single most memorable echo of the reverberations of this ancient schism between technology and the impacts of it application is in the words recalled by Robert Oppenheimer on witnessing the first nuclear explosion at the Trinity Site on July 16, 1945: "Now I am become Death, the Destroyer of worlds." Oppenheimer was quoting the god Vishnu from the *Bhagavad Gita*, spoken through the mouth of his avatar Krishna, upon revealing to the warrior Arjuna the full, cosmic compass of his divine state in the course of their dialogue on right action in the world, especially in the midst of the inescapable evils of war (Temperton, 2017). The overwhelming nature of this state has a Sanskrit name: *Viratswaroop*. It expresses the unimaginable scope of the power of gods, far beyond the reach of the human mind—very much like the specter of the first mushroom cloud and the first real intimation of its horrific destructive capacity.

Artificial intelligence is not a new idea. The writings of Homer and Hesiod (c. 8th to 10th centuries BCE) tell us the blacksmith god Hephaistos created robots: girl forge assistants made of gold, with "voice and strength" and the intelligence of living women, the bronze man Talos who patrolled King Minos's vast estates on Crete, undying golden dogs protecting the palace of King Alcinous. Hephaistos also fashioned from clay the first human of biotechnological origin: Pandora, also mythically the first woman, who was given various powerful 'gifts' by the other gods, including, notably, the ability to lie and dissimulate (De Ciantis, 2019). Fast-forward 28 centuries: artificial intelligence is already deployed in reality, often in the form of digital avatar assistants and customer service representatives, like Pepper, "the world's first social humanoid robot able to recognize faces and human emotions" (Soft Bank Robotics). Avatar versions living in digital windows and VR environments are increasingly lifelike, and their overt and subliminal behavioral affects accurately mimic natural characteristics such as dilation of the pupils as an expression of interest, driven by human behavior sets in an autopoietic learning mode. The assistant becomes both more friendly and more efficient as the interactions progress (Gell, 2019). CRISPR gene editing technology has already created potential new species, well in advance of policy and legal safety barriers. Scientific communities trust their members not to violate common standards, but Chinese scientist He Jiankui, who created the first gene-edited human babies, "did so through forgery and subterfuge, deliberately skirting the proper channels in the pursuit of personal fame," according to Chinese officials (Weisberger, 2019). Current plans by the Saudi Arabian government for the development of a new city called Neom, just beginning construction, include blanket digital surveillance and partnership with a Japanese tech conglomerate which will create "a new way of life from birth to death reaching genetic mutations to increase human strength and IQ," along with "flying cars, robot dinosaurs and a giant artificial moon" (Scheck, Jones, & Said, 2019). Isaac Asimov's Prime Directive for AI (1950), "No Robot shall do anything that hurts a human" (p. 40), has already been challenged by the 'decisions' that self-driving cars will have to make in certain accident situations: whom to sacrifice when necessary among its passengers, those in other vehicles and pedestrians, and on what bases. Supposedly value-neutral technologies are already in a position to create direct impacts on what we have persisted in thinking of as a solely human domain, the domain of values and ethics, the domain of our *choice* of one outcome over another.

Back to our runner in Singapore who is about to receive a delivery of gummy bears: if we can monitor heart rates, we can also stop them; we are already past the point of no return for certain technologies with regard to embedded values. Among others, Joy Buolamwini, MIT Media Lab Research Assistant and 'poet of code,' has spoken out on the dangers of facial recognition technologies, which are increasingly used bypolice agencies and governments, as racially biased, unable to recognize black faces (Buolamwini, 2016). "Research conducted by the National Institute of Standards and Technology (NIST) in the US tested AI software from more than 50 companies across the globe," finding that the false match rate (FMR) for black women was 10 times higher than for white women. At settings where the number one facial recognition technology company's (Idema, of France) algorithms gave an FMR of one in 10,000 for white women, the software had an FMR of one in 1,000 for black women—10 times more often. "White males ... is the demographic that usually gives the lowest FMR." In 2019, MIT researchers announced a new algorithm that scans for recognition "but also evaluates the training data supplied to it" (Collins, 2019). Buolamwini has established the "Safe Face Pledge" as "an opportunity for organizations to make public commitments towards mitigating the abuse of facial analysis technology. This historic pledge prohibits lethal use of the technology, lawless police use, and requires transparency in any government use" (Safe Face Pledge, 2018).

Coder, journalist and blogger Zeynep Tufecki insists that "Machine intelligence makes human morals more important," pointing to current use of AI in business such as informing hiring decisions. In a TED talk, she recounts a too-brief conversation with an unnamed high-level tech executive about bias encoded in the 'black box' of hiring applications that her female interlocutor abruptly ended by turning on her heel, saying, "I don't want to hear another word about this" (Tufecki, 2016). If artificial intelligence is not new, what is also not new are our persistent biases and our persistent blindness to them. Our ingrained cultural assumptions persist, and thus our biases persist as well, the true 'ghost in the machine.'

Companies seeking to develop products and services with AI components need to build trust in their transparency, accuracy and reliability, "yet some machine-learning models that underlie AI applications qualify as black boxes, meaning we can't always understand exactly how a given algorithm has decided what action to take" (Rao & Golbin, 2018). When a mortgage application is processed, or a hiring decision is made, or a medical diagnosis is obtained using AI, it may also be hard for consumers to forget that racial discrimination and medical mistakes have been widespread and perennial. It not only becomes imperative for companies to open the black box, but also to establish and maintain transparency with regard to the qualifications, rationale for judgments and the ethics of the human contributors to the underlying assumptions. Both Tufecki and Buolamwini assert the necessity of auditing code in artificial intelligence applications, which currently fall outside any regulatory oversight. Worry about the security of US elections in 2020, based on sure intelligence that the 2016 elections were interfered with, largely through context-effaced disinformation disseminated via Facebook using false accounts, has not yet resulted in any legislation aimed at protecting the ballot box. This is the case even though comprehensive Russian hacking interference in the 2016 national elections has been well-documented and publicized, and as US federal prosecutor Robert Mueller insisted in his testimony before the US Congress, interference aimed at the 2020 presidential election is happening "as we sit here" (Davis & Mazzetti, 2019).

The Value of Trust

Organizations of all kinds claim 'trust' as an institutional value. What trust really means, however, is not by nature something that can be cut in stone in a building lobby. The nature of human values is that their definitions are naturally and appropriately subject to change given the demands of context and in the course of personal development. Values 'live' within the ethos of the individual, and each person defines the same value differently (Hyatt & De Ciantis, 2014, pp. 54–55). What 'trust' really means can only be established through dialogue, both intra- and interpersonal. We all know it is easier to claim trust as a value than to actually behave in the myriad potential ways, within the widely varying interpersonal contexts, that make it reality in any given set of relationships. In the course of consulting in Silicon Valley, we have heard managers say, "Our engineers are very collaborative." So, why were we hired to solve a silo problem?

Trust, as it turns out, is necessary for collaboration to occur. And what is necessary for trust? Many more 'foundational' values have to be in place and behaviorally exhibited in order for trust to be formed and maintained. This track of values winds back to listening, not for evaluation but for comprehension; on openness to sources of information from diverse sources, which is in turn dependent on voluntary sharing of information with others (yes, "you first"); also on honesty and responsibility for due diligence with regard to the reliability of information that one shares; and trust thrives only in environments where respect is mutually expressed in ways that are understandable to the respective recipients. All of these values require the most foundational values of safety and security to be in place (Hyatt & De Ciantis, 2014, pp. 105–109). In other words, you won't be sidelined, fired or killed because of what you say. Professor Amy Edmundson of Harvard Business School defines safety in the business world "in a negative way." It means, simply that "you *won't* be humiliated" for bringing forward your idea, concern or feedback at work (Ruettimann, 2019). Diversity comes highly into play in this lineup of needed values, since all other qualifiers aside (such as gender identity, skin color, age, ethnic identity, religion), or indeed because of the sum of all other qualifiers, we each see and make meaning of things uniquely. Zeyneb Tufecki (2016) points out that what routinely goes into the 'black box' of, for example, AI-assisted vetting for hiring decisions is the (largely unconscious) determiner: "we need someone like us," with the inevitable limited horizon of understanding group-think brings us. In this sense, the old saw still applies: "garbage in, garbage out." The greatest advantage will still come from ancient wisdom—know thyself. And, we have learned, knowing oneself is a psychological precondition to acceptance of others; especially others whose life experiences and thus viewpoints and opinions differ from our own.

Phronesis

This brings us into the territory of phronesis, Aristotle's concept of social wisdom. For centuries, we in the West have retained Aristotle's three ways of knowing as discretely separated and hierarchically ranked concepts. Episteme, knowledge, derived through logic and mathematics, of the unchanging essences and forms of Reality, was, and is, esteemed as the highest and most valuable way of knowing. *Technê*, from which we derive 'technology,' is knowledge derived through interaction and manipulation of physical things. Aristotle viewed *technê* as a step removed from the ideal world (recall Plato's metaphor of the cave), and though practical, was capable at best of producing a series of poor copies of the unchanging Ideal forms, whether through art or manufacture. Phronesis, social intelligence, the knowledge obtained through interaction with other people and the body politic at large, has been least valued and most suspect in that it is subjective, and further, subject to sophistry and manipulation. In an era where it is increasingly difficult to tell fact from opinion, and charges of 'fake news' are leveled willy-nilly by the president of the US, it seems reasonable to agree with Aristotle.

But the social arena is in fact where we live, trade and prosper, or otherwise. Social scientist Bent Flyvbjerg has situated Aristotle's concept of phronesis centrally into his rationale for revitalized social and workplace practices. Flyvbjerg (2001) argues that all envisioned interventions must begin with the key questions: Where are we going? Is this desirable? and What should be done? (p. 60). These are very different questions from: How much will it cost? How much profit is there in it? Like the questions we ask when doing values work with groups, these questions require human engagement in the form of dialogue.

Our Western habits of discrete and categorical thinking have also resulted in a void in some of our best efforts at dialogue, because, as Flyvbjerg reminds us, we tend to think of power as a sort of undifferentiated mass, which tends to keep real discussions about real power off the table. Instead, we need reminding that power is ultradynamic: "not only something one appropriates, but also something one reappropriates and exercises in a constant back-and-forth movement in relations of strength, tactics, and strategies." Moreover, "power is studied with a point of departure in small questions"—looking at the details, the consequences of small, ordinary interactions—"not only, nor primarily, with a point of departure in 'big questions'" (p. 131). We need to look at not only who has power and why, but how it is used. "It is only when participants see themselves as potentially, personally powerful and capable of influencing that they may become part of an actual, informal power node or a more formal power structure. This is how things change" (De Ciantis & Grant, 2019, p. 135). Phronesis requires *experience*—lived knowledge of contexts and situations that involve ethical reflection, judgment and choice. What we call 'common sense' is learned through lived experience. That is the difference between theoretical knowledge (episteme) and practical wisdom: our actions are dictated by and tempered through our value system, our moral code. The practical and, more importantly, the ethical has been frequently overlooked by modern science. We cannot avoid context when making decisions. In our age of Industry 4.0, ethics are more important than ever.

And this is why we can understand the need to add additional questions to our phronetic dialogues:

- Who gains, and who loses?
- Through what kinds of power relations?
- What possibilities are available to change existing power relations?
- And is it desirable to do so?
- Of what kinds of power relations are those asking questions themselves a part? (Flyvbjerg, 2001, p. 131).

It can be easy to lose sight of the overall goals—or in fact to understand what the overall goals are. Are they solely for profit? Are they intended to benefit the largest number of people without undue prejudice towards others? Are those aims in conflict or harmony? In what ways? How do we go about designing the most appropriate solutions?

We are not advocating a return to the philosophies of ancient Greece, but instead to learn from the past in order to create a future that includes practical wisdom alongside our advances in technology. Perhaps the rise of movements such as conscious capitalism reflect this growing awareness that we are responsible for our creations. Incorporating questions of power makes the move towards building a bridge between our advances in science and technology and values-driven social innovation as our new public philosophy.

Radical Creativity

In his book *Radical Creativity*, Kenton S. Hyatt observes that creativity has been defined too restrictively. In fact, its single defining characteristic is that it exceeds any definitions we try to place on it. Our cognitive bias favors Cartesian, categorical thinking and our habits of 'either/or' hyper-rationality have habituated us to thinking of creativity as a measurable and somehow manageable quantity (Hyatt, 2019, p. 81). C.G. Jung recognized creativity as a human instinct (p. 57). Depth psychologist

James Hillman added, "As an instinct, the creative is a necessity of life, and the satisfaction of its needs a requirement for life (Hillman, 1976, as cited in Hyatt, 2019, p. 104). Moreover, insists Hyatt, creativity is essentially *relational*: we are, in effect, always in dialogue with three large domains independent of our egoic selves, which Hyatt terms context, medium and content. "Having a context implies we are joined to influences from historical, cultural, social, physical, geographic, linguistic, interpersonal, organizational, religious, political, socio-economical dynamics" (Hyatt, 2019, p. 192), and that these and other factors are both internal, as experiences and personal history, and external to ourselves, in society and interpersonal relationships. Medium is the how: tools, materials, and the know-how we bring to bear or acquire in the process of making; what Aristotle would term our *technê* (pp. 196–197). Content, in simple terms, is the subject matter we engage with. One of our habitual misconceptions of creativity is that we create content *ex nihilo*. We impose on creativity our chimerical notions of originality. "Created content is the result of rearrangement, of finding or developing new or different connections, of adaptation to existing conditions which might include messy, chaotic or even catastrophic conditions and realignments" (p. 203). Creativity cannot be limited to what is 'new and useful'; it is better expressed with Hyatt's concept of relationship. As neuroscientist Iain McGilchrist explains,

> the qualities of what we bring to this relationship matter a great deal and have implications: "The kind of attention we pay actually alters the world: we are, literally, partners in creation. This means we have a grave responsibility, a word that captures the reciprocal nature of the dialogue we have with whatever it is that exists apart from ourselves."
> *(McGilchrist, 2009 as cited in Hyatt, 2019, p. 164)*

We are by definition creative, and we are makers—of tools and of meaning. Aristotle in fact recognized *technê* as a powerful way of knowing: our ability to interact with matter in an instrumental way that leads to understanding. Significantly, the products of the archetypal maker gods such as Greek Hephaistos include the warrior's sword, the needle used to make garments and close wounds, the farmer's plow, and the ruler's scepter and regalia of office. It was traditionally at the smithy located at the commercial crossroads which could be said to have represented the meeting place of market segments whose purposes were often at odds and who viewed each other with suspicion and distaste, where oaths were taken on the blacksmith's anvil—a recognition that wild, human impulses can be contained, transformed, balanced and civilized through the ability to tolerate and contain the seeming contradictions we encounter as humans making our mark on the world. Not unlike Crawford's motorcycle mechanic, who needs to be both analytically detached when identifying the problem and passionately motivated to solve it.

Breakout Innovation

Joanna Levitt Cea and Jess Remington, writing in *Stanford Social Innovation Review* (2017, pp. 32–39), found five practices of breakout innovation that rest on the principle of co-creativity. They constitute a "self-evaluation tool," and we invite you to consider them in light of what has been raised in the foregoing pages. These practices emerged from observations impelled by Cea and Remington's "surprise" finding that "many of the big names in co-creation" were not actually significantly departing from the status quo, particularly when it came to generating a shift in power, voice and ownership. Cea and Remington stipulate that these practices were observed in the interactions of actors "on the fringes," able to operate "without the constraints or judgment of existing systems," and that they offer ways for to get beyond "the self-imposed limits of business as usual." They emphasize that these are not a prescriptive recipe; instead, "each of these practices is about continually striving to strike the right balance."

Practice 1: Share Power. Power is rarely shared among stakeholders beyond soliciting or mandating input. Instead, what is advocated is regular shifting of roles to ensure the widest range of perspectives. From the beginning, problem definition should be shared with involved parties and all players given access to full information about the project. An environment that "incentivizes decentralization of creative input" (p. 35) needs to be created and ownership shared, including returns.

Practice 2: Prioritize Relationships. "Co-commitment" needs to be prioritized at the outset, and agreements returned to as a "touchstone." The importance of fostering community includes cultivating bonds that outlast the project, with each participant learning by cultivating curiosity and striving for a relational worldview. Caring for everyone in the process is vital and requires the devotion of both ongoing attention and time.

Practice 3: Leverage Heterogeneity. This means creating designs that are "powerfully aligned with the needs and possibilities of the system they are addressing" (p. 34), and rapid delivery of solutions "from concept to real world implementation and wide uptake" (p. 34). Shifting power structures becomes a central driver for changing dynamics and getting a much greater number of actors into creative leadership roles.

Practice 4: Legitimize All Ways of Knowing. "It can be challenging for many people to accept that all types of knowledge are legitimate" (p. 36). Creating a safe space for new approaches is fundamental. Activities that foster mindfulness are recommended, as well as engagement in non-traditional modalities such as movement, arts, music and nature to awaken innate creativity. Value and invite "knowledge from nonformal sources" (p. 37), such as seeking advice and learning from the life experiences of others, in other words, storytelling and story-sharing. Successfully innovative groups reported the importance of seeking sources of inspiration that acknowledge "insight from a greater power" (p. 37), whether social or spiritual. We would also add: the perennial wisdom sources of myth.

Practice 5: Prototype Early and Often. "A prototype is a draft, model, or mock-up of an idea" (p. 37). It is vital to start the process by prototyping it by defining problems, identifying goals and finding the best processes to achieve them, and to reiterate prototyping at every stage of the process. All participant ideas should be viability tested before moving to the next idea, placing a positive value on the sheer work, time and energy it requires to consolidate many ideas into a robust prototype. Transparency and open discussion need to take place, "about what input was incorporated into a prototype, what didn't make it in, and why" (p. 37). Finally, encourage all participants to "let go of perfectionism" (p. 37) and contribute any and all ideas they can come up with.

Cea and Remington acknowledge that "breakout innovation is hard" (p. 37). And, success enables participants in myriad ways and builds confidence that can open the door to more paradigm-shifting the next time around. You may note if you re-read the Practices listed above, that none mentions numbers. Instead, the language is of iteration and extension, diversity, inclusion and power-sharing: the language of phronesis.

Pepper may learn quickly. We may feel that as a species, we have little time to waste, but even though we may be best at slow and iterative learning, with more neurological potential—Nobel Prize–winning biologist Gerald M. Edelman notes, "there are more possible connections in the brain than there are particles in the known universe" (Hyatt, 2019, p. 77)—we also have access to unquantifiable psychic reserves of instinctive creativity. As Joseph Campbell (1968) observed of the functions of human myth, it is paradoxically both conservative *and* creative—mythopoetic (p. 5)—and phase shifts of enormous magnitude that fundamentally change how we derive meaning from life can happen quickly. The collective network of Pepper's is autopoietic. We humans are also; and in addition, perhaps uniquely, mythopoetic. Heraclitus (540–480 BCE) said, *You cannot discover the depths of the psyche, even if you travelled every road to do so, such is the depth of its meaning.*

References

Asimov, I. (1950). Runaround. In *I, Robot*. The Isaac Asimov Collection. New York, NY: Doubleday.

Buolamwini, J. (2016, November). *How I'm fighting bias in algorithms* [Video file]. Retrieved from www.ted.com/talks/joy_buolamwini_how_i_m_fighting_bias_in_algorithms

Campbell, J. (1968). *The masks of God: Creative mythology*. New York, NY: Penguin.

Cea, J. L., & Rimington, J. (2017, Summer). Creating breakout innovation. *Stanford Social Innovation Review*, 32–39.

Collins, T. (2019, July 23). World's best facial recognition AI systems STILL struggle to tell black people apart—particularly women. *Daily Mail.com Science and Tech*. Retrieved from www.dailymail.co.uk/sciencetech/article-7275897/Worlds-best-AI-algorithms-struggle-detect-faces-black-people.html

Crawford, M. B. (2010). *Shop class as soulcraft: An inquiry into the value of work*. New York, NY: Penguin.

Davis, J. H., & Mazzetti, M. (2019, July 24). Highlights of Robert Mueller's testimony to congress. *New York Times*. Retrieved from www.nytimes.com/2019/07/24/us/politics/mueller-testimony.html

De Ciantis, C. (2019). *The return of Hephaistos: Reconstructing the fragmented mythos of the maker*. Tucson, AZ: Kairios Press.

De Ciantis, C., & Grant, G. (2019). Awakening leadership: The outer reaches of inner space. In J. Marques (Ed.), *The Routledge companion guide to management and workplace spirituality* (pp. 124–139). New York, NY: Routledge.

Design Management Institute. (2014). *Design driven companies outperform S&P by 228% over ten years*. Retrieved from www.dmi.org/blogpost/1093220/182956/Design-Driven-Companies-Outperform-S-P-by-228-Over-Ten-Years—The-DMI-Design-Value-Index?hhSearchTerms=%22design+and+value+and+index%22&terms=

Flyvbjerg, B. (2001). *Making social science matter: Why social inquiry fails and how it can succeed again*. Cambridge, UK: Cambridge University Press.

Galloway, S. (2017). *The four*. London: Penguin Random House UK.

Gell, A. (2019, July 11). Facing the future. *The Medium*, OneZero. Retrieved from https://onezero.medium.com/facing-the-future-1962abacf3b1

Grant, G. (2018). The untapped power of imagination in the workplace. In J. Neal (Ed.), *Handbook of personal and organizational transformation*. Berlin: SpringerMeteor AG.

Harari, Y. (2018). *21 lessons for the 21st century*. Toronto: Penguin Random House.

Hillman, J. (1976). *Re-visioning psychology*. New York, NY: HarperCollins Publishers.

Hughes, C. (2019, May 9). It's time to break up Facebook. Op-Ed. *New York Times*. Retrieved from www.nytimes.com/2019/05/09/opinion/sunday/chris-hughes-facebook-zuckerberg.html

Hyatt, K. (2019). *Radical creativity*. Tucson, AZ: Kairios Press.

Hyatt, K., & De Ciantis, C. (2014). *What's important: Understanding and working with values perspectives*. Tucson, AZ: Integral Publishers.

Kharpal, A. (2017, November 6). Stephen Hawking says A.I. could be "worst event in the history of our civilization." *CNBC, Tech Transformers*. Retrieved from www.cnbc.com/2017/11/06/stephen-hawking-ai-could-be-worst-event-in-civilization.html

McGilchrist, I. (2009). *The master and his emissary: The divided brain and the making of the Western world*. New Haven, CN: Yale University Press.

Mezher, M. (2018, May 22). Singapore eases registration requirements for some devices. *RAPS Regulatory Affairs Professionals Society: Regulatory Focus*. Retrieved from www.raps.org/news-and-articles/news-articles/2018/5/singapore-eases-registration-requirements-for-some

Norman, D. (2005). *Human centered design considered harmful* [PDF file]. Retrieved from www.researchgate.net/profile/Donald_Norman/publication/200086092_Human-centered_design_considered_harmful/links/0c9605208fca197c2e000000.pdf

The Ontario Public Service. (2016, Winter). *21st century competencies: Foundation document for discussion*. Phase I: Towards defining 21st century competencies for Ontario [PDF]. Retrieved from www.edugains.ca/resources21CL/About21stCentury/21CL_21stCenturyCompetencies.pdf

Pinkel, S. (2015, November 23). Stem, steam, steams. *Leonardo*, *49*(1), 2. doi:10.1162/LEON_e_01161

Rao, A., & Golbin, I. (2018, May 15). What it means to open AI's black box. *PwC, Next in Tech*. Retrieved from https://usblogs.pwc.com/emerging-technology/to-open-ai-black-box/

Rodriguez, S. (2019, July 22). Facebook user engagement keeps growing despite numerous scandals. *CNBC*. Retrieved from www.cnbc.com/2019/07/22/facebook-user-engagement-grew-through-first-half-of-2019-tools-say.html

Romm, T. (2019, July 24). U.S. government issues stunning rebuke, historic $5 billion fine against Facebook for repeated privacy violations. *The Washington Post*. Retrieved from www.washingtonpost.com/technology/2019/07/24/us-government-issues-stunning-rebuke-historic-billion-fine-against-facebook-repeated-privacy-violations/?noredirect=on&utm_term=.e9fb3ea56272

Roochnik, D. (1996). *Of art and wisdom: Plato's understanding of techne*. University Park, PA: Pennsylvania State University Press.

Ruettimann, L. (2019, March 4). *Defining psychological safety in the workplace with Professor Amy Edmondson* [Video podcast]. Retrieved from https://laurieruettimann.com/letsfixwork-49/

Rychen, D. S. (2003). Key competencies: Meeting important challenges in life. In D. S. Rychen & L. H. Sagalnik (Eds.), *Key competencies for a successful life and a well-functioning society* (pp. 63–107). Göttingen: Hogrefe & Huber Publishers.

Safe Face Pledge. (2018, December 1). *Joint project of the algorithmic justice league and the center on privacy & technology at Georgetown law*. Retrieved from www.safefacepledge.org/

Scheck, J., Jones, R., & Said, S. (2019, July 25). A Prince's $500 billion desert dream: Flying cars, robot dinosaurs and a giant artificial moon. *The Wall Street Journal*.

Schwab, K. (2016). *The fourth industrial revolution*. New York, NY: Penguin Random House.

Sheppard, B., Sarrazin, H., Kouyoumjian, G., & Dore, F. (2018, October). *The business value of design*. McKinsey Quarterly Reports. Retrieved from www.mckinsey.com/business-functions/mckinsey-design/our-insights/the-business-value-of-design

Small, M. F. (2008, November 7). How great leaders evolved. *LiveScience*. Retrieved from www.livescience.com/3018-great-leaders-evolved.html

SoftBank Robotics. Pepper. Retrieved July 20, 2019, from www.softbankrobotics.com/emea/en/pepper

Temperton, J. (2017, August 9). Now I am become death, the destroyer of worlds: The story of Oppenheimer's famous quote. *Wired*. Retrieved from www.wired.co.uk/article/manhattan-project-robert-oppenheimer

Tufecki, Z. (2016, June). *Machine intelligence makes human morals more important* [Video file]. Retrieved from www.ted.com/talks/zeynep_tufekci_machine_intelligence_makes_human_morals_more_important

UN Report. (2019, May 6). *Nature's dangerous decline 'unprecedented': Species extinction rates 'accelerating'*. Retrieved from www.un.org/sustainabledevelopment/blog/2019/05/nature-decline-unprecedented-report/

Uptis, R. (2014, November 8). Creativity: The state of the domain. *People for Education, Measuring What Matters*. Retrieved from http://peopleforeducation.ca/measuring-what-matters/domain/creativity-and-innovation/

Wagner, T. (2010). *The global achievement gap*. New York, NY: Basic Books.

Weisberger, M. (2019, January 22). Chinese scientist who created gene-edited babies lied and skirted regulations, officials say. *LiveScience*. Retrieved from www.livescience.com/64561-gene-edited-babies-scientist-defied-bans.html

World Economic Forum. (2015, September). *Deep shift: Technology tipping points and society impact*. Survey Report [PDF]. Retrieved from http://www3.weforum.org/docs/WEF_GAC15_Technological_Tipping_Points_report_2015.pdf

3

LEADING AS ONE

Inclusive Leadership Through Unity Consciousness and the Act of Oneness

Duysal Aşkun

Introduction

The world today has immense problems, ranging from physical, societal, political, economic and climatic to, finally, consciousness-related. The tip of the iceberg that represents those problems we see as climate change, terrorism, economic downfalls, massive attacks, educational shortcomings and political turmoil all have underlying mechanisms that sometimes feel invisible but remain strong and active. All of us as human beings inhabit this planet earth. As individuals, we bring what we have to this life as single personalities, then as societies and cultures. What we believe, think, feel and behave all have consequences for life on earth. Although seemingly we might be very consumed with our own individual lives and how we will overcome our individual problems, our social standing is always there. No matter what we do on a small or a larger scale, there is always a consequence. Although why and how we do things remain a little bit out of the scope of this paper, we can assume with confidence that the whys and hows also matter to a large extent.

Among nations, societies, cultures and small groups like families, there's always been a person who assumes a role that has more influence than that assumed by the rest of the group that they represent. Over centuries of human existence, this role has extended far beyond its planned course of action. The most extreme cases are represented by such legendary leaders as Alexander the Great, Augustus Caesar, Napoleon Bonaparte, Cleopatra, Jesus Christ, John F. Kennedy, Mahatma Gandhi, Joan of Arc, Hitler, Martin Luther King and many others. I'm confident that none of us would say we've never heard of any of those figures while we were growing up. Through storytelling, history class or any kind of educational program, we were introduced to these leaders in one way or the other. Although the way we might have coded their presence may differ, there's been a standard way of getting to know them, usually through their actions and the changes they have made in their societies.

That is what a leader does—they take action, and changes follow those actions. The actions may include written codes of conduct, meeting reports, starting a new constitution or conquering a new land. No matter what the changes are, they have been made possible by the influential role that the leader took at that period of time and space. As time passed, the circumstances might have changed and the outcomes might not be as valid as they once were, but the influence is there.

How does the leader create those actions? What is the underlying mechanism that we talk about today?

There is a simple psychological mechanism that might serve very well in terms of explaining it. Everyone takes action, and so does the leader. The actions are tangible and visible motions that carry energy. Their visible nature comes from the energy that lies within the actor. That energy is rooted in consciousness. But what is consciousness?

We may not yet say that consciousness lies at a specific location in the brain. Despite new scientific discoveries, it is still somewhat of a mystery. However, we can try to define it, as nowadays many researchers are working on the construct which is defined as

> the state or quality of awareness, or, of being aware of an external object or something within oneself. It has been defined variously in terms of sentience, awareness, qualia, subjectivity, the ability to experience or to feel, wakefulness, having a sense of selfhood or soul, the fact that there is something "that it is like" to "have" or "be" it, and the executive control system of the mind.
>
> *(Wikipedia: Consciousness)*

In other words, consciousness is awareness of that which happens inside.

How about those actions that stem from the level of consciousness? Meaning, what do the actions look like when there is less consciousness, more consciousness or somewhere in between? Is there still an action? Are we able to create actions even if we are less conscious?

The answer might be "Yes," as we can observe children, who are less conscious at a certain age, but can still create a course of action. Don't they? They are active from day 1, and their actions might differ as they mature over the years. As an example, in the first 3 to 5 years of life, a child may not always calculate the consequence of his/her actions and therefore might get involved in aggressive acts, without understanding the consequences of them, either for his/her own self or for the other.

As we age, we learn by experience that our actions have consequences and that we might be punished for harmful acts. However, this "way of knowing" doesn't always lead to zero aggression. In fact, the world is increasingly suffering from violent acts. Therefore, we might conclude that "knowing" in the sense of change in cognition doesn't always lead to "a positive behavior."

Similar observations can be made in the current world of business. There are many leaders with names like CEO, COO, general manager, manager and supervisor. Yet there are also many people who might get hurt, feel left out, underperform, feel demotivated or might finally decide to leave the organization because of certain leader actions. Those actions can be in the form of decisions, verbal acts or manners. However, they come into existence as a result of the "leader's level of consciousness" that determines the day-to-day maneuvers of the leader.

With many things going on, leaders may or may not be fully aware, meaning their consciousness might not have evolve to the extent that they are completely in control of their decisions, words and manners. As the world of business becomes more complex, therefore more demanding, the goals and immediate pressures might make things worse for leaders to grasp and take control of what is happening inside, outside and in between, and the calculation of some outcomes becomes even harder.

In this "state of ambivalence," leaders choose the actions that are most readily available to them, usually automatic reactions that they generates in times of stress. These automatic reactions are the ones to which we usually refer depending on our "level of consciousness." And that might be a key term that might help us define both the problem and the solution for our work life today.

Consciousness and Leadership Behavior

Kirkpatrick and Locke (1991) argued that although leadership study has moved beyond traits to behaviors and situational approaches, a shift back to a modified trait theory involving the personal qualities of leaders is occurring. Theories of who the leader is help us understand one important aspect of leadership—the character of the individual leader. These theories do not do much to predict future leaders or any kind of leader behavior. They also do not help in leadership development training. New, more operationally specific theories were needed, and theorists turned their attention to another thread, focusing on the leader's behavior.

To cope with this lack of certainty about what makes an effective leader, some researchers began to rethink leadership as something distinct from leaders and rather start to reconceptualize it as a theory of social interaction which involved follower dynamics, relationships, intrinsic and extrinsic motivation, organizational culture, organizational change and power that would help us to understand what variables were of influence in terms of the effectiveness of leaders (Fairholm & Fairholm, 2009).

Leadership Happens in Relationships

Leadership is relational. It is an interpersonal connection between the leader and the followers based on mutual needs and interests (Fairholm & Fairholm, 2009). Kouzes and Posner (1990) argued that leadership is a reciprocal relationship between those who choose to lead and those who choose to follow. Unless there is a relationship, there is no venue within which to practice leadership. It is something we experience in an interaction with the other. Leadership is a form of consciousness in which people are aware that they exist in a state of interconnectedness with all life and seek to live in a manner that nourishes and honors that relationship at all levels of actions. Jacobsen (1994) indicated that the leader's values and leadership itself are related and that leaders view the personal and group values and the secular world as inherent in each other—that is, all leadership is values driven and relationship based.

An Important Tool: Relational Consciousness

Coined by Hay and Nye in 1998, relational consciousness refers to the ability of children to perceive the world in relational terms. The consciousness here is mainly relational, existing in the intra- and the interpersonal domain. More than being simply alert and attentive, relational consciousness represents being aware of one's cognitive activity with regards to a certain context. Mainly rooted in Nye's observations with children, relational consciousness was classified usually along four dimensions, between the self and the God, the self and other people, the self and the world, and finally the children's consciousness of a relationship with their own selves (Hay, 2010).

Although this concept has been discovered through studies with children, as I mentioned in the beginning of this chapter, consciousness is something that might not change according to age; in fact, there are studies that demonstrate that some people can become even more "egocentric" as they age (McDonald & Stuart-Hamilton, 2003; Salthouse, 1991; Desrocher & Smith, 1998). And how to cultivate more consciousness so as to include the other in one's world remains an important topic to explore and research. As no two people perceive and understand the world in the same way, it becomes a mystery how to reconcile those cognitions to come up with positive outcomes, as is the case of organizations with a positive climate, positive conflict resolution, effective and productive teamwork, positive leader-member interactions, citizenship behaviors, etc.

In line with our topic here, the leader and the follower form a dyad in which they share a space, where they might have problems stemming from different perceptions, understandings and behaviors that might lead to negative outcomes. Here, the space that they create might be large or small, accessible or inaccessible, easy to enter or not so easy. I call this space the "area of interpersonal consciousness" which might serve for both, for one only or for no one.

What Is a Consciousness Gap?

When two individuals interact, each chooses a way of communication or an action that reflects the level of consciousness one possesses. And in between those two individuals, *an area of interpersonal consciousness* is formed. Each person in the dyad has access to that area and an understanding of it. Having more access reflects one's level of interpersonal consciousness that involves:

- Awareness of the possible effects of one's actions/words
- Understanding and a sensitivity towards the other's feelings and cognitions
- A felt need or an interest to better understand what the other is really feeling/thinking

A consciousness gap forms and unfortunately widens when:

- Personal awareness does not expand (expanding self) towards a more interpersonal consciousness
- A personal need/interest/problem gets in the way of mutual fulfillment and an experience of interpersonal consciousness
- A selfish orientation that stems from fear, anxiety or a desire for getting more of each interaction that leads the individual to pull more of him- or herself towards his/her own self (contracting self)

What Are Some of the End Results of the Consciousness Gap?

Unfortunately, experiencing a consciousness gap is common in organizations because of the following end results experienced:

- Reported feelings of being hurt, misunderstood and resentful after certain actions/words are expressed by the other party (coworker, manager, client, etc.)
- Demotivation related to certain types of mistreatment by a manager or a related party
- Increased mobbing rates reported or unreported
- Decisions made about leaving the organization, in other words, increasing turnover rates
- Break-up of teamwork because of increased conflicts
- Escalating dysfunctional conflict between several work dyads

If we depict this as a series of figures:

Figure 3.1 Area of interpersonal consciousness

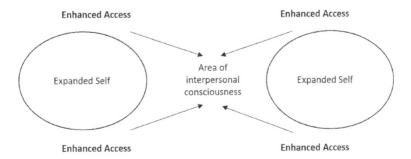

Figure 3.2 Expanded self

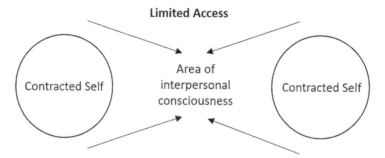

Figure 3.3 Contracted self

Limited Access

Depending on the expansiveness of the self, which is enabled through the level and type of consciousness, the area between the two individuals either becomes a "oneness zone" or a "war zone.". Here, the important thing is to understand how to use some tools to enhance that level of understanding; hence, how to reduce the gap in consciousness between the two.

Using Awareness as a Tool

Being aware, both internally and externally, is an important tool to consider. Awareness, if implemented in the right way and at the right time, can be a crucial tool to enhance our consciousness level and type. Here a popular term, mindfulness, comes into the picture with certain definitions, rules and practices that follow. Representing nonjudgmental awareness of the present moment and what it all brings (Brown & Ryan, 2003), mindfulness, even with all the criticisms associated with its highly popularized notion without any guarantee for positive outcomes, especially at the level of employee well-being and life standards (Purser, 2019: McMindfulness), could still be considered a viable tool for enhancing personal awareness. However, mindfulness alone, without the necessary awareness work carried out at the cognitive (mind), emotional (soul) and behavioral (body) levels, would not be an adequate tool, as enhancing one's consciousness needs awareness work at all levels of being, which involves all parts: mind, body and soul. As much as possible, all need to be in sync to benefit from the process of awareness in any part.

The Individual as One

"The individual," coming from the Latin root "*individuum*," means indivisible, united, integrated, whole and actually One. Oneness is not the same thing as sameness, as sameness implies "no difference between the parts of a whole." As Atkinson (2011, p. 3) points out, "Unity in diversity is not just a slogan or buzz phrase. It is a way of explaining the principle of humanity's oneness with itself and the entire creation." As has already been put forward many times, the individual is composed of body, mind and soul. And the well-being associated with the individual is reflected in connection between those three parts, which should be working in harmony with each other without any energy leakage from any part.

It is hard to be a human. Because we are born with our flesh, it naturally reminds us of our mortality and the fact that we are separate from others. This constantly leaves us with the separate body-related consciousness that has needs on a daily and hourly basis. It is our body that needs to be fed, needs to go to bed and needs to feel good all the time. It sometimes may function so independently that we may forget what our soul yearns for. The needs of the soul can in fact be quite different. Instead of bodily needs, the soul may want to go to places, to experience different things with different people. Instead of the security of a job, the soul may want to do whatever it wants at that moment or place. The soul has a complete need to be free, whereas the body by nature is trapped in the here and now, in this house, city or country.

Where does mind fit in this picture? Between the needs of the body and soul, the mind, if it is healthy and functional, tries to find the common solution and the middle ground. However, if the individual loses access to either body or soul or both, the mind starts to dominate. It creates enormous amounts of unnecessary thought, worry, duty, needs and all sorts of dysfunctional things. Because of its busy nature, the mind usually stays in the moment for only very short intervals, and goes to the past or future. The mind's way of going to the past manifests as recurrent regrets, sadness over the past and remembrances that are often negative. These involvements with the past are carried over into the future as worries, fears and all different sorts of anxieties of what might happen next (expectation that the past may repeat).

However, if the individual manages to access both the body and soul, his or her mind has a chance to function in the present, working out many solutions related to needs, desires, visions and dreams. And this leads to being able to receive gifts, untie knots, solve many issues and take a different perspective related to problems in life.

Having or Not Having Access to Body and Soul

How does an individual achieve having access to both body- and soul-related consciousness? For example, how do you know whether you need to rest or work at a given time and place? How do you know whether it is now time to leave your current job and move on to a different one? How do you know when it is time to end this relationship/worry/thought/dysfunctional pattern of being? How can you manage stress regarding your busy workload? Where does it all fit in?

As listed earlier, these types of problems can be resolved only if the individual has access to body and soul with the help of momentary awareness, now usually called mindfulness. As the term itself implies, mindfulness has been widely researched in the literature, with many studies exploring the concept from both theoretical and practical perspectives. There have been findings related to mindfulness training, meditations as a tool for mindfulness, mindfulness as a state of mind, as a skill of staying in the moment, etc. Brown, Ryan, and Creswell (2007) have defined mindfulness as being rooted in the fundamental activities of consciousness: attention and awareness. Mindfulness was also associated with flexibility, being as actively engaged with the observed experience. In short, mindfulness is noticing what is present, including noticing that one is no longer present. Recognizing that one is not being attentive and aware is itself considered to be an indication of mindfulness, which can be considered a quality of consciousness.

This means that with the help of consciousness, you can see the current desirous states of the body and the soul, which have special ways/styles of communicating with the individual.

Conversely, when you do not have access to any of them, such as to the soul, you may feel one or more of the following:

- Life making no sense to you—frequent feelings of boredom and emptiness
- Chronic depressive mood
- No feelings of life satisfaction even with worldly achievements or considerably high income
- Dependent or shallow relationships
- Not being able to stay alone for a certain period
- Constant need for communication with others or shutting down all types of communication
- Chronic physical symptoms, and even physical dysfunction requiring constant medical care

- People complaining about you from behind, for example your family members, your subordinates
- Feelings of anger even with little daily hurdles
- No or very little motivation to work and do things

And when you do not have access to the body, these are possible:

- Prolonged or acute obesity
- Rapid weight loss
- Catching flu easily
- Few or no leisure activities
- Workaholic or type A behavior
- Constant feelings of fatigue
- Unwanted life conditions such as uncomfortably small house, noisy city or workplace and even uncomfortable bed
- Insomnia or too much need for sleep
- Acute or chronic medical conditions (any part of the body)
- Unhappiness and lack of energy for daily endeavors

Any of the preceding are possible when you lose access to body or soul. And the mind cannot do anything to help, but instead will worsen or help create these situations. As for the root of the word psychology, it comes from the Greek word "*psyche*" meaning "the reason for the soul." It is no coincidence that when people have certain psychopathologies or pathologies of any kind, they have a sense of "no purpose."

Balance the Body and Soul, Wants and Goals, Shoulds and Is's, Wishes and Fears...
"Watch out! Open your eyes; perceive the trap of the carnal self. Move on to the station of the Beloved; what better station could there be?"
Yunus Emre, Turkish Sufi Poet (by Grace Martin Smith, 1993)

With the help of awareness, the individual can be aware of all the different forces, needs, desires, wishes, goals and musts coming from different sources. And the first reaction is "surprise, not knowing what to do" which is quite normal. But sometimes the reaction might also be "fear," and when this is felt, the person can only go directly to protect oneself in the situation, nothing else. To keep one's integrity or wholeness, in other words, to keep it altogether, the individual might lose his or her mind (sanity), and this can be destructive to both oneself and others. Sometimes it is that one wish that might create the reaction. Freud talked a good deal about this. There are many writings and practical methodologies regarding one's self dealing with one's unwanted, threatening wishes. And yes, wishes can create a fear reaction inside of us, as well as a real-life horrifying situation. What is true for us can be very frightening and, thus, we might hide it, even from ourselves. Thus, awareness can create a lot of discomfort, a lot of confusion. But think of it as a necessary step to enhance your consciousness at the mind, body and soul levels. Between worries of the future and regrets and frustration from the past, you feel trapped. Let me stop at this point and tell you a story of the old man and his grandson.

One day the grandson says to his grandfather:
"Granddad, you have a long beard. I wonder something about it. During the night while at sleep, do you hide your beard underneath your sheets, or do you take your beard out?"
Granddad puzzled, gets upset with his grandson's stupid question and says:
"What is in it for you? Why do you wonder about such a thing?"

Grandson stays silent and the Grandfather forgets about it during the day. Then, at night, when the old man was happily going to sleep, remembers the conversation about the beard. He hides it and then tries to go to sleep. . . . Some moments pass. No sleep. And then he does the opposite. Moments pass. No sleep. Granddad goes back to hiding it again, time passes, and he starts counting the sheep. . . . No use.

The next day, after a night of insomnia, the first thing he does in the morning is to go to the barbershop. He has his beard shaved off completely.

(Wholey, 2016)

This is what awareness can do to us. It might come in many different forms and in such abrupt moments that we might end up with a serious change to stop our discomfort without knowing what to do with the current situation. In any case, our consciousness helps with our balance in the long run, whatever the cost is in the short run.

Moving From One-Self to the Other: The Invisible Space Between Us

A girl and a boy are suddenly in love. They are in Vienna, Austria. They talk endlessly about life, relationships and people. And during one conversation about where God may be, the girl says to the boy: "There is no one place to locate God, but if I had to locate God, I would say, it is in the space, that exists between you and me, space filled by our common effort to understand each other."

(Linklater, Krizan & Brandenstein, 1995)

Osho (2011) says, if we are neurotic, our relationships will be more neurotic, and the world neuroticism will be multiplied because of those relationships. This might be translated as "losing our self-balance leading to imbalanced relationships." As relationships are strong means to create our world, what we create with that imbalanced state would not be very attractive, but destructive. From the smallest type of organizational entity like a nuclear family to the largest one like a giant organization, company or governmental entity, it is evident that "interdependence" is the most important asset, since no one alone can accomplish a goal just by him- or herself anymore. The world is way too complicated to do things alone now.

However, when there are individual goals and accomplishments existing side by side with group goals and organizational vision, conflict inevitably occurs. Our fragile selves and our individual needs and desires sometimes interfere with our organizational goals and vision. Throughout that conflict, the following might occur:

- Chronic and unresolved interpersonal disputes
- Negative group dynamics
- Hurt feelings.
- Dysfunctional teamwork
- Nonproductive work processes
- Miscommunication
- Negative rumors
- Fear inside the organization
- Decreasing levels of individual and group motivation
- Decreasing levels of job satisfaction
- Mobbing-related issues
- Low performance levels
- Increasing turnover and turnover intentions

In the short run, these types of organizational outcomes lead to distress and uneasy feelings, negative climate inside the organization and finally, the organizational breakdown by losing market share, losing members or followers, diminishing levels of competitive power in the long run. As for interdependence to happen between individuals, groups, departments and the whole organization, the following has to be there:

- Whole individuals
- Individual and collective consciousness
- Fearless workplace
- Information and resource sharing
- Open communication and trust for the other
- Free but respectful individual expression
- Positive approach to relationships
- Showing empathy for oneself and for the others
- Listening to others with true interest and respect
- Ownership of organizational problems and tasks
- Value for both the individual and the team and none of them sacrificed for the other
- Humiliating no one
- Hurting no one
- Individual and relational honesty
- Objective performance appraisals
- Elimination of any kind of injustice and prejudice
- Harmony inside the teams/departments
- Collaboration and consensus between groups and individuals
- Citizenship behavior
- Helping/supporting behaviors
- Rewarding success and recognizing individual achievements
- Leader bringing out the best in subordinates
- Work and family life balance at all levels of the organization
- No workaholics, but a self-disciplined workforce
- Problem solving and conflict resolution approach
- Both individual and team orientation balancing each other
- Individuals working to their fullest potentials
- Working for the same vision held by all parties
- Personal and group awareness of common goals
- Acknowledgment of the interdependency between the parties
- Commitment to learning and change at all levels
- Positive approach to double loop learning

Actually, more can be added to this list, but these are some basic principles if one wants to create oneness inside an organization. As can be seen, a lot of effort needs to be spent on the part of individuals to share, communicate, reach out, help and support, co-create, evaluate, collaborate and come together with others so that the organization is healthy and functional.

Leading as One

As we follow from the unity of mind-body and soul inside the individual, it is of enormous importance to look at some leadership perspectives that define and depict that kind of unity concerning the leader as an "individual."

States of Being

Initially, Graves (1970) had talked about "states of being" or "levels of existence" that represented the power of individual values and personal perception in shaping thoughts and actions. Graves's work reflects the understanding that a certain level of existence one holds has a determining power over our values and then our actions and relationships. Operating at a certain level uses a related mindset for problem solution and a certain choice of action, especially in our relationships with other people. Another state of being would lead to acting differently, using different values and ethics that would lead to judging the appropriateness of a certain behavior.

Therefore, a leadership mindset can be conceptualized as complex levels of mental, emotional and even behavioral awareness. Here, leadership could even be described as a holarchical system (Koestler, 1970) of transcendent perspectives of social interaction based on values, vision, direction of action and, obviously, free choice.

Here, a more recent and a relevant approach to this type of leadership comes from Egel and Fry (2017), who explicitly articulated the achievement of "being-centered" leadership.

Being-Centered Leadership With a Global Mindset

As the world of work is becoming more diverse each day, the idea of "global leadership" comes to the fore even more than in the past. As we have more enhanced levels of technology and working capabilities enabled through increased levels of skill, knowledge and abilities, the management and leadership of a highly diverse and skilled workforce becomes even more fundamental than before. According to Egel and Fry (2017), global leadership requires leaders to have the specific capability of integrating the needs of diverse stakeholders while balancing the goals of economic profits, social impact and environmental sustainability, referred to as the *triple bottom line*, or *3 Ps* denoting people, planet and profit (Fry & Nisiewicz, 2013; as cited in Egel & Fry, 2017).

Here, the idea of "being-centered" leadership incorporates multiple levels of knowing and being that stems mainly from the global mindset and its core properties, which are existentialist, cognitive and behavioral (Levy, Beechler, Taylor, & Boyacigiller, 2007; as cited in Egel & Fry, 2017). In terms of its conceptualization, the cognitive component involves knowledge structures, the ability to interpret and develop, attention, sense making and conceptualization. The existentialist component represents state of mind, way of being, orientation, awareness and openness. And the behavioral component, which we focus most on here, represents the ability to adapt, curiosity, seeking opportunities and a propensity to engage. Here Egel and Fry (2017) suggest that global leaders with a global mindset must be conscious, self-aware and also self-transcendent. And in contrast, an unconscious, self-centered mindset reflects biased interpretations that would naturally lead to stereotypical behaviors towards other cultures and groups. In other words, this type of mindset would lead to "not seeing the other as is, but through one's own personal restricted lenses." This is very similar to the idea of "contracted self," which we discussed briefly earlier.

Fry and Kriger (2009) explain fives levels of knowing and being that lead to different leadership approaches. At level 5, we mainly talk about leadership that is based on leader traits and behavior that are appropriate to the context. This is the type of leadership we commonly observe today in many cultures, societies, and workplaces. At level 4, leadership is based on images and a social construction of reality. At level 3, leadership is based on the individual being conscious and self-aware moment to moment in relation to others. At level 2, there is a spiritual leadership that is based on love and service and presence in the now. At level 1, leadership is based on oneness and constant reconciliation of apparent opposites. At level 1, there is a transcendent unity that represents transcendence of all opposites and the realization of self-actualization. This level of being is very *inclusive* in that it might contain both pure emptiness and pure completeness. This type of being goes beyond all types of distinctions, even the distinction between leader and follower. Here the experience of duality (in other words, separation) is said to dissolve, and the potential of being the leader or the follower resides in each person at each moment in time. The roles could be reversed if the situation would call for it. This type of being is defined as being more aspirational rather than reflecting the current reality in organizational settings today.

Another related and inspiring leadership type comes from Fairholm and Fairholm (2009), who put forward the concept of "whole-soul" leadership.

Whole-Soul Leadership

As we are all made up of mind-body and soul, the interaction of those parts of us and operation of the self beyond the sum of those parts is imperative to the idea of "wholeness." By increased self-awareness, acceptance and related action, less fear thus a less "contracted self" would be the outcome (Aşkun, 2015). According to Fairholm and Fairholm (2009), the whole-soul leadership concept involves certain key elements below:

1. Showing concern for and integration of the whole-soul of leader and followers
2. Setting individuals free so they can grow constantly
3. Enabling individual wholeness in one's community
4. Developing an intelligent organization
5. Setting moral standards
6. Inspiring
7. Freeing followers to build communities of stewardship
8. Modeling a service orientation

These types of leaders appreciate and cherish what is happening at the moment and look for what is best in every person or situation. This is about leading not just from one's personality but also from a connected awareness. In relation to this understanding, Schaetti, Ramsey, and Watanabe (2009), in their discussion on "intercultural competencies of leaders," outline six practices for personal leadership:

- Attending to judgment
- Attending to emotion
- Attending to physical sensation
- Cultivating stillness
- Engaging ambiguity
- Aligning with vision

Here, right action represents a sense of wholeness and completion instead of ultimate or absolute truth. As the leader practices personal leadership, mindfulness and creativity require us to find that one right action according to that moment in time, which may not be so right in another moment in time. This type of choice to act in the right way is said to come with practice.

Inclusive Leadership and Oneness

As a term coined by Nembhard and Edmondson (2006), inclusive leaders are those who demonstrate openness, accessibility and availability in their interactions with their followers (Carmeli, Reiter-Palmon, & Ziv, 2010; as cited in Choi, Tran, & Kang, 2017). These reflect the leaders' care and concern for others as well as their willingness to communicate their expectations to the other party, such as followers (Choi et al., 2017). Inclusive leadership was also defined as a form of relational leadership (Carmeli et al., 2010), which means availability and willingness to listen, while paying attention to followers' needs (Choi et al., 2017).

In their discussion related to diversity management vs. diversity leadership, Asumah, Nagel, and Rosengarten (2016) argued that diversity leadership is all about redefining and rethinking problems in creative ways and taking transformational approaches to overcoming difficult dialogues while raising human consciousness to implement goals and policies to reach inclusive excellence. They stress that the leaders of diversity must walk their talk. Using the social change model, they talk about the importance of the 7 Cs of leadership: citizenship, collaboration, common purpose, controversy with civility, consciousness of self, and congruence (Komives, Wagner, & Associates, 2009; as cited in Asumah et al., 2016).

Coming to behavioral aspects of inclusive leadership, Bilimoria (2012) identified two sets of behaviors:

1. Authentically value and respect all individuals for their talents and contributions, which require leaders to behave and communicate in a way that represents authentic appreciation for diverse populations, including their skills and abilities, while being aware of their own stereotypes, biases and mental models. While appreciating all around them, they should be able to hold others accountable for any kind of disrespectful behavior. They should commit to diversity in their hiring, compensation, advancement and retention practices while maintaining a willingness to learn from diverse perspectives.
2. Actively create a high-engagement culture by encouraging the input and initiative of all employees. Leaders should constantly monitor their own behaviors, so they treat everyone and every opinion equally with respect. They should be able to cultivate a shared purpose and common vision with shared values. They should be able to create a work environment where everyone feels ok to share their viewpoints and raise their voice while feeling psychologically safe. The leaders should be able to create a fair, democratic, supportive, welcoming environment where there is transparent team decision-making and processes.

According to Bilimoria (2012), ensuring these practices will eventually help organizations transform from an exclusionary and stagnant culture, which is de-motivating and de-energizing, to an inclusive and open culture which brings out the best in people, while energizing them through encouraging collaboration and welcoming innovative approaches to problems. This way, inclusive leadership becomes the agent of an inclusive culture enriched by the diverse contributions of its members at every level of operation.

Appreciative Inquiry as an Imperative Tool for an Inclusive Organization

When we go into the root meaning of *appreciative*, it means valuing, the act of recognizing the best in people or the world around us and affirming strengths and potentials. *Inquiry* means the act of exploration and discovery, asking questions while being open to seeing new potentials and possibilities (Krahnke & Cooperrider, 2008). Cooperrider and Srivastva coined the term "appreciative inquiry" in 1987 because they were unsatisfied with relying solely on the "problem solving approach." Therefore, they replaced it with a term representing finding new ways and new methods of inquiry towards any type of organizational change that is needed (Wikipedia: Appreciative Inquiry).

Its premise rests on the infinite possibilities of the future, which connotes infinite potentials that an entity can realize. It could be a person, an organization, a department or any other. The premise is that the reality could change at any moment, depending on how you approach the issue/problem/solution. Here, the approach to time is nonlinear, as we transcend a linear understanding of time, such as that in the endless present moment. Here the power of thought as well as no-thought and stillness is being stressed, while individuality as well as interdependence are important. Dialogue, where two individuals participate with equal respect and concern for one another, replaces debate and discussion where listening is not prominent and the focus is on who wins the game. Dialogue, by definition, means common meaning and developing something without competing, which allows both parties to see the issues from both angles while they both suspend their assumptions to allow for an open exploration (Krahnke & Cooperrider, 2008).

As they discuss this important tool that serves to open the path towards inclusive and transformative organizations, Krahnke and Cooperrider (2008) also mention the *power of wholeness*, an idea standing in contrast to the world of fragmentation, which creates so much dysfunctional conflict by the endorsement of competition and is enabled through so much "disconnection from what surrounds us." Instead, exploring the inherent wholeness in all systems, including all living creatures and thus organizations themselves, would open up the opportunity for a healthier functioning in an open, accepting and inclusive environment. Here, appreciative inquiry is offered as an important tool that helps enable the collaborative capacities of a mixture of individuals across all levels and teams participating and exchanging ideas with diverse perspectives. Finally, appreciative inquiry is also defined not just as a technique or a tool but a way of being that leads us to see the world differently while acknowledging the good and the possible in everything and everyone.

Leading as One Through the Expanded Self and Oneness Behaviors

As a leading philosopher and scholar in oneness theory and hypothesis, Ivanhoe (2017) draws a picture of oneness that involves the nature of the relationship between oneself and others, including not only human beings but also all different sorts of creatures, such as animals, plants, mother earth, planets and even galaxies. The main premise of oneness hypothesis is that we are all interrelated. In other words, we are all interconnected at some level with each other. As an alternative to individualistic definitions of self, which is more of a Western conception, Ivanhoe (2017) talks about the relational nature of the self as part of the oneness hypothesis. Through enhanced connections with others, the self has the potential to lead a healthier and a happier life, and so do others. This way of positive connection with others might lead to even more care and compassion for all that is around us. This kind of connection with others cultivates and enhances an expanded sense of self, which does not see the others as separate but as related to one's own self, meaning, in oneness with the personal self.

Relatedly, in line with the oneness hypothesis and conceptualization, Aşkun and Çetin (2017), in their study that described what our acts of oneness might look like, came up with two types of behavioral tendencies in people: focus on one's self vs. consideration of the other. The first dimension reflects a tendency to behave according to one's own self-interests, needs, goals and preferences. The second reflects behaving while considering who else is also present in one's social environment. As an example, let's say a leader or a manager is trying to quickly finalize a task as he or she is missing his/her own deadline. And while having this personal goal in his/her focus, he or she may ignore a subordinate's concern about another important issue in the department. Here the manager may decide not to listen or not to respond to an urgent email, etc. Depending on his or her urgency and level of interest, he or she might even say or do things that might even harm or hurt the subordinate or colleague. Another example might be a situation where the manager is trying to plan for his/her own vacation time and might not read an email or any other kind of communication from a subordinate who might be, for example, having a family issue and would understandably like priority in terms of vacation planning. As a result of not communicating or responding, there might be related consequences for the subordinates, such as decreased motivation, feeling hurt and not valued, etc. We might think of even more examples concerning the workplace. But more important is the fact that "not considering the other" in one's social environment might lead to behaviors that might produce negative and dysfunctional outcomes.

How would a leader change a behavior or adopt a different behavior concerning others in the social environment? What would be an antecedent to this type of behavior so that it produces more positive and healthy results for the dyad, for the department and for the organization as a whole?

Path to Oneness and Inclusiveness: Unity Consciousness

Hollick (2006) described unity consciousness as the awareness of all that is. It is transcendental, in the sense that this type of consciousness goes beyond our own personal experience, knowledge and such. In unity consciousness, there is now a blurred boundary between the self and the non-self, where separate awareness of the subject and the object is no longer present. It is important to note, however, that self as an entity would not disappear here. The self, instead, is expansive (Ivanhoe, 2017) and expands towards all (Aşkun, 2019). This is like a flexible entity that has the capability of expansion and contraction, such as the universe, which is declared to be an expansive entity.

In this unity consciousness state, there is no separate me or other, but all is one. This means not only perceiving and understanding the other as one, but also treating the other as one. This translates into several skills to develop such as:

- Empathy
- Emotional intelligence
- Altruism
- Courtesy
- Active listening
- Appreciative inquiry
- Ethical approach
- Holistic approach to self and others
- Mindfulness
- Oneness behaviors

As discussed earlier, today's leadership approaches in theory and practice need to provide certain guidelines concerning how effective leadership should be best cultivated through training, coaching practices and consulting. It seems like unity consciousness, oneness behaviors, holistic and being-centered leadership and appreciative inquiry enriched with related skills could all be considered practical and tangible steps to take while not necessarily requiring a sequential approach.

Conclusion

Leadership has been and is still an important area for research and practice today. If we think about the influential role and power of leaders for shaping our future in business, in politics, in the economy and in all areas of life, we must stop and rethink what it entails and what it should encompass in more detail, albeit in a different way. In a holographic understanding of the world and the universe, each leading entity creates a ripple effect which might in fact go very far in terms of its impact, be it positive or negative. Today, many countries and societies suffer because of negative leadership behaviors and/or lack of conscious leaders. As is outlined in this chapter to some extent, conscious leadership starts from within. For leaders to enable impactful and transformational change, they should be able to change their level and type of consciousness. To be able to lead from the top level beingness state, in other words, to be able to operate and manage in transcendence, the leader has to go beyond time and space, the duality of existence, and try to perceive, understand and treat the other with unity consciousness. It is this type of existence that will change our world towards a healthier and a more positive state of being.

References

Aşkun, D. (2015). Whole soul leadership: A new approach for the world's diverse make up //Dukhovnist osobystosti: Metodologiya, teoriya i praktyka (*Spirituality of a personality: Methodology, theory and practice): Collection of research materials/materials of the VIth International Scientific and Practical Conference* "Dukhovno-kulturni tsinnosti vykhovannya lyudyny" ("Spiritual and cultural values of upbringing of the person") (pp. 203–222), Kyiv, May 27, Galyna P. Shevchenko (Ed.), *3*(66). Severodonetsk: Publishing House of the Volodymyr Dahl East Ukrainian National University.

Aşkun, D. (2019). Organizational oneness: A possible vision or an inescapable reality? In J. Marques (Ed.), *The Routledge companion to management and workplace spirituality*. New York, NY and London: Taylor & Francis Group.

Aşkun, D., & Çetin, F. (2017). How do we demonstrate oneness as a behavior: Operationalizing oneness through scale measurement. *Journal of Spirituality in Mental Health*, *19*(1), 34–60, doi:10.1080/19349637.2016.1184998

Asumah, S. N., Nagel, M., & Rosengarten, L. (2016). New trends in diversity leadership and inclusive excellence. *Wagadu: A Journal of Transnational Women's & Gender Studies*, *15*.

Atkinson, R. (2011). Toward a consciousness of oneness. *Institute of Noetic Sciences Newsletter*, *9*, 1–5.

Bilimoria, D. (2012). Inclusive leadership. *Leadership Excellence*, *29*(3), 13.

Brown, K. W., & Ryan, R. M. (2003). The benefits of being present: Mindfulness and its role in psychological well-being. *Journal of Personality and Social Psychology*, *84*(4), 822.

Brown, K. W., Ryan, R. M., & Creswell, J. D. (2007). Mindfulness: Theoretical foundations and evidence for its salutary effects. *Psychological Inquiry*, *18*(4), 211–237.

Carmeli, A., Reiter-Palmon, R., & Ziv, E. (2010). Inclusive leadership and employee involvement in creative tasks in the workplace: The mediating role of psychological safety. *Creativity Research Journal*, *22*(3), 250–260.

Choi, S. B., Tran, T. B. H., & Kang, S. W. (2017). Inclusive leadership and employee well-being: The mediating role of person-job fit. *Journal of Happiness Studies*, *18*(6), 1877–1901.

Desrocher, M., & Smith, M. L. (1998). Relative preservation of egocentric but not allocentric spatial memory in aging. *Brain and Cognition*, *37*(1), 91–93.

Egel, E., & Fry, L. W. (2017). Spiritual leadership as a model for Islamic leadership. *Public Integrity*, *19*(1), 77–95.

Fairholm M., & Fairholm, G. (2009). *Understanding leadership perspectives: Theoretical and practical approaches*. New York, NY: Springer.

Fry, L. W., & Kriger, M. (2009). Towards a theory of being-centered leadership: Multiple levels of being as context for effective leadership. *Human Relations*, *62*(11), 1667–1696.

Fry, L. W., & Nisiewicz, M. S. (2013). *Maximizing the triple bottom line through spiritual leadership*. Redwood City, CA: Stanford University Press.

Graves, C. W. (1970). Levels of existence: An open system theory of values. *Journal of Humanistic Psychology*, *10*(2), 131–155.

Hay, D. (2010). Spirituality vs. individualism: Why we should nurture relational consciousness. *International Journal of Children's Spirituality*, *5*(1), 37–48.

Hay, D., & Nye, R. (1998). *The spirit of the child*. London: HarperCollins.

Hollick, M. (2006). *The science of oneness: A worldview for the twenty-first century*. Hants, UK: John Hunt Publishing.

Ivanhoe, P. J. (2017). *Oneness: East Asian conceptions of virtue, happiness, & how we are all connected*. New York, NY: Oxford University Press.

Jacobsen, S. E. (1994). *Spirituality and transformational leadership in secular settings: A Delphi study* (Doctoral Dissertation), Seattle University.

Kirkpatrick, S. A., & Locke, E. A. (1991). Do traits matter. *Academy of Management Executive*, *5*(2), 48–60.

Koestler, A. (1970). Beyond atomism and holism—the concept of the Holon. *Perspectives in Biology and Medicine*, *13*(2), 131–154.

Komives, S. R., Wagner, W., & Associates. (2009). *Leadership for a better world: Understanding the social change model of leadership development*. San Francisco, CA: Jossey-Bass.

Kouzes, J. M., & Posner, B. Z. (1990). The credibility factor: What followers expect from their leaders. *The National Magazine of Business Fundamentals C&FM. Business Credit*, *92*(5), 24–28.

Krahnke, K., & Cooperrider, D. (2008). Appreciative inquiry: Inquiring new questions and dreaming new dreams. In L. Tischler & G. Biberman (Eds.), *Spirituality in business: Theory, practice, and future directions*. New York, NY: Palgrave Macmillan.

Levy, O., Beechler, S., Taylor, S., & Boyacigiller, N. A. (2007). What we talk about when we talk about "global mindset": Managerial cognition in multinational corporations. *Journal of International Business Studies, 38*(2), 231–258.

Linklater, R., Krizan, K., & Brandenstein, G. (1995). *Before sunrise*. New York, NY: St. Martin's Press.

McDonald, L., & Stuart-Hamilton, I. (2003). Egocentrism in older adults: Piaget's three mountains task revisited. *Educational Gerontology, 29*(5), 417–425.

Nembhard, I. M., & Edmondson, A. C. (2006). Making it safe: The effects of leader inclusiveness and professional status on psychological safety and improvement efforts in health care teams. *Journal of Organizational Behavior: The International Journal of Industrial, Occupational and Organizational Psychology and Behavior, 27*(7), 941–966.

Osho. (2011). *Living dangerously-ordinary enlightenment for extraordinary times*. London: Watkins Publishing Ltd.

Purser, R. (2019). *McMindfulness: How mindfulness became the new capitalist spirituality*. London: Repeater.

Salthouse, T. A. (1991). Mediation of adult age differences in cognition by reductions in working memory and speed of processing. *Psychological Science, 2*, 179–183.

Schaetti, B. F., Ramsey, S. J., & Watanabe, G. C. (2009). From intercultural knowledge to intercultural competence: Developing an intercultural practice. In M. A. Moodian (Ed.), *Contemporary leadership and intercultural competence: Exploring the cross-cultural dynamics within organizations* (pp. 125–138). Thousand Oaks, CA: SAGE Publications.

Smith, G. M. (1993). *The poetry of Yunus Emre, a Turkish Sufi poet* (Vol. 8). Berkeley, CA: University of California Press.

Wholey, K. (2016). *Your first step to re-create your life in oneness: Awareness*. Bloomington, IN: Balboa Press.

Wikipedia on Consciousness. Retrieved from https://en.wikipedia.org/wiki/Consciousness

Wikipedia on Appreciative Inquiry. Retrieved from https://en.wikipedia.org/wiki/Appreciative_inquiry

4
INCLUSIVE LEADERSHIP
People, Engagement, and Performance

William A. Guillory

Introduction

Inclusive leadership has been a continually evolving approach to facilitating the achievement of organizational inclusion. There are literally as many definitions of inclusion as there are organizations researching and executing it. Some organizations have a serious intent to *integrate* inclusion as an embedded part of their culture, but most fall short, primarily because of an unwillingness to seriously experience personal and organizational transformation.

At Innovations International, we have always believed that there are two key elements in the serious implementation and achievement of inclusion, *cultural transformation* and *cultural integration*. Transformation involves an "irreversible change" in the dominant individual and organizational mindset from *human superiority* to *human equality*. Integration involves the systematic process of instituting policies, practices, and procedures which create a holistic culture of inclusion. Cultural integration is not possible without personal and organizational transformation. Inclusion is an environment where:

1. *An experienced sense of equality* exists between and among *all* employees,
2. *Equitable opportunity* for success exists among *all* employees, and
3. *An integrated, evolving culture* reflects a continually changing workforce driven by the values of Generations X, Y, and next generation born after 2012.

An experienced sense of equality is an environment where *all* employees are:

1. *Wanted* for their diverse membership
2. *Valued* for the unique, creative perspective they bring
3. *Respected* as a person and for their unique cultural contribution

Equitable opportunity for success means that inclusion is an interwoven part of the culture, in terms of:

1. Mentoring, coaching, and career development
2. Visible opportunities, continuous learning, and advancement
3. Education, training, and the expectation of exceptional workplace performance

An integrated, evolving culture is the recognition that the US 2020 Generation (Gen Z) is the most diverse (45% persons of color) of the generational groups and most educated.

Therefore:

1. Technology integration is a way of life for these digital natives
2. Radically changing beliefs and expectations with respect to leadership will continue to evolve, based upon the five principles of engagement
3. A culture where inclusion evolves into *compatibility* will be essential for attracting future generations

Compatibility is an environment of mutually supportive relationships wherein *differences* are viewed as the "creative tension" necessary for breakthrough innovation of new products and services, and modes of operation on behalf of customers and performance, respectively. Compatibility evolves from and builds upon inclusion. It is the next organizational paradigm for exceptional performance. A clear understanding of the growing diverse workforce, evolving generational compositions, and the present and future cultural paradigms provides the basis for a holistic discussion of inclusive leadership.

Inclusive Leadership

Inclusive leadership is the ability and intention to facilitate the achievement of an inclusive culture—or inclusion. In this discourse, intention is confirmed as the *irreversible achievement* of cultural transformation and integration. Mastery of inclusive leadership is achieved by:

- *Exploring* one's inner self to continually acquire greater awareness, knowledge, and wisdom. (*Self-Mastery*)
- *Influencing* others in accepting and valuing differences in people, thinking, and cultures. (*Develops Others*)
- *Ensuring* a culture of equality, equitable access, and opportunity for mainstream participation and success. (*Drives Inclusion*)
- *Managing and engaging* a wide array of people, competencies, and styles for exceptional performance. (*Manages Performance*)
- *Producing* business and performance results by utilizing the full participation and contribution of all employees. (*Delivers Business Results*)

The following sequential model illustrates the competencies of inclusive leadership for leading and managing a (global), diverse, multicultural high-performance workforce in the 21st century.

Demonstrates Self-Mastery	Develops People	Drives Inclusion & Manages Performance	Delivers Business Results

This sequence covers the range from relationship-orientation (on the left side) to task-orientation (on the right side). The corresponding critical competencies to master, in terms of skillsets, include:

1. Self-Mastery—through personal exploration, introspection, and awareness.
2. Develops People—through teaching, coaching, and mentoring a diverse workforce.
3. Drives Inclusion & Manages Performance—through creating an engaging and inclusive environment.
4. Delivers Business Results—through creating a culture of creativity, innovation, and exceptional performance.

The focus of achieving inclusive leadership is on people, engagement, and performance.

People

Demographics

The first place to begin, in terms of people, is a brief discussion of those who are led, whether it involves the public, private, or academic sector. One of the most influential demographics with respect to leadership is generations. There is general agreement by most demographers and those involved in cultural transformation that the various generational categories include the following approximate time frames:

1. The Traditionalists or "Wisdom Carriers" (before 1946)
2. The Baby Boomers (1945–1964)
3. Generation X (1965–1975)
4. Generation Y or Millennials (1976–1996)
5. Generation Z or 2020 Generation (1997–2010)

Although the various time frames are variable and somewhat arbitrary, it is generally agreed that a major change in trust of political leadership began during the Generation X era. This shift was strongly influenced by the inconsistency—truth telling—of the accounts and the decisions relating to the Vietnam War (1954–1975). This mistrust further permeated the societal and corporate worlds. In corporations, millennials began to associate leadership with competency and the five principles of engagement rather than position and/or title—and correspondingly, *influence* rather than *power*.

Presently, this conception of leadership is beginning to influence *all* sectors of the corporate world. It is reflected in the present and projected 2020 workforce composition.

1. Traditionalists   2%
2. Baby Boomers   21%
3. Generation X   20%
4. Generation Y   50%
5. Generation Z   7%

It is important to note that Generations X, Y, and Z will comprise 77% of the US workforce by 2020 and are highly aligned in terms of organizational governance. In addition, many of them will have moved into highly influential leadership and management positions. Most of the millennials have also been educated in racially and ethnically mixed grammar and college school systems. The point is any leadership program designed to *influence* the emerging generations must take into account not only the cultural diversity of their composition, but also the population demographics of the constituent groups. They will undoubtedly have a significant influence over the emerging organizational culture of the coming generations.

The 2018 US population was:

1. 61.3% White, Non-Hispanic Americans
2. 17.8% Hispanic Americans
3. 13.3% African Americans
4. 3.5% Asian Americans
5. 4.1% Other

This distribution closely mirrors the 2018 US workforce. For example, the population projection for 2020 is approximately 60% white, non-Hispanic and 40% nonwhite—excluding recent immigrants who declare as white.

The most important demographics where engagement and performance involve the greatest number of people through underutilization are women, who comprise 47% of the workforce and persons of color, who will comprise 40% by 2020. These two areas, alone, represent a major challenge to creating an inclusive culture.

Culture

The US is the most ethnically and culturally diverse *developed* country on the planet. It is the "great experiment" with respect to the true integration of such a wide variety of people in learning how to compatibly live and work together. The most fundamental barriers to cultural compatibility, by sheer number of people affected, are *ethnocentrism, racism,* and *sexism.* Ethnocentrism is the comprehensive belief that one's culture and way of life is superior to all existent forms. Comprehensive, because ethnocentrism is inclusive of language, religion, values, race/ethnicity, sex, and customs. The result is not only a superior attitude relative to others and their way of life, but also a driving desire to convert others to their way of thinking and living.

Whereas true *inclusion* is, first and foremost, incorporating a process of achieving an "experienced" environment of human equality, which is followed by reinforcing policies, procedures, and behaviors for ensuring equitable opportunity—not simply mixing people together with a *presumed* hope that somehow a miracle will occur resulting in personal and organizational transformation and compatibility.

The most dominant form of ethnocentrism, globally, is Eurocentrism (Peer Advisory Groups for CEOs, 2019), particularly among former colonies derived from England and Western Europe. The most prominent examples where ethnocentrism was imposed upon the existent populations are the US, Canada, Australia, India, New Zealand, and South Africa.

Eurocentrism is practicing a worldview from a European cultural perspective. It is based upon an implied and practiced belief in the preeminence of basic European cultural values. These include:

Individualism	Standard British English
Competition	Judeo-Christian Beliefs
Dualistic Thinking	Task-Orientation
Rigid Time Orientation	Objective/Rational Thinking
Hierarchical Thinking	Control of Feelings/Emotions
Newtonian-Cartesian View	Patriarchy

In contrast, the historical values of non-Eurocentric countries include:

Group	Teamwork
Interpersonal Compatibility	Expressed Feelings/Emotions
Inclusive Viewpoints	Holistic, Context-Thinking
Empowerment Through People	People-Oriented
Relationship-Oriented	Experiential Learning
Collaboration	Flexible Time Orientation

The distribution of values of women and people of color in Eurocentric cultures is strongly inclusive of those from non-Eurocentric cultures. In spite of the global dominance of Eurocentric practices and wealth, the population of Eurocentric cultures, globally, is less than 10% of the world's population.

The crucial point of these discussions relating to culture is that today's leaders and managers must have the knowledge, experience, and skills to manage the complete spectrum of values inclusive of Eurocentric (task-oriented) and non-Eurocentric (relationship-oriented) cultures, often referred to as cultural competency. This ability is significantly more challenging for global leaders and managers who have to acclimate to radically different cultures relative to their own.

Information Technology and Generations

One of the continuing challenges for leadership in today's workplace is bridging the gap between younger and more mature workers in terms of information technology. This is a critical area that leadership must bridge in an inclusive way as we progress through the coming decade. There is little doubt that the advances in technological devices and instrumentation are essential for improved workplace functioning, such as new software programs, smart phones, social networking and media, and storage and retrieval of large databases, to name a few. Many of the advances are operated from smartphones, laptops, and desktop computers. Facility with a personal computing system is an *essential* tool for functioning in today's workplace—anytime and anyplace.

We have learned from our leadership courses that the major difficulty which maintains this divide is not employees' ability to learn to use such technology, but a *mindset* which is based upon the *fear of change*—and often transformation—of how things are done. This fear is anchored by a deeper realization that the mastery of one device is simply the "doorway" into a whole new reality of future workplace functioning at an incredible rate of speed. For example, communication using texting simply because it is popular is preferred, even if a telephone conversation is more efficient and effective in getting work done. Bridging the mindset gap will, of necessity, have to begin by establishing constructive human relationship and communication to set the new rules for the way things are done based upon efficiency and effectiveness of operation; in essence, productivity.

In our courses, we begin with establishing the experiential process of identifying barriers across generations, not only with respect to technology, but of basically working together in a constructive way. What has emerged are the major "clashpoints" across generations. These include:

1. Thinking Styles—old way *and* new of doing things
2. Communication Styles—verbal, interpersonal, *and* social networking, IT
3. Technology Integration—technology averse *and* digital natives
4. Learning Styles—classroom, interpersonal, *and* social learning, IT
5. Decision-Making—hierarchical (position) *and* democratic (consensus)
6. Management Styles—hierarchical *and* democratic
7. Workplace Etiquette—work ethic, communication, dress, personal appearance, serving customers, etc.

Notice in our descriptions we identify the conjunction "and" with the assumption that nothing is automatically thrown away. We also observe that technology integration is related to practically all of the clashpoints identified. Resolving the barriers to relationship and communication creates a process for establishing the most important criteria for exceptional performance. These criteria are simply the most *efficient use of resources, e.g., people, money, time, or technology* and the most *effective system of operation, e.g., collaboration, empowerment, or self-management*, which maximize performance and productivity. When these criteria are applied to the use of a smartphone, where a verbal exchange of five minutes can avoid 15 to 20 minutes of texting, it's obvious what should be the most productive mode of communication. I emphasize here that a mindset resistant to change is irrespective of age or generation—although, as a group, there *are* generational trends with respect to age.

A few of the technological trends that must be managed for greater effectiveness include communications, virtual teams, analytical skills, and presentation formats. Speed of communications and information dissemination is one of the essential factors for productive business operation and is made possible through technology integration. The most important point to be made in this section is that *people* are the most important factor in technology integration. That is, until robotics and artificial intelligence begin to comprehensively replace them, which will hopefully be in primarily human-directed functions.

Engagement

Performance-Oriented Inclusion Survey Analysis

Innovations International has been conducting performance-oriented cultural surveys for more than 25 years. A few of our clients have included Kellogg, Genentech, Merck & Company, Brambles of Australia, Pricewaterhouse Coopers (Canada), NASA, and more than 150 other organizations over that 25-year period. When engagement began to emerge, we decided to reexamine our most recent surveys based upon this high-employee involvement initiative, which we noticed was very similar to the basics of empowerment. We had written a very popular book on that subject in 1996—*Empowerment for High-Performing Organization* (Guillory & Galindo, 1996).

Instead of focusing mainly on the survey questions, we decided to closely examine the more than 5,000 comments, accumulated for each of the questions on a survey, as well as two open-ended questions, by demographic age breakdown. More specifically, we decided to focus on the millennials because we believed that their comments and expectations were the forerunner of today's emerging workplace culture; particularly since their workforce composition, at that time, was projected to be 50% by 2020 (Meister & Willyerd, 2010). As such, it was expected, and presently confirmed, that their "imprint" would strongly influence present workplace trends.

As we began our analysis, we noticed that most of the comments fell into five major categories having the following themes:

1. Performance of work, with the least oversight and management
2. Extensive involvement of employees in workplace governance
3. Open relationships and communication
4. Work which creates passion, creativity, and meaning
5. An engaging and inclusive environment

We assumed—like the discovery of Post-it Notes (Silver & Fry, 2011) by the 3M Corporation from chemical reaction residue—the harbinger of the future workplace culture was the written comments and suggestions of the millennials. *Democracy* and *transparency* were terms they suggested throughout their written comments.

An additional component of the Innovations' analysis of the survey data is the fact that we were also able to measure organizational inclusion. We applied several demographic breakdowns to *every* question on a survey. The most popular demographics selected by most organization were race/ethnicity, sex/gender, and generations. Hence the composite overall survey result, using a Likert-type scale, in terms of strongly agree/agree for positively stated questions, is a measure of performance and the various disparities for *each* question as a function of dimension is a measure of inclusion. Thus, only *one* well-designed performance-oriented inclusion survey is able to comprehensively measure both performance and inclusion. Two self-explanatory examples are shown below.

Visible/High Profile/Leadership Opportunities

In this organization, the perception exists that women are equally competent as men.

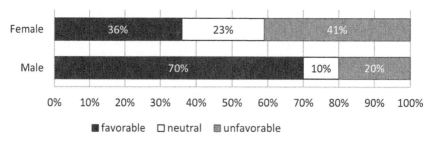

Figure 4.1 Perceptions on competencies women vs. men

Managing Performance

I receive sufficient coaching and mentoring for my career development.

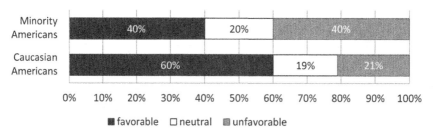

Figure 4.2 Perceptions on career development mentoring

The most important requirements of this process are *knowledge* and *experience-based questions* about the initiatives being measured—inclusion and performance in this case. In the case of inclusion, disparities are measured for every question on a survey rather than four or five questions described as an "inclusion index." The reason the latter measurement is meaningless is that inclusion must be comprehensively embedded into every aspect of organizational functioning or every question on a survey. It must be an inseparable part of the "promoted *and* practiced culture" in order to become a reality.

Defining the Principles of Engagement

It is fairly obvious from the results of the previous section that the five themes correspond to the five major principles of engagement listed below:

1. *Empowerment*—the capacity to perform, inclusive of an individual's present and potential capability.
2. *Democracy*—the proactive involvement of employees in policies, decisions, and practices that affect them and the organization's operation.
3. *Transparency*—an open, honest, and shared system of communication which engenders trust, confidence, and commitment of employees.
4. *Innovation and Corporate Responsibility*—the creation of cutting-edge processes, products, and services that *anticipate* the expectations of internal and external customers, as well as the *impact* on people and locales of operation.

5. *Inclusion*—an employee-supportive workplace environment where equitable opportunity exists for all employees to experience personal success and fully contribute to the organization's success.

It is commonly assumed, by most organizations implementing high-employee involvement initiatives, that there is a common definition of important terms such as those listed above. This assumption is not valid. Therefore, I'd like to clearly define three of the terms which comprise the engagement principles as suggested by the millennial comments: empowerment, democracy, and transparency.

Empowerment is the capacity to perform. It is not the act of delegation. An individual is not empowered because he or she "showed up" or "declares it to be so." Empowerment, as a noun, is performance-oriented. As such, delegation or to empower (as a verb) someone is granted in proportion to an evaluation of his or her competency, demonstrated performance, and potential. Two measurements of performance are the present "ability" one demonstrates on a given project and the "capability" one displays at full potential. And finally, it is *not* possible to empower or enable someone with competence. Competence is acquired by an experiential learning process resulting in expanded performance potential.

Democracy is the proactive involvement of employees in the assignment of work projects and the degree of unmanaged operation. Thus, it entails establishing a balance between independence and interdependence in team assignments as well as agreed-upon coaching for assignments which exceed an employee's proven capability. Most challenging of this high-involvement mode of operation is the necessity for personal growth in terms of ensuring constructive interpersonal relationships. Required courses on emotional intelligence, mindfulness, and personal counseling are designed to balance task-oriented mastery with mastery of relationship-orientation.

Transparency is an open, honest, and mutually supportive system of operation which engenders trust, confidence, and commitment of employees. It is probably strongly influenced by the popularity of the various social networking sites. The effect of open communication has not only created the expectation of open relationships and decision-making processes but to some extent the necessity for professional trust. The essence of these expectations is really the establishment of open and honest channels of communication relating to promotions, advancement, and visible opportunities, particularly by employees who have been traditionally overlooked by group identity.

The principles of engagement appear to fit perfectly the stated definition by the US Merit Systems Protection Board—a federal agency established to protect an effective federal workforce free of prohibited personnel practices.

> *Engagement refers to a high level of motivation, commitment, and passion for one's work in collaboration with others.*
> —Managing for Engagement U.S. Merit Systems Protection Board

The Engagement Agreement

The Engagement Agreement is a mutual agreement between leadership and employees to create an environment where passion, innovation, and exceptional performance prevail. First and foremost, the agreement establishes the fact that conceiving and achieving engagement—as an initiative—is a joint effort involving both leadership and the workforce. It is *not* an agreement where leadership *solely* establishes an environment which is conducive and acceptable for high-employee involvement. There is a specific role for each component.

The excerpted phrase from the aforementioned engagement definition, "passion for one's work" implies the necessity for employees to discover and communicate their passion to their managers in order to actively set the process into motion. In response, managers must understand the changing nature and expectations of the younger driving generations. In truth, engagement can only be successful where there is a realization of the necessity of a mutual agreement, setting aside position, title, and presumed authority.

This agreement gives rise to the roles of leadership/management and employees, respectively, as outlined next.

The Role of Leadership/Management

1. *Empower* employees in proportion to competency, demonstrated performance, and potential.
2. *Establish*, by example, an open and honest environment for dialogue and transformation among all employees.
3. *Provide* mentoring and coaching based upon an employee's career development and workplace responsibilities.
4. *Learn* the backgrounds and professional aspirations of those you manage in order to engage their passion, creativity and innovation, and commitment.
5. *Establish* an inclusive workplace based upon a cultural measurement instrument, employee feedback, and equitable opportunity for success.

The Role of Employees/Individual Contributors

1. *Acquire* the skills and competencies necessary to be empowered based upon performance and potential.
2. *Learn* the interpersonal skills necessary to engage in challenging dialogue and feedback for professional development and success.
3. *Design and proactively implement* a career development plan inclusive of critical learning experiences.
4. *Request, design,* and *ensure* engaging work that requires creativity, innovation, and meaning.
5. *Establish inclusive relationships* among coworkers based upon trust, acceptance, and mutual support.

Performance

Performance is the final *measurable output* for which one can apply a judgment of its value. The most obvious judgment in the business world is monetary profit. (In other areas of activity, it is aesthetics, learning, and just personal satisfaction, to name a few.) The process of creating high performance in the business world might be modeled as the confluence of empowerment, inclusion, and engagement—all integrating to synergize the outcome from each contribution. What they all have in common are people who are *different* in every conceivable way: human, cultural, and systems dimensions, reflected by race, sex, and generations; language, religion, and work style; and teamwork, empowerment, and quality, respectively. That diversity is an inherent part of anything people attempt to accomplish together; it is a common ingredient of the confluent initiatives.

The *pièce de résistance*, or masterpiece, is the creative artistry of the conductor who brings together the various initiatives in a symphony of harmony resulting in inclusive leadership. It is the driving force that resolves the resistance to the harmony necessary for high or exceptional performance. The major resistances are commonly differences in human perceptions, such as resistance to *transformation* (mindset) and *change* (the way things are organized and done). Leadership's ability and intention are the key (cognitive) competencies in prevailing for success.

Workshop experience has shown that diversity and inclusion are the most challenging initiatives in this capacity. After all, diversity's official entre was in 1985, almost 35 years ago with the publication *Workforce 2000* (Johnston, 1987), and inclusion's was circa 2000. They are probably the reason that very few, if any, organizations, have transitioned from high to exceptional performance—where both monetary success *and* people's well-being have been preserved and enhanced in the process of achieving inclusion.

An overall model of high performance and its various constituents are shown next.

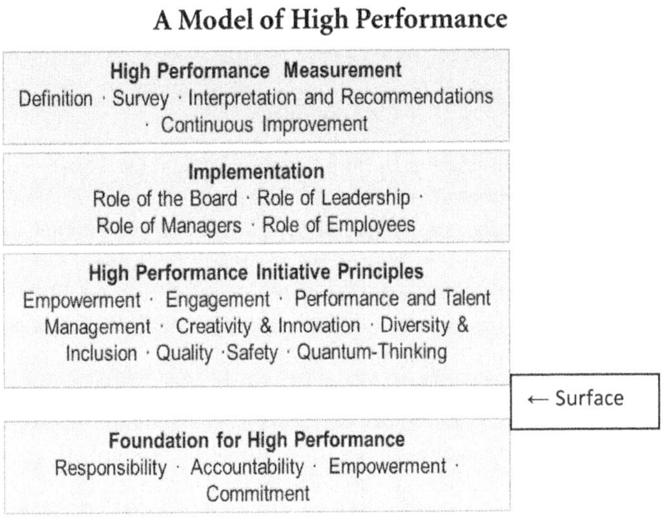

A Model of High Performance

High Performance Measurement
Definition · Survey · Interpretation and Recommendations · Continuous Improvement

Implementation
Role of the Board · Role of Leadership · Role of Managers · Role of Employees

High Performance Initiative Principles
Empowerment · Engagement · Performance and Talent Management · Creativity & Innovation · Diversity & Inclusion · Quality · Safety · Quantum-Thinking

← Surface

Foundation for High Performance
Responsibility · Accountability · Empowerment · Commitment

Figure 4.3 A model of high performance

The foundation components of this model are the basic necessities for *any* high-employee-involvement initiative and are *assumed* to exist. Most of these initiatives have never reached their potential in organizational performance because a critical mass of the foundation components have *not* been dominantly accepted by the workforce and embedded into the organization's culture—particularly a very high degree of responsibility and accountability. All four of the foundation components are cognitive predispositions programmed individually and collectively within an organization's culture.

The present challenge of inclusive leadership is transitioning from high to exceptional performance. The next organizational paradigm for exceptional performance is *compatibility*, the evolution from inclusion, as defined in the first section of this chapter. This paradigm also provides an environment for *synergism* and *synchronicity* to occur as natural components of exceptional performance. Compatibility is characterized by the following working principles of operation:

1. *Collaboration*—working with others in a mutually respectful, trusting, and supportive way.
2. *Reconciliation*—working with others to amicably resolve and synergize differences.
3. *Receptiveness*—working with others with openness, transparency, and the creative exchange of ideas.
4. *Resilience*—working with others to proactively respond to conflict, adversity, and change as learning experiences.
5. *Cohesiveness*—working with others as a connected, united, and aligned organization of One.

Synergism is the interaction or cooperation of two or more organizations or individuals (of a team) to produce a combined effect greater than the sum of their individual effects. An example is the spontaneous realization of a transcendent solution of a dichotomy, such as superior/inferior individuals, by personhood. The transcendent resolution is the *self-realization* of one's inherent equality and the simultaneous falsity of the dichotomy.

Synchronicity is the simultaneous occurrence of events which appear to have no discernable causal relationship; such as the simultaneous imagination of similar or connected thoughts or images by two different individuals, commonly in totally different locations. An example is the simultaneous discovery of a scientific proposition, such as the debate over the origin of the species between Darwin and contemporaries.

Conclusion

Leadership takes on a completely different meaning when modified by the adjective inclusive. Most of all, leadership, in the 21st century, is not simply a process of designing traditional generic skills for the presentation to a practically homogeneous group with common values, and then adding a module about diversity at the completion to acknowledge that it might have some impact on implementation. The entire conceptual framework, principles of operation, and implementation process take on a much more complex nature when differences are an integral part of every module of a leadership learning experience for a diverse, multicultural, and global workforce. An example of synergism is the design of a case study exercise where the characters are different by sex, race, culture, and work styles. Then have them organized as a team to design an implementation plan for compatibility to be integrated into their existing culture of inclusion. The resulting plan, by nature, will be inseparable from their integrated human and cognitive differences. Conclusion: *Diversity is an inherent part of the human experience.*

This chapter has shown how such differences are involved with the transition of inclusive leadership, with present emphasis on inclusion, to the next organizational paradigm of compatibility. The achievement of compatibility will require the mastery of expanded skills focused equally on relationship and task orientation. The major elements for integration include people, engagement, and performance.

The prominent relationship-oriented differences include race/ethnicity, sex/gender, culture/ethnocentrism, and a variety of other dimensions in order to effectively lead and manage today's highly diverse workforce. Leadership requires mastery of self, unconscious bias, cultural competence, mindfulness, and emotional intelligence in addition to mastery of the implementation skills associated with the five principles of engagement and compatibility.

References

Guillory, W. A., & Galindo, L. (1996). *Empowerment for high-performing organizations.* Salt Lake City, UT: Innovations Publishing.

Johnston, W. B. (1987). *Workforce 2000: Work and workers for the twenty-first century.* Washington, DC: The Hudson Institute.

Meister, J. C., & Willyerd, K. (2010). *The 2020 workplace.* New York, NY: HarperCollins Books.

Peer Advisory Groups for CEOs. (2019). *Eurocentrism.* Retrieved from https://science.jrank.org/pages/7680/Eurocentrism.html

Silver, S., & Fry, A. (2011). *Post-It note origin.* Retrieved from www.snopes.com/fact-check/sticking-with-it/

5
STAKEHOLDER ENGAGEMENT AS AN INCLUSIVE PRACTICE

Robert S. Fleming

Introduction

The various chapters in this collection are intended to challenge the reader to become both a student and practitioner of inclusive leadership. Sound leadership is recognized as a crucial factor in determining the success of any contemporary organization. This leadership must rise beyond the mere enactment of the recognized management functions of planning, organizing, directing, and controlling to skillful leadership practice that ensures success and survival of an organization.

An important point of departure in our journey is to recognize that the work of an organization is usually performed by individuals working in groups or teams on behalf of that organization. Thus the role that individuals play in organizational success cannot be overstated. It is also important to acknowledge that employees of an organization typically follow the direction that they receive from their supervisor or manager because they are required to, whereas they follow that of a leader because they want to. This illustrates the importance of an organization's managers also possessing the knowledge and skills required to function as skilled leaders, capable of nurturing followers.

Our focus in this chapter will thus be on leadership and how "inclusive leadership" can contribute to an organization's success. While when you first picked up this book, you may not have been fully familiar with the phrase "inclusive leadership," we trust that by this point you understand what is meant by inclusive leadership and are continually gaining the knowledge, skills, confidence, and will to become an inclusive leader. It is our desire that you will not merely view "inclusive leadership" as the new buzz or in-vogue word for leadership, but will fully comprehend and appreciate the power of this leadership approach when skillfully utilized in a contemporary organization.

You may be familiar with the significant difference in leadership practice and outcomes between "transactional leadership," which basically concentrates on keeping the trains running as they always have, and "transformational leadership," which focuses on taking one's organization to a new level. These two contrasted leadership approaches differ significantly in both their approach and outcomes. Managers have also been categorized in terms of their leadership style, with some managing organizational members in an authoritarian manner whereby the input of others is not valued, while others function as leaders and seek to engage others and afford them opportunities to participate and contribute in their organization's decision-making processes and success.

While many delimit their view of inclusive leadership to the role of a leader in working with the team members under his or her direction with a focus on workplace diversity and inclusion, enlightened leaders and their organizations can realize significant benefits from an expanded approach to inclusive leadership that reaches well beyond the normal bounds considered in inclusive leadership practice. We thus advocate that, rather than limiting our application and practice of inclusive leadership to only the employees of an organization, we expand our horizons and practice to the application of inclusive leadership when also working with other stakeholder groups. Organizational leaders recognize that, while organizations have numerous stakeholder groups with which they interact, there are three primary groups that are considered most important to the success and survival of an organization. These stakeholder groups are an organization's employees, its customers, and its owners. We will advance the concept that practicing inclusive leadership is valuable when interacting not only with an organization's employees, but also with its customers and owners.

Each set of these organizational stakeholders is positioned to contribute in many ways to the future success of the organization. The practice of inclusive leadership is the key to unlocking the potential ways in which all three stakeholder groups can contribute more fully to the success of an organization. In today's fast-paced and challenging world, an organization and its leaders must continually strive to gain and sustain the organization's competitive advantage. Through a genuine commitment to inclusive leadership accompanied by skillful leadership practice, an organization can position itself for present and future success.

Using "stakeholder analysis," organizational leaders can identify the various stakeholders with which their organization interacts, as well as the expectations of each group with respect to the organization. These expectations must be evaluated in terms of whether they are realistic and how they should be prioritized. An organization will want to meet and ideally exceed the reasonable expectations of stakeholders—particularly those of employees, customers, and owners. There is worth in valuing the views and potential contributions that not only our employees but also customers and owners can make.

Our pilgrimage in this chapter will begin with a discussion of this expanded view of inclusive leadership and how inclusive leadership can contribute to organizational success. It will challenge readers to commit to the practice of inclusive leadership and provide guidance on how one can prepare to serve an organization as an inclusive leader. We will next turn our attention to a discussion of the stakeholder concept and why engaging stakeholders and understanding their expectations are important in determining organizational success. Lastly, we will discuss the importance of aligning inclusive leadership practice with stakeholder expectations and how an inclusive leader can successfully engage stakeholders.

Inclusive Leadership

The genesis of inclusive leadership is the increasing diversity of our world and workplace. Astute organizations and their leaders recognize the value of workplace diversity and how a diverse cadre of workers can contribute to an organization's success in understanding, meeting, and ideally exceeding the expectations of its stakeholders. These enlightened leaders are committed to recognizing, valuing, and utilizing the talents of each and every member of their organizations through affording all employees opportunities to contribute in their unique way to the success of the organization.

The concept of inclusive leadership thus had its origin in light of the growing diversity in today's organizations and a desire to involve and engage all of an organization's employees through affording them opportunities to contribute to the success of their organization in both common and unique ways. While inclusive leadership represents a significant advancement and builds on the leadership theories and practices that preceded it, this enlightened approach to leadership is distinctive in that it is grounded on the premise that everyone has value and successful leaders will enhance their effectiveness through recognizing this value and affording organizational members opportunities to fully utilize their unique talents in support of achieving their organization's goals and mission.

Leaders of successful contemporary organizations recognize the importance of being proactive, rather than reactive, as they lead their organizations in the present and seek to position them for enhanced success in the future. The prevalence of strategic planning activities in most contemporary organizations attests to the fact that astute managers and executives recognize the importance of a proactive management and leadership approach. These leaders acknowledge the essential role that an organization's most important resource—its people—plays in determining its success, and similarly that proactive leadership practice is essential to the recruitment, motivation, empowerment, and retention of the employees necessary for an organization to excel and achieve its goals and mission.

Effective organizational leaders have many useful tools in their leadership toolbox, including those designed to enable them to motivate and empower others to commit and contribute fully to the work of their organization. Among the various leadership techniques in a seasoned leader's tool kit should be the relatively new tool of inclusive leadership. The power of this leadership approach has been demonstrated in leading an organization's employees and likewise has significant potential as a valuable tool also to engage an organization's customers and owners. While the idea of engaging other stakeholder groups through inclusive leadership may be new, successful organizations and those that lead them have long recognized the importance of engaging their customers and owners.

While inclusive leadership may actually be practiced by some enlightened leaders, it is not the customary leadership approach of others. The suggestion that inclusive leadership has value when attempting to engage employees and fully avail an organization of their talents should not be a hard sell; the notion that inclusive leadership could also serve a useful purpose in engaging an organization's customers and owners may be less apparent to some organizational leaders. While that may be a reality in some situations, every individual that has been afforded the opportunity to manage and lead their organization, regardless of the management level at which they currently serve, has a responsibility to their organization and its various stakeholders to consider how this expanded application of inclusive leadership could benefit their organization.

The successful practice of inclusive leadership is best accomplished when an organization, rather than only select managers, adopts this leadership approach. Doing so requires a change in mindset and oftentimes organizational culture. While a change in mindset may seem less than a formidable challenge, it must be recognized that realizing the full potential of the implementation of inclusive leadership necessitates that all of an organization's managers, regardless of their specific roles and responsibilities or the level of management at which they serve, fully commit to and engage in the practice of inclusive leadership. In many organizations this will represent a genuine change in an organization's culture that will often take time to be fully implemented, in that an organization's culture is neither formed nor changed overnight but rather develops over time and is influenced by an organization's members and work practices.

Creating a culture that values inclusion of employees, as well as other stakeholder groups such as customers and owners, may obviously require both individual and organizational change. This must begin with the commitment of an organization's senior management to inclusive leadership and their articulation to other organizational stakeholders why such a proactive stance is prudent and consistent with fully achieving the organization's mission. Their words must be supported by actions and behaviors that reinforce their commitment to practicing inclusive leadership and creating an inclusive culture. The actions of senior leaders demonstrate to the organization's employees and other stakeholders the organization's commitment to inclusive leadership and stakeholder engagement.

By their very nature, the individuals that comprise an organization's stakeholders—whether employees, customers, or owners—often desire to have their "voice" heard by the organization and are willing to take the time to share their ideas, thoughts, and opinions with the organization. Their engagement with an organization through participation and involvement typically contributes to them having authorship and commitment to related resulting decisions that the organization subsequently makes. Such engagement supports an organization's recruitment and retention of not only employees, but also customers and owners. It should be understood that, while inclusive leadership seeks to afford employees and other stakeholders opportunities to contribute to the success of an organization through their input, and it is imperative that organizational leaders be committed in words and practice to listening and considering their "voice"; it is those individuals charged with managing and leading an organization that are ultimately responsible for making the actual decisions, ideally with the benefit of engaged stakeholder input.

Importance of Inclusive Leadership

The concept of organizational stakeholders will be introduced later in this chapter along with a discussion of the importance of understanding and responding to stakeholder expectations. While a number of internal and external stakeholder groups will be introduced at that juncture, the focus of discussion will be on understanding, meeting, and ideally exceeding the realistic expectations of an organization's employees, customers, and owners, since these are typically considered the most important stakeholders in determining an organization's success.

While there are many measures of success that are applicable for any organization, these measures can vary based on organizational mission. Some organizations are created to yield a profit that in turn benefits the owners of an organization who have invested their resources in the organization; while others operate as nonprofits that strive to fulfill the mission for which they were established. Organizations thus may or may not have "owners" as such, with for-profit businesses operating under various legal forms where their owners are considered proprietors, partners, or stockholders. While nonprofit organizations typically do not have "owners," they usually rely on benefactors or supporters of their operations. In addition to various financial metrics intended to measure the success of an organization, effectiveness, efficiency, and productivity of both labor and capital are often utilized, as is whether the organization accomplishes its goals and attains its mission.

By definition, organizations are collections of people, typically working in groups or teams, to perform the collective work necessary to support their mission. As such, organizations rely on people as their most important resource as they seek to fulfill their mission. An organization cannot survive, succeed, and ideally realize its full potential while accomplishing its mission and goals without the necessary cadre of qualified, motivated, and empowered people. While we will refer to these individuals as "employees" from this point forward, it should be acknowledged that there are some individuals who volunteer their time in service to an organization rather than being compensated, particularly in nonprofit organizations.

As previously related, inclusive leadership had its origin in the leadership of organizations comprised of diverse groups or teams of employees. It is paramount that workplace diversity plays an instrumental role in the success of contemporary organizations and thus should be desired and valued by organizational leaders. Most individuals affiliate with an organization with a desire to make a difference in that organization. They seek to be valued and respected for the knowledge and skills that they bring to an organization. They have various expectations, and seasoned organizational leaders recognize the importance of understanding and responding to the expectations of their employees.

An integral strength of successful contemporary organizations is their ability to recruit, and more importantly retain, employees that are highly qualified, motivated, and empowered. The interaction that ideally exists between job satisfaction and job performance further illuminates the challenges inherent in personnel recruitment and retention, and the importance of motivation and empowerment. Employees realize job satisfaction when their expectations for their job and organization are realized. When this happens they tend to be more productive, which in turn continues to contribute to their satisfaction regarding the job they hold, how they are valued and treated, and their organization.

Employees need and want to feel that their talents and efforts are recognized, valued, and appreciated by their organization. This has been documented and has informed the management/leadership practices and cultures of many contemporary organizations. While many leadership approaches incorporate this reality and its role in motivating employees and consequently in the retention of employees, inclusive leadership has the potential of further motivating employees as well as empowering them. Although empowerment incorporates many recognized principles and practices including participation, involvement, motivation, and effective delegation, it further advocates that employees should be afforded opportunities and autonomy to make or contribute to certain decisions within the scope of their role and responsibilities and that they should have access to appropriate information that will enable them to make informed decisions. While this may seem to be a fairly simple addition to the aforementioned list of traditional management practice, it can truly represent the difference between motivating and empowering employees.

Just as involvement in decision-making and trusting employees to provide them with the information that they will need to enact their roles and responsibilities successfully can make the difference between simply motivating employees and empowering them, so too can inclusive leadership contribute to significant increases in employee commitment, loyalty, job satisfaction, and job performance. A hallmark of inclusive leadership is fostering an organizational culture that encourages employees to become highly motivated and empowered contributors to the success of "their" organization. This innovative and promising leadership approach seeks both solicited and unsolicited input from organizational members as organizational leaders engage in decision-making activities. An organization that is genuinely committed to practicing inclusive leadership not only welcomes the ideas of employees but should make provision to hear and listen to these "voices" in their decision-making processes.

The enhanced involvement and participation of employees that can be facilitated through the practice of inclusive leadership, while of significant merit in determining the success of an organization, could in reality be only the tip of the iceberg of the practice and benefits of inclusive leadership in today's organizations. While we have focused on employees in our discussion thus far, we must not forget the other two stakeholder groups that organizational leaders delineate in the set of three most important stakeholder groups. Inclusive leadership also has a rightful place when dealing with these additional stakeholder groups.

While we will further consider the expectations of customers and owners later in this chapter, suffice it to say that the recruitment and retention of both customers and owners is essential to the continued survival and success of any contemporary organization. Through inclusive leadership practice that involves the appropriate shift in the organizational mindset and that of its leaders, as well as a supportive, inclusive culture, an organization can similarly motivate and empower its customers and owners to continue to support the organization. This commitment to inclusivity should likewise incorporate a proactive sharing of appropriate information with customers and owners, as well as actively and genuinely soliciting their ideas through listening and valuing their "voices."

As with employees, affording both customers and owners an opportunity to be heard by an organization with which they are engaged in an exchange relationship will motivate and empower these individuals based on being afforded appropriate participation and involvement opportunities. Their resulting commitment to the organization can prove of great value as the organization navigates the often challenging waters of a dynamic business environment. The power of inclusive leadership can be fully realized through incorporating all three stakeholder groups in its practice.

The Inclusive Leader

While the successful implementation of inclusive leadership ideally emanates from an organization's senior leaders, its successful practice and attainment of its full potential results when managers throughout an organization develop the desire to commit to and practice inclusive leadership as they enact their particular roles and responsibilities within the organization. While the scope and specifics of their roles and responsibilities will vary, the active involvement of each and every member of an organization's management team comprises the requisite puzzle pieces necessary to fully realize the potential of inclusive leadership.

By this point we trust that you recognize the merit of inclusive leadership and are interested in enhancing your individual effectiveness, as well as that of those that you lead, through the skillful practice of inclusive leadership. We will thus now consider how one prepares to be an effective inclusive leader and provide some practical guidance to assist you in becoming an inclusive leader. Ideally you have the full support of a visionary senior management team that have recognized the benefits of inclusion fostered and facilitated through inclusive leadership, are committed to this shift in mindset, and are through their words and behaviors creating the necessary organizational culture to realize fully the potential that can be achieved through the practice of inclusive leadership.

Your success in becoming an effective inclusive leader must begin with an honest, realistic assessment of your current leadership style and approach. If you commonly involve others by offering them opportunities to participate through effective delegation, rather than retaining all decision-making authority, you will have a less challenging pilgrimage towards becoming an effective inclusive leader. Similarly, if your leadership approach has traditionally been transactional, in contrast to transformational, you likewise will have some challenges to overcome. The starting point in your journey must thus involve making a genuine professional commitment to gain the knowledge, skills, and attitude necessary to succeed as an inclusive leader.

You may find it necessary to change your mindset and purpose to enable others to do likewise. It is important to realize that as more managers in an organization commit to inclusive leadership practice and the organizational culture evolves accordingly, the easier it will be to practice inclusive leadership and realize its power in terms of organizational outcomes. You should also bear in mind that if this leadership approach is a new challenge for you, it may also be challenging for those with whom you interact, and they too may need time to adjust to this new leadership approach. While they will likely come to appreciate this new approach that more fully values the additional ways in which they can contribute to the success of the organization, they may need time to trust and feel comfortable if the introduction of inclusive leadership represents a new world order in their organization. Just as it may take you time to adjust to this leadership approach, so too may it take time for employees and other stakeholders of your organization to adjust.

As part of your organization's leadership team, you will want to support the development of the inclusive culture, both in your words and actions. It is imperative that you recognize that your actions and those of other organizational managers will prove instrumental in the successful fostering of the inclusive culture. All of your dealings with involved stakeholders must incorporate the honesty, integrity, and credibility that all successful relationships are built and sustained on. Courage, fortitude, and humility may also be required as you transition from your current leadership style and approach to the practice of inclusive leadership.

Transparent communication in seeking the ideas and opinions of others must underpin inclusive leadership practice. It is likewise imperative that all interactions with stakeholder groups be conducted in a manner that demonstrates the utmost respect and value for other people and their points of view. While you will likely find yourself in many situations where you will have the opportunity to practice the art and skill of inclusive leadership with the employees of an organization, whether you have similar interactions with customers and/or owners will depend on your position and its accompanying roles and responsibilities.

While perfecting your skill as an inclusive leader may take time as the development of any professional competencies does, it will be well worth your effort in terms of the potential results that the skillful use of inclusive leadership can yield. You will benefit from always remembering that the individuals with whom you will be dealing from one or more stakeholder groups will welcome opportunities to provide input to your organization. The key is to be respectful and continually seek, always welcome, actively listen to, and value and acknowledge the "voices" of your stakeholders. Doing so begins with understanding your organization's stakeholders and the expectations that they have for your organization. We will now turn our attention to how organizations and their leaders can understand and respond to the expectations of their stakeholders.

Why Stakeholder Engagement Matters

The sustainable success of any contemporary organization demands that its leaders fully understand, embrace, and address the expectations of its stakeholders. Stakeholders are individuals, groups, or organizations that have an interest, claim, or stake in what an organization does, as well as in its success. Anyone that is engaged in an exchange relationship with an organization is thus a stakeholder of that organization and will have expectations regarding that organization's actions and outcomes. Organizations and those who lead them must recognize the importance of continued stakeholder support and that a loss of such support could compromise the future success and survival of the organization.

An organization's stakeholders can be categorized as internal or external stakeholders, and as primary or secondary stakeholders. Internal stakeholders include an organization's employees, managers, executives, owners, and board members, whereas external stakeholders include customers, suppliers, creditors, the general public, local communities, and governments. Employees, customers, owners, and suppliers are considered primary stakeholders in that they have a vested interest in an organization's actions and success given that they can benefit from an organization's successes as well as be negatively impacted by an organization's business activities and conduct. The remaining stakeholder groups are considered secondary stakeholders in that they are only indirectly affected by an organization's actions and success.

Customers, employees, and owners are typically viewed as the most important stakeholder groups to consider as an organization conducts its present operations and plans and implements its strategic direction for the future. Astute organizational leaders recognize the integral role that an organization's stakeholders play in their organization's present and future success. Understanding the expectations of an organization's various stakeholder groups and prioritizing these expectations is crucial in determining the present and future success and, at times, survival of the organization that they have been afforded the opportunity to lead and navigate through a dynamic and challenging business environment. As inclusive leaders these organizational leaders must be committed to understanding stakeholder expectations and positioning their organizations to meet and ideally exceed all reasonable and realistic stakeholder expectations. The inclusive leadership approach must incorporate an understanding of relevant stakeholder expectations along with a commitment to conscientiously consider these expectations through inclusive practice.

Understanding Stakeholder Expectations

Understanding stakeholder expectations is necessary if an organization intends to respond to these expectations. Therefore, before an organization can appropriately address the various expectations of its stakeholders, its leaders must identify the relevant stakeholder groups and the expectations that each group has with respect to their organization. This insight is a necessary prerequisite as an organization seeks to respond to the various expectations and strives to meet and ideally exceed the expectations of its various stakeholders.

A process called stakeholder analysis can be used to discern the stakeholder groups with which organizational leaders should concern themselves and the expectations that each group has for the organization. An effective stakeholder analysis process incorporates a series of sequential steps, beginning with the identification of the various stakeholder groups that are likely to have an interest in and corresponding expectations for the organization. The interest, claims, and expectations of each stakeholder group are then determined. This serves as a basis for discerning the "realistic" expectations of each stakeholder group for the organization. The most important stakeholder groups, from the standpoint of contributing to organizational success and survival, are identified. This information, provided through a comprehensive, conscientious stakeholder analysis, will serve an organization and its leaders well as they subsequently seek to address the expectations of their organization's stakeholders appropriately.

As stated earlier, most organizations determine that their employees, customers, and owners represent their most important stakeholder groups and concentrate their greatest attention on addressing the expectations of these groups. It should be noted that balancing the expectations of these differing stakeholder groups can sometimes be challenging, in that meeting the expectations of one group may make it more difficult to meet expectations of another group. This can be vividly illustrated by considering the expectations of the three stakeholder groups on which we are focusing in our discussion. Each of these stakeholder groups plays an integral and essential role in an organization's success. An organization cannot survive and succeed without dedicated, qualified employees and loyal customers. Its success is similarly underpinned by the continued commitment of the organization's owners to provide essential resources. The expectations of customers typically relate to the price and/or differentiation of the organization's products and services. Employee expectations include receiving appropriate wages and benefits, fair treatment, job security, and advancement opportunities. Owners expect that their financial investment in an organization will yield anticipated returns.

If an organization fails to meet the expectations of its employees, the consequences will be a workforce that is not highly motivated or empowered and in turn employee retention problems. Likewise, if the wants, needs, and expectations of customers are not met, they may take their business elsewhere. Last, but certainly of no lesser importance, is that owners whose expectations are not realized often withdraw their support from an organization. Maintenance and enhancement of the essential exchange relationships between an organization and its employees, customers, and owners represent the lifeblood of any organization and consequently its future survival and success.

While the specific expectations of each of these three essential stakeholder groups will vary based on the nature of their exchange relationship with the organization, there are some common "interests," if not expectations, that these seemingly divergent stakeholder groups have for an organization with which they are engaged in a business relationship. Each group is clearly interested in the present and future success of the organization, with employees desiring the resulting continued employment opportunities, customers hoping to continue to purchase products and/or services that meet their wants and/or needs from the organization, and owners realizing a return that justifies their continued investment in the organization.

The common interests or expectations that all three stakeholder groups may routinely possess relate to their interest in and willingness to contribute to the continued success of the organization. They desire to know more about the organization and welcome receiving timely information about the organization. They are also interested in having avenues whereby they can communicate with the organization, at times offering their thoughts, ideas, and suggestions. These common interests or expectations could be generalized as an interest in being afforded opportunities to be involved and participate as the organization makes the necessary decisions to chart its present and future course. The fact that many decisions that an organization's leaders will make have the potential of impacting stakeholders, should make the importance of two-way communication and opportunities for participation and involvement convincingly clear. Inclusive leaders recognize the potential benefits of valuing and listening to the "voices" of organizational stakeholders and incorporate active listening as they seek to respond to stakeholder expectations.

Addressing Stakeholder Expectations

While in a perfect world an organization could benefit from fully addressing the expectations of all of its stakeholder groups, this is usually not feasible. It is thus necessary for an organization to prioritize the various stakeholder groups during the stakeholder analysis process. As stated earlier, three stakeholder groups—employees, customers, and owners—usually emerge as the most important stakeholder groups on which an organization should concentrate its attention. While primarily focusing on the expectations of these three stakeholder groups is constructive, the reality is that their divergent interests and expectations often present challenges to organizational leaders.

As important as this prioritization of stakeholders is, so too is discerning if the expectations of each group are realistic and whether it is reasonable for the organization to seek to address each particular expectation. While the success of an organization can be greatly enhanced through meeting and ideally exceeding reasonable stakeholder expectations, organizational leaders have a responsibility to use proper discernment and stewardship as they attempt to do so.

The engagement of organizational stakeholders through inclusive leadership can prove beneficial from the standpoint of developing relationships of mutual respect between organizational leaders and members of these stakeholder groups. Valuing their "voice" will motivate and empower employees, customers, and owners to help organizational leaders definitively understand their expectations and how, through the involvement and participation of these key stakeholders, an organization can understand and meet if not exceed their appropriate expectations while collaboratively contributing to the present and future success of the organization.

Engaging Stakeholders Through Inclusive Leadership

By now we trust that you acknowledge the merit of practicing inclusive leadership within a contemporary organization, as well as the importance of stakeholder engagement, and that you are committed to applying what you have learned to enhance your effectiveness as a leader, as well as the present and future success of your organization.

Inclusive leadership is a powerful tool in the hands of skillful leaders working in an inclusive culture. It requires a change in mindset and a supporting inclusive organizational culture. This chapter was intended to convince you to commit to becoming an inclusive leader and to provide some guidance that will enable you to do so. It likewise sought to make you a committed believer in the importance of engaging organizational stakeholders. When paired together these two concepts are essential tools of any effective organizational leader.

If you are an astute reader who seeks to understand the connections that exist between things, you may have already realized that inclusive leadership is both a leadership approach practiced by inclusive leaders and, equally if not more important, a desired organizational outcome or reality resulting in an inclusive organization. Similarly, stakeholder engagement is not only an action of successful leaders, but also a highly valued outcome deriving from the mindset, commitment, and practices of an organization's leaders facilitated by a supporting inclusive organizational culture.

It all comes down to recognizing the value of others and being willing to solicit their active involvement and participation in an organization. While this mindset is fairly prevalent with respect to affording an organization's employees involvement and participation opportunities, many organizations and their leaders fail to adopt the same philosophy and practice when it comes to their customers and owners. Today's organizations have much to gain from rethinking their often limited practices in the essential area of stakeholder engagement.

By combining the two related concepts of inclusive leadership and stakeholder engagement, you will be adding two invaluable tools to your toolbox as a leader. Rather than view inclusive leadership and stakeholder engagement as separate and unrelated tools, we challenge you to consider them as companion tools that should be used together.

In closing, we challenge you to become the inclusive leader profiled throughout this chapter and incorporate stakeholder engagement in your leadership practice. In doing so, you will be contributing to the building of a successful organizational future that values and respects the various others who are also architects of that organizational future. Together, you can and must start building a successful future for the benefit of all organizational stakeholders. Are you ready to grab your tools and start building?

6
BEING MINDFUL OF CHANGE

Kennedy Muema Musyoka, Susan K. Lewa, Catherine W. Maingi, and Sarah M. Mutuku

Introduction

The purpose of this chapter is to discuss the paradigm of change management and put into context the issue of how to be *mindful of change*. The authors accomplish this through a presentation of the key theories/models of change management; some of which are being critically challenged today due to the unprecedented changes affecting the way leadership, as traditionally known and practiced, is expected to change. Before new models emerge in the near future, it suffices at this point in history and in our view to have a good record and summary of the various models of change management for scholars in universities and colleges to make reference to; to present issues relating to resistance to change; to discuss how to be mindful of change, and to present a case study on how a major statutory body in the telecommunications sector of Kenya, Telcom Kenya Ltd, has managed to deal with change in the ICT sector, which has faced disruptive technology in recent years.

Meaning and Scope of Change Management

Change management is a phenomenon to behold. It can be described as the tool that prepares us for an uncertain future by enabling us to create it and by empowering the organization to take responsibility for their future. It is the task of managing change or an area of professional practice where change is planned or as a body of knowledge where the content or subject matter, that is models, methods and techniques, tools, skills and other forms of 'change knowledge' are studied. Change is a reality that we all need to be comfortable with, because we have little or no control over it (Mutuku, 2005). In an MBA term paper at Allaint International University in San Diego California (US), Sarah M. Mutuku, one of the contributors to this chapter, makes the following observations that capture the aspect of change management very well.

> Change always starts with the 'how' question, for instance how do we get people to be more creative and responsible? Or how do we raise more effective barriers to market entry by our competitors? The initial formulation of a change problem is means centered with the goal state more or less implied according to many authors. We then have the 'what' question, for instance, what are we trying to accomplish? Or what are the changes necessary? Here the ends sought are not discussed since diagnosis is assumed or not performed. Lastly, we have the 'why' question, for instance why do people need to be more creative today? Or why do

we have to change the way we do things today. I like the way Nickols puts it, "the ends and means are relative notions, not absolutes; that is why I find the 'why' question most useful. I think that these questions lead to the ultimate purpose of the organization and lead the way to better performance. Change management is embraced herein."

(Mutuku, 2005, p. 2)

Managing change today requires engagement and inclusion of all stakeholders in a given context. Failure to do this would lead to mismanagement of change and bad consequences. Thus, the application of the tenets of inclusive leadership is a must today.

Theories of Change Management: How Organizations Really Work

Cameron and Green (2015) posit that we all have our own assumptions about how organizations work that have developed through a combination of experience and education. The use of metaphor is an important way in which we express these assumptions. Some people talk about organizations as if they were machines. This metaphor leads to talk of organizational structures, job design and process reengineering. Others describe organizations as political systems. They describe the organization as a seething web of political intrigue where coalitions are formed and power rules supreme. They talk about hidden agendas, opposing factions, negotiation, control and political maneuvering. Organizational metaphors are a good starting point for understanding the different beliefs and assumptions about change and change management. All the different aspects here can be addressed fairly well through inclusive leadership.

Organizations as Machines

The machine metaphor is a well-used metaphor which is worth revisiting to examine its implications for organizational change. When we think of organizations as machines, we begin to see them as rational enterprises designed and structured to achieve predetermined ends (Morgan, 1998).

Organizations as Organisms

This metaphor of organizational life sees the organization as a living, adaptive system. Organizations are legally taken as artificial human beings with motives and goals that they pursue in their organizational lives. Morgan (1998, p. 96) says, "The metaphor suggests that different environments favor different species of organizations based on different methods of organizing . . . congruence with the environment is the key to success." For instance, in stable environments, a more rigid bureaucratic organization would prosper. In more fluid, changing environments, a looser, less structured type of organization would be more likely to survive. This metaphor represents the organization as an 'open system.' The needs of individuals and groups and those of the environment are balanced by viewing organizations as groups of interconnected sub-systems. This approach implies that when designing organizations and also when managing change, we should always do this by keeping in mind the environment and what is happening in it. Emphasis is placed on scanning the environment and developing a healthy adaptation to the outside world. Individual, group and organizational health and happiness are essential ingredients of this metaphor. The interaction with stakeholders in the environment is a key tenet of inclusive leadership.

Organizations as Political Systems

When we look at organizations as political systems, we are drawing clear parallels between how organizations are run and systems of political rule. We may refer to 'democracy,' 'autocracy,' 'dictatorship' and even 'anarchy' to describe what is going on in a particular organization. The orientation adopted by the leaders of organizations may as well determine the kind of approaches to change management that are adopted. Political systems thrive on negotiation for control of resources and other organizational inputs. Here, the style of power rule employed in an organization matters. Conflict, competing interests and power plays are key in organizational life, and therefore the political metaphor factors in all of these. Morgan (1998, p. 133) comments,

> Many people hold the belief that business and politics should be kept apart.... But the person advocating the case of employee rights or industrial democracy is not introducing a political issue so much as arguing for a different approach to a situation that is already political.

Competing interests in political systems are best handled through inclusion of key stakeholders and especially interest groups.

Organizations as in Flux and Transformation

Viewing organizations as in flux and transformation takes us into areas such as complexity, chaos and paradox. Rather than viewing an organization's life as different from the environment, this metaphor allow us to see it as a part of the environment. Organizations are seen as simply part of the ebb and drift of the entire environment and not as a separate system that adjusts to it. In order to acquire a certain identity, organizations are characterized by the ability to change, to self-organize and to self-renew. This metaphor is the only one that begins to shed some good light on how change happens in a turbulent world. This view implies that managers can nudge and shape progress, but cannot ever be in control of change. Morgan (1998, p. 182) says, "In complex systems no one is ever in a position to control or design system operations in a comprehensive way. Form emerges. It cannot be imposed."

Models of Change Management

Several models of change management have been developed and implemented in the current century. Many of them have assumptions that are being challenged, especially in emerging countries where many scholars see them as based on Western theories of change which may not always adequately address change in emerging economies. This is especially true in the African context, where social, economic and political systems do not always follow Western models of business practice. What follows next is a review of each of the key models of change.

Lewin's Three-Step Model

Kurt Lewin (1951) defined organizational change from the viewpoint of the organism metaphor. His model of organizational change is well known and much quoted by managers and academics today. He is responsible for bringing into the limelight force field analysis, which scrutinizes the resisting and driving forces in any change situation. The driving forces must be greater than the resisting forces in any condition if change is to occur. This is the underlying principle. His traditional model has three steps: unfreeze, moving/change and freeze. At each step the inclusion of key stakeholders becomes a must.

Unfreezing—refers to diminishing the forces that keep things inside an organization the same, i.e. creating dissatisfaction with the status quo. Unfreezing occurs through supposed "mental disconfirmation"; for instance, running an organization-wide advancement survey and assessing the outcomes or benchmarking organization operations.

Moving/Changing—refers to moving the organization's conduct or behavior. This includes redesigning organizational roles, responsibilities and relationships and training for newly required skills in preparation for the new organizational equilibrium. This can also be enhanced by promoting supporters of change and getting rid of resisters within the organization.

Refreezing—refers to balancing out the organization in another condition of equilibrium. This progression is impossible without a support mechanism; for instance, constructing strong and supportive corporate systems and structures such as reward systems, pay alignment, measurement reengineering, control systems and a new organizational structure.

Bullock and Batten, Planned Change

Bullock and Batten's (1985) phases of planned change draw on the disciplines of project management. There are many similar 'steps to changing your organization' and models to choose from. For example:

- *Exploration*: for the change to occur, change and the acquisition of any specific resource necessary for managing the change, such as expertise, must first be verified.
- *Planning*: whereby technical experts and key decision makers are involved. The plan is signed off by management before moving into the action phase after completing a diagnosis and sequencing actions in a change plan.
- *Action*: must be done as per the plan. In case things go off track, a feedback mechanism must come into play to allow some re-planning.
- *Integration* is the final phase and is started once the change plan has been fully actioned. It is through this phase whereby established mechanisms such as company updates, rewards and policies allow alignment of changes with other departments in the organization and are made formal in some way.

This particular approach implies the use of the machine metaphor of organizations. The model assumes that change can be defined and moved towards a planned way. A project management approach simplifies the change process by isolating parts of the organizational machinery in order to make necessary changes; for example, developing leadership skills in say, middle management, or reorganizing the sales team to give more engine power to key sales accounts.

Kotter's Eight-Step Model

Kotter's (1996) 'Eight Steps to Transforming Your Organization' goes a little further than the basic machine metaphor. Kotter's eight-step model derives from his experience and analysis of his consulting practice with 100 different organizations that went through change management. He translated the highlighted eight key lessons in his research into a useful eight-step model. The model highlights the significance of a 'felt need' for change in the organization, addresses some of the power challenges which engulf the change management process and emphasizes the importance of communicating the vision and keeping the communication levels tremendously high throughout the course of change management. The eight steps by Kotter (2009) are outlined as follows:

1. *Establishing a sense of urgency*. This step entails discussing current competitive truths and detecting potential future scenarios. Increasing the 'felt need' for change.
2. *Forming an influential guiding coalition*. This step entails bringing together a powerful group of people who can work well as a team.
3. *Creating a vision*. In this step, strategies for achieving the vision are put in place. A vision is key in guiding the change effort.

4. *Communicating the vision.* Emphasis on the need to communicate at least 10 times the amount you expect to have to communicate is key in this step. A variety of different ways need to be adopted to communicate the vision and associated strategies and expected new behaviors.
5. *Empowering others to act on the vision.* This step involves doing away with obstacles which may prevent change, such as unsupportive structures or systems. At this stage, individuals are allowed to experiment.
6. *Planning for and creating short-term wins.* This step allows searching for and advertising short-term noticeable developments.
7. *Consolidating improvements and producing still more change.* This step encompasses promoting and rewarding individuals who are able to promote and work towards the set vision.
8. *Institutionalizing new approaches.* This step ensures that every individual is made to understand that the new expected behaviors will translate into the success of the organization.

Beckhard and Harris's Change Formula: Organism

Beckhard and Harris (1987) developed their change formula from some original work by Gelicher. For the change to occur, they posit that the process of change and the identification of factors that are required to be intensely put in place can be captured in a concise way by the following formulae:

$C = (ABD) > X$
$C = $ Change
$A = $ Level of dissatisfaction with the status quo
$B = $ Desirability of the proposed change or end state
$D = $ Practicality of the change (minimal risk and disruption)
$X = $ Cost of changing

The formula is sometimes written as $(A \times B \times D) > X$. This adds something useful to the original formula. The multiplication implies that if any one factor is zero or near zero, the output will also be zero or near zero and the resistance to change will not be overcome. This means that if the vision is not clear, dissatisfaction with the current state is not felt or the plan is obscure, the likelihood of achieving change is severely reduced. These factors (A, B, D) do not compensate for each other if any one of them is low. All factors must be assigned weights based on critical analysis. The model comes from the organism metaphor of organizations, although it has been adopted by those working with a planned change approach to target management effort. Beckhard and Harris emphasized the need to design interventions that allow these three factors to surface in the organization.

Nadler and Tushman, Congruence Model: Political, Organism

Nadler and Tushman's congruence model takes a different approach to looking at the factors influencing the success of the change process (Nadler, Tushman, Tushman, & Nadler, 1997). This model aims to help us understand the dynamics of what happens in an organization when we try to change it. This model depends on the conviction that organizations can be seen as sets of connecting sub-frameworks that scan and sense changes in the outer condition or external environment. This model sits solidly in the open frameworks way of thinking, which uses the life-form illustration to comprehend organizations' conduct. In this case, the political background isn't disregarded; it shows up as one of the sub-frameworks. This model perceives the organization as a framework that draws contributions from both inside and outside sources (technique, assets, environment condition) and changes them into yields (activities, conduct and execution of the framework at three levels: individual, gathering and aggregate). The core of the model is the open door. It offers to break down the change procedure in a manner that does not offer prescriptive responses; rather it invigorates contemplations on what requirements may occur in a particular hierarchical setting. David Nadler in (Nadler et al., 1997, p. 82) observes that it is critical to see

> the consistency model as an instrument for sorting out your deduction ... as opposed to an inflexible layout to dismember, arrange and compartmentalize what you observe. It's a way of making sense out of a constantly changing kaleidoscope of information and impressions.

The model draws on the sociotechnical view of organizations that looks at managerial, strategic, technical and social aspects of organizations, emphasizing the assumption that everything relies on everything else. This means that the different elements of the total system have to be aligned to achieve high performance as a whole system. Therefore the higher the congruence, the higher the performance. Achieving congruence is a big challenge in change management. It requires the inclusion of all the sub-systems in the environment where change is occurring.

William Bridges's Model—Managing the Transition: Machine, Organism, Flux and Transformation

Bridges (1991) makes a reasonable qualification between arranged change and progress. He argues and marks change as the more unpredictable of the two, and focuses on upgrading our comprehension of what continues during progress and of how we can deal with this procedure more viably. In this way, he manages to separate the mechanistic functional changes from the natural human process of becoming emotionally aware of change and adapting to the new way of things. Bridges argues that transition is about letting go of the past and taking up new behaviors or ways of thinking. Planned change is about physically moving office, installing new equipment or restructuring. Transition lags behind planned change because it is more complex and harder to achieve. Transition is psychological and less easy to manage, whereas change is situational and can be planned. Bridges's ideas on transition, once embraced in an organization involved in change management, lead to a deeper understanding of what is going on when an organizational change takes place. While focusing on the importance of understanding what is going on emotionally at each stage in the change process, Bridges also provides a list of useful activities to be attended to during each phase. Transition consists of three phases: ending, neutral zone and new beginning. Each of these is outlined as follows:

Ending

Before you can begin something new, you have to end what used to be. You need to identify who is losing and who is gaining what, expect a reaction and acknowledge the losses openly. Repeat the information to all the stakeholders in question about what is changing, for it will take time to sink in; ensure that you mark the endings.

Neutral Zone

In the neutral zone, people feel disoriented. Motivation falls and anxiety rises. Consensus may break down as attitudes become polarized. It can also be quite a creative time. The leader's and manager's job is to ensure that people recognize the neutral zone and treat it as part of the process. They need to be educated on this and have information provided to them. Temporary structures may be needed—possibly task forces and smaller teams. The manager needs to find a way of taking the pulse of the organization on a regular basis. William Bridges suggested that we could learn from Moses of the Bible and his time in the wilderness to really gain an understanding of how to manage people during the neutral zone. The story of Moses of the Bible teaches a lot about some aspects of change: hardship, shared vision, patience, risk/danger, impatience of followers, need for a higher calling in change management, inclusivity, hope, strategy, polarization, information management, consensus building and servant leadership, engaged leadership and spiritual leadership.

New Beginning

Change engenders new beginnings. Beginnings should be nurtured carefully. They cannot be planned and predicted, but they can be encouraged, supported and reinforced. Bridges suggests that people need four key elements to help them make a new beginning:

- The purpose behind the change;
- A picture of how this new organization will look and feel;
- A step-by-step plan to get there; and
- A part to play in the outcome.

The beginning is reached when people feel they can make the emotional commitment to doing something in a new way. Bridges makes the point that the neutral zone is longer and the endings are more protracted for those further down the management hierarchy. This can lead to impatience from managers who will have emotionally stepped into a new beginning, and in most cases with their people or followers/subordinates lagging behind, seemingly stuck in an ending.

Carnall's Change Management Model: Political, Organism

Carnall (2007) produced a useful model that brings together a number of perspectives on change. He says that the effective management of change depends on the level of management skill in the following areas:

- Managing transitions effectively;
- Dealing with organizational cultures; and
- Managing organizational politics.

A manager who is gifted in overseeing advances can help individuals learn as they change and create an atmosphere of transparency and hazard taking. A manager who manages culture in an organization must analyze the current organizational culture and begin to create what Carnall (2007, p. 64) calls "a progressively versatile culture." This implies, for instance, growing a better data stream, more transparency and more prominent local self-governance. It is not easy to achieve, though, because changing culture is a difficult process even when it is clear that certain cultural ethos and nuances need to be changed.

A manager must also be able to oversee the organization's governmental issues and interactions and comprehend and perceive various groups and various motivation. He/she should create aptitudes in using and perceiving different political strategies, for example, building alliances, utilizing outside specialists and controlling the motivation. He/she should be good at applying stakeholder management theory and the demands of inclusive leadership.

Senge, Kleiner, Roberts, Ross, Roth, Smith and Guman (1999): Systemic Model (Political, Organism, Flux and Transformation)

If you are interested in sustainable change, then the ideas and concepts in Senge et al. (1999) will be of interest to you. This excellent book, *The Dance of Change*, seeks to help "those who care deeply involved in or about building new types of organizations" (p. 56) to understand the challenges ahead. Senge et al. (1999) observe that many change initiatives fail to achieve hoped-for results. They reflect on why this might be so by commenting, "To understand why sustaining significant change is so elusive, we need to think less like managers and more like biologists." Senge et al. (1999) talk about the myriad 'balancing processes' or forces of homeostasis which act to preserve the status quo in any organization. These need to be well understood by the top management team and the internal as well as the external stakeholders.

Senge et al. (1999) observe,

> Most genuine change activities in the long run face issues inserted in our predominant arrangement of the management. These include managers' commitment to change as long as it doesn't affect them; 'undiscussable' topics that feel risky to talk about; and the ingrained habit of attacking symptoms and ignoring deeper "systemic causes of problems".

Their guidelines are as follows: Start small. Grow steadily. Don't plan the whole thing. Expect challenges—it will not go smoothly! Senge et al. use the principles of environmental systems to illustrate how organizations operate and to enhance our understanding of what forces are at play. Business and other human endeavors are also systems and do borrow a lot from environmental systems (Senge, Kleiner, Roberts, & Smith, 1994). They are also bound by imperceptible textures of interrelated moves which regularly take a long time to completely play out their consequences for one another. Since we are a piece of that lacework ourselves, it's doubly difficult to see the entire patterns of change. Instead we will generally focus on depictions of confined pieces of the frameworks, and marvel why our most profound issues never appear to get ironed out. The approach is noticeably different from much of the other work on change, which focus on the early stages such as creating a vision, planning, finding energy to move forward and deciding on first steps (Senge et al., 1999). They look at the longer-term issues of sustaining and renewing organizational change. They examine the challenges of first initiating, second sustaining and third redesigning and rethinking change. Their book does not give formulaic solutions, or 'how to' approaches, but rather gives ideas and suggestions for dealing with the balancing forces of equilibrium in organizational systems. A key question is, What are the balancing forces that those involved in change need to look out for? The key challenges of initiating change are the balancing forces that arise when any group of people starts to do things differently (Senge et al., 1999). Some arguments advanced by those resisting change include:

- 'We don't have time for this stuff!' People working on change initiatives will need extra time outside of the day-to-day activities to devote to change efforts, otherwise there will be pushback.
- 'We have no help!' There will be new skills and mindsets to develop. People will need coaching and support to develop new capabilities.
- 'This stuff isn't relevant!' Unless people are convinced of the need for effort to be invested, it will not happen.
- 'They're not walking the talk!' People look for reinforcement of the new values or new behaviors from management and especially their leaders and supervisors. If this is not in place, there will be resistance to progress. The authors of the book go on to say that the challenges of sustaining change come to the fore when the pilot group or change champions (those who start the change) become successful and the change begins to touch the rest of the organization.
- 'This stuff is. . .!' Anything can be advanced here as an argument. This challenge concerns the discomfort felt by individuals when they feel exposed or fearful about changes. This may be expressed in a number of different ways, such as 'This stuff is taking our eye off the ball' or 'This stuff is more trouble than it's worth.'

- 'This stuff isn't working!' People outside the pilot group, and some of those within the pilot group, may be impatient for positive results. Traditional ways of measuring success do not always apply under the circumstances and may end up giving a skewed view of progress.
- 'We have the right way!'/'They don't understand us!' The pilot group members become evangelists for the change, setting up a reaction from the 'outsiders.' The challenges of redesigning and rethinking change appear when the change achieves some visible measure of success and starts to impact on ingrained organizational habits.
- 'Who's in charge of this stuff?' This challenge is about the conflicts that can arise between successful pilot groups, who start to want to do more, and those who see themselves as the governing body of the organization.
- 'We keep reinventing the wheel!' The challenge of spreading knowledge of new ideas and processes around the organization is a tough one. People who are distant from the changes may not receive high-quality information about what is going on.
- 'Where are we going and what are we here for?' Senge et al. (1999, p. 57)says, "engaging people around deep questions of purpose and strategy is fraught with challenges because it opens the door to a traditionally closed inner sanctum of top management."

The arguments listed imply the need for coming along with everyone and hence the need for inclusive leadership.

Stacey and Shaw, Complex Responsive Processes: Political, Flux and Transformation

Stacey (2003) and Shaw (2002) view organizations by utilizing the metaphor of flux and transformations. The ramifications of this method of intuition for those keen on overseeing and enabling change are huge:

- Change, or a new order for things, will develop normally from clean correspondence, strife and strain (not all that much).
- As a manager, you are not outside of the framework, controlling it or wanting to adjust it; you are a piece of the entire environment.

Shaw (2002) addresses the traditional inquiries of 'How would we oversee change?' by tending to the inquiry, 'How would we take an interest in the manners in which things change after some time?' This composition manages the oddity that "our cooperation, regardless of how considered or enthusiastic, is continually developing in manners that we can't control or anticipate in the more drawn out term, regardless of how refined our planning instruments" (p. 102).

ADKAR Model (Awareness, Desire, Knowledge, Ability, Reinforcement)

ADKAR is a foundational tool for understanding "how, why and when" to use different change management tools. ADKAR is useful for individual change management and also for supervisors, managers and employees involved in a change management process. The key elements of the model are:

- Awareness of the need for change.
- Desire to participate and support the change (our choice).
- Knowledge on how to change.
- Ability to implement required skills and behaviors.
- Reinforcement to sustain the change.

Before moving to the next section of this chapter, it suffices to observe that it is useful to understand your own assumptions about managing change, in order to challenge them and examine the possibilities offered by different assumptions and models. It is useful to compare your own assumptions with the assumptions of others with whom you work. This increased understanding can often reduce frustration. Organizational metaphors provide a useful way of looking at the range of assumptions that exist about how organizations work. The four most commonly used organizational metaphors already discussed are the machine metaphor, the political metaphor, the organism metaphor, and the flux and transformation metaphor. The machine metaphor is deeply ingrained in our ideas about how organizations run, so it tends to inform many of the well-known approaches to organizational change, particularly project management, and planning-oriented approaches. Models of organizations as open, interconnected, interdependent sub-systems sit within the organism metaphor. This model is very prevalent in the human resource world, as it underpins much of the thinking that drove the creation of the HR function in organizations. The organism metaphor views change as a process of adapting to changes in the environment. The focus is on designing interventions to decrease resistance to change and increase the forces for change. The political map of organizational life is recognized by many of the key writers on organizational change as highly significant. The metaphor of flux and transformation appears to model the true complexity of how change really happens. If we use this lens to view organizational life, it does not lead to neat formulae or concise how-to approaches. There is less certainty to inform our actions. This can be on the one hand a great relief, and on the other hand it can be quite frustrating.

There are many approaches to managing and understanding change to choose from, none of which appears to tell the whole story, and most of which are convincing up to a point. To be an effective manager, leader or consultant engaged in change management, you need to be able to flexibly select appropriate models and approaches for particular situations. Addressing change today requires total inclusion of all the variables in the dynamic way in which things are happening. A good piece of advice to change champions today is to consider the application of inclusive leadership, because this improves the chances of success.

Being Mindful of Change

By this time, you are aware that change can originate from external sources through technological advances, sociopolitical or economic pressures. Or it can come from inside an organization as a management response to a range of issues, for example, customer needs, costs or human resource or performance issues. Change can affect a small area in the organization, e.g. a department, or the entire organization. There are essential principles and practices that help individuals and organizations to accept change. Change is an inherent characteristic of any organization, and all organizations, whether in the public or the private sector, must undergo change in order to remain relevant. In today's turbulent environment of organizations, change has become synonymous with standard business practices, as long-term organizational ends have to be reformulated on an ongoing basis (Volberda, 1996).

The models reviewed so far have given lots of information on how to be mindful of change. Change management is the process, tools and techniques to manage the people side of business to achieve the required business outcomes and to realize that business changes effectively within the social infrastructure of the workplace (Nadler, 2001). Change in attitudes and behaviors can build a culture based on open communication, interpersonal trust, constructive handling of conflict, teamwork and collaborative problem solving. Organizations that have successfully managed change have been able to link strategic change with operational change and every aspect of the organization in relation to a dynamic external environment. For an organization, change management means defining and implementing procedures and/or technologies to deal with changes in the business environment and to profit from changing opportunities.

Change management requires tools, processes, skills and principles to be effective. The responsibility for managing change is with the management and executives of the organization; they must manage the change in a way that employees can cope with. This means employees have to be included in the process. The manager has a responsibility to facilitate and enable change by understanding the situation from an objective standpoint (to 'step back' and to be nonjudgmental), and then to help staff/people understand reasons, aims and ways of responding positively according to employees' own situations and capabilities (Yazici, 2009). A good change management practice strategy is a critical success factor in implementing changes in organizations. Effective change management practices, therefore, require being approached from both an individual and an organizational perspective. In order to successfully manage change processes, managers need to know what changes to expect and the nature of change, and situations as well as possible problems likely to be experienced, including causes of resistance and possible solutions. Successful change management strategies and practices, therefore, must include the people's component of change. Changes become successful when each employee who must do things differently has awareness, desire, knowledge, ability and reinforcement. Training in the dynamics of change management using the models already discussed can be very enriching in a change management process.

Resistance to Change

There are two types of resistance to change: behavioral and systemic. Resistance to change is a common problem in almost all organizations. It impairs concerted efforts to improve performance. All changes involve loss, and they require that individuals give up familiar routines. In some cases, loss is substantial, affecting position, power, networks of friends and colleagues.

Reason for Resistance to Change

Many reasons have been advanced in almost every piece of literature on change management. The key ones are:

Parochial self-interest—Some employees have more concern with the implication of change for themselves and their interests than for the effects on the success of the organization.

Low tolerance to change—Some people are very keen on feeling secure and having stability in their work.

Different assessments of the situation—Some employees may disagree with the reasons for the change and with the disadvantages of the change process.

Misunderstanding about the need for change/when the reason for the change is unclear—On the off chance that staff don't comprehend the requirement for change, you can anticipate resistance particularly from the individuals who firmly accept the present method for doing things/functions admirably/status quo/etc. and have accomplished for a long time.

Fear of the unknown—One of the most widely recognized purposes behind resistance is dread of the obscure. Individuals will possibly step toward the obscure in the event that they truly accept—and maybe more significantly feel—that the dangers of stopping are more noteworthy than those of pushing ahead toward another path. This helps make resistance natural.

Lack of competence—This is a dread people will only occasionally concede. However, here and there, change in organizations requires changes in aptitudes, and a few people will feel that they won't likely make great progress with their limited skills and competencies.

Connected to the old way—In the event that you ask individuals in an association to get things done in another manner, as objective as that new way may appear to you, you will find yourself facing such hard wiring or what we might call deeply ingrained ideas, in each one of those passionate organizations with the individuals who showed your group of spectators the old way—and that is not a minor thing.

Low trust—At the point that individuals don't accept that they, or the organization, can ably deal with the change, there is probably going to be opposition.

Temporary fad—This is the point where and when individuals believe that the change activity is just a brief trend.

Not being consulted—On the off chance that individuals are permitted to be included in the change, there is less opposition. Individuals like to realize what's happening, particularly if their jobs might be affected. Educated representatives will in general have more elevated amounts of occupation fulfillment than uninformed workers.

Poor communication—Many people in many quarters argue, 'It's self-evident, isn't it?' With regards to change management, there's no such thing as an excess of correspondence. All stakeholders need well-articulated and repeated messages.

Changes to routines—When we talk about comfort zones, we're truly alluding to schedules that people/staff are used to. We cherish them. They make us secure. So there will undoubtedly be resistance at whatever point change expects us to do things another way or is based on new paradigms.

Exhaustion/Saturation—Try not to confuse consistency with acknowledgment. Individuals who are overpowered by nonstop change leave themselves to it and give in to the flow. You have the staff in body; however, you don't have their hearts. There is low motivation in this case. You have to lead from the heart (Margues & Dhiman, 2018).

Change in the status quo—In many cases, opposition can likewise originate from the impression of the change that individuals hold. For instance, individuals who feel they'll loose in the process are probably not going to give it their full help. Also, if individuals believe that the change supports another department/group, there might be (implicit) outrage and disdain. Human beings are selfish by their very nature.

Benefits and rewards—At the point when the advantages and rewards for rolling out the improvements through change management are not seen as sufficient, there will be resistance to change.

Other reasons—In today's highly turbulent and globalized business environment, we would like to suggest in this chapter that there are new business "bugs" or "negative changes" occurring at an unprecedented scale. Leaders, managers and staff need continuous education and training in order to expose them to the new changing elements in today's business environment.

Overcoming Resistance to Change

Many strategies and suggestions for addressing resistance to change have been suggested in current literature by practitioners, leadership gurus, management theorists and academics. The interventions required to address resistance to change all point to the need for practicing the principles of inclusive leadership. The key ones are outlined as follows:

Education and communication—This tactic assumes that the source of resistance lies in misinformation or poor communication. It is best used where management assesses that there is lack of information or inaccurate information in the organization.

Participation and involvement—Prior to making a change, those opposed can be brought into the decision process. Many of the models considered in this chapter have suggestions on how this can be achieved. This approach is best where initiators lack information, and others have the power to resist. In emerging economies, power to resist is exercised by trade unions, civil society organizations and religious bodies to the chagrin of the political class.

Facilitation and support—The provision of various efforts to facilitate adjustment helps a lot. This is best used where people resist because of adjustment problems.

Negotiation and agreement—Leaders and the change champions must provide something of value to lessen resistance. This occurs best where one group will lose and has considerable power to resist.

Manipulation and cooperation—Twisting and distorting facts to make them appear more attractive is a common technique mostly used in emerging economies where institutions are weak and citizens' have a muzzled voice in challenging executive and political decisions. But it can also be used anywhere when other tactics won't work or are too expensive.

Explicit and implicit coercion—The application of direct threats or force upon resisters is most useful where speed is essential and initiators have power.

Conclusion

The environment is dynamic and the demands of people are changing, therefore organizations need to be cognizant of these changes. Change agents and champions have to think on their feet in answer to the strategic imperatives of the moment. Today, organizations know that they need a sustainable competitive edge in order to achieve their goals and satisfy their customers so that they don't find it necessary to go to the competition. Hence they need concepts that transcend any boundaries, and that is why it is advisable to welcome change with open arms. There is always a 'change facilitator' who is in charge of managing people and in charge of the change management strategy. The communication plan and expertise for how to manage the resistance to change is important too. Change can be planned and managed in a systematic way where the goal is to implement new methods and systems in an organization, or it can be a response to changes where the organization has little or no control over the actions of competitors or shifting economic events. This is the reactive approach, while the former is more anticipative because the change lies within and is controlled by the organization. The change process can be viewed as a problem-solving template, where a solution is sought and the organization is brought to the future state they want to be in. The main goal is to empower the organization to take responsibility for their future.

Telkom Kenya Limited: A Case Study on Change Management in an Emerging Economy

Telkom Kenya Limited was established by the government of Kenya as a telecommunications operator under the Companies Act in April 1999 to provide integrated communications solutions in Kenya, which include a wide range of voice and data services as well as network facilities for residential and business customers. In 2008, France Telecom acquired 51% shares in Telkom Kenya Limited under its brand name Orange. Telkom Kenya Limited is the only integrated telecommunication solutions provider in Kenya with services such as a fixed 5G network, mobile and internet services. As of 2012, the company had 2,200 staff after restructuring (Muteti, 2013). Despite this advantage, a major competitor known as Safaricom Ltd increased competition by leaps and bounds and made Telkom think of managing change in a new way.

Telkom Kenya Ltd thought of implementing various changes in order to increase efficiency and remain competitive in the telecommunication sector. The changes which had taken place in Telkom Kenya Ltd were informed by serious preparation of staff and stakeholders, including the government, which previously had majority shares in the company. The activities engendered by change included downsizing, acquisition, structural changes, strategic changes and restructuring, among others. The company was forced to change its organizational structure, its strategic focus, its employee size and composition and also its management orientation. Various studies identified key factors in the strategic change management practices adopted by Telkom Kenya Limited. They included a scientific approach for managing planned change, diagnosis, analysis, feedback, action and evaluation utilizing Kurt Lewin's model and Kotter's model as well as the ADKAR model.

The company practiced unfreezing the status quo, moving to a new state and refreezing the new change to make it permanent. Another strategic change management practice adopted was the systematic collection of data and selection of a change action based on analysis. Data and information was shared liberally and communication was pitched at very high levels.

The Telkom Kenya Limited change management process was executed in a systematic order to guarantee the desired smooth transition of the company. It defined the internal context as well as external very well and identified key success factors in the change management process. It required the inclusion of as many stakeholders as possible; inclusive leadership, in essence. There was success, but the entry of Safaricom and other key players in the ICT sector has complicated matters for the organization. A key problem appears to be resistance to change from government circles. However, it is envisaged that allowing private equity in the ownership of the company will increase its competitiveness.

Key Takeaways

1. Many models on change management have been very useful traditionally but are being challenged today by turbulence in the business environment.
2. Change management can be done successfully by those who accept change and learn how to manage it.
3. Very good strategies exist for managing resistance to change. They all involve shared vision and frequent communication of critical messages.
4. Sociocultural, economic and political systems in emerging economies may not always follow Western-centric theories.
5. Telkom Kenya Ltd provides a good case study on change management (initial success but later facing serious competition, which engenders the need for continuous change management).

References

Beckhard, R., & Harris, R.T. (1987). *Organizational transitions: Managing complex change*. Reading, MA: Addison-Wesley Publishing Company.
Bridges, W. (1991). *Managing transitions: Making the most of change*. New York, NY: Perseus Books.
Bullock, R., & Batten, D. (1985). It's just a phase we're going through: A review and synthesis of OD phase analysis. *Group & Organization Studies*, 10(4), 383–412. doi:10.1177/105960118501000403
Cameron, E., & Green, M. (2015). *Making sense of change management: A complete guide to the models, tools and techniques of organizational change*. London: Kogan Page Publishers.
Carnall, C.A. (2007). *Managing change in organizations*. London: Pearson Education.
Kotter, J.P. (1996). *Leading change*. Brighton, MA: Harvard Business Press.
Kotter, J.P. (2009). Leading change: Why transformation efforts fail. *The Principles and Practice of Change*, 113–123. doi:10.1007/978-1-137-16511-4_7
Lewin, K., University of Michigan. Research Center for Group Dynamics. (1951). *Field theory in social science: Selected theoretical papers*. New York: Harper.
Margues, J., & Dhiman, S. (2018). *Engaged leadership: Transforming through future-oriented design thinking*. Cham: Springer International Publishing.
Morgan, G. (1998). *Images of organization*. Oakland, CA: Berrett-Koehler Publishers.
Muteti, M.N. (2013). *Management of strategic change at the Telkom Kenya Limited* (Master's thesis, University of Nairobi, Nairobi, MA). Retrieved from http://erepository.uonbi.ac.ke/bitstream/handle/11295/60130
Mutuku, Sarah Mutheu. (2005). *MBA Term Paper*. San Diego, CA: Alliant International University, Scripts Ranch.
Nadler, D. A. (2001). *Champions of change: How CEOs and their companies are mastering the skills of radical change*. San Francisco: Jossey-Bass.

Nadler, D. A., Tushman, M., Tushman, M. L., & Nadler, M. B. (1997). *Competing by design: The power of organizational architecture*. New York, NY: Oxford University Press.

Senge, P., Kleiner, A., Roberts, C., Ross, R., Roth, G., Smith, B., & Guman, E. C. (1999). The dance of change: The challenges to sustaining momentum in learning organizations. *Performance Improvement, 38*(5), 55–58. doi:10.1002/pfi.4140380511

Senge, P. M., Kleiner, A., Roberts, C., & Smith, B. J. (1994). *The fifth discipline fieldbook: Strategies and tools for building a learning organization*. New York, NY: Crown Business.

Shaw, P. (2002). *Changing conversations in organizations: A complexity approach to change*. London, England: Psychology Press.

Stacey, R. (2003). *Complex responsive processes in organizations: Learning and knowledge creation*. London: Routledge.

Volberda, H. W. (1996). Toward the flexible form: How to remain vital in hypercompetitive environments. *Organization Science, 7*(4), 359–374.

Yazici, H. J. (2009). The role of project management maturity and organizational culture in perceived performance. *Project Management Journal, 40*(3), 14–33.

7
FOSTERING INCLUSIVE ORGANIZATIONS THROUGH VIRTUOUS LEADERSHIP

Aikaterini Grimani and George Gotsis

Introduction

In recent years, there has been an increasing interest in the field of virtue theory and organizational behavior. The concept of virtue is a term denoting universal standards of correctness, rectitude and goodness (Antunes & Franco, 2016). Virtues are "contextual, learned habits that reflect and involve discriminating moral judgment and deliberation" (p. 75) (McLaughlin & Cox, 2015). For Aristotle, virtues developed or were cultivated over time through habituation, which led to stable characteristics or traits (Aguirre-Y-Luker, Hyman, & Shanahan, 2017). Aristotelian virtue theory asserts that the purpose of life is to maximize flourishing and overall well-being by living in balance or harmony (eudaimonia, happiness) (Neubert, 2011). At the core of his system of moral virtues and emotions lie three of the four fundamental virtues as known from Plato: courage, self-control, and justness. The fourth Platonic cardinal virtue, wisdom, is an intellectual virtue with significant implications for diversity management (Bachmann, 2019). Virtuousness encompasses the best of the human condition, assuming that it is inherent (McLaughlin & Cox, 2015). Several aspects of virtues described in the existing literature include the distinction between right and wrong in the leadership function, taking measures to ensure justice and honesty, influencing and allowing others to morally follow fair objectives for themselves and their organizations, and helping others to interconnect with a higher purpose (Cameron, 2011; Pearce, Waldman, & Csikszentmihaly, 2006; Rego, Cunha, & Clegg, 2012).

Whereas the general definition of virtues can be established with reference to its origins in Aristotle, virtues as they apply to organizations and the disciplines of management, organizational behavior, psychology, organization theory, and strategy need further discussion of their relation to core constructs (Neubert, Carlson, Kacmar, Roberts, & Chonko, 2009). On an individual level, virtue ethics can provide insight into how managers and business leaders behave and make decisions. Individuals not only produce goods and services, transforming their environment through their job, but also develop a series of abilities and competences that shape their personality. Virtue ethics also give them a chance to consider the business environments and cultures they should build, as well as how business goals, policies, and procedures foster positive or negative learning in their employees (Fontrodona, Sison, & de Bruin, 2013). Identified virtues pertaining to positive business practices include caring, compassion, conscientiousness, empathy, forgiveness, gratitude, inspiration, integrity, making work meaningful, optimism, respect, trust, warmth, and zeal (Aguirre-Y-Luker et al., 2017).

However, organizations continue to be challenged and enriched by the diversity of the workforces. Researchers are increasingly focusing on inclusion to enhance work environments by supporting a diverse workforce (Shore, Cleveland, & Sanchez, 2018). A broad definition of inclusion indicates the following, according to Ferdman (2017, p. 235), "In inclusive organizations and societies, people of all identities and many styles can be fully themselves while also contributing to the larger collective, as valued and full members." In addition, the existing literature commonly defines inclusion as "minority members' insider status, belongingness, full contribution, engagement, voice, and participation in the organizational decision-making process, as well as the means to draw out minority members' unique perspectives and to integrate differences within a workplace" (Fujimoto, Azmat, & Subramaniam, 2019, p. 714). According to Shore et al. (2018, p. 177), inclusion involves

> equal opportunity for members of socially marginalized groups to participate and contribute while concurrently providing opportunities for members of non-marginalized groups, and to support employees in their efforts to be fully engaged at all levels of the organization and to be authentically themselves.
>
> *(p. 177)*

In the workplace, inclusion is based on a pluralistic value frame that respects all cultural perspectives among workers (Shore et al., 2018).

Virtuous leadership and inclusion in the workplace have become important themes for both academic theory and business practice. Although we know a great deal about virtuous leadership, scholarship focused on inclusion is still in the initial stages, while there has also been precious little research exploring the relationship between them. The aim of this chapter is to provide an integrative framework of virtuous behaviors and inclusion in organizations. It is also intended to explore precisely how virtuous leadership can claim conceptual distinctiveness with respect to related values-based leadership theories and to emphasize how leaders enact virtuous behaviors from which a diversity of organizational stakeholders can significantly benefit. The structure is as follows: the first section will present a theoretical framework concerning virtuous leadership and values-laden leadership types. The following section will concentrate on the inclusive leadership and workplace diversity. A discussion and conclusion section will close the chapter.

Virtuous Leadership: The Quest for Conceptual Distinctiveness

Virtuousness is a term denoting universal patterns of correctness, rectitude, and goodness. The aggregate of virtues includes the following aspects: distinguishing between right and wrong in the leadership function, taking measures to ensure justice and honesty, influencing and allowing others to morally follow fair objectives for themselves and their organizations, and helping others to interconnect with a higher purpose (Antunes & Franco, 2016). Virtuous leadership has been considered conceptually synonymous with or highly similar to moral, ethical, servant and spiritual, inclusive, transformative, transformational, and paternalistic leadership, while others have treated virtuous leadership as a component of ethical, servant, charismatic, transformational/authentic, and responsible leadership (Wang & Hackett, 2016).

The concept of leaders' virtue derives from Aristotelian logic and Confucian perspectives which indicate that virtue is a character trait. According to Pearce et al. (2006), virtuous leadership can be displayed and formally designated as covering vertical leaders who operate through shared leadership. Hence, virtuous leadership can be perceived as an important facilitator of learning in organizations, allowing the formation of the necessary trust and openness fundamental for the creation and transformation of knowledge in organizations. For instance, sharing ideas and concerns strengthens leadership around a common goal.

According to Cameron, Donaldson, Csikszentmihalyi, and Nakamura (2011), managers should be guided by organizational virtues, such as purpose, safety, fairness, humanity, and decency, that are interlinked with subjective experiences (such as happiness, pleasure, fulfillment, and well-being) and with the positive strength of individual traits (such as character, interests, talents, and values). One of the great advantages of practice founded on virtue is that it evokes an alternative vision to the dominant practice, and that option is extremely necessary in organizations nowadays. This vision incorporates a characteristic of carrying out business with virtue. In addition, virtues create a determining point in decision-making and increase performance. In this aspect, organizations scoring highest in virtue demonstrated significantly higher productivity, higher quality, and better employee retention than did other organizations (Cameron, 2011). Existing literature, especially in the last decade, has significantly contributed to virtuous leadership theory. In Table 7.1, the main varieties of virtuous leadership styles are presented.

Table 7.1 Main Varieties of Virtuous Leadership Types

Source	Publication	Construct under examination	Contribution to Virtuous Leadership theory:
(Bauman, 2018)	*Business Ethics Quarterly*	Virtuous Leadership	Plato's model of virtuous leadership centered on cardinal virtues and ideal virtuous leaders is applied to inform leader development and selection in the contemporary corporate world, explaining how this model is expected to guide leaders, board members, and investors.
(Bohl, 2019)	*Philosophy of Management*	Global Leadership	The authors argue in favor of an underlying philosophy supportive of leadership as an emergent social phenomenon and suggest that recent work in virtue epistemology, along with the theory of communicative praxis and transversal rationality, can facilitate a better understanding of leadership. Viewing leadership as an emergent and complex social phenomenon changes our attitude regarding the roles that leaders play in the creation of leadership.
(Bragues, 2006)	*Journal of Business Ethics*	Virtues-Based Leadership	The intellectual virtues of prudence and wisdom, manifest in the leadership of organizations and in the philosophic quest for truth, are viewed as an ethical imperative for business. Affording individuals the opportunity to apply their leadership competences and engage in philosophic reflection constitutes the most important mission of Aristotelian business ethics.
(Bragues, 2010)	*Journal of Business Ethics*	Virtues-Based Leadership	The paper demonstrates the mechanisms through which worldly success in leadership is complemented by the practice of virtue, by elaborating a procedural framework to properly analyze ostensible conflicts between the beneficial and the honorable, manifest in Cicero's philosophical reasoning.

(*Continued*)

Table 7.1 (Continued)

Source	Publication	Construct under examination	Contribution to Virtuous Leadership theory:
(Caldwell, Hasan, & Smith, 2015)	Journal of Management Development	Virtuous Leadership	Virtuous leadership integrates the abilities required for leader excellence as integral to leaders displaying a commitment to the pursuit of the social welfare and success of others. Such positive outcomes appear as a by-product of the cultivation of leader personal virtues, namely character (honesty and integrity), competence, commitment, courage, clarity, and compassion.
(Cameron, 2011)	Journal of Business Ethics	Responsible Leadership	Virtuous leadership entails desirable ends. Among them, flourishing is defined as having people experience positive emotions, engagement, meaningfulness in their activities, and achievement. Responsibility implies the pursuit of the ultimate best—eudaemonism—and secondarily, the creation of advantages for constituencies: organizations nurturing virtuousness exhibit beneficial outcomes.
(Cameron et al., 2011)	Applied Positive Psychology: Improving Everyday Life, Schools, Work, Health and Society	Virtuous Leadership	Virtuous leadership is in a position to mitigate various manifestations of negative organizational phenomena (worsening morale, degradation of trust, emergence of negative organizational politics, scapegoating effect with respect to leaders, increasing conflict, and lack of communication).
(Campbell, 2015)	Journal of Business Ethics	Virtues-Based Leadership	Leader virtue and moral discipline in considering the interests of others and acting in service to those interests above self-interest can significantly affect risk management effectiveness.
(Crossan et al., 2017)	Journal of Management Studies	Virtues-Based Leadership	Leader character is essential for effective leadership. The authors extend the virtues-based approach to ethical decision-making to the broader domain of judgement and decision-making in view of pursuing individual and organizational effectiveness. The pursuit of sustained organizational excellence requires an emphasis on character dimensions (such as transcendence, courage, and drive), as well as on justice, humility, and humanity. Leader character is inserted into the judgement process to ensure the harmonic behavioral display of these resources in ever-shifting business contexts.

(Continued)

Table 7.1 (Continued)

Source	Publication	Construct under examination	Contribution to Virtuous Leadership theory:
(Crossan, Mazutis, Seijts, & Gandz, 2013)	Academy of Management Learning and Education	Virtues-Based Leadership	Focusing on leadership character at the individual, group, and organizational levels, the paper theorizes on character development in leadership training programs and elaborates on character strengths as intertwined with virtues, values, and ethical decision-making.
(Del Baldo, 2016)	Corporate Governance: Principles, Practices and Challenges	Virtues-Based Leadership	Virtues-based leadership is in a position to foster a cultural reorientation by valorizing humanity and personal relationships between all organizational stakeholders. Focusing on the factors affecting moral and virtues-based leadership and governance, the author addresses the need for a balance between the particular conditions under which different strategies are carried out.
(Flynn, 2008)	Journal of Business Ethics	Virtues-Based Leadership	The paper seeks to reconstruct Aristotle's views on virtue and moral character and argues for their relevance to modern management and corporate leadership practices.
(Gini & Green, 2014)	Business and Society Review	Ethical Leadership	All forms of ethical leadership are based on three elemental ingredients: character, stewardship, and experience. More importantly, ethical character, stewardship, and experience through trial and error are characteristics of good leadership.
(Hackett & Wang, 2012)	Management Decision	Virtuous Leadership	Drawing on Aristotelian and Confucian literatures on virtue ethics and considering seven leadership styles (moral, ethical, spiritual, servant, transformational, charismatic, and visionary leadership), the authors identify a comprehensive list of virtues commonly associated with leadership effectiveness in view of providing a model relating leader virtues to particular outcomes (ethics, happiness, life satisfaction, leader effectiveness). Four Aristotelian cardinal (courage, temperance, justice, and prudence) and two Confucian principal virtues (humanity and truthfulness) were found to underlie all seven leadership styles examined.
(Hannah & Avolio, 2011b)	Leadership Quarterly	Character-Based Leadership	Character is viewed as an indispensable component of leadership, as well as an antecedent to exemplary leadership styles.
(Hannah & Avolio, 2011a)	Leadership Quarterly	Character-Based Leadership	Character is considered to be an integral part of the leader's self-system, with ethos viewed as integral to leader character and as related to extra ethical virtuous behaviors.

(Continued)

Table 7.1 (Continued)

Source	Publication	Construct under examination	Contribution to Virtuous Leadership theory:
(Karakas & Sarigollu, 2013)	Journal of Business Ethics	Benevolent Leadership	Benevolent leadership is deemed an important factor in creating virtuous and compassionate organizations and promoting common good through spiritual depth, ethical sensitivity, positive engagement, and community responsiveness.
(Ko & Rea, 2016)	Advances in Global Leadership	Virtuous Leadership	The authors assert that developing virtuous global leaders who are in a position to help others demonstrate the seven virtues of wisdom, temperance, courage, hope, trust, justice, and compassion are expected to help create a more aligned and clear workforce, guide ethical behaviors, and manage cultural differences in the case of cross-border mergers and acquisitions.
(Lemoine, Hartnell, & Leroy, 2019)	Academy of Management Annals	Authentic Leadership	This is an integrative literature review that unravels the interrelationships between management ethics and moral philosophy and provides a valuable framework which can help to better differentiate the specific underlying moral foundation (deontology, virtue ethics, consequentialism) of ethical, authentic, and servant leadership, respectively.
(Manz & Manz, 2014)	Journal of Management, Spirituality and Religion	Virtuous Leadership	Intro to a special issue of JMSR
(Manz, Manz, Adams, & Shipper, 2011)	Canadian Journal of Administrative Sciences	Virtues-Based Shared Leadership	Shared leadership contributes to sustainable performance in organizations displaying virtuous behaviors through an ongoing creative process, as well as through recognition of every organization member as a valuable resource.
(Martínez, 2018)	Routledge Handbook of Organizational Change in Africa	Virtuous Leadership	The author elaborates a model of ethical leadership based on virtues and character development. Virtuous leadership has to properly consider both task-oriented and person-oriented skills, in view of leveraging excellent outcomes centered on higher follower commitment and loyalty. More importantly, virtuous leadership fosters personal excellence through a deep transformation of attitudes, which serves as a condition for sustainable organizational and societal transformation.

(Continued)

Table 7.1 (Continued)

Source	Publication	Construct under examination	Contribution to Virtuous Leadership theory:
(Meara, 2001)	*Journal of Vocational Behavior*	Virtuous Leadership	Justice is viewed as integral to virtuous leaders, primarily as a virtue entwined with the respective virtues of veracity, prudence, humility, compassion, and respect.
(Meyer, Sison, & Ferrero, 2019)	*Canadian Journal of Administrative Sciences*	Virtuous Leadership	Positive and neo-Aristotelian leadership are motivated from goals and benefits shared by both leaders and followers. These commonalities serve as the pillars of virtuous leadership and should be considered when defining ethical leadership. Flourishing (eudaimonia) remains the ultimate neo-Aristotelian leadership goal and as such, it is path-dependent upon virtue. Practical wisdom, virtue or excellence, and goodwill are elevated to essential personal qualities in neo-Aristotelian leadership. The authors suggest the adoption of practical managerial procedures from Positive Leadership, making them dependent upon the virtues to achieve organizational, as well as societal flourishing.
(Morales-Sánchez & Cabello-Medina, 2015)	*Business Ethics: A European Review*	Competence Management	A set of moral competencies should be implemented in competency-based human resource management: amiability, empathy, affability, gentleness, meekness, cordiality; commitment, responsibility; courage, fortitude, bravery, magnanimity, ambition, audacity, initiative; environmental responsibility, sustainability, stewardship; generosity, liberality; gratitude; honesty, integrity, truthfulness, transparency; humility, self-assessment, modesty; justice, equity, fairness; optimism, positive outlook, self-confidence; perseverance, constancy, resistance, resilience, patience; prudence, practical wisdom, decision-making, good sense; self-control, moderation, temperance; service to others, developing others, willingness to serve, service orientation; solidarity, teamwork, citizenship, loyalty; transcendence, spirituality, religiousness, religiosity, meaning of life.
(Morales-Sánchez & Cabello-Medina, 2013)	*Journal of Business Ethics*	Competence Management	Moral character affects the ethical decision-making process through four main moral competences understood as moral virtues: prudence, justice, fortitude, and temperance.

(*Continued*)

Table 7.1 (Continued)

Source	Publication	Construct under examination	Contribution to Virtuous Leadership theory:
(Neubert et al., 2009)	Journal of Business Ethics	Ethical Leadership	Ethical leadership involves shaping perceptions of ethical climate, in particular when interactional justice is experienced to be high; managers can thus virtuously influence such perceptions, which in turn will positively impact employees' flourishing and thriving.
(Palanski & Vogelgesang, 2011)	Journal of Business Ethics	Ethical Leadership	Drawing on a virtue ethics framework, the authors found that subordinates' perceptions of their leader's behavioral integrity positively predicted their sense of psychological safety that in turn influenced followers' intention to think creatively and to take risks.
(Palanski, Cullen, Gentry, & Nichols, 2015)	Journal of Business Ethics	Virtuous Leadership	Managing behavioral courage may originate in managing behavioral integrity. As a leader places an emphasis on her/his values enactment and overt promise keeping and more specifically in the face of adversity, she/he is more likely to be perceived as courageous and concomitantly effective.
(Pearce Waldman, & Csikszentmihalyi, 2008)	The Virtuous Organization: Insights From Some of the World's Leading Management Thinkers	Virtuous Leadership	Organizational virtue plays a critical role in creating holistic, healthy, and humane work environments. Virtuous organizations fill a need for humanistic management that functions as a paradigm shift in management theory and practice. In advancing this paradigmatic shift, concepts such as efficiency, return on investment, and competitive advantage should not be given priority to the detriment of the virtuous concerns for caring, compassion, integrity, and wisdom.
(Pearce & Csikszentmihalyi, 2014)	Journal of Management, Spirituality and Religion	Virtuous Leadership	Drawing on positive organizational behavior and positive psychology, the authors seek to examine the mechanisms through which virtuous leadership is expected to manifest and perpetuate itself in modern organizations, in particular with relation to organizational learning.
(Pearce et al., 2006)	Journal of Management, Spirituality and Religion	Virtuous Leadership	The authors identify two potential antecedents of virtuous vertical leadership and, more specifically, the personal characteristic of responsibility disposition as well as environmental cues (e.g., code of ethics), as potential predictors of subsequent virtuous leadership. Moreover, the authors articulate the mechanisms through which virtuous vertical leadership might result in virtuous shared leadership and demonstrate how both vertical and shared virtuous leadership can act as pivotal factors in the creation of organizational learning.

(Continued)

Table 7.1 (Continued)

Source	Publication	Construct under examination	Contribution to Virtuous Leadership theory:
(Rego, Clegg, & Cunha, 2012)	The Oxford Handbook of Positive Organizational Scholarship	Global Leadership	The authors explore the mechanisms through which the character strengths and virtues of global leaders can make them more effective in developing flourishing organizations that help stakeholders' thriving in the contexts in which they operate. Global leaders invested with such positive qualities are more motivated to seek global leadership development opportunities, as well as more able to capitalize on these learning opportunities.
(Rego, Cunha et al., 2012)	The Virtues of Leadership: Contemporary Challenges for Global Managers	Virtuous Leadership	Taking for granted that virtues represent the golden mean between two extremes, those of excess and deficiency, the authors explore the ways through which virtues and character strengths induce positive organizational performance. Business leaders, aspiring to self-enlightenment in seeking to follow a values-based capitalism paradigm, will have to adopt meaningful practices that are in a position to help them fulfill three primary conditions: obey laws and regulations, act in conformity to enlightened self-interest, and be motivated by values that stimulate them to make a positive difference.
(Rego, Júnior, & Cunha, 2015)	Journal of Business Ethics	Authentic Leadership	The authors demonstrated that authentic leadership and organizational virtuousness were potential facilitators of group success. Authentic leadership was found to predict sales achievement via the mediating role of positive constructs such as store virtuousness and store potency.
(Riggio, Zhu, Reina, & Maroosis, 2010)	Consulting Psychology Journal	Ethical Leadership	An ethical leader is defined as one who adheres to the four cardinal virtues of prudence, fortitude, temperance, and justice, in conformity to the Aristotelian and Thomistic traditions. The authors introduced an instrument for assessing leader virtues that was found to be highly positively correlated with transformational, authentic, and ethical leadership, such an instrument, combined with the virtues approach to ethical leadership, provides us with a valuable tool in view of assessing leader virtues and ethics.

(Continued)

Table 7.1 (Continued)

Source	Publication	Construct under examination	Contribution to Virtuous Leadership theory:
(Sinnicks, 2018)	*Journal of Business Ethics*	Servant Leadership	The author challenges earlier views of management as neutral and value free, even amoral and manipulative, as incorrect. The paper highlights the affinities between MacIntyre's political philosophy and Greenleaf's concept of servant leadership.
(Sison, 2006)	*Responsible Leadership*	Virtues-Based Leadership	The author proposes Aristotelian rhetoric as a model pertinent to the art of leadership, a fact that necessitates professional competence and moral integrity. Leadership delineates a sphere of relationships that results not only in the achievement of noble goals, but also in the moral growth and flourishing of both leaders and followers. Authentic leadership requires trustworthiness, a main virtue or combination of virtues.
(Sosik & Cameron, 2010)	*Consulting Psychology Journal*	Authentic Transformational Leadership	The authors present a framework for examining how character, conceived in terms of inherent moral beliefs, intentions, and predispositions plays an integral role in the display of authentic transformational leadership under individual and situational constraints. Leaders shape an ascetic self-construal that derives from character strengths and virtues and then manifest this self-image through transformational leadership's main components: idealized influence, inspirational motivation, intellectual stimulation, and individualized consideration. The authors identify 23 specific character strengths reflecting six universal virtues (wisdom, courage, humanity, justice, temperance, and transcendence), as well as suggest paths for assessing and developing leader behavior consistent with virtue and transformational leadership.
(Sosik, Chun, Ete, Arenas, & Scherer, 2018)	*Journal of Business Ethics*	Ethical Leadership	Character strengths play a pivotal role in fostering leader in-role performance and psychological flourishing. Leaders have to possess high levels of honesty, humility, empathy, and moral courage, but also high self-control which appears to enhance the effectiveness of these character strengths. Organizations that can select and/or train leaders to possess these character strengths are more likely to yield performance excellence and psychological well-being through enacting such character strengths and virtues.

(*Continued*)

Table 7.1 (Continued)

Source	Publication	Construct under examination	Contribution to Virtuous Leadership theory:
(Sosik, Gentry, & Chun, 2012)	*Leadership Quarterly*	Character-Based Leadership	The authors explore behavioral manifestations of the character strengths of integrity, bravery, perspective, and social intelligence as exerting influences on executive performance in the context of top-level executive leadership of both for-profit and not-for-profit organizations, with integrity found to have the most significant contribution in explaining variance in executive performance.
(Sturm, Vera, & Crossan, 2017)	*Leadership Quarterly*	Character-Based Leadership	The authors introduce the concept of character-competence entanglement, which reflects the entwinement between character and competence: high character-competence entanglement will lead to extraordinary performance over time. Relying on naturally occurring learning opportunities and the process of learning-by-living is expected to positively affect the development of character-competence entanglement.
(Thun & Kelloway, 2011)	*Canadian Journal of Administrative Sciences*	Virtuous Leadership	In three empirical studies, character-based leadership was supportive of relationships between leader wisdom and employee affective commitment, leader humanity and employee well-being, organizational citizenship behaviors, and cognitive and affective trust, as well as between leader temperance and employee trust.
(van Dierendonck & Patterson, 2015)	*Journal of Business Ethics*	Servant Leadership	The authors employ a virtues perspective in demonstrating how servant leadership will encourage a more meaningful human functioning with a strong sense of community in today's organizations. In essence, leaders' propensity for compassionate love is expected to encourage virtuous attitudes driven by humility, gratitude, forgiveness, and altruism: such virtuous attitudes will in turn foster servant leadership behaviors epitomized in empowerment, authenticity, stewardship, and providing direction.
(Wang & Hackett, 2016)	*Journal of Business Ethics*	Virtuous Leadership	Drawing on both Confucian and Aristotelian traditions, virtuous leadership is distinguished conceptually from related perspectives, such as virtues-based leadership in the positive organizational behavior literature, as well as from ethical and value-laden (spiritual, servant, charismatic, transformational, and authentic) leadership styles.

(*Continued*)

Table 7.1 (Continued)

Source	Publication	Construct under examination	Contribution to Virtuous Leadership theory:
			The paper identifies specific virtues exemplified by virtuous leaders, the contexts in which virtuous leadership is embedded and the perceptual and attributional underpinnings to virtuous leadership. Virtuous leadership predicted a wide range of desirable leader and follower outcomes, including ethical conduct, general happiness, life satisfaction, and job performance.
(Whetstone, 2005)	*Business Ethics: A European Review*	Virtuous Leadership	Virtuous leadership is integral to efforts intended to implement a principled virtue-based organizational ethic. The interrelated aspects of mission, organizational culture, and leadership shape the intermediary components of a virtue-based framework for an ethical organization.
(Yuan, 2013)	*Wise Management in Organizational Complexity*	Wise and Virtuous Leadership	The author enumerates a list of Confucian virtues relevant to leadership that are interwoven with the ideals of Confucian excellence and meritocracy: benevolence, trustworthiness, the doctrine of the mean, and communal harmony are deemed as normative criteria of evaluating effective leadership.

Virtuous behaviors are associated with both ethos and praxis of individuals acting in specific contexts. Virtuousness, however, may be located at three interrelated yet distinct levels: the individual, the organizational, or the societal level. Virtue can be located at the micro-individual level, the sphere of more innate experience, motives, and proclivities. Virtuousness may also arise from the interactive effect of various agents operating within teams, groups, and organizations in conformity to the precepts of virtue. Organizational-level virtue may be the distinctive feature of a virtuous organization that supports and encourages the enactment of virtues through vision, culture, and leadership. Beyond the meso-organizational level, virtuousness can be situated at the intersection of an organizational entity with its surrounding societal environment. Virtuousness is then viewed in relational terms in that it informs the design and implementation of policies aiming at fostering the common good and enhancing social welfare through interventions originating in and justifying organizational and individual level virtue (Gotsis & Grimani, 2015).

The role of virtues in the framing of decisions is very important, as the fundamental virtues can be seen as authentic moral competence, namely fortitude, prudence, the habit of self-control, and justice. Leaders can exhibit virtuousness through the particular way they embody the practice of virtues in their leadership style. Managers can espouse virtuousness through attitudes and behaviors by which they cultivate specific virtues and embrace and value certain character strengths. Virtue theories reflect an attempt at reconciling and unifying strategic and normative excellence, rational self-interest, and business virtues. Virtues may further entail excellence in meeting investment advising functional goals, by both increasing the professional skills of the advisor and by fostering quality of relationships and practical engagements.

Virtuous Leadership and Values-Laden Leadership Styles

Virtues underpinned a wide range of leadership styles (ethical, transformational, authentic, servant, benevolent, and responsible leadership). Certain emerging leadership theories have a potential in promoting virtue. Neubert et al. (2009) showed that ethical leadership exemplified through virtuous behaviors was in a position to influence perceptions of ethical climate that were in turn expected to generate positive experiences in terms of enhanced follower job satisfaction and affective commitment. Some virtues are more basic and important in the workplace, such as good judgment, justice, and self-control. Moreover, Riggio et al. (2010) defined an ethical leader as one who adheres to the four cardinal virtues (prudence, fortitude, temperance, and justice) founded in Aristotelian and Thomistic frameworks. The authors developed a leadership virtues questionnaire that was found to be positively correlated with trans-formational and authentic, as well as ethical leadership styles.

Sosik and Cameron (2010) highlighted the important role of self-construal in the display of a transformational leadership behavior. They identified 23 specific character strengths reflecting six universal virtues (wisdom, courage, humanity, justice, temperance, and transcendence) as potential antecedents of an ascetic leader self-image enacted through idealized influence, inspirational motivation, intellectual stimulation, and individualized consideration, supportive of transformational leadership styles. In addition, Sosik et al. (2012) demonstrated the role that behavioral manifestations of three character strengths, such as integrity, bravery, and social intelligence, play in improving executive performance in the upper echelons of organizations.

Authentic leadership styles may also exert a strong positive effect on virtuous behaviors. Rego et al. (2015) suggested that in acting authentically and fostering team virtuousness, leaders are more able to promote pragmatic outcomes such as team affective commitment and team potency, thus increasing team performance. In addition, Palanski and Vogelgesang (2011) revealed positive relationships between team virtues and team performance. In addition, the authors indicated that leader behavioral integrity facilitates a sense of psychological safety on the part of followers that appears to positively predict their willingness to take risks and to think creatively.

Servant leadership may urge a more meaningful and optimal human functioning with a strong sense of community in organizations. In particular, a leader's propensity for compassionate love encourages a virtuous attitude in terms of humility, gratitude, forgiveness, and altruism. This attitude gives rise to servant leadership behavior, such as empowerment, authenticity, stewardship, and providing direction (van Dierendonck & Patterson, 2015). Leaders of organizations and political institutions are able to create healthy and productive workplaces for workers, placing more emphasis on positive psychology and developing philosophies, such as servant leadership, and methods, such as foundational principles based on education and communication. Servant leadership displays a virtuous cycle which maintains a culture of trust, service, quality, and learning that is linked with positive micro (through hope) and macro (through organizational virtuousness and happiness) behaviors (Rego, Clegg et al., 2012).

Regarding benevolent leadership, Karakas and Sarigollu (2013) explored its role in creating virtuous and compassionate organizations, contributing to their long-term health and sustainability through spiritual depth, ethical sensitivity, positive engagement, and community responsiveness.

Cameron (2011) developed responsible leadership on the grounds of virtuousness as a meaningful activity in pursuit of the ultimate good (eudaimonic well-being) that generates benefits for all stakeholders. Responsible leadership involves three core assumptions: the eudaimonic assumption, the inherent value assumption, and the amplification assumption. According to the eudaimonic assumption, all human beings are afforded an inherent inclination toward moral goodness, while the inherent value assumption posits that virtuousness is an end in itself. Finally, the amplification assumption denotes the efficacy of virtuousness in fostering an elevating and self-perpetuating effect. Manz et al. (2011) contend that a virtuous organization is grounded in shared leadership construed as a dynamic process that secures sustained performance while adhering to virtuous organizational practices.

Workplace Diversity and Inclusion

There has been an explosion of ideas as to what specific practices and behaviors contribute to inclusive workplaces. However, many of these ideas have not been clearly defined in a set of constructs with associated empirical analysis. In the current literature, several different inclusion constructs have been presented, such as work group inclusion, leader inclusion, perceived organizational inclusion, organizational inclusion practices, and inclusive climate. Nevertheless, more advanced inclusionary organizational goals and enhanced experiences of inclusion among workers are needed (Shore et al., 2018).

A key issue in the diversity and inclusion literature is to increase understanding of the role of human resources practices in creating experiences of inclusion for workers. Organizations that seek to enhance inclusion should have a strong and visible commitment among top managers. It is vital to know how to develop and promote the many types of individuals within the organization who are capable of holding leadership positions (Theodorakopoulos & Budhwar, 2015).

Defining diversity is not straightforward, as it can be understood as an evolving concept. Diversity recognizes that everyone is unique and that each individual may have different personal needs, values, and beliefs. It focuses on significant differences that distinguish one individual from another, such as personality (e.g., traits, skills, and abilities), internal characteristics (e.g., gender, race, ethnicity, intelligence, and sexual orientation), external characteristics (e.g., culture, nationality, religion, and marital or parental status), and organizational characteristics (e.g., position, department, and union/nonunion) (Kreitz, 2008).

In addition, inclusion goes beyond just recruiting and retaining a diverse workforce. It is about the creating of an environment where difference is seen as a benefit and perspectives and differences are shared, leading to better decisions. An inclusive environment is one in which everyone feels valued, that their contribution matters, and that they are able to reach their full potential no matter where they come from, who they might be, or what their circumstances are.

Considering the definitions of inclusion in the exciting literature, two general themes are apparent—belongingness and uniqueness. To fulfill a fundamental need for belongingness, individuals choose social identities with particular groups and seek acceptance into those groups. Belongingness has been defined as the need to form and maintain strong, stable interpersonal relationships. There are many advantages associated with being an accepted member of a group, as individuals attribute positive characteristics to other members of their in-groups. The loyalty, cooperation, and trustworthiness among group members enhance individuals' security. Nevertheless, if members of groups are perceived as too similar, then individuals become interchangeable and a need for uniqueness is being essential. Consequently, individuals define themselves in terms of category memberships that distinguish themselves from others by making comparisons within their group (e.g., I am different from others) or to others outside their group (e.g., our group is different from others). Optimal distinctiveness theory suggests that both needs (belongingness or uniqueness) are important and can vary depending on the context in which an individual is situated (Randel et al., 2018; Shore et al., 2011).

Being inclusive takes time, discipline, and commitment. Yet, there are significant benefits regarding employees. Minority members, who are unique, with developed networks and thus a sense of belongingness, report a high level of career optimism. At the group level, inclusive work groups incorporate both uniqueness (through viewing diversity as a resource) and belongingness, since members feels valued and respected (Shore et al., 2011). Employees have become more confident to challenge inappropriate behaviors, excited to be inclusive, and less willing to accept dated leadership styles.

Diversity vs Inclusion

The terms diversity and inclusion are often treated as interchangeable. However, both academics and practitioners have attempted to disentangle the meanings of those two terms, suggesting that there are mainly practical differences (Roberson, 2006). Diversity management practices have focused on bringing women and individuals of marginalized groups into the workplace, while inclusion practices have sought to create equal access to decision-making, resources, and advancement opportunities at work for these individuals (Shore et al., 2018).

Research on diversity and inclusion also suggests a distinction between the concepts of these terms. Definitions of diversity focused primarily on heterogeneity and the demographic composition of groups or organizations, whereas definitions of inclusion focused on employee involvement and the integration of diversity into organizational systems and processes (Roberson, 2006; Theodorakopoulos & Budhwar, 2015). The Office of Personnel Management (2011) defined diversity as

> characteristics such as national origin, language, race, color, disability, ethnicity, gender, age, religion, sexual orientation, gender identity, socioeconomic status, veteran status, and family structures. The concept also encompasses differences among people concerning where they are from and where they have lived and their differences of thought and life experiences.
>
> *(p. 5)*

This same strategic plan defines inclusion "as a culture that connects each employee to the organization; encourages collaboration, flexibility, and fairness; and leverages diversity throughout the organization so that all individuals are able to participate and contribute to their full potential" (p. 5). Likewise, Hays-Thomas and Bendick (2013) define diversity as "the mixture of attributes within a workforce that in significant ways affect how people think, feel, and behave at work, and their acceptance, work performance, satisfaction, or progress in the organization." In contrast, they indicate that inclusion "focuses new attention on the policies, practices, and climate of the workplace (the workplace culture) that shapes the experiences of employees with those characteristics" (p. 195). In addition, Shore et al. (2011) defined inclusion as "the degree to which an employee perceives that he or she is an esteemed member of the work group through experiencing treatment that satisfies his or her needs for belongingness and uniqueness" (p. 1265).

Although Winters (2014) pointed out that diversity is much more easily achieved than inclusion, it does not always bring beneficial outcomes to organizations, as it can increase conflict and turnover and decrease cohesion and job performance. Thus, focusing on inclusion practices can foster the potential advantages and opportunities of having a diverse workforce (e.g., greater innovation) (Shore et al., 2018).

Inclusive Leadership

Researchers and practitioners have increasingly looked to inclusion in order to achieve more complete involvement of diverse individuals in the workplace and to provide the opportunity for all organizational members to reach their full potential. However, experiencing inclusion in the workplace is dependent in part on effective leadership. Inclusive leadership is beneficial for diverse teams through its focus on accepting women and minorities while simultaneously valuing all members for their unique attributes, perspectives, and contributions, ultimately leading to higher performance (Shore et al., 2011).

Inclusive leadership is described as leaders who exhibit openness, accessibility, and availability in their interactions with employees and is a leadership that emphasizes participative and open leader behaviors. These participative and openness behaviors send a clear signal that innovation is welcome and appreciated (Carmeli, Reiter-Palmon, & Ziv, 2010; Ye, Wang, & Guo, 2019). Initial research on inclusive leadership shows generally positive results. Inclusive leadership, characterized by openness, accessibility, and availability, increases psychological safety, which, in turn, increases employee creativity and innovative work behavior (Carmeli et al., 2010; Javed, Naqvi, Khan, Arjoon, & Tayyeb, 2017). In particular, Javed et al. (2017) indicate that inclusiveness is key in providing leadership support for innovative work behavior, because it cultivates high-quality relationships that further augment a sense of psychological safety. Psychological safety is a vital social psychological mechanism that creates conditions where individuals feel safe to bring up ideas, voice opinions, and to question. Environmental complexity with new changes has made creativity and innovation important sources to compete in the market. Thus it is practically important for leaders to socialize and initiate training programs to cultivate a close relationship with employees (Javed et al., 2017). Similarly, Ye et al. (2019) found that inclusive leadership elicited and contributed to team innovation indirectly through team voice.

In addition, Carmeli et al. (2010) indicated that inclusive leaders recognize and respect individual differences between group members, encourage them to express their opinions and concerns, listen to their ideas and suggestions, and support them to try different approaches without worrying that they might be criticized and punished. Moreover, Hirak, Peng, Carmeli, and Schaubroeck (2012) found that leaders who display a high level of inclusiveness play a major role in cultivating psychological safety and facilitating learning from failures, thereby enhancing subsequent unit performance. Furthermore, Choi, Tran, and Park (2015) found a positive relationship between inclusive leadership and employee work engagement, mediated by affective organizational commitment and employee creativity. Inclusive leaders are always supportive of followers and maintain open communication to invite input, at the same time exhibiting availability, willingness, and concern about their interest, expectations, and feelings.

Several specific leader behaviors are likely to facilitate belongingness such as supporting group members, ensuring that justice and equity are part of each member's experience, and providing opportunities for shared decision-making on relevant issues. Supporting group members involves leaders making members feel comfortable and communicating that they have the members' best interests in mind. Ensuring justice and equity allows inclusive leaders to demonstrate fair treatment of group members and thus to indicate to members that they are a respected part of the group. Finally, shared decision-making with an emphasis on sharing power, broadening consultation on decisions, and helping decide how work is conducted is also important to creating a sense of belongingness. Although the existing literature on inclusion has tended to emphasize belongingness more than uniqueness, leader behaviors regarding uniqueness, such as encouraging diverse contributions to the work group and helping group members fully offer their unique talents and perspectives to enhance the work of the group, are equally important. An inclusive leader can encourage diverse contributions by creating a working environment that acknowledges, welcomes, and accepts different approaches, styles, perspectives, and experiences. In addition, a leader might ask group members to share their ideas, ensuring that all voices are heard, understanding and taking into account their strengths and preferences and also recognizing, for example, the different ways in which group members with disabilities can contribute (Randel et al., 2018).

Inclusive Leadership and Other Styles of Leadership

Several existing leadership styles have the potential to incorporate an inclusive component to facilitate commitment to a common goal; however, they are not necessarily inclusive in nature (Randel et al., 2018). For instance, transformational leadership as a vision-based leadership may enhance members' commitment to common organizational goals. However, it is focused on motivating and developing members based on the organization's needs, while inclusive leadership is focused on accepting members for who they are and allowing them to contribute their unique abilities and perspectives. In addition, empowering leadership relies on the sharing of power, teaching, and coaching, while inclusive leadership fosters belongingness and uniqueness. Similarly, leader-member exchange (LMX) is based on the quality of relations between leaders and members. Although a manager who has an LMX relationship with all the members of the group might be thought to be inclusive, this relationship does not necessarily imply inclusive leadership. Moreover, servant leadership focuses on developing and creating success for the members, but not necessarily on tending to member needs for work group belonging or uniqueness. Finally, authentic leadership may have some overlap with inclusive leadership, as well as having many aspects that are distinct. As a self-based approach, the leaders are authentic to who they are in their interactions with others, rather than focus on encouraging authenticity in others (Gotsis & Grimani, 2016; Randel et al., 2018).

Although key tenets of inclusive leadership are not fully captured by the leadership styles presented earlier, virtuous leadership is in a position to fulfill individuals' need for uniqueness, an important dimension of inclusive leadership. Virtuous leadership, as has been previously presented, encapsulates behaviors and attitudes that empower group members to experience feelings of thriving and flourishing, cultivate their innate potential, and display their inner capabilities. This approach integrates virtues, such as integrity, humility, and benevolence, with follower-oriented processes involving intrinsic motivation, follower mindfulness, moral emotions, and encouragement underlying work-related well-being. Virtuous leaders are expected to display inclusive behaviors by treating others with dignity and respect, engaging in fair decision-making processes, refraining from discriminating against disadvantaged groups, having concern for the welfare of society in its entirety, and shaping trustful relationships (Gotsis & Grimani, 2015, 2016).

Discussion and Conclusions

An inclusive organization is one in which a set of inclusion practices and processes (psychological safety, involvement in the work group, feeling respected and valued, influence on decision-making, authenticity, and recognizing, honoring, and advancing diversity) are consistently shown at all organizational levels and manifested in all aspects of inclusion: inclusive climate, inclusion practices, perceived organizational inclusion, leader inclusion, and work group inclusion (Shore et al., 2018). More specifically, inclusive leadership embodies a unique potential in both facilitating belongingness (mainly through supporting individuals as group members, ensuring justice and equity within a work group, and sharing decision-making) and indicating value for uniqueness (by encouraging diverse contributions, as well as helping group members fully provide their unique perspectives and abilities to the work group).

Inclusive leadership encompasses behaviors that collectively facilitate all group members' perceptions of belongingness to the work group and that encourage group members to contribute their uniqueness for achieving positive group outcomes (Randel et al., 2018). In a nutshell, inclusive leadership focuses on facilitating a group environment in which members experience the fulfillment of belongingness and uniqueness needs within the work group. Worth noticing is that humility, a core virtue in both the positive organizational and the virtue ethics literature, appears as a significant predictor of inclusive leadership (Randel et al., 2018).

Inclusive leadership is enacted through specific behaviors that facilitate belongingness and indicate value for uniqueness. Virtuous leadership, as demonstrated earlier, encapsulates behaviors and attitudes that empower group members to experience feelings of thriving and flourishing, cultivate their innate potential, and display their inner capabilities: in this respect, virtuous leadership is in a position to fulfill individuals' need for uniqueness, an important dimension of inclusive leadership. Furthermore, virtuous leaders enable their subordinates to cultivate their potential as valued members of a community of friendship, a moral community founded in interpersonal justice and fairness. In such a framework, individual identities are shaped through their embeddedness in this community, and individuals feel as constituents of relations of interconnectedness, in a way that their needs for belongingness are appreciated and fulfilled.

Leader virtues in particular, such as humility, forgiveness, compassion, and affability, may be thought of as antecedents of inclusive workplaces. Virtuous leadership is more holistic, contextual, and relational: dependent upon the specific context, virtuous leadership is viewing people as ends in and by themselves, and primarily not as means to satisfy organizational ends. Virtuous leadership develops leader moral reasoning and encourages employees' positive affect, intrinsic motivation, and meaningful and prosocial behaviors, thus nurturing strong psychological safety climates indicated by trust and forgiveness, conducive to human flourishing and well-being. In a community of friendship, group members are more prone to exhibit purposeful and helping behaviors that mitigate the negative effects of stereotypes and prejudice for outgroup members. Through their participative practices, virtuous leaders recognize that all subordinates are worthy of equal dignity and respect, deserving respectful treatment, thus honoring and affirming their distinctive needs for uniqueness and belongingness, respectively.

This chapter provided an integrative framework of virtuous leadership and inclusion in organizations, giving emphasis on how leaders enact virtuous behaviors from which a diversity of organizational stakeholders can significantly benefit. Virtuous leadership generates multilevel beneficial outcomes, indicating that it is inherently inclusive.

References

Aguirre-Y-Luker, G., Hyman, M. R., & Shanahan, K. J. (2017). Measuring systems of virtue development. In A. J. G. Sison, G. R. Beabout, & I. Ferrero (Eds.), *Handbook of virtue ethics in business and management*. Amsterdam, Netherlands: Springer.

Antunes, A., & Franco, M. (2016). How people in organizations make sense of responsible leadership practices: Multiple case studies. *Leadership Organization Development Journal, 37*(1), 126–152.

Bachmann, C. (2019). Practical wisdom: Revisiting an ancient virtue in the context of a diverse business world. In M. Stangel-Meseke, C. Boven, G. Braun, A. Habisch, N. Scherle, & F. Ihlenburg (Eds.), *Practical wisdom and diversity* (pp. 23–40). Berlin: Springer.

Bauman, D. C. (2018). Plato on virtuous leadership: An ancient model for modern business. *Business Ethics Quarterly, 28*(3), 251–274.

Bohl, K. W. (2019). Leadership as phenomenon: Reassessing the philosophical ground of leadership studies. *Philosophy of Management,* 1–20.

Bragues, G. (2006). Seek the good life, not money: The Aristotelian approach to business ethics. *Journal of Business Ethics, 67*(4), 341–357.

Bragues, G. (2010). Profiting with honor: Cicero's vision of leadership. *Journal of Business Ethics, 97*(1), 21–33.

Caldwell, C., Hasan, Z., & Smith, S. (2015). Virtuous leadership—insights for the 21st century. *Journal of Management Development, 34*(9), 1181–1200.

Cameron, K. S. (2011). Responsible leadership as virtuous leadership. *Journal of Business Ethics, 98*, 25–35.

Cameron, K. S., Donaldson, S. I., Csikszentmihalyi, M., & Nakamura, J. (2011). Effects of virtuous leadership on organizational performance. In S. I. Donaldson, M. Csikszentmihalyi, & J. Nakamura (Eds.), *Applied positive psychology: Improving everyday life, health, schools, work, society* (pp. 171–183). London: Routledge.

Campbell, K. A. (2015). Can effective risk management signal virtue-based leadership? *Journal of Business Ethics, 129*(1), 115–130.

Carmeli, A., Reiter-Palmon, R., & Ziv, E. (2010). Inclusive leadership and employee involvement in creative tasks in the workplace: The mediating role of psychological safety. *Creativity Research Journal, 22*(3), 250–260.

Choi, S., Tran, T., & Park, B. (2015). Inclusive leadership and work engagement: Mediating roles of affective organizational commitment and creativity. *Social Behavior and Personality: An International Journal, 43*, 931–944.

Crossan, M. M., Byrne, A., Seijts, G. H., Reno, M., Monzani, L., & Gandz, J. (2017). Toward a framework of leader character in organizations. *Journal of Management Studies, 54*(7), 986–1018.

Crossan, M., Mazutis, D., Seijts, G., & Gandz, J. (2013). Developing leadership character in business programs. *Academy of Management Learning Education, 12*(2), 285–305.

Del Baldo, M. (2016). An ethical and virtues-based model of leadership for a good governance insights and reflections between theory and practice. In E. Klein (Ed.), *Corporate governance: Principles, practices and challenges* (pp. 85–107). New York, NY: Nova Science Publishers.

Ferdman, B. M. (2017). Paradoxes of inclusion: Understanding and managing the tensions of diversity and multiculturalism. *The Journal of Applied Behavioral Science, 53*(2), 235–263.

Flynn, G. (2008). The virtuous manager: A vision for leadership in business. *Journal of Business Ethics, 78*(3), 359–372. doi:10.1007/s10551-006-9331-y

Fontrodona, J., Sison, A. J. G., & de Bruin, B. (2013). Editorial introduction: Putting virtues into practice. A challenge for business and organizations. *Journal of Business Ethics, 113*(4), 563–565.

Fujimoto, Y., Azmat, F., & Subramaniam, N. (2019). Creating community-inclusive organizations: Managerial accountability framework. *Business & Society, 58*(4), 712–748.

Gini, A., & Green, R. M. (2014). Three critical characteristics of leadership: Character, stewardship, experience. *Business Society Review, 119*(4), 435–446.

Gotsis, G., & Grimani, K. (2015). Virtue theory and organizational behavior: An integrative framework. *Journal of Management Development, 34*(10), 1288–1309.

Gotsis, G., & Grimani, K. (2016). Diversity as an aspect of effective leadership: Integrating and moving forward. *Leadership Organization Development Journal, 37*(2), 241–264.

Hackett, R. D., & Wang, G. (2012). Virtues and leadership: An integrating conceptual framework founded in Aristotelian and Confucian perspectives on virtues. *Management Decision, 50*(5), 868–899.

Hannah, S. T., & Avolio, B. J. (2011a). Leader character, ethos, and virtue: Individual and collective considerations. *The Leadership Quarterly, 22*(5), 989–994.

Hannah, S. T., & Avolio, B. J. (2011b). The locus of leader character. *The Leadership Quarterly, 22*(5), 979–983.

Hays-Thomas, R., & Bendick, M. (2013). Professionalizing diversity and inclusion practice: Should voluntary standards be the chicken or the egg? *Industrial and Organizational Psychology, 6*(3), 193–205.

Hirak, R., Peng, A. C., Carmeli, A., & Schaubroeck, J. M. (2012). Linking leader inclusiveness to work unit performance: The importance of psychological safety and learning from failures. *The Leadership Quarterly, 23*(1), 107–117.

Javed, B., Naqvi, S. M. M. R., Khan, A. K., Arjoon, S., & Tayyeb, H. H. (2017). Impact of inclusive leadership on innovative work behavior: The role of psychological safety. *Journal of Management Organization*, 1–20.

Karakas, F., & Sarigollu, E. (2013). The role of leadership in creating virtuous and compassionate organizations: Narratives of benevolent leadership in an Anatolian tiger. *Journal of Business Ethics, 113*(4), 663–678.

Ko, I., & Rea, P. (2016). Leading with virtue in the VUCA world. In J. S. Osland, M. Li, & M. E. Mendenhall (Eds.), *Advances in global leadership* (pp. 375–397). Bingley, UK: Emerald Group Publishing Limited.

Kreitz, P. A. (2008). Best practices for managing organizational diversity. *The Journal of Academic Librarianship, 34*(2), 101–120.

Lemoine, G. J., Hartnell, C. A., & Leroy, H. (2019). Taking stock of moral approaches to leadership: An integrative review of ethical, authentic, and servant leadership. *Academy of Management Annals, 13*(1), 148–187.

Manz, C. C., & Manz, K. P. (2014). Virtuous leadership made manifest through education-focused philanthropy: An introduction. *Journal of Management, Spirituality Religion, 11*(3), 194–195.

Manz, C. C., Manz, K. P., Adams, S. B., & Shipper, F. (2011). Sustainable performance with values-based shared leadership: A case study of a virtuous organization. *Canadian Journal of Administrative Sciences, 28*(3), 284–296.

Martínez, S. (2018). Enhancing change implementation through virtuous leadership: A philosophical discourse. In F. Ovadje & S. Aryee (Eds.), *Routledge handbook of organizational change in Africa* (pp. 210–224). London: Routledge.

McLaughlin, M., & Cox, E. (2015). *Leadership coaching: Developing braver leaders*. London: Routledge.

Meara, N. M. (2001). Just and virtuous leaders and organizations. *Journal of Vocational Behavior, 58*(2), 227–234.

Meyer, M., Sison, A. J. G., & Ferrero, I. (2019). How positive and Neo-Aristotelian leadership can contribute to ethical leadership. *Canadian Journal of Administrative Sciences, 36*(3), 390–403.

Morales-Sánchez, R., & Cabello-Medina, C. (2013). The role of four universal moral competencies in ethical decision-making. *Journal of Business Ethics, 116*(4), 717–734.

Morales-Sánchez, R., & Cabello-Medina, C. (2015). Integrating character in management: Virtues, character strengths, and competencies. *Business Ethics: A European Review, 24*, S156–S174.

Neubert, M. J. (2011). Introduction: The value of virtue to management and organizational theory and practice. *Canadian Journal of Administrative Sciences, 28*(3), 227–230.

Neubert, M. J., Carlson, D. S., Kacmar, K. M., Roberts, J. A., & Chonko, L. B. (2009). The virtuous influence of ethical leadership behavior: Evidence from the field. *Journal of Business Ethics*, *90*(2), 157–170.

Office of Personnel Management. (2011). *Government-wide diversity and inclusion strategic plan*. U.S. Office of Personnel Management, Office of Diversity and Inclusion.

Palanski, M. E., Cullen, K. L., Gentry, W. A., & Nichols, C. M. (2015). Virtuous leadership: Exploring the effects of leader courage and behavioral integrity on leader performance and image. *Journal of Business Ethics*, *132*(2), 297–310.

Palanski, M. E., & Vogelgesang, G. R. (2011). Virtuous creativity: The effects of leader behavioural integrity on follower creative thinking and risk taking. *Canadian Journal of Administrative Sciences*, *28*(3), 259–269.

Pearce, C. L., & Csikszentmihaly, M. (2014). Virtuous leadership revisited: The case of Hüsnü Özyeğin of FIBA Holding. *Journal of Management, Spirituality Religion*, *11*(3), 196–207.

Pearce, C. L., Waldman, D. A., & Csikszentmihaly, M. (2006). Virtuous leadership: A theoretical model and research agenda. *Journal of Management, Spirituality Religion*, *3*(1–2), 60–77.

Pearce, C. L., Waldman, D. A., & Csikszentmihaly, M. (2008). Virtuous leadership: A theoretical model and research agenda. In C. C. Manz, K. S. Cameron, K. P. Manz, & R. D. Marx (Eds.), *The virtuous organization: Insights from some of the world's leading management thinkers* (pp. 211–230). Singapore: World Scientific Publishing.

Randel, A. E., Galvin, B. M., Shore, L. M., Ehrhart, K. H., Chung, B. G., Dean, M. A., & Kedharnath, U. (2018). Inclusive leadership: Realizing positive outcomes through belongingness and being valued for uniqueness. *Human Resource Management Review*, *28*(2), 190–203.

Rego, A., Clegg, S., & Cunha, M. P. (2012). The positive power of character strengths and virtues for global leaders. In K. S. Cameron & G. Spreitzer (Eds.), *The Oxford handbook of positive organizational scholarship* (pp. 366–381). Oxford: Oxford University Press.

Rego, A., Cunha, M. P., & Clegg, S. R. (2012). *The virtues of leadership: Contemporary challenges for global managers*. Oxford: Oxford University Press.

Rego, A., Júnior, D. R., & Cunha, M. P. (2015). Authentic leaders promoting store performance: The mediating roles of virtuousness and potency. *Journal of Business Ethics*, *128*(3), 617–634.

Riggio, R. E., Zhu, W., Reina, C., & Maroosis, J. (2010). Virtue-based measurement of ethical leadership: The leadership virtues questionnaire. *Consulting Psychology Journal: Practice Research*, *62*(4), 235–250.

Roberson, Q. M. (2006). Disentangling the meanings of diversity and inclusion in organizations. *Group Organization Management*, *31*(2), 212–236.

Shore, L. M., Cleveland, J. N., & Sanchez, D. (2018). Inclusive workplaces: A review and model. *Human Resource Management Review*, *28*(2), 176–189.

Shore, L. M., Randel, A. E., Chung, B. G., Dean, M. A., Holcombe Ehrhart, K., & Singh, G. (2011). Inclusion and diversity in work groups: A review and model for future research. *Journal of Management*, *37*(4), 1262–1289.

Sinnicks, M. (2018). Leadership after virtue: MacIntyre's critique of management reconsidered. *Journal of Business Ethics*, *147*(4), 735–746.

Sison, A. J. G. (2006). Leadership, character and virtues from an Aristotelian viewpoint. In T. Maak & N. M. Pless (Eds.), *Responsible leadership* (pp. 128–141). London: Routledge.

Sosik, J. J., & Cameron, J. C. (2010). Character and authentic transformational leadership behavior: Expanding the ascetic self toward others. *Consulting Psychology Journal: Practice Research*, *62*(4), 251–269.

Sosik, J. J., Chun, J. U., Ete, Z., Arenas, F. J., & Scherer, J. A. (2018). Self-control puts character into action: Examining how leader character strengths and ethical leadership relate to leader outcomes. *Journal of Business Ethics*, 1–17.

Sosik, J. J., Gentry, W. A., & Chun, J. U. (2012). The value of virtue in the upper echelons: A multisource examination of executive character strengths and performance. *The Leadership Quarterly*, *23*(3), 367–382.

Sturm, R. E., Vera, D., & Crossan, M. (2017). The entanglement of leader character and leader competence and its impact on performance. *The Leadership Quarterly*, *28*(3), 349–366.

Theodorakopoulos, N., & Budhwar, P. (2015). Guest editors' introduction: Diversity and inclusion in different work settings: Emerging patterns, challenges, and research agenda. *Human Resource Management*, *54*(2), 177–197.

Thun, B., & Kelloway, K. (2011). Virtuous leaders: Assessing character strengths in the workplace. *Canadian Journal of Administrative Sciences*, *28*(3), 270–283.

van Dierendonck, D., & Patterson, K. (2015). Compassionate love as a cornerstone of servant leadership: An integration of previous theorizing and research. *Journal of Business Ethics*, *128*(1), 119–131.

Wang, G., & Hackett, R. (2016). Conceptualization and measurement of virtuous leadership: Doing well by doing good. *Journal of Business Ethics*, *137*(2), 321–345.

Whetstone, T. (2005). A framework for organizational virtue: The interrelationship of mission, culture and leadership. *Business ethics: A European Review, 14*(4), 367–378.

Winters, M. F. (2014). From diversity to inclusion: An inclusion equation. In B. M. Ferdman & B. R. Deane (Eds.), *Diversity at work: The practice of inclusion* (pp. 205–228). San Francisco, CA: Jossey-Bass.

Ye, Q., Wang, D., & Guo, W. (2019). Inclusive leadership and team innovation: The role of team voice and performance pressure. *European Management Journal, 37*(4), 468–480.

Yuan, L. (2013). Wise and virtuous leadership: The contribution of Confucian values to business leadership. In M. J. Thompson & D. Bevan (Eds.), *Wise management in organisational complexity* (pp. 106–121). Berlin: Springer.

8

INCLUSIVE LEADERSHIP AND EMOTIONAL INTELLIGENCE

Juanita Coleman-Merritt

Introduction

Exclusivity in the workplace has been a hallmark of the working world in America for most of its existence. Beginning with its long and tawdry history of slave labor, the country has experienced a distortion in the way that our labor system has developed. Unfair treatment of participants in the work environment throughout American history has been primarily based on skin color and gender. However, many ethnic and language groups, including Germans, the Irish, Italians, various Asian peoples and Latinos have also taken turns bearing the burdens of economic exclusion and workplace discrimination. European ethnic groups have sometimes evened the playing field by masking their backgrounds: changing their names, dropping their accents—even hiding their grandparents, in order to fit in and be included.

Given this history and the extent of cultural and ethnic diversity in America, modern American work environments have had much to learn about inclusion. The Second World War that caused women to enter the work world in droves; the civil rights movements of the 1960s, which resulted in the passage of many federal and state anti-discrimination laws across America; and eventually the economic imperatives of the technological revolution and globalization have driven American employers to increasingly embrace nondiscriminatory practices. Gradually, over the last 50 years, and because of the great effort of many determined individuals, this kind of overt disregard and disrespect for employees has diminished.

Since this doorway to inclusive practices was opened, it has become obvious to more and more employers that businesses become more competitive and successful as they become more inclusive—hiring based on individual talent, then recognizing and taking greater advantage of the diverse perspectives and individual strengths available to them. Many employers have implemented diversity training programs at all levels of their businesses in order to improve the work environment, so that all workers can contribute to the success of the enterprise. The wisest of employers and managers have gone beyond the prevention of workplace conflict and actively sought to promote the well-being and efficacy of each employee.

What Is Inclusive Leadership and Why Has It Become a Desirable Quality in Today's Workplace?

The term "inclusive leadership" has come to characterize the organizational approach of business leaders who truly recognize the value of every employee and seek to enhance each person's capacity and opportunity to contribute. Inclusive leaders use a system of evaluation and promotion based on merit. They are not personally threatened by the abilities or strengths of coworkers or subordinate employees. They actively try to learn about and harness such strengths and abilities because they understand that each worker's best effort enhances the outcome of the common product.

In their article "Inclusive Leaders: Why Are Inclusive Leaders Good for Organizations and How to Become One," Bourke and Espedido state that research on workplace performance shows that businesses that consciously promote inclusive leadership practices tend to outperform those that do not: they are 17% more likely to report high performance; 20% more likely to have a high quality of decision-making and 29% more likely to have workers that exhibit collaborative behavior. They also tend to have a higher level of attendance.

Bourke and Espedido surveyed 4,100 businesses identified as having highly inclusive work environments and highlighted six categories of behaviors or traits that are characteristic of leadership in these organizations:

- Visible commitment to diversity and inclusion
- Humility—modesty regarding capabilities and admission of mistakes
- Awareness of bias
- Curiosity about others—open mindset
- Cultural intelligence—adaptive
- Collaboration—willingness to empower others

According to these practitioners, inclusive leaders actively show their interest in promoting diversity and implementing strategies/activities that encourage appreciation for diversity.

They exhibit their humility by being modest about their own capabilities, admit their mistakes and encourage others to shine, as well as acknowledge their own need to grow. They actively work to discourage bias and support meritocracy in the organization. Because they are curious about others and open to learning about them, they develop cultural intelligence and adaptability to different perspectives. They tend to be collaborative in their approach to organizational activities because this approach utilizes the varied strengths and abilities of the workers they seek to lead.

Bourke and Espedido comment that if a leader is indeed, inclusive, "[the workers will] agree that they are being treated fairly, respectfully, are valued, have a sense of belonging and are psychologically safe."

Delores's Experience

Let's continue our exploration of inclusive leadership with the story of a worker—we'll call her Delores. Delores immigrated to the United States from Jamaica as a young woman—she was anxious to make a life in her new country and she was determined to find a "good job" and do a "good job" wherever she worked. She lived in New York City and found her first job in the jewelry industry in the heart of the city. Delores was happy to board the bus each morning, making her way to the shop before 8 am, where she served at the pleasure of her managers as a "Girl Friday." Her job was whatever the bosses asked her to do: run out to get coffee, deliver materials or finished products wherever they were needed, staff the telephones, write up orders for products.

Delores didn't mind her job title; she felt she was learning about a new business and she believed that learning all she could about the company would make her a valuable employee. She worked for the company 10 years and, when she left there, she was actually doing the work of a senior clerk who provided quality control, handled inventory and purchases of materials, helped to settle disputes and disagreements among staff, kept track of product inventory and interacted with retail store managers regarding the sale of products; however, her title was still "Girl Friday."

When Delores moved to Los Angeles, California, she had already made the acquaintance of several sales managers in the industry on both coasts. She was a single parent who had a young son to raise and needed a job right away. Her contacts helped her land a job in a small company that actually created a position for her because she was so highly recommended. The owner was looking for ways to make the company grow. Within two years, she was sought after by a company where the owner and manager were both new to the jewelry business and offered her a position, again because of her reputation with retail managers in the business. Delores, whose salary had barely increased in over two years, accepted a position as a quality control clerk.

At that point, Delores was knowledgeable about the business she had set out to learn. She felt accomplished and she liked her job. Over the years, she designed trainings for all workers to help them see themselves as part of a team. She helped improve working conditions and retain skilled workers by speaking up and letting her employers know when the staff was disgruntled about concerns such as overtime or lack of vacation. She advised her bosses when products needed to be improved or changed to better serve the market. She negotiated prices with suppliers of precious metals and stones to her employer's advantage. Delores worked for the company for 20 years and was never promoted to a management position.

When the owner decided to hire another manager, he brought in a young white woman and told Delores to train her. Delores resigned. She felt abused, undervalued and discriminated against.

Delores's story is a classic case. Unfortunately, it is terribly typical of the experiences of countless numbers of people in our society who have been excluded and denied fair opportunity to reap the benefits of their efforts in the workplace—their genuine desire to contribute to the growth and development of the institutions and businesses where they work. This denial of opportunity, respect and financial benefit has been based on race, ethnicity, gender, sexual preference and religious affiliation or lack thereof.

How might inclusive leadership have improved Delores's experience as a dedicated employee?

Actually, Delores probably encountered a higher level of inclusive leadership in her first workplace than in her other work experiences. In that setting, she was able to learn about all of the activities involved in jewelry-making and wholesale operations. She was hired as a "Girl Friday"—a somewhat demeaning job description that we no longer hear in the workplace. Yet, the position allowed for Delores, a curious and quick learner, to become a skilled worker who carved out areas of interest, and no doubt found mentors who informally shared their expertise and encouraged her development. But Delores's supervisors were not inclusive leaders—in spite of her obvious leadership qualities and drive to improve work performance, they did not look for ways to show appreciation for her initiatives, nor did they compensate her through regular pay increases.

In Delores's second position, an inclusive leader might have determined that Delores was really no longer just a clerk—an appropriate job title and an increase in pay could have helped persuade her to continue working with the company and support its growth. However, it was in the third position that Delores's supervisors clearly behaved in an exclusive manner.

Over 20 years of service, the owner and managers showed little recognition of her value to the organization. While they benefitted from her leadership, organizational skills, creativity and work ethic, they too did not compensate her in terms of promotion or pay. And they added insult to injury by requiring that she provide the knowledge and skills that she had earned during her long service to an inexperienced but ethnically acceptable person. She perceived that the newcomer would then become her superior in title, earn greater compensation—and probably continue to use her expertise in order to do the job that should have been offered to her.

Delores felt that because she was a woman of color and had a foreign accent, she was not valued and would never be appreciated, no matter how hard she worked, no matter what she accomplished on behalf of the company.

Inclusive leadership would have taken note of Delores's leadership ability, initiative and, most important, her obvious inclusive tendencies. Her development of trainings to help other workers see themselves as team members who would benefit from the success of the organization was collaborative. She shared her understanding of the business with the whole staff—including her superiors. Since the workers were not organized, Delores stepped up to speak with her supervisors when she felt there were conflicts brewing that should be resolved in order to improve the work environment. She listened carefully to her fellow workers and made suggestions that she thought would work well for both employees and management.

Michael's Experience

Michael is an officer on a large city police force with 20 years of experience. When he completed his initial training, he was immediately assigned to a precinct in the African American community. He was one of only two African Americans in the division. From the beginning of his career, he looked for opportunities for advancement. He talked with his sergeant about his interests and asked about opportunities that might be suitable for him. He stayed abreast of upcoming exams. And he made every effort to demonstrate his dedication to his work. None of his efforts resulted in new assignments or promotion. Over the next few years, he noticed that others with less experience were given opportunities for which he had expressed an interest in or applied to. Michael felt that his efforts and talents were being deliberately overlooked because of racial bias.

There were other incidents that reinforced his sense that he was being discriminated against. He was aware that the other African American officer in the division had been accused of failing to support his partner during an arrest. The officer explained to him that during the arrest the suspect was assaulted by his partner. He had put the handcuffs on and considered the suspect to be his prisoner, so he objected to his partner beating him up. Michael was shocked to find that the accused officer, who was still on probation, was summarily fired.

Michael experienced a similar incident when he and his partner investigated some activities in the park. While they were there, his partner shined a light on a couple who were sitting on a bench kissing and hugging. The man was African American and the woman was white. Michael's partner said, "Let's stop them." When Michael asked, "Why—what's the charge?" his partner had no answer for him and walked away in disgust. He believed that if he had not been African American that couple would have been roughed up or maybe even arrested just because they were a racially mixed couple. What was most disturbing was that when such incidents took place, supervisors seemed to "look the other way."

Michael found himself in an extremely uncomfortable work environment. Some of his fellow officers regularly made racist jokes; others may not have approved but laughed and went along with the program. Even ranking officers heard the comments and made no effort to intervene.

Michael wanted to be reassigned. He spoke to his sergeant about what he was seeing and feeling. He noted that he had tried to seek new assignments but had been turned down for vague reasons. The sergeant signed documents to have Michael transferred within the week.

Michael felt that the sergeant transferred him because he considered him a "troublemaker."

Michaels's new assignment was under the only African American lieutenant on the police force. His experience was entirely different. The lieutenant was demanding—he required his staff to set goals and meet them. But Michael felt that all officers were treated fairly and were held accountable for their interactions with each other and the community they served. Individual officers may have had racist attitudes, but they didn't feel free to make disrespectful comments to others. Officers were there to protect the community from criminals and to ensure a safe community. It was clear that harassment of community members would not be tolerated, so the kind of "rogue" police behavior he had witnessed on his first assignment was rare and quickly deterred.

Yet, Michael felt constrained in his efforts to advance his career. He approached his supervisor about applying for positions where he could specialize—for example in gang operations or internal affairs—and was told that it was "very difficult for black officers to specialize." Still, he had had excellent evaluations for several years at that point, so he went ahead and took the requisite exams. Having passed the exam for a specific position that he knew to be open, he approached his supervisor again and was told that the division "already had one black officer" and would not take another. Because of his determination to fight for what was considered "elite" status, Michael found himself transferred again and placed under the first African American to become a captain in the entire police force. Working under that captain, he finally began to get assignments that led to the promotions he was seeking.

Michael subsequently became a detective in gang operations. He was the only African American working on the floor of the administrative building where elite units were housed. He eventually was promoted to Detective 3 in the Internal Affairs Division—the investigative division that was tasked with making sure that police officers conducted themselves appropriately and were held accountable for criminal or corrupt activities. Michael's long struggle to become a leader in his career of choice had taught him a great deal about how poor leadership can waste an organization's talent and prevent it from becoming a successful enterprise.

Anthony's Experience

Anthony is an educational technology professional. He has worked in two government offices and has faced challenges in his effort to practice inclusive leadership. His first experience was as the lead manager for a team of computer engineers under a government contract with ABC Company. Anthony was tasked with setting up the computer systems and providing training for a group of federal government sites. Having come out of an educational work environment, Anthony was used to being part of an integrated group of practitioners who functioned as a team to assist educational institutions as they developed their capacity to use technology more effectively.

He was surprised to find that his team did not function as an integral part of the department in which they worked. As a manager, he continually had to exert pressure on the departmental heads to meet with the members of his team and to share vital information, so that they would be appropriately informed of the scope of work projects, changing priorities or changes in scheduling. There didn't seem to be any key executive who was aware of the disconnect and prepared to initiate or facilitate a change in this relationship.

Anthony was confronted with a culture that had developed a separation between contracted staff and the host staff they supported. He often felt that he and his team were operating "in the dark." He sometimes moved forward with what he believed to be a good plan of action—given the information he had—but had to abort or change operations based on new information or a seemingly sudden change of plans "from above."

Anthony noted that at one point his team was assigned a project—he was assured that he had adequate personnel for the assignment and that they would be provided with all the necessary resources to get the job done. Midway through the assignment, he was told that his technology staff was being reduced. He had to designate workers to be laid off and adjust the project because of limited resources. These circumstances caused the remaining staff to become uncertain and distrustful. They felt they were expendable and their morale suffered.

While he was aware that his best workers were looking for an "exit strategy," he couldn't blame them—he also was looking for other positions himself, and when he found one, he resigned!

Kevin's Experience

As a newly graduated electrical engineer, Kevin did not immediately find a position directly related to his training. But he had a flexible approach to career development and took a position as a service provider with a company that contracts to develop computer software. The software is designed to meet the specifications of business clients. Then, members of the service team supervise its installation, present it to the staff who will use it and provide them with training. Kevin was hired to work with the staff of 15 to 20 people who were engaged in different aspects of the project. His role was to understand the software and its relationship to the clients' computer systems currently in place in order to foster a smooth transition as the staff learned to use the new product.

Kevin was the newest member of his team. He found that his work environment was constantly shifting because he was servicing businesses in different settings depending on the kind of software, the experience of the staff and the size and structure of the business. He might be assigned to a company that was as large and complicated as an urban school district or to a single real estate office with 8 to 10 employees. He was expected to be comfortable meeting new clients and their workers, quick to learn the intricacies of new software and the systems for which they were intended and confident in presenting training, troubleshooting and finding out how to remedy problems that might arise during a software transition. In spite of the challenging nature of his work, he expressed his sense of feeling supported and appreciated by his team.

Kevin attributed his success during that early stage of his working life to Jim, a leader who recognized his capacity to learn and to relate well to others. He was aware of this good opinion of his potential because Jim told him of his observations. In other words, he let Kevin know of his high expectations when he hired him. Kevin felt that his ability to contribute was respected and that he was included as a full member of the team from the beginning. He was given the information and the tools that he needed, and as he learned, he was encouraged to ask questions, offer opinions and help plan strategies and work schedules in order to effectively and efficiently service clients.

When Jim was recruited to build a new service department with a similar company, he offered all team members, including Kevin, positions in his new operation. Kevin noted that Jim was a leader who protected his staff, recognized their individual talents and skills and looked for ways to offer promotions and/or pay increases based on growth and work output. In the four years that he worked with Jim, he became a successful project manager.

Each of the subjects whose experiences were described in the preceding sections has become an organizational leader. Each of them has endeavored to develop a leadership style (Sadri, 2012) that embraces the practices of inclusive leadership. As they discuss the hallmarks of their practice, we can discern the relationship of high levels of emotional intelligence in the way they interact with coworkers, whether they are followers or leaders in the organization.

What Are the Characteristics Evident in a Leader With High Levels of Emotional Intelligence?

In his seminal book, *Emotional Intelligence: Why It Can Matter More Than IQ*, Goleman (1995) describes emotions as a powerful force in human beings, driven by primal instincts buried deep within our brains. From the verb, *motere*—to move—the word emotion refers to bodily reactions designed to drive a person's movement for the purpose of survival (Goleman, 1995, p. 6). Emotions emanate from the oldest parts of our brains, now layered over by our imposing cortex. Goleman notes that under demanding or stressful situations, the amygdala—the brain's "emotional sentinel"—can "hijack" the brain and take control of the unsuspecting human being (Goleman, 1995, pp. 24–26).

Goleman (2002) tells us that in order to be successful in working with groups of people, whether workers, students, customers or clients, leaders must be able to exercise high levels of self-management and relationship management—in other words, emotional intelligence (EI).

Goleman's model for EI has four domains: self-awareness, self-management, social awareness and relationship management. A person who is self-aware recognizes his or her own bodily reactions to situations and owns them. Self-management requires the development of emotional balance, a positive outlook even in the face of adversity, a drive to achieve and adaptability in difficult or perplexing circumstances—the understanding and strength to master and control one's self regardless of outer conditions. The third domain is social awareness—which Goleman explains as empathy—the ability to understand and feel what others are experiencing—and organizational awareness or sensitivity to the needs of the group as a whole. The fourth domain is relationship management reflected in influence, coaching and mentoring, inspiration, teamwork/team building and conflict management (Goleman, 2011).

Let's look at how each of our four subjects manifest the characteristics and competencies of emotional intelligence.

Delores as an Inclusive Leader

Delores was already acting as an inclusive leader in her capacity as a jewelry shop worker. Aware of her value as an employee, she was devastated by her employer's disregard of her dedication to her work and to the business where she had worked diligently for so long. She was determined to improve her prospects for a career where her abilities would be appreciated and rewarded. Undaunted by her age, she decided to go to college and graduated with a degree in communications. As she networked with colleagues in social organizations and the entertainment industry, she discovered that there were training programs and funding for those who were interested in developing their own organizations that could provide services for underserved communities.

Today, Delores is executive director of a small but significant organization that provides opportunities for young people to engage in cultural and artistic activities that might not ordinarily be available to them. She has a staff of eight, who she encourages to reach out and connect with as many influential individuals and organizations in the surrounding community as possible. In this way, the reach and influence of her programs are far greater than they would otherwise be.

Delores's EI operated in her favor in several ways. First, she was self-aware: she realized that she would probably continue to feel anger and frustration in her position at the jewelry shop. Her positive outlook, desire to achieve and adaptability caused her to seek another pathway in life. She had learned a great deal about running a business and organizing a group of workers to accomplish goals and work as a team. She had learned to listen carefully to her coworkers and help them resolve conflicts with management. She knew how to give constructive criticism in ways that encouraged her colleagues to try harder rather than become resentful. Her study of communications led her to use those insights and skills in building her own organization.

Delores believes in mentoring young people who may have the talent to achieve but need help recognizing their opportunities or seeking out people with experience who can open doorways.

Michael as an Inclusive Leader

Michael's experience in a highly exclusive workplace and his sense of being disrespected and unappreciated heightened his awareness of unfair and biased practices. His EI is evident in his willingness to press his case for access to promotions and coveted assignments in spite of the toxic environment in which he worked. He noted the obvious differences between the practices he faced in his first assignment and those he encountered in the department led by the African American lieutenant where bias, openly racist comments and corrupt behavior were not tolerated.

As Michael was gradually promoted and became a supervisor of others, he thought deeply about the importance of inclusive leadership. He did not want officers under his command to feel the anger, disappointment and hurt that he had experienced so often, earlier in his career.

He made every effort to stay aware of the needs of officers who reported to him—whether it was for training, supplies, constructive criticism, a sympathetic ear or resolution of a problem or conflict. Michael explained that he felt it was extremely important to listen carefully to everyone's concerns—employees all needed to know that they had a voice, so he set aside time for candid communication.

Michael was particularly sensitive to the women under his command. He knew that they felt vulnerable and sometimes unwelcome. They needed for him as a leader to model respect, appreciation and the expectation that they would give excellent service and be rewarded with all the same opportunities as the men. He noted that in all the years he worked with women as officers, he had been especially impressed with their effort and work ethic.

Michael's goal as a leader was to make sure that his officers had all the necessary tools to be successful—he felt that successful employees are what make a supervisor successful. Over his years on the police force, he found that inclusive leadership practices were increasingly promoted and the police force gradually became more diverse. He was eventually promoted to lieutenant and earned the reputation of running the most outstanding unit in his division.

Anthony as an Inclusive Leader

In his previous workplace, Anthony exhibited the understanding and EI to be an inclusive leader, but worked under conditions that caused his staff to become distrustful and unmotivated. He was unable to encourage their confidence and good faith effort because he was excluded by his superiors and therefore uninformed himself.

When he left that work setting, Anthony took a similar position as a lead customer support in another department. In this setting, he and his team have full access to the resources and information that they need to service their clients. Initially, Anthony felt he was facing a steep learning curve because of the large number of clients in four different locations, but he became confident in his ability to be successful because of his supervisors' openness and supportive approach.

Anthony's EI is evident in his analysis of how the two work environments differ. He notes that his new leadership promotes collaborative practices. He has daily interaction with the leadership team and he understands the guidelines within which his service team operates. He has been asked to assist in planning and setting priorities, which allows him to help his team execute their tasks smoothly and to experience greater satisfaction in his role as a team lead.

Because Anthony recognizes and appreciates his own positive reactions and improved performance in an open, inclusive setting, he has been able to enhance the performance of team members who report to him as well. For example, supervisors and employees are evaluated according to "smart objectives" in his department—each individual discusses the scope of his/her work within the department with a supervisor, considers areas of strength and areas for growth, then chooses goals for the next evaluation cycle accordingly. Everyone is included in this process.

Anthony has found that some of his team members are not comfortable with this collaborative approach to evaluations. They want him to tell them what they need to do. He has decided that he needs to show his understanding of their apprehensions and provide them with an orientation that helps them see how they can participate in the process and what the benefits would be for them in the long run. He has been able to show them that "smart objectives," when practiced effectively, can help them develop greater self-awareness and self-management objectives. In essence, Anthony is not only leading based on his own EI but is helping his team members activate and improve on their use of EI as well.

Anthony expresses his appreciation of being in a work environment where colleagues communicate openly and respectfully and are able to make connections with each other on all levels. He strives to learn about each team member and understand their individual concerns, motivations and modes of functioning so that he can recognize opportunities for them to grow. He is also able to recognize challenges/problems/conflicts early and help resolve the issues they encounter effectively.

Kevin as an Inclusive Leader

Kevin is our subject who has experienced the most inclusive work settings throughout his career. He was most familiar with the terms inclusive leadership and emotional intelligence.

Kevin describes inclusive leaders in these terms: they are collaborative and interested in their employees' unique perspectives, especially when making important decisions; they try to get everyone's buy-in for new initiatives or changes in ongoing projects; they share information; they believe that collaborative practices develop a stronger and more successful organization.

Kevin found such a leader in his supervisor, Jim. He describes Jim as a person who was "cool under pressure"—he seemed able to calm others under stressful circumstances. Team members trusted him—they felt that he looked for opportunities to increase their effectiveness and promote them. He had a great deal of understanding for team members' concerns and communicated it to them. These were the elements of EI that Kevin identified in his former supervisor.

Kevin has now become a director of originations for an investment management firm that deals in commercial real estate. His team seeks out businesses that are looking for loans to reposition or expand their markets, analyzes whether they are suitable investment opportunities for their group of investors, and then processes and manages the loans. Kevin supervises a group of 11 employees.

Although operating in a very different work setting, Kevin continues to find that people with a high level of EI are important for success in his business. He notes that leaders who have a deep understanding of human beings combined with emotional stability have the greatest success managing others. In his practice, he tries to harness elements of EI that he first admired in Jim and has developed as he progressed through his career and eventually transitioned to the investment business. He finds them essential as he works with both clients and staff.

Kevin strives to maintain a keen awareness of himself and his body. He explains that he practices yoga and meditation regularly to gain control over his emotions and his ability to center himself so he remains calm under pressure. He sees empathy as a key element that helps him to "read people and situations"—this is the foundation for building relationships and "closing the deal." He sees confidence as an important outcome of high EI. Kevin is metacognitive about his feelings and thoughts and consciously strives to increase his emotional competence.

Kevin looks for the characteristics reflected in EI as he works with his team.

He believes in spending time with them reviewing past successful and unsuccessful client relationships and talking through the clients' circumstances, characteristics and business knowledge—having them ask questions and share their opinions. When a team member finds a potential client and proposes an investment, rather than simply rejecting or accepting the proposal, he helps them think through important aspects of the proposal and how well it fits or doesn't fit the company's criteria. He also believes in seeing them in social settings to learn more about them as individuals. He is keenly aware of those who build relationships with clients easily and those who are better at analyzing proposals/reports and crunching the numbers related to a prospective investment.

Enhancing the Effect of EI in the Workplace

We have seen how each of these four leaders have developed their leadership skills and become increasingly committed to inclusive leadership. We have also examined the ways that their varying levels of EI have enhanced their abilities to implement inclusive practices in different workplace environments. Delores and Anthony found that they had to leave the non-inclusive setting in which they were unable to effect positive changes. Each created a space where she/he could foster more satisfying working relationships. Michael was able to use his EI to gradually maneuver his way through a decidedly toxic environment, until he achieved the longevity and status in the organization to create an inclusive work setting in his sphere of influence. There he could demonstrate the effectiveness of his practices and set an example for other leaders to do the same. Kevin, who had the good fortune to work in inclusive settings and be mentored by a leader with EI, has consciously modeled ways for his team members to increase their level of self-awareness, self-management and relationship awareness.

Goleman devotes a chapter in *Emotional Intelligence*, his first definitive treatise on the concept, to the importance of fostering high EI in children. In Chapter 16, "Schooling the Emotions," he describes a class in self-science at the Nueva Learning Center, a private school. The self-science curriculum was developed by the school's founder and director, Karen Stone McGowan—versions of this kind of "emotional literacy training" has spread to a number of schools across the country as intervention/prevention programs for teen smoking, drug abuse, pregnancy and dropping out of high school (Goleman, 1995, ch. 16).

Goleman believes that such classes should be offered regularly to entire school populations. In 1995, when he published *Emotional Intelligence*, such training was still rarely offered as a part of the regular curriculum, but there were several studies that showed positive outcomes for students, such as better understanding of others, more pro-social strategies for interpersonal problem solving, better self-control, assertive (rather than aggressive) social skills, decreases of self-reports of sadness and depression, and even improved scores on standardized achievement tests (Goleman, 1995, p. 263).

Though he notes that such results are generally more pronounced in children than adults, Goleman suggests that elements of EI can be developed and consciously promoted in work environments by leaders who themselves function with a high level of EI and understand the tools they have at their disposal. Michael and Kevin clearly found that some of their reports have learned from and emulated their behavior. Becoming attuned to one's own feelings and to others' feelings, finding ways to handle disagreements or deescalate conflicts, and possessing the art of persuading others to work together toward a common goal are skillsets that can be developed (Goleman, 1995, pp. 149–151). Employees can be given the space to air grievances freely and respectfully in a supportive setting. They can be trained in the art of giving and receiving constructive feedback, which helps to build self-awareness. Everyone in a work setting can be helped to develop networking skills so that they become better at building relationships with their colleagues. Employees can be encouraged to examine and discuss their own strengths, weaknesses and areas for growth (Smiglia & Patoria, 2000). Several organizations now offer training in EI, among them American Management Association, Genos International and Mainstream Corporate Training (Bandura, 1995, 1977).

References

Bandura, A. (1977). Self-efficacy: Toward a unifying theory of behavioral change. *Psychological Review, 84*, 191–215.
Bandura, A. (1995). *Self-efficacy in changing societies*. Cambridge, UK: Cambridge University Press.
Goleman, D. (1995). *Emotional intelligence: Why it can matter more than IQ*. New York, NY: Bantam.
Goleman, D. (2002). *Working with emotional intelligence*. New York, NY: Bantam.
Goleman, D. (2011). *Are women more emotionally intelligent than men?* Retrieved from www.psychologytoday.com/blog/ the-brain-and-emotional-intelligence /201104/are-women-more-emotionally-intelligent-men
Sadri, G. (2012). Emotional intelligence and leadership development. *Public Personnel Management, 41*(3).
Smiglia, J. E., & Patoria, G. (2000). Emotional intelligence: Some have it, others can learn. *CPA Journal, 70*(6).

9
INCLUSIVE LEADERSHIP AND RESPONSIBLE INNOVATION

Toward a Contingency Perspective of Leader-Follower Dynamics in Work Integration Social Enterprises

Susanna L. M. Chui

Introduction

Inclusion within organizations holds great promise in creating dynamic leadership processes. A climate perceived as inclusive by employees can motivate employee commitment and creativity (Choi, Tran, & Park, 2015). This kind of inclusion that serves to generate a motivating and resilient employee phenomenon is emerging especially within the work integration social enterprise (WISE) context. This is because most WISEs are founded to provide a prosocial and supportive work environment for marginalized individuals, with the goal of helping them achieve self-reliance and reintegration into society through job employment (Bode, Evers, & Schulz, 2006).

Building an inclusive organizational climate hinges on a coherent integration of leadership, organizational climate of fairness, perceived organizational inclusion and work group commitment (Shore, Cleveland, & Sanchez, 2018). Social constructionist approaches to leadership emphasized a context where leaders and followers cooperate and collaborate to achieve organizational goals as part of the inclusive leadership process (Hollander, 2009). Hollander (2009, p. 3) describes 'inclusion' as a phenomenon having the essence of "doing things with people, rather than to people" as a kind of fair exchange. Inclusive leaders create, shape and build an environment for active followership and followers' participation for pursuing and accomplishing group, organizational and community goals. As part of this inclusive environment building, responsible innovation is an important strategy for empowering and motivating collective efforts.

This chapter aims at theorizing inclusive leadership with a contingency perspective. It is divided into five sections. First, multiple factors that contribute towards inclusive leadership are put forth. Second, how inclusive leadership is played out in the WISE context is elaborated. Third, the concept of responsible innovation is introduced. Fourth, the relationship between inclusive leadership and responsible innovation is discussed through the illustration of a WISE case. Finally, the chapter concludes that inclusive leadership contextualized in the WISE context deserves more research attention.

Inclusive Leadership—Definitions and Contingency Factors

Inclusive leadership puts 'inclusion' at the centre of the leading and collaborating processes amongst leaders, followers and informal leaders who do not hold formal leadership positions. Inclusion can be fostered by leader inclusiveness, which is described as the encouragement and empowerment of different viewpoints of diverse members by leaders (Mitchell et al., 2015). In such a way, the hierarchical approach of leading is diminished to make space for more participation and self-organization of followers. Hence, the definitions of inclusive leadership being advanced depart from the traditional single leader or 'great men theories' leadership' perspective. Instead, the concept of a more participative, distributed and bottom-up approach of leading with formal leaders making space and time for informal leaders to contribute in the leading process has been put forth by scholars.

To understand inclusive leadership, a holistic view on processes that can bring about a collaborative and cooperative work group environment is required. Hollander (2009) described inclusive leadership as the relationships that facilitate the accomplishment of organizational performance for mutual benefits. Randel et al. (2018) conceptualized inclusive leadership as a set of positive leader behaviours that aim to fulfil two work group needs—(i) members' perceived belongingness and (ii) perceived group uniqueness. These theoretical perspectives assert a social constructionist approach in conceptualizing inclusive leadership as a shared and dynamic phenomenon that relies not only on formal leaders in the leadership process. They assert that inclusive leadership requires a contingency approach in understanding how factors related to the situation and other players within and outside organizations could impact on leadership and leadership effectiveness.

As inclusive leadership is a collaborative and contingent process that binds leaders and followers in acting dynamically towards common goals, what fosters the emergence of inclusion involves five situational factors (Shore et al., 2018). First, work group inclusion involves the experiences of an individual within his or her group and of having one's sense of belonging anchored within that group (Shore et al., 2011). Second, inclusive leadership also refers to the role of the leader or immediate supervisor in creating and fostering experiences of inclusion, especially for organizational members of marginalized social groups, and thus can collectively build an inclusive organization. Research has revealed that inclusive leadership has a positive relationship with psychological safety and employee engagement and involvement in creative work (Carmeli, Reiter-Palmon, & Ziv, 2010). Third, perceived organizational inclusion on the part of the employee perceptions is crucial for fostering proactive followership which is an essential outcome, directly related to the social mission of raising up the marginalized (Avery, McKay, Wilson, & Volpone, 2008). Studies have implicated the importance of the exchanges between the leader and the employees for the employee to experience perceived organizational inclusion (Shore et al., 2018). Fourth, organizational inclusion practices stress the role of top management and refer to the practices that would enhance inclusion, such as enhancing the retention of diverse talent and leveraging diversity to enhance organizational performance, developing accountability systems for inclusion and using peer support for inclusion etc. Last but not least, organizational climate is considered the perceptions of the practices, organizational procedures and behaviours that employees observe getting rewarded (Schneider, Ehrhart, & Macey, 2013). Thus, inclusive climate refers to the collective perceptions that the norms that guide employee behaviours are consistent with the employees' self-concept, along with their various identities, and that the norms are included in the decision-making process (Nishii, 2013). Research on inclusive climates reveals that they have positive effects on the organization and decrease the possible problems that arise from diversity, such as high turnover and conflicts (Holvino, Ferdman, & Merrill-Sands, 2004). In summary, the discussed factors of inclusive leadership facilitate the process towards building the desired positive selves of employees in general. The way these five situational factors play out in WISE will be further discussed in the next section.

Inclusive Leadership at WISEs

WISEs provide a meaningful work environment for marginalized individuals, such as people with disabilities (PWDs), ex-inmates, deviant youth and the elderly, with the goal of supporting them to reintegrate into society through job employment. The opportunity to gradually attain a positive self-identity through work role enactment is crucial for these WISE employees. Work engagement and interaction with colleagues and customers create avenues for social acceptance, through which their socially marginalized or stigmatized identity could be healed and/or reverted. These employees, when empowered, also develop a positive work attitude as they experience psychological safety within an inclusive environment. By internalizing a work role while simultaneously honing their work skills, they can gradually assert self-confidence, self-efficacy and self-esteem. Members of disadvantaged groups can go through reintegration into society as employees in WISEs. The opportunity to contribute to their social enterprises further deepens their work motivation, which directly helps them pursue self-determination.

The intrinsic nature of WISEs is about social inclusion where inclusive leadership is typically found. WISEs have been considered as the emerging engine that promotes social inclusion, equality and diversity (Vidal, 2005; Tuner & Martin, 2005). WISEs create an inclusive environment for job training and placement for the marginalized communities who find it difficult to find jobs in the mainstream job market (Vidal, 2005). The following sections will elaborate further on how the five inclusion factors discussed before are found in WISEs.

Work Group Inclusion

With work engagement, WISEs provide work roles and emotional support for social beneficiaries who have suffered from prior marginalization and stigmatization to restore positive psychology (Rothbard & Patil, 2012). Structural discrimination occurs when stigmatized groups are discriminated by institutional practices over time (Link, Phelan, & Hatzenbuehler, 2015). The way individuals can derive subjective vitality at WISEs come from three areas of need fulfilment, including the needs for belongingness, competence and autonomy, which has been elaborately explained and discussed by the self-determination theory (Ryan & Deci, 2000). The work opportunity given at WISEs to the marginalized, who are otherwise deprived of such an opportunity, creates a spontaneous sense of inclusion and belongingness for these employees as they occupy a work role. Through work engagement, they gain respect from different communities, from colleagues to customers. More importantly, they regain and rebuild a new sense of self with new work skills and capacity. Competence is developed as they are trained up to appropriate skill levels to handle job roles. As social enterprises are created voluntarily with a social mission to benefit the community, this kind of prosocial environment within WISEs which are people-oriented also provides a context for the marginalized to secure autonomy in regaining personal growth, social acceptance and self-worth while being a part of society. Moreover, the within-group shared identity of employees with similar backgrounds form a new energy resource to establish a new positive work identity, creating a collective upward spiral effect of positive psychology.

Leader Inclusion

Social enterprises are defined as an 'extreme case' of hybridization, where a social mission is housed within a commercial operation, financed by a business model (Battilana & Lee, 2014). As part of the hybrid organizing, WISE founders and leaders provide the appropriate environment for the beneficiaries to thrive by addressing the states of underemployment and poverty. These leaders model inclusiveness through a contingency perspective by responding to the beneficiaries' needs and deploying strategies in constructing a positive workplace with the appropriate situational forces.

To implement this contingency approach, inclusive leaders at WISEs exercise flexibility and experimentation with the aim to find a person-role fit for the underemployed individuals. Very often, the internal training of these beneficiaries requires extra efforts because of the need to meet the commercial expectation and standard of customers. Nonetheless, this integration of organizational activities that balance the social and commercial goals can create organizational tensions for leaders as they face potential paradoxes in the allocation of "human, financial, and attentional resources" (Battilana & Lee, 2014, p. 413). More attention or resources need to be assigned to look after the emotional stability, professional standard of services, job-related skillsets and commercial mindsets of these employees in order to run a commercial business that generates revenue effectively and to achieve financial sustainability.

Leader inclusion in WISEs, depending on the scale and nature of businesses, can involve an intensive process of appealing to the multiple audiences of different sectors, business and social, to seek legitimacy, expert advice and resources. This is part of the situational nature of inclusive leadership at WISEs. With a conscious awareness of balancing the social and commercial objectives, WISE leaders respond to this kind of hybrid organizing and balancing with proactive behaviours in creating an inclusive but also financially sustainable environment for the healthy personal development of the beneficiaries. Discussed by institutional scholars who considered WISEs as a kind of hybrid organizations, the building of an inclusive workplace involves paradoxes and tensions in serving the social and commercial objectives (Battilana & Lee, 2014). Thus, to avoid mission drift towards either the social or the commercial goals, leaders have to exercise discipline in achieving the integration of organizational activities.

Perceived Organizational Inclusion

WISE employees' first-hand experience that contributes to their sense of independence is a significant element and is evidence of inclusive leadership being exercised. WISE employees were reported to have moved away from welfare dependency to self-reliance through wage-earning (Ho & Chan, 2010). The active employee participation in the WISE operation facilitates their job satisfaction and happiness. These employee outcomes are social impacts in realizing the goal of social integration and social cohesion. In another study, WISE employees reported work motivation and self-efficacy, which were predicted by work role salience, perceived organizational support and servant leadership (Chui, 2018). WISE employees who perceived to receive support from the organization and the leaders identify with not only their work roles but also their organizations. These identifications developed within them can lead to positive work motivation and self-efficacy as they become driven towards learning, training and role performance. The related research findings have shown that inclusive work engagement can foster the disadvantaged to secure not only wages but also a sense of empowerment and encouragement. These employees can develop perceived job satisfaction, work motivation and, over time, positive work role salience. Moreover, these employees' or followers' positive work identity can be associated with the relational aspect of the leadership process.

Leadership is a socially constructed process during which leaders influence followers' self-concept (Lord & Brown, 2004). The WISE leaders possibly are behaving and strategizing in a way with a goal to serve the needs of their beneficiaries. As employees interact with caring and fair leaders and are trained in a way that empowers them, they are naturally put under the kind of moral influence that promotes a strong sense of inclusion. Research of servant leadership as a positive, morally ethical and other-directed behavioural scale has been empirically examined and is related to positive individual and teamwork outcomes, including work performance, organizational citizenship behaviour (OCB) and job satisfaction (Donia, Raja, Panaccio, & Wang, 2015; Hu & Liden, 2011). Therefore, perceived organization inclusion in WISEs which are running for the genuine benefit of their employees can positively impact their beneficiaries, who develop a positive perception of inclusion.

Organizational Inclusion Practice and Climate

As leaders can shape culture, the influence of leadership goes beyond making a dyadic impact to creating a norm that individuals and groups find meaningful to follow. Culture of a group is defined as

> a pattern of shared basic assumptions that was learned by a group as it solved its problems of external adaptation and internal integration, that has worked well enough to be considered valid and, therefore, to be taught to new members as the correct way to perceive, think, and feel in relation to those problems.
>
> *(Schein, 2004, p. 17)*

This shared experience requires the consistent practice of behaviours and a shared purpose that followers find aspirational. At WISEs, the superordinate goal of achieving social inclusion and creating workplaces for the disadvantaged become a prosocial norm that employees and subordinates look up to. Research has also shown that the emergence of a serving culture is related to servant leadership (Liden, Panaccio, Meuser, Hu, & Wayne, 2014). It is expected that followers who are under the ethical influence of leadership at WISEs can become prosocial and may be actively engaged in co-leading the social inclusion mission.

While WISE leaders work to create internal social value, they also have a duty to manage financial sustainability. This balancing act urges them to explore and experiment with innovative ideas in the process of managing the financial bottom line. The hybrid nature of the integrated organizational activities forces them to innovate without creating trade-offs for their beneficiaries. Moreover, very often, a high degree of care, sensitivity and responsiveness are involved in designing new areas of business lines that can integrate the talents of these beneficiaries. It is this kind of responsible consideration in the process of introducing innovations that link 'responsible innovation' to WISEs.

Responsible Innovation

Responsible innovation is defined as "a collective commitment of care for the future through responsive stewardship of science and innovation in the present" (Owen, Bessant, & Heintz, 2013, p. 36). With the goal of building a better society, concepts of "responsible innovation" (RI), "responsible research and innovation" (RRI) and "responsible development" emerged at the dawn of the new millennium, creating new concepts for responsibility and innovation (Guston et al., 2014). At the core of RI is the collective enactment of care and responsiveness in addressing social issues that propel the continuous stream of strategic innovation. RI also requires the convergence of values, cognition, adaptive behaviours and leader-based agentic dynamics of institutional actors. Therefore, the concept of responsible innovation when applied in WISE operations can be considered as innovative product or service offerings that fully deploy, match and maximize the potentials of the social beneficiaries working in the respective social enterprises. Moreover, these innovative offerings are also required to answer the financial bottom line. Therefore, responsible innovation is also a survival strategy for the hybrid organizing in WISEs.

Organizational innovation and change are part of the hybrid organizing of social enterprises (Battilana & Lee, 2014). The hybrid organizing in fulfilling both the social and the commercial bottom line produces stretch goals that require constant adaptation and experimentation. This is because new opportunities linked to financial revenue sources or new ways of providing solutions that meet beneficiaries' needs can be constantly changing. This requires corresponding adjustment to ensure sustainability of these social enterprises. To justify this line of discussion, a WISE case is presented in the next section. It illustrates how inclusive leadership is strongly linked to responsible innovation for attaining both social and financial goals over the course of its 10 years since inception.

A WISE Case of Inclusive Leadership and Responsible Innovation

Founded in 2009 as Dialogue in the Dark Hong Kong (DIDHK), DIDHK commenced its start-up as mobile workshops in 2009 to test the market and their business model. DIDHK is a privately owned enterprise funded entirely by individual shareholders. It has grown from a social enterprise that provides experiential tours in darkness to a corporate training partner, providing training workshops to business organizations in Hong Kong. They grew from a team of less than 10 people in 2009 to 40 full-time staff with a team of 25–30 full-time and part-time visually impaired (VI) and hearing-impaired (HI) trainers. Over 50% of the core management team members are PWDs. As a social enterprise, the board sets aside a percentage of their profit in the DID Foundation for supporting the personal development of their PWD employees.

Interviews with the previous general manager and the current CEO have provided the narratives of how DIDHK's organizational development has moved from a critical state of constrained resources to achieving not only the equilibrium of meeting the double bottom line but also the complex dynamics of allowing self-organization and innovation to co-exist and co-evolve. The organizational development is divided into four phases—(i) disequilibrium, (ii) amplifying action to facilitate responsible innovation, (iii) recombination of resources to integrate strengths, and (iv) continuous responsible innovation beyond stabilization. These phases depict how the organization experienced financial struggle. However, through the empowerment of bottom-up self-organization, innovative service offerings emerged to create new business opportunities. The seamless integration of the talents of PWD allowed them to charter new stages of responsible innovation, one after another. Moreover, the case illustrates how inclusive leadership and responsible innovation can be closely integrated for sustaining the creation of both social and financial values.

Phase One—Disequilibrium Before Financial Breakeven

Much as DIDHK had attracted attention and sales revenue since 2009, the operation was still running at a loss financially six months into its opening at a fixed location in 2010 because of its high operational and maintenance costs. The previous general manager (GM) came on board in June 2010. Although the GM understood that the financial shortfall was normal for a new start-up, he did not allow himself to be complacent and set the goal of seeking revenue increase but also by providing the conditions to facilitate bottom-up dynamics. He stated that they had no specific strategy but they tried everything in order to achieve financial viability. Identifying that the corporate workshops achieved a higher profit margin, he mobilized two levels of members to act. First, he promoted one junior member of the sales team to head up the team as a manager and set a sales target to be achieved. Second, he appealed to the board to facilitate referral of potential corporate clients for the sales team to follow up on. 'Opportunity tension' was heightened at this stage of disequilibrium in such a way that every staff worked hard in attaining financial breakeven. The organization, including the founders, were not imposing the urgency of revenue increase. Seeing that it was a natural course for building up clientele, however, the GM, new then in 2010, turned the imbalance of the financial situation into a positive tension, putting different functional systems, such as the sales team, the board and the educational team of the visually impaired trainers on the their toes and seeking solutions for achieving financial stability. The result was almost immediate, with the following month witnessing income exceeding expenditures in July 2010, although the financial breakeven was not yet to be achieved until the end of the following year in 2011. The previous GM turned the financial shortfall into a stretch goal and motivated collective efforts towards the problem-solving process.

Phase Two—Amplifying Action in Bringing About Responsible Innovation

In order to find more revenue sources, the small team at DIDHK constantly sought new product ideas for experimentation, including 'Birthday in the Dark' and 'Dating in the Dark.' When the company came up with the concept of 'Concert in the Dark' and realized its potential of generating a sufficiently large audience, they started to look for collaborators in terms of singers and musicians. They successfully found a mobile phone operator to be a major sponsor as the corporation's corporate social responsibility programme. This not only allowed the costs of the event to be absorbed, it also started to extend the advantage of social capital and continued to propel staff to seek more opportunities with corporate collaborators.

'Concert in the Dark' was an innovation, because this was the first live concert ever held in the dark, putting all the musicians, singers and audience in complete darkness. The success of the event helped DIDHK gain popularity; it also boosted the morale of the staff internally to continually seek innovation. Their satisfaction came from the complete ownership of the innovative idea and the successful implementation. Through interviews with the two team heads of the education team who were both visually impaired, they described the process of creating 'Concert in the Dark' as a continuous process of testing and experimentation, as there was no prior reference or people with the same experience. This process helped both the education and the operation teams to reach higher levels of competence. Therefore, impacts of DIDHK accomplished by the end of 2011 were achieved not only within but also outside the enterprise. The success of the 'Concert in the Dark' experiment was only made possible by the bottom-up efforts of the VIs and performers. It was not a top-down instruction but came from a new idea borne from dynamic internal experimentation and adaptation. Because of its pioneer nature, the birth of the event had to be borne from nonlinear interactions and the work of different parties who were ready to enter an experimental mode. The result was an outcome that was unpredictably well received. Its success required close working of all the parties following paths, rules and prudence to allow the operation in darkness to take place without mistakes.

In the meantime, DIDHK continued to attract volunteers to pour in both their time and their expertise to the enterprise because they trusted that their contribution would be meaningful in helping the visually impaired and found that the enterprise was innovative and revolutionary in welcoming new attempts. At this time, they attracted a creative designer who was interested in developing a new business opportunity with DIDHK. This designer explored how to unleash the potential of the hearing-impaired community and therefore worked on products based on using silence and body language as the only form of expression. As a result, a new innovative franchised arm, Dialogue in Silence, was granted by Dialogue in the Dark (Germany) and formed in 2011. This represented a new diversified product of the enterprise. The evolvability has been obvious at DIDHK as they found that while they thrived in seeking innovation, their financial return was also raised. By the end of 2011, the enterprise achieved profitability. DIDHK was also recognized for its performance by obtaining four different awards recognizing its performance in innovation, being a successful social enterprise and promoting the rights of persons with disabilities.

Phase Three—Recombination of Resources to Integrate Strengths

In 2012, DIDHK took the venture to another new height through two major steps.

First, they integrated the dark and silent experiences in their corporate executive workshops to maximize learning for corporate trainees. At the same time, Dialogue in Silence continued to experiment to provide 'entertaining' products which could attract more participants. This gave birth to the new idea of Silence le Cabaret, a dinner with silent entertainment.

Second, DIDHK opened a second location for their new 'Dialogue Experience Square.' This allowed the corporate training workshops to take up more space and cater to more participants.

Phase Four—Sustained Responsible Innovation Beyond Stabilization

In the second quarter of 2012, DIDHK conducted a soul-searching exercise by gathering all staff members together to orchestrate a rebranding exercise. They sought the opinions of all staff members in terms of the social mission, future direction and how to achieve the double bottom line. That paved the way for DIDHK's rebranding and redefining their mission statement. They put more emphasis on empowering the physically challenged and broadening the enterprise's social role to "inspire people to take positive actions to transform the world to a better one" (DIDHK, 2013, pp. 6–9). In an interview, the GM described this as "a major realignment within the organization" and said, "we could move forward with a common ground and a united goal."

The importance of tracking how DIDHK went through the four phases of emergence was to unfold the complexity the enterprise had gone through in meeting its double bottom line. There were obvious bottom-up dynamics validated in how the enterprise had moved from disequilibrium to financial stability. However, the enterprise in many ways never operated with complacency. It consistently faced a number of challenges including high staff turnover; the imminent expiry of the rent-free arrangement in their second location; and the constant and hostile criticism and scepticism coming from the social sector that their profit-making output outweighed their social impact outcomes. Much as the enterprise has emerged to be financially viable, it is thriving on the edge of chaos within and without. DIDHK remains in an operational journey that requires continuous seeking of stabilization in a complex and dynamic environment.

In 2016, in order to address the neglected faculty of PWDs in the job market, a program called DE Empower (DEE) was conceptualized in 2015 as a social innovation initiative in empowering PWD university graduates to be recruited by mainstream employers. The program includes a six-month immersion, embedding a three-month internship in a real workplace. It aims at enabling these PWD trainees with business skills and work experience to enhance their employability in the business world. DEE plays the role of a catalyst in honing the skills and unleashing the potential of PWDs so that they are better prepared for job placement in the business world. The funding for the successful launch of the DEE program in 2016 came from the CSR sponsorship of a major developer who supported the first three years of training and job placement for six cohorts of DEE trainees. However, corporations tend to rotate their CSR funding targets. Therefore, relying on CSR funding does not provide a permanent and self-reliant funding source to sustain the DEE program. Following its launch in 2016, although the DEE program has already equipped five cohorts of 32 trainees, with over 80% of them under sustainable employment, DEE as a social innovation was facing a survival issue, risking the lack of funding for its continuity.

Over the course of the last 10 years, the products and services of the company have diversified. They serve commercial clients to provide dark and silent workshops in order to develop employees' empathy, communication skills, teamwork and heightened awareness of self-competence. Moreover, they develop a number of innovative, cultural and experiential offerings including 'Concert in the Dark,' 'Birthday in the Dark,' 'Love in the Dark,' 'Dinner in the Dark,' 'Silence le Cabaret' and 'Dialogue Experience Silence Yum Cha.' Concert in the Dark and Silence le Cabaret obtained innovative awards in recognition of their excellence in quality and innovativeness. In further advocating the concept of diversity in workplaces, DEE has initiated an iCorp certification program that provides systematic learning processes for corporations that aim at building a 'diverse and inclusive culture.' Still at its inception stage, DEE is constrained by the limited resources to maximize the promotion and advocacy of this program to business organizations in Hong Kong. Hence, the iCorp program has yet to gather momentum and interest from corporations. At the point of completing this chapter, DIDHK remains as a WISE that is yet to stabilize in terms of its financial viability. However, it presents how inclusive leadership in a WISE persists in unleashing the talents of PWD concurrent with the efforts committed to responsible innovation. Hence, it makes a strong case that inclusive leadership within a WISE context can face different challenges at different times. Only with a dynamic and resilient commitment to responsible leadership and innovation can a hybrid organization continue to attain its balancing act of sustainable social-financial value creation.

Conclusion

Research has shown that a leadership process that involves supportive, open-minded and responsive leaders who are ready to listen produces an inclusive environment that facilitates creativity and innovation (Choi et al., 2015; Carmeli et al., 2010). WISEs create an exemplary environment for showing not only inclusive leadership but also a nourishing ground for responsible innovation within which both formal and informal leaders can be engaged in producing new ideas for the benefit of social-financial value creation. As this kind of hybrid organizing is pursued in WISEs, leaders who can manage the process are not only inclusive leaders but also have to be a good team player who can empower team leadership. This is because WISEs require multiple expertise and stakeholders to be part of the innovative process. Their complexity lies in the integration of both social and commercial logics to be sustainable.

References

Avery, D. R., McKay, P. F., Wilson, D. C., & Volpone, S. (2008). Attenuating the elect of seniority on intent to remain: The role of perceived inclusiveness. Presented at the annual *Academy of Management Conference*, Anaheim, CA.

Battilana, J., & Lee, M. (2014). Advancing research on hybrid organizing – Insights from the study of social enterprises. *The Academy of Management Annals*, 8(1), 397–441.

Bode, I., Evers, A., & Schulz, A. (2006). Work integration social enterprises in Europe: Can hybridization be sustainable? In M. Nyssens (Ed.), *Social enterprise: At the crossroads of market, public policies and civil society* (pp. 237–258). London: Routledge.

Carmeli, A., Reiter-Palmon, R., & Ziv, E. (2010). Inclusive leadership and employee involvement in creative tasks in the workplace: The mediating role of psychological safety. *Creativity Research Journal*, 22, 250–260.

Choi, S. B., Tran, T. B. H., & Park, B. I. (2015). Inclusive leadership and work engagement: Mediating roles of affective organizational commitment and creativity. *Social Behaviour and Personality*, 43(6), 931–944.

Chui, S. L. M. (2018). *Construction and impact of leader identity of dynamic work selves at social enterprises: Linkage of the intrapersonal and interpersonal processes with motivation to lead* (Unpublished doctoral dissertation, Durham University Business School, Durham, UK).

DIDHK, 2013–2014: Annual Report of DID HK. Retrieved from https://issuu.com/dialogueexperience/docs/annual_report_2013-14_final_version, pp. 6–9.

Donia, M. B. L., Raja, U., Panaccio, A., & Wang, Z. (2015). Servant leadership and employee outcomes: The moderating role of subordinates' motives. *European Journal of Work and Organizational Psychology*, 25(5), 722–734.

Guston, D. H., Fisher, E., Grunwald, A., Owen, R., Swierstra, T., & van der Burg, S. (2014). Responsible innovation: Motivations for a new journal. *Journal of Responsible Innovation*, 1(1), 1–8.

Ho, A. P., & Chan, K. T. (2010). The social impact of work-integration social enterprises in Hong Kong. *International Social Work*, 53(1), 33–45.

Hollander, E. P. (2009). *Inclusive leadership: The essential leader-follower relationship*. New York, NY: Routledge.

Holvino, E., Ferdman, B. M., & Merrill-Sands, D. (2004). Creating and sustaining diversity and inclusion in organizations: Strategies and approaches. In M. S. Stockdale & F. J. Crosby (Eds.), *The psychology and management of workplace diversity* (pp. 245–276). Malden: Blackwell Publishing.

Hu, J., & Liden, R. C. (2011). Antecedents of team potency and team effectiveness: An examination of goal and process clarity and servant leadership. *Journal of Applied Psychology*, 96(4), 851–862.

Liden, R. C., Panaccio, A., Meuser, J. D., Hu, J., & Wayne, S. J. (2014). Servant leadership: Antecedents, processes, and outcomes. In D. V. Day (Ed.), *The Oxford handbook of leadership and organisations* (pp. 357–379). Oxford: Oxford University Press.

Link, B. G., Phelan, J. C., & Hatzenbuehler, M. L. (2015). Stigma and social inequality. In J. D. McLeod, E. J. Lawler, & M. Schwalbe (Eds.), *Handbook of the social psychology of inequality* (pp. 49–64). Heidelberg: Springer.

Lord, R. G., & Brown, D. J. (2004). *Leadership processes and follower self-identity*. Mahwah, NJ: Lawrence Erlbaum Associates.

Mitchell, R., Boyle, B., Parker, V., Giles, M., Chiang, V., & Joyce, P. (2015). Managing inclusiveness and diversity in teams: How leader inclusiveness affects performance through status and team identity. *Human Resource Management, 54*(2), 217–239.

Nishii, L. H. (2013). The benefits of climate for inclusion for gender-diverse groups. *Academy of Management Journal, 56*(6). https://doi.org/10.5465/amj.2009.0823

Owen, R., Bessant, J., & Heintz, M. (2013). *Responsible innovation: Managing the responsible emergence of science and innovation in society.* West Sussex, UK: John Wiley & Sons, Ltd.

Randel, A. E., Galvin, B. M., Shore, L. M., Ehrhart, K. H., Chung, B. G., Dean, M. A., & Kedharnath, U. (2018). Inclusive leadership: Realizing positive outcomes through belongingness and being valued for uniqueness. *Human Resource Management Review, 28*, 190–203.

Rothbard, N. P., & Patil, S. V. (2012). Being there: Work engagement and positive organizational scholarship. In K. S. Cameron & G. M. Spreitzer (Eds.), *The Oxford handbook of positive organizational support* (pp. 56–69). New York, NY: Oxford University Press.

Ryan, R. M., & Deci, E. L. (2000). Self-determination theory and the facilitation of intrinsic motivation, social development, and well-being. *American Psychologist, 55*(1), 68–78.

Schein, E. H. (2004). *Organizational culture and leadership.* San Francisco, CA: Jossey-Bass.

Schneider, B., Ehrhart, M. G., & Macey, W. H. (2013). Organizational climate and culture. *Annual Review of Psychology, 64*, 361–388.

Shore, L. M., Cleveland, J. N., & Sanchez, D. (2018). Inclusive workplaces: A review and model. *Human Resource Management Review, 28*, 176–189.

Shore, L. M., Randel, A. E., Chung, B. G., Dean, M. A., Ehrhart, K. H., & Singh, G. (2011). Inclusion and diversity in work groups: A review and model for future research. *Journal of Management, 37*, 1262–1289. http://dx.doi.org/10.1177/0149206310385943

Tuner, D., & Martin, S. (2005). Social entrepreneurs and social inclusion: Building local capacity or delivering national priorities. *International Journal of Public Administration, 28*, 797–806.

Vidal, I. (2005). Social enterprise and social inclusion: Social enterprises in the sphere of work integration. *International Journal of Public Administration, 28*, 807–825.

PART II

Inclusive Intersections

10
INCLUDING EVERYONE WITH RESPECTFUL PLURALISM

Debra J. Dean

Introduction

In theory, diversity and inclusion sound like good things. The idea is to include everyone, regardless of their difference. However, many employees are finding that diversity and inclusion exclude their specific difference. This chapter will introduce the reader to the concepts of cultural dimensions, followership, and respectful pluralism to explain that each and every single human being is a unique and different masterpiece. Additionally, discussion of immigration and finding an agreed-upon moral code of conduct is discussed to aid in the explanation of how public and workplace incivility has risen to some of the highest levels of the century. Finally, practical tips to develop a culture of respectful pluralism are provided to promote respect for human dignity.

Cultural Differences

When first introduced to Geert Hofstede's efforts, Dean worked in the heartland of America. According to City-Data (http://www.city-data.com/city/Cedar-Rapids-Iowa.html), the demographics of the town showed 99% white residents; however, the landscape was very different due to the local business community pulling actuarial, engineering, and information technology contractors into the historically corn- and soybean-laden farmland. In the early 2000s the churches, grocery stores, neighborhoods, schools, workplaces, etc. were witnessing a rise in diversity like never seen before.

Hofstede (2001), a Dutch social psychologist and former IBM employee, spent much time researching cross-cultural groups and organizations. The Cultural Dimensions Theory developed by Hofstede reviews power distance, individualism, uncertainty avoidance, masculinity, long-term orientation, and indulgence. At a high level, Hofstede sought to understand if people from different geographical locations behaved the same. For Dean, this study was just what she needed to personally understand why certain people acted in certain ways, and it enabled her to embrace, empathize, and support the differences. Hofstede's work is truly a turning point in understanding how and why people groups behave the way they do. From this fact-based approach, it is easy to teach others about cultural dimensions, and ultimately, the result is more understanding and better relationships. In the following paragraphs, each dimension is discussed in more detail.

Power distance is the dimension focusing on a culture's preference of dispersion of power. For example, India scored a 77 on the power distance dimension. Hofstede (2001) wrote that this score indicates the need for a top-down hierarchical structure and the Indian "employees expect to be directed clearly as to their functions and what is expected of them"; in return, "managers count on the obedience of their team members." This is a different way of thinking from the American employee.

The United States scored a 40 on the power distance dimension. According to Hofstede (2001), this score indicates that Americans are less dependent on direction from management. Americans, instead, value equality and their constitutional right to have "liberty and justice for all." In comparison to the Indian culture, Americans will have a significant comfort level for communicating across hierarchical boundaries and questioning authority. In short, if working on a team with people from India and America, one can expect that the team member from India will do as they are told without much confrontation or questioning. However, the American team member may question why they need to do what was assigned or they may even brainstorm ways to do the task better.

Individualism is the dimension that examines the interdependence of a society (Hofstede, 2001). There are two basic types of society, according to Hofstede. The individualist society is one where people look after themselves more than those in their society. The collectivist society is the opposite, whereas one looks after their society and is less concerned with self. The United States scores the highest of any country in the world as an individualistic society. The score of 91 indicates that Americans are concerned with self more than others. Americans are comfortable with doing business with strangers. India scored a 48 on this dimension, indicating they are a collectivist society. In comparison to India, employees in the United States display initiative and are self-reliant. Americans are typically more mobile than Indians are, since American society is loosely knit. Indians, on the other hand, have deeper relationships and are a tight-knit society. Indians value relationships and are loyal to their groups(s). Rejection in a collectivist society is difficult, as one perceives it as being lowly or unworthy of their peer group. In the workplace, Dean saw this collectivist versus individualist philosophy as she witnessed large groups of Indian contractors meet in the cafeteria for lunch on a routine basis. They appeared to have planned their meal, and each person brought a family-style dish to share with the group. This was very different from the American that either worked through their lunch or sat alone at a table surfing the internet on their phone.

The masculinity dimension indicates the measurement of competition within society (Hofstede, 2001). The more masculine a society, the more they focus on success and achievements. The competitive nature of the masculine dimension pushes members to be a "winner" or "the best in the field." A people group is either masculine or feminine, which does not reflect gender but preferences of how they display competitive actions. While masculine societies are motivated by being the best, feminine societies are motivated by liking what they do and not necessarily standing out in the crowd. India and the United States are relatively close with their scores on this dimension. India scored 56 and the United States scored 62. India displays its success and power through designer brand labels and other self-advertising methods. Americans display their masculinity via their behavior. For example, in school, work, and play, Americans strive to be the best. They have a "can-do" attitude and are always seeking a faster, better, healthier, more efficient way of doing something. Americans "live to work," in other words, they work hard to show others how successful they are. On the other hand, the country of Estonia scored 30, which represents they prefer fairness and modesty as a feminine society. Hofstede (2019) explained, "Estonians do not boast about their achievements. Instead, they enhance their character through hard work and diligence and show their competition by letting the results speak for themselves." Hofstede furthered that masculine countries will allow conversations to overlap as people compete with words, "Estonians prefer to take turns out of fairness and consideration of the other person's time."

Uncertainty avoidance is the next dimension, and it revolves around the need of the society to have security or know what their future will be (Hofstede, 2001). Some societies try to control the future, while others just let it happen. Countries with high scores for uncertainty avoidance are usually emotionally expressive and fearful of the unknown. They like to have plans and take great strides to forecast their future. India scored a 40 on uncertainty avoidance and the United States scored 46, both of which are fairly low scores. With a low to medium tolerance for uncertainty, societies often are tolerant of imperfection (Hofstede). The scores for India and the United States indicate they have "acceptance for new ideas, innovative products, and a willingness to try something new or different" (Hofstede, 2019). A low score also permits opinions and freedom of expression. An example of a country with a high score is Egypt with 80. In other words, they prefer to avoid uncertainty and maintain rigid codes of belief and behavior. They are intolerant with unorthodox behavior. In Egypt, people have an "inner urge to be busy and work hard" because people see time as money (Hofstede, 2019).

The long-term orientation dimension describes how people relate to the unknown (Hofstede, 2001). Pragmatic societies are content with not knowing everything, whereas normative societies have a strong desire to understand as much as possible. India scored 51 on the long-term orientation dimension and the United States scored 26. The low score indicates that the United States is a normative society and India is a pragmatic culture. India prefers a long-term orientation. The members of the Indian culture intertwine their relationship between karma and long-term orientation. In other words, "those who believe more strongly in karma are less influenced by disconfirmation sensitivity and therefore have higher expectations" (Kopalle, Lehmann, Farley, & Deighton, 2010, p. 251). They are not as worried about what is going on today as they are with how it will affect their future (as in generations ahead). Americans, on the other hand, are short-term oriented. Some manage their money by the day, if at all. The savings rate in the United States is much lower than that of India. Compared to the American gross savings rate of 17.3% in 2018, the national savings rate in India was 30.5% in 2018 (Ceic, 2019).

Another cultural dimension is indulgence. India scored a 26 and the United States scored 68. The indulgence score reflects the degree that people try to control their impulses or desires (Hofstede, 2001). If one indulges, they are thought to be weak and have little self-control. Restrained cultures are the opposite of indulgent. Restrained societies are more content and do not see the need for leisure or luxuries. Some cultures perceive indulgence as sinful. Americans are known to work hard and play hard. They work to live, spending their money on things they want and not necessarily on what they need.

Followership

Dean embarked on a study in 2015 to evaluate the followership styles of people from different cultures. Chaleff, Kellerman, and Kelley are pioneers in the study of followership. Their work is truly changing the way practitioners and scholars think about leaders in organizations, and rightfully so. Since most organizations have on average 80% more followers than leaders, it just makes sense to spend more time on followers than it does to spend on leaders. However, the word follower has historically and unfortunately been perceived with a negative connotation. Think about how many times one may have heard, "Don't be a follower—be a leader." But, the reality is that each and every single human being on the planet is a follower. The study of followership has led to several different lists of follower types. Chaleff (1995, 2003, 2008) identified four types of followers, including implementer, partner, individualist, and resource. Kellerman (2008) found five types of followers, including isolate, bystander, participant, activist, and diehard. Kelley (1992) also discovered five types of followers, including exemplary, alienated, conformist, pragmatist, and passive.

Dean used Kelley's (1992) Followership Questionnaire to examine if different cultures may lean towards one type of follower more than another culture. One of the caveats of this study is the specificity of culture. From a research perspective, one could classify their culture based on the current location, birthplace, or where they have spent the most time. The belief is that those basic assumptions in answering the question of nationality, ethnicity, or race can alter a person's thinking in regards to norms, values, beliefs, customs, and traditions. For this study, Dean asked specifically for ethnicity. For clarification purposes, nationality identifies the country that a person originates from (Pariona, 2017). Ethnicity describes the culture of a particular people group. Generally, ethnicity refers to commonalities of ancestry, clothing, cuisine, heritage, language, and religion. Although nationality remains the same, ethnicity can change if a person assimilates with another people group.

As the globe has seemingly become more traveled, where transient humans migrate from one continent to the next in search of work or happiness, the question of innate cultural tendency is one that surfaced with much interest. In her study, she collected data from 324 participants around the globe using a random sample, of which only 287 surveys were completed. Based on the responses, she had 0 alienated, 4 conformists, 132 exemplary, 1 passive, and 150 pragmatists. When asked how long the participant had lived in their current location, she found a variety of responses with the majority saying more than 20 years (28%) and the second majority representing the least number of years (15%). There was not a clear connection between the type of follower and where the person lived and/or worked. The participants self-reported their ethnicity as 71 Caucasian, 40 Irish, 8 Indian, 6 African American, and 6 French. Other cultures were also represented, including Filipino, Latino, Polish, African, British, Indonesian, Italian, Lithuanian, Malay, Mexican, New Zealander, Nigerian, Pacific Islander, Puerto Rican, Russian, South African, Spanish, and Vietnamese. Ultimately, this research showed that culture is not representative of the type of follower. In other words, a particular geographical location will not dictate the type of follower a person is. This research contributes to the concept of respectful pluralism in finding that culture does not dictate the followership type. Therefore, practically speaking, if one human being is searching for a particular type of follower, they should not disregard any particular ethnicity; all people should be treated equally. From a cultural dimension perspective, this research contributes to the body of literature in that cultural dimensions found by Hofstede seem to be consistent within the geographical location; however, follower type is not consistently based on location. Future research on this topic may include an additional examination of cultures and followership types using Chaleff's and/or Kellerman's tools as well as increasing the number of participants in various geographical locations.

In pursuit of this research, Dean questioned if a person born in one location would carry with them character traits to another location. As an example, if a young woman was born and raised in the Philippines but moves to the United States, will she continue to reflect the same cultural norms as a Filipino or alter her characteristics to be more of an American? This question started to bubble to the surface after Dean noticed many people moving to the same town where she worked in the heartland of America. And, in the one company she worked for, more than 60 languages were spoken. Some people groups seemed to gather together and cultivate a family unit of sorts with other people that were from their same country. Meanwhile, some isolated themselves from their past and seemed to have a mission to recreate their identity as an American.

This was also seen as some continued to speak their native language and subsequently teach their language to their American-born children, whereas others did not teach their children their native language at all and never spoke it in the home. When asked why they would not encourage their children to be bilingual, Dean was told that some immigrants believe it is a weakness if their children are taught to cook, dress, or speak like their ancestors. So, the question became, will people groups maintain their native cultural dimension once they migrate to the United States or will they assimilate entirely? And, if they change, how fast or slow is the process?

For most if not all Native American Indians, their native language was forbidden between the last part of the 1800s and into the 1970s due to a government-forced assimilation policy. Language was likely low on their list of worries during that time. Ehle (1989) explained that the American Indian encounter with white people resulted in a bitter and shameful removal of more than 18,000 Cherokee from their homelands. Specifically, the Treaty of New Echota was signed on December 29, 1835, and became the legal document for the forced removal of Indians from their southeastern homeland, known as the Trail of Tears. The removal focused on the Five Civilized Tribes and their relocation to Oklahoma. During this forced removal, Native American Indians encountered disease, hunger, freezing temperatures, snowstorms, and pneumonia, leading to 4,000 to 15,000 deaths. As part of this forced assimilation, if anyone was caught speaking their native language they were met with harsh punishment. As a result, many native languages have been lost. Some dialects are already extinct, some are considered severely endangered, and others are considered definitely endangered. According to Hirata-Edds (2011), only 10% of the 115,026 registered members of the Cherokee Nation are fluent in their native language. The fear is that if more people do not learn the language, it may disappear within 50 years.

Respectful Pluralism

Hicks's (2003) concept of respectful pluralism focused mostly on religion; however, there is no reason it should not include all sorts of differences. The main idea is to tolerate at minimum, embrace and encourage at best, the uniqueness of each and every human being so long as their difference is not threatening to society as a whole and so long as their difference is not against some form of a moral code. Hicks (2003) explained that certain religions are not allowed in Singapore and India because they are viewed as a threat to the general public. This same concept can be used for all sorts of differences. But, the question then becomes, what moral code are we all to abide by? In the United States, that moral code has been Christian scripture found in the Holy Bible. The Ten Commandments and doctrine of virtuous behavior essentially tells us what is acceptable and what is not.

Unfortunately, mainstream media encouraged people of all ages to behave immorally and to shout their immorality from the rooftops. Behavior such as having multiple sexual partners is viewed as attractive and popular on television shows and in books. Profanity and disrespect are common in children's cartoons. And, same-sex couples have become all the rage in 2019 as movies, commercials, television, and even laws have changed to promote a lifestyle one could be "proud" of. But such behavior is against Christian scripture. And, political correctness has essentially silenced Christians from speaking of the moral code and additional rhetoric has blamed Christians for hate crimes when they do speak up and say that certain behavior is inappropriate or wrong. Without an agreed-upon moral code, incivility will continue to rise because the basic starting point is not agreed upon. The majority of people must agree on a basic moral code for civility to be reintroduced into society.

Hicks (2003) stated that many people's view, "religion is an inappropriate topic altogether for the workplace (and for other spheres of public life), thus reinforcing the view of religion as a private matter" (p. 23). In the past religion and other topics such as salary amount and politics were private. The question now becomes, should religion remain a private matter in the 21st century, purely from the viewpoint of finding an agreed-upon moral compass for what we deem as acceptable behavior? In the past, maintaining privacy about one's faith was acceptable because the majority of citizens in the United States were Christian. Essentially, all had the same foundation or moral compass and they did not need to discuss it. However, since so many other faiths are now in the United States, this discussion simply needs to be had.

Respectful pluralism is a constructive approach proposed as an alternative to the "generic-spirituality approach or a Christian establishment approach" (Hicks, 2003, p. 25). Hicks acknowledges that the workplace is comprised of human beings with a variety of religious interests, including Buddhists, Christians, Hindus, Jews, and Muslims (p. 26–27). His approach involves a discussion of religious symbols, clothing, and holiday time; which has been primarily Christian based in the United States (Hicks, 2003). The discussion could go further with a review of laws that allowed or forbid immigration; they each played a part in where we are today, especially with the religious landscape.

Hicks (2003) wrote, "when scholars of organizational leadership discuss diversity in the workplace, they most often refer to gender, race, ethnicity, nationality, age, ability-disability, and sexual orientation as principal categories" (p. 23). Historically, religion has not received significant attention in diversity and inclusion literature. Diana Eck, a founding member of the Harvard Pluralism Project, published a book titled *A New Religious America*, in which she notes that the United States is now one of the most religiously diverse nations on the planet. Pew Forum (2015) reported 70.6% of Americans as Christian and 5.9% as Jewish, Muslim, Buddhist, Hindu, or belonging to another world religion. The Harvard Pluralism Project maps out the religious landscape in the United States (Eck, 2019). As an example, a Hindu temple can be found in Houston, Texas; Nashville, Tennessee; and Lemont, Illinois, and a mosque is located in Toledo, Ohio. And, within one building at the United States Air Force Academy, Protestant, Catholic, Jewish, and Buddhist services are held.

As an example of respectful pluralism, a Taiwanese American woman, age 68, wrestled with a relationship at work. The issue is that the manager is Hindu and the subordinate is Christian. The Hindu manager continues to open the door and push her agenda on the Christian. Every day, the Hindu finds an opportunity to express how her religion is superior or better in some way. She inserts her comments when a discussion about food is had. If a conversation about sleep or rest surfaces, the Hindu inserts her comments there too. The Christian woman tries to be nice and listen, but the Hindu seems agitated if the Christian does not agree. Eventually, the Christian had to assert herself and tell the coworker that she did not want to discuss religion at work. Since then, she walks away every time the Hindu tries to talk about it, which is still daily. From a respectful pluralism perspective, both women could have a mutual agreement to work together and get along. There is no need to try to push an agenda on another person, especially in the workplace. However, since one person is continuing to push, even after the other has said to stop, this relationship is not healthy. For respectful pluralism to work, Hicks (2003) mentions that "workers must be treated fairly" (p. 169). Hicks explains that certain behavior could be seen as divisive and even hostile to some employees. Therefore, it is necessary to have a clearly articulated plan and continuous training to help employees know that some certain signals or conversations should give warning signs or red flags and prevent the behavior from happening in the future.

Immigration

The United States of America was declared independent on July 4, 1776. Since then, immigration laws have tightened and released for various reasons throughout history. The laws have considered certain people inadmissible based on literacy, health, and country of origin. This section briefly covers some of the law over the years to explain how and why the country has struggled with immigration in the past, how and why the country is now one of the most religiously diverse nations on the planet, and why we must understand our past in order to comprehend our current and future state of affairs.

Just 22 years after the birth of the country, the 1798 Naturalization Act authorized the president of the United States to deport any resident immigrant deemed "dangerous to the peace and safety of the United States." The president could also deport resident aliens if their home country was one actively at war with the United States. The Page Act of 1875 prohibited entry of immigrants deemed "undesirable." The 1882 Chinese Exclusion Act restricted immigration of Chinese laborers for 10 years. The 1891 Immigration Act was the first comprehensive immigration law for the United States and enabled enforcement of immigration laws. The 1903 Immigration Act refused citizenship to anarchists, beggars, people with epilepsy, and prostitutes. In 1906 the fires in San Francisco allegedly burned birth certificates and opened the door for American citizenship of Chinese immigrants. The Bureau of Immigration and Naturalization was established in 1906 and documented that citizens should speak English. The 1952 McCarran-Walter Act allowed people into the country based on skills needed. The 1954 Operation Wetback was a roundup and deportation of illegal immigrants. And, on July 4, 1965, President Lyndon Johnson signed the Immigration and Naturalization Act.

Each of these laws represents a handful of laws that have attempted to allow people into the country for one reason or another or to forbid their entry.

Respect for Human Dignity

Hicks's (2003) concept of respectful pluralism "focuses on whether the content of the message itself reflects respect or disrespects human dignity" (p. 177). If each person took a stance to look at human dignity as the ultimate goal of a comment, a stare, a decision, etc., the world could be a better place. Each and every single human being has a purpose. We each have special gifts and talents. And, we each have our unique strengths. It does not make sense for a team to be comprised of people with all of the same strengths. However, attaining the beautiful process of a well-performing team requires a leader who can see the strengths, skills, gifts, and talents of each team member and place them in the position where they will thrive. Along those same lines, a leader that develops a culture where every person is recognized for their positive asset to the team should do well developing high-performing teams. This includes having the training, processes, and procedures documented for each person on the team. Far too often, teams fail because they do not have the proper infrastructure in place for all team members (representing all differences) to survive, let alone thrive.

Microsoft advertises that they are a workplace where persons of differing abilities can do well. Specifically, they advertise their autism program where they "recruit, onboard" and offer "development of individuals on the autism spectrum." This type of hiring process respects human dignity, whereas other companies may not hire someone with a disability or may fire them because they cannot perform as expected. As an example of a toxic workplace that disrespects human dignity, a middle-aged man tried his best and ultimately lost his job. His team, unfortunately, did not provide proper training. He desperately wanted training and continuously asked for help. He has a non-verbal learning disability. He is eager to learn and does a good job when given the right tools. Mostly, this person has a can-do attitude and is responsible. Unfortunately, in the work environment where he served for more than 10 years, his self-esteem diminished and he lost confidence. Why do companies do this? If the mindset changed to focus on whether the actions taken in the workplace reflected respect or disrespect for human dignity, it would become clear to see that this man was not in the right environment, but he was a good worker. He just needed a different seat on the bus with proper infrastructure (Collins, 2001).

In addition to discrimination based on physical or mental ability, discrimination based on age seems to still be alive and well; just ask any job applicant over the age of 40 how their job search is going. The Age Discrimination in Employment Act of 1967 reached a milestone birthday in 2017. In 2018, AARP surveyed working adults age 45 and older to see how the law is protecting the aging American population (Perron, 2018). They found that 9 in 10 people thought age discrimination occurred regularly and more than 60% said they saw age discrimination or had experienced it themselves. The type of discrimination observed included qualified applicants not hired for a job or promoted due to their age, overhearing negative remarks regarding age from colleague or supervisor, denied access to professional development or training, and termination of a job.

> Older workers do not think it is fair for the courts to treat age discrimination as more acceptable than other forms of discrimination, and they strongly support strengthening the age discrimination laws to ensure equal opportunity and a respectful work environment for employees of all ages.
>
> *(Perron, 2018, p. 11)*

As an example, after a series of events, an older woman was let go from her job after more than a decade. Sadly, she was singled out as the only black female over the age of 60 in the department. At the time of her termination, she was also battling breast cancer. The team had a history of dysfunction even before she was promoted to the team, but the manager did not handle the dysfunction at all. This employee needed training and she asked for training on multiple occasions. But, she was not given the tools she needed and was not set up for success. Sadly, this is another example where the environment did not focus on respect for human dignity.

In recent years, political discrimination has become a major issue. Historically, most Americans just did not talk about religion and politics to a broad audience. Those two topics were considered private. However, when President Trump took office, the act of political discrimination took on a whole new lifeform. In one example, a female cashier at an organic grocer said she had to quit her job because if her coworkers found out she had voted for Trump they would make life very difficult for her. And, they obviously already had made life challenging, which lead her to terminate employment with tears streaming down her face. In other examples, groups of coworkers were found bashing Trump while the one lonely Trump supporter sat quietly at her desk hoping to not be discovered. Several people have commented that in their lifetime, no other president ever incurred such scrutiny as Trump. And, this incivility and division within the United States has caused major issues. On social media, the following post circulates:

> Sad day in America!!! I am ___ years old. I offer no apology for what I am posting for this is truly how I feel. I'm going to vent here. I have lived through Presidents Kennedy, Johnson, Nixon, Ford, Carter, Reagan, George H. Bush, Bill Clinton, George W. Bush, and Obama. In my lifetime, I have never seen or heard of a president being scrutinized over every word he speaks, humiliated by the public to the point of wanting to hurt someone, slandered, ridiculed, insulted, lied to, threatened with murder, threatened to rape our beautiful First Lady, and have his children also insulted and humiliated. I am truly ashamed of the people of this country. I am ashamed of the ruthless, hating, cruel, Trump haters who have no morals, and news reporters who feel they have the right to purposely lie and do the things they are doing. Every other president after they were elected and took the oath of office were left alone, they weren't on the news 24/7 being dissected by every word out of their mouth, always being pressured to do this or that and never being given the support to do anything. Now, we have Tax Reform, Every President in recent history has talked about tax reform, we hear about this for a week or two and it's over for a couple of years. With President Trump we have been hearing about this for months, it started even before he was elected. *enough is enough is enough, leave the man alone and let him do his job for god's sake! doesn't matter if you are republicans or democrats.*

Sadly, this is another example where fellow humans are not focused on the respect for human dignity. And, this matter seems to have a huge stronghold on the American public. If this single matter can be addressed with the adage of "If you don't have anything nice to say, don't say anything at all," a big step for respect and civility may be made.

An even more controversial topic than politics may be sexual orientation. The rise of lesbian, gay, bisexual, transgender, and queer (LGBTQ) acceptance in recent years is likely not an accident. GLAAD is an organization that states they are "a dynamic media force" that is rewiring the "script for LGBTQ acceptance" (Ellis, 2019, p. 5). In their 2018–2019 report, GLAAD explains that they have been tracking the presence of LGBTQ on television for 23 years and "there is still much work to do before television reflects the full diversity of our community" (p. 11). The report states,

> while year over year the numbers of LGBTQ characters on broadcast have risen significantly … Hollywood should be sure that they are including lead LGBTQ characters whose stories are told with nuance and depth that reflects the real world that audiences know.
>
> *(p. 9)*

From a respectful pluralism perspective, the question here should be, does the LGBTQ movement focus on respect or disrespect for human dignity? And, this question cannot be answered without an agreed-upon moral code of conduct. The reality is that Americans are now in situations where they are at churches, grocery stores, neighborhoods, schools, workplace, etc. and they are encountering the LGBTQ movement in some way, shape, or form. Perhaps it is a server at a restaurant that is gay or a transgender employee at a beauty counter. Or, perhaps it is an older woman working for a gay manager. In this example, a 70-year old woman has worked for the same manager for 40 years. She is a Christian and he is gay. In years past, he kept his private life private. But, as he ages, he is becoming more outspoken and has asked her to do work for his private business. This includes organizing "pride" events, writing letters and emails about such topics, and more. It appears that he has no issue with asking his employee to do this work, although none if it is the work she was hired to do 40 years ago. For years, she has continued to do the work as he asked. After all, he is the boss. But, when a colleague was let go from the company for speaking up and asking to be taken off of company emails promoting the "pride" agenda, she had to put her foot down too. Her manager asked her to write a scathing email retaliating against the man that professionally expressed his lack of interest in the topic and she finally said no. She explained to her boss (with tears flowing down her face) that this topic is one she does not agree with based on her Christian values, and she asked him to have someone else write his email. For this 70-year-old woman, she was heartbroken, stressed, and distraught to have to stand up to her boss. She feared she would lose her job too. And, this one event gave her medical issues for quite some time resulting from the stress of it all. Why does this have to be this way? At what point in history did someone's private life become so public? And, in speaking of respectful pluralism, does this situation reflect the respect for human dignity of all involved?

Chapter Takeaways

How did we get to where we are today? How did the greatest nation on the planet become so confused about how to respect the human dignity? Whose fault is it? And, what are we going to do about it? Can't we all just get along? The following section will give practical tips to help individuals and groups move forward. Hicks (2003) wrote, "to achieve morally acceptable working conditions and employee health, it is necessary to discuss the proper role of religious, spiritual, political, and cultural expression by individuals while at work" (p. 171).

The first and most obvious step to pursue respect for human dignity through respectful pluralism is to talk about it positively and productively. Use the concepts of cultural dimensions, followership, and respectful pluralism as training topics. Leaders of an organization, families, school administration, and any other leadership group need to start talking about how we can respect the human dignity of all people regardless of their ability, age, ethnicity, gender, immigration, nationality, political, race, religion, and/or sexual orientation. The conversation needs to include a discussion of an agreed-upon moral code of conduct and boundaries to ensure a safe and healthy environment.

The second step to encourage respectful pluralism is to include everyone, not just one particular group. In one organization, they received accolades for being named to the Diversity Best Practices Inclusion Index two years in a row. However, their focus is primarily on the LGBTQ movement. When employees of faith asked about hosting a prayer group on company property during lunch, they were told no. And, when an employee asked the same company to investigate ways for people of all faiths to celebrate holidays, they were told it was not part of their agenda. It is vitally important that all people receive equal investment by their organization, meaning if one group receives company-funded events, all groups should receive the same. And, if one group is receiving awards, all groups should receive awards.

The third step to encourage respect of human dignity through respectful pluralism is to establish the bumpers for the boundary of what is acceptable and what is not acceptable. In other words, it will be necessary to discipline some employees because they go too far. For example, it is common for Americans to have a flag in their workplace. However, what will happen if someone claims the flag upsets them? And, what will happen if an employee displays a Nazi swastika on their desk? It is vitally important that leaders think about these issues ahead of time and decide on an agreed-upon solution. Otherwise, every employee could say that something distresses them.

The fourth step is to encourage a positive and proactive approach to respectful pluralism. Hicks (2003) wrote, "all employees bring some set of values and some wider worldview with them when they enter the workplace" (p. 107). This can be a very good opportunity when we look at the strengths, skills, gifts, and talents of every single person, without focusing on anything negative (unless it is a threat to safety). Shifting the mindset of a workplace, school, church, or family culture to focus on strengths is new and can be very powerful. The question needs to move from "how do we work well together despite our differences?" to "how do we use our differences to work better together?"

References

The 2019 Diversity Best Practices Inclusion Index. (n.d.). Retrieved from www.workingmother.com/diversity-best-practices-inclusion-index-2019

Ceic. (2019). *Gross savings rate [1951–2019]* [Data & Charts]. Retrieved from www.ceicdata.com/en/indicator/india/gross-savings-rate

Chaleff, I. (1995). *The courageous follower: Standing up to and for our leaders.* San Francisco, CA: Barrett-Koehler Publishers, Inc.

Chaleff, I. (2003). *The courageous follower: Standing up to and for our leaders* (2nd ed.). San Francisco, CA: Berret-Koehler Publishers, Inc.

Chaleff, I. (2008). Creating new ways of following. In R. Riggio, I. Chaleff, & J. Lipman-Blumen (Eds.), *The art of followership: How great followers create great leaders and organizations* (pp. 67–87). San Francisco: Jossey-Bass.

Collins, J. C. (2001). *Good to great.* New York, NY: Harper Business.

Eck, D. (2019). Retrieved from http://pluralism.org/

Ehle, J. (1989). *Trail of tears: The rise and fall of the Cherokee nation.* New York, NY: Anchor Books.

Ellis, S. (2019). *Where we are on TV.* Retrieved from https://glaad.org/files/WWAT/WWAT_GLAAD_2018-2019.pdf

Hicks, D. (2003). *Religion and the workplace: Pluralism, spirituality, leadership.* New York, NY: Cambridge University Press.

Hofstede, G. (2001). *Culture's consequences: Comparing values, behaviors, institutions, and organizations across nations* (2nd ed.). Thousand Oaks, CA: SAGE Publications. ISBN 978-0-8039-7323-7. OCLC 45093960. Retrieved from http://geert-hofstede.com/india.html

Hirata-Edds, T. (2011). Influence of second language Cherokee immersion on children's development of past tense in their first language, English. *Language Learning, 61*(3), 700–733. doi:10.1111/j.1467-9922.2011.00655.x

Hofstede, G. (2019). *Country comparison.* Retrieved from www.hofstede-insights.com/country-comparison/

Kellerman, B. (2008). *Followership: How followers are creating change and changing leaders.* Boston: Harvard Business Press.

Kelley, R. E. (1992). *The power of followership.* New York, NY: Doubleday Business.

Kopalle, P., Lehmann, D., Farley, J., & John Deighton served as editor and Jennifer Aaker served as associate editor for this article. (2010). Consumer expectations and culture: The effect of belief in karma in India. *Journal of Consumer Research, 37*(2), 251–263. doi:10.1086/651939

Microsoft. (2019). *Inclusive hiring at Microsoft.* Retrieved from www.microsoft.com/en-us/diversity/inside-microsoft/cross-disability/hiring.aspx

Pariona, A. (2017, September 13). *What are the differences between nationality and ethnicity?* Retrieved from www.worldatlas.com/articles/what-are-the-differences-between-nationality-and-ethnicity.html

Perron, R. (2018). *The value of experience study: AARP's multicultural work and jobs study.* Retrieved from www.aarp.org/ValueofExperience

Pew Forum. (2015). *Religion in America: U.S. religious data, demographics and statistics.* Retrieved from www.pewforum.org/religious-landscape-study/

11

EVERYDAY LEADERSHIP

How Can Anyone Be a Leader Every Day?
Examples of Amish Leadership and Japanese
Corporation Leadership Training

Sunny Jeong

Introduction

More often than not, a leadership role is believed to be a reserved position or status attainable only for those who hold extraordinary performance records and special characteristics. As such, most leadership literature focuses on distinct leader skills, behaviors, and characteristics of leaders distinct from other roles, including followers. Different leader-related skills, personal characteristics, and behaviors, therefore, define leadership styles into sub-categories such as transformational leadership (Bass, 1985; Yammarino & Bass, 1990), charismatic leadership (Conger & Kanungo, 1994), and authentic leadership (George, 2003; George & Sims, 2007; Gardner, Avolio, Luthans, May, & Walumbwa, 2005; Walumbwa, Luthans, Avey, & Oke, 2009). A vast amount of literature on leadership underscores a dichotomy between leaders and followers, confirming that different qualifications are needed to become a leader. This chapter challenges the distinction of leaders from followers and helps an organization discover a leader within anyone who plays a critical leadership role every day. It requires a new definition of everyday leadership, and this chapter suggests ways to embrace, practice, and train an everyday leader.

In this chapter, inclusive leadership is redefined on the liberating tenet of shared individual and collective responsibility under the concept of everyday leadership. Examples of inclusive everyday leadership are provided in the contexts where everyone can be and is trained to become a leader. Everyday leadership at the workplace occurs when employees, including the CEO, managers, and even receptionists, janitors, general laborers, and warehouse workers take intentional and daily action to make a positive impact on other stakeholders (other employees, customers, community, environment, etc.) within the boundary of the organization's shared core vision. A new definition of everyday leadership allows us to celebrate intentional leadership as the everyday act of improving others' lives, including those of colleagues, coworkers, customers, and stakeholders of any business, as well as the community. Everyday leaders are found in schools, homes, and communities beyond the management field. They are agents of positive change in our society who create an authentic and humanistic way of creating value. There are numerous examples of everyday leadership in action in our daily works where people make the extra effort to make a conscious and an unconscious impact on others' lives. One home improvement store staff made the extra inquiry to a vendor to order a sought-after item, a customized bracket of blinders that is only possible to purchase from a special vendor. She made several phone calls to a vendor and managed to get it delivered directly to the customer's house with no charge. This is beyond the duties listed on her job description, and her vision is bigger than her current role. She wants to keep customers satisfied and play her part so that customer ratings on the company improve and the company can grow. One of my business students, Sabrina, while working as a water polo instructor, made a great impact on her student's life. Her student Emma was about to quit water polo because of a lack of self-confidence and one game in which she performed poorly. With every day's practices alongside Emma, with Sabrina's positive reinforcement, teaching necessary skillsets and work ethics, Emma is not only enjoying her newly found favorite sport, but now considers water polo as her career path to pursue. Then there is the manager who motivates employees to work seamlessly as a team. She makes sure they feel appreciated by visiting their workplace to converse in person and address any daily challenges instead of sending orders via an email. Everyday leaders work alongside others regardless of their corporation rank and status. Many employees often simply need to be heard; the act of listening drives commitment to an organization/team and builds trust among them.

This chapter will demonstrate ways to cultivate a culture of everyday leadership that benefits employees and organization alike. Everyday leadership allows organizations to empower their employees to make decisions that contribute to their company's success. Retention of employees will improve as they feel appreciated and trusted to make their own decisions to support others and be supported themselves. A higher retention rate means the organization will save the cost of recruiting, training, and onboarding. Empowered employees are more committed to their company's vision and success. They become more productive. In addition, they become the organization's best ambassadors to spread the organization's vision to their friends, family, and entire network.

The benefits of implanting everyday leadership into an organization's culture and everyday practice far outweigh the costs.

Leadership Development

Leadership narratives have changed over time, from directing individuals with vision to facilitating the process of reaching goals collectively. Current leadership focuses less on answering questions such as where do we need to go and how do we get there. More discussion on leadership takes place concerning the facilitation process within the wider relational context in order to address "what's getting in your way to go where you think we should head to." Leadership failure in this regard is ascribed not to a lack of vision but to a lack of facilitation and interpersonal competence. The new leadership narrative justifies that leadership development is more than just focusing on a skillset of an individual. Leadership development is conceptualized as a social process, therefore it focuses on the wider social context in which leadership takes place (Day, 2001). According to Schyns, Kiefer, Kerschreiter, and Tymon (2011), the social context (leadership development) has received considerably less attention in research and practice than the individual leader (leader development). Along this line, Iles and Preece (2006) argue that self-awareness is a part of leader development and that social awareness is a facet of interpersonal competence for leadership development. With respect to social awareness in leadership development, empathy, service orientation, and developing others are included as a part of leadership development. Bolden and Gosling (2006) support the differentiation between leader development and leadership development, stressing that leadership has to move from individualistic to collective forms. Everyday leaders are people who, in connection with others, serve and develop others and create the alignment of shared norms and values with their daily tasks.

What Everyday Leadership Looks Like

There are numerous examples of ways that everyday leadership is nurtured and developed. In particular, the Amish community demonstrates everyday leadership, which takes intentional and daily action to make a positive impact on others within the boundary of a shared core vision and value in their community. What makes them act as everyday leaders is not individual roles that they are assigned to play. Instead, collective norms, values, and faith in a broader social context are guiding them to carry out tasks that support others and the community. They play parts in the bigger picture of their faith community and carry out the tasks that serve their purpose.

Amish Philosophy of Sharing: Everyone Has Something to Share

Kraybill, Nolt, and Wesner (2011a) stated that Amish businesses have a much higher five-year survival rate, between 90% to 95%, than the average 50% survival rate of all US small businesses. Approximately 10,000 Amish-owned enterprises operate in North America, and it is not rare to hear about the many Amish millionaires who are successful in their businesses. In line with the self-sustaining and higher success rate of Amish business, the Amish business community does not depend on government programs such as food stamps, litigation of business conflicts and bankruptcy law, and insurances to protect their businesses. Officials in Ohio noticed that the food stamp participation rate was unusually low in a few of the state's counties. They eventually pinpointed the reason—the counties had high numbers of Amish, who are unlikely to use the government-sponsored program. Many Amish families with seven or eight kids often live below the poverty line, based on the amount of income they bring in. Regardless, they don't like to turn to the government for a hand, and they work hard until seeking help from their church is inevitable.

Financial Advisor Group and Community Aid

Personal and business bankruptcies are very rare in the Amish business community. Bankruptcy is not only considered a financial failure but also a moral affront, because creditors might not be repaid in full (Kraybill, Nolt, & Weaver-Zercher, 2012). The Amish view bankruptcy as not consistent with the values they hold regarding honesty and integrity, because bankruptcy is a dishonorable discharge of debts. A church-imposed taboo on litigation prohibits owners from using the force of law to protect themselves in corporate competition, sue debtors, or make other legal claims. Amish entrepreneurs are permitted to hire attorneys to create articles of incorporation, handle real estate transactions, and attend to legal matters that do not involve litigation. If a business is struggling financially due to mismanagement, failure to adapt to ever-changing market conditions, or some other reasons, the church appoints trustees of three men to step in and oversee the daily operation in order to avoid legal bankruptcy and attempt to ensure that creditors are fully paid and that employees (church members) are not losing their work, so that many families are not facing financial hardships at home. In terms of the church-appointed trustees, three men are appointed by the church to manage the operation back to the profitable stage or sell it if necessary. The local church district appoints a trustee, the owner in trouble invites a trustee, and those two select a third one. Three trustees compose a temporary management team that provides not only advice but executes corrective measures of everyday operation, including finances and payments to make the business survive. Leadership in this regard is expected to be played by any member of the Amish community, as other members seek their advice. Their support of others is not based on any financial return nor recognitions. It is seen as a voluntary act of kindness to offer others what they can to help their community members.

Many Amish communities also have low-interest loan programs (4%) out of a community fund to help young adults buy their own land or house and get their start in the business world. Again, people voluntarily contribute to these funds, and funnel their financial resources back into the community, and don't ask for high payoffs in return. At the same time, 1% of any contribution made to the fund goes to the community fund to address any distress—fire or flood that causes property loss, medical expenses, or personal hardship of any church members that a member can't pay by herself/himself.

The Amish do not believe in insurance and do not purchase any life, medical, home, or business insurance or even pension plans. Two Amish businessmen that I met made this point clear:

> I don't own my life or my house or my car or anything. The Lord does. And he doesn't need me insured. He's quite capable of taking care of that. So we believe if we trust the Lord, and if he does allow something to happen, he's allowed it to happen to teach us. . . . We try to again be good stewards of what the Lord has given us so that in case of emergencies of our own, then we should be able to help in some way.
>
> *(Troyer, Amish family, personal conversation).*

An Amish family who used this fund described it as, "we have something called mutual aid where if there is a need . . . you pay everything you could, and do everything you could to pay your own. And then over and above that then the church would help" (Troyer, Amish family, personal conversation).

The same goes for the payment of social security. Amish business owners and their Amish employees are exempt from paying into social security or tapping its benefits. Some states also exempt them from participation in workers' compensation. Amish people will be covered and supported by the community when it is needed. Private church aid covers the costs of Amish members' job-related injuries. When somebody has a tragedy, people come together and give of themselves to help those people get back on their feet again. However, this mutual aid for ailing businesses is never forced as rules but rather as voluntary roles to play within the shared boundary of the core value of faith. Amish faith cites biblical teaching about church members' moral responsibility to help each other in time of need. Amish businesses draw on a readily available pool of church and community support with such shared values and faith. It underscores the fact that any member can play a role as a trustee, a community supporter, and an advisor as necessary. Everyday leadership in this regard is played not based on rules and roles but on shared value and necessary tasks that can be carried out by anyone in the community.

The Amish philosophy of sharing is not limited only to the form of financial support. A committee of business mentors is made up of senior Amish business people who take on advisory and mentoring roles when their businesses reach a certain level of achievement. Informal mentoring is a vital enterprise success in Amish communities. A producer of vinyl windows, citing the crucial advice he garnered from his father-in-law, concluded that mentors "mean the difference between being successful and failing." An Amish mentoring network in one community consists of small, informal clusters of owners from different industries who gather occasionally for breakfast or coffee to share ideas and support. Young Amish business members can tap into the wisdom of trusted mentors and peers who foster a positive business environment for others. When Amish business people reach a certain level of achievement, they may take on advisory and mentoring roles, fostering a positive business environment for others. In order to make themselves available to young mentees, often their own children, Amish senior business people limit the growth of their businesses. This explains the following aspects of thriving together on a small scale instead of winning on a larger scale.

Limit of Business Growth: Thrive Together

Amish businesses self-impose limits to their business size, which is in contrast to the typical growth orientation of non-Amish businesses. Amish leaders hold a deep bias against large-scale operations. A church-imposed limitation on business size restricts growth so that well-to-do business owners do not disrupt the egalitarian balance of power and wealth in their communities. A 30-employee operation is considered very large. Limiting the scale of business keeps business manageable, sparing time for mentoring and training their children and young business people to start their own businesses and allowing other Amish businesses to run similar operations in a limited market region with no hostile competitions. Allen Miller, an Old Brethren business owner, commented his intention of keeping his business small so that he can find time to work with his children.

> We have a tractor salvage yard for farm tractors and we started getting combines in, harvesting combines. And tearing those apart for parts and selling those parts, too. But it got to the place where it was too much. We needed more buildings and we needed more employees and I think the main reason why we quit is because I wanted to be able to work with my children. I didn't want to manage a corporation. And so we decided we would just stick to tractors and get out of the combines. Because to me making money wasn't the most important thing. I wanted to raise my family too.

It is common for owners of growing businesses to divide their companies or spin off certain product lines to their family members or other employees in order to keep a business in a scale. A harness and leather shop owner, who received help to start his business from another Amish businessman, has passed on the favor. Rather than focusing on expansion and growth, he has helped to start three nearby enterprises that produce similar products. He explained,

> I keep saying I can't do it all, so why not let the other people work, too? If God gave me a chance . . . I'm here to help. I'm not here to turn anybody down. Although Amish manufacturers do compete for sales, it rarely becomes cutthroat or a hostile competition.

Peachey (Amish businessman, personal conversation) underscored the importance of collaboration with other competitors in business.

> One contractor avoids bidding a job if he knows a neighboring business is already competing for it. Gauging a potential client, he'll contact a competitor who he knows did previous work for the person . . . this prevents infringing on foreign turf but also allows him to learn of any problems with the customer . . . as far as really getting competitive and getting nasty, I don't see any of that.

Such practice allows hundreds of Amish entrepreneurs of small family businesses to thrive together with other similar businesses instead of only a handful of large corporations enjoying the wealth.

Again, limiting business size and emphasizing collaboration have a lot to do with the context of their faith, which sets shared norms and values. While one Amish man says he's proud of the fact that "we're making a lot of money," he notes that elders in his church worry about the growth. "They discourage us getting too big," he adds. This can also mean that with the guidance of the Ordnung, oral and written histories and rules of local churches, and the advice of their ministers, Amish church members of the same district will stand up for what is right against injustice and make decisions that limits business success like higher recognition, advancement, and pay. All members feel it is their duty to rebuke anyone who appears to be straying from church standards, although such admonishment is to be undertaken with great humility and in a spirit of love. Yoder (Amish business owner, personal conversation) reiterated the Amish value of humility by saying,

> It's not money that's evil, it's the love of money that's the root of all evil. So if it manages you instead of you managing it then you've lost your spiritual self. And there's a lot of wealth because a lot of our parents owned land. And this land sold and went to children's hands. But we have to adapt and be cautious. There's no big "I's" and little "You's" of it. And so

finances isn't what distinguishes from one another. That's the reason for the simple common dress, that we don't put on a show to show someone that we're better.

Small changes in dress code, including hooks, buttons, colors of pants, and width of hat brim are often main discussion topics during church meetings on Sunday. In sum, the shared cultural values (humility, honesty, trust, and service to others) taught by the Amish religion enhance cooperation within business networks. However, those rules are unwritten norms that are shared among members. An everyday leader is a proactive player in a community or an organization to support others' success within the boundary of shared values and norms.

Work Alongside Others

Kraybill (2001) attributes the Amish's success to staying personally invested in their enterprises. Amish business owners build positive relationships with their vendors, customers, and employees. First of all, they are willing to work alongside the average employee and care for them. Wesner (2010) described it as a key factor to Amish business owners' success, "Often, the owner is not off bossing everyone around . . . he's working there . . . I think it builds credibility and they appreciate that" (Dursin, 2014). Taking it further, one Amish man commented that he would never sell his business regardless of the amount that is offered only because of his employees, who are often fellow church members, family members, and friends.

> If somebody would come and ask us to buy our business . . . it's really not for sale, . . . a lot of people say, well anything is for sale if you give enough money, but we have so many people that depend on us for their income, it's more than just making money . . . we feel it's a service to the community.
>
> *(Miller, Amish businessman, personal conversation)*

On top of working alongside their employees, Amish business owners understand that creating relationships with their customers is key. An Amish lumber business in Ohio hung a framed statement about his customer orientation. It says,

> A customer is the most important visitor on our premises: She is not dependent on us. We are dependent on her. He is not an interruption in our work. He is the purpose of it. She is not an outsider in our business. She is part of it. We are not doing him a favor by working with him. He is doing us a favor by giving us an opportunity to do so.

He once faced bankruptcy due to a major contract that took the majority of his stock with no payment following. He recalled it as the hardest time during his business cycle but explained he did not resort to or consider a litigation process. He added, "we don't believe in confrontation and legal action is a form of aggression." He added, "Bible says agree with your adversary quickly. The quicker you find common ground, or find something you agree on, and try and dwell on that, then the other [issue] will start going away." Instead of seeking a legal solution, he emphasized ethical practices guided by his value-garnered respect from other businesses as well as from customers. There was an Amish businessman who stated firmly, "If there's gonna be swearing, dishonesty inside this contract, then I'm out. . . . Principle trumps extra profit ten times out of ten" (Lapp, Amish businessman, personal conversation).

Forgiveness

Consider another aspect of everyday leadership: the forgiveness that is practiced by the Amish community. The *New York Times* on February 25, 2012, reported a rare case in the Amish community, a

Ponzi scheme of the accused Monroe Beachy, who was a respected financial figure for decades in the Amish and Mennonite communities of rural Sugarcreek, Ohio. Mr. Beachy, a 78-year-old investment broker, pleaded guilty to defrauding 2,700 clients of an estimated $16.8 million. Prosecutors contended that, from 1990 to 2010, Beachy raised an estimated $33 million from an estimated 3,200 investors from 29 states. Many of the investors were from the Amish communities in Holmes and Tuscarawas counties. More than a dozen churches, church building funds, fellowships, and ministries lost money in Mr. Beachy's downfall. On September 15, 2011, Monroe Beachy filed for bankruptcy, and federal prosecutors announced that he had been indicted on mail fraud charges arising from a "scheme to defraud" that they said dated back to 1990 (McCarty, 2012). While the unusual nature of the offense is noteworthy, so too is the reaction of the victims. Within weeks of Mr. Beachy's bankruptcy, religious leaders urged the judge to put the case into the hands of the church where it belonged. The judge received letters from nearly 75 investors and members of the Amish community who proposed to handle the settlement of claims outside the court process, using the cash remaining in the estate, as well as donations from Amish and Mennonite communities nationwide. That would accomplish three worthy goals, they said. It would allow a less expensive, more advantageous financial workout "based on Christian principles of love and care for the poor and needy." It would create a setting in which "Biblical forgiveness and restoration can be found between Monroe Beachy" and those he is accused of betraying. And it would repair "the tarnished testimony and integrity of the Plain Community" (Henriques, 2012). Mr. Beachy told the judge he has confessed his sins to God and his church, and he sent letters to every investor seeking their forgiveness. Only two wrote back asking the judge to sentence Beachy to prison. The other 75 said it was more important for them to forgive Beachy than to recover their lost money.

What's intriguing in this story is how different Monroe Beachy's story is from Bernie Madoff's—and from almost every other story with a "Ponzi scheme" headline over the years (Henriques, 2012). While victims of Mr. Madoff's fraud, like most Ponzi victims, condemned their accused betrayer in court as a monster, many of Mr. Beachy's investors have said in court that it is more important to forgive him than to recover their money. And while Mr. Madoff's wife and sons instantly became social pariahs in Manhattan, Mr. Beachy's wife and his five children, 16 grandchildren, and 11 great-grandchildren remain at his farmstead in Ohio, living peacefully with their neighbors. "A hundred years from now, what will be the difference about how much money we had here?" asked Emery E. Miller, a village resident and a proponent of the alternative plan, at the first creditors meeting. "But a hundred years from now, there will be a difference in how we responded to this from our moral being, from a moral level—the choices we made to forgive or not to forgive" (Henriques, 2012).

The following story highlights the magnitude of forgiveness practiced in the Amish community beyond business practices. It is a story told by Marie Monville, wife of Charlie Roberts who entered an Amish schoolhouse and shot 10 girls before turning the gun on himself. Marie, in her book *One Light Still Shines: My Life Beyond the Shadow of the Amish Schoolhouse Shooting*, acknowledged the power of love and forgiveness that she received from the Amish community. On October 2, 2006, at approximately 10:26 AM, Charles Roberts entered an Amish schoolhouse in the rural Pennsylvania hamlet of Nickel Mines. He rapped on the door armed with chains, clamps, and guns...then he shot 10 girls—aged 6 to 13—killing five, before taking his own life. Marie recalled,

> On Charlie's funeral...I was devastated. This intrusion into our privacy by reporters only added to the agony. I wanted to shout, "*Let my children weep by the grave of their father in private!*"...One after another, the line of Amish men and women walking in our direction.... I watched unbelieving, tears streaming down my face, as that line of Amish formed a wall in front of us, hiding the grave site from our view—and from the view of the reporters and photographers.... The Amish were shielding the family of Charlie Roberts. The cameras of the world could see only one thing—the backs of the Amish people. The Amish do not

have their pictures taken. To do so violates their belief that picture-taking creates a graven image.... This act was a true sacrifice, unconditional love poured out upon the wife and children of the man who had taken their daughters from them. That they would choose to give such a gift to us was beyond comprehension.

(Monville, 2013, pp. 159–161)

Amish Church and Church Leadership

Amish communities are located in 425 geographic settlements in 28 US states and the Canadian province of Ontario. Amish life is organized around 1,825 local church districts, composed of 25 to 35 households (Kraybill et al., 2011b). Each church district has its own Ordnung, guidelines for daily living. The Ordnung, from a German word meaning "order" or "discipline," is unwritten set of rules and regulations that guide the Amish to live a proper Christian life. It is reviewed orally twice per year at special church services. It varies among the many different church districts, with different technology adoption and use and dress standards, for example, among other things. It can change and does so over time.

The Amish church plays a key role in any individual Amish business to define its success, what new practices to adopt, growth orientation, better stewardship of financial resources, and more. Amish business owners are expected to follow the regulations of the church, which may curtail some business activities. Church rules forbid business owners from producing or selling certain products, traveling by airplane, and conducting business on Sundays. Industries related to alcohol, entertainment, computers, electronic communications, gambling, and theater are all off-limits. Television and radio ads are prohibited, as are promotions that feature photographs of the business owner. Church regulations also restrict certain types of technology for Amish businesses. These include prohibitions on owning and operating motor vehicles, tapping electricity from the public power grid, freely using telephones, owning computers, and using the internet. Moreover, entrepreneurs who violate regulations by selling goods on Sunday or by purchasing a motor vehicle, for example, face censure by the church and, if unrepentant, excommunication from the Amish community.

All of those principles are communal decisions that are different from one church district to the other. The Amish don't automatically embrace what's new; they evaluate it and decide if it's a good fit for the lives they want to lead. Every new idea is examined carefully to consider how it will affect their cherished lifestyle and purpose. The deliberation takes place before deciding whether to embrace any new way of living. Among Amish businesses, adopting business technology, including a computer and cell phone, has been a heated topic. Kraybill, Johnson-Weiner, and Nolt (2018) underlined questions that the Amish ask themselves as a community before adopting anything new, including technology, or changing their lifestyle. They ask if the new technology is going to bolster their life together as a community or if this new technology would hurt the Amish way of life. The Amish tend to stick with "the way we've always done it," rather than rush into adopting ever-changing styles and unproven new theories.

Considering the importance of the church's role in a community, the way that Amish choose their spiritual leaders truly represents the concept of everyday leadership. Spiritual leaders in the Amish community are chosen when needed and only during a communion service, which occurs twice a year. According to Wagner (2012), the bishop and/or ministers go into a side room to listen as each member walks up to the door, one by one, to whisper the name of their nominee. They tally up the numbers and call for those who have received three or more votes to come sit in a row in front of the congregation. Meanwhile, the bishop picks up as many hymnbooks as there are nominees and slips a piece of paper with a verse written on it into one of the hymnbooks. He shuffles the books into a different order before each nominee comes forward to pick up one of these hymnbooks. One by one, they open the hymnbooks until the paper is discovered, and the one holding it is the chosen leader. Becoming a leader in the Amish community is never perceived as a prideful status. Instead, Amish people see leadership as something to dread. The thought of having to stand before the others and expound on the scriptures is terrifying to them. It is a time-demanding job—preparing sermons and counseling those who are out of line with the rules. (Confronting each other is not their forte.) It also puts pressure on them, as they do not want to appear more prideful or spiritual than the others; however, they are expected to set a spiritual example. Upon finding the piece of paper in his open book, the chosen one begins to weep along with his wife due to the amount of responsibility that lays before him. Church members spend the evening consoling and encouraging the new leader at his home. It is nothing similar to any typical occasion of celebration. Church leaders recognize their responsibilities more than any other benefits that come with a leadership position, such as privilege and pride.

Teaching and Development of Everyday Leadership

Learning Everyday Skills by Doing Everything

Four values in particular energize the vitality of Amish business: a vigorous work ethic, practicality, honesty, and frugality (Dana, 2007, 2009). The Amish amplify these values in the socialization of their children and promote them throughout adulthood. Hard work and a strong work ethic are integral parts of Amish life. It is one of the key factors to Amish business success. A strong work ethic is manifest in every aspect of Amish life and emphasized from a very young age. That strong work ethic builds a positive brand of Amish products. Many of the Amish who choose not to farm go into skilled trades like furniture building, construction, and metal parts manufacturing. These products are often sold to those outside the Amish community. Amish businesses benefit from an "in-born brand," since people appreciate the quality that comes with Amish products. Amish business people -do good work and it kind of feeds itself (Wesner, 2010). It is noteworthy to acknowledge that financial achievement is never the ultimate goal of an Amish person's life. Instead, it is one outcome where faith and work are interwoven through hard work, where hour after hour, day after day, good work is evident to all (Peabody, 1974). The work ethic is developed to run a successful business but also taught in a pragmatic, common-sense attitude of finding ways to make things work despite obstacles (Kraybill et al., 2011a). Amish people have to juggle many different tasks, including growing crops, managing and feeding herds, building, mending and maintaining facilities, and cleaning house. Those practical skills are easily transferable from farming to business and from business to problem solving in any situation. In particular, farmers always face contingencies such as weather, fluctuating crop prices, machinery breakdown, and vendor reliability. The agrarian heritage and limited education of Amish people foster a pragmatic, common-sense attitude of finding creative ways to make things work despite obstacles. This inventive approach to solving problems characterizes Amish business owners and employees. An entrepreneur touting the virtue of practical hands-on education said, "You can be taught it, you can see it, you can know how it feels, but you can never learn it, until you actually do it." This disposition toward practicality empowers Amish entrepreneurs as they face challenges that require innovation, flexibility, creativity, and risk taking.

Learning Skills That Can Be Applied to Everyday Work Situation: Japanese Corporate Training

In a similar vein of Amish training drawn from all aspects of life experiences, in the Japanese corporate training program, job rotation is a unique example of everyday leadership development, in which employees are exposed to every aspect of a business operation. Job rotation refers to the systematic movement of employees from one job to another or any change in assignment, job content, or department within the organization. American and European corporations also have programs of job rotation to broaden the experience and training of their managers. But the Japanese-style shuffling of people into new disciplines every few years is a practice that is rare in other corporations. Japanese firms regularly transfer employees to different departments repeatedly during one's career, at intervals ranging from two to seven years. For instance, after being initially assigned to a sales department, they could be transferred to the product development department, and then to the human resources department after that. "In his 26 years with the Toyo Kogyo Company, Mitsuji Muraoka has been an accountant, a plant designer, an efficiency watchdog, a materials-handling specialist and a computer systems manager. The zigzagging career that Mr. Muraoka, a 50-year-old division manager, has experienced at Toyo Kogyo, the producer of Mazda cars and Japan's third-largest auto maker, is not unusual in Japan" (Lohr, 1982, P.1). Job rotation is one of the distinctive features of Japanese management. Cosgel and Miceli (2000) found that the practice of job rotation contributed to the success of Japanese firms. From the view of human resource management, many researchers have described job rotation in a broader perspective. Noe and Ford (1992) described job rotation as opportunities for employees to gain an overall appreciation of organizational goals, to generate a broader knowledge of different functional areas, to develop a network of organizational contacts, and to enhance employee skills. This is based on the argument that employees can use the information and skills acquired at one task to improve their performance at other tasks (Lindback & Snower, 2000). Much of this "inter-task learning" takes place through job rotation within and between teams of workers in production, management, and marketing departments in an organization. Developing broad-gauged generalists instead of training a specialist in designated fields such as sales, legal affairs, engineering, or accounting makes Japanese corporations more cohesive and smoother-working organizations. In contrast to senior executives in the United States, the Japanese top executive is more likely to have experience in operations and manufacturing. At the same time, the benefits of frequent job rotation include a close working association with many workers in a variety of areas. This enhances communication and mutual understanding of the company's problems. The value of job rotation has long been espoused in promoting employee learning and career development (Campion, Cheraskin, & Stevens, 1994). Numerous firms have used job rotation as a tool to motivate employees by providing task variety and enhancing employee socialization (Susan, 1996).

Job rotation creates a strong identity of employees with the values of the corporation generally, rather than the values of a given specialty or profession. This makes finding a job in other companies harder, as they are not trained and placed in one specialty. At the same time, an unsatisfied Japanese worker, knowing that his position will change before long, is less likely to leave the company. It contributes to a reduced risk of losing skilled personnel.

In short, regular job rotation is a typical part of the lifetime employment system that is unique to the Japanese business culture. The job rotation system decreases the rate of turnover of their employees and increases the likelihood that the employee will stay at the company for many years, recouping the investment the company made in training the employee. To some extent, frequent job rotation is both a reflection of Japanese culture and possible because of it. Historically, Japan has been a collectivist, group-oriented society. In feudal times, the group that gave one's life meaning and identity was the clan. Today, it is the corporation.

Everyday Leadership Development in a Classroom

Everyday leadership development can be incorporated in business courses. Team leader rotation is one of the ways that allows each student to play a leadership role in their coursework. In all of my business courses, including international business, business ethics, and business leadership, I developed a team contract, which teams of three to five students read together and agree to the terms. Terms include that every member rotates their role as a leader defined by tasks, coordination of meetings and team communication, facilitation of team meetings and allocations of individual tasks, control of the quality of group work, and organizing order and content to present. Each team defines their needed tasks and they rotate the leadership task from one to the other throughout the semester. Constant feedback and coaching are critical for the activation of everyday leadership development in a classroom. When an instructor provides the coaching necessary for successful execution of their rotated leadership roles, students are far more capable, more willing to seek help when necessary, and better able to identify and correct errors and problems than if they're left to figure things out on their own. At the same time, everyday leadership can be practiced in any class session when an instructor empowers (weak) students to present their opinions and endorse their ideas, which create a more inclusive and supportive class culture for all.

Conclusion

When it comes to inclusive leadership, in many workplaces, it is the members of small dominant identity groups (e.g., white men in North American and European contexts) who are most likely to feel included (Mor Barak, Cherin, & Berkman, 1998). They are typical organizational leaders who attain positions of power and influence, participate in decision-making, and gain access to organizational resources (Acker, 1990; Carter & Silva, 2010; Findler, Wind, & Mor Barak, 2007; Silva, Carter, & Beninger, 2012). These inequities result in conflict, attrition, and underutilization of skilled talent (Holvino, Ferdman, & Merill-Sands, 2004). To avoid these ill effects, organizations are increasingly recognizing the need to cultivate inclusive leaders—leaders who can help ensure that irrespective of identity, all employees have opportunities for advancement, have access to resources, and can participate in decision-making. Taking the inclusive leadership further, this chapter argues that inclusive organizations should activate everyday leadership where everyone can be and should be a leader. Inclusive organizations are fundamentally shared ventures, individually and collectively under the foundation of shared visions, norms, and values. An inclusive organization activates a culture of flourishing everyday leaders, as illustrated by the Amish community in this chapter. When we involve everyone in leadership, only then we can hope for a totally inclusive organization, where everyone takes responsibility for organizational success by serving others. Such structural design of everyday leadership provides the felicitous space for creative work that is mind enriching, heart fulfilling, soul satisfying, and financially rewarding for both employees and organizations.

References

Acker, J. (1990). Hierarchies, jobs, bodies: A theory of gendered organizations. *Gender and Society*, 4: 139–158.
Bass, B. M. (1985). *Leadership and performance beyond expectations*. New York, NY: Free Press.
Bolden, R., & Gosling, J. (2006). Leadership competencies: Time to change the tune? *Leadership*, 2, 147–163.
Campion, M. A., Cheraskin, L., & Stevens, M. J. (1994). Career-related antecedents and outcomes of job rotation. *Academy of Management Journal*, 37, 1518–1542.
Carter, N. M., & Silva, C. (2010). *Pipeline's broken promise*. New York: Catalyst. Retrieved from http://www.catalyst.org/publication/372/pipelines-broken-promise
Conger, J. A., & Kanungo, R. N. (1994). Charismatic leadership in organizations: Perceived behavioral attributes and their measurement. *Journal of Organizational Behavior*, 15, 439–452.
Cosgel, M. A., & Miceli, T. J. (2000). Job rotation: Costs, benefits and stylized facts. *Journal of Institutional and Theoretical Economics*, 21, 234–257.
Dana, L. P. (2007). A humility-based enterprising community: The Amish people in Lancaster County. *Journal of Enterprising Communities: People and Places in the Global Economy*, 1(2), 142–154.
Dana, L. P. (2009). Religion as an explanatory variable for entrepreneurship. *Entrepreneurship and Innovation*, 10(2), 97–109.
Day, D. V. (2001). Leadership development: A review in context. *Leadership Quarterly*, 11, 581–613.

Dursin, M (2014). *13 Money secrets from the Amish*. Retrieved from https://www.businessinsider.com/money-secrets-of-amish-people-2014-4/commerce-on-business-insider

Findler, L., Wind, L. H., & Mor Barak, M. E. (2007). The challenge of workforce management in a global society: Modeling the relationship between diversity, inclusion, organizational culture, and employee well-being, job satisfaction and organizational commitment. *Administration in Social Work, 31*(3), 63–94.

Gardner, W., Avolio, B., Luthans, F., May, D. R., & Walumbwa, F. (2005). Can you see the real me? A self-based model of authentic leader and follower development. *Leadership Quarterly, 16*, 343–372.

George, W. (2003). *Authentic leadership: Rediscovering the secrets to creating lasting value*. San Francisco, CA: Jossey-Bass.

George, W., & Sims, P. (2007). *True north: Discover your authentic leadership*. San Francisco, CA: Jossey-Bass.

Henriques, D. B. (2012). In Amish country, accusations of a Ponzi scheme. *The New York Times*. Retrieved from www.nytimes.com/2012/02/26/business/in-amish-country-accusations-of-a-ponzi-scheme.html

Holvino, E., Ferdman, B. M., & Merrill-Sands, D. (2004). Creating and sustaining diversity and inclusion in organizations: Strategies and approaches. In M. S. Stockdale & F. J. Crosby (Eds.), *The psychology and management of workplace diversity* (pp. 245–276). Malden, MA: Blackwell.

Iles, P., & Preece, D. (2006). Developing leaders or developing leadership? The academy of chief executives' programmes in the North East of England. *Leadership, 2*, 317–340.

Kraybill, D. B. (2001). *The riddle of Amish culture*. Baltimore: The Johns Hopkins University Press.

Kraybill, D. B., Johnson-Weiner, K., & Nolt, S. M. (2018). *The Amish*. Baltimore: Johns Hopkins University Press.

Kraybill, D. B., Nolt, S. M., & Weaver-Zercher, D. (2012). *The Amish way: Patient faith in a perilous world*. New York, NY: Wiley.

Kraybill, D. B., Nolt, S. M., & Wesner, E. (2011a). Sources of enterprise success in Amish communities. *Enterprising Communities: People and Places in the Global Economy, 5*(2), 112–130.

Kraybill, D. B., Nolt, S. M., & Wesner, E. (2011b). *Sources of enterprise success in Amish communities*. Bingley: Emerald Publication Group.

Lindback, A., & Snower, D. J. (2000). Multi-task learning and the reorganization of work from Tayloristic to holistic organization. *Journal of Labor Economics, 18*(3), 353.

Lohr, S. (1982, July 12). How job rotation works for Japanese. *New York Times*, p. 1. Retrieved from www.nytimes.com/1982/07/12/business/how-job-rotation-works-for-japanese.html

McCarty, J. F. (2012). *Ohio's "Amish Bernie Madoff" gets prison term for bilking investors*. Retrieved from www.cleveland.com/metro/2012/06/ohios_amish_bernie_madoff_gets.html

Monville, M. (2013). *One light still shines: My life beyond the shadow of the Amish Schoolhouse shooting*. Grand Rapid, MI: Zondervan.

Mor Barak, M. E., Cherin, D. A., & Berkman, S. (1998). Organizational and personal dimensions in diversity climate: Ethnic and gender differences in employee perceptions. *The Journal of Applied Behavioral Science, 34*(1), 82–104.

Noe, R. A., & Ford, J. K. (1992). Career building: Learning from cumulative work experience. *Career Development in Organisations, 7*, 45–52.

Peabody, L. D. (1974). *Secular work is full-time service*. Christian Literature Crusade.

Schyns, B., Kiefer, T., Kerschreiter, R., & Tymon, A. (2011). Teaching implicit leadership theories to develop leaders and leadership: How and why it can make a difference. *Academy of Management Learning & Education, 10*(3), 397–408.

Silva, C., Carter, N. M., & Beninger, A. (2012). Good intentions, imperfect execution? Women get fewer of the "hot jobs" needed to advance. New York, NY: Catalyst.

Susan, S. D. (1996). The new story about job rotation. *Academy of Management Executive, 10*(1), 86–88.

Wagner, C. (2012). *How do the Amish choose their ministers and bishops?* Retrieved from www.mapministry.org/articles/2012/10/31/how-do-the-amish-choose-their-ministers-and-bishops

Walumbwa, F. O., Luthans, F., Avey, J. B., & Oke, A. (2009). Authentically leading groups: The mediating role of collective psychological capital and trust. *Journal of Organizational Behavior, 30*, 1–21.

Wesner, E. (2010). *Success made simple: An inside look at why Amish businesses thrive*. New York, NY: Jossey-Bass.

Yammarino, F. J., & Bass, B. M. (1990). Transformational leadership and multiple levels of analysis. *Human Relations, 43*(10), 975–995.

12
INCLUSIVE LEADERSHIP AND RELIGION

Sarah M. Mutuku, Faith Mutuku Muna, Rachel Mwende M. Murigi, and Miriam M. Mutuku-Kioko

Introduction

This chapter discusses inclusive leadership within the broader paradigm of religion. It starts with an introduction, then goes on to examine the meaning of leadership; the meaning of inclusive leadership and its common traits and principles; and the concept of inclusive leadership and religion. The main religious persuasions are made reference to. The key takeaways, reflective questions, and a featured case on how a growing consulting firm operating in Kenya and in the other East African Community (EAC) countries practices inclusive leadership in its operations are presented.

It is widely acknowledged and accepted everywhere that leadership is about influence (Bass, 1990; Rost, 1991). There is, however, no agreement on the best way to influence followers. It is commonly known that no one is born a leader; a leader is someone that has a position of influence; it is the role one grows into; some people seek leadership but others have it thrust upon them. However, today because of the dynamic changes taking place in the political, economic, technological and especially social-cultural arenas, leaders are expected to become more engaging and inclusive. Inclusive leadership has become a key concern today. This is the case in every sector of society, including in every religious persuasion. It is our key focus in this chapter.

Meaning of Leadership

There exist so many books, articles and authors on leadership, but there has never been any consensus on the concrete meaning of this intricate concept. The concept continues to develop, and so it is a changing paradigm. Leadership is indeed a complex phenomenon and intricate. However, there is a consensus that leadership is about influence and that it involves the leader, followers and a context in which it occurs. Leadership occurs in all groups of people regardless of religion, geographical context, nationality, culture or formal or informal situations (Rost, 1991; Bass, 1990).

Leaders influence and motivate their followers to move towards certain goals and in the process attempt to achieve constructive change. Historical records provide us with examples of men and women of influence who impacted their societies and organizations positively through their leadership influence. Some famous leaders include United States of America leaders such as George Washington, Abraham Lincoln, John F. Kennedy and Martin Luther King. Famous leaders from other continents include Mahatma Gandhi of India and Nelson Mandela of South Africa. They also include great leaders from the continent of Africa such as Jomo Kenyatta of Kenya, Kwame Nkrumah of Ghana and Mwalimu Julius Nyerere of Tanzania.

John Walsh of General Electric and Anne M. Livermore of Hewlett-Packard are renowned for their successful leadership that led to marked improvements in the performance of their organizations through the application of business strategies and strategic thinking, as well as their personal influence that involved what is today described as inclusive leadership. It is often argued that Livermore exceptionally inspired, influenced and motivated her staff to achieve constructive change in Hewlett-Packard. She had an inclusive leadership orientation.

Many theories of leadership have been developed over time. They include trait theory, the earliest leadership theory that focused on differing categories of traits or characteristics such as looks, size, ability to fight enemies etc.; behavioral theory, whose key concern is the behavior of leaders; contingency theories that focused on situations and context as key influencers on leadership; modern day or contemporary theories primarily focusing on organizational changes from the conviction that change is a constant reality of life; strategic leadership theories focusing on the creation of meaning and purpose for the organization; and the new leadership theories that have developed to address the changing dynamics in today's turbulent world of business. These new theories include charismatic, transformational and visionary leadership. We also have emergent leadership theories that deal with behavioral and cognitive complexity as well as social and emotional intelligence and their influence on leadership effectiveness.

The aforementioned theories of leadership all emphasize that the leader and followers have to be consciously connected. This is the case no matter what style of leadership is considered. A key issue in leadership development, because of the unprecedented changes of today, is that leaders have to increasingly include their followers in the leadership process. Some leaders may use force, the carrot and stick, persuasion, charisma and other means of influence, but at the end of the day the followers must consider themselves part of the leadership effort. This is the essence of inclusive leadership. But what exactly is inclusive leadership?

Inclusive Leadership

Our view is in agreement with many writers' views that in the leadership process inclusion is about making sure everyone is on board with participating in an organization for the common good. Sturm (2006, p. 249) defines inclusion as "identifying the barriers to full participation and the pivot points for removing those barriers and increasing participation." Inclusion can be looked at from many perspectives. Some researchers choose to take a psychological approach to inclusion, defining it as "the degree to which an employee is accepted and treated as an insider by others" (Pelled, Ledford, Jr, & Mohrman, 1999). Other definitions focus on a sense of belonging, having voices heard and feeling as though their organization values their perspectives and seeks their engagement (Wasserman, Gallegos, & Ferdman, 2008). This is close to the religious view, where in every known religion on earth everyone belonging to a particular religion or sect is embraced as a member of the particular religious family under consideration. The practice part of inclusion in religion may and sometimes does differ greatly between and within religions, as religious beliefs and practices may not always be in congruence. However, the belief in and focus on a deity or deities by religious leaders and their followers is the one common factor that greatly engenders inclusion.

The terms 'inclusive leadership' and 'inclusive leader' are already in common use today by researchers, academicians, practitioners and policymakers, meaning that different definitions are available and are in use. What is commonly known in leadership literature is that all the definitions of leadership have some commonalities. However, they all center on human relationships and the valuing of personal differences. In other words, everyone is important in spite of his/her position in the organization. One type of leadership, known as servant leadership, first brought out by Robert K. Greenleaf (1977, 2002), provides many of the concepts of inclusion. Transformational leadership too provides some insights into what inclusion requires in several of its aspects. These concepts of leadership put the individual human being at the center of the organization's aspirations and moves.

Common Traits in Inclusive Leadership

Identifying key characteristics or traits relating to a particular concept is one good way of shedding light on the critical aspects of the particular concept, given that some conceptual meanings may be shared with many other concepts. Substantial research on inclusive leadership carried out in different contexts has the consensus that this type of leadership enhances performance significantly and assures that all team members feel they are treated respectfully and fairly, are valued and sense that they belong, and are confident and inspired, and this motivates them naturally to perform highly. It can be distinguished from other types of leadership even though it shares some characteristics especially with servant leadership and transformational leadership. With the increasing importance of diverse, multidisciplinary teams in today's organizations, one requires the application of inclusive leadership in order to enhance effectiveness and high performance. Changing dynamics demand that this be the case.

Various research efforts appear to have reached a consensus that there are basically six traits or behaviors that distinguish inclusive leaders from others. Literature from different sources generally supports the six traits as the key characteristics of inclusive leadership. The six traits are outlined as follows.

Visible commitment: Inclusive leaders articulate authentic commitment to diversity, challenge the status quo, hold others accountable and make diversity and inclusion a personal priority. We can posit that such leaders are engaged.

Humility: Inclusive leaders are modest about capabilities, admit mistakes and create the space for others to contribute. They are open to suggestions and constructive criticism and value these, as they add value to their leadership.

Awareness of bias: Inclusive leaders are very much aware of personal blind spots as well as flaws in the system and work hard to ensure meritocracy. Through inclusion and openness, they are able to mine useful gems concerning new and novel ideas from their followers and their peers.

Curiosity about others: Inclusive leaders demonstrate an open mindset and deep curiosity about others, listen attentively without judgment, pay due regard to their followers' ideas and seek with empathy to understand those around them. They realize that they are not sufficient by themselves and do need others to come along with them in their leadership efforts.

Cultural intelligence: Inclusive leaders realize that people come from different cultures and have different orientations as a result, and for them to succeed they must consciously remain attentive to the cultures of the people they interact with and be able to adapt as required. We can also add that they have to appreciate differences in culture and especially those brought about by cultural nuances and ethos.

Effective collaboration: Inclusive leaders empower their followers through different ways, pay attention to diversity of thinking and psychological safety and focus on team cohesion.

Principles of Inclusive Leadership

Principles in this context tell us how to put into practice the theory and philosophy of inclusive leadership. Many writers and researchers, including those from salesforce.com (2017), have identified the key principles of inclusive leadership. These are presented in the following sections.

Lead With Equality

Leading with equality means ensuring that all the members of the organization are accorded the same status as far as possible and are accorded their due rights and responsibilities. Inclusive leaders attempt to integrate equality into everything they do. They keep equality at the forefront of everything they do. Leading with equality has many dimensions. They include:

- Adding equality to all the plans and goals of the organization. This should be reflected in the organization's vision, mission, values and philosophy.
- Practicing inclusive hiring, which goes hand in hand with diversity considerations.
- Leaders always predisposing themselves as allies to the followers. They must make employees feel valued and ensure they are heard and empowered in order to be able to function unfettered. This includes asking, listening, showing up and speaking up as important guidelines for dealing with employees with empathy. Inclusive leaders always try to be present, engaged and committed.

The previous principle requires that the inclusive leader understands his/her own team's unique strengths, supports flexibility and encourages active leadership, growth and development.

Having Brave, Authentic Conversations

Having brave and authentic conversations is a key principle that requires inclusive leaders to host brave and authentic conversations with their stakeholders, particularly their internal stakeholders, including employees. It is envisaged that this can be achieved through listening with empathy, telling your story as a leader, creating a culture of transparency, encouraging healthy discourse and emphasizing accountability and forgiveness.

Practicing Inclusive Meetings

This is what we call the principle of meetings. Meetings bring people together to discuss and make decisions on issues. They are a key ingredient in the modern workplace. They are indeed a hard fact of the workplace today, especially in today's horizontal, flexible and team-oriented structures. Meetings can sometimes have casual invitations and can be selective, time wasting and unproductive (Schermerhorn, 2010, p. 378). To make meetings more meaningful, the inclusive leader must ensure that everyone is heard, everyone is invited to have a seat at the table, remote employees are not forgotten, credit and recognition are given where due and note taking even though seemingly a mundane issue is given due consideration with initiation of a rotation of note taking. Experience shows that some leaders pick on some able people, especially women, and perpetually condemn them to note taking without a care that they too need to be heard in meetings.

Being Fair in Assignments and Promotions

This is an important principle concerning fairness and justice. The way that leaders assign work and approach the promotion process is important in inclusion. Sometimes biases, stereotypes, halo effects and selective perception may trickle in and cloud the judgment of the leader in work assignments and promotions. To attempt to avoid these and other problems, the inclusive leader is required to spread high-visibility projects so that there is inclusion, consider giving everyone equal opportunity in promotions and ensure that the promotion process is transparent.

Celebrating and Bonding With Everyone in Mind

Celebration and team-bonding activities are important parts of culture and life at work. They bring colleagues closer and enhance work relationships. This is an important principle that should incorporate social activities.

The previous principles of inclusion are significant when looked at in the context of different religions.

Inclusive Leadership and Religion

In religious leadership circles, the term inclusion means influencing followers to move towards a certain vision based on a calling from a higher authority or deity or deities. Every organized religion in the world has leaders who occupy positions of influence to guide congregations of followers as per the tenets of their faith. Such leaders perform the rites and ceremonies that a particular religion demands, such as established and accepted religious celebrations and others such as birth rituals, coming-of-age rituals and marriage and death rituals. Religious leaders are also the keepers of religious tradition and often take on the role of moral leader as well as teacher or 'guide.' Generally speaking, they have the key role of creating other leaders. This is true of most religions. Religious leaders are given the name 'clergy' that describes the official religious leadership in a religion. For example, titles such as ayatollah, allamah, elder, apostle, bishop, archbishop, canon, pastor, caliphate, deacon or deaconess (Christian), overseer, guru (each of the first 10 leaders of the Sikh religion), mufti of Saudi Arabia, imam, lay leader, murshid, kahen (Beta Israel), mahdi and vardapet are common and well known in today's different religious persuasions. Religious leaders are assumed to occupy positions of inclusion on behalf of higher authorities. It suffices at this point to examine the key religions and how each handles inclusion.

Buddhism is both a religion and a philosophy. It was founded around the 5th century BC in India by Siddhartha Gautama, the Buddha. Buddhism teaches that someone who becomes enlightened without instruction is a Buddha. The goal of Buddhism is the attainment of 'nirvana,' a state where cravings, desires and even 'egos' cease and where, because of the associated merit, one can hope to be freed from the endless chain of rebirths into suffering lives. This state enables adherents to do good to humanity through works of charity. The Five Precepts are the basic rules of living for lay Buddhists—refrain from harming living beings, taking what is not given, sexual misconduct, harmful speech and drink or drugs which cloud the mind. Those who ascribe to these precepts are accepted as belonging to Buddhism and are included in all its operations.

Hinduism is another major world religion that is an ancient tradition of related beliefs and practices that developed in the Indian subcontinent. Core ideals and values shared by most Hindus would include respect for elders, reverence for teachers, regard for guests and tolerance of all races and religions. The teachers or leaders have the important role of ensuring that followers are included in the teachings of the faith with the aim of making sure that they can transcend the materialistic and physical things and go for higher things (spiritual) that really matter in life. Just as Hinduism includes a variety of religious traditions, it also has a variety of different types of religious leaders. According to the strict interpretation of the caste system, all priests must come from the highest, or Brahman, caste. Throughout his life, a person is included and remains included in the same caste into which he was born throughout his life, with the possibility to be born into a higher caste at his next reincarnation, which means in many cases, the priesthood is hereditary. Besides the priests, Hinduism also has ascetic monastic orders, referred to as *Sannyasa*, members of which are also primarily from the Brahman caste. *Acharya* or *gurus*, teachers of divine personality who have come to the earth to teach by example and to help ordinary adherents to understand the scriptures, make up a third category of religious leaders in Hinduism. Since Hinduism includes a variety of gods, religious practices and religious leaders, each person's faith is an individual matter, and each will choose a form of devotion and a spiritual leader that suits the goals and nature of his faith. Those who share a common orientation are automatically included in the particular order. All of the religious leaders have a responsibility to guide those who follow them and look to them as examples, to live and teach an upright and holy life. The caste system, a hierarchy of socioeconomic categories called varnas (colors), is made up of priests, warriors and commoners as recorded in the Rigveda. The Rigveda describes four varna:

- Brahmas, the priests and religious officials, teachers of the sacred knowledge of the Veda.
- Rajanyas, composed of rulers and warriors.
- Vaishyas, who were farmers, merchants, traders and craftspeople.

People in these three varnas are permitted to study the Vedas and have the possibility to be reborn into a higher caste, eventually reaching enlightenment or *moksha*.

- Shudras, the lowest caste, were not permitted to study the Vedas and had their own religion and priests.

Later another caste was added:

- Untouchables, who performed tasks too dirty for others, including hunting and butchering.

Christianity is a widespread religion in the world. It has many religious persuasions and sects. But generally, in the Christian faith true religion occurs when a human being attains a personal relationship with God and practices God's law based on the teaching of Jesus Christ. Christian groups and sects differ in their interpretation of his teaching, life, death and resurrection, but these matters are at the heart of the way of life of all of them. Those who accept Christ and the example he gave for service are considered as belonging to the faith and are included in the fellowship of brothers and sisters. The attainment of eternal life with God is the ultimate goal in Christianity. It is reflected through the behavior of those included in the fellowship of believers, no matter what religious orientation or sect is considered. Through inclusion, Christian leaders ensure that all believers play a role in their communities. The idea is to ensure that inclusion helps followers to grow spiritually while aiming at making them 'disciples' of Jesus Christ who then assume the responsibility of going throughout the world preaching and baptizing people and helping them become disciples of Jesus Christ (Matthew 28, p. 19 in The Reformation Study Bible, New King James Version, 1995).

Islam is revealed in its final form by the Prophet Muhammad. Islam has two main sects, each with its own separate but similar beliefs. The essentials of Muslim practice are summarized in the five pillars of Islam—declaration of faith, ritual prayer, welfare, a month of fasting during Ramadan and pilgrimage. Islam, the complete code of life, declares leadership as a trust (*Amanah*) and gives a detailed description of it. According to the Islamic view, leadership is a sacred position that can solve the problems of humanity and guide them to the eternal betterment in the here and the hereafter. It involves a person or a group of people who guide and lead the followers and the rest of humanity from the brink of destruction to the way of Allah. Giving preference to human welfare, Islam defines leadership as a psychological contract between a leader and his followers that he will try his best to guide them, to protect them and to treat them fairly and with justice. Those who accept the tenets of the particular Islamic sect in consideration are included wholly as members of the particular sect.

Judaism is based on the Jewish people's covenant relationship with God. Jews believe they are challenged and blessed by God. Love of one's neighbor is the great principle of social life and the founding inspiration of the Jewish community. Those who are included in the community are only those who prescribe to the beliefs and way of life of Judaism.

Jainism is the religion of the followers of Mahavira, the 24th Tirthankara, or the 24th in a line of teachers espousing Jain principles. It is an ancient philosophy and ethical teaching that originated in India. The main principle is *ahimsa*—the avoidance, where possible, of physical or mental harm to any living being. Jainism is a religion without a belief in a creator god. Jains reject the Vedas and highlight the practice of austerity. Jain philosophy states that the *jiva*, or soul, can escape the cycle of rebirth and death through strict ethical behavior. When nothing remains but the purity of the *jiva*, that person is called a *jina*, or winner, and demonstrates high spiritual maturity. Jainism requires a strict vegetarian lifestyle, avoiding hurting animals, birds and other organisms if used for food. Members included in the Jain community are only those who accept the precepts of the faith.

Sikhism is a religion that began in Punjab in Northern India. It was founded by Guru Nanak in India in the 15th century. The key belief supposed to be held by those included in the faith is that there is one God, and that followers should serve by leading a life of prayer and obedience. Sikhs believe that their souls pass through various existences and become one with God. The Gurū Granth Sāhib are the central scriptures intended to preserve hymns and the teachings of the Sikh gurus and other saints from Hindu and Sufi traditions. Those included or to be included in the faith must embrace the tenets of Sikhism. The tenets include achievement of honest living (and earning as well), tithing and giving alms to the needy and chanting on God, the giver of life. A follower who practices the tenets is wholly included in the faith.

Zoroastrianism is a religion founded in ancient times by the prophet Zarathushtra, who taught that Ahura Mazda (Lord of Wisdom), the all-powerful and perfect creator, grants humans *Vohu Manah*—a clear rational mind with which to dispel ignorance.

East Asian religions or philosophies are many and they share the concept of Tao. The Taoic faiths claim more than 500 million followers worldwide. Taoism, also known as Daoism, comprises a variety of related religious and philosophical traditions. Categorization of Taoist sects and movements is very controversial. Taoist propriety and ethics places an emphasis on love, moderation and humility. These qualities lead followers to practice charity and acts of mercy. Only those who practice these are accepted wholly or included in the community of faith. The best Tao leader maintains clarity of mind, simplicity, balance and Yinyang, stoops low in their influence and lets go and hence allows the followers who have been included in the community of faith to do their works and to let nature take its course.

Key Takeaways

- Many approaches and theories to leadership exist, and they all attempt to prescribe how to be an effective leader.
- Inclusive leadership has established characteristics and principles that must be understood by those who practice or ought to practice it.
- Every major religion attempts to achieve inclusion through education and training of members on its key doctrines and beliefs. Those who ascribe to these are automatically included in the faith.
- Nearly every major religion builds its inclusion of members through a common vision pegged on a deity or deities.
- Servant leadership provided key contributions to the development of inclusive leadership.

Conclusion

Many theories exist on leadership. Most of them mainly focus on the organization. However, the concept of leadership has been undergoing a paradigm shift over time. Robert Greenleaf (Greenleaf, 2002) initiated a new approach to efficient leadership, known as servant leadership, that provided important insights into inclusive leadership. This leadership style mainly focuses on the interests and needs of the followers and hence their inclusion in the leadership process. Thus, the needs and wants of followers concerning belonging are central in this type of leadership. Consultancy, Research & Training Associates (CORETRA) Limited, a medium-sized consulting firm in Kenya, practices inclusive leadership to the core. Inclusive leadership is about making sure every single person in an organization feels like they belong. When they walk through the organization's doors, they should feel certain that they are supported and valued. "We are building a culture—what we call Ohana—that represents everyone and welcomes all" (Cindy Robbins, President and Chief People Officer, Salesforce, 2017). Inclusive leadership involves intrinsically motivating and inspiring workers through hope/faith in a vision of service to followers and other key stakeholders and a corporate culture based on inclusion.

Featured Case

Consultancy, Research and Training Associates (CORETRA) Limited

CORETRA Limited was established in 1998 and registered by the Registrar of Companies in Kenya as a Private Limited Company. It was founded by six directors, one male and five females. The company represents a broad range of knowledge and expertise, particularly in the areas of organizational review, audit, and organizational restructuring; information technology; public and corporate governance; organizational development; strategic management and strategic thinking; program management; systems development; capacity and institution building; resources distribution; financial and economic management; development studies, human resource management and health systems management; among other related ones.

CORETRA has over 20 regular consultants who operate in Kenya and in a number of East African Community (EAC) countries. Occasionally the consultants carry out assignments in other African countries. The consultants come from the company's pool of both full-time and associate consultants.

At the start of company operations, the directors agreed to model their operations on engagement and inclusion. They had the conviction that in order to achieve high performance and sustainability, the individual workers and other stakeholders who would work for the company would be placed at the forefront and would be given an opportunity to be heard.

To actualize inclusion, the company developed a method of involving both internal and external stakeholders. Whenever the company decides to respond to a request for proposal (RFP), the directors and the top managers invite the associate consultants to discuss the RFP and, through some brainstorming, reach a consensus on the mode of response in the context of the company's modus operandi that is well established. The beginning point is to request permission from a client who has requested the RFP to carry out limited interviews in order to understand the 'client as it is now' and make a judgment on 'where it ought to be.' Some clients do not allow this, as they see it as an undue advantage to CORETRA since competing companies would rarely ask for this opportunity. Where there is rejection, the company writes a polite note to the CEO of the client organization excusing itself from participating. Where permission is granted, it becomes easier for CORETRA to identify the needs of the client as well as that of the key managers. This also provides an opportunity to begin building an environment for inclusion much later if CORETRA wins the final bid for the assignment.

The next step usually involves writing a proposal in response to the RFP. The RFP is structured around the following key considerations.

Phase 1: Clarify the Scope of the Proposed Project

This phase would be essential to the overall project, as it would formalize the project scope, project objectives, specific requirements, participant roles and responsibilities, and overall project control and reporting procedures. Once this is done, it would ensure that the various participants would have a clear understanding of exactly what activities are included in the project, their involvement in and accountability to the project management, as well as what would be expected to be delivered.

A committee structure is always recommended for managing the project for the consultancy assignment. Generally, the proposed structure consists of:

i. Project steering committee (client's representatives)
ii. Project team (consisting of CORETRA and the client's representatives)
iii. Project team leader/manager (CORETRA) and assistant project team leader (CORETRA)

Role of the Project Steering Committee

- Provide project progress and feedback to the client
- Monitor progress
- Discuss and gain acceptance from the client and its stakeholders
- Resolve critical issues
- Approve or reject recommendations

Role of the Project Team

- Delivery and facilitation of work according to agreed project plan
- Communicate progress to steering committee
- Ensure conformance to terms of reference
- Provide guidance on key aspects

Role of the Project Leader

- Act as spokesperson for steering committee
- Schedule, convene and co-ordinate meetings
- Manage progress against plan
- Ensure conformance to terms of reference
- Ensure full involvement of stakeholders in the client
- Keep steering committee up to date with developments
- Ensure quality and also complement the work of the consultant

Phase 2: Agreement on the Approach to Use

The approach proposed for assignments is always strictly consultative. The client undertakes in writing that it would allow CORETRA access to documents, the board members and the staff. In order to reach all the staff, CORETRA arranges for meetings with subordinate staff, supervisory staff, middle-level staff and the top management team.

Phase 3: Jointly Developing the Technical and Financial Proposals

All the consultants for a particular proposed project meet together to develop the financial proposal and the technical proposal. This is a very important stage as the consultants work with the CEO to work out the figures including taxes, rates to individual consultants depending on the specific assignments they would undertake in the project, and administrative expenses. Everyone involved contributes to the writing of the proposals. Once the financial proposal is finalized based on the technical proposal, it is clear on how finances would be handled. All the writers of the financial proposal sign off the document to signify their agreement.

Phase 4: Writing the Inception Report Once Award Has Been Given

This is written by all the consultants to be involved in the assignment under the leadership of the CEO or his representative. The CEO models inclusion as far as possible and takes the opportunity to discuss with every consultant—aspirations, fears, gaps in skills of consultants and how each may wish to be assisted to help fill them.

Phase 5: Implementation Phase

Implementation usually follows a carefully phased action plan agreed and signed off by the client's CEO and CORETRA's CEO.

Phase 6: Continuous Monitoring and Evaluation (M&E)

This is always part of any project undertaken by CORETRA Limited. CORETRA always proposes a joint team constituted by the client and CORETRA that is usually given full mandate to carry out M&E unfettered.

Phase 7: Putting Money Where CORETRA's Mouth Is

Profits from a particular project are shared by all the consultants involved in conjunction with the CEO based on the financial plan. This is seen as a transparent process that makes people very happy and excited to work with CORETRA. People, not money, are the top priority in CORETRA.

The story of CORETRA appears to provide important lessons for inclusive leadership. It shows that consultants and staff are given an opportunity to be heard; an inclusive environment is built; the top management tries to identify the needs of individual consultants particularly in regard to skills sets; the CORETRA CEO attempts to model the way; innovation and creativity are allowed and possibly given space to thrive, and this is especially so for new recruits; and a well-established methodology is shared with all the consultants and the clients. This is used in order to encourage the inclusion of all the stakeholders involved in a given project. One can argue that the theory of inclusive leadership comes alive in CORETRA Limited.

References

Bass, B. M. (1990). From transactional to transformational leadership: Learning to share the vision. *Organizational Dynamics, 18*(4), 19–31.

Greenleaf, R. K. (1977). *Servant leadership: A journey into the nature of legitimate power and greatness.* Mahwah, NJ: Paulist Press.

Greenleaf, R. K. (2002). Essentials of servant-leadership. In L. C. Spears & M. Lawrence (Eds.), *Focus of leadership: Servant leadership for the 21st century* (pp. 19–25). New York, NY: Wiley.

Pelled, L., Ledford, G. E. Jr., & Mohrman, S. (1999). Demographic dissimilarity and workplace inclusion. *Journal of Management Studies, 36*(7), 1013–1031.

The Reformation Study BIBLE (The New King James Version). Nashville, 1995.

Rost, J. C. (1991). *Leadership for the twenty-first century.* New York, NY: Praeger.

Salesforce's Dreamforce Equality Summit. (2017). San Francisco. Retrieved from https://www.salesforce.com

Schermerhorn, R. J. (2010). *Introduction to management* (10th ed.). International Student Version. Hoboken, NJ: John Wiley & Sons, Inc.

Sturm, S. (2006). Architecture of inclusion: Advancing workplace equity in higher education. *The Harvard Journal of Law & Gender, 29,* 247.

Wasserman, I. C., Gallegos, P. V., & Ferdman, B. M. (2008). Dancing with resistance: Leadership challenges in fostering a culture of inclusion. In Kecia M. Thomas (Ed.), *Diversity resistance in organizations* (pp. 175–200). New York, NY: Taylor & Francis Group/Lawrence Erlbaum Associates.

13
VEDANTIC LEADERSHIP

Glen Callahan and Subhasis Chakrabarti

Introduction

The philosophy of Vedānta presents a theory and practice of spiritual development. With spiritual maturity comes commensurate changes in both one's sense of self and relationship with the world, improving one's capacity to act in a leadership role.

This chapter presents a definition of spiritual maturity and explains the subjective changes and personality traits that develop in its wake. It draws on an aspect of Vedānta's extensive metaphysical underpinnings to explain these changes and to describe the normative case of a Vedantic Leader (VL). The Indian poem Bhagavad Gītā, a philosophical dialogue between the military leader Arjuna and his advisor Kṛṣṇa, is explored for practical examples of spiritual maturity.

Vedānta is a millennia-old wisdom tradition, with a long lineage of past and present teachers, authors, and commentators. It is a living tradition, which continuously has been and is adapting to the challenges of the respective time. This chapter draws its references primarily from the work of contemporary Indian philosopher, author, and educator Swami A. Parthasarathy.

Metaphysical Perspective and Inclusiveness

Defining Spiritual Maturity

The Bhagavad Gītā presents a clear definition of spiritual maturity. Within the narrative, Arjuna directly asks, "What is the description of one of steady wisdom?" (Gītā: II.54. Trans. A. Parthasarathy, 1992, p. 129). Kṛṣṇa responds in the subsequent verse (Gītā: II.55. Ibid.):

> When one completely casts off, O Pārtha, all desires of the mind, and is satisfied in the Self by the Self, then one is said to be of steady wisdom.

To better understand Kṛṣṇa's response, the Vedantic conception of ego and desire is presented here. Vedānta conceptualizes the human personality as comprising two aspects, Spirit and matter (note that to denote the Absolute, explained later, capitalization is always used). The term 'matter' refers to the various personality layers. A. Parthasarathy (2008) presents these as:

- the physical body (action and perception; sensory)
- the mind (impulse, attachment, desire, emotion; non-rational)

- gross intellect (finite reasoning; rational)
- subtle intellect (positing the Absolute; contemplative)

The body-mind-intellect (BMI) are of course inherently relational in their activity. That is, their activities are always in relation to a reality external to them; the BMI influence the world and are influenced by it. The body relates to the sensible world, receiving stimuli as raw material for experience; the mind-intellect reacts with stimuli based on memory, meaning structure, and analysis. Action is the response, communicating the reaction to the world. Throughout this cascading series of experiences, the BMI is always in relation.

'Spirit' refers to the essential yet unknown inner Self, the Subject of all experiences delivered by body-mind-intellect. It denotes an identity that does not depend upon the matter layers for its definition. Crucially, It is never in relation to either the matter layers or to external reality. It does not influence the world, nor is It influenced by the world. It is Absolute.

The term 'ego' in this context refers to the identification of one's Self with the matter layers. In short, the individuality. One identifying with BMI thus ascribes physical, emotional, and cognitive states to their own Self and not to the personality layers themselves. For example, when the body is cold, it is experienced and expressed as '*I am cold,*' not '*The body is cold.*' Similar first-person assertions are made about one's mind and intellect. Self-analysis of these experiences reveals an underlying belief of oneself as the body-mind-intellect. This assumption is ego. Vedānta philosophy claims that this is an error in identity due to lack of wisdom, insight, and spiritual maturity (e.g. Ātmabodha: 19, 21. Trans. A. Parthasarathy, 2011).

Ego is responsible for the feeling of separateness between individuals, the sense of duality. This is the implicit assumption and feeling that oneself and others exist as wholly independent/separate entities. If I claim to be 'this' (body-mind-intellect), then I cannot be 'that' (world). Ego thus tends to objectify others, regarding them solely as worldly objects that may impede, advance, or be neutral towards one's wish-fulfilment. This is true even for altruistic motivations, where the object of desire is others' well-being. However, as ego-involvement intensifies around selfish motivations, the fact of another as the inherent subject of their experiences is entirely forgotten. Attitudes and behaviors that arise from this lack of regard further isolate individuals from each other.

From ego arises desire. Accompanying the ego will be an inherent sense of constraint and limitation, as one assigns the BMI's inherent constraints and limitations to him- or herself. The dissonance of this egoistic feeling elicits desire, "a plan or scheme entertained . . . to set right an imperfection felt within yourself" (A. Parthasarathy, 1990, p. 3). The individual then initiates a course of action to fulfill the desire, with the hope of eradicating the sense of incompleteness. However, even when action successfully gains the object, such ego-driven behavior is ultimately futile, as desire-fulfilment does not address the underlying causes of either desire or ego.

Thus, Kṛṣṇa's description in II.55 of spiritual maturity (wisdom) encompasses the reduction and eradication of ego-centered desires. While the verse describes an absolute State, it can (like many verses in the text) also be construed as presenting the path or process of developing spiritual maturity: working to gain Self-knowledge so that ego and desires fall away. One of the three methods presented in Vedānta for gaining wisdom is philosophical inquiry. (The other two are gratitude/devotion and selfless action). In this regard, the knowledge offered by the philosophy is an antidote to the implicit assumption of separation. It presents instead the theory of non-duality, advaita in Sanskrit. It asserts that there exists an inner Reality or Identity that is never in relation to anything in the way that the BMI is (Ātmabodha: 7, 36). One of Its many designations is Ātman.

While the previous list of personality features (BMI) is described in order of increasing subtlety, Ātman transcends all of these (e.g. Kaivalya Upaniṣad: I.21–23; Gītā: III.42, VII.4–5, XIV.19, XV.18; Ātmabodha: 14, 18, 31–33, 60). It is important to note that, technically, Ātman is not 'subtler than' the BMI. This would indicate that It occupies the same relative scale of subtlety. However, Ātman being

Absolute, It transcends the BMI and all qualitative and quantitative categories. It thus transcends the dualistic nature of the personality layers and ego; It is non-dual.

Vedānta philosophy asserts further that this Reality is each one's own Self (e.g. Kena Upaniṣad: IV.9; Kaivalya Upaniṣad: I.6, I.23; Ātmabodha: 7, 34–36, 56–57, 64; Gītā: XIII.3). As A. Parthasarathy (2011, p. 85. Ātmabodha: v.3 commentary) explains, "The Self is the core of your personality. Your essential Being." The notion of an 'essential Being' implies a non-essential being. Non-essential beings or selves refer to the compartmentalized roles and relationships that each one adopts in life, none of which wholly defines the individual. For example, one may be simultaneously a mother, daughter, wife, sibling, friend, coworker, etc. Yet no single one of these identities wholly defines the individual. The role and identity of wife is suspended (in some cases entirely forgotten) when she enters the workplace and assumes the role and identity of boss. One's essential Being is that identity which remains present and unchanged through all other roles.

Thus Ātman is said to pervade all experiences as the unchanging medium in which they take place. The analogy of space is used to convey this idea (Gītā: IX.6; Ātmabodha: 10, 35). Just as space accommodates all physical objects, Ātman accommodates all objects of experience. Thus the ground of one's individual, dualistic consciousness is an absolute, non-dual Consciousness. This is conveyed through the well-known Vedic aphorism, Prajñānam brahma, Consciousness is Brahman (Aitareya Upaniṣad: III.i.3).

Vedānta thus states that the separation seemingly inherent in reality is in fact not so. Separation only appears to be the intractable reality of experience from the limited perspective of ego. As egocentric desires reduce, so does the egocentric perspective of experience. This shift in worldview and self-identity is spiritual growth.

Effects of Spiritual Maturity

Among the expressions of spiritual maturity is an enhanced vision of unity *within* diversity, and feeling of unity *across* diversity. Others are experienced as not separate from oneself. This cognitive and affective inclusiveness is designated as oneness. It is important to note that oneness is not fusion with others, in which one's own sense of self and recognition of individual differences are lost. Oneness implies the capacity to retain autonomy while at the same time experiencing unity. The ancient Sanskrit texts refer to this experience of perceiving unity in diversity at length (e.g. Iśāvāsya Upaniṣad: 6; Kaivalya Upaniṣad: I.11, 16; Bhagavad Gītā: IV.35; V.7, 18; VI.9, 29–31; X.20; XIII.16–17, 27–29, 31; XIV.25; XV.15; XVIII.20, 61; Ātmabodha: 47, 48; Bhaja Govidam: 25).

Everyday scenarios reveal relative degrees of oneness. For example, discovering another person shares the same religious or political belief, has a common ancestry or cultural history, supports the same sports team, etc. The realization collapses a perceived distance, and within that context there is shared ground, inclusiveness. The individuals' shared ground is the vision of unity, the greater comity between them is the feeling of unity.

However, such examples are limited in their scope. While individuals may feel closeness because of their shared religion, distance opens up again when they discover they support opposite political ideologies. True Oneness must be unassailable, remaining untouched across all other differences. It would therefore arise from realizing the common Ground of experience that transcends and pervades all differences/dualities.

The gradual realization of the Self as a true common ground of experience is spiritual maturity. Growth culminates in the permanent apperception of the non-dual Ground of individual experience and of the falsity of separateness. This is not merely an academic acceptance or emotional appreciation of an idea. Experience itself is no longer split along the subject-object dichotomy. Kṛṣṇa presents this State as being "without the sense of 'I' and 'mine'" (Gītā: II.71. Trans. A. Parthasarathy, 1992, p. 151). This insight is also seen in the words of Swami Rama Tirtha. Many of his public addresses were transcribed, and they invariably begin with him addressing the audience with greetings such as "My own Self in the form of brothers and sisters" (Tirtha, 2005, vol.6, p. 65); or "Rama's own Self in the form of Audience" (Tirtha, 2005, vol.6, p. 91). All beings are recognized as expressions of the non-dual Subject that is one's own Self. Thus, the ideal Vedantic Leader is perfectly inclusive.

The Ideal Vedantic Leader Is Perfectly Inclusive

A Vedantic Leader is one whose natural style of relating is informed by their wisdom, their spiritual maturity. It is important to note that according to Vedānta, one's state of spiritual maturity is only defined by the reduction and eventual elimination of egocentric desire. Wisdom is not differentiated according to the means of having achieved it. Hence, the Vedantic idea of wisdom is independent from the religious and ideological background of the practitioner.

Spiritual maturity finds its culmination in the Self-realized soul: one who has eradicated all desire, transcended ego, and realized the non-dual Self as the subjective Reality in one and all. Such a person would be the ideal Vedantic Leader. Having recognized the underlying Ground of experience, unity is sustained throughout the diversity of others' physical, psychological, cognitive, and cultural qualities. Other beings are not seen as fundamentally different to one's own Self. This is love, described as "realising your identity with the world. Your oneness with the whole" (A. Parthasarathy, 2004, p. 62), and it promotes inclusivity and harmony with all.

The impossibility in conveying the abstract concept of Self-realization is highlighted by the texts' liberal use of literary and philosophical devices including metaphor, simile, paradox, deliberate contradiction, and negation. However, the expressions of this State can be more directly conveyed and are often done so in the form of lists that span several verses. Specifically, there are three lists of qualities from the Bhagavad Gītā that warrant investigation:

35 qualities of a person endowed with devotion
(Ch. XII, verses 13–20)
20 qualities of a person endowed with knowledge
(Ch. XIII, verses 8–12)
26 qualities of a divine human being
(Ch. XIV, verses 1–3)

This state of Self-realization is attributed to Kṛṣṇa in the allegory of the Bhagavad Gītā. Thus, his use of first-person pronouns does not denote the individuality, the body-mind-intellect-ego of Kṛṣṇa. Instead, 'I' and 'Me' refer to the Self. A reader not understanding this may confuse first-person claims such as those found in Gītā X.20 as describing his own BMI, and advice such as that found in Gītā IX.34 as inciting personal obeisance to himself. Such misunderstandings will limit the effectiveness of spiritual practice and can contribute to cults of personality. These statements are descriptions of the non-dual Self and methods to achieve it for each and every person who wishes to pursue the same State:

> I am the Self, O Guḍākeśa, seated in the heart of all beings; I am the beginning, the middle and also the end of all beings.
>
> (Gītā: X.20. Trans. A. Parthasarathy, 1994, p. 153)

> Fix your mind on Me, be devoted to Me, sacrifice to Me, bow down to Me; thus uniting yourself to Me, taking Me as the supreme Goal, you shall come to Me.
>
> (Gītā: IX.34. Trans. A. Parthasarathy, 1994, p. 126)

Kṛṣṇa is also friend, counsellor, and military advisor to Arjuna, the commander whose ego-centered perspective on the cusp of battle has rendered him paralyzed with confusion and sorrow. Thus, the qualities are also embedded within the narrative itself, revealed through the relationship between Kṛṣṇa and Arjuna. Kṛṣṇa being an embodiment of Vedāntic wisdom, his reactions to Arjuna, and the strategy behind his guidance reveal the principles of a VL in practice.

To simplify the discussion, the 81 qualities were grouped under 13 sub-headings. They are listed as follows, along with the number of mentions they receive in the earlier described verses.

Sākṣī	14
Compassion	12
Seeing unity in diversity	10
Humility	8
Emotional maturity	8
Visionary	5
Non-preferential	5
Selfless	4
Being without attachment	4
Forgiving	3
Honest	3
Healthy emotion regulation	3
Physical grace	2

This discussion focuses on the top four headings, those that encompass over 50% of the qualities listed. Each heading is briefly defined and its aetiology from spiritual maturity described. The narrative of the Bhagavad Gītā is then explored for examples of the quality in the relationship between Kṛṣṇa and Arjuna.

Sākṣī

Leadership and guidance of others can only be effective when they arise from one's own intellectual and emotional stability. Just as in-flight safety demonstrations advise donning one's own oxygen mask before helping others, Vedānta insists primarily on developing oneself first, to gain stability of mind-intellect and inner well-being. The VL's role in society is to then extend this to others. This stability is referred to here as Sākṣī, which translates as 'witness.' However, this translation does not convey the full scope of its meaning, thus the Sanskrit word is retained.

Definition and aetiology: Sākṣī refers to a sense of fulfillment irrespective of the changing perception-emotion-thought; a permanent freedom from the constraints and limitations imposed by ego. A. Parthasarathy describes this state:

> When you identify with . . . the Self within you, you become neutral and unaffected by the trials and tribulations of the world. You become a Sākṣī, a witness of all that happens here.
>
> *(A. Parthasarathy, 1994, p. 97. Gītā: IX.9 commentary)*

> inwardly he has become a Sakshi Witness of the entire phenomena of life. Nothing in the world can either enhance or diminish his State of absolute fulfilment.
>
> *(A. Parthasarathy, 2004, p. 237)*

This absolute definition can also be applied to the relative perspective, there describing a stability that waxes and wanes depending upon circumstance but which is widening in its scope with spiritual practice.

The common understanding is that a 'witness' to an event is not directly engaged in it but simply observes from a safe vantage point. The VL could thus be misunderstood as holding a disconnected or indifferent stance toward their environment. This is not how a Sākṣī functions. The Gītā describes a steady-minded and peaceful Sākṣī "moving among objects with his senses under control" (Gītā: II.64. Trans. A. Parthasarathy, 1992, p. 143). This indicates one's full engagement with the world while mental peace and intellectual balance remain undisturbed. The phrases "disinterested interest, dispassionate passion" (A. Parthasarathy, 2004, p. 211) are used to convey this stance: engagement in and enthusiasm for action in the world, while not depending upon it for satisfaction or being affected by its changes.

Importantly, the fulfillment experienced by the Sākṣī does not preclude experiences that are otherwise generally regarded as diminishing it, such as sadness, sorrow, grief, fear, etc. The Vedāntic conception of fulfillment expands beyond the common understanding. As A. Parthasarathy describes:

> Your mind would still feel joy and suffer sorrow. But your intellect [i.e. wisdom] would not allow the feelings of joy or sorrow to victimise you, to overpower you.
>
> *(1992, p. 133. Gītā: II.56 commentary)*

A. Parthasarathy (2004, p. 220) presents a powerful analogy to illustrate this state of fulfillment, posing the question, "How does a sad movie make millions happy?" When done well, a movie can convey directly to the viewer emotions such as sadness, sorrow, loss, disgust, outrage, grief etc. A harrowing or tragic film can win accolades for its cinematic and human achievements. However, throughout the fluctuating emotions, there is an untouched enjoyment. The viewer's fulfillment is not defined by the fluctuating emotions.

> On a careful study you find that the enjoyment arises from one's aloofness from the happenings on the screen. It is one's detachment from it. Not being involved or entangled in it.
>
> *(Ibid.)*

Sākṣī develops in direct correlation with the absence of desire. Desire constitutes a specific mode of relating with circumstances, characterized by a personal sense of lack, and initiating individual action to assuage it. As desires increase in strength, so does one's dependency upon objects and circumstances for stable satisfaction. However, a Self-realized soul's identity remains anchored in Spirit rather than matter, and thus experiences no sense of lack and has no desires to fulfill. Therefore, external and internal conditions cannot augment or diminish their well-being.

Sākṣī also extends greater freedom to one's scope of action. For one caught in the demands of a particular desire, actions are limited to those that will satisfy it. One without any dependency or demand has a wider latitude for action—they can act according to the principle of lokasa'graham, the welfare of the world (Gītā: III.25. Trans. A. Parthasarathy, 1992, p. 189). The needs of the moment dictate action, not the internal forces of desire. Kṛṣṇa describes this state directly:

> For him there is no interest whatever here in what is done or what is not done, nor does he depend upon any being for any object.
>
> *(Gītā: III.18. Trans. A. Parthasarathy, 1992, p. 181)*

Examples: This quality is seen in Kṛṣṇa's response to the abject and despondent condition of his lifelong friend. As A. Parthasarathy notes (1992, p. 64, Gītā: II.2 commentary), "[s]ignificantly,

Kṛṣṇa remains silent" throughout Arjuna's emotional outburst. Kṛṣṇa recognizes Arjuna's need to fully express himself, to know that his doubts and fears have been heard and understood. Only after Arjuna becomes receptive (as evidenced by his active participation in questioning) does he speak. Importantly, Kṛṣṇa does not lack feelings of love and compassion for Arjuna (as discussed under Compassion later), yet the absence of personal desire here is complete. He is filled with compassion, yet unmoved. He feels, yet the feeling does not initiate any action until it is clearly called for. As a Sākṣī, he is without the pressure to satisfy personal desire and motivations. This too despite understanding the cause of Arjuna's condition, and having the prescription to dispel it, indicated by Kṛṣṇa "smiling as it were" as he begins his sermon (Gītā: II.10. Trans. A. Parthasarathy, 1992, p. 75).

A more common response to a loved one's distress would spring from a personal desire to assuage their (and one's own) feelings. The personal, emotional need to speak and advise would result in one rushing in prematurely with words and gestures of solace and understanding. Instead, Kṛṣṇa offers Arjuna the space to speak uninterrupted, to externally process his internal confusion and come to a point of receptivity.

Kṛṣṇa's inner poise is shown further through his remarkable patience with Arjuna's condition. The entire allegory of Gītā takes place in the midst of a battle that has just been enjoined. Arjuna has petulantly refused to fight, and then begins to ask questions of a highly speculative and philosophical nature. They are wholly inappropriate for their environment and circumstances, yet Kṛṣṇa duly responds to the queries undisturbed, never losing the thread of patience for his friend.

A leader must possess this quality of a disinterested interest. Dealing with the myriad interpersonal and environmental challenges of a dynamic workplace can result in emotional fatigue and frustration. By taking the stance of a Sākṣī, a leader remains attentive and poised in all circumstances. And because there is no personal interest to be frustrated, worry and anxiety, fatigue, and burnout are eliminated. The VL's responsiveness, respect, and support for their team members remain at their peak throughout the work environment, promoting successful leadership outcomes. As Hollander (2006) states:

> Support is an essential element in the leader-follower bond. It can be considered as credit followers can accord or withhold from their leaders, as part of a personal bond that extends to loyalty and trust.
>
> *(p. 14)*

> Listening is respectful.... Two-way communication, including listening, is also significant for recognition and responsiveness. Listening also facilitates communication and influence and is therefore vital to effective leadership and critical when absent.
>
> *(p. 4–5)*

Compassion

Definition and aetiology: Compassion is described by A. Parthasarathy as "[i]ntellect supporting the mind to favour the well-being of all beings" (1998, p. 116. Gītā: XVI.2 commentary) and "not weak pity [but] a feeling of sympathy towards others" (1994, p. 255. Gītā: XII.13). Compassion can be considered the emotional aspect of Oneness. For the VL, others are viewed as expressions of their own Self. And, just as an individual feels a natural duty of care towards the well-being of their own body-mind-intellect, the VL naturally seeks to extend their feeling of well-being to all.

Complete compassion expresses at all levels of the personality. The mind resonates with the other's feelings, experiencing life as they do; another's joy or sorrow is one's own. However, the intellect understands the other's condition and retains objectivity (Sākṣī) throughout. This protects the VL from becoming emotionally overwhelmed by the intensity of others' experiences and ensures an appropriate and beneficial response. Third, there is the conscious intent to act in the service of the other's genuine well-being.

Ego-centered desires limit one's capacity for compassion, as they limit the attention only to the benefits that will accrue to one's own BMI. They collapse the 'we' of social living down to the 'I' of self-absorption. As ego-centered desires reduce, there is diminished attention on one's own BMI as the sole beneficiaries of action. The feeling of care naturally extends to others' BMI.

As with many of the concepts presented in Vedānta philosophy, compassion describes both a state of being and a practice. Throughout the text, Kṛṣṇa advises Arjuna to act with compassion as a means of fulfilling his duty and rising to greater spiritual maturity. In one example he notes that Arjuna should act "unattached, wishing the welfare of the world" (Gita: III.25. Trans. A. Parthasarathy, 1992, p. 189).

Examples: Examples of Kṛṣṇa's compassion abound in the text. As discussed earlier, Kṛṣṇa shows remarkable patience with his friend's condition. Kṛṣṇa's feelings are also revealed in the many personal names by which he addresses Arjuna, using 21 different monikers. Each one has a specific meaning and is used as a means of eliciting a subtle idea or feeling within Arjuna. For example, the names Pārtha and Kaunteya indicate Arjuna's relationship to his mother (Pṛtha, Kuntī). They are used as a reminder of his filial obligation and to elicit feelings of devotion. The name Mahābāho means 'mighty-armed' and is used to bolster his flagging self-confidence.

Kṛṣṇa indicates his warmth in other ways also, for example, by using personal phrases such as "O beloved" (Gītā: VI.40. Trans. A. Parthasarathy, 1992, p. 351); by advising him to do "good to himself" (Gītā: XVI.22. Trans. A. Parthasarathy, 1998, p. 139); by assuring Arjuna that he is dear to him (e.g. Gītā: IV.3; X.1; XVIII.64); and by indicating that all he says is "for your welfare" (Gītā: X.1. Trans. A. Parthasarathy, 1994, p. 131).

However, Kṛṣṇa's compassion is not limited to positive affirmations. In his earliest response to Arjuna's despondency, Kṛṣṇa refers to his stance as "klaibyam," translated by A. Parthasarathy as "unmanliness" (Gītā: II.3. Trans. A. Parthasarathy, 1992, p. 351). This direct confrontation to Arjuna's identity as a warrior presents a different view of his refusal to fight, which Arjuna claims to be the honorable course of action (Gītā: I.36–46).

Kṛṣṇa's ability to identify with Arjuna's position is essential for the success of the psychological techniques designed to work with the contours of Arjuna's personality and steer him towards understanding and conviction. In chapter III, Kṛṣṇa first deploys logic and reason to address Arjuna's concerns (III.4–19), and then follows up with six emotion-based appeals to act (III.20–24). A. Parthasarathy (1992, p. 188) summarizes Kṛṣṇa's strategy as eliciting Arjuna's devotion to other great men of action; persuading Arjuna to fight for society's welfare; exploiting Arjuna's vanity over potential loss of reputation; a personal appeal to follow Kṛṣṇa's own example; initiating fear of the dire consequences of inaction; presenting the threat of societal annihilation. The success of his efforts is seen in Arjuna's ultimate response: he rises up, filled with enthusiasm and conviction towards fighting the righteous war that faces him.

The feeling of inclusion is a natural human need. It is "the degree to which an employee perceives that he or she is an esteemed member of the work group through experiencing treatment that satisfies his or her needs for belongingness and uniqueness" (Morgan, 2017, p. 11). A leader lacking compassion will not be able to fulfill these needs. As a result, they will not garner the esteem and support of their team members. Compassion shows the VL's recognition and respect of an individual's specific nature. The recipient of genuine compassion feels the individual respect and recognition that is essential for healthy team membership.

Unity in Diversity

This may be considered the intellectual aspect of Oneness. It is insight into the Truth of beings' various experiences—that they all draw from a non-dual Reality that is Consciousness. Gītā: IV.34–35 (Trans. A. Parthasarathy, 1992) describes the method of practice for gaining this knowledge, and the effect of the insight developed:

> Know that by prostration, by questioning and by service, the wise who have realised the Truth will teach you the knowledge.
>
> *(IV.34, p. 261)*
>
> Knowing which you shall not again get deluded thus, Pj,·ava, by which you will see all beings in the Self, also in Me.
>
> *(IV.35, p. 263)*

Every person inherently claims a first-person perspective on the perceptions-emotions-thoughts delivered through the body-mind-intellect. All beings share this sense of 'self-ness' at the core of their experiences. However, involvement in desire creates a sort of narcissism in which the shared nature of this experience goes unrecognized and only one's own needs and demands are considered. Others are forgotten, not just in their needs but even in the fact of the existence of an inner, first-person dimension. They are thereby reduced to objects, and this objectification of others is what permits harmful or discordant behavior.

With the reduction of desires, involvement in the ego-centered perspective diminishes. This brings a growing realization of the shared quality of subjective experience. Once this unity of experience is seen, it cannot be unseen, and one's attention and sense of community naturally shift onto the wider circle's experiences and needs. By seeing one's own Self in others, intentionally harmful actions and deceit are eradicated, and action naturally reflects Rabbi Hillel's Golden Rule, "What is hateful to yourself, do not do to your fellow man."

Seeing unity in diversity reduces inferiority and superiority complexes, both expressions of ego, "an exaggerated projection of oneself over others" (A. Parthasarathy, 2010, p. 92). With an identity defined only by the qualities of one's BMI, comparison with others lead to feelings of superiority or inferiority. With a growing recognition of a unity within the diversity of life, the plurality of beings is seen as a single organism with many different parts. The ego's exaggerated emphasis on oneself diminishes with this recognition of all beings—including oneself—as spokes in the wheel of life. The Vedantic Leader's vision penetrates beyond the matter layers into the unifying Self and relates to differences from that basis. Individual differences then cease to initiate comparison and complex.

Seeing unity in diversity also eliminates any bias due to personal preference or attachment. Egocentric desires exert a great deal of influence over one's attitudes and choices. As they reduce, so too does the leverage that external actors and circumstances would otherwise have. This optimizes impartiality and fairness, as well as clearer strategic and logical thinking.

Examples: Within the narrative of the Bhagavad Gītā, Kṛṣṇa and Arjuna are the only two protagonists. The Gītā is embedded within the broader epic, Mahābhārata. It narrates the episodes surrounding the Kurukṣetra war, and thus offers further insight into Kṛṣṇa's relationships with others.

In the narrative preceding the battle at Kurukṣetra, Kṛṣṇa is sent as an emissary from the Pj,·ava family to negotiate with the Kaurava clan. As he states when speaking to King Virāṭa, "our relationship to both the Kurus and the Pandus is equal, howsoever these two parties may behave with each other" (Mahābhārata, 5.V. Trans. Haldar & Roy, 1955, p. 6). His statement reveals his impartiality, since Arjuna (from the Paṇḍava family) is a lifelong friend. This non-preferential relationship implies being poised in a worldview that exists outside the duality of virtue (Paṇḍava clan) and vice (Kaurava clan). This is the vision of unity in diversity.

This perspective of an underlying unity beyond opposites is shown again later in the same text. The leaders of the two warring armies simultaneously approach Kṛṣṇa to ask for his help in the upcoming war. Kṛṣṇa's impartiality and accurate assessment of the others' natures is revealed by his response (Mahābhārata, 5.VII. Trans. Haldar & Roy, 1955, p. 9):

> I shall, no doubt, lend my assistance, O [Duryodhana], to both. But it is said that those who are junior in years should have the first choice. Therefore, [Arjuna], the son of Kunti, is entitled to first choice. There is a large body of cowherds numbering ten crores, rivalling me in strength and known as the Narayanas, all of whom are able to fight in the thick of battle. These soldiers, irresistible in battle, shall be sent to one of you, and I alone, resolved not to fight on the field, and lying down my arms, will go to the other. You may, O son of Kunti, first select whichever of these two commends itself to you. For, according to law, you have the right to the first choice!

Kṛṣṇa's adherence to legal statutes shows an easy integrity uninfluenced by preference. And by offering support to both sides, he reveals a sense of fairness, since both leaders asked at the same time. Crucially, the choice he offers ensures that both are satisfied, avoiding the zero-sum mentality. Arjuna chooses Kṛṣṇa's assistance; Duryodhana is delighted with the boost in troops. This indicates the accuracy with which he assessed the supplicants' respective natures.

The impartiality necessary here is impressive: there are lifelong personal relationships to overlook, and the stakes are staggeringly high—the future of the kingdom and its inhabitants. His solution to the problem of being asked to support two sides of a war reveals his ability to view beyond culture, genealogy, emotional connection, and ideology. By never losing sight of the non-dual Reality beyond any opposites, Kṛṣṇa remains mentally poised above the warring sides. His actions come from an objective stance that lies outside the fratricidal war.

By remaining outside the influence of different relationships, the VL's assessments of others' temperaments and conduct will be free of bias and misperception, a vital element in successful leadership. As Hollander (2006) states:

> *How leaders and followers mutually perceive and respond to each other's personal qualities and actions is crucial to their relationship.*
>
> (p. 13)

Further, remaining without complexes becomes increasingly difficult where there is sustained pressure to perform, combined with elements such as comparison-based social media platforms. Thus, there is a greater need for leaders to free themselves from these artificial constraints by adopting a unifying vision beyond personal differences and individual success.

> *Rather than be separate, leadership and followership exist in a reciprocal, interdependent system as a unity.*
> (Hollander, 2006, p. 14)

A VL's established vision of a unity underlying all transactions in life puts them in precisely this position. This vision pervades all relationships, and thus while the surface duality of the leader-follower dynamic is recognized as a necessary operating system, it is never taken as defining the reality of their situation. Their relationship is bracketed within a larger unity. It is much like a sportsperson seeing the opponent-opponent dynamic as describing their bodily activity, but never losing sight of the unifying truth that they are both players striving together to deliver a single spectacle of skill and tenacity.

Humility

Humility is described in the Gītā through negation: "having no pride" (Gītā: XIII.8. Trans. A. Parthasarathy, 1998, p. 17). Humility is the conscious recognition of the limitations of one's claimed knowledge. It is significant that humility is mentioned first in the list describing a person endowed with knowledge, and that this list emphasizes humility more strongly than the other two in sheer frequency of mentions. This highlights the powerful relationship between knowledge and humility. Humility accompanies genuine insight in any field of study. New understanding reveals one's erstwhile ignorance, and through analysis of this experience recognition dawns on the vast, unknown ignorance that underlies present knowledge. Thus, the liberal study of any subject can bring a general attitude of humility.

Humility is also a necessary condition for gaining knowledge (e.g. Gītā: II.6–7), for drawing expertise and wisdom from others. As the educator Laurence Musgrove puts it (2008, p. B28), humility is "that premier scholarly virtue" and arises from accepting and embracing "the limited nature of human understanding." Thomas Szasz (1973, p. 18) similarly points out,

> Every act of conscious learning requires the willingness to suffer an injury to one's self-esteem. That is why young children, before they are aware of their own self-importance, learn so easily; and why older persons, especially if vain or important, cannot learn at all.

Expecting oneself to be the sole repository of knowledge isolates the leader from their teams and ensures that better solutions go unrecognized. For a leader to be effective, they must be able to accept criticism of their own ideas and actions and look to find better ones from others. The recognition of one's ignorance and the absence of vanity promotes curiosity, the impersonal search for better answers—even ones that come at a perceived cost to ego. This highlights "the principle of education that knowledge is taken, never given" (A. Parthasarathy, 1992, p. 241. Gītā: XVIII.63 commentary).

Adhering to this principle is also essential if one wishes to convey knowledge. The backfire effect refers to the phenomenon in which an opinion contradicted by facts is strengthened rather than weakened. This is due to the absence of receptivity: if one is not ready to have their knowledge changed, then being exposed to knowledge can be too confronting to the identity upon which it depends, and is counter-productive. Kṛṣṇa makes note of this truth twice in the text, stating:

> Let not the wise man unsettle the minds of the ignorant.
> *(Gītā: III.26. Trans. A. Parthasarathy, 1992, p. 191)*

> the one of perfect knowledge should not unsettle the dull-witted whose knowledge is imperfect.
> *(Gītā: III.29. Trans. A. Parthasarathy, 1992, p. 194)*

Humility is also essential for efficient and productive teamwork. Author David Brooks defines humility as "having an accurate assessment of your own nature and your own place in the cosmos" (2015, p. 263). Any overemphasis on one's strengths or shortcomings is an expression of ego or superiority or inferiority complex. The ego thus "creates waves of disparity and disharmony in the society" (A. Parthasarathy, 2010, p. 93). The effect on teamwork is significant. Creative energies are spent on managing personal interests and interpersonal interactions as various complexes jostle for position. The free exchange of knowledge is inhibited, impeding the successful realization of team goals.

Within the spiritual context, humility naturally arises as an effect of "true knowledge of life" (A. Parthasarathy, 1998, p. 17. Gītā: XIII.8 commentary). Knowledge does not refer to merely acquired information, but rather insight, the Aha! effect or eureka moment. Against the recognition of a unifying Self, the plurality of beings is seen as a single organism with many different parts. The ego's exaggerated emphasis on oneself diminishes with this recognition of all beings—including oneself—as spokes in the wheel of life. A. Parthasarathy (ibid.) develops this idea poetically:

> As you gain true knowledge of life, you begin to realise the divine scheme of nature and that you are here to play your role in the world. You then develop humility.

As ego and desires reduce, a subtler and more stable identity is realized, based less on the changing equipment and more on one's essential Self. With the absence of a BMI-centered identity, there is an honest acceptance of oneself and one's place in the world. This is not the end of striving for greatness nor the suppression of identity, but rather growth beyond current self-limiting ideas. Negating the BMI as defining one's essential identity allows them to be seen as tools or equipment for the achievement of ideals and obligations.

Examples: A single episode that exemplifies humility and its effects is in fact displayed by Arjuna and Kṛṣṇa's earliest interaction. Initially, Arjuna felt "an intellectual vanity that he could handle his complex situation himself" (A. Parthasarathy, 1992, p. 71. Gītā: II.7 commentary). Not until II.6–7 does he admit his ignorance and confusion and ask for guidance. This is the moment of receptivity that Kṛṣṇa had waited for, and it signals the beginning of his sermon on Vedānta. Kṛṣṇa's humility counseled him not to impart knowledge to Arjuna, but to wait until it was taken; Arjuna's humility drew the knowledge from Kṛṣṇa when he was ready to receive it.

This episode also reveals Kṛṣṇa's humility in his display of active listening, the ability to fully capture, understand, and appropriately respond to what is being said. Active listening requires recognizing that the other's communication has intrinsic value and is worth taking seriously. It does not preclude disagreement or dissent; it merely means presupposing that listening to the speaker may fill a lacuna in one's own understanding. The impediments to active listening are expressions of ego: the vanity of 'I-know'; shifting the focus of attention back to one's own perspective; and misperceiving what has been said due to implicit bias.

Kṛṣṇa's sensitivity to Arjuna's communication permits responses that appropriately guide the latter's conviction regarding his obligations. This is typified by Kṛṣṇa's reaction to one of Arjuna's objections, a rejection of Kṛṣṇa's claim that the mind can be controlled (Gītā: VI.33–34). Rather than dissenting, Kṛṣṇa signals his agreement, responding with "Doubtless" (Gītā: VI.35. Trans. A. Parthasarathy, 1992, p. 345). This immediately brings Kṛṣṇa and Arjuna onto the same side—Kṛṣṇa removes the barrier of ideological opposition by siding with Arjuna's claim. It is important to note that this is not merely a pedagogical tool, cajoling, or a condescending agreement. Kṛṣṇa has taken to heart Arjuna's very real predicament and the firmness of his conviction that emotional control is beyond him. Having met Arjuna on his ground, Kṛṣṇa then proceeds to guide him towards his own higher perspective.

Further evidence of Kṛṣṇa's humility is the non-arrogation of the knowledge he is delivering. Throughout the text he refers to the declarations of great thinkers and teachers as the source of his knowledge (e.g. Gītā: XVII.17–19). As a Self-realized soul, he is acclaimed as having gained perfect Knowledge, and yet he does not arrogate the knowledge as his own.

Finally, Kṛṣṇa ends his oration and guidance with a remarkable show of humility. Having exhaustively imparted the knowledge and its practical application designed to clear Arjuna's despondency and confusion, he concludes by saying, "having reflected on this fully, act as you wish" (Gītā:

XVIII.63. Trans. A. Parthasarathy, 1998, p. 241). The commentary (ibid.) to this verse interprets these words:

> It establishes Kṛṣṇa's liberal attitude in giving Arjuna the choice of action. A guru follows the principle of education that knowledge is taken, never given. . . . Kṛṣṇa now upholds the Vedāntic tradition wherein knowledge is not imposed on others. "Reflect upon these truths," appeals Kṛṣṇa, "and act as you wish". Such an appeal reveals humility and liberality of a spiritual master.

Like all relationships, the leader-follower relationship is "a set of *mutual expectations* about each other's future behavior based on past interactions with one another" (Schein & Schein, 2018, p. 22). Unrealistic expectations arise from viewing others through the lens of bias and preconceived ideas. A humble leader's enhanced clarity of assessment comes from their absence of assumed knowledge. With ego-centered expectations defused, the leader maintains a charitable disposition, "accept[s] each one's service at the level of one's competence" (A. Parthasarathy, 2010, p. 100). The recognition of, respect for, and responsiveness to the different qualities and characteristics of team members builds openness and trust.

A humble leader also permits the sharing of power, responsibility, and success. As Hollander states:

> On balance, we found that by sharing power and allowing followers to influence them, leaders foster leadership skills in others, as well as achieve other gains through their greater participation and involvement.
>
> *(2006, p. 14)*

The ego's tendency to grasp for and aggrandize individual knowledge, success, and power is counter-productive to these ends. No one person can harbor sufficient knowledge and skill to be highly successful and productive. Humility's capacity to organically enlist the trust and cooperation of others renders it essential for the survival and growth of teams and organizations.

Concluding Remarks

Oneness is a vantage point occupied by the spiritually mature, one in which inclusive leadership behavior becomes the default state. The ideal leader naturally displays virtues such as being a Sākṣī, compassion, seeing unity in diversity, and humility. Such a Vedantic Leader innately experiences Oneness with all and acts accordingly. Before embodying this ideal State, striving to understand and integrate these qualities can be used as a practice to gradually develop them. Trying to cultivate and live these virtues improves inclusive day-to-day leadership. Thus, it becomes the obligation of leaders in all fields (professional and personal) to embark upon a path of Self-inquiry and Self-discovery.

References

Brooks, D. (2015). *The road to character*. New York, NY: Random House.
Haldar, H. (Ed.), & Roy, P. C. (1955). *The Mahabharata of Krishna-Dwaipayana Vyasa,* Vol. IV, Udyoga Parva. Kolkata: Oriental Publishing Co.
Hollander, E. P. (2006). *Inclusive leadership: The essential leader-follower relationship*. New York, NY: Routledge.
Morgan, E. (2017). Breaking the zero-sum game: Transforming societies through inclusive leadership. In A. Boitano, R. Lagomarsino Dutra, & H. E. Schockmann (Eds.), *Breaking the zero-sum game: Transforming societies through inclusive leadership* (pp. 5–27). Bingley: Emerald Publishing Limited.
Musgrove, L. E. (2008). Mystery and humility in general education. *The Chronicle of Higher Education, 54*(36), n.p. Retrieved from www.chronicle.com/article/MysteryHumility-in/2975
Parthasarathy, A. (1990). *Atmabodha*. Mumbai: A. Parthasarathy.

Parthasarathy, A. (1992). *Śrīmad Bhagavad Gītā Vol. 1*. Mumbai: A. Parthasarathy.
Parthasarathy, A. (1994). *Śrīmad Bhagavad Gītā Vol. 2*. Mumbai: A. Parthasarathy.
Parthasarathy, A. (1998). *Śrīmad Bhagavad Gītā Vol. 3*. Mumbai: A. Parthasarathy.
Parthasarathy, A. (2004). *Vedanta treatise: The eternities*. Mumbai: A. Parthasarathy.
Parthasarathy, A. (2008). *The fall of the human intellect*. Mumbai: A. Parthasarathy.
Parthasarathy, A. (2010). *Governing business & relationships*. Mumbai: A. Parthasarathy.
Parthasarathy, A. (2011). *Bhaja Govindam & Atmabodha*. Mumbai: A. Parthasarathy.
Schein, E. H., & Schein, P. A. (2018). *Humble leadership: The power of relationships, openness, and trust*. Oakland, CA: Berrett-Koehler.
Szasz, T. (1973). *The second sin*. Garden City, NY: Doubleday & Co.
Tirtha, R. (2005). *In woods of god-realization or the complete works of Swami Rama Tirtha (*Vol. 6). Lucknow: Swami Rama Tirtha Pratisthan.

14
INCLUSIVE LEADERSHIP AND WORK-LIFE BALANCE

Wanda Krause

Introduction

In 2016, the World Health Organization for the first time included burnout in its handbook *International Classification of Diseases and Related Health Problems*. In 2019, burnout is again included in the 11th revision of the *International Classification of Diseases (ICD-11)* as an "occupational phenomenon" that stems directly from our collective crisis of workplace stress (World Health Organization, 2019). The World Health Organization (WHO) defines burnout as "a syndrome conceptualized as resulting from chronic workplace stress that has not been successfully managed" (para 4). Burnout is a psychological syndrome emerging as a prolonged response to chronic interpersonal stressors on the job (Maslach & Leiter, 2016, p. 103). The WHO further characterized burnout by three dimensions: (a) feelings of energy depletion or exhaustion; (b) increased mental distance from one's job, or feelings of negativism or cynicism related to one's job; and (c) reduced professional efficacy (2019). The significance of this definition is that it clearly places the individual stress experience within a broader context and involves the person's conception of both self and others (Maslach & Leiter, 2016, p. 103).

The need for better work-life balance is an increasingly discussed topic because it is a serious challenge in many workplace environments for individuals. There is a small percentage of forward-thinking organizations that understand and value work-life balance to their own success and the changes they are trying to make in the world. However, there is also an enormous gap in understanding the long-term importance of work-life balance for most organizations. The attainment of work-life balance cannot be the sole responsibility of the employee or individual. There is an urgency for a more comprehensive form of leadership—inclusive leadership—to lead the kind of changes we need, as the workplace and the world place expectations on human beings to work more effectively and efficiently, as if humans were mere machines. The dominant paradigm is one where individuals are expected to adapt to working longer, faster, and harder and become ever more resilient to these pressures and consequences of stress.

Why Work-Life Balance

The countries performing the highest have the shortest workdays. Seven countries among those with the highest GDP rank have the fewest working hours. They include Luxembourg, and then Norway, Switzerland, the Netherlands, Germany, Denmark, and Sweden. We still live in a culture of bragging about how hard we work and how little we sleep to work. Bragging might reflect the need to compensate for the feeling of underperformance (Wadors, in Huffington, 2017). So, what does work-life balance in the workplace have to do with harmony and equilibrium in the world? Everything.

In 2013, Gallup gathered data from 230,000 full- and part-time workers in 142 countries. According to the 2013 Gallup poll, in the US more than two in three workers are unhappy in their jobs. Gallup found that 52 percent of US workers are not engaged, meaning that even if they don't actively hate their jobs they're unhappy and don't invest themselves in their job. Gallup found that another 18 percent are what they call 'actively disengaged,' meaning they can't stand their jobs and sometimes even sabotage coworkers or their companies.

It is clear that employee burnout is having a significant impact to the bottom line, including through attrition. Burnt-out employees are over 30 percent more likely to leave their jobs. It's the reason nearly a third of caregivers have had to leave their jobs to care for someone. It's also why over 75 percent of expecting mothers say they're excited to go back to work after giving birth, but 43 percent of them will quit their jobs at some point after that. Employee attrition costs, with some estimates suggest the costs can be as high as 1.5 or 2 times the departing employee's annual salary (Huffington, 2019).

I am concerned about the micro level or how well and balanced we are in our work and life just as much as I am concerned about what concerns civilization (the macro level) and the future. The broader perspective is developed through concepts involving interpersonal relations, so, for example, how people perceive and respond to others. Engagement and the large gap in engagement is a key concern for work-life balance and wellbeing because these are about detached concern, dehumanization in self-defense, and attribution processes. Viewing work-life balance from broader dimensions and concepts helps us also understand the role of motivation and emotion.

The clinical literature has also dealt with motivation and emotion, but framed these more in terms of psychological disorders, such as depression. Subsequent researchers came from industrial-organizational psychology, and this perspective emphasized work attitudes and behaviors. It was also at this point that burnout was conceptualized as a form of job stress (Maslach & Leiter, 2016). However, Hartney (2018) argued this to be the case even in the healthcare system:

> The healthcare system exists to improve the health of individuals, families, and populations, yet often its functioning contradicts everything we know about what enhances health. Instead of being a nurturing safe haven, where patients can feel cared for as they recuperate and recover from their injuries and illnesses, it is often an overcrowded, dehumanizing, confusing maze of fragmented silos, where patients frequently feel fearful, frustrated, and humiliated, as they are passed through a series of burnt-out staff.
>
> (p. 81)

The rate of burnout among those employed in the health care field tends to be reported in the moderate to high levels, and it is generally believed that the burnout risk in health care is higher than in the general working population (Maslach & Leiter, 2016).

My work and interest in work-life balance comes from a global or systems perspective, the study of organizational impact on civil society, gender and women's inclusion, and the evaluation of their impact, all of which has lead me to understand the critical role of self in systems. I realized in much of my work that some of the women (and men) in the organizations were successful in leading change, and some were not (Krause, 2008, 2012). Many who were leading change could no longer do so in the long run. Some took on other interests and goals, but many were burnt out; thus, ensuring that whatever initiatives or work they were doing, regardless of how passionate, motivated, and inspired they were, it ended.

Unfortunately, too many of us can identify. For me, family is priority. I also take my health and wellbeing seriously. I also love to spend time in the outdoors. For the first time in months, I was lying on the beach in the sun. I was watching my daughter, then 7 years old, on the water during her sailing lesson while I was holding a book called *Everyday Grace* by Marianne Williamson. After another stressful and empty day, I was really soaking up the seaside peace, laughter, and beauty, despite the heat of +40 degrees Celsius of Doha, Qatar. I looked up several times as my daughter came in closer waving, and then waving again, not holding back her enthusiasm that I was in fact there. Each wave was also probably to get confirmation that I was watching; mommy was finally present. I had actually left my office to come watch, only to return back to my office after. But this day marked an intense wake-up call. Williamson's words drew me in—to the bigger picture. I flipped to the next page and read her quote to an opening chapter:

> "You would rather be anywhere than going into this meeting. You think about being at the movies, being on the beach, being with your kids—being anywhere but here. The people waiting on the other side of that door don't know who you are or even seem to care. You don't have the feeling they really want you to succeed. You can't believe you work here. Welcome to your career."

I was not remotely living work-life balance. I was not practicing being present with my family. I had imposed an ideal of success on myself that was career driven. But while I was achieving some great milestones in my career at the time, I was exhausted and feeling extreme guilt about missing key milestones in my children's lives—here my daughter developing in her sailing skills and the fun she was having that wanted me to witness.

Numerous studies have emerged connecting burnout to health issues (Maslach & Leiter, 2016). Burnout, in fact, is used as a predictor of work disability and health problems (Leiter, Backer, & Maslach, 2014). Burnout and stress often result in poorer decisions, deteriorating health, and aggressive leadership (Krapivin, 2018). It can take over one's life with depression, anxiety, concentration and illness, heart disease, high cholesterol, obesity, and substance abuse (Stahl, 2016). Work-life imbalance leads to the imbalance of responsibilities shared with significant others outside of the workplace. Stahl asks, "Put yourself in your partner's shoes: would you want to be completely responsible for all the housework, chores, and errands because your spouse or significant other is chronically absent, whether physically or mentally or both?" (ibid.) Such imbalance is also the cause for stress on and deterioration of relationships. In fact, "[t]he greatest threats to a thriving future of global sustainability and collective well-being are cynicism and resignation" (Steffen & Rezmovits, 2019, p. 5).

If people are unable to work in a way that is honoring of wellbeing, their significant others, children, those for whom they are caregivers, and overall work-life balance, despite their own attempts for greater equilibrium between work and home or personal life, then the responsibility to address this situation isn't simply theirs. Leaders at both the organizational and policy levels have a responsibility to ensure that wellbeing and work-life balance is a value in their organizations, communities, and countries—*any* sphere of influence a leader has is the work of the inclusive leader. It is critical that leadership studies and leaders in countries that have such high levels of burnout, as the WHO describes, or disengagement as Gallup has found, identify work-life balance as the key area to focus. It is critical that leaders see work-life balance as a core aspect to wellbeing, that wellbeing correlates to effectiveness, efficiency, and performance, and that this addresses an even broader and shared issue of global wellbeing, stability, and peace. It is time they see that we are speaking of a civilizational issue when the whole person is not seen. The whole person is a person that has rights and needs, such as time for sleep and time for family and connections. Inclusivity, as a leadership imperative, can significantly advance how an individual is seen and valued and how our civilization is flourishing.

Work-life balance is a collective issue. Work-life balance is a shared interest and responsibility (People Diagnostics, 2019, p. 3). The individual must be seen not merely as an instrument for organizational goals, but also as part of a larger systems whole. When people are excluded, they often do not have the resources, tools, or skills to create their own wellbeing, or the means to acquire them—including balance between work and other priorities (Ryan, 2006, p. 6). The implications to ensuring work-life balance are significant to global wellbeing and harmony. Inclusive leadership, through intentionality, specifically to be inclusive and integrative, can best support the carving out of work-life balance as key to individual and global wellbeing.

Inclusive Leadership

It is a critical time for leadership studies and organizational leaders to shift focus from effectiveness, efficiency, and performance to work-life balance. The whole person has been forgotten and marginalized in the quest for hitting greater performance targets and profits. The whole being has great implications to a positive workplace, institutional, or communal environment, that in turn feeds into productivity and potential positive implications to global wellbeing. Such requires an expanded and integral way of thinking and approaching leadership.

Inclusive leadership is concerned first and foremost with inclusion, both in its processes and the ends for which it strives (Ryan, 2006, p. 3). Inclusive leadership has seen its pivotal development as a theory of leadership in education, often in discussion around pedagogies for including the marginalized (see Stefani & Blessinger, 2017; Komives, 2013; Mcleskey & Waldron, 2000). Inclusive leadership has occasionally been used to emphasize the need for more diversity and better leader-follower relationships (Wuffli, 2016, p. 2; see Hollander, 2009). It has been useful for understanding inclusion, access, and equity challenges in social work (Hafford-Letchfield et al., 2014; Vogel, 2013) As such, inclusive leadership has provided a framework to think about gender inclusion (Adapa & Sheridan, 2018).

Significant for advancing how an individual is seen and valued and how our civilization is flourishing, inclusive leadership focuses on relationships that promote mutual benefit (Hollander, 2009, p. 3). It has developed to not simply be concerned with leading others, or even just about including people. Wuffli (2016) argues for an inclusive leadership concept that "incorporates bridge-building and provides holistic perspectives and orientations" which takes us further beyond an understanding of inclusive leadership that is about including people (p. 4). This understanding includes their perspectives, relations, and orientations (p. 5), which is no longer about counting who is in and who is out but now allows us to consider inclusiveness in a larger systems framework of people tied to and in relation to others, their families, and their various responsibilities.

The interconnections matter as much as the constituent parts because inclusive leadership is premised on engagement and collaboration. Inclusive leadership is relational and contextual, involving relations with people within and without the organization. A key lesson is for responsibility across contexts (Leibowitz, 2017, p. 138). Key principles of inclusive leadership, therefore, are working 'with' others; actively involving others in decision-making; and strengthening and valuing relationships and connections, social justice, plurality, fairness, and welfare.

Inclusive leaders ask how they lead themselves, first and foremost. If a leader is driving herself into the ground from overwork, she cannot give herself what she needs to thrive and flourish, and she cannot be the pillar for those around her, in *both* her private and public life. Hardy points out, "what you do outside work is just as significant for your work-productivity as what you do while you're working." Self-leadership will be a key challenge for leaders as they assume higher-level leadership that involves being inclusive, aware of the whole, and aware of the broader system (Krause, 2018).

Leading Work-Life Balance Inclusively and Integrally

To address work-life balance effectively requires using an integral approach. A suitable model is the integral approach, based on integral theory, as originally developed by Ken Wilber (2000). This approach rests on the theory of including everything to understand and work with key dimensions of reality. It is, thus, a key approach I include under any conception of inclusive leadership. "Integral" means comprehensive, balanced, and inclusive (Wilber, Patten, Leonard, & Morelli, 2008, p. 27). As a life practice, it is

> founded in deep care—care for ourselves, for others, and for this mysterious existence. This care inspires us to want to make a difference, to give more, to cut through the bullshit of narrow and fragmented views and to magnify the freedom, love, openness and depth in us, in others, and in this beautiful, terrible world.
>
> *(Ibid., p. 4)*

As such, this approach sees (a) the whole individual (states of being, health), (b) the behaviors and actions of the individual, (c) the collective (including process of inclusion, marginalization, or culture of the organization), and (d) the context (rules, policies and sociopolitical and economic structures) in which the individual or the organization is embedded, influenced by, or subject to.

This model, thus, seeks to include the individual interior or 'self-change,' collective interior or 'cultural change,' individual exterior or 'behavioral change,' and collective exterior or 'systems change' (Hochachka & Thomson, 2009, p. 4). What is significant to recognize is that this approach to work-life balance allows one to measure and deliberate on leadership techniques around the inner dimension of the individual (mental, emotional, physical, and spiritual states) without losing sight of the inner dimension of the collective or what often translates to culture of an organization. The latter are the hidden rules and norms, although sometimes made explicit through expectations. Yet, this approach and framework calls us to notice the external and what are the more easily measurable performance indicators and related behaviors associated with performance or engagement. A fourth dimension is within the exterior and, also, more easily measurable in comparison to individual states and collective culture. This includes the structures, policies, laws, and directives.

Regarding the whole individual, dimension category a, an inclusive leader can help individuals learn to value work-life balance, be attuned to their states or wellbeing, as well how to experience engagement, commitment, and motivation within the individual interior. Employees who eat healthy and exercise are less at risk of getting sick and missing days from work, which could ultimately detract from the organization's productivity. In a 2015 interview, LinkedIn's chief human resource officer, Pat Wadors, says,

> Trust me, it's not a badge of honor to brag that you can get by on 4 hours or 5 each night. . . . You intimate that with fewer hours 'wasted on sleep' you are more productive. Nope. Can't buy that. When you brag about that, you are telling me that it's ok for you to harm your health and not perform your best at work or at home. Is that something to brag about?
>
> *(in Huffington, 2017)*

Good cognitive functioning, including decision-making under conditions of uncertainty, are directly correlated to sleep (Killgore, Balkin, & Wesensten, 2006). Good cognitive function is critical for good leadership and performance. Mowbray (2013) argues, "if [people] cannot focus and concentrate on completing a task, they are not performing effectively." Mbaabu found that "that majority of employees who participated in physical fitness programs had above average performance, lower rates of absenteeism, higher commitment to work, and lower employee turnover" (p. 15). Huffington (2017) argues, "If performance at your job or in your life involves focus, attention, decision-making, productivity, creativity, resilience or learning, sleep can be just as effective as a performance enhancer in your life." Studies show that individuals who have a healthy work-life balance do better at work. As such, promoting this balance is of benefit to individuals and the organization (Bradley et al.,

2006). It must be recognized that individual work-life balance and wellbeing can be impacted from the individual dimension (e.g. practicing individual care, nurturing positive relationships, enjoying positive experiences).

As for behaviors, or category b, employees regard the attitudes of management as a key factor contributing to their work-life balance. The extent to which management was open to negotiation with individual workers on work-life balance issues was positively associated with employee wellbeing, satisfaction, and organizational commitment (Bradley et al., 2006). In addition, management's acknowledgment of the importance of employees' non-work activities, willingness to introduce formal work-life balance initiatives (e.g. changes in working hours to a five-day week), and adaptation to 'traditional' ways of working were also identified as factors promoting work-life balance. The findings reinforce the important role the project manager has in supporting and promoting team development and challenging standard industry working conditions, traditionally regarded as essential to individual and organizational productivity (ibid.). The inclusive leader can shift focus, using this approach to hone in on the behaviors, actions, and choices that contribute to or sabotage work-life balance and harmony.

For culture, or dimension category c, the inclusive leader can seek to better understand the culture of an organization for why collectively people tend to overwork themselves to a state of burnout and exhaustion, and how to shift that culture to value work-life balance. The inclusive leader does not neglect the broader environment or context. The inclusive leader will even go outside the organization to inquire about what economic, political, or social pressures exist that might contribute to a culture of burnout. It is here that the inclusive leader might find leverage points to effect change towards greater balance to create work-life balance in the organization or institution. This is what many leaders in Scandinavian countries have done, through research, policy, and educational initiatives, to address challenges to work-life balance and, in fact, enhance wellbeing and productivity.

Changing organizational culture is one of the hardest tasks for any leader. However, workplace or organizational culture around work-life balance and wellbeing is a key determinant of how valued and supported people feel in their roles and how productive the organization becomes. Employee relationships are much like any personal relationship. When there is a sense that the employer or leadership and staff at all levels invest in building trust and belonging, employees or individuals are inspired to reciprocate with greater investment in the organization. When individuals feel they have contributed to shared objectives that address essentially how well they feel in their workplace, leaders will have greater success at creating a culture of wellbeing and sustained productivity. Inclusive leaders can do that by including everyone's ideas, input, experiences, and ideas for how they can get on board with their own wellness, and also how to support each other in creating that shared objective for wellness (Krause, 2017a). Studies illustrate the connection between reciprocity and performance that organizational leaders might want to consider. Economists show that employers who are perceived as distributionally fair by their employees generate comparatively more value due to the positively reciprocal behavior of those employees (Bosse, Phillips, & Harrison, 2009). Hence, values of belonging, fairness, and equality are essentials in an inclusive leader's toolbox.

Engagement is considered to be the opposite of burnout and is defined in terms of the same three aspects of burnout, but the positive end of those dimensions rather than the negative (Maslach & Leiter, 2016, p. 105). From this perspective, engagement consists of a state of high energy, strong involvement, and a sense of efficacy (Maslach & Leiter, 1999, in ibid.). In the *Harvard Business Review*, Friedman (2015) says that we need to reframe why we are disengaging at the end of the day. He explains, it's much like exercise where we are doing something that is not just for your own personal, selfish benefit, but rather something that can help us be more effective at work. He emphasized that the people who don't disengage, the people who are constantly checking their emails on evenings and on weekends, are the ones who tend to be less engaged a year later—because they're burnt out. Engagement is a critical value to inculcate, especially given the consequences of disengagement and the high levels of disengagement cited by Gallup. All cultures are based on value systems, and to create change in any value system takes a common framework, institutional and social support, and discipline until work-life balance, engagement, and, thus, wellbeing is an intrinsic value (Krause, 2017b).

Regarding systems, or category d, leaders need to provide the environment for wellbeing. They need to include effective policies and programs for sustainable and long-term work-life balance. Physically, an enhanced environment can include anything from beautiful colors on walls, plenty of plants, pictures, a lot of natural light, adequate space for individuals and shelving, offices that offer privacy and confidential conversation, proximity for colleagues to engage so that they do not have to go far distances, or alternatively flexibility in workspace so that individuals do not need to do long commutes and go through expense for travel. Inclusive leaders need, however, to be attuned to the needs of individuals for working happily and healthily, and these might differ in some respects. Individuals may find daycare facilities close to the organization an enormous help to save time and be close to young children. A gym membership or facility close to the organization might boost individual health if they take advantage of the gym. It must be recognized that individual work-life balance and wellbeing can be impacted at work from both the environment and design of work (e.g. workload, coworker and supervisor support, autonomy).

Inclusive leaders need to work with the different aspects that relate to work-life balance. In other words, they need to lead with an inclusive and integral understanding of work-life balance that includes but is not limited to the workplace, organization, or institution in question. They need to see the whole individual, the individual in relation to others inside the organization but significantly also outside the organization. They need to understand the practices that are normalized as culture and the larger system that holds a situation of imbalance and overwork in place, before they can strategize how and where to shift change.

Further, in linking individual wellbeing to collective wellbeing, it is also important to consider such imbalance between one and the other. The culture of the collective could be such that burnout is ignored and performance targets are valued as the most important goal, a culture likely created through sometimes more punishments than rewards in a less inclusively oriented or flat organization where decision-making power is spread throughout the organization. An authoritarian style leadership often uses language that aims to have the individual sacrifice her work-life balance and wellbeing for the good of the collective. Therefore, while individual wellbeing is important for the health of the whole organization, this is not yet fully recognized in most organizations. The inclusive leader must be mindful not to tip the balance in favor of the collective wellbeing where authoritarian managers see individuals merely as instruments for the collective, or the organization, to hit targets that rely on overworked individuals, a method that is unsustainable. The idea here is that inclusive leaders are not merely inclusive of top management priorities where these are not based on inclusivity, but are also mindful of inclusive processes, policies, and structures for individual empowerment.

Conclusions

Engaging in inclusive leadership and work-life balance is timely and critical. Progressive leaders are recognizing that the old business model is not working. They are in desperate need to change the way they live and work in order to not just survive, but thrive. They also know they can't really afford to be putting off addressing underlying causes for burnout, the related retention issues, and lack of engagement, and that individuals they lead also need a more peaceful, productive, and healthy work environment. When leaders help people feel valued and supported, they facilitate belonging, trust, and reciprocity. Practices that support belonging, trust, and reciprocity in turn boost productivity and impact. The inclusive leader understands that when an individual is viewed as a whole person and supported, the whole system is impacted because the individual is part of the system.

Inclusivity is the key to creating thriving and flourishing organizations that have the potential to have greater impact in performance and in the world. The move from the minimalist and reactionary leadership approach to health and investment in individual work-life balance and wellbeing requires a leadership approach that is integral and inclusive—inclusive leadership. When a part or dimension of the system is supported and enhanced, the whole system can reach balance and harmony too. When the individual suffers for the organization, this is an unsustainable scenario. The inclusive leader sees no separation between the parts and strives to include harmony, health, and equilibrium everywhere. Ensuring inclusive leadership at the individual level, organizational level, and within communities is a key step toward creating a healthier, more secure, civil, and peaceful world. To identify and create the opportunities for individual work-life balance becomes a central concern for leaders, the concept of inclusive leadership, and our civilization.

References

Adapa, S., & Sheridan, A. (Eds.). (2018). *Inclusive leadership: Negotiating gendered spaces*. Cham, Switzerland: Palgrave Macmillan. doi:10.1007/978-3-319-60666-8

Bosse, D. A., Phillips, R. A., & Harrison, J. S. (2009). Stakeholders, reciprocity, and firm performance. *Strategic Management Journal, 30*(4), 447–456.

Bradley, L. M., Bailey, C., Lingard, H. C., & Brown, K. A. (2006/2014). Managing employees' work-Life balance: The impact of management on individual well-being and productivity. In K. Brown, K. Hampson, & P. Brandon (Eds.), *Clients driving construction innovation: Moving ideas into practice* (pp. 220–224). Brisbane: CRC for Construction Innovation.

Friedman, R. (2015, March). *Your brain's ideal schedule*. Retrieved from https://hbr.org/ideacast/2015/03/your-brains-ideal-schedule.html

Gallup. (2013a). *State of the global workplace*. Retrieved from www.gallup.com/topic/STATE_OF_THE_GLOBAL_WORKPLACE_2013.aspx

Gallup. (2013b, October). *Worldwide, 13% of employees are engaged at work*. Retrieved from www.gallup.com/poll/165269/worldwide-employees-engaged-work.aspx

Hafford-Letchfield, T., Lambley, S., Spolander, G., and Cocker, C. (2014). *Inclusive leadership in social work and Social Care*. Bristol: Policy Press.

Hardy, B. (2016, August). This morning routine will save you 20+ hours per week. *The Mission*. Retrieved from https://medium.com/the-mission/how-to-structure-your-day-for-optimal-performance-and-productivity-dcbf0665e3f3#.cmq1lmhw7

Hartney, E. (2018). A three-step model of stress management for health leaders. *Healthcare Management Forum, 31*(3), 81–86.

Hochachka, G., & Thomson, S. (2009). Developing capacity and community well-being: action research on an integral capacity development approach in the Mapacho River Watershed, Peru. *IDRC Project*. Retrieved from https://idl-bnc-idrc.dspacedirect.org/bitstream/handle/10625/45038/131492.pdf?sequence=1&isAllowed=y

Hollander, E. (2009). *Inclusive leadership: The essential leader-follower relationship*. New York, NY: Routledge.

Huffington, A. (2017). *10 years ago I collapsed from burnout and exhaustion, and it's the best thing that could have happened to me*. Retrieved from https://journal.thriveglobal.com/10-years-ago-i-collapsed-from-burnout-and-exhaustion-and-its-the-best-thing-that-could-have-b1409f16585d

Huffington, A. (2019, June). Burnout is now officially a workplace crisis. *Thrive Global Journal*. Retrieved from https://thriveglobal.in/stories/burnout-is-now-officially-a-workplace-crisis/

Killgore, W. D., Balkin, T. J., & Wesensten, N. J. (2006, March 15). Impaired decision making following 49 h of sleep deprivation. *Journal of Sleep Deprivation*, 7–13.

Komives, S. (2013). *Exploring leadership: For college students who want to make a difference* (3rd ed.). San Francisco, CA: Jossey-Bass.

Krapivin, P. (2018, October). The deadly cost of employee burnout. *Forbes*. Retrieved from www.forbes.com/sites/pavelkrapivin/2018/10/10/the-deadly-cost-of-employee-burnout/#653b719c68c7

Leibowitz, B. (2017). Inclusive leadership: Lessons from South Africa. In L. Stefani & P. Blessinger (Eds.), *Inclusive leadership in higher education: International perspectives and approaches*. New York, NY: Routledge.

Krause, W. (2008). *Women in civil society: The state, Islamism, and networks in the UAE*. New York, NY: Palgrave Macmillan.

Krause, W. (2012). *Civil society and women activists in the Middle East*. London: I.B. Tauris.

Krause, W. (2017a). Why a culture of well-being is critical for performance in the workplace. *Thrive Global Journal*. Retrieved from https://medium.com/thrive-global/why-well-being-has-everything-to-do-with-productivity-bc89ecc09959

Krause, W. (2017b). Wellbeing is correlated to higher performance. *Thrive Global Journal*. Retrieved from https://medium.com/thrive-global/why-well-being-has-everything-to-do-with-productivity-bc89ecc09959

Krause, W. (2018). 3 leadership mistakes that keep you stuck. *Thrive Global Journal*. Retrieved from https://medium.com/@wandakrause_80255/3-leadership-mistakes-that-keep-you-stuck-d1ee5de0499d

Leiter, P., Backer, A., & Maslach, C. (Eds.). (2014). *Burnout at work: A psychological perspective*. New York, NY: Taylor & Francis.

Maslach, C., & Leiter, M. P. (1999). Burnout and engagement in the workplace: A contextual analysis. In T. Urdan (Ed.), *Advances in motivation and achievement* (pp. 275–302). Stamford: JAI Press.

Maslach, C., & Leiter, M. P. (2016, June). Understanding the burnout experience: Recent research and its implications for psychiatry. *World Psychiatry, 15*(2), 103–111. doi:10.1002/wps.20311

Mbaabu, C. (2013). *Effect of workplace recreation on employee wellbeing and performance: A case of the commission or university education (CUE)*. Research project report submitted to School of Business Kenyatta University. Retrieved from http://irlibrary.ku.ac.ke/bitstream/handle/123456789/10165/Effect%20of%20workplace%20recreation%20on....pdf?sequence=1

McLeskey, J., & Waldron, N. (2000). *Inclusive schools in action: Making differences ordinary*. Alexandria, VA: Association for Supervision and Curriculum Development.

Mowbray, D. (2013). Performance is all about wellbeing. *Training Journal*. Retrieved from www.trainingjournal.com/articles/feature/performance-about-wellbeing

People Diagnostics. (2019). *Flourishdx: A comprehensive approach to workplace psychological health, safety, and wellbeing: An implementation guide*. Retrieved from file:///Users/Wanda/Downloads/flourishdx_guide.pdf

Ryan, J. (2006). *Leadership and policy in schools* (pp. 3–17). New York, NY: Taylor & Francis Group 5. doi:10.1080/15700760500483995

Stahl, A. (2016, March 4). Here's what burnout costs you. *Forbes*. Retrieved from www.forbes.com/sites/ashleystahl/2016/03/04/heres-what-burnout-costs-you/#4bc1d15e4e05

Stefani, L., & Blessinger, P. (Eds.). (2017). *Inclusive leadership in higher education: International perspectives and approaches*. New York, NY: Routledge.

Steffen, S. L., & Rezmovits, J. (2019). Introduction. In S. L. Steffen, J. Rezmovits, S. Trevenna, & S. Rappaport (Eds.), *Evolving leadership for collective wellbeing*. Bingley, UK: Emerald Publishing.

Vogel, N. (2013). Inclusive leadership: Individuals with disabilities. *Profiles in Diversity Journal, 15*(6).

Wilber, K. (2000). *A theory of everything: An integral vision for business, politics, science, and spirituality* (1st ed.). Boston: Shambhala.

Wilber, K., Patten, T., Leonard, A., & Morelli, M. (2008). *Integral life practice: A 21st century blueprint for physical healthy, emotional balance, mental clarity, and spiritual awakening*. Boston: Integral Books.

World Health Organization. (2019). *Burn-out an "occupational phenomenon": International classification of diseases*. Retrieved from www.who.int/mental_health/evidence/burn-out/en/

Wuffli, P. (2016). *Inclusive leadership: A framework for the global era*. Cham: Springer. doi:10.10037/978-3-319-23561-5

15

AN AMERICAN KALEIDOSCOPE

Rethinking Diversity and Inclusion Leadership Through the Prism of Gender and Race

Seth N. Asumah and Mechthild Nagel

Introduction: First Thoughts, The Great Man Theory, and Leadership Demographics Today

In this chapter, we offer a pathway out of the traditional and heteropatriarchal hegemonic deficit model of leadership prevalent in corporate America and institutions of higher learning. We do this by interrogating some of the traditional leadership models through the prism of gender and race and analyze two different leadership paradigms. One is concerned a with gendered and racialized pattern of leadership styles and the other deals with the broader diversity and inclusion process of leadership, as the process of leadership is more important in a relational democracy than is a position, per se. We argue that these different approaches and processes ought to be subjected to an intersectional analysis, which foregrounds gender and racial equity, inclusive excellence, and social justice considerations. Furthermore, it is our contention that in the American polity, gender and race have structured our lives with deeper implications and impacts on women and people of color because of the historical contradictions of American life and the enduring agency of heteropatriarchal leadership in these changing times. Gender and racial stratifications, formations, and oppression continue to shape our leadership approaches and models, and how they affect diversity, inclusion, equity, and social justice is important to our work.

The recent emergence of the global #MeToo and #Blacklives Matter movements have given rise to a critique of racialized institutions and toxic masculinity and their articulations in organizational mismanagement, insensitivity to oppressed groups, and missed opportunities in responding to sporadic crisis and patterns of abuse of power. Our focus will be on effective diversity and inclusion leadership and on dealing with gender and racial crises in academic institutions in the United States. To that end, we interrogate the transactional approach frequently associated with business models of leadership and suggest a social change model that rests on the pillars of transformation, supported by the combined metaphoric forces of the leadership qualities of the eagle and the crow—powerful vision, fearlessness, nurturing, strength, adaptability, intelligence, and inclusion.

The euphoric prognosis about the state of diversity and inclusive leadership by the appointments of chief diversity officers (CDOs) on all of the 64 campuses of the State University of New York (SUNY) in the past three years seems to have subsided, as a plethora of issues involving diversity mismanagement affecting several college and university presidents and others in leadership roles have resulted in many resignations and expulsions. Among the college presidents, provosts, or deans whose leadership authorities were challenged recently were the president of Ithaca College, Tom

Rochon; Tim Wolfe of the University of Missouri; and Jack Thomas of Western Illinois University. And, colleges and universities, including Duke, South Carolina, Syracuse, Binghamton University, the University at Albany, UCLA, Nebraska, Arizona State, Florida, San Jose UC-Irvin, Connecticut, and Alabama, have problems associated with diversity mismanagement on their campuses (Cole & Harper, 2017).

What is interesting about the majority of these leadership positions in higher education is that most of the presidents and their cabinets are mostly White traditional heteropatriarchal leaders, who have accumulated and consolidated power in the academy for years despite this era of diversity and inclusion. Many of these leaders are mostly removed from their students and faculty, depending strictly on a transactional leadership style, which, like the traditional Great Man model, is lineal, hegemonic, risk-abatement, masculinist, rational, practical, and uni-directional. Furthermore, a basic course on Diversity Leadership 101 could have informed these college and university leaders about three important elements/tests for leadership success: one, diversity leadership work must be intentional; two, diversity leadership work should be about human relations and not about "things," and three, during crisis management, one's rhetoric must contain an alignment between intent and impact. The college and university leaders in most of the aforementioned institutions failed these tests (Cole & Harper, 2017). The leadership qualities mentioned earlier, which do not seem to work in institutions filled with Generation Z students and millennials, have been ingrained in our minds since the body of knowledge in leadership studies was propounded in the 1800s. Nonetheless, many institutions still operate on the Great Man leadership model in the 21st century. Is this leadership model and its concomitant application a product of unconscious bias?

We teach courses on diversity, inclusion, and leadership. We also direct and co-facilitate diversity and inclusion professional development institutes in the United States and around the world. In our workshops and classes, when we ask participants and students to engage in an exercise called "first thoughts," what one thinks first of when, for instance, manager or leader is mentioned, we receive a long list of stereotypes and archetypes: men, White males, competitive, strict, businesslike, boss, WASPs, head, chairman, administrator, master, taskmaster, in charge, head honcho, and boss man, to name a few. Our students and participants represent a cross-section of Americans in higher education or in the general populace. Some of these stereotypes and archetypes may not have validity, but most of them are products and images of the old records that constantly play in our minds. Yet, we know that not all leaders and managers in the United States are White males or boss men, but these images become the narratives, the narratives become our realities, and the perceived realities are turned into policies, hiring practices, and programs—in short, we are dealing with a White Racial Frame (see Feagin, 2014).

Mapping Out Gender, Race, and Leadership

Before we map out the traditional transactional management and leadership styles, let us look at the state of senior leadership demographics in US-based Fortune 500 companies and the academy. We might also ask what changes, if any, have occurred since the civil rights revolution of the 1950s and 60s. What are the prevailing changes in leadership in the post-civil rights era and the recent period of the politics of inclusion or the illusion of inclusion?

While women from all ethnic/racial backgrounds and people of color have entered the workforce in record numbers, they have not really broken the glass ceiling and the leadership color line respectively. Why do men who enter "pink-colored" careers still get a male privilege of riding the glass escalator? People of color who, per chance, enter leadership positions are mostly in an auxiliary capacity, such as chief diversity officers (CDOs) with little or no power for policymaking, if they do not serve on the president's cabinet, and most CDOs do not. Furthermore, with reference to leadership positions in our world today, we cannot ignore the forces of intersectionality of gender and race. Omi and Winant (2015) assert:

> The intersectionality of race and gender gains particular importance because sex/gender also is a corporal phenomenon. The chattelization of the body has been a common experience for both people of color and women. In many ways racial differences and sex/gender-based differences resemble each other and women. Gender differentiation resembles racial differentiation in numerous discomfiting ways.
>
> *(Omi & Winant, 2015, p. 258)*

Our observations and informed opinions in leadership discourses is that what affects most people of color have a similar trajectory for women, and an approach to mitigating the inequities in leadership both in higher education and diversity categories all over the world is long overdue.

A decisive change in leadership demographics is only apparent in countries where decisive affirmative action, mentoring, and quota systems are in place to diversify company boards and executive chambers as well as members of parliament and ministers. Of course, structural equity measures to enhance leadership advancement for people who have been historically disadvantaged, such as legal instruments regulating pay equity, work family balance, and parental/family leave benefits, accompany such quota policies. However, in the United States diversity hiring is based on the pool of applicants that apply and not quotas, since the case of *Bakke vs. Regent University of California* (1978) made quotas illegal but affirmative diversity based on percentages acceptable.

The measure of all (heterosexist) things still seems to be Aristotle's natural complement theory. The philosopher and scientist seems to defend all that is noble and good for mostly White men and relegates women to undesirable aspects of the masculinist self-expression and social identity. It reinforces a reasoning/body dichotomy, whereby "reasoning" is reserved for White males and "body" for Black men and all women. The woman's body is objectified and Black bodies are sanctioned for physical labor and athleticism in this perspective. Aristotle's misogynist ideology has had lasting effects through the millennia. Table 15.1 gives us a clarification of masculine and feminine ideal attributes that differentiate personality dispositions, skills, and interests within the heteronormative, *White* American nuclear family:

It is a binary table of ideal dispositions; i.e., they are mutually exclusive and as thus reinforcing differences. The ideological claims of such biologically based, essentialist complement theory are expressed in a rigid gender (and sexual) division of labor: cis-gendered men and women have biologically different capacities and interests; the social cohesion will be guaranteed when each gender accomplishes tasks that they are best suited for. Finally, women and men are "separate but equal." That means that men have power in the public sphere, pertaining to the economic and political order,

Table 15.1 Gender Stereotypes

Masculine	*Feminine*
Active	Passive
Independent	Dependent
Assertive	Receptive
Self-interested	Altruistic, caring
Physically competent	Physically weak
Rational	Intuitive
Emotionally controlled	Emotionally open
Self-disciplined	Impulsive

while women have power in the private sphere (domestic life, family). In the end, such a biologically determinist theory suggests that gender roles and the division of labor are not sexist (i.e., they are not unequal, unfair, and discriminatory towards women).

Of course, such claims are easily debunked. The cultural traits defined as masculine are seen as positive in a dominant heteropatriarchal society, while the traits defined as feminine are negative, specifically inappropriate for the public domain. The same cultural traits that refer to heteropatriarchal masculinity apply specifically to White males in powerful positions. Second, biology does not determine social destiny: male aggression and female submission and maternal "instincts" are products of society, not biology. Therefore, gender expression is on a continuum, where masculinity does not necessarily exclude femininity. Racial categories are also socially constructed and are not biologically structured, and race projects intersect with all the diversity categories of gender, class, religion, disability, and sexual orientation. Race projects are socio-political identities based on phenotypes, combined with social agendas and structures to enhance racial groups' representation and struggle for rights and resources within a polity. Omi and Winant (2015) maintain that a "racial project is simultaneously an interpretation, representation, or explanation of racial identities and meanings, and an effort to organize and distribute resources" (Omi and Winant, 2015, p. 125). Finally, in reality, women and men actually do not play in a "separate-but-equal" realm. Separate but equal did not start with *Plessy vs. Ferguson* (1896)—affirming segregation; nor did it end with *Brown vs. Board of Education of Topeka* (1954)—undoing segregation. We continue to struggle with both equality and equity even today.

Despite equal protection and anti-discrimination gains in the workforce, women still have less economic and political power than men do; there still is a glaring pay equity gap; in a heterosexual relationship, a woman still does much more unpaid care labor than her partner does, which increases with parental responsibilities. Arlie Hochschild's (1989) extensive studies on the second, unpaid shift describe it as the upstairs-downstairs division of labor: the male partner is responsible for basement activities (e.g., light household repair, but the laundry machine, which may also be deposited in the basement, is her responsibility. He gets to do glorified public chores such as taking out the garbage and mowing the lawn, and she gets to do everything else (behind the scenes)! Another analysis gives us an even clearer picture of the *structural* inequity of unpaid domestic labor: "Feminine chores are mainly indoor and done frequently: cooking, cleaning, laundry and child care. Masculine chores are mostly outdoor and less frequent: taking out the trash, mowing the lawn or washing the car" (Miller, 2018). What are the psychological effects of such unequal task sharing in this cis-gendered heterosexual matrix? Women get anxious and resentful and men do *not* see themselves as overempowered, enjoying the benefits of male unearned privilege. As Aristotle would remark on this distribution of goods: "it is the natural order of the oikos."

Such reified binary disposition of "public man, private woman," in the famous words of Jean Bethke Elshtain, is so powerful that it seems even today that working men or women have difficulty accepting the fact of competent leadership from a woman CEO, college president, or head of state, let alone general secretary of the United Nations. In the workforce, gender essentialism means that women are pegged into secretarial, supportive social roles even where it is incongruent with their professional disposition. A natural science researcher boasts about having achieved gender parity in his lab; the advantages being that women do the meticulous, detailed-oriented experimental work, whereas men are the decision makers and grant writers who have the birds-eye view and put teams together; however, men are incapable of doing "more routine work for a longer period" and it's best to delegate such work to women (Linkova, 2017, p. 58). Marcela Linkova notes that this male team leader displays benevolent sexism of typecasting women into performing analytic support work and leaving the big picture, synthetic cognition to male researchers. The latter style is more valuable because it leads to successful grant writing. We note that his unconscious bias is also a case of microaggression, namely one of microinvalidation with clearly punitive consequences for women researchers, condemned to a life of data entry. It is clear that the prized good is grant writing, and women would lose out on bonuses and other types of compensation and leadership recognition.

Black and Latinx people are entrapped in a similar quagmire. Whether it is acquiring a PhD or becoming a corporate executive, dean, provost, or president of a college, the achievement gap is real. Miseducation of the Black elites, diseducation of the Black masses (to serve capitalistic needs), White syllogism that casts Black and Brown folks out as failed races; White solipsism, which sustains White privilege; cultural imperialism and the mindset that whiteness is the norm; and stereotype threat, which sets Black and Brown people up for failure are all programmatic through social engineering. We can add to the awful list: Black immiseration—the part of the foundation of the capitalism that detains Black people in the bottom billion and helps to promote material fetishism of Black folks for the marketplace; Black and Brown infantilization, a childlike position placed on Black and Brown folk by the dominant culture which reduces their anthropomorphic status; and post-traumatic slave syndrome—the lack of clinical healing for the Black race since slavery and Jim Crow are some of the reasons for lack of Black leadership in corporate America and academia. Of cause, race is a major category in America and racism is the elephant in the room.

Needless to say and without getting into an oppression Olympics (oppressed groups competing for medals for who have suffered most), it is evident that White women are the prime beneficiaries of affirmative action and White male veterans are the fastest-growing group for affirmative action benefits, not Blacks. So, the lights and reflections on the leadership kaleidoscope is not only genderized but highly racialized. Racial categories and racialized bodies are contained in workplaces and spaces, where Black bodies run an unequal opportunity race to the top without much success. When spaces are given authoritative meaning in terms of leadership and management, they become mostly White heteropatriarchal places and spaces. Black bodies were "questioned" in our history for personhood and leadership. "Questioned personhood" did not start with disability studies, because we can travel as far back as the Supreme Court decision of *Dred Scott vs. Sanford* (1857), where Black bodies were not regarded as fully human, but as properties. Founding fathers like Thomas Jefferson believed Blacks were "dumb," "have very strong and disagreeable odor," and were "unable to utter their thoughts in plain narration" (Smith, 1998). Yet Jefferson cherished Sarah Hemings in order to have a relationship with her for over 30 years (ibid.). Paternalism and heteropatriarchy shaped Jefferson's mindset to group women and Black folk in a category that would always be subjugated and yet protected for economic benefits of the system.

Joe Feagin's (2014) White Racial Frame theory encapsulates the saga of America's racial formation, racial project, and race relations that reduce Black Americans to servitude and minoritized positions. In this White Racial Frame, which supports and sustains White privilege, the unearned advantage of Whites because of history and skin color and White racial stereotypes of Black people (lazy, childlike, predator) are turned into racial narratives and interpretations loaded with negative images of Black folk. Racial images are transformed into racialized emotions. Racialized feelings are transformed into racist perceptions, and these perceptions are turned into public policy and discriminatory actions combined with lethal social trust that prevent Black folks from securing leadership positions (Feagin, 2014).

However, interlocutors of the racial project and leadership may question the election of the first African American president of the United States, even with an Islamic name—Barak Hussein Obama as *primus inter pares* of world leaders. Racial projects shape American lives through the connections of structural entities, systems, and racial representations. These racial projects facilitate the nature of racial formations and a racial group's ability to lead or rule (Omi & Winant, 2015). Obama's election was a test case for the American presidency and the United States' racial projects. This test case included Obama's mixed race identity; a challenge to White heteropatriarchal hegemony of the United States political establishment and the presidency, and the extent to which "no drama Obama" could remain racially neutral in a racialized society. In the assessment of White supremacists and heteropatriarchal masculinists, Obama failed all three of those measures (cf. Asumah, 2015).

Dealing with the dynamics of the White Racial Frame for Black and Brown folk and women leadership is one thing; the other thing that, from time immemorial, has threatened Black and Brown leadership efforts is the concept and effects of social trust. Social trust is the precepts, norms, and beliefs associated with integrity, honesty, and reliability of a group of people or a nation state (Putman, 1993). Social trust sounds simple, but its impact on Black and Brown leadership and African nation states is devastating. When a group of people is perceived to be deviants and deficient in social trust, they are not given the opportunity to aspire to be leaders, managers, or administrators of programs, institutions, or nation states. The PEW Social Trends Survey indicates that in the United States, Whites are more trusted than Blacks and Latinos (PEW Research Center, 2007). This distrust is also translated in leadership roles and responsibilities. Who would entrust a leadership position in the hands of a distrustful person? This might be a rhetorical question, but the answer is an important one when studies about distrustful groups and nations point to the Black community in the United States and Africa (ibid.).

On the global scene, studies conducted in the West indicate Black/African countries and their leaders are more distrusted than Scandinavians and Americans (ibid.). Does White solipsism, the epistemological and cognitive position that since Black knowledge base is outside White spheres of reasoning and behavior, mean that Black folks cannot be successful leaders? Does it tickle our moral consciousness that in American football—the National Football League (NFL), a sport populated by 65% Black men—the most important positions that involve leadership, quarterbacks and center positions, are 23 out of 32 and 82% White, respectively, in the 2013 season? (Mudede, 2017; Ralston, 2019). The narrative is not different in corporate America. According to *Fortune* magazine (2018), there are only three Black CEOs in the Fortune 500 companies. This number is down from six CEOs in 2012 (McGirt, 2018). In academia, the American Council on Education (ACE) 2017 Report indicates that African Americans make up 8% of all college presidents, and women of color make up only 5% of this leadership position (ACE, 2017 Report). Women of color are the most underrepresented group in university and college leadership.

Social trust and implicit bias are powerful motivators to maintain the status quo. The Harvard-based Project Implicit self-testing exercise serves the purpose of unearthing our deep-seated unconscious fears about women and Blacks in the workforce, in White male-dominated careers; they also offers testing about disability, racism, and many other diversity indicators. As we will show in the section on transformative ethical leadership, only through conscious effort and repetition can old habits can be broken and an equity mindset and habitus start to germinate in each of us and our lifeworld, and, in an enduring sense, in the institutions where diversity educators and thought leaders are able to report directly to the top leadership. We have heard many times in the diversity and inclusion institute that we co-direct at SUNY Cortland the frustration of White colleagues about their inability to deal with their biases if these prejudices are "unconscious" in the first place. Our answer to such a perspective is that we must work smarter and inclusively to make the unconscious conscious, so that the personal and institutional cycles of oppression can be broken.

Furthermore, breaking discrimination patterns at the individual (conscious) level is necessary but not sufficient. If it were sufficient, anti-discrimination policies and procedures (de jure legislation) would have immediate deterrent effects and persuasive power. As we have seen, the legacies of White supremacy, including chattel slavery, convict lease system, Jim Crow, and the perpetuation of a racial caste system in the carceral system are lingering on. Astoundingly, Black Americans have one tenth of the average wealth accumulated by Whites in 2019. In response to federal pressure, southern states enacted their own anti-lynching laws during the height of lynch terrorism of African Americans. However, state actors (sheriffs, etc.) never bothered to enforce the laws, and the White lynch mob was never indicted, prosecuted, or convicted of the thousands of deaths they committed during the Jim

Crow era. The enduring effects of the Jim Crow era was a mass exodus, dubbed the Great Migration, of hundreds of thousands of Black Americans to northern states. But accumulation of networks did not ensure generational wealth there either, thanks to redlining enshrined in the "Whites only" New Deal legislation of the 1930s. In this perspective, race, a master category, strengthened systemic oppression and provided ample space also for resistance. Racialization facilitated superordination and subordination with leaders and the led. Yet, the led was not dormant. Resistance, matches, rallies, protests, and insurgencies were all part of the struggle for democracy and inclusive leadership. Finally, the civil rights moral revolution and legal changes were supposed to present a break from a White supremacist past: the universal right to suffrage, integration of schools, and even Affirmative Action federal policies went beyond formal anti-racist measures to endorse substantive educational and economic opportunities for Black people.

Or, so it seemed. As we mentioned earlier in this chapter, with the US Supreme Court decision of *Bakke vs Regent University of California* (1978), it was made clear that any race-based policies that favored Black applicants for universities or employment, i.e., had the tinge of a "quota" system, would be abolished. In the end, the Kennedy initiative of Equal Opportunity and Affirmative Action to undo the racist legacies of the past benefited another group of people: White women; decades later, they found themselves displaced by veterans of war. And today, redlining continues to be the status quo—residential segregation is as prominent as it had been in the 1950s, and many African American children now (again) are educated in schools that have fewer than 10% White children. The difference is that today most of them are educated by Whites and no longer have Black role models as teachers, guidance counselors, or principals (hooks, 1994). White teachers teach most Black students, and those who control institutions and processes of education can easily use them to maintain their leadership roles and superordination, while subordinate cultures are enmeshed into subservient and not leadership roles. Many African American males are sadly placed in special education programs, and these boys by the fourth grade are set up for failure. Kunjufu (1995) calls this process that kills the educational enthusiasm of Black boys the "fourth grade syndrome," a stage where Black boys begin to lose enthusiasm in education and leadership. White teachers are unprepared to assist them, and at the age 9, these boys are seen as a burden to society (Kunjufu, 1995, p. 33; Asumah & Perkins, 2001). We are hopeful that recent inclusive educational practices would counter the process of miseducation, diseducation, fourth grade syndrome, inadequate educational financing in public schools and mitigate the forces of the stereotype threat to enable Black students to be fully prepared to enter college and be ready to take up leadership roles.

The topic of women of color, specifically of Black girls and women, continues to be systematically excluded from gendered equity discussions in educational institutions. Over and over, Black feminist testimonies deride the fraudulent claims of the Moynihan Report, which was supposed to present a status report on the Black American Family. What Senator Moynihan's study effectively does is resort to a "blame the victim" gendered-racist framework (Davis, 1981). Moynihan resorts to the tired mammy stereotype and opines that Black women as mothers and wives are simply out of step with the normative (i.e., White, patriarchal) ideology of cult of domesticity and therefore ill-equipped to deal with rearing their sons and providing proper (domestic) moral support for Black men. However, the Black man is characterized as a caricature, predator, and destroyer of the Black family. The Black man was emasculated through a reduced alpha image, vacant esteem, and nihilism—the feeling of hopelessness and nothingness because he cannot fully provide for the Black family. The Moynihan Report emasculates the Black male by citing matriarchal family structures of the Black community and their demerits vis-à-vis heteropatriarchal White family structures as the normative measure of the American family. Astoundingly, he concludes that Black women are to blame for the lack of educational and employment opportunities of Black boys and men. Thus, in one magic trick relying on historical amnesia, all racist, sexist, systemic, oppressive inequities are disappeared from the political landscape and (White, male supremacist) policymakers are offered assurances to treat the ailments of the Black family with "benign neglect" (sic). Thus, the Black family's enduring struggle is as much about coping with the post-traumatic slavery syndrome, as DeGruy Leary (2005) notes, which continues to be an irrepressible racial and gendered apparitional structure that haunts Blacks in the American society. So, "what originally began as an appropriate adaptation to an oppressive and danger-filled environment has been subsequently transmitted down through generations" (DeGruy Leary, 2005, p. 15). Angela Y. Davis (1981) notes, what also disappears from such racist framing is the fact that through the centuries, the Black family has enjoyed a much more egalitarian and supportive gendered relationship than what was offered to White middle-class women with the allure of the cult of domesticity. To patriarchs (such as Moynihan), such egalitarianism is deliberately misread as a threat to the power structure, and Black women are deemed to diminish the ideal of (toxic) masculinity prescribed by Aristotle some 2,500 years ago.

A common complaint of scholars of color who work in the White ivory tower is that their service expectations are monumental, creating a racial-gendered fatigue syndrome for cis and trans women and men of color. Such unfair service burden is coupled with a perennial suspicion that their scholarship is just not good enough—again, a serious case of microinvalidation. This cultural taxation, the invisible labor of faculty of color (unpaid service), is concomitant with the exacerbation of enrollments of students of color without adequate support systems and limited hiring of faculty of color. As Audrey Williams (2015) notes, "Professors who carry heavy service loads do it at the risk to their careers." In academe, being perceived as a productive scholar is often an entrance ticket to respectable leadership positions such as dean or provost.

Rethinking Leadership Models for the Disadvantaged

Like any valuable commodity, leadership is highly sought after in both corporate America and academia. While good leadership is a *sine qua non* in any successful business, institutions of higher learning have recognized that fact and have developed many leadership courses and programs. Research in the area of leadership continues to grow, examining the theoretical frameworks and processes of leadership. Even the basic definition of leadership runs the gamut from "the ability to impress the will of a leader on those led and induce obedience, respect, loyalty, and cooperation" (Moore, 1927, p. 124) to "Leadership is a process whereby an individual influences a group of individuals to achieve a common goal" (Northouse, 2018, p. 7) to "Leadership is concerned with effecting change on behalf of others and society" (Komives, Wagner, & Associates, 2009, p. xii). Nevertheless, very little research and few books address the emerging field of diversity and inclusive leadership. As far back as the Great Man Theory of leadership in the 19th century was propounded by White historians such as Thomas Carlyle, who had the idea that leaders were born and not made, women and people of color were absent in this school of thought. Great men—heroes—were prophets like Jesus; poets, such as Shakespeare; kings as Napoleon; and philosophers, such as Rousseau, were the leaders of the time. We wonder where Yaa Asantewaa, the most eminent African queen mother, leader, and warrior of the Ashanti Empire, who fought against British colonialism, and Frederick Douglass, the African American scholar and philosopher, would place in Carlyle's mind.

The evolution of leadership theories has circled around mostly White male traits, those who are born to lead and those who are "natural" leaders. Process-orientated leadership places emphasis on the interaction between the leader and the led. Here, leadership is seen as something that could be learned and behavioral. In recent times few Black, Brown, and women leaders have risen to the occasion. Martin Luther King Jr., a civil rights leader, Nelson Mandela, former president of South Africa, who brought apartheid to its knees, and Oprah Winfrey, a television talk show host who rose from rags to riches, are some of the leaders who combined traits and behavior in their leadership style.

While traits and behavior seem to dominate the theoretical framework of leadership, one should not be surprised to learn from many corporate and higher education leaders that they admire

Greenleaf's work on servant leadership. "A servant leader is servant first.... It begins with the natural feeling that one wants to serve, to serve first," Greenleaf notes (1977, p. 27).

Transactional and Transformational Paradigms in Leadership Development

As we have mentioned earlier in this chapter, there are many theories about leadership; the dominant ones have crystallized as theories on transactional versus transformational leadership. A growing body of literature tackles the thorny issue of leadership styles with respect to racial and gendered stereotypes and stereotype threat (Rudman & Glick, 2001; Eddy & VanDerLinden, 2006; Madden, 2011; Ellemers, Rink, Derks, & Ryan, 2012). With reference to gendered stereotypes, they argue that the agentic style is congruent with expectations of male leadership while women are expected to lead using a collaborative style. Building on Eagly and Karau's (2002) role congruity theory of prejudice, Margaret Madden, former provost at SUNY Potsdam, notices that when a woman leader adopts an agentic style, direct reports (i.e., subordinates) have more difficulty accepting her leadership, because she does not fit into the expected supportive, caring, collaborative mold of femininity. Whenever women are in senior leadership positions, their work tends to be devalued. As soon as she retires and a (White) man, *usually*, is hired, power and legitimacy again are vested with that office.

For a Johns Hopkins study done in 2002, senior women faculty/administrators were asked the following, "Are women faculty attracted to leadership positions as currently designed?" Francesca Dominici and her team found that women are systematically devalued in the academy; they lack informal networks and mentoring that prepare them for the traditional advancement (from department chair to dean, etc.). Furthermore, the Hopkins study notes that "[s]uccess in such positions often seems to depend on having a spouse who can shoulder domestic responsibilities—often on a full-time basis" (Dominici, Fried, & Zeger, 2009). Surprisingly, the Hopkins study also notes that where women have focused a lot of energy is on building interdisciplinary centers that "address important unmet needs." They labor to find office space, have scarce internal resources, and build these centers with external grants because they often have a national/international reputation, yet these center directors find only tacit approval by department chairs and deans, even though the university's reputation is greatly enhanced due to an increase in research productivity (ibid.). Here then is a paradoxical situation: women find traditional leadership workload onerous but do not mind spending equally endless hours building centers, running conferences without any compensation, or doing administrative office support! Again, aspiring women leaders are supposed to enjoy service work without demanding the appropriate compensation or rewards afforded to similarly positioned male leaders. Here, the books of feminist economists Linda Babcock and Sara Laschever (2007) still have salience: *Women Don't Ask: The Hight Cost of Avoiding Negotiations—and Positive Strategies for Change* and their sequel: *Ask for It: How Women Can Use the Power of Negotiations to Get What They Really Want* (2009).

Table 15.2 shows an overview of the differentiating traits in leadership.

There are three important aspects to this model: first, in this schematic version, we disagree with Margaret Madden and others who wish to synthesize the transactional with the transformational ideal of leadership. Some might wonder why academic excellence, a hallmark of most mission statements, should be attached to transactional leadership. Inclusive excellence in leadership involves the intentional strategies in higher education that are aimed at connecting diversity, inclusion, and equity variables, units, and programs to the vital educational vision and mission of any institution. Inclusive excellence leadership should be a value-laden, behavioral, attitudinal, and policy-goal attainment process in our daily undertakings. However, many other characteristics denote that a unity of opposites is not desirable. For instance, the sociocentrist, relational ideal of transformational leadership is starkly oppositional to the transactional model that is described as egocentric. So, rather than arguing

Table 15.2 Model of Transactional and Transformational Leadership

Transactional Leadership	Ethical, Transformational Leadership
Fear-based	Hope-affirming
Power and control	Empowerment, collaboration, and equity
Scarcity and deficit model	Abundance model (trust in creative process)
Egocentric	Sociocentric, altruistic
Information control and secrecy	Info. sharing, transparency, collegiality
Rigid adherence to hierarchy	Flat hierarchy and service-leadership ideal
Risk management	Diversity leadership
Monochromatic, homogeneous culture	Commitment to intercultural competence
Academic excellence	Inclusive leadership: inclusive excellence and strategic mentoring/pipeline/bridge initiatives
Cloaked in mantle of invincibility	Accountability and genuine peace-making culture

for an integrative model that adopts the best traits of transactional and transformational leadership, we argue for a defense of the transformational theory.

Second, the transactional model seems to have many of the features of toxic masculinity—a topic spearheaded by the popular #MeToo movement, engendered by sexual assault survivor Tawana Burke and which rose to a global social justice movement after female Hollywood celebrities broke the Weinstein scandal in 2017. In fact, Weinstein's company excelled in secrecy, manipulation, and massive cover-ups of sexual assault. Such practices are exemplified by legal non-disclosure agreements, and Harvey Weinstein amassed quite a few of them, but the majority of his accusers never even bothered to sue him, because his control over Hollywood was massive and his bullying was legendary.

It is important to note that we worry about gender essentialism when it comes to effective and ethical leadership. We speculate that it is quite possible that women who adopt the (masculinist) transactional leadership style do so as a coping mechanism or to overcompensate in order to attain worth and credibility among peers and their direct reports. Furthermore, most White women who adopt transactional leadership styles are mentored and nurtured in the heteropatriarchal system similar to White males. However, it is unclear whether this "iron lady" image works to their advantage. A Hillary Clinton, who was perceived as "bossy," ended up losing to a Donald Trump, who seems to be the cliché of toxic masculinity.

Third, we insist on describing the combined transformational and social change models as an ethical leadership model. Following Christine M. Allen (2018), ethical leadership has several qualities: humility, role-modeling behavior that emphasizes giving credit to others, and a focus on a culture of integrity, not compliance. Her sixth quality is crucial: "Senior leaders should focus on reinforcing integrity in lower-level management." This means (applied to our model) that it is quite meaningless if the CEO has high-minded visionary transformational commitments when their vision is not implemented throughout the organization or company, who, in fact, may just work in transactional, self-serving manner.

The Social Change Model (SCM) of leadership challenges our diversity leaders to maintain congruence in their utterance and deeds, not just in window dressing events. As diversity and inclusion advocates, we are tired of being tired of what our colleagues of color call "food, fun and festival" and "organized happiness" to fulfill the institutional needs for the "appearance" of diversity and inclusion. Are our colleges and university presidents walking the talk? Collaboration is primary to the dynamics of producing social change. Diversity demands collaboration as stakeholders bring their agendas to the table—they must have a place at the table, but oftentimes the voices of minoritized groups and women are silenced by hegemonic powers at the table. Nonetheless, diversity leadership is human work, which is "grounded in relationships between people; in these relationships one develops the ability . . . to work collaboratively with others that is essential to the leadership process" (Komives et al., 2009, p. 195). Commitment enables transformational leadership to reach a point of sustenance. If college and university leadership is about stewardship, then commitment enables the leader to have a responsibility to service, to be an advocate for all the people regardless of their minoritized status on campus, and common purpose trumps it all. Common purpose is an essential element for diversity leadership for a shared vision, inclusive meanings, democracy, and organizational success.

Next, we will explore what counts as ineffective risk leadership and decision-making when intercultural competence is lacking and diversity leadership only means "managing diversity."

Failure in Diversity Management: What Happened to the Eagle and the Crow?

In researching and working on many college campuses and on our own campus, we continue to explore the predictable administrative reactions to a sporadic campus crisis and develop a (cultural) competence analysis at the organizational level. With the intelligence of the crow, it is natural to respond to or defuse, diminish, or trivialize racist incidents. Yet, the nurturing ability, humanity, strength, and endurance of the eagle in diversity and inclusion are missing in this leadership model. We argue that the crow model alone corresponds to our transactional model, whereas the combined forces of the eagle and crow represent the ethical, transformational leadership paradigm. Combining the social change leadership model and transformational leadership model for diversity leadership is the best approach for modern institutions that seriously make diversity and inclusion part of their *modus operandi*. In our previous work on diversity leadership, we have proposed the following:

> A core demand of diversity leadership, as opposed to diversity management, is to evaluate and validate the work of faculty of color [and women] as change agents in terms of inclusive academic excellence standards. The caged bird is indeed free to leave the cage and soar in community-engagement praxis, which will "count" towards valuable research, elevating the academy as a place that is accountable to its diverse residents.
>
> *(Asumah, Nagel, & Rosengarten, 2016)*

Interestingly, while White women leaders in general are often called upon to serve and "save" a financially struggling company (without receiving credit), Black and Latinx leaders are usually neglected (Bruckmüller, Ryan, Rink, & Haslam, 2014; Cook & Glass, 2014). Cook and Glass use the concept of the glass cliff (instead of glass ceiling) to assert that women need to prove themselves in very stressful leadership roles, i.e., managing organizations in crisis. In such moments, relying on the short-term semi-transformational approaches to "save" the organization seems a wise investment in organizational leadership, requiring such leaders to adopt a collaborative, non-agentic, non-transactional style. Eddy and VanDerLinden (2006) hold out hope for community colleges for favoring transformative leadership. When Harvard Business School starts adopting such leadership philosophy without any hint of racism and benevolent sexism, perhaps we could say that the "crow paradigm" is being considered the dominant leadership theory—the crow and eagle must join forces for diversity leadership to be transformative. Until then, the road to diversity leadership would remain undulating, rough, and filled with obstacle courses for Black and Latinx folks, women, and minoritized groups in the academy.

Conclusion

In this chapter, we have argued that the traditional heteropatriarchal leadership models on our college and university campuses have failed to serve the needs of women and Black and Brown people and their aspiration for leadership roles in the academy. The transactional, big man trait and situational theories are White male orientated, and the changes that are needed based on the preponderance of evidence in the #MeToo and #Black LivesMatter movements require transformative and social change leadership. These two models require leaders who are ready to alter the dominant culture of society in order to effect institutional behavioral and procedural changes. Intentionality, pervasiveness, and human consciousness are inevitable in this leadership process. Educational leadership must be inclusive, hope affirming, and inextricably linked to our social responsibilities and civil rights in order for diversity leadership to be successful.

References

Allen, C. M. (2018, January 17). Keys to ethical leadership in corporate culture. *RANE (Risk Assistance Network + Exchange)*. Retrieved June 10, 2019, from https://insightbusinessworks.com/keys-to-ethical-leadership-in-corporate-culture-a-critical-opportunity-in-enterprise-risk-management/

American Council on Education (ACE). (2017). *Annual report*. Retrieved July 16, 2019, from https://www.acenet.edu/Documents/Annual-Report-2017-final.pdf

Asumah, S. N. (2015, Summer). Race, immigration reform and heteropatriarchal masculinity: Reframing the Obama presidency. *Wagadu: Journal of Transnational and women's Studies*, 13. Retrieved July 16, 2019.

Asumah, S. N., Nagel, M., & Rosengarten, L. (2016). New trends in diversity leadership and inclusive excellence. *Wagadu: A Journal of Transnational Women's and Gender Studies*, 15. Retrieved July 16, 2019, from http://sites.cortland.edu/wagadu/v-15-summer-2016-new-trends-in-diversity-leadership-and-inclusive-excellence/

Asumah, S. N., & Perkins, V. C. (2001). *Educating the black child in the black independent school*. New York, NY: Global Publications.

Babcock, L., & Laschever, S. (2007). *Women don't ask: The high cost of avoiding negotiations—and positive strategies for change*. New York, NY: Bantam.

Babcock, L., & Laschever, S. (2009). *Ask for it: How women can use the power of negotiations to get what they really want*. New York, NY: Bantam.

Bruckmüller, S., Ryan, M. K., Rink, F., & Haslam, S. A. (2014). Beyond the glass ceiling: The glass cliff and its lessons for organizational policy. *Social Issues and Policy Review*, 8(1), 202–232. doi:10.1111/sipr.12006

Carlyle, T. (1840). Heroes and hero worship, and the heroic in history. *The Project Gutenberg*. Retrieved July 2, 2019, from www.gutenberg.org/cache/epub/1091/pg1091.txt

Cole, E. R., & Harper, S. (2017). Race and rhetoric: An analysis of college presidents statements of campus racial incidents. *Journal of Diversity in Higher Education*, 10(4), 318–333.

Cook, A., & Glass, C. (2014). Women and top leadership positions: Towards an institutional analysis. *Gender, Work & Organization*, 21(1), 91–103. doi:10.1111/gwao.12018

Davis, A. Y. (1981). *Women, race and class*. New York, NY: Random House.

DeGruy Leary, J. (2005). *Post traumatic slave syndrome: America's legacy of enduring injury and healing*. Upton, MA: Upton Press.

Dominici, F., Fried, L. P., & Zeger, S. L. (2009). So few women leaders. It's no longer a pipeline problem, so what are the root causes? *Academe*, 95(4), 25–27. Retrieved June 10, 2019, from www.aaup.org/article/so-few-women-leaders#.XP31ji2B3d8

Eagly, A. H., & Karau, S. J. (2002). Role congruity theory of prejudice toward female leaders. *Psychological Review*, 109(3), 573–598. doi:10.1037/0033-295X.109.3.573

Eddy, P. L., & VanDerLinden, K. E. (2006). Emerging definitions of leadership in higher education: New visions of leadership or same old "hero" leader? *Community College Review*, 34(1), 5–26. Retrieved from http://crw.sagepub.com/cgi/content/abstract/34/1/5

Ellemers, N., Rink, F., Derks, B., & Ryan, M. K. (2012). Women in high places: When and why promoting women into top positions can harm them individually or as a group (and how to prevent this). *Research in Organizational Behavior*, 32, 163–187.

Elshtain, J. B. (1980). *Public man, private woman*. Princeton: Princeton University Press.

Feagin, J. (2014). *Racist America: Roots, current realities and future reparations*. New York, NY: Routledge.

Greenleaf, R. K. (1977). *Servant leadership: A journey into the nature of legitimate power and greatness*. New York, NY: Paulist Press.

Hochschild, A., & Machung, A. (1989). *The second shift: Working parents and the revolution at home*. New York, NY: Viking Penguin.

hooks, bell. (1994). *Teaching to transgress: Education as the practice of freedom*. New York, NY: Routledge.

Komives, S., Wagner, W., & Associates. (2009). *Leadership for a better world: Understanding the social change model of leadership development.* San Francisco, CA: Jossey-Bass.
Kunjufu, J. (1995). *Countering the conspiracy to destroy Black boys.* Series. Chicago: African American Images.
Linkova, M. (2017). Academic excellence and gender bias in the practices and perceptions of scientists in leadership and decision-making positions. *Gender and Research, 18*(1), 42–91.
Madden, M. (2011). Gender stereotypes of leaders: Do they influence leadership in higher education? *Wagadu, 9,* 55–88. Retrieved from http://sites.cortland.edu/wagadu/wp-content/uploads/sites/3/2014/02/genderStereotypes.pdf
McGirt, E. (2018, March 1). Raceahead: Only three black CEOs in Fortune 500. *Fortune Magazine.* Retrieved June 2019, from http://fortune.com/2018/03/01/raceahead-three-black-ceos/
Miller, C. C. (2018, May 16). How same-sex couples divide chores, and what it reveals about modern parenting. *New York Times.* Retrieved from www.nytimes.com/2018/05/16/upshot/same-sex-couples-divide-chores-much-more-evenly-until-they-become-parents.html?action=click&module=RelatedLinks&pgtype=Article
Moore, B.V. (1927). The May conference on leadership. *Personnel Journal, 6,* 124–128.
Mudede, C. (2017, September 25). Why the overrepresentation of Black Americans in professional sports is not a good thing. *The Stranger.* Retrieved July 20, 2019, from https://www.thestranger.com/slog/2017/09/25/25432524/why-the-over-representation-of-black-americans-in-professional-sports-is-not-a-good-thing
Northouse, P. (2018). *Introduction to leadership: Concepts and practice.* Los Angeles, CA: Sage.
Omi, M., & Winant, H. (2015). *Racial formation in the United States.* New York, NY: Routledge.
PEW Research Center. (2007). Americans and social trust: Where and why. Retrieved from https://www.pewsocialtrends.org/2007/02/22/americans-and-social-trust-who-where-and-why/
Putman, R. D. (1993). *Making democracy work: Civic traditions in modern Italy.* Princeton: Princeton University Press.
Project Implicit. Retrieved May 21, 2019, from https://implicit.harvard.edu/implicit/
Ralston, M. (2019). Why there aren't more Black quarterbacks in the NFL: *Matt Ralston's Blog: Everything Explained in 500 Words.* Retrieved June 26, 2019, from http://mattralston.net/sports/the-unimpressive-rise-of-black-quarterbacks-in-the-nfl/
Rudman, L. A., & Glick, P. (2001). Prescriptive gender stereotypes and backlash toward agentic women. *Journal of Social Issues, 57,* 743–762.
Smith, D. (1998, November 7). The enigma of Jefferson: Mind and body in conflict. *The New York Times.*
Williams, A. (November 8, 2015). *The invisible labor of minority professors.* Faculty. Washington, DC: The Chronicle of Higher Education.

16
DIVERSITY AND WELL-BEING
An Interactive Qualitative Perspective From India

Akanksha Jaiswal and Lata Dyaram

Introduction

Extant literature highlighting the normative importance of diversity explicates proportion of diversity representation and its effects on minority groups and on the morality/constitutionality of demographic diversity. It becomes necessary to comprehend how and why diversity matters, so as to enable organizations to prioritize diversity. At both descriptive and normative levels, the extant literature on diversity cites its intersection with organizational productivity spanning several decades. Exploring this body of work echoes the significance of diversity in organizations, highlighting the need for its continued research.

Diversity breeds a multitude of ideas requiring the intentional inclusion of underrepresented individuals to contribute to an organization's effectiveness. Some researchers believe that by increasing demographically underrepresented members, barriers associated with these groups are minimized and productivity of all individuals is maximized. While women and religious minorities are often underrepresented in the organizational workforce, it may be necessary for organizations to go beyond proportional representation despite its notable positive effects for the underrepresented individuals. Organizations often resort to intentional diversification, seeking unique demographic qualifications towards expanding their demographic and knowledge heterogeneity. It is important to recognize that these strategies are limited in curbing workplace discrimination. Several firms witness issues related to tokenism and polarization among their members owing to a poor diverse mix. Organizations need to continually innovate on how diversity (i.e. balanced organizational demography) can eliminate several negative phenomena for them. If not addressed, these issues can stimulate feelings of inadequacy and alienation among the organizational members.

Towards equality, anti-discrimination initiatives spanning decades are witnessed. Affirmative action and equal opportunities (AA/EO) gained heightened eminence in Western countries during the 1960s–1980s. Concurrently, India developed the constrained legislation of 'reservations' defining quotas for minority groups in higher education and mainstream public sector jobs. However, a mere representation of diversity in organizations does not guarantee social equality. Stereotypes emerging from differences in power, authority, and social roles inevitably invoke social categorization at the workplace. Hence, organizations must expend effort on changing the power dynamics among employees towards seeking value in diversity. If diversity embraces and balances minority/majority demographics and includes similar and dissimilar individuals, such a diversity agenda helps uphold the values of democracy and promotes inclusion.

Gradually, the discourse towards diversity shifted from social equality to a competitive advantage for businesses. Diversity assumes the existence of a multitude of differences, with valuing and celebrating differences as an essential tenet of diversity management. Proponents promulgated the significance of diversity management recognizing and accommodating the differential needs of different groups, towards attaining competitive advantage. What matters primarily to organizations is talent, despite the diversity in demographic attributes and/or social strata. Thus, the workforce in contemporary organizations is a representation of diversity in various attributes, and this employee potpourri is not a result of a transient fashion but a trenchant formulation.

The changing demographic workforce composition continues to provide an important opportunity for researchers to advance diversity management theory (Jackson & Joshi, 2004; Mannix & Neale, 2005). This is because, when managed well, diversity promotes performance, creativity, and innovation. However, its mismanagement undermines social integration and performance (Guillaume et al., 2014; Jackson & Joshi, 2004). While enhanced creativity and performance are the key desired outcomes of diversity, employee affect-related outcomes such as job satisfaction, commitment, cohesion, and well-being are often disregarded (Jackson, Joshi, & Erhardt, 2003). Well-being is what individuals and society are interested in ultimately (Ng, 2015). As people spend more time on work-related activities, how employers demonstrate their commitment to the well-being of their workforce becomes important. Contemporary organizations are actively creating positive and enriching work environments; however, diversity's impact on well-being has received scant scholarly attention. Further, not much is known on *how* and *when* diversity's affective effects become evident. Thus, to promote diversity and concurrently facilitate employee well-being, diversity needs to be examined contextually (Joshi & Roh, 2009).

Diversity is the hallmark of Indian society, representing a plethora of cultural patterns. Likewise, well-being, as construed by Indians, differs significantly from the conceptualization in Western countries. Further, scholarly attention to diversity's impact on well-being is scant, despite known multiculturalism's influence on individuals and communities in India (Das, 2014). Thus, the aim of this chapter is two-fold: (a) what comprises the diversity and well-being of Indian employees, and (b) how diversity relates to employee well-being.

What We Know About Diversity

Diversity Types and Theories

In recent years, diversity has become increasingly relevant in organizations, owing to an overwhelmingly mobile workforce. There are prominent typologies in literature categorizing different types of diversity. Diversity based on readily detectable demographic attributes such as gender and age is referred to as *surface diversity*, while diversity based on less observable attributes such as personality or values is called *deep-level diversity* (Guillaume, Brodbeck, & Riketta, 2012; Milliken & Martins, 1996; Phillips & Loyd, 2006). Another diversity type based highly on job-related attributes such as skills and functional background is *knowledge diversity* (Pelled, 1996; Webber & Donahue, 2001).

Social categorization theory (Tajfel, Billig, & Bundy, 1971) and similarity/attraction paradigm (Byrne, 1971) are often considered as theoretical underpinnings for diversity research. Social categorization theory suggests that individuals have a natural tendency to categorize themselves and others into 'us' versus 'them' based on some salient characteristic such as age or gender. Commonality with similar others builds mutual trust and facilitates smooth group functioning. Likewise, the similarity-attraction paradigm theorizes that similarity with others increases interpersonal liking and attraction such that 'in-group' members are viewed more favorably, perceived to be more trustworthy, and are included in various organizational processes. On the other hand, dissimilarity evokes prejudices, biases, and stereotypes which reduce trust, cohesion, and cooperation while increasing conflict and employee turnover.

Diversity Effects

Extant literature illustrates performance benefits of a diverse workforce such as improved decision-making, enhanced productivity, creativity, innovation, reduced litigation, and a better corporate image (Cox & Blake, 1991; Jackson, May, & Whitney, 1995; Kunze, Boehm, & Bruch, 2011; Milliken & Martins, 1996; Shore et al., 2011; Williams & O'Reilly, 1998). In their seminal review of diversity literature, Williams and O'Reilly (1998) observe performance as a function of three criteria: productivity, social processes, and affective experiences. Much of the scholarly works examining the diversity-performance link have focused solely on productivity. Social processes are often cited to explain such findings, whereas affective experiences have received minimal scholarly attention. Likewise, Jackson et al. (2003) in their meta-analysis of diversity research highlighted performance as a preferred outcome for researchers, while there was a dearth of studies on affect-related diversity effects. Furthermore, despite social processes and affective reactions being conceptually distinct, some diversity researchers employed these concepts interchangeably to extend the negative effects of diversity on social processes to predict negative affective reactions. Jackson and colleagues (2003) cautioned against such an extension of findings. As a result, critical yet unanswered questions have emerged regarding how diversity impacts the affective experiences of employees. With rapid changes in occupational demography, the organizational compositional mix has changed. Employees of varied characteristics, backgrounds, and experiences have varied needs and expectations. Moreover, dissimilar employees often experience feelings of worthlessness, exclusion, and lack of respect and acceptance, thus influencing their well-being (Daya, 2014; Findler, Wind, & Mor Barak, 2007). Thus, in the present inquiry, we explore the lesser-known affective effects of diversity, specifically, employee well-being.

The Case of India

India has attracted the attention of entrepreneurs and multinational corporations all over the world as a promising economy. Since companies are expanding their global footprint to establish recognized operations in India, an understanding of various aspects of the Indian context, business needs, and workforce requirements is essential. Diversity is the hallmark of the Indian milieu, and just a handful of countries in the world may be as diverse as India. Indian demography is a potpourri of cultural, linguistic, educational, socioeconomic, and lifestyle differences. Further, the world acknowledges that Indian human capital is of high potential. Thus, the nature of the Indian workforce warrants a comprehensive understanding before companies invest in diversity management. Ancient Indian scriptures and philosophy emphasize that attaining well-being is the ultimate goal of life. The *Indian National Pledge* highlights India's pride in its rich and varied heritage and emphasis on the well-being of Indians.

Much of the discourse on diversity in India is at the juncture of equal opportunity and legal compliance. India is a large country, comprising 29 states and seven union territories with a variety of languages, dialects, and cultures. While the Indian Constitution recognizes 23 major languages, discrimination based on region/state of origin is prevalent across India. Diversity based on religious beliefs adds to the plethora of existing issues, as about 20% of Indians belong to religious minority groups such as Christianity, Islam, or Sikhism. The Hindu Indian society is divided into four castes: Brahmins, Kshatriyas, Vaishyas, and Shudras (Shudras have been historically most discriminated). As the caste system was followed in India since ancient times, there is still a prevalence of both overt and covert caste-based discrimination in social and employment matters, despite reservation/quota for shudras in educational institutes and government jobs. There is further inequity when it comes to the disabled and women, owing to their differential needs and vulnerabilities. While the Indian Constitution has enacted laws to protect the interests and civil rights of all minority groups, their integration in the social fabric is not seamless yet. Organizations draw their members from social demography and, thus, societal concerns drip into organizational functioning as well. Discrimination, stereotyping, biases, and perceived unfairness create a lot of dissatisfaction among employees. When organizational members feel ostracized, excluded, or mistreated owing to being different from most others, their self-esteem and overall well-being are often compromised. Thus, organizations need to proactively manage diversity to not only curb feelings of ill-being but also to accomplish solidarity and competitive advantage.

About the Study

The present study aimed to explore how contemporary organizations in India viewed dissimilarity among employees with respect to diversity attributes, their notion of well-being at work, and how diversity relates to well-being. Interactive qualitative analysis (IQA) design with focus groups was used in this inquiry (Northcutt & McCoy, 2004). IQA is a qualitative research technique built on ideas from systems theory, which explores phenomena through the socially constructed reality of participants. The purpose of IQA is to develop a pictorial representation of the study phenomenon through the lens of a group. IQA enables the group to create its own 'interpretive quilt,' i.e. individual quilts of meaning represented as a collection of patches (affinities) held together by stitches (relationships among affinities).

The key difference between IQA and other qualitative methods is that in IQA, the participants themselves analyze and interpret the data that they generated during the focus group while the researcher facilitates the process. Since the researcher is not the sole analyst and data interpreter, IQA reduces erosion of original data by the researcher, thus enhancing research rigor. The aim of IQA is to ensure that participants create a shared understanding of the phenomena by collectively developing causal relationships between the themes referred to as affinities. The outcome of IQA is a graphic illustration of the phenomena and the interrelationships between various affinities, called the system influence diagram (SID).

Procedure and Data Source

Two interactive focus group sessions focusing on the key research question, "how diversity relates to employee well-being," were conducted by following the subsequent protocol:

1. Silent brainstorming: Each participant contemplated the research question and wrote down thoughts on a plain sheet of paper. Then, participants listed keywords related to their thoughts on note cards.
2. Inductive coding: Individuals were instructed to stick the note cards on the wall. Then, as a group, they were asked to create clusters of thoughts such that a shared meaning was generated from each cluster. The cards could be moved to other clusters based on group consensus.
3. Axial coding: These sets of clusters (called affinities) were then named by the participants.
4. Affinity relationship table (ART): The final step reverted to individual participants who indicated relationships among the affinities in an affinity relationship table. For instance, for any two affinities A and B, participants indicated either A influenced B or B influenced A or there was no relationship between A and B (Northcutt & McCoy, 2004). An affinity relationship table is illustrated in Figure 16.1.

Affinity Name		Possible Relationships
1.		A → B
2.		A ← B
3.		A <> B (No relationship)
4.		
5.		
6.		

Affinity Pair Relationship	
1	2
1	3
1	4
1	5
1	6
2	3
2	4
2	5
2	6
3	4
3	5
3	6
4	5
4	6
5	6

Figure 16.1 Affinity relationship table
Source: Interactive Qualitative Analysis, Norvell Northcutt & Danny McCoy, 2004, p. 151

We initiated the IQA process with a brief discussion on the purpose of the inquiry. Participants were assured of confidentiality and anonymity of their response. Two IQA focus groups were conducted with a total sample of 20 participants working in a large information technology firm in India. The first focus group consisted of 10 senior-level managers, seven males and three females, having more than 15 years of work experience and working in different domains such as human resource management, research and development, and finance. The second group had 10 employees, five females and five males, having an experience ranging from one to three years and currently working in different domains such as product management, delivery, and design and marketing. To ensure a comparable IQA process experience for both groups, the steps followed were as described earlier: silent brainstorming, note card writing, inductive and axial coding, and completing an affinity relationship table. For both groups, the IQA process lasted for 150 minutes as the participants were actively involved and engaged.

Analysis

Participants of Groups 1 and 2 clustered their individual thoughts written down on note cards. Five affinities each emerged from the discussions in both groups. Inductive coding and axial coding outputs for Group 1 and Group 2 are presented in Table 16.1a and Table 16.1b respectively:

Table 16.1a Summary of Group 1 Focus Group Discussion

Inductive coding output	Axial coding output
Mother tongue, foreign language, local language, official language, language-based clusters	Language
Diversity culture, move out of comfort zone, break stereotypes, work culture, mindset, varied thoughts	Culture
Adaptability, friendly work environment, recognition of different others, cohesive support systems, makes people more tolerant, facilitates open work culture, learn to become unbiased, positive attitude, motivates learning new things, open-mindedness, facilitates exposure and education, broadens perspectives, generates new ideas	Diversity affecting employee well-being
Gender, mother tongue, marital status, age, religion, caste, physically challenged	Types of diversity
Area of interest, personality, personal well-being, leverage diverse knowledge and educational backgrounds	Need for uniqueness

Table 16.1b Summary of Group 2 Focus Group Discussion

Inductive coding output	Axial coding output
Cultural background, upbringing, varied life experiences, culture of different states, festivals celebration, food habits	Culture
Common language, regional language, accent	Language
Gender diversity, millennials and other generations, cross-department diversity, native, region, attitude, skillset	Diversity types
Rewards and recognitions, transparency, organizational support to the family, ethics, career growth, fair salary structure, workplace safety, cordial relationships, and challenging work	Factors influencing employee well-being
Good and bad learning experiences, professional attitude, enables growth and learning, new techniques and thinking, varied experiences, develop self-confidence, physical and mental strength	Diversity influencing well-being

After the IQA process, the following steps comprise the analysis—

1. *Creating a group composite*: Group composite represents the group's consensus on the analysis of relationships. Towards this, we used the statistical method of *Pareto principle*, which states that 20% (or 30%) of the variables in a system account for 80% (or 70%) of the total variation in the outcomes. To create a statistical group composite, we crafted the Pareto cumulative frequency chart.

The Pareto composite requires determining the frequency of each relationship and recording on a Microsoft Excel spreadsheet by tallying all the relationships from the affinity relationship tables. Subsequently, the relationships were sorted in descending order, and cumulative percentages were calculated for each relationship. Cumulative frequencies help in determining the optimal number of relationships comprising the composite system and resolving ambiguous relationships (relationships that attract votes in either direction). Finally, the Pareto chart was constructed (Figures 16.2a and 16.2b). For Group 1, power (24.04) reached a maximum at the ninth relationship, accounting for 69.04% of the variation in the outcomes. Likewise, for Group 2, power (24.23) reached a maximum at the ninth relationship, accounting for 69.23% of the variation in the outcomes.

2. *Rationalizing the system*: An interrelationship diagram (IRD) is a matrix containing all the perceived relationships in the system. The IRD displays arrows demonstrating whether each affinity in a pair is perceived as a cause or an effect, or no relationship. Arrows either point to the left or

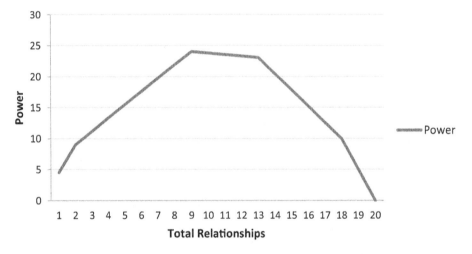

Figure 16.2a Power analysis of Group 1

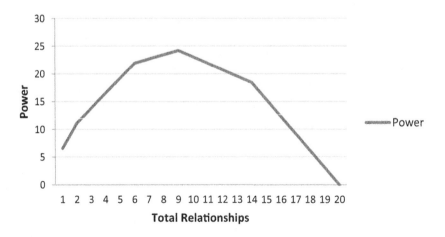

Figure 16.2b Power analysis of Group 2

Diversity and Well-Being

up, and each relationship is recorded twice in the IRD. For instance, if a relationship was determined between 2 and 1, it might be noted as 2 ← 1 and read as *1 influences 2*. Two arrows will be indicated in the IRD representing this relationship. The number of up arrows (↑) is referred to as *Outs* while the number of left arrows (←) is referred to as *Ins*. Subtracting the number of *Ins* from the *Outs* determines the (Δ) *deltas*. Finally, the table is sorted in the descending order of deltas.

Delta values mark the relative position of an affinity within the system. Affinities with positive deltas are considered as drivers or causes, while those with negative deltas are considered as effects or outcomes. An affinity with a high positive delta resulting from many Outs but no Ins is called a *Primary Driver*. The *Secondary Driver* is identified with more Outs than Ins. If an affinity has an equal number of Ins and Outs, it is a *pivot* in the final representation of the system. Likewise, when there are more Ins than Outs, the affinity is a *Secondary Outcome*, while an affinity with a high negative number resulting from many Ins but no Outs is a *Primary Outcome*. Tables 16.2a and 16.2b demonstrate the interrelationship diagrams for Group 1 and Group 2 respectively.

3. *System influence diagram (SID)*: SID is an illustration of the mind map developed from the data in the interrelationship diagram. Graphic representation highlights the relationships among affinities that may be accountable for the dynamics of the system. The first version of the system influence diagram called cluttered SID contains all of the links identified by participants leading to the interrelationship diagram. Figures 16.3a and 16.3b demonstrate the cluttered system influence diagrams for Groups 1 and 2 respectively.

Since a cluttered SID is difficult to interpret, redundant links are removed to obtain an uncluttered or clean SID. For instance, if A → C and A → B → C are the two links in a cluttered SID, in an uncluttered SID, we remove the A → C direct link, as it is deemed redundant. Thus, we achieve

Table 16.2a Interrelationship Diagram for Group 1

Axial coding output		1	2	3	4	5	Out	In	Δ	Driver/Outcome
Language	1	-	↑	↑	-	-	2	0	2	Primary Driver
Culture	2	←	-	↑	↑	↑	3	1	2	Secondary Driver
Types of diversity	4	-	←	↑	-	↑	2	1	1	Secondary Driver
Need for uniqueness	5	-	←	↑	←	-	1	2	-1	Secondary Outcome
Diversity affecting employee well-being	3	←	←	-	←	←	0	4		Primary Outcome

Table 16.2b Interrelationship Diagram for Group 2

Axial coding output		1	2	3	4	5	Out	In	Δ	Driver/Outcome
Culture	1	-	↑	↑	↑	↑	4	0	4	Primary Driver
Language	2	←	-	-	↑	↑	2	1	1	Secondary Driver
Diversity types	3	←	-	-	↑	-	1	1	0	Secondary Driver
Factors influencing employee well-being	4	←	←	←	-	↑	1	3	-2	Secondary Outcome
Diversity influencing well-being	5	←	←	-	←	-	0	3	-3	Primary Outcome

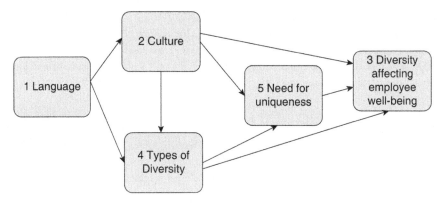

Figure 16.3a Cluttered system influence diagram for Group 1

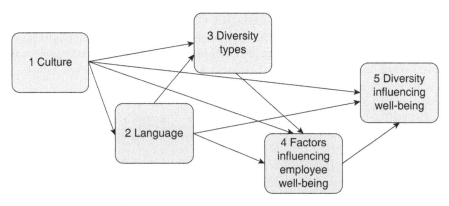

Figure 16.3b Cluttered system influence diagram for Group 2

a simpler model having an optimum explanatory power. Figure 16.4 demonstrates the clean system influence diagrams for Groups 1 and 2 respectively.

Emerging Perspectives

The present study that aimed to delve into how diversity relates to employee well-being unraveled some important aspects. Since the extant literature is highly West-centric, some indigenous aspects emerged from the interactive qualitative analysis process such as the nature of a diverse Indian workforce, what entails employee well-being, and how diversity relates to employee affective experiences. Next we discuss some insights drawn from the relationships derived from the IQA process.

> *Culture ↔ Language*: Although it was noted that language and culture emerged as two affinities in both the groups, language caused culture only in one group. After closer examination of how the two groups had characterized language and culture, the language seemed to refer to mother tongue, local/regional language, or official language with linguistic clusters in organizations. The junior employees group referred to culture as an amalgamation of cultural differences in states, varied backgrounds, upbringing, life experiences, festivals, and food. Regional/

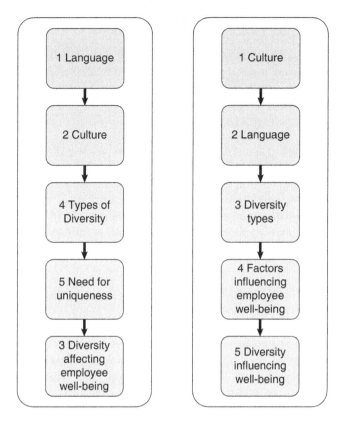

Figure 16.4 Uncluttered system influence diagrams for Groups 1 and 2

native language emerged as a salient marker of cultural diversity among Indian employees. India has 23 officially recognized languages (Census of India, 2011), and most state boundaries have been organized based on linguistic differences. Language-based clusters deep-rooted in cultural differences are often evidenced in organizations.

The senior managers group referred to language playing a pivotal role in the formation of an organizational culture of diversity in order to reap the potential benefits of diversity. This culture referred to overcoming prejudices, biases, and stereotypes, accepting and valuing varied thoughts, perspectives, and mindsets, and building an open and cohesive culture. This consideration perhaps could be owing to challenges experienced in dealing with unfamiliar native languages spoken at the workplace. Organizations seek improved functional efficiency through a standardized official working language in order to provide a common platform by integrating diverse organizational members. Although English is widely spoken at most workplaces in India, communication in English is not strictly followed. Critical information, ideas, and resources unique to employees may not always be translatable in a common language. While it is easier to express oneself in their native language, language can become a basis for divisions. Even momentary swapping of language was noted to divide and create feelings of dissimilarity among multilingual employees (Kulkarni, 2015). Thus, it is imperative for organizations to develop language-related policies in order to develop a close-knit organizational membership.

Culture/Language → Diversity types: Several characteristics form the basis of dissimilarity among Indian employees which have not been examined in other cultural contexts. Besides culture and language, the diversity attribute that was commonly and spontaneously alluded to in both groups was *gender*. Participants also mentioned generational, religious, regional, caste, marital status, and disability diversity. Cultural differences with respect to language, food habits, celebration of festivals, and regional uniqueness surfaced as markers of dissimilarity. Besides these demographic diversity attributes, diversity based on attitude, skillsets, and functional background emerged as salient in the Indian context.

Diversity types → Need for uniqueness: While people may be different or dissimilar based on demographics, knowledge levels, or personalities, organizations seek cohesion and social integration towards effective organizational functioning. In addition, individuals have a fundamental need to maintain good and stable interpersonal relationships, identify with certain social groups, and seek acceptance from others in the group. Nevertheless, the need for uniqueness is a remarkable aspect that arose from the interactive qualitative analysis process. Inclusion is a key component of diversity training and programs. Rather, inclusion is deemed to be the most critical component of diversity culture (Shore et al., 2011). India is a collectivistic country where the sense of belongingness, cohesion, and integration form the basis of social functioning. However, it was noteworthy that Indian employees voiced their need to maintain a unique identity, differentiated sense of self, and individual distinctiveness. It was noted that an individual's uniqueness based on differences in demographics, personality, educational backgrounds, or areas of interest must be identified and leveraged upon in a diverse work environment.

Diversity → Employee well-being: Some of the key determinants of well-being in Indian organizations as reported by the participants included aspects such as rewards and recognition, fair and transparent systems, organizational support to the family, avenues for career growth and development, workplace safety, cordial relationships, and challenging work. While these factors may significantly contribute to the well-being of employees, types of diversity will also contribute to their well-being. This is because employees seek fairness and transparency in all human resource practices regardless of their diversity characteristic. Employees want equitable treatment with respect to practices such as pay, promotion, opportunities for development, and inclusion in decision-making, notwithstanding their categorical differences such as those based on gender, age, first language, or religion. This relationship signifies a level playing field among organizational members. Diversity has the potential to enhance learning experiences, sharing of varied thoughts and techniques, generation of new ideas, and broadening of perspectives. As expressed by the participants, diversity will boost self-confidence and mental strength of employees through the building of positive and professional attitude, increased recognition of different others, and tolerance among organizational members.

The Road Ahead

The business case for diversity purports that a diverse workforce will deliver positive outcomes such as improved performance and creativity. This line of thought comes with a caveat that workforce diversity will deliver benefits *only* if it is effectively managed (Jaiswal & Dyaram, 2019). Extant literature is rife with evidence indicating a negative impact of diversity on commitment, satisfaction, and even performance. Thus, effective diversity management is the key to leveraging the potential benefits of diversity. This is easier said than done. Professionals championing the diversity management agenda face an uphill task of managing its complex and dynamic components: diversity paradigms, policies, programs, practices, and climate (Kulik, 2014).

The present study participants shared their interpretations of diversity and its influence on employee affect. Kulik (2014) refers to this shared perception as a *diversity climate*, which is the lowest component of the diversity management system of an organization. The group comprising senior-level managers expressed *diversity practices* through their experiences reflecting the organization's diversity management programs. However, these experiences may not necessarily be consistent with the spirit of the *diversity program*. Senior manager groups' need for identity and uniqueness emerging as a striking aspect of the analysis, indicates a gap between the diversity program and practice. This implies that managers need to clearly specify *diversity policies* for managing diversity alongside lucid *diversity paradigms* about how diversity should be managed in organizations. Study participants indicated several aspects influencing the diversity well-being relationship such as fair and transparent systems, avenues to share varied thoughts, enhanced tolerance, and acceptance of different others. We believe that these factors will draw favorable results only when diversity climate, practices, programs, policies, and paradigms, i.e. the diversity management system, is seamlessly integrated.

While the present study was limited to focus group discussions, there is scope for further work to strengthen the findings. Interactive qualitative analysis is a systems approach to qualitative research with the primary purpose of demonstrating a phenomenon through its affinities and the relationships among those affinities. The aim of the focus group is to inform and shape questions for deeper exploration. Hence, the protocol of the in-depth interview is determined by the affinities emerging out of the focus group. Interview participants are first asked to define the affinities and then reflect on the perceived cause-and-effect relationships that emerged from the researcher's analysis. Thus, conducting rigorous and systematic one-to-one interviews with the focus group participants is the next logical step towards enhancing the robustness of the findings of the present study.

Final Comments

Owing to increasing caution regarding the universal applicability of Western conceptualizations and findings, the present study began a systematic investigation of how diversity relates to employee well-being in India, thus contributing to indigenous scholarship. Extant literature highlights several paradigms of diversity such as social and occupational equality, the business case for diversity, or value-in-diversity perspectives. However, scholarly work is rampant with equivocal findings on the effects of diversity. The purpose of this chapter was to explore diversity effects in the Indian context using interactive qualitative analysis as the research design. Employing a systems approach to qualitative research, the study construed the diversity and well-being phenomenon culminating into a mind map of how diversity relates to employee well-being among Indian employees. While the study has initiated the development of indigenous knowledge for diversity management, much scholarly work in this direction is needed, to generate contextualized understanding to inform theory and practice.

References

Byrne, D. E. (1971). *The attraction paradigm.* New York, NY: Academic Press.
Census of India. (2011). *Office of the registrar general & census commissioner.* Ministry of Home Affairs, Government of India.
Cox, T. H., & Blake, S. (1991). Managing cultural diversity: Implications for organizational competitiveness. *Academy of Management Executive, 5*(3), 45–56. http://doi.org/10.5465/AME.1991.4274465
Das, S. K. (2014). Governing cultural diversity and the question of well-being in India. *Indo-Swiss 2014 Seminar,* 1–5. http://doi.org/10.1093/0198288352.001.0001
Daya, P. (2014). Diversity and inclusion in an emerging market context. *Equality, Diversity, and Inclusion: An International Journal, 33,* 293–308. http://doi.org/10.1108/EDI-10-2012-0087
Findler, L., Wind, L., & Mor Barak, M. E. (2007). The challenge of workforce management in a global society: Modeling the relationship between diversity, inclusion, organizational culture, and employee well-being, job satisfaction and organizational commitment. *Administration in Social Work, 31*(3), 63–94. http://doi.org/10.1300/J147v31n03

Guillaume, Y. R. F., Brodbeck, F. C., & Riketta, M. (2012). Surface- and deep-level dissimilarity effects on social integration and individual effectiveness related outcomes in work groups: A meta-analytic integration. *Journal of Occupational and Organizational Psychology, 85*(1), 80–115. http://doi.org/10.1111/j.2044-8325.2010.02005.x

Guillaume, Y. R. F., Dawson, J. F., Priola, V., Sacramento, C. A., Woods, S. A., Higson, H. E., ... West, M. A. (2014). Managing diversity in organizations: An integrative model and agenda for future research. *European Journal of Work and Organizational Psychology, 23*(5), 783–802. http://doi.org/10.1080/1359432X.2013.805485

Jackson, S. E., & Joshi, A. (2004). Diversity in social context: A multi-attribute, multilevel analysis of team diversity and sales performance. *Journal of Organizational Behavior, 25*, 675–702.

Jackson, S. E., Joshi, A., & Erhardt, N. (2003). Recent research on team and organizational diversity: SWOT analysis and implications. *Journal of Management, 29*(6), 801–830. http://doi.org/10.1016/S0149-2063

Jackson, S. E., May, K. E., & Whitney, K. (1995). Understanding the dynamics of diversity in decision-making teams. In R. A. Guzzo & E. Salas (Eds.), *Team effectiveness and decision making in organizations* (pp. 204–261). San Francisco, CA: Jossey-Bass.

Jaiswal, A., & Dyaram, L. (2019). Towards well-being: Role of diversity and nature of work. *Employee Relations, 41*(1), 158–175. http://doi.org/10.1108/ER-11-2017-0279

Joshi, A., & Roh, H. (2009). The role of context in work team diversity research: A meta-analytic review. *Academy of Management Journal, 52*(3), 599–627. http://doi.org/10.5465/AMJ.2009.41331491

Kulik, C. (2014). Working below and above the line: The research-practice gap in diversity management. *Human Resource Management Journal, 24*(2), 129–144.

Kulkarni, M. (2015). Language-based diversity and faultlines in organizations. *Journal of Organizational Behavior, 36*(1), 128–146. http://doi.org/10.1002/job

Kunze, F., Boehm, S. A., & Bruch, H. (2011). Age diversity, age discrimination climate and performance consequences: A cross-organizational study. *Journal of Organizational Behavior, 32*, 264–290. http://doi.org/10.1002/job

Mannix, E., & Neale, M. A. (2005). What differences make a difference? The promise and reality of diverse teams in organizations. *Psychological Science in the Public Interest, 6*(2), 31–55.

Milliken, F. J., & Martins, L. L. (1996). Searching for common threads: Understanding the multiple effects of diversity in organizational groups. *Academy of Management Review, 21*(2), 402–433. http://doi.org/10.2307/258667

Ng, Y-K. (2015). *Happiness, life satisfaction, or subjective well-being? A measurement and moral philosophical approach.* Working paper, Nanyang Technological University, Singapore.

Northcutt, N., & McCoy, D. (2004). *Interactive qualitative analysis: A systems method for qualitative research.* Thousand Oaks, CA: Sage.

Pelled, L. H. (1996). Demographic diversity, conflict, and work group outcomes: An intervening process theory. *Organization Science, 7*(6), 615–631.

Phillips, K. W., & Loyd, D. L. (2006). When surface and deep-level diversity collide: The effects on dissenting group members. *Organizational Behavior and Human Decision Processes, 99*(2), 143–160. http://doi.org/10.1016/j.obhdp.2005.12.001

Shore, L. M., Randel, A. E., Chung, B. G., Dean, M. A., Holcombe Ehrhart, K., & Singh, G. (2011). Inclusion and diversity in work groups: A review and model for future research. *Journal of Management, 37*(4), 1262–1289. http://doi.org/10.1177/0149206310385943

Tajfel, H., Billig, M. G., & Bundy, R. P. (1971). Social categorization and intergroup behavior. *European Journal of Social Psychology, 1*(2), 149–178.

Webber, S. S., & Donahue, L. M. (2001). Impact of highly and less job-related diversity on work group cohesion and performance: A meta-analysis. *Journal of Management, 27*, 141–162.

Williams, K. Y., & O'Reilly, C. A. I. (1998). Demography and diversity in organizations: A review of 40 years of research. *Research in Organizational Behavior, 20*, 77–140.

17
TRANSITION FROM DIVERSITY TO INCLUSION
Auditing the Pulse From an Indian Perspective

Aneesya Panicker and Rakesh Kumar Agrawal

Introduction

Globalization has posed no alternative for today's organizations but to pay heed to the incessant market demands. Organizations of today are required to be agile and revamp themselves as per technological advancement and customer needs. Diverse and inclusive workplaces help businesses reap the benefit of innovation, improved bottom lines and access to diverse talent. Thus, embracing and fostering the diverse traits of the workforce has emerged as one of the top priorities for leaders. Diversity management has evolved from being a mere legal compliance to an indispensable business strategy. Research studies in the field of workplace diversity have suggested that organizations with a diversified workforce perform better than organizations with a homogeneous workforce. Implicit bias, cross-cultural barriers and lack of prospects for growth and advancement are some of the major challenges faced by organizations managing, engaging and retaining the diverse workforce. Since 1950, organizations, ranging from public to private enterprise, academic institutions to government organizations, have assimilated diversity awareness programs in their human resource practices to avoid lawsuits and ensure organizational success and transformation.

Contemporary organizations have to ponder the developing trend of multiculturalism, which includes understanding the perceptions of employees towards the degree of prejudice and discrimination, equality in the reward management system, equal access to significant information and justifiable prospects for career advancement (Comer & Soliman, 1996). An organization's diversity consciousness adds increases its pace in this area, yet not much research exists that appraises diversity for developing training interventions (Dahm, 2003). The work of E. Miller in 1994 revealed that the very few organizations that have attempted to train and educate diversified workforce have ignored the human element in terms of behavior and developing the human capital needs and motivation level of employees.

As we observe, the future of diversity is in a transition stage across our country and the world, thus we have to acknowledge that priorities may change from one organization to another. Nonetheless, inclusion will always take the front seat for both employees and organizations, since inclusion is as indispensable and inevitable as diversity in today's globalized world. Workplace inclusion is the hidden asset and the goal is use it as a tool for organizational success.

Over the years, primacies for workplace diversity and inclusion have been changing for every organization, company, academic institution, community and individual specifically with respect to their geographical location or the year of establishment. Hitherto, many organizations and certain select group members are wrestling with the issues of equality, affiliation, growth and above all retention of a diversified workforce. Over the years, landmarks reflect the treads and brawls of advancement and acceptability of the concept diversity and inclusion at the workplace. Considering the brawls and transition, diversity can present many opportunities and benefits to the organizations, but not without inclusion. That is, mere diversity will not reap real benefits until and unless it is mixed with inclusion. Success lies in how well we are establishing and balancing the mix. Thus, the bottom line is that organizations must move from diversity to inclusion through diverse leadership (McKinsey, 2018). In fact, diversity and inclusion are integral parts of organizational culture which foster innovative idea generation, enhanced financial performance and a contented workforce. As diversity brings in other perspectives, inclusion empowers employees to give voice to their opinions, so as to nurture and bring prosperity at workplace.

The word 'diversity' at the workplace stirs up a range of feelings, in fact mixed emotions; people either accept diversity or reject it, irrespective of its adverse effects on them or others. Further, regular assessment of employee attitude and perception towards issues related to diversity has become a stepping-stone in organizational success (Erasmus, 2008). But the topic which often arises from the conversation is workforce inclusion, the better half of diversity, a necessity leading to organizational effectiveness and success. Despite its similarity, the concept of workplace inclusion is different from diversity. On one hand, diversity at the workplace refers to "situations that germinate when employees differ in terms of age, gender, ethnicity, education etc." (Mor Barak, 2005). These dimensions of diversity present an affirmative basis for the social categorization of Indian society (Shenoy-Packer & Myers, 2013). On the other hand, inclusion at the workplace means eliminating the barriers and fostering an inclusive environment for its employees, where every individual has equal rights to participate in the organization's decision-making process and advance organizational success.

Managing diversity at national and international levels has been examined in a significant number of research studies, specifically in the context of the United States and Europe (Ferner, Almond, & Colling, 2005; Sippola & Smale, 2007). However, very few studies have explored the integration of workplace diversity and inclusion with strategic human resource management, and even fewer in the less-developed regions of Asia, which encompass a rich cultural and historical heritage (Cooke & Saini, 2010; Syed & Özbilgin, 2009). In this chapter, we first elucidate the concept of diversity and inclusion. This is followed by an outline of the literature on diversity and inclusion. After outlining the categories that affect diversity and inclusion programs in India, we finally mull over the various issues leading to the journey of diversity and inclusion programs, especially in the Indian scenario.

Conceptualizing Diversity and Inclusion

Expanding workforce diversity in India Inc. was an urgency created by globalization. The 1991 balance of a payment crisis led to a multitude of structural reforms popularly known as liberalization, privatization and globalization (LPG). According to an IMF report, "India's economy is set to grow at 7.0 percent in 2019, picking up to 7.2 percent in 2020" (Business Standard, July 23, 2019). As a result, the Indian economy is the seventh largest growing economy in the world today with a GDP growth rate of 7.0% (Asian Development Bank. Asian Development Outlook, 2019). It stands second in Asia in 2019.

Globalization, in the last 28 years or so, has been linked to intra-industry and intermediate goods trade and greater global competition. With the expansion of the customer base, large-scale employment opportunities are mushrooming. India has a very large pool of an English-speaking and scientifically and technically sound HR base. Because of this, even youngsters and recent graduates are finding gainful employment. Most of the professionally qualified Indian women are at par with any women in the world, and they are employed in a multitude of occupations like nursing, teaching, medicine, science, and even as airplane pilots and bus conductors.

One of the highlights of globalization across the world was the migration of workforces, which created the need for rational strategies and development of approaches to facilitate harmonious relationships in a diversified workplace. This was necessary, since workforce diversity is critical for the growth and expansion of organizations along with a stimulating, conducive work environment for all (Hansen, 2003). Past studies on diversity mainly centered on the problem areas concerning diversity, like bias, discrimination, tokenism and affirmative behavior (Shore et al., 2009). The field of diversity is now attracting researchers and scholars to work on various strategies and ways through which synergy can be obtained by integrating the diverse individuals in the organization as well as enhancing the work mechanism and organizational processes (Thomas & Ely, 1996; Homan et al., 2008; Gonzalez & DeNisi, 2009).

Another research stream evolving along this line is integrating diverse individuals with a feeling of inclusion by creating and developing a conducive and cooperative work environment (Roberson, 2006; Bilimoria, Joy, & Liang, 2008). Inclusion, as a concept, is of recent origin. It has marked its place in the organizational literature over the last decade (Roberson, 2006). This concept, however, lacks consensus, because of which inclusion's utility is hampered on practical as well as theoretical ground.

Diversity: Uniqueness in Differences Matter

When employees work together for a common goal, there exist various factors within the work environment that lead them to incline towards a similar group—the insiders (Lefkowitz, 1994)—and less towards outsiders, especially if they assume the outsiders might harm them negatively (Bowen & Blackmon, 2003). If this feeling prevails in a workforce, the diversity strategies in that organization are likely to fail. The applicability of diversity programs by employers also depend on the existing organization's performance as well as awareness about situations and circumstances, since these factors predict the way employees are going to receive this program. Companies that are going for downscaling usually face resistance when introducing diversity programs, while those that are experiencing growth and expansion will monitor minimal resistance for these new diversity programs. While fostering programs on diversity, an enterprise must work in association with prevalent labor laws and as per the ethical standards of the industry and nation. Timely evaluation and integrated feedback facilitates the success of implementation process.

Inclusion: State of the Art

Inclusion is considered a separate field of study, and many researchers have talked about it as the working environment prevailing in the organization that stimulates employees to interpret work-related information (Mowday & Sutton, 1993; Weick, 1979; Bilimoria et al., 2008). Although inclusion is an integral part of diversity acceptance and has to be built on sound moral grounds (Pless & Maak, 2004), it was found that there exists a considerable amount of inconsistency among researchers with respect to the definition of inclusion. Inclusion is about the way an employee's diversity is being acknowledged as a part of a whole working system by others. It is about how the social identity of groups is formed. Providing equal opportunity to be heard and appreciating employees' contributions by removing obstacles for full participation thereby establishes a sense of belongingness, and exhibiting inclusive behavior entails eliciting and valuing contributions from all employees (Holvino, Ferdman, & Merrill-Sands, 2004; Roberson, 2006).

Measuring inclusion unveils not only the "what" but also the "why" about organizational culture. Inclusion satisfies the need for belongingness and uniqueness of a member of the work group. Pelled, Ledford, and Mohrman (1999, p. 1014) defined inclusion as "the degree to which an employee is accepted and treated as an insider by others in a work system." They said the there are three important indicators of inclusion: first, to be able to influence decisions; second, accessibility towards work-related facts; and third, job stability. Result of this work laid emphasis on the positive association of dissimilarity of tenure and education and the negative association of dissimilarity of race and gender on these indicators.

Framework of Inclusion

The framework as proposed by Shore et al. (2011) signifies that to create feelings of inclusion, uniqueness and belongingness should work together. Belongingness facilitates the acceptability of an individual in the group while uniqueness provides opportunities to improve group performance. In the framework, "Inclusion" refers to a high level of both belongingness and uniqueness. There is evidence in support of advantages of belongingness and uniqueness in the diversity literature; for example, unique minority members with good networks and contacts revealed a high level of career opportunities and advancements (Friedman, Kane, & Cornfield, 1998).

The opposite end of the spectrum is labeled as "Exclusion," which represents the amalgamation of low uniqueness and low belongingness. In this situation, an individual because of lack of uniqueness is not treated as an insider, but other employees are considered insiders. This leads to harmful emotional, cognitive, psychological and physiological results (Baumeister, DeWall, Ciarocco, & Twenge, 2005; Blackhart, Nelson, Knowles, & Baumeister, 2009; DeWall, Maner, & Rouby, 2009). In the opinion of Hitlan, Clifton, and DeSoto (2006), workplace rejection, especially by peers and the boss, have a higher detrimental effect on the work attitude and psychology of men than women.

"Differentiation" refers to low belongingness and a high level of uniqueness. Work groups with these perspectives value diversity at a superficial level. They consider it as a means to attain a specific marketplace, leading to a feeling of isolation among minority group members as a result of racial and ethnic discrimination (Ely & Thomas, 2001). Organizations make use of this differentiation by hiring diverse, highly talented and competent individuals so as to cater to specific organizational issues by offering them permanent employment (Riley & Buckley, 2008).

Opposite to Differentiation is "Assimilation," which is the amalgamation of low uniqueness and high belongingness. In this situation, individuals are treated as insiders because they conform to the dominant cultural norms.

	Low Belongingness	High Belongingness
Low in Uniqueness	**Exclusion** Individual is not treated as an Organizational insider with unique value in the work group but there are other employees or groups who are Insiders	**Assimilation** Individual is treated as an insider in the work group when they conform to organizational/dominant culture norms and downplay uniqueness.
High in Uniqueness	**Differentiation** Individual is not treated as an Organizational insider in the work group but their unique characteristics are seen as valuable and required for group/organization success.	**Inclusion** Individual is treated as an insider and also allowed/encouraged to retain uniqueness

Figure 17.1 Workplace inclusion framework
Source: Shore et al., 2011, p. 1266

Relevance of Diversity and Inclusion in Indian Context

India is a culturally diversified country rich in customs and a civilization which has a glorious heritage of more than 5,000 years. Its unity in diversity embraces a variety of cultures, traditions, customs and languages. India is the seventh largest country in the world in area and the second largest in terms of population (World Atlas, June 6, 2019). In terms of religious orientation, Hindus comprise 79.80% of the population, Muslims 14.23%, Christians 2.30%, Sikhs 1.72%, Buddhists 0.70%, Jains 0.37% and Adivasi 0.90% (Census, 2011). All five major ethnic groups find are represented in India's population, namely Australoid, Mongoloid, Europoid, Caucasian, and Negroid (Ministry of Environment, NITI Aayog, Ministry of Health, Press Information Bureau, Census of India, Ministry of External Affairs, Union Budget, Reserve Bank of India). There are 450 ethno-linguistic variations and over 2,295 ethnic groups in terms of caste, religion and culture. The prime working age is above 15 years and the labor force participation rate (LFPR) stood at 49.8% in 2017–18 (Economic Times, February 4, 2019). The present working population constitutes about 35.4% of the total population, which is expected to increase to 63.9% around 2020. This expansion of diversity in all spheres ranging from age, education, sex, caste, birthplace, language, ethnicity and race puts immense pressure on employers of India to arrange, compete and develop the requisite skills among the employees.

Diversity Dimensions and Organizational Challenges in Indian Context

India is a multicultural and multidimensional society and one of the most diverse nations in the world (Sowell, 2002). Historically, India is a proud country with diversified cultures, traditions, religious orientation, languages, caste, creed, identities and financial status. Remarkably, our Indian mythologies also celebrate liberal instances of homosexuality. Our ancient temples and monuments, constructed between the 6th and 14th centuries, show explicit examples of unconventional couples. Later in the 19th century, the Britain's archaic Victorian rule laid down Section 377 which criminalized homosexuality; this was denounced in 2018. This law led to deteriorating outlooks and non-acceptance of the LGBTQ community in India. Sociocultural and demographic factors represent its diversity dimensions. India's demographic and sociocultural diversity dimensions are classified into four categories, namely deep, partially deep, visible and partially visible (Harrison, Price, & Bell, 1998). Another way of categorization is deep-level and surface-level diversity. Deep-level diversity comprises vague characteristics that cannot be perceived directly, like sexual orientation, caste, etc. Whereas surface-level diversity refers to the manifest biological traits that are overtly visible, like physical features (Mor Barak et al., 2016).

Sex, age and physical disability are the visible or demographic dimensions of diversity. Religious orientation, place of birth, ethnicity, experience and sexual orientation are the partially visible or sociocultural dimensions of diversity (see Figure 17.2). Among the various dimensions of diversity discussed in the previous paragraph, the most significant dimensions in the context of Indian organization are gender, place of origin (region), religious orientation, language, ethnic background, socioeconomic status, caste and food habits. Thus, in order to build a culture receptive to diversity, an organization must build sensitivity towards local norms and traditions, recognize and appreciate the 'hidden' dimensions of diversity and combine them with broad organizational values. Both visible and invisible dimensions of diversity result in positive outcomes, such as organizational commitment, satisfaction with the job and coworkers, and an intention to stay with the organization, and negative outcomes, such as interpersonal conflict and an intention to quit (Mor Barak et al., 2016).

Every dimension has a significant impact on the individuality, work values, work style and behavior of individuals at their workplace and pose various challenges to the organization. Organizations that address these challenges with appropriate diversity management practices and policies foster inclusion among the diverse workforce that makes them able to survive in this competitive era. A summary of the diversity dimensions and organizational challenges in the Indian context are presented in Table 17.1.

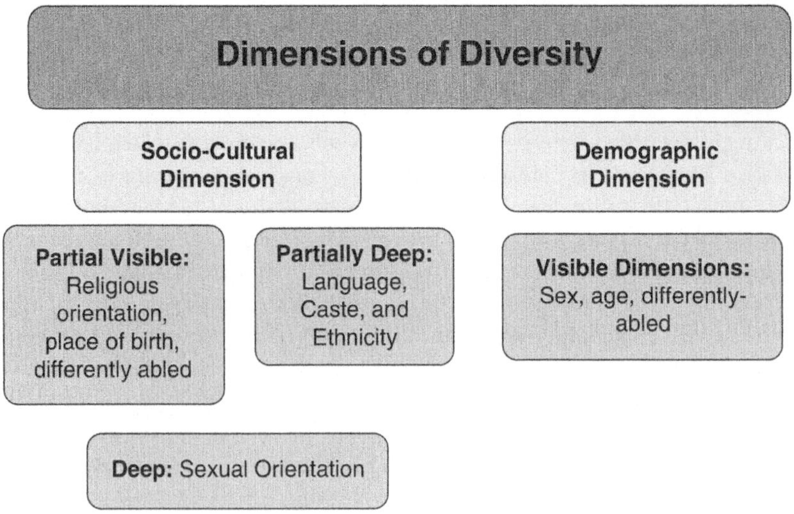

Dimensions of Diversity

Socio-Cultural Dimension
- **Partial Visible:** Religious orientation, place of birth, differently abled
- **Partially Deep:** Language, Caste, and Ethnicity
- **Deep:** Sexual Orientation

Demographic Dimension
- **Visible Dimensions:** Sex, age, differently-abled

Figure 17.2 Dimensions of diversity in an Indian context

Table 17.1 Diversity dimensions and Organizational Challenges in Indian Context

Diversity Dimensions	Organizational Challenges in Indian Context
The socio-cultural dimension of diversity	
Caste	Caste-based Nepotism
	Discriminatory advantages for high caste people
	Discriminatory disadvantages for low caste people
	Discrimination on the basis of Stereotypes
Religious orientation	Organizational culture and work behavior
	Management philosophy, policy and decision making
	Direct and Indirect discrimination
	Religious Stereotypes
	Employee Harassment- calling names, religious jokes etc
Language	For informal communication use of mother tongue leading to barriers in relationship building and communication among various groups
Demographic dimensions of diversity	
Sex	Glass ceiling Work-life balance issues
	Role stereotypes
	Gender stereotypes
	Inequity in pay and career progression
	Harassment
Age	Differences in work values and work- styles among various dimensions
	Challenges of Generation-Y
	Age stereotypes
Place of birth	Favoritism on the basis of regional identity Discrimination on the basis of place of origin Cultural shock leading to the acceptability of people from different regions Prejudice on the basis of cultural stereotypes
Physical disability	Physical facilities and infrastructure for differently-abled peoples
	Stereotypes on the basis of physical disability
	Underestimating their potential
	Belief and attitude of colleagues and seniors towards them
Sexual orientation	Taboo in the Indian context
	Non-acceptability of their identity by family values and religious values
	Discrimination on the basis of sexual orientation
	Bullying at workplace

Source: Meena, K. (2015). Diversity Dimensions of India and Their Organization Implications: An Analysis. *International Journal of Economics and Management Sciences*, 4, 261.

Along this line, the following paragraphs will elucidate how inclusion is and can be managed in India. The point is to treat the categories discussed as an asset through inclusion:

Categories to Be Considered During Diversity and Inclusion Programs

I. Categories Identified by the Indian Constitution

- *Schedule Caste (SC)/Schedule Tribe (ST)/Other Backward Class (OBC)*
  Articles 16(4) and 335 of the Indian Constitution govern the entire reservation of appointments and posts of this section of the population so as to protect them from social injustice and all types of exploitation. While Articles 341 and 342 of the Constitution defines the meaning of Scheduled Castes and Scheduled Tribes with respect to any State or Union Territory (DoPT, Chapter VI).

- *Immigrants*
  In India, the law and provisions relating to nationality or citizenship of people is majorly governed by the Constitution of India. Part II of the Constitution of India contains provisions related to immigration in Articles 5 to 11. The Immigrants (Expulsion from Assam) Act and The Immigration (Carriers' Liability) Act, 2000 govern immigration law in India.

- *Ex-Defense Personnel, Ex-Servicemen and Parliamentary Personnel*
  The Government of India has made certain provisions in the form of concessions to senior citizens worked in the defense forces and parliament. Retired defense and parliament personnel are eligible for special cost benefits in the areas of housing facility, health, travel, reemployment and pension facility. Further, a specific percentage of posts in government jobs are specially allotted to ex-defense personnel. The central government has reserved 10% of posts in the Group "C" category and 20% in the Group "D" category for ex-servicemen. In case of public sector units and nationalized banks, the reservation is 14.5% in Group "C" and 24% in Group "D," and 10% of the assistant commandant posts are reserved in the paramilitary forces for ex-servicemen (National Portal of India).

- *Differently Abled Personnel*
  The Personnel with Disabilities Rules of 1996 made by the Government of India cover aspects related to equal opportunities, protection of rights and full participation. The term "differently abled" personnel refer to "physically challenged" or "mentally challenged" persons. The Government of India under the flagship of Department of Empowerment of Persons with Disability, in the Ministry of social Justice and Empowerment also provide "Unique Disability ID" to such individuals. By means of these IDs, such individuals can avail various benefits sanctioned by the government.

- *Displaced Personnel*
  Factors triggering displacement of individuals in India are development projects, political clash, establishing protected area networks and conservation areas, natural calamities and other such situations. The Government of India has framed rehabilitation policies for such individuals.

II. Categories Identified by India Inc.

- *The partially and differently abled group*
  This group comprises physically disabled and some visually challenged employees. This is considered as diversity because they can also function perfectly well if just little changes are made. A small change in the infrastructure will help these physically challenged people, like ramps to accommodate wheelchairs, talking elevators, computers with translators of speech and many others.

- *Marital status of employees; no bar*
  It is because of government initiatives through various enactments and company polices that women are breaking through the glass ceiling. The concepts of work from home and flexible work schedules have helped working female professionals balance their work as well as personal life. This flexibility saves costs and time as well. But still today, it is difficult for females to obtain or sustain their job if they declare they are getting married or becoming pregnant. So, these sensitive issues need to be dealt with sensitively.
- *Post-retirement or silver category*
  There is a category of people who want to reenter corporate life because either they need money or they want to utilize their time. In fact the attrition rate of this category of people is much less in comparison with the younger employees
- *Cultural diversity*
  The Indian theme of unity in diversity must be addressed because every culture has some unique traits that can be used for the benefit of the organization.

Diversity and Inclusion Go Hand in Hand!

After reviewing the literature on diversity and inclusion, it is evident that it is next to impossible to think about the success of any diversity program without considering inclusion programs. Inclusion programs here refer to the acceptability of a diverse workforce through their full participation in various organizational activities, ranging from decision-making to its implementation. We have already defined diversity, which means the presence of a heterogeneous workforce in an organization in terms of religion, ethnicity, cultural origin, age, gender, educational background, economic status, etc. Some of the diversity theories and the constructs are associated with the benefits of similarity rather than the uniqueness of the workforce. For example, racial similarity is often associated with a higher level of satisfaction, favoritism during employment interviews and better interpersonal communication and cooperative behavior with reduced conflict and less employee turnover (Tsui, Egan, & O'Reilly, 1992; Wiersema & Bantel, 1992; Riordan & Shore, 1997; Chatman, Polzer, Barsade, & Neale, 1998; Chattopadhyay, 1999; Godthelp & Glunk, 2003; Buckley, Jackson, Bolino, Veres, & Feild, 2007). Gender similarity is also positively associated with trust, enhanced leader-member exchange (LMX), group cohesiveness, feelings of contentment, psychological affection and an intention to stay (Tsui et al., 1992; Mellor, 1995; Pelled & Xin, 2000; Shapcott, Carron, Burke, Bradshaw, & Estabrooks, 2006). To foster inclusion in the perceptions of employees, not only belongingness but also the worth of uniqueness must also be realized. Such perceptions have a positive impact on organizational attitudes and behaviors.

According to Nirmala Menon, CEO of Interweave,

> Inclusion is one way of ensuring your employees are working at their optimum. Since there is a war for talent, you are looking for skills. It is not important anymore in what form, shape, size these come packaged in. So you're getting a very diverse group of people at the workplace.
> *(yourstory.com, June 2012)*

Without inclusion, synergy cannot be obtained from a diverse workforce. It is imperative that members of the diverse group feel accepted by the other group members.

Problems That Companies Face While Tackling Diversity and What Can Be Done for Inclusion

- *Risk and return factor:* The bigger the risk the bigger the return. So it is easier for big companies to accommodate the changes required to bring about diversity than it is for smaller ones.

Diversity requires sensitizing people regarding this through inclusion, which requires altering the infrastructure and making various other changes.
- *Sector or industry differences:* Inclusion classically features on the schema of particular sectors—like the service sector and nursing—where females are more acceptable than are males, but it is not the same in the manufacturing sector, where it is difficult for females and physically challenged people to tackle the physical stress of the job.
- *Differences persevere:* In the previous section, we talked about a partially and differentially abled group. The problem lies with the fact that most of these physically challenged individuals are educated and trained by nongovernmental organizations (NGOs), where they were treated differently. So, they expect the same in a corporate scenario, but it's a normal human tendency to challenge differences.

Organizations must start their diversity efforts with some specific purpose, followed by creating and enhancing a supportive work environment and respecting the organizational values to create a high work-performing culture. This means that from top to bottom, everyone must be involved in the practice. It is important that not only a company's leadership views diversity as a value, but also that everyone sees why it makes a better work environment for employees and a better business environment for customers.

Issues Leading Towards the Journey of Diversity and Inclusion

To extract benefits from this diversity, it becomes a necessity for businesses organizations to develop a strategic competitive business model that ensures compliance with employment laws and regulations but that doesn't increase business risks. This model should respond to economic and social changes, and as such will ensure overall success in business (SHRM, 2008). The cultural background of employees working in organizations with a diversified workforce has a significant impact on their expectations, motivation, morale and satisfaction at large (West & Frances, 2007). People from different national, regional, cultural and social backgrounds with different levels of education, ages, genders and mental and physical abilities positively affect the organizational environment and ensure increased returns on investment based on equal pay, providing opportunities to showcase the talent and motivation of employees (Watson et al., 1993).

The critical issue in today's organizations is that of talent attraction and retention. Organizations that adopt sound diversity management strategies by properly addressing the issues of minority employees can have control over employee turnover, which will not only preserve money but talents too and will enhance the goodwill of the organization in the global as well as domestic market (Richard, 2000). Sustainable competitive advantage can be gained through competent employees who can neither be copied nor obtained by competitors from the labor market. As such, organizations should strive to develop and foster a knowledge-based diverse culture (Sacco & Schmitt, 2003).

Diversity training and development enhance the overall process of diversity management. A culturally diverse environment provides tremendous avenues for growth opportunities for the human resource working in an organization, who are provided with the opportunity to exchange their knowledge and diverse and valuable experiences, which ultimately make them more integrated and committed towards sharing with their subordinates and colleagues. When employees with different backgrounds are acknowledged and included, they tend to solve specific problems with enhanced creativity and innovation (Grimes, 2002). Cross-cultural training enhances the way employees relate with each other and therefore increases team effectiveness. As a result, there is improvement in service and the relationship with customers as well. Training on cross-cultural functioning gained significant impact on contemporary studies because the findings of these works indicate that culturally diversified employees presume conditions and situations differently and they have a very different style of learning as well.

Conclusion

Today, organizations are significantly emphasizing workplace diversity by fostering a supportive, inclusive and respectful work environment where all the employees have equal opportunity to contribute in the workplace. Irrespective of the size and domestic or international status of the companies, HR professionals everywhere are concerned with the impact of change being placed on workplace diversity because of significant global demographic changes. With this fact, organizations are evolving various innovative ways to attract and retain the best and most qualified worker by providing opportunities for showcasing their talent. People from diverse backgrounds bring differences in their style of working, thought processes, work ethics, value systems, etc., so enabling them to adjust in a new setting by facilitating cross-cultural training, especially with an orientation towards communication across cultures, if done effectively can contribute tremendously to organizational success. These drastic changes in workplaces require HR professionals and leaders to come up with new concepts, strategies, diversity- and inclusion-oriented HR practices, policies and programs to craft an organizational culture that best fits in with today's challenging marketplace.

The time has come to realize that diversity and inclusion are a necessity.

References

Baumeister, R. F., DeWall, C. N., Ciarocco, N. J., & Twenge, J. M. (2005). Social exclusion impairs self-regulation. *Journal of Personality and Social Psychology, 88,* 589–604.

Bilimoria, D., Joy, S., & Liang, X. (2008). Breaking barriers and creating inclusiveness: Lessons of organizational transformation to advance women faculty in academic science and engineering. *Human Resource Management, 47,* 423–441.

Blackhart, G. C., Nelson, B. C., Knowles, M. L., & Baumeister, R. F. (2009). Rejection elicits emotional reactions but neither causes immediate distress nor lowers self-esteem: A meta-analytic review of 192 studies on social exclusion. *Personality and Social Psychology Review, 13,* 269–309.

Bowen, F., & Blackmon, K. (2003). Spirals of silence: The dynamics effects of diversity on organizational voice. *Journal of Management Studies, 40*(6), 1393–1417.

Buckley, M. R., Jackson, K. A., Bolino, M. C., Veres, J. G., & Feild, H. S. (2007). The influence of relational demography on panel interview ratings: A field experiment. *Personnel Psychology, 60,* 627–646.

Chatman, J. A., Polzer, J. T., Barsade, S. G., & Neale, M. A. (1998). Being different yet feeling similar: The influence of demographic composition and organizational culture on work processes and outcomes. *Administrative Science Quarterly, 43,* 749–780.

Chattopadhyay, P. (1999). Beyond direct and symmetrical effects: The influence of demographic dissimilarity on organizational citizenship behavior. *Academy of Management Journal, 42,* 273–287.

Comer, D. R., & Soliman, C. E. (1996). Organizational efforts to manage diversity: Do they really work? *Journal of Managerial Issues, 8*(4), 470–484.

Cooke, F. L., & Saini, D. S. (2010). Diversity management in India: A study of organizations in different ownership forms and industrial sectors. *Human Resource Management, 49*(3), 477–500.

Dahm, M. J. (2003). *The development of needs analysis instrument for cultural diversity Training: WDQ-II.* UMI Microform 3081485 by Pro Quest Information and Learning Company.

DeWall, C. N., Maner, J. K., & Rouby, D. A. (2009). Social exclusion and early-stage interpersonal perception: Selective attention to signs of acceptance. *Journal of Personality and Social Psychology, 96,* 729–741.

Ely, R. J., & Thomas, D. A. (2001). Cultural diversity at work: The effects of diversity perspectives on work group processes and outcomes. *Administrative Science Quarterly, 46,* 229–273.

Erasmus, L. J. (2008). *The management of workforce diversity and implications for leadership at financial asset services* (Doctoral dissertation).

Ferner, A. M., Almond, P., & Colling, T. (2005). Institutional theory and the cross-national transfer of employment policy: The case of 'workforce diversity' in US multinationals. *Journal of International Business Studies, 36*(3), 304–321.

Friedman, R., Kane, M., & Cornfield, D. B. (1998). Social support and career optimism: Examining the effectiveness of network groups among Black managers. *Human Relations, 51*, 1155–1177.

Godthelp, M., & Glunk, U. (2003). Turnover at the top: Demographic diversity as a determinant of executive turnover in the Netherlands. *European Management Journal, 12*, 614–636.

Gonzalez, J. A., & DeNisi, A. S. (2009). Cross-level effects of demography and diversity climate on organizational attachment and firm effectiveness. *Journal of Organizational Behavior, 30*, 21–40.

Grimes, D. S. (2002). Challenging the status quo? Whiteness in the diversity management literature. *Management Communication Quarterly, 15*(3).

Hansen, F. (2003). Diversity's business case doesn't add up. *Workforce*, pp. 28–32.

Harrison, D. A., Price, K. H., & Bell, M. P. (1998). Beyond relational demography: Time & the effects of the surface & deep-level diversity on work group cohesion. *Academy of Management Journal, 41*, 96–107.

Hitlan, R. T., Clifton, R. J., & DeSoto, M. C. (2006). Perceived exclusion in the workplace: The moderating effects of gender on work-related attitudes and physical health. *North American Journal of Psychology, 8*, 217–235.

Holvino, E. H., Ferdman, B. M., & Merrill-Sands, D. (2004). Creating and sustaining diversity and inclusion in organizations: Strategies and approaches. In M. S. Stockdale and F. J. Crsoby (Eds.), *The psychology and management of workplace diversity* (pp. 245–276). Malden, MA: Blackwell.

Homan, A. C., Hollenbeck, J. R., Humphrey, S. E., van Knippenberg, D., Ilgen, D. R., & Van Kleef, G. A. (2008). Facing differences with an open mind: Openness to experience, salience of intragroup differences, and performance of diverse work groups. *Academy of Management Journal, 51*, 1204–1222.

Lefkowitz, J. (1994). Sex related differences in job attitudes and dispositional variables: Now you see them. *Academy of Management Journal, 37*, 323–349.

Meena, K. (2015). Diversity dimensions of India and their organization implications: An analysis. *International Journal of Economics & Management Sciences, 4*, 261.

Mellor, S. (1995). Gender composition and gender representation in local unions: Relationships between women's participation in local office and women's participation in local activities. *Journal of Applied Psychology, 80*(6), 706–720.

Mor Barak, M. E. (2000). Beyond affirmative action: Toward a model of diversity and organizational inclusion. *Administration in Social Work, 23*(3–4), 47–68.

Mor Barak, M. E. (2005). *Managing diversity: Toward a globally inclusive workplace.* Thousand Oaks, CA: Sage.

Mor Barak, M. E., Lizano, E. L., Kim, A., Duan, L., Rhee, M. K., Hsiao, H., Brimhall. K. C. (2016). The promise of diversity management for climate of inclusion: A state-of-the-art review and meta-analysis. *Human Service Organizations: Management, Leadership and Governance, 40*(4), 305–333.

Mowday, R. T., & Sutton, R. I. (1993). Organizational behavior: Linking individuals and groups to organizational contexts. *Annual Review of Psychology, 44*, 195–229.

Pelled, L. H., Ledford, G. E., & Mohrman, S. A. (1999). Demographic dissimilarity and workplace inclusion. *Journal of Management Studies, 36*, 1013–1031.

Pelled, L. H., & Xin, K. R. (2000). Relational demography and relationship quality in two cultures. *Organization Studies, 21*(6), 1077–1095.

Pless, Nicola M & Maak, Thomas. (2004). Building an Inclusive Diversity Culture: Principles, Processes and Practice. *Journal of Business Ethics, 54* (2), 129–147.

Richard, O. C. (2000). Racial diversity, business strategy, and firm performance: A resource based view. *Academy of Management Journal, 43*, 164–177.

Riley, P. G., & Buckley, P. R. (2008). The best scientists are becoming free agents. *Research Technology Management, 51*(3), 9–12.

Riordan, C. M., & Shore, L. M. (1997). Demographic diversity and employee attitudes: An empirical example of relational demography within work units. *Journal of Applied Psychology, 82*(3), 342–358.

Roberson, Q. M. (2006). Disentangling the meanings of diversity and inclusion in organizations. *Group and Organization Management, 31*, 212–236.

Sacco, J. M., & Schmitt, N. W. (2003). *The relationship between demographic diversity and profitability: A Longitudinal study.* Paper presented at the 18th Annual Conference of the Society for Industrial and Organizational Psychology, Orlando.

Shapcott, K. M., Carron, A. V., Burke, S. M., Bradshaw, M. H., & Estabrooks, P. A. (2006). Member diversity and cohesion and performance in walking groups. *Small Group Research, 37*(6), 701–720.

Shenoy-Packer, S., & Myers, K. (2013). Challenges to organizational assimilation: Experiences of white women and people of color in the U.S. workforce. *The International Journal of Organizational Diversity, 12*(2), 1–15.

Shore, L. M., Chung, B., Dean, M. A., Ehrhart, K. H., Jung, D., Randel, A., & Singh, G. (2009). Diversity and inclusiveness: Where are we now and where are we going. *Human Resource Management Review, 19*, 117–133.

Shore, L. M., Randel, A. E., Chung, B. G., Dean, M. A., Holcombe Ehrhart, K., & Singh, G. (2011). Inclusion and diversity in work groups: A review and model for future research. *Journal of Management, 37*(40), 1262–1289.

Sippola, A., & Smale, A. (2007). The global integration of diversity management: A longitudinal case study. *The International Journal of Human Resource Management, 18*(11), 1895–1916.
Sowell, T. (2002). Those who gush about 'diversity' never want to put their beliefs to the test. *The Enterprise, 31*(38), 22–32.
Syed, J., & Özbilgin, M. (2009). A relational framework for international transfer of diversity management practices. *The International Journal of Human Resource Management, 20*(12), 2435–2453.
Thomas, D. A., & Ely, R. D. (1996). Making differences matter: A new paradigm for managing diversity. *Harvard Business Review, 74*(5), 79–90.
Tsui, A. S., Egan, T. D., & O'Reilly, C. A., III. (1992). Being different: Relational demography and organizational attachment. *Administrative Science Quarterly, 37*, 549–579.
Watson, W. E., Kumar, K., & Michaelsen, L. (1993). Cultural diversity's impact on interaction process and performance: Comparing homogeneous and diverse task groups. *Academy of Management Journal, 36*(3), 590–602.
Weick, K. E. (1979). Cognitive processes in organizations. *Research in Organizational Behavior, 1*, 41–75.
West, B., & Frances, T. M. (2007). *G'Day Boss: Australian Culture and the Workplace*. Abbotsford: Tribus Lingua.
Wiersema, M. F., & Bantel, K. A. (1992). Top management team demography and corporate strategic change. *Academy of Management Journal, 35*(1), 91–121.

Websites

www.adb.org/countries/india/economy
www.business-standard.com/article/international/imf-scales-down-india-s-gdp-growth-rate-by-0-3-each-for-fy20-and-fy21-119072301227_1.html
www.business.mapsofindia.com/globalization/impact-employment-india.html
http://censusindia.gov.in/Census_And_You/religion.aspx
www.citeman.com/12552-workforce-diversity/#ixzz1YI29cID4
www.connect.in.com/workforce-diversity/profile.html
www.diversityworking.com
https://economictimes.indiatimes.com/articleshow/67830482.cms?from=mdr&utm_source=contentofinterest&utm_medium=text&utm_campaign=cppst
https://economictimes.indiatimes.com/jobs/50-indias-working-age-population-out-of-labour-force-says-report/articleshow/67830482.cms?from=mdr
www.epi.org/publications/entry/webfeatures_viewpoints_21st_century_workplace_testimony/
http://EzineArticles.com/4202403
www.shrm.org/hr-today/trends-and-forecasting/special-reports-and-expert-views/Documents/HR-Strategy-Globalization.pdf
www.fibre2fashion.com, Impact of globalization on Indian economy- An overview, Tanveer Malik
www.india.gov.in/people-groups/life-cycle/senior-citizens/defence-personnel
https://knowindia.gov.in/profile/india-at-a-glance.php
www.mckinsey.com/business-functions/organization/our-insights/delivering-through-diversity
www.nitjsr.ac.in/Circulars&Orders/Circulars&Orders/Brochure%20on%20Reservation%20DOPT.pdf
www.scribd.com/doc/43863942/HRM-Workplace-Diversity
https://yourstory.com/2012/06/interweave-provides-diversity-management-and-inclusion-solutions-for-your-workplace
www.weforum.org/gendergap, November 2010 report
www.worldatlas.com/articles/the-largest-countries-in-the-world-the-biggest-nations-as-determined-by-total-land-area.html

18
CROSS-CULTURAL DIFFERENCES IN INCLUSIVE LEADERSHIP PERCEPTION AND APPLICATION

Mike Szymanski, Komal Kalra, Evodio Kaltenecker, and Anna Olszewska

Introduction

Inclusive leadership, i.e., leading people in such way that all team members feel treated respectfully and fairly, are valued, and sense that they are important elements of the team, is becoming a popular approach in multinational companies where a majority of projects is conducted by multicultural, highly diverse teams. This new reality is not only limited to multinational companies but is rather becoming a norm for all companies, both big and small. While the overarching question of inclusive leadership of how to make everyone feel treated fairly is universal across the world, the routes to inclusiveness may differ significantly as each country, culture, and society struggles with its own challenges.

In what follows, we discuss the meaning of inclusive leadership in various cultures. To understand the essence of inclusive leadership, we analyze some challenges posed by diversity and how to tackle them. We then move on to examine challenges for inclusive leadership in the context of a developed, multicultural economy such as Canada. We continue with four examples (Mexico, Brazil, India, and Poland) of developing economies to illustrate how their challenges might differ from the ones discussed previously. The chapter concludes with a short summary.

Leadership and Diversity Across the World

Leadership is usually defined as the art of motivating a group of people to act together towards achieving a shared goal. It is a challenging task as it involves balancing the needs and acts of the leader, the organization, and each of the team members. What does it take to be an effective leader? There is a variety of definitions, but Brake (1997) proposed a leadership triad: (1) business acumen, i.e., the ability to pursue and apply appropriate professional knowledge and skills to achieve optimal results for the company; (2) personal effectiveness, i.e., the ability to attain increasing levels of maturity to perform at peak levels under strenuous conditions; and (3) relationship management, i.e., the ability to build and influence collaborative relationships. The last skill is of particular importance for those who want to become inclusive leaders, that is who want everyone on their team to feel appreciated and valued. Bourke and Espedido (2019) propose a set of behaviors that may lead to building perception of inclusion in the team. They advise the leaders to share personal weaknesses, acknowledge team members as individuals, and to learn about cultural differences, as leadership is perceived differently in various cultures (House, Hanges, Javidan, Dorfman, & Gupta, 2004). Leader effectiveness is embedded in the societal and organizational norms, values, and beliefs of the people being led. In other words, two people coming from different cultures may have completely different expectations for their team leaders. For instance, in Anglo-Saxon cultures, people prefer performance-oriented leaders, while Latin Americans prefer team-oriented leaders (House et al., 2004). But even individuals coming from the same country may have various, often conflicting, expectations.

Diversity has recently become a buzzword that is present across all social media, public debate, and academic discourse. However, most public debate in the United States and Canada revolves around ethnic and racial diversity, with little to no concern for other forms of diversity. It must be stressed that diversity does not end at ethnic and racial backgrounds. While these two are undoubtedly important, they are not the only types of diversity. In most companies, one can find also generational diversity, linguistic diversity, educational diversity, and political diversity. Briefly, diversity is the presence of individuals with a range of different, often conflicting, characteristics. Such a situation may lead to an internal team conflict, miscommunication, lack of mutual trust, and emergence of serious faultlines across the team. However, if managed well, diversity can be a great source of competitive advantage, as individuals coming from different backgrounds bring a plethora of experiences, insights, and ideas, leading to higher levels of creativity and better organizational performance. However, the catch is that diversity must be *managed* well. If managers want to be true and *inclusive leaders*, they must understand the true nature of diversity in their teams. For example, a group of seven Caucasian men may seem to be homogeneous on the surface. It may seem that making everyone included is an easy task as there are no visible differences between team members. Thus, a one-size-fits-all leadership style might be sufficient. However, diversity faultlines in this group may lie much deeper, for instance at the religious or political beliefs level. What happens if five of the members graduated from Ivy League schools and two come from public colleges? Such faultlines are more difficult to spot but are critical for the sense of inclusion in the whole team. In the next part of this chapter, we build on this argument and illustrate what faultlines are most profound in Canada, Mexico, India, Brazil, and Poland.

Inclusive Leadership in Canada

Canada is the world's second largest country, with an area of 9.98 million km^2. Although it is sparsely populated, with a total population of 37 million people, it has a GDP of US$1.6 trillion. It has been consistently ranked as one of the most livable (Madden, 2019) and immigrant-friendly (Cocking, 2018) countries in the world. Nevertheless, inclusive leadership in Canada faces numerous challenges. First, Canada is a highly multiethnic, multicultural, and multilingual society.

Historically, Canada has been influenced by British and French cultures. While very often ignored in the United States, the indigenous communities of Canada (called First Nations) have significantly influenced the Canadian identity. Furthermore, over the past few decades, there has been large immigration from South Asia, specifically China, India, and the Philippines. Between 1999 and 2009, there were an average of 138,389 economic immigrants admitted per year to Canada (Jackson & Girard, 2011). As a result, Canada is one of the most diverse countries in the world. Cultural diversity and multilingualism, because of immigration policies and the emphasis on preserving individual and social identities, manifests itself clearly in the multitude of languages used in Canada, with English and French being the native tongues of, respectively, 56% and 21% of Canadians (Census, 2016). It means that almost a quarter of Canadians use a non-official language at home. Some of the non-official languages used in Canada include Cantonese, Punjabi, Spanish, and Arabic.

This multiethnic, multicultural, and multilingual mosaic poses a great challenge for Canadian inclusive leaders (Hrenyk et al., 2016). The GLOBE leadership study (House et al., 2004) results suggest that the desired style in Canada is charismatic and participative leadership, where leaders involve their followers in the decision-making process. However, an analysis of cultural dimension scores (Hofstede, 2011) sheds more light on potential challenges. In terms of power distance (i.e., the extent to which the followers accept and expect that power is vested in the leader), Canada in general scores 39/100. On the other hand, India and China (i.e., the country of origin of the two largest ethnic minorities in Canada), score 77/100 and 80/100, indicating very hierarchical social structure expectations. In other words, the immigrant followers may expect the leader to make the decision and thus to take the responsibility.

Canada is very proud of its multiculturality and social diversity climate where everyone's cultural and ethnic heritage is respected and valued. This attitude of a cultural mosaic where cultures are preserved as opposed to the approach of a melting pot where all new comers should blend into the existing norms creates a significant challenge for leaders. They need to be aware of the cultural orientations of their peers and subordinates who come from different cultural backgrounds. There is definitely no one-size-fits-all way to inclusive leadership.

Inclusive Leadership in Mexico

With a population of around 130 million people, Mexico is the 10th most populous country and the most populous Spanish-speaking state in the world. Additionally, Mexico is the world's 13th largest state, with an area of 1,972,550 km^2, and because of its GDP of US$1.2 trillion, has the world's 15th largest nominal GDP. Unlike many countries in Latin America, two-thirds of Mexico's exports are manufactured. Additionally, Mexico's industrial base is firmly connected to the US-based manufacturing environment. Finally, the unique Mexican culture reflects the complexity of the history of the country, which is a blend of indigenous and Spanish cultures and attracted 39 million international arrivals in 2018, which allowed the country to be the sixth most-visited nation in the world (UNWTO, 2019).

In Mexico, the dominant form of inclusion is the increase in Mexico's female labor force participation. Although the nation is often viewed as a stronghold of a machismo culture with a strong separation between the roles of men and women, Mexican women have made significant progress in labor force participation, education, and political representation in recent years. For instance, 42.6% of the seats in Mexico's national parliaments are held by women (OECD, 2017a), and a number of powerful and influential businesswomen and executives have emerged in Mexico (Wood & Young, 2017). Despite these gains, Mexico's female labor force participation rate remains among the lowest in The Organisation for Economic Co-operation and Development (OECD), the gender gap in workforce participation is high, and Mexican women generally have lower-quality jobs than have their male counterparts (OECD, 2017b). However, changes are expected to slowly occur in the country, as public opinion polls reveal that society's expectations and attitudes towards women are changing, as younger Mexicans take a more egalitarian view towards women's roles. Moreover, it is important to mention the asymmetric characteristic of acceptance of diversity in Mexico. While in the large centers and multinational companies the acceptance of diversity in senior managerial roles is improving, the same cannot be said in smaller cities and small and mid-sized enterprises.

The leadership model in Mexican businesses can be described as autocratic and paternalistic. On the one hand, the Mexican leadership style is autocratic because as Mexico presents a high power distance culture, instructions should be given clearly and precisely, while subordinates are expected to follow those instructions without much questioning. On the other hand, leadership in Mexico tends to be paternalistic because the apparent rigidity of hierarchy and formalism is tempered to some degree by a relatively casual approach to rules and regulations. Paternalism and a sense of "extended family" are important factors of Mexican management styles; as a consequence, instructions cannot be given to subordinates with no concern about politeness and respect to the subordinates.

Mexico is a high power distance nation, which means that Mexican firms are likely to use hierarchical structures with power vested at the top of the pyramid. In a traditional, hierarchical structure of Mexican business organizations, there is typically a "director-general," or "president," or "CEO" who has come up through the ranks to assume that position and who generally deals only with a small group of senior managers who report to the executive and are expected to show respect to him/her (Gómez, 2004). Therefore, according to Hofstede's (1980) rankings of power distance, Mexico is a culture that accepts large power differences. Moreover, Mexico ranks high on uncertainty avoidance (Hofstede, 1980), meaning that Mexicans feel uncomfortable with ambiguous and uncertain situations. Mexico's values of high power distance and high uncertainty avoidance would appear to make it a less than ideal culture to implement a learning strategy focused on employee involvement and empowerment (Gómez, 2004). Therefore, the consultative management style is not very common in Mexico, even in multinational companies with operations in the Mexican market.

There are several takeaways for inclusive leaders in Mexico. First, they must remember that the manager-subordinate relationship is viewed as reciprocal. As relationship bonds are important to the Mexican culture, the manager expects loyalty and in return, team players expect that leaders will look after the interests and the well-being of employees. Second, inclusive leaders should be authoritative but not authoritarian. It is important to show that you are in control but at the same time have a warm, human touch. Third, as Mexicans want to get to know you better when doing business, leaders should understand that the concept of time is different from the one seen in other cultures; therefore, they should understand that their teams do not always embrace the "time is money" mentality from other cultures. Inclusive leaders know best that relationships are more important than time.

Inclusive Leadership in India

India is the world's largest democracy and the second most populous country with a population of over 1.2 billion. It is the seventh largest economy in the world, with a GDP of US$2.6 trillion. Since 2014, India's economy has been the world's fastest growing major economy, surpassing China (IMF, 2019). The long-term economic perspective of the economy is estimated to be positive because of its young population and English proficiency ratio (CIA, 2019).

India is a country of great diversity. Being a country with a large population, India presents endless varieties of cultural, ethnic, and linguistic features and patterns. Historically, India has been colonialized by people from different societies, and each left its own mark on the culture and language of present-day India. Due to this wide range of variation, it is difficult to generalize about the leaders and leadership practices in India. In fact, it is impossible to determine the dominant form of diversity in India because of its unique ethos. However, management and organizational studies scholars have noted the negative effects of ignoring cultural and linguistic diversity (e.g., Dheer, Lenartowicz, & Peterson, 2015; Kulkarni, 2015), largely because cultural diversity encompasses ethnic and regional differences. For instance, in order to understand the implications of linguistic diversity, one has to understand that the ethos of language use in India is different from the rest of the world. There are 22 official languages in India and over a million speakers of at least 30 regional languages (Registrar General and Census Commissioner, India, 2011). In fact, India follows a three-language formula, which instructs the teaching of three languages in the school curriculum. The teaching of Hindi and English is mandatory, but the choice of the third language (usually the regional language) is left to the discretion of the state governments. In addition, there are nine different subcultural regions in India, each with its own set of dominant cultural values, which have further implications for the multinational organizations operating in the India (Dheer et al., 2015).

Such diversity poses tremendous challenges for leaders in India. Most organizations and individual leaders assume that India is a homogenous nation, therefore they do not adapt to the changes in the different regional environments. Second, inclusive leaders need to learn to manage relationships, no matter which region they are located in. Despite the subcultural and linguistic differences, India is a high power distance country (Hofstede, 1980), therefore firms in India are likely to use strict hierarchical structures and the senior management is responsible for making the crucial decisions.

Lower-level employees do not open up and voice their concerns to the management, therefore inclusive leaders will have to speak on the behalf of their subordinates. However, despite the high power distance, India is a collectivist society and, therefore, leaders are expected to be supportive and considerate, along with being compassionate and generous. Furthermore, according to Hofstede's cultural dimensions (1980), India is a masculine country, therefore visible symbols of workplace success are very important. Therefore, it is vital for inclusive leaders to display the individual and team success to others in their organization, as this can motivate employees to perform better.

There are several takeaways for inclusive leaders in India. First, they must remember that India is a collectivist country, and the concept of saving face is quite important. Therefore, it is a common practice to think of the common good and not to mention one's mistakes in front of their peers. Inclusive leaders will have to learn to manage their relationships with low-performing employees by talking to them in private without letting their peers know of their low evaluations. Second, inclusive leaders must be visionaries who can effectively build teams by taking advantage of the individuals' collectivist cultural orientations and giving the team a sense of a common goal or purpose. Third, similar to Mexico, relationships outside the work are quintessential in the Indian context. Indians want to know their managers and peers better and, therefore, inclusive leaders should understand the importance of relationship building. In addition, Indians are ambivalent about time and punctuality. This can be attributed to the fact that the word for tomorrow and yesterday is the same in many Indian languages (*kal*); therefore, inclusive leaders must be sensitive to the ambiguity surrounding the notion of punctuality and not evaluate their subordinates harshly because of their notions of time.

Inclusive Leadership in Brazil

Brazil is the eighth largest economy in the world, with a nominal GDP of US$1.9 trillion. The country is home for 210 million people, being the fifth most populous nation. Regarding its territory, Brazil is the fifth largest country due to its area of 8.5 million square kilometers. Although the country is one of the most important exporters of commodities in the world, the Brazilian economy is somewhat closed to the rest of the world compared to other emerging markets.

Ethnic diversity is the main form of diversity in Brazil, and it is caused by the confluence of different populations that form the Brazilian society, which is based on Native Brazilians, descendants of the Portuguese colonists, African descendants, and European, Arab, and Japanese immigrants. Other significant groups include Koreans, Chinese, Paraguayans, Bolivians, and more recently, Venezuelans. To understand the ethnic diversity in Brazil, take the example of African descendants. Brazil was the last country in the Western world to abolish slavery in 1888. Forty percent of the total number of slaves brought to the Americas arrived in Brazil, around four million people. This population was ten times bigger than the population of slaves that arrived in the United States, which makes Brazil the home of the largest African-descendant community in the world outside Africa. Another example comes from the Italian-Brazilian community. Brazil is the home of the largest number of people with full or partial Italian ancestry outside Italy, with São Paulo being the most populous city with Italian ancestry in the world. Brazil also possesses the largest Japanese community outside Japan, the largest Lebanese community outside Lebanon, and a significant presence of Germans and Swiss in the southern part of the country. Therefore, the main challenge to diversity and inclusive leaders in Brazil is to deal with team members from a different background, such as country of origin, religion, and ethnicity.

An effective business leader in Brazil faces several challenges. First, there is the complexity of the business environment. The Brazilian scenario is typically volatile, uncertain, complex, and ambiguous (VUCA), which causes leaders to develop a sensitivity to context, flexibility judgment, and influencing skills (Senosiain, 2012). Second, inclusive leaders' main challenge comes from managing relationships, which are of key importance in the country. Business leaders need to foster a relationship based on trust and respect with his/her team. Third, a manager's personal style is considered to be of great significance, and the respect afforded to the manager by subordinates is directly proportionate to the personality of the boss. Fourth, managers need to master diversity. Successful managers must understand the similarities and differences of the various ethnic groups that exist in the country to be accepted by locals as a leader. Finally, a highly informal, ambiguous, and indirect communication style characterizes the Brazilian business environment. Brazilians are not normally explicit in their arguments; instead, they might use informal gatherings and usually opt for the indirect message. In order to deal with the informal organization and have an influence on it, global leaders need first to take their time and dig into the deeper levels of the Brazilian cultural iceberg.

There are several takeaways for diversity and inclusive leaders in Brazil. First, be comfortable with ambiguity. In order to survive hyperinflation, the frequent ups and downs of the economy, and a complex regulatory environment, Brazilian learned the hard way to become ambiguous. So, their diversity and inclusive leaders must act accordingly. Second, inclusive business leaders must deal with the diversity of his/her team, given the diversity of the Brazilian population. Finally, be open and get the team onboard. Share goals, objectives, and challenges with employees.

Inclusive Leadership in Poland

"Poland stands out as a European growth champion" (Fredriksson, 2019), demonstrating a steady growth for the past 28 years. Poland is the only country in the EU which didn't suffer recession after the 2008/2009 financial crisis and is the seventh largest economy within the EU. The GDP of Poland as of 2017 amounts to US$524.5 billion (World Bank, 2019) and is expected to reach US$605 billion by the end of 2019 (Trading Economics, 2019). With its 38 million people, Poland has a very good domestic consumption, a dominant service sector, strong trading ties, and a focus on the support and development of small and medium-sized enterprises.

Over the last decade, Poland has been experiencing a global exposure like never before, attracting investors, capital, and talent from around the world. Culturally speaking, Poland has always been rather monolithic, with a majority of the population speaking the same language (Polish) and sharing the same values and religious beliefs. It should be pointed out that 91.9% of the population is Catholic, and 97% identify themselves as Polish nationals, ethnically speaking. In terms of Hofstede's cultural dimensions, Poland scores extremely high on uncertainty avoidance, which means that people feel generally better when implementing mechanisms, codes, and rules that prevent any unexpected events. That suggests a landscape that is highly intolerant, rigid, and careful. Moderately high scores on dimensions of power distance, masculinity, and individualism show Poland as a work-driven, hard-working, and focused society. It seems in the workplace people are individualistic but feel good with hierarchy and a centralized management style. Low long-term orientation means a respect of traditions, tried solutions, and norms. On the indulgence scale, Poland comes across as rather pessimistic and restrained.

In Poland, there are three recent yet big challenges for leadership. First, Poland is one of the most rapidly aging societies in Europe. In the workplace, there is a clear divide between the "old guard" and the "young wolves." Currently, the number of employees aged over 50 amounts to 40% of the workforce and will increase to 55% within the next decade (IBS, 2017). At the same time, a large number of employees aged 35–45, who are well educated, dynamic, and career oriented and may at times perceive their older colleagues as obstacles to own career growth. Whereas, more experienced colleagues may perceive young ones as incompetent and arrogant. Second, sexual diversity in the workplace has not really been a part of the debate for a long time because Poland comes across as a rather conservative and intolerant society. Although we don't know the numbers of LGBTQ community participation in the labor market as such, the social presence and visibility of this group is high. An objective measure of an increasing importance of this community can be seen in number of devoted events. In 2018 there has been 14 equality marches and parades, and 2019 will aim to double this number. This shows the scale of the community and how crucial it is for leaders to be sensitive and inclusive to these important economic contributors. And finally, a recent and rapid increase of foreign labor, especially in the service and construction sectors, from Ukraine, Belarus, India, Nepal, and Turkey is causing challenges. According to various sources, there are between 800,000 and 1.2 million workers from just Ukraine in Poland. The number of employees from Ukraine is expected to increase by 25%–30% by the end of 2019 compared to 2018. Naturally, this is due to language, culture, and demographic proximity. Interestingly, the number of immigrants from India has also increased four times from 2014. Altogether, the Polish workforce is far from being homogeneous.

Speed of action and ability to deal with ambiguity, improvisation, and resistance to change were always amongst the competencies Polish management has been known for (Koźmiński, 2014). Polish leaders used to be characterized as visionary, diplomatic, and administratively capable, with tendencies to an autocratic leadership style (den Hartog, Van Muijen, & Koopman, 1997). This is the "old and tried" leadership style, based on hierarchy, rules, and "do's and don'ts." Nowadays, on the GLOBE Leadership visualization scale, it is depicted that Poles value charismatic, team, and humane oriented as well as participative leadership. This is an important shift, happening in a relatively short time period (of 30 years), which can't be ignored. Leadership happens in the context of boundaries, such as political, cultural, ethical, emotional, motivational, competence based, and cognitive (Koźmiński, 2015). It seems that inclusive leadership can be a remedy to these limitations. So especially in the light of the aforementioned three faultlines, Polish leaders should inspire their organizations to cherish cooperation and trust within their teams. Strongly diversified employees crave leaders who have exceptional "soft skills," are good communicators and listeners, and who would mentor them, while taking care of their career and well-being in the organization. Polish employees desire leaders who provide a sense of belonging, safety, as well as feeling of respect, to which they can respond with unlimited levels of loyalty and engagement.

Summary

Motivating a group of people to act towards achieving a common goal is in itself a challenging task. Doing so in such way that every group member feels "they are treated respectfully and fairly, are valued and sense that they belong" (Bourke & Espedido, 2019) is even more challenging. In today's business organizations, teams comprise individuals of various ethnic or social backgrounds, who speak different languages, or who grew up in completely different political contexts. Cross-cultural differences add yet another layer of complexity to this already demanding task.

The first step for leaders to be inclusive is to understand the type of diversity they face in their teams, because even groups that appear to be relatively homogeneous on the surface may be torn by deep-level differences difficult to spot by outsiders. Therefore, leaders who strive to be inclusive must first identify all potential faultlines in the team, understand their impact, and seek to address them in such a way that all team members feel respected. Without a doubt, it is an enormous challenge, but it will pay off with high team morale, motivation, and, eventually, superior team performance.

References

Bourke, J., & Espedido, A. (2019, March). Why inclusive leaders are good for organizations, and how to become one. *Harvard Business Review*. Retrieved from https://hbr.org/2019/03/why-inclusive-leaders-are-good-for-organizations-and-how-to-become-one

Brake, T. (1997). *The global leader: Critical factors for creating the world class organization*. New York, NY: Irwin Professional.

CIA. (2019). *The CIA World Factbook*. New York, NY: Central Intelligence Agency. Skyhorse Publishing.

Cocking, L. (2018, August 7). These are the 11 best countries to immigrate to. *Culture Trip*. Retrieved from https://theculturetrip.com/europe/articles/these-are-the-11-best-countries-to-immigrate-to/

Den Hartog, D. N., Van Muijen, J. J., & Koopman, P. L. (1997). Transactional versus transformational leadership: An analysis of the MLQ. *Journal of Occupational and Organizational Psychology*, 70(1), 19–34.

Dheer, R. J., Lenartowicz, T., & Peterson, M. F. (2015). Mapping India's regional subcultures: Implications for international management. *Journal of International Business Studies*, 46(4), 443–467.

Fredriksson, E. (2019, June 25). How Poland's "golden age" of economic growth is going unreported. *Euronews*. Retrieved from www.euronews.com/2019/06/25/how-poland-s-golden-age-of-economic-growth-is-going-unreported-view

Gómez, C. (2004). The influence of environmental, organizational, and HRM factors on employee behaviors in subsidiaries: A Mexican case study of organizational learning. *Journal of World Business*, 39(1), 1–11.

Hofstede, G. (1980). Motivation, leadership and organization: Do American theories apply abroad. *Organization Dynamics*, 9, 42–63.

Hofstede, G. (2011). Dimensionalizing cultures: The Hofstede model in context. *Online Readings in Psychology and Culture*, 2(1). https://doi.org/10.9707/2307-0919.1014

House, R. J., Hanges, P. J., Javidan, M., Dorfman, P. W., & Gupta, V. (Eds.). (2004). *Culture, leadership, and organizations: The GLOBE study of 62 societies*. Thousand Oaks, CA: Sage Publications.

Hrenyk, J., Szymanski, M., Kar, A., & Fitzsimmons, S. R. (2016). Understanding multicultural individuals as ethical global leaders. In *Advances in Global Leadership* (pp. 57–78). Bingley, United Kingdom: Emerald Group Publishing Limited.

International Monetary Fund. (2019). *World Economic Outlook update, January 2019*. Washington, DC: International Monetary Fund. Retrieved from https://www.imf.org/en/Publications/WEO/Issues/2019/01/11/weo-update-january-2019

Jackson, T., & Girard, E. (2011, February 21). Cross-cultural leadership skills for a multicultural Canada. *People Talk*. Retrieved from https://peopletalkonline.ca/cross-cultural-leadership-skills-for-a-multicultural-canada/

Koźmiński, A. K. (2014). *Czas pokera*. Warsaw, Poland: Wolters Kluwer.

Koźmiński, A. K. (2015). Bounded leadership: Empirical study of the Polish Elite. *Polish Sociological Review*, 192(4), 425–453.

Kulkarni, M. (2015). Language-based diversity and faultlines in organizations. *Journal of Organizational Behavior*, 36(1), 128–146.

Kwiatkowska, B., & Baran, J. (2017, February 13). Population ageing, labour market and public finance in Poland. *The Institute for Structural Research (IBS)*. Retrieved from http://ibs.org.pl/en/events/population-ageing-labour-market-and-public-finance-in-poland/

Madden, D. (2019, March 28). Ranked: The 10 happiest countries in the world in 2019. *Forbes*. Retrieved from www.forbes.com/sites/duncanmadden/2019/03/28/ranked-the-10-happiest-countries-in-the-world-in-2019/#7b7952ba48a5

OECD. (2017a). *Better policies towards a stronger and more inclusive Mexico an assessment of recent policy reforms: An assessment of recent policy reforms*. Paris: OECD. https://doi.org/10.1787/9789264189553-en.

OECD. (2017b). *Building an inclusive Mexico: Policies and good governance for gender equality*. Paris, France: OECD. https://doi.org/10.1787/9789264265493-en.

Registrar General and Census Commissioner. (2011). *Census of India*. New Delhi, India: Office of the Registrar General. Retrieved from www.censusindia.gov.in/2011Census/Language_MTs.html

Senosiain, M. (2012). Managing in Brazil a guide for American managers. *HIM 1990–2015*. 1302. Retrieved from https://stars.library.ucf.edu/honorstheses1990-2015/1302

Statistics Canada. (2016). *The 2016 census*. Ottawa, Ontario. Retrieved from https://www12.statcan.gc.ca/census-recensement/2016/dp-pd/prof/details/page.cfm?Lang=E&Geo1=PR&Code1=01&Geo2=PR&Code2=01&Data=Count&SearchText=canada&SearchType=Begins&SearchPR=01&B1=All&TABID=1)

Trading Economics. (2019). *Poland*. Retrieved from https://tradingeconomics.com/poland/gdp

Wood, D., & Young, G. K. (2017, June 12). A U.S.-Mexico women's Business Council: Let's get women to drive the bilateral relationship. *Forbes*. Retrieved from www.forbes.com/sites/themexicoinstitute/2017/06/12/a-u-s-mexico-womens-business-council-lets-get-women-to-drive-the-bilateral-relationship/#5e89ca4e5726

World Bank. (2019). *World development indicators*. Washington, DC: The World Bank Group. Retrieved from www.google.com/publicdata/explore?ds=d5bncppjof8f9_&met_y=ny_gdp_mktp_cd&idim=country:POL:SWE:UKR&hl=en&dl=en

World Tourism Organization UNWTO. (2019). *International tourism highlights, 2019 Edition*. Madrid: UNWTO. https://doi.org/10.18111/9789284421152.

PART III

Inclusive Leadership Practices

19
AWAKENED LEADERSHIP
A Roadmap to Inclusion and Morality

Joan Marques

Introduction

Today's leaders are expected to excel in different ways than their predecessors did. Given our fast-paced times, they are continuously facing, (a) shifts in societal values, leading to greater employee awareness and greater need for involvement (Higgs, 2003); (b) changes in investor focus—from sheer shareholder advancement to increased stakeholder involvement (Jennings, 2005); (c) needs for significant organizational change (Gordon & Pollack, 2018; Sakhartov & Folta, 2013), and (d) increased stress on employees, requiring steadfast human resource guidance to curtail excessive turnover (Raza, Khan, & Mujtaba, 2018). These are just a minor selection of the leadership challenges in our times. Additionally, leaders should not underestimate that today's followers are, on average, more educated and more independent in their thinking. They expect more input, appreciate inclusion, and get demoralized when they are summoned to follow their leaders mindlessly. Today's leaders are therefore expected to have some psychological foundations that can assist them in critical areas such as humanism, moral awareness, and a communal approach. (Marques, 2015). To address issues that epitomize the spirit of our times, this chapter describes the awakened leader.

Leadership: A Fascinating Phenomenon

Leadership has been described, studied, and applied in numerous ways. The fact that this is the case implies the fascination that scholars and practitioners generally have with the subject. It also demonstrates that leadership is a frequently implemented phenomenon. Actually, there are conflicting opinions about the meaning of leadership. A large group of leadership authors feels that we can only speak of leadership when people exert leadership behavior in a formal, hierarchical setting toward others. Others broaden this scope and include informal settings to the picture, but they maintain that "others" have to be involved before we can speak of leadership. And then there are those, such as the author of this chapter, who feel that leadership should be considered from an even broader scope: as a behavior we exert throughout the many decisions we make and the many actions we take, whether others are involved or not. It is our personal leadership that drives us to make the strategic choices in our lives, for instance, whether we will continue our study or find a job right after college, or whether we should invest our savings in a new car or a long overdue paint job of the house.

Seen from a positive angle, the fact that opinions differ so broadly about leadership indicates the vitality of this phenomenon, for whenever people passionately differ in opinion about something, it means that they *think* about it and consider it important enough to take a stance. However, whether we consider leadership a behavior in which others should be involved is of less importance to this chapter. The *quality* of the leadership we choose to exert today—regardless of the setting—is of much higher urgency and importance, as it will determine the difference between self-centeredness and selflessness, exclusion and inclusion, and ultimately, between leading failing and flourishing organizations.

The Quality of Our Leadership

As theories around leadership continue to advance, there seems to be one theme that encompasses all: cognizance, or the very act of being awake. One only has to review the currently supported leadership styles, such as "team leadership," "strategic leadership," "symbolic leadership," or "servant leadership" (Pierce & Newstrom, 2003, p. 9), to realize that the foundation to successful implementation of all these styles is *applicability*. Dion (2012) adds some additional leadership styles to this enumeration, such as "self-leadership," "authentic leadership," "shared leadership," and "transformational leadership," pointing out that several of these leadership styles place an emphasis on the moral issue, thus unveiling the basic link between a given leadership style and what could be considered as "ethical leadership."

Many authors have exclaimed for quite some time now that there is no single leadership style that proves to be successful under all circumstances. In an interview with Paul Cavanagh of Cisco Ireland, he emphasized that there is no one leadership style that is universally applicable, because different people will respond to different approaches ("There is no single leadership style. . .," 2017). Concurring with this perspective, Hughes, Ginnet, and Curphy (2002) avowed, "[L]eadership depends on several factors, including the situation and the followers, not just the leader's qualities or characteristics" (p. 23). These authors then elaborated,

> When you see a leader's behavior . . . you should not automatically conclude something good or bad about the leader, or what is the right way or wrong way leaders should act. You need to think about the effectiveness of that behavior in that context with those followers.
>
> *(p. 45)*

Bennis (2003) underscored this vision in his assertion, "Genuine leaders empathize with others, engage them in shared meaning, and make them feel essential. No single style has a lock on the ability to win others to a vision" (p. 4). In an interview with professor Rosenbach, the Evans Professor of Eisenhower Leadership Studies and Professor of Management at Gettysburg College, published in the 2003 edition of the *New Zealand Management*, this perception was also accentuated in the statement, "What leaders do is important, but how they do it is of equal concern. Although much research has focused on identifying the one best style, no single style or personality is best for all situations" ("NZIM: William Rosenbach on The Essence of Leadership," p. 18). Madsen and Hammond (2005) added, in that regard, "The monolithic, one-size-fits-all theory of leadership that is a result of globalization and the primacy of the American management model must be broken. It doesn't work anywhere; it doesn't work in the US" (p. 71). The previous may illustrate, hence, that there has been, for quite some time now, general unanimity about the insight that the situation and the type of followers involved play a significant role in the leadership style that will be successful.

If, then, one considers "awakened" or "wakeful" leadership as a multifaceted way of leading (to be explained next in this chapter), precisely based on the prerequisites mentioned earlier—the situation and the followers—it can be inferred that this could be the single leadership style that will work in all scenarios. As Madsen and Hammond (2005) stated it, "Emergence is a self-organizing process for taking local actions to achieve global impact" (p. 71). It is this self-organizing process, this all-inclusive and well-considered specific strategy tailored to local circumstances, that can be considered the foundation for awakened leadership. In essence, when we evaluate the quality of our leadership, we have to include our values and moral convictions. What do we believe in? What do we consider important? What is acceptable to us and what is not?

It should be noted that many people have a tendency to just adopt mindsets and behaviors from others because they simply don't think about the option of developing their own. And as they engage in this mindless adoption process, they fail to question the reasons and motives behind those others' actions, or the circumstances under which those mindsets and behaviors were developed. This act of mindlessly following trends and behaviors has been the plight of humanity for the longest time. Mindless behavior is when rules and routines are more likely to govern our behavior, irrespective of the current circumstances (Langer & Moldoveanu, 2000). Mindless people have a tendency to tune out and ignore new information (Cram & Newell, 2016). The major problem we are facing today is that we have progressed—or regressed—too far in our so-called civilized pattern to further uphold any form of mindlessness. In our local and global society of today, we are too connected, too informed, and too interdependent to continue hiding behind a mask of ignorance and mindless behavior. Aside from the numerous alerts on global warming, pollution, extinction of species, and forest and water decline, we are dealing with inevitable interdependencies, inexorable cause and effect trends, which demand urgent attention to the decisions we make from here onward. Some recurring interdependencies in business leadership that require strict caution are:

- Short-term profit-based decisions. On one hand, these hit-and-run type decisions benefit a small cluster of affluent individuals, but on the other hand, they cause escalating levels of poverty and anger among large human communities.
- Downsizing workforces to safeguard corporate continuance. These processes often happen without considering constructive and creative alternatives, such as proposing a temporary collective salary reduction. Downsizing sets a tone of despair and destroys morale, which in turn negatively affects perceptions of the company and its leaders, since they are ultimately responsible for these actions. A company with a harsh reputation may rest assured that this will eventually result in declining performance.
- Starting businesses with a sheer profit motive rather than a socially oriented motive. This egocentric model may have worked in the 20th century, but in today's day and age, the model and its success rate are just as unsustainable as the mindset behind them.
- Lack of transparency within the business. Leaders who try to maintain this, now obsolete, model of "divide and conquer" will soon find that today's educated workforce has neither patience nor appreciation for such insecure strategies. These leaders may find that their employees will display lack of transparency about their opinions and preferences, which may lead to painful and embarrassing findings in vulnerable times.
- Underpaying field-level employees in order to pay out gigantic bonuses, salaries, and dividends to strategic-level stakeholders. Leaders who see themselves as "higher" and "better" than their workforce will not find empathy when they need it most (Marques, 2015).

As we move toward an increasingly interdependent and vulnerable global, mental, and emotional climate, it is critical to adopt wisdom and empathy as dominant virtues to ends that justify means.

So, which mindsets and behaviors are causing the previously described behaviors? Here are some:

- Lack of reflection, which can drive us into self-centeredness and failure to consider the effects our decisions have on others.
- Mindless performance, which is the immediate manifestation of a lack of reflection.

- Change aversion, which is a problem many people struggle with, because we are creatures of habit, even when those habits have lost their constructive use.
- Blindly adhering to traditions, which is one of the most common drivers behind mindless behavior: we often get stuck in doing things that were traditionally done this way without reflecting or questioning whether they still make sense today.
- Lack of broad view, which lies at the foundation of many a disastrous decision. Till today, when deforestation practices are implemented, they are done with a deliberate blind eye to the massive damage this practice does, not only to wildlife, which is robbed of its habitat, but also to humanity, which is systematically stripped of its oxygen.
- Too much detail focus, which is a more focused approach to the issue mentioned earlier: we can get so lost in details—a problem that is visible in many workplaces—that we waste precious time on nitpicking, at the expense of the bigger picture and its impact.

Awakened Leadership

As is the case with most inclusive leadership approaches, the urge to inquire about awakened leadership arose from the earlier described trend of massive interconnectedness, triggered by globalization and the consequential exposure to increasingly diversifying work settings. The name "awakened leader" was inspired by a story of Gautama Siddhartha's enlightenment, which established him as "the Buddha" (the awakened one) afterwards. Upon a lengthy insight meditation, Siddhartha was walking up a road, when he encountered a passerby, who was stunned by his radiance and asked him whether he was a wizard, a God, or some other kind of other upper being. The Buddha simply responded that he was "awake."

When considered in light of the most dominant leadership theories, we find that awakened leadership is very situational oriented. In the situational leadership theory, leaders adapt their leadership style by assessing their employees, evaluate the critical factors in their workplace, and then choose the leadership style that best fits their goals. Awakened leadership, however, reaches beyond the distinction of the conventional tasks and relationship orientation, given the range of circumstances and stakeholders today's work environments deal with (Marques, 2008). Awakened leaders are aware that, while the situational theory remains useful, there is more to leadership today than leaders, followers, and a work-based situation (Northouse, 2018), so awakened leaders cannot merely base their decisions on those parameters only. They have to consider critical contemporary factors such as shifts in societal values, changes in investor focus, needs for significant organizational change, increased stress on employees and the guidance this requires, as well as the urge of employees to acquire more ownership in decision-making. Most importantly, awakened leaders need to remain in touch with their conscience, and identify reflective practices that enhance their mindfulness, so that they can maintain their inner balance. The strategies that these leaders may choose for mindfulness maintenance and enhancement may vary widely. Some leaders will gravitate to meditation, while others may engage in prayer, yet others turn to trusted mentors, and some take to walking, yoga, or reading. The strategies unto themselves don't matter, as long as the leader feels that deep reflection occurs and wakefulness is attained and maintained.

Foundational Structures of Awakened Leaders

The logical question that emerges when mentioning awakened leadership is, what exactly does this phenomenon comprise? The simplest answer to this question would be, every possible leadership style, trait, and skill developed so far, as well as those still to be developed in the future, as long as these styles, traits, and skills meet the criteria of being constructive and applicable to all parties involved.

Style Inclusions

Awakened leadership entails a comprehensive consideration of various leadership styles, which are at the disposal of every leader. Yet, the key factor is that awakened leaders are conscientious in their consideration and application of any leadership style, whether autocratic, democratic, laissez-faire, transformational, participative, servant, authoritarian, situational, or other (Hussain & Hassan, 2016). Given today's fast-changing performance climate, awakened leaders may display a fondness of servant leadership, as this style invites an approach of yielding and sharing responsibility.

> Servant leadership can be defined as a multidimensional leadership theory that starts with a desire to serve, followed by an intent to lead and develop others, to ultimately achieve a higher purpose objective to the benefit of individuals, organizations, and societies.
> *(Coetzer, Bussin, & Geldenhuys, 2017, p. 1)*

This behavior can also be related to the phenomenon "situational leadership," which Northouse (2018) explains as matching the leader's style to the competence and commitment of subordinates.

Trait Inclusions

McCrae and Costa (1990) describe traits as "dimensions of individual differences in tendencies to show consistent patterns of thoughts, feelings, and actions" (p. 23). In a study amongst 195 participants, Nichols (2016) found that as their leadership experience grows, leaders gain better insight in what it takes to be a good leader. With that, they also change the traits they desire to cultivate. Some of the dominant traits that emerged from Nichols's study were helpfulness, kindness, support, agreeableness, cooperation, fairness, self-confidence, self-assuredness, goal-orientation, ambition, dominance, and assertiveness. In the case of awakened leaders, mindfulness is eminent. "Mindfulness likely supports positive affect because it consists of being focused on the present moment and [is] deeply engaged with present experiences" (Carleton, Barling, & Trivisonno, 2018, pp. 186–187). Other scholars, such as Secretan (2001), prefer the term "consciousness." He asserts, "Consciousness is being awake to the mystical and ineffable aspects of being alive. The rational mind sees a world of scarcity and responds with fear. The conscious mind sees a world of abundance and responds with love" (p. 19). In Figure 19.1, the concept of mindfulness/consciousness is captured as "conscious mind."

Balance

Along with the cautious selection of the appropriate style and the development of distinctive traits, awakened leadership still requires a responsible balance between task and relationship behavior, since these remain the drivers of performance toward a required goal. Leaders that focus strongly on task behavior are mainly concerned with getting the job done and don't engage too much with the individuals involved and their perceptions about the job. In relationship behavior, the opposite happens: leaders are more concerned with the employees' well-being and less with the task at hand. Awakened leaders maintain a careful balance between these two extremes, in that they are concerned and supportive toward stakeholders (not merely employees), but also ensure that performance does not suffer.

Emotional Intelligence

In the performance of awakened leadership, special emphasis should be laid on the aspect of emotional intelligence. EI has been defined as the ability to perceive emotions, access and generate emotions to assist thought, understand emotions and emotional meanings, and regulate emotions reflectively to promote both better emotion and thought (Mayer & Salovey, 1997). Goleman (1998) defined emotional intelligence as "the ability to rein in emotional impulses, to read another's innermost feelings and to handle relationships and conflict smoothly" (p. 36). Pointing out the importance of developing and sustaining this quality, Goleman (1998) explained, "These emotional aptitudes can preserve relationships, protect one's health and improve success at work" (p. 36). Goleman divided emotional intelligence into the following five emotional competencies: (1) "The ability to identify and name one's emotional states and to understand the link between emotions, thought and action" ("Emotional Intelligence," para. 11); (2) "The capacity to manage one's emotional states—to control emotions or to shift undesirable emotional states to more adequate ones" ("Emotional Intelligence," para. 11); (3) "The ability to enter into emotional states (at will) associated with a drive to achieve and be successful ("Emotional Intelligence," para. 11); (4) "The capacity to read, be sensitive to, and influence other people's emotions" ("Emotional Intelligence," para. 11); and (5) "The ability to enter and sustain satisfactory interpersonal relationships" ("Emotional Intelligence," para. 11). More recently, Mayer, Roberts, and Barsade (2008) have described EI as "the ability to carry out accurate reasoning about emotions and the ability to use emotions and emotional knowledge to enhance thought" (p. 515). While there is still no unified definition of EI, the previously provided explanations underscore strongly enough that emotional intelligence is of high eminence in the performance of awakened leadership.

Authenticity

The final attribute mentioned in this chapter, although not the final quality involved in awakened leadership, is authenticity. George (2003) refers to authentic leadership as "driven by passion and purpose, not greed" (p. 6). It is George's opinion that "there are five essential dimensions to authentic leaders: purpose, values, heart, relationships, and self-discipline" (p. 6). George (2003) perceives authentic leadership as "the only way to build lasting value [by focusing] on the company's missions, customers, and employees" (p. 30). George further explains the creation and sustenance of lasting value by focusing on various aspects, which the author of this chapter divided into two distinctive categories: the people and the organization. Pertaining to the people aspect, George mentions, "Connecting every day with your employees"; "Being out with your customers looking for great ideas for growth"; and "Getting results for all your stakeholders, not just the shareholder of the past five minutes" (p. 32). Pertaining to the well-being of the organization, George lists the following procedures, "Building your business by pursuing your mission with a passion"; "Being true to your core values in every decision"; and "Building an enduring organization of authentic leaders from top to bottom" (p. 32).

Bonau (2017) adds to the aforementioned that authenticity is a crucial trait for inspirational leaders. She stresses that while not all authentic leaders may be inspirational in nature, it remains a fact that leaders would not be able to genuinely inspire followers if they were not true to their values and goals. Bonau also stresses that authentic leaders are a greater asset to humanity as a whole, due to the positive development they aim to bring, than inauthentic leaders are.

Based on the styles and behaviors listed in this chapter for the awakened leader, the following working definition can be formulated: awakened leadership is the all-encompassing leadership approach, involving the leader's awareness to incorporate the appropriate style given the followers and the situation; the leader's capacity to sharpen the skills necessary for guiding him- or herself, his or her followers, and the organization in its entirety toward advancement; and the leader's ability to remain emotionally attuned to the self, the stakeholders, and the environment, thereby maintaining the highest level of authenticity possible.

Dimensions of the Wakeful Approach

As extensively explained previously, a wakeful approach begins with awareness—of our values and moral convictions, as mentioned earlier, of our beliefs, priorities, boundaries, and behavioral tendencies. It really catalyzes when we start accepting that many of our traditionally held beliefs may need serious re-evaluation, so that we refrain from mindlessly following existing patterns, but instead formulate our own opinions, based on our own, contemporary insights.

Reflection is a fairly simple activity, yet many people forget to engage in it regularly. Frequent reflection can help us stay alert of our decisions, because we dare to question them. It can also enable us to see the wider scope of our actions and motivate us to reconsider first impulses. Reflection can help us understand that each choice we make is actually based on insufficient information, and that much of the course of our life depends on the actions we take after our decisions are made. What this means is that we may sometimes make poor decisions, but we can correct them if we reflect and find that the direction in which things are developing is unsatisfactory.

Wakeful leaders reflect in three dimensions: personal, relational, and professional (Marques, 2015).

- Personal reflection solidifies the relationship we have with ourselves. It can be achieved and maintained through self-imposed questions such as (a) how do I differ today from the person I was last year? (b) have I changed for better or worse in moral regards? and (c) how can I (further) improve my moral performance from here onward?
- Relational reflection evaluates our connections with others and the nature of those connections. It can be practiced through insight-enhancing contemplations such as (a) what does this relationship mean to me? (b) what constructive actions have I taken in recent months to nurture this relationship? and (c) what constructive effects has this relationship had on me in recent months?
- Professional evaluation considers our connection with our formal activities. Some reflective questions we could ask in that regard are (a) what am I passionate about professionally? (b) is what I do today related to my passion? and (c) is my professional activity a constructive one to me and to society? (Marques, 2015).

Allocating regular time to reflect helps us gain more influence of our past (because we get to appreciate it more), the present (because we experience it more intensely), and the future (because we consider it more deliberately). Self-reflection is a guaranteed way of staying mindful and preventing ourselves from mindless actions. Self-reflection is therefore not something we should only do once. It has to become a regular part of our life. Self-reflection can serve as a powerful thread that weaves our past, present, and future together: we see the bigger scheme better and realize that many of your setbacks are necessary parts in the puzzle that is our life. More importantly, self-reflection helps us make different decisions, based on broader considerations, thus elevating our moral and mental spectrum from merely the here and now toward inclusion of the well-being of those that come after us.

The Dimensions of Wakefulness

Wakefulness may not immediately sound like a leadership skill of any prominence, but the more one contemplates on it, the more it will. Based on observations of multiple remarkable leaders over the course of two decades, each in a different type of environment, a number of perceived traits and behaviors emerged, which are presented in this chapter. Wakefulness, as a significant leadership trait, has been explained before (see earlier cited statements from Secretan (2001) and Harung, Heaton, and Alexander (1995). Carson (2016) agrees with those statements about consciousness and the importance of wakefulness in leaders by affirming, "Conscious leading is taking consistent actions that make a positive difference for your people, family, friends, community, organizations and environment, while making the world a better place to live" (p. 301).

Wakefulness—or consciousness—could therefore also be described as the way of an awakened leader. Hence, the simplest explanation of an awakened leader—if we want to concisely capture the essence of the previously presented working definition—is "a leader who is awake." Not just in the factual sense of the word, but in every way. An awakened leader maintains a high level of alertness in every regard: toward him- or herself and his or her driving motives in various matters; toward the people he or she guides; toward the organization he or she leads; toward the environment in which his or her organization operates, and toward the entire universe.

Wakefulness, in the case of a leader, can be segmented into many dimensions. For the purpose of conciseness, only the three basic areas shall be reviewed here:

- Internal wakefulness
- External wakefulness
- Integrated wakefulness

Each of these layers could, in turn, be subdivided further.

Internal Wakefulness

Internal wakefulness pertains, in foundation, to the leader's connection with his or her inner source of wisdom. It could be subdivided into two main segments, which are (a) rational wakefulness, which pertains to areas such as intellectual skills, ethical sense, and beliefs; and (b) emotional wakefulness, which touches on areas such as emotional intelligence, intuition, morals and values, self-perception, and passion. Regardless of whether one chooses to consider the following a form of rational or emotional wakefulness, or a combination of both, it is prudent to underscore, within this context, spiritual wakefulness. Living a righteous life, thus remaining wakeful, is largely a consequence of being in tune with one's spiritual side. The spiritual aspect is a common factor among the majority of religious and spiritual teachings as well. While it's important to not confuse spirituality with religion, there is something to say about the general mutuality in teaching acceptance, understanding, and goodwill among both spiritual and religious streams (Marques, 2008). The growing availability of Buddhist literature, for instance, reveals an interesting similarity with spiritual behavior, especially amongst leaders in today's increasingly interconnected global professional community. The Vietnamese Buddhist monk Nhat Hanh (2003) illustrates this in his statement, "When we practice mindfulness in our daily life, we cultivate the foundation of peace, sowing seeds of understanding in ourselves and others" (p. 56). Nhat Hanh further asserts, "If we transform our individual consciousness, we begin the process of changing the collective consciousness. Transforming the world's consciousness is not possible without personal change" (p. 56). These teachings, although stemming from a religious leader, are independent of any particular religious cluster. They are based on purely spiritual practices, regardless of one's affiliation with any religious congregation. It is generally known, however, that all major religions, including Christianity, Hinduism, Islam, Buddhism, and others, teach similar values as the ones previously described by Nhat Hanh. It is also commonly accepted that the factors involved in these teachings are very much in line with the ideal of enlightenment, which is generally ascribed to deeply religious individuals or high-ranking congregational officers. This might be a wrong perception, however. Enlightened perspectives are very well within the reach and practices of any internally wakeful individual who participates in the daily sequence of working, socializing, and maintaining a family. In support of the this, Rahula (1974) reminds his readers of a statement made many centuries ago by Sariputta, Buddha's chief disciple. It was Sariputta's opinion that you can have ascetics living in the forest with "impure thoughts and defilements," (p. 77) while you can have other individuals living in a village or town, "practicing no ascetic discipline, yet with a mind that is pure and free from defilements." Rahula (1974) further cites Sariputta's establishment that the regular town person, in such a case, is "far superior to, and greater than, the one who lives in the forest" (p. 77). With Sariputta's example in mind, we can draw the conclusion that enlightenment is not necessarily reserved for those who seclude themselves. As an extension to this insight, we can surmise that acting as "a good person" is not demonstrated by either going to church every Sunday or reading the Bible or Koran every night—particularly if one continues to submit to dark habits and customs the rest of the time. Being spiritual has little to do with one's external rituals and everything with one's internal wakefulness. The spiritual mindset comes about through internal growth: nurturing one's emotional intelligence (EI), as mentioned before, and relating to others in an empathetic way.

External Wakefulness

External wakefulness pertains to the leader's awareness of the world around him or her. Not just the environment within the organization, but also within the industry in which the organization operates; outside of this industry toward other, potentially new industries to enter once an operational change comes about; and in the world at large.

External wakefulness can be subdivided into three basic segments: (a) close external wakefulness, which pertains to the leader's behavior within the organization and the way he or she treats the people and processes around him or her. Elements such as continuous questioning of processes in order to establish upward spiraling organizational learning will be involved in this area; (b) medial external wakefulness, which involves skills such as a vision for the organization; one or more strategies toward realizing the vision; and the continuous alertness necessary to analyze trends and to use them to the advantage of the organization's future. The awakened leader will most apparently use his or her wakefulness in this regard to alter the perceived trends in order to become the change agent in the organization's industry: and (c) distant external wakefulness, which pertains to global effects of the activities of the organization and the industry in which it operates. The awakened leader will, at this level, consistently attempt to decrease harm done to environments due to this industry and increase advantages for as many and as wide a range of stakeholders as possible.

Integrated Wakefulness

Integrated wakefulness pertains to the way the leader intertwines his or her internal and external wakefulness attributes. It gets into areas of combining the leader's values, intuition, emotional intelligence, intelligence quotient, beliefs, ethics, self-perception, and passion, with the given circumstances of the organization; its workers; its current direction; its potential; its industry, including all stakeholders; and the world at large. The integrated wakefulness is the most complicated part of being a leader, because it pertains so much to action through perceived compatibility. If there is no compatibility between the leader's internal qualities and his or her external environment, there will not be any integration. Either the leader will exit this organization, or the organization will undergo some sort of change in order to establish equilibrium between its operations and the leader's perspectives.

Within the context of acquiring wakefulness, there are some aspects to keep in mind: first and foremost, the fact that "Achieving [any] transformation requires the creation of commitment" (Guillory, 2004, p. 24). It is Guillory's opinion that "commitment begins with realizing that one is not superior or inferior to anyone else—by race, sex, ethnicity, ability, or culture" (p. 24). In his argumentation of applying a wakeful-based transformation, Guillory continues, "Creating an environment of inclusion also requires education, sensitivity and awareness, and suggested behavioral changes" (p. 27).

Important to keep in mind is also that—being human and, thus, receptive to things that happen to us—awakened leaders are constantly changing. And so may some of their internal pillars of wakefulness. Fortunately, the changes are usually not too tremendous unless something life changing occurs in the leader's personal or professional life, for instance, death, birth, intense exposure to another culture, or a great loss affecting the business. If such is the case, the leader will probably reevaluate his or her areas of wakefulness and calibrate them again toward the external circumstances, which also change continuously, in order to determine the possibility of continued integrated wakefulness, altered integrated wakefulness, or separation.

Characteristics of Awakened Leaders

As could already be gathered from the previous section, awakened leaders share some powerful characteristics, in addition to those already mentioned. They exert adaptability to different circumstances, drive, passion, and commitment to achieve their goals, resilience, willpower to use failures as lessons for growth, clear vision of the bigger picture and the future, and a clear formulation of their values. Through their flaws, they also develop emotional intelligence, which enables them to compassionately relate to even the most downtrodden among their followers. Awakened leaders further share qualities such as courage, inspiration, and the ability to instigate positive change. In the following section, we will take a closer look at some specific skills, strategies, and qualities of awakened leaders.

As a leader who aims to attain positive results and well-being for all stakeholders, human and non-human, an awakened leader consciously examines and cultivates a series of responsibility-based qualities, such as,

- Morals and values, often coming forth from past challenges and deep self-reflection in order to become more aware of the type of decisions to make.
- Ethics, with an emphasis on the understanding that diverse environments oftentimes harbor people with very diverse ethical insights, and that ethical decisions are not always the most positive ones. This may lead to having to explain and defend courses of actions to stakeholder groups on a regular basis.
- Integrity, honesty, and trust, an interrelated set of qualities and behaviors that very much influence the way employees will consider such a leader.
- Vision, which requires clear and open communication with stakeholders, in order to help them understand the reasons behind actions and inspire them toward the common goal.
- Respect, which these leaders know to make all the difference in interactions of any kind. One earns respect by giving it.
- Passion, which doesn't only drive the leader, but inspires followers to perform optimally and enthusiastically.
- Commitment, which is one of the foremost role model qualities. Awakened leaders know how important walking the talk is and how well employees gravitate to that behavior.
- Compassion, which entails the leader's ability and desire to understand the circumstances that others are subjected to and work with them, yet in such a way that they are not blatantly taken advantage of.
- Justice, which is not always a broadly appreciated quality, but nonetheless one that awakened leaders know they should implement in order to keep matters fair and acceptable.

- Kindness, which goes so much further than arrogance, autocracy, and negativity. Oftentimes, it is the experience of kindness in their lives, and the recollection of how good this experience felt, that triggers awakened leaders to be kind to others as well.
- Forgiveness, which is a quality that is also acquired through experience, but becomes very important in establishing and maintaining a positive work environment. It expresses itself in workplaces by not holding grudges and moving on from conflicts once those have been settled.
- Courage, a must-have in leadership, not only to develop a vision, but also to stand up for what one believes and to lead the way in moving toward it.
- Love, in the sense of making stakeholders—coworkers, customers, shareholders, suppliers, community members, and all others that are affected by the organization's actions—understand that their well-being is at the core of decisions made, and that the aim is to advance all parties as much as possible, and to harm as little as possible.
- Deep listening, a quality that many leaders still have to learn, as assertiveness seems to be a higher regarded leadership trait, especially in Western societies. Yet, those who practice deep and empathetic listening know how much it is appreciated and what bond it can help create.
- Inspired and inspiring, which is almost like two sides of the same coin: a leader cannot inspire others without first being inspired. Yet, even then, it takes clear communication and many of the traits discussed here to win followers and exude genuine good intention.
- Authenticity, which was discussed earlier, which entails critical awareness to personal values and adherence to integrity, honesty, and mindfulness.
- Spiritual connection, in which there is a clear and present focus on the connection with the source inside, instigating frequent reflections on actions, thoughts, and decisions.
- Multidimensional, which pertains to both the leader's focus on multiple stakeholders and aspects in the performance realm and his or her style of leading, which integrates the proper behavior given the situation and the followers.
- Fulfillment, entailing the deep understanding of attaining positive outcomes for as many stakeholders, to ensure longitudinal personal and professional gratification.
- Initiative, which is what leaders need to get into action toward accomplishments. Initiative also entails inclusion of others, in order to share ownership of processes, and team spirit.
- Change, a quality that is rooted in the understanding that we are not the same on a moment-by-moment basis, and that others, as well as the circumstances we deal with, are also subject to change (Marques, 2010).

A 2012 study of 69 leaders yielded that awakened leaders emphasize their focus on the well-being of stakeholders; doing the right thing, even if that means a reduction in the bottom line; family, which also encompass those they spend time with away from home (colleagues); enjoying their work; showing appreciation; understanding the self; earning trust; and providing recognition to those that conducted extraordinary accomplishments. Three main focus areas for awakened leaders emerged from this study: a focus on personal mastery (internal), relationships (integrated), and professional growth (external) (Marques, 2012).

A Roadmap to Inclusion and Morality

As can be concluded from this extensive overview and from Figure 19.1, awakened leadership is a very intuitive leadership style that requires continuous internal, integrated, and external calibration of circumstances and needs, in order to apply the most proper and mindful approach, thereby doing as much good and reducing as much harm as possible. Awakened leadership is based on the human sense of connecting, empathizing, and understanding and may not be the easiest leadership style to

Joan Marques

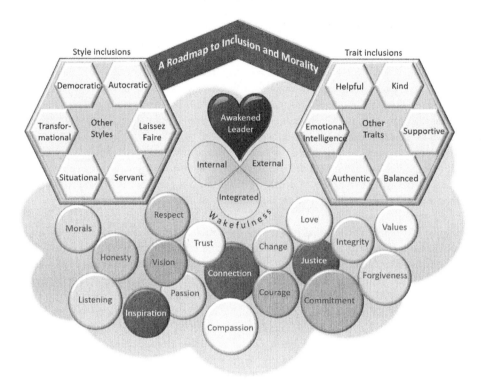

Figure 19.1 A roadmap to inclusion and morality

outline in terms of predictable outcomes. Because it is so intuitive, it is hard to measure, and may therefore not be easy to pin down as some more straightforward leadership styles. However, in favor of awakened leadership, it has to be stated that it is optimally attuned to inclusion and highly geared toward doing the right thing.

References

Bennis, W. (2003). Flight of the Phoenix. *Executive Excellence, 20*(5), 4.
Bonau, S. (2017). How to become an inspirational leader, and what to avoid. *The Journal of Management Development, 36*(5), 614–625.
Carleton, E. L., Barling, J., & Trivisonno, M. (2018). Leaders' trait mindfulness and transformational leadership: The mediating roles of leaders' positive affect and leadership self-efficacy. *Canadian Journal of Behavioural Science/Revue Canadienne Des Sciences Du Comportement, 50*(3), 185–194.
Carson, F. (2016). Why personal change is important for a conscious leader. *Industrial and Commercial Training, 48*(6), 300–302.
Coetzer, M. F., Bussin, M., & Geldenhuys, M. (2017). The functions of a servant leader. *Administrative Sciences, 7*(1), 5.
Cram, W. A., & Newell, S. (2016). Mindful revolution or mindless trend? examining agile development as a management fashion. *European Journal of Information Systems, 25*(2), 154–169.
Dion, M. (2012). Are ethical theories relevant for ethical leadership? *Leadership & Organization Development Journal, 33*(1), 4–24.
George, B. (2003). Authentic leadership. *CMA Management, 77*(8), 6.
Goleman, D. (1998). The emotionally competent leader. *The Healthcare Forum Journal, 42*(2), 36–38.

Gordon, A., & Pollack, J. (2018). Managing healthcare integration: Adapting project management to the needs of organizational change. *Project Management Journal, 49*(5), 5–21.
Guillory, W. A. (2004). The roadmap to diversity, inclusion, and high performance. *Healthcare Executive, 19*(4), 24.
Harung, H. S., Heaton, D. P., & Alexander, C. N. (1995). A unified theory of leadership: Experiences of higher states of consciousness in world-class leaders. *Leadership & Organization Development Journal, 16*(7), 44–59.
Higgs, M. (2003). How can we make sense of leadership in the 21st century? *Leadership & Organization Development Journal, 24*(5), 273–284.
Hughes, R. L., Ginnett, R. C., & Curphy, G. J. (2002). *Leadership: Enhancing the lessons of experience*. New York, NY: McGraw-Hill.
Hussain, M., & Hassan, H. (2016). The leadership styles dilemma in the business world. *International Journal of Organizational Leadership, 5*(4), 411–425.
Jennings, M. M. (2005). Ethics and investment management: True reform. *Financial Analysts Journal, 61*(3), 45–58.
Langer, E. J., & Moldoveanu, M. (2000). The construct of mindfulness. *Journal of Social Issues, 56*(1), 1–9.
Madsen, S. R., & Hammond, S. D. (2005). "Where have all the leaders gone?" An interview with Margaret J. Wheatley on life-affirming leadership. *Journal of Management Inquiry, 14*(1), 71–77.
Marques, J. (2008). Spirituality at work: Internal growth with potential external challenges. *The Journal for Quality and Participation, 31*(3), 24–27.
Marques, J. (2012). Achievements that matter: Perspectives of awakened leaders. *Journal of Management Policy and Practice, 13*(5), 103–115.
Marques, J. F. (2010). Awakened leaders: Born or made? *Leadership & Organization Development Journal, 31*(4), 307–323.
Marques, J. F. (2015). Why wakeful leadership is more important now than ever. *Development and Learning in Organizations, 29*(3), 18–20.
Mayer, J. D., Roberts, R. D., & Barsade, S. G. (2008). Human abilities: Emotional intelligence. *Annual Review of Psychology, 59*, 507–536.
Mayer, J. D., & Salovey, P. (1997). What is emotional intelligence? In P. Salovey & D. J. Sluyter (Eds.), *Emotional development and emotional intelligence* (pp. 3–31). New York, NY: Basic Books.
McCrae, R. R., & Costa, P. T. Jr. (1990). *Personality in adulthood*. New York, NY: Guilford Press.
Nhat Hanh, T. (2003). *Creating true peace*. New York, NY: Free Press, a division of Simon and Schuster, Inc.
Nichols, A. L. (2016). What do people desire in their leaders? The effect of leadership experience on desired leadership traits. *Leadership & Organization Development Journal, 37*(5), 658–671.
Northouse, P. G. (2018). *Leadership theory and practice* (8th ed.). Thousand Oaks, CA: Sage Publications.
NZIM: William Rosenbach on The Essence of Leadership. (2003). *New Zealand Management*, 18.
Pierce, J. L., & Newstrom, J. W. (2003). *Leaders and the leadership process*. New York, NY: McGraw-Hill.
Rahula, W. (1974). *What the Buddha taught*. New York, NY: Grove Press.
Raza, M. A., Khan, M. M., & Mujtaba, B. G. (2018). The impact of organizational change on employee turnover intention: Does stress play a mediating role? *Public Organization Review, 18*(3), 313–327.
Sakhartov, A. V., & Folta, T. B. (2013). Rationalizing organizational change: A need for comparative testing. *Organization Science, 24*(4), 1140–1156.
Secretan, L. (2001). The conscious leader. *Industry Week, 250*(2), 19–20.
There is no single leadership style that is universally applicable. (2017, July 8). *Sunday Business Post*, Cork.

20
SPIRITUAL LEADERSHIP
Leading While Spiritual

Sylvia W. Burgess and Karen Martin-Jones

Introduction

The phenomenon of what leaders do is complex. There is a myriad of responses for the definition of leadership. When adding spirituality to leadership, the complexity is more obvious. Often people think that spirituality and leadership cannot operate in the workplace at the same time. There are also differing opinions about what is meant by spirituality, making this as difficult to define as leadership. For the purpose of this writing, the authors are adopting a combined definition taken from work by Delbecq (1999) and Conger (1994). Collectively, these authors define spirituality as a universal energy of an individual's lived experiences that have transcendental qualities that lift us beyond ourselves and our personal interests. From a Christian perspective, we define the transcendental as God. Others may define this phenomenon in other ways that may or may not have a religious connection.

Ultimately, the foundation of spiritual leaders is based on their value system. According to Burgess (2011), the value system is spiritual capital. Spiritual capital is the value system that is an asset everyone possesses. Spiritual capital allows people to have trust and faith in each other that goes beyond just working together (Lloyd, 2010). When coupled with spirituality, it creates a foundation for understanding the meaning of how the capital is sustainable for leaders. Since leaders then possess spiritual capital, they are already well placed in using their values to work with others. When we add spirituality to this process, it provides a multifaceted dimension to a leader's capacity to lead.

Spiritual leaders are not just ministers, preachers, or pastors. Spiritual leaders can lead people who are not God's people as well as people who are (Blackaby & Blackaby, 2006). Thus, the idea of spiritual leaders in the workplace is gaining momentum. People who embrace their capacity as spiritual leaders in the workplace base their success on the idea that what they do is a calling or vocation. They view it as something greater than themselves. Additionally, they see the workplace in a holistic manner as opposed to a means to an end, such as income or lifestyle. Spiritual leadership requires that leaders are open-minded and inclusive. When spiritual leaders walk in this approach, their perception of the individual is viewed holistically, thus giving way to an organization that warrants and embraces diversity and inclusion.

Inclusion and Spirituality

As organizations evolve and become ever increasingly diverse, the need to embrace the whole person has become vital to organizational sustainability. Despite small gains in organizations shifting to a more diverse workforce, much work is still needed in this area. After all, many organizations view diversity and inclusion as one and the same; they are, however, very different. There is a distinct difference between inclusivity and diversity. Many organizations have incorporated diversity to satisfy the status quo. However, these underrepresented individuals are poorly represented in upper management or other leadership capacities. Diversity is, in effect, something that is forced or seemingly mandated upon an organization. However, inclusivity is making a conscious and intentional effort to view the differences of individuals as organizational assets, not mandates. It is the ability to acknowledge the value of the whole person, thus leading to the importance of inclusive leadership as an integral component of the organization's mission and vision.

Inclusive leadership is an important concept for leaders in organizations. Bilimoria (2012) described inclusive leadership as the ability to create a diverse, respected, and motivating environment that encourages the input of all individuals, while Shore, Cleveland, and Sanchez (2018) defined inclusion as "organizations and societies, people of all identities and many styles that can fully be themselves while also contributing to the larger collective, as valued and full members" (p. 176). If people are not allowed to bring their whole selves to work, then organizations are ultimately employing a less productive and partial individual. Implying or requiring one to leave their whole selves results in either a reluctant conformity to the organizational norms and or low employee retention. One losing themselves as a result of conformity stifles an individual's ability to contribute their creative, authentic selves to the overall success of the organization, all of which ultimately impact the bottom line.

An integral part of oneself is their soul or human spirit, which is in effect their spirituality. One's spirituality is associated with their inner calling. Religion has been a cultural aspect, and countless variations of its practices exist, however, common to all, religion is an appeal for meaning beyond the empty varieties and sufferings to something greater. The terms religion and spirituality, though often used interchangeably in much of the literature, are distinctly different. Although different, they both affect the physical and mental well-being of an individual.

Spirituality and Religion

Many people confuse religion with spirituality and often view their spirituality through a religious framework. Often the line between religion and spirituality is so close that no one definition adequately delineates the two. Webster defines spirituality as the quality of being concerned with the human spirit or soul as opposed to material or physical things. Newman (2004) stated, "to be spiritual or have spirituality, persons attempt to live a life guided by the spirit of their faith" (p. 105). This is evidenced in prayer and or meditation. Religion, however, is defined as either the belief in and worship of a superhuman controlling power, especially a personal God or gods and or a system of faith and worship. Worthington, Hook, Davis, and McDaniel (2011) defined religion as adhering to a belief system and practices related to traditions where there is agreement about beliefs and practices. They defined spirituality on the other hand as a more general feeling of closeness and connectedness to the sacred (Worthington et al., 2011). For the purposes of this writing, we will refer to God as the supreme being, providing the caveat that others may believe differently. In summary, Newman described spirituality as a state of "being" and religion as a state of "doing" (i.e. attending church, fasting, praying). Both require the act of preparation in some manner.

Preparation for Spiritual Leadership

While the ideology of being a spiritual leader sounds great, how does this manifest in the workplace? First, as individuals, we must become comfortable with who we are as both spiritual beings and leaders. The notion that one can be a successful leader and not have to leave their spirituality at the door requires intentional preparation. The successful spiritual leader must be prepared in several ways. These ways include being transparent, authentic, grateful, self-aware, and engaging and having a mindset for change. Transparency as a leader involves being honest in both success and failure. It also requires a degree of humility on the part of the leader. Lastly, the leader is pushed to transparency through honor, faith, and belief that there is more to the process than just individual success. Transparency is part of the foundation of spiritual capital. It provides an avenue for trust to be built and groomed among people who are working towards a common goal. Spiritual leaders who practice transparency welcome open communication, input, and feedback from the team. They tend to not withdraw when difficulties arise, and they practice telling the truth.

Second, authenticity is a critical component of preparation for a spiritual leader. Being real with self and others is significantly important to success. Aviolio, Gardner, Walumbwa, and May (2004) indicated that authentic leaders tend to be people who have a deep awareness of their thoughts and behaviors. They are perceived by others as being self-aware, value-oriented, moral, knowledgeable, and strong. Being real allows leaders to know how they operate and in what context they are operating. The notion of being authentic or real takes a serious look at one's values and moral perspectives. Authenticity in conjunction with spirituality points to leaders with strong character. These leaders do not say things they do not mean. They are deemed as trustworthy because they keep their word no matter what it requires. Lastly, spiritual leaders who practice authenticity believe in open communication and showing empathy towards others. You can expect these leaders to portray similar behavior in both their private and public lives. These leaders have the courage to admit when they are right or wrong.

Spiritual leaders also prepare themselves by having a heart of gratitude. Spiritual leadership involves intentionally being grateful. Even though gratitude seems simple, leaders must consciously cultivate it. We must train our minds to see situations as good instead of as disappointments. Showing gratitude is a choice that a leader makes when engaging others and making decisions in the workplace. Sometimes during change, trouble, or difficult times, when dealing with others it is hard to show gratitude. However, if we can show gratitude, it opens space for light to come into difficult situations.

When spiritual leaders remember to show gratitude, it provides the energy that elevates and expands others to a place for success. As leaders practice gratitude, it can turn challenges into opportunities, turn denial into acceptance, and turn confusing situations into clear paths for action. Leaders who engage with an attitude of gratitude are intentionally giving this area attention with the goal of having a positive impact. These leaders create an atmosphere where gratitude is deemed important and does not happen by accident. This allows for the creation of new energy for leaders and followers.

Further, spiritual leadership requires self-awareness. Self-aware spiritual leaders are intentionally conscious of their feelings, thoughts, ideologies, and experiences. When leaders can tune into these areas, they realize that their thoughts, beliefs, and ideologies are only one frame from which things can be seen or decisions made. Having a focus on self-awareness and how one's behaviors impact others causes spiritual leaders to think more about the shared well-being of others and how a more collaborative approach leads to greater success.

In addition, self-awareness is fundamental to the success of any leader. From a spiritual leadership perspective, self-awareness is even more important. With the constant changes in the workplace, spiritual leadership allows leaders who are self-aware to be more flexible. The choice to be flexible provides leaders a means by which to be resilient and stable. Lastly, self-awareness can be fostered by leaders to help them understand how their personal values play out in the workplace with others. Once leaders understand their own values and views, they are more likely to be receptive to others and to various viewpoints. Self-awareness in union with spirituality creates a more holistic way of engaging with others. The engagement process becomes more open and authentic.

Another way to prepare as a spiritual leader is to develop a mindset for change. When leaders are inflexible, it can create roadblocks to success. As often noted, as a leader, all that you know is not all there is to be known. Spiritual leadership requires that the leader understands that change is a way of life in the workplace and a rigid mindset will impede success. Growth without change is impossible. Blackaby and Blackaby (2011) noted that as leaders grow in their capacity, it creates growth in the organization. Accordingly, this requires that leaders should grow personally in order to impact change in the organization.

Finally, preparation for spiritual leadership involves leaders who are engaging. One cannot be a spiritual leader and be closed off to others. The ability to engage with others creates the community within organizations that fosters collaboration and teamwork. There has been a big shift in where and how individuals find and participate in community. In recent years, people tend to congregate less in formal religious settings where community has traditionally been built. This is particularly true for younger generations. Also, the change in living communities where people do not necessarily know or interact with their neighbors as was common in the past has created another missed opportunity for engagement. All of which have had significant implications in the need for individuals to desire community within the workplace.

Thus, people are more likely to build community among work colleagues. Being engaged is necessary to support employees' needs to belong and connect to something and to others. While engagement is not an exclusive characteristic for spiritual leaders, it is certainly important. Spiritual leadership requires that leaders be able to engage with others. The way this happens is when leaders can incorporate both individual and organizational success together. These leaders focus on praising and showing appreciation to others. It is essential to give credit and share the success. Successful engagement requires the leader to be willing to learn and to listen to others. Most important is the ability to promote and foster loyalty and trust. Engagement is a two-way process. The leader must be willing to allow others to engage with them as a leader.

In summary, spiritual leadership involves leaders who are prepared both inwardly and outwardly. The inward preparation is a personal journey that includes understanding who you are and your tolerance for acceptance of other people, other opinions, and behaviors that may vary from yours. The outward process is based on how the leader responds to the call for action. According to CACE (2015), this means that spiritual leadership requires leaders to learn, live, and lead. As spiritual leaders learn who they are and live who they are, they can in effect lead others to be who they are as well. This methodology leads to a more focused and intentional approach to spiritual leadership.

Intentional Approach to Spiritual Leadership

How does intentionality impact leadership? Intentionality is often linked with leaders who are decisive or assertive. According to Bates (2017), leaders are intentional when they remain focused on the results. The focus is on what is important and has a purpose for the organization. Intentional leaders tend to be deliberate and they work with a clear plan. For spiritual leaders to be successful, there must be an intentional approach to their leadership. Without intentionality, any focus on spirituality might get lost in the many other aspects of workplace leadership. Intentionality with spiritual leaders requires that we do our work with regard to one another. This again points us back to our values system or spiritual capital.

Many individuals struggle to find balance with how spirituality plays out in the workplace. We spend most of our lifetime working, and thus it is not possible for our spirituality to not infiltrate our work lives. As such, leaders are becoming more interested in how to integrate spirituality with work. As leaders seek to find more meaning in what they do, integrating spirituality into every part of their life is becoming an intentional strategy. This strategy allows leaders to be more intentional about how their spirituality impacts what they do and how they represent their actions.

Leaders who can intentionally focus on integrating their spirituality with work tend to have less fear about decisions, to be more ethical, and to be more committed to organizational values. When we can think about spirituality as an asset and not about specific religious affiliations or behaviors, we can better enmesh it with our work and leadership style. An intentional approach to spirituality and leadership in the workplace allows leaders and followers to think about themselves as spiritual beings who have a purpose that permits them to fulfill their calling here on earth without fear of reprisal.

Intentionally integrating spirituality in the workplace allows us to create a sense of community and belongingness that is vital for human survival. It permits us to be okay with bringing aspects of our inner self into the workplace. We have inner and outer components that make us who we are. When leaders feel compelled to separate their inner being from their outer being in the workplace, it creates an inner turmoil that will erupt at some place and time. The eruption might occur at work or outside of work. Therefore, intentionally allowing our spiritual self to help guide us in every aspect of our lives is critically important to a leader and to the overall organization.

An intentional approach also allows spiritual leaders to help create vision and experiences within the work environment that permits followers to connect with a sense of purpose and outcomes that create paths for success. It also sends a message to followers that they matter, that their lives have purpose and meaning, and that who they are and how they approach the work matters. Further, it creates an environment that fosters a mindset that the work we do matters and is for a greater good. Next, allowing spirituality to intentionally influence one's behavior creates a work culture that is based on values, and both leaders and followers can connect and belong in community together.

Further, an intentional approach to incorporating spirituality into the workplace lets leaders and followers have space for their inner life practices. These practices may vary from leader to leader and may include but are not limited to prayer, reading, yoga, journaling, meditation, or practicing mindfulness. This behavior allows spiritual leaders to intentionally build an organization's culture that includes using spiritual capital to impact the organizational outcomes. This requires that leaders and followers are more intentional about how they work together and what they allow as part of the workplace culture and community.

The last important aspect of spiritual leadership is the enhancement and focus on building community that is not leader-centric. This means that both leaders and followers play an essential role in the climate and culture of the workplace. There is an intentional engagement of all members of the organization and an appreciation of what each member contributes to the community and the organization's success. This type of spiritual leadership influence creates a positive work environment and a collective approach to how successful the organization is. The leaders who emerge from this process can come from anywhere in the organization. The focus of leadership is removed from just the titled or positioned leaders. It includes leaders who can use their experiences to gain results that impact the bottom line of the organization. Between the experiences and the results are the components of spiritual leadership.

Model of Spiritual Leadership

The spiritual leadership components build a model for spiritual leadership consideration. The spiritual leadership model suggests that experiences are influenced and shaped by intentional spirituality, spiritual capital, leadership, and inclusivity, all of which are working in concert to produce the fruit or results of one's experiences. Although personal, spirituality is directly impacted by one's experiences, which shape their responses to each of the components outlined in the model.

As shown in the model, the leaders' experiences are the beginning point for spiritual leadership. The goal is to get to the results or the "fruit." One's experiences are the building blocks for the foundation of the person's spirit. An individual's experiences dictate who they become as a person. Each person has multiple types of experiences that influence who they become. The experiences

Spiritual Leadership

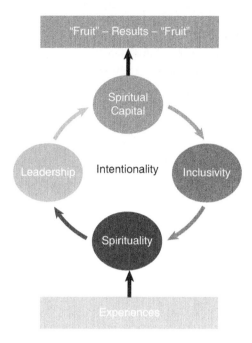

Figure 20.1 Spiritual leadership components

begin as early as one's childhood and in family systems. Growing up, we have both tacit and overt social experiences. The tacit socialization comes from those things we saw and followed, although no one said out loud that it was required. The overt socialization involved the good and bad things we were trained to do, and we choose to follow them.

Further, failures and successes both shape a leader's experiences. The difference between spiritual leadership and non-spiritual leadership is how we use failures and successes to shape our behavior as a spiritual leader. Spiritual leadership looks at failures as a stepping-stone to the next level. It is less about personal failure than about experiences that make you stronger and what lessons you can learn from them. Success is also a stepping-stone to growth. While different from the lessons learned from failure, successful experiences can help spiritual leaders to get to the next level as well. Successes do not encourage a sense of self-importance, but more as an example to others that they too can be successful and move to the next level. Both failures and successes are growth opportunities. The key is the response, which is the most important component for how experiences shape the leader.

Experiences that we have shape our level of spirituality. According to Burgess and Martin-Jones (2019), spirituality is that interconnected duality between the leader's intrinsic value system (spiritual capital) and the world in which they live. Spiritual capital reflects what is valued by a leader. When leaders focus on how their spirituality plays a significant role in both their private and public lives, spirituality will manifest itself in how the leader works with others, builds trust in relationships, and who they are fundamentally as people. Spiritual leadership is an asset that requires nurturing and attention to be sure that it remains an integral part of who we are as leaders.

Another component is inclusivity. Inclusivity is necessary to promote and enhance spiritual leadership. Gotis and Grimani (2017) noted that spiritual leadership creates opportunity for equitable and fair practices that encourages followers to resist being marginalized and status focused. Instead, spiritual leadership helps followers focus more on collective well-being, because they are paying attention to how their attributes are not posing problems but are integrating success in the workplace. In terms of relating, spiritual leadership and the need to be more inclusive are essential to healthy workplaces. This can only be accomplished when everyone is included and engaged in accomplishing the goal. Spiritual leadership, if manifested correctly, must embody being inclusive and valuing diversity. Spiritual leaders who engage in inclusive leadership emphasize being change oriented and engage in building cultures that shift the focus from individual success to a more collaborative and team approach. The goal is to ensure less isolationism and more collaboration through the development of psychological safe spaces (Carmeli, Reiter-Palmon, & Ziv, 2010). Using an inclusive approach creates a climate for participation, growth, and learning more than individual success does.

Spiritual leadership empowers practices that allow employees to work in a unified manner and collaborate on ideas with an inclusive mindset. According to Gotis and Grimani (2017), spiritual leadership supports the following inclusive propositions:

- Supports empowering practices
- Nurtures practices of equality
- Facilitates inclusive decision-making
- Informs productive conflict resolution processes
- Encourages training that produces appreciation of diversity

Spiritual leadership further fosters an atmosphere where anyone's contributions are weighed on merit and value versus who made the contribution. Spiritual leaders support inclusive behavior both in acceptance of others and in personal behavior. They are willing to promote belonging and connectivity.

There is no doubt that spiritual values operationalize spiritual leadership. The spiritual values of a leader related to respect, fairness, honesty, and care and concern for others are at the foundation of how spiritual leadership is played out in organizations. Often these soft skills are not looked upon favorably, but they do create an opportunity for leaders to use their "whole being" to lead. This use of spiritual capital as defined by Lloyd (2010) and Burgess (2011) is when leaders can use their intrinsic value system which are aligned with trust, culture, and relationship building to serve society and to fulfill our internal human need to serve. Again, spiritual capital does not take into consideration religious constructs. The focus is on individuals having faith in one another that is not bound by traditions or contractual agreements and that allows us to work together for a common goal.

Spiritual capital is directly aligned with the willingness to engage and participate. Spiritual capital is an asset that spiritual leaders use to build organizational participation among team members. Burgess (2011) designated spiritual capital as being universal and necessary for spiritual leadership. When leaders recognize the value of spiritual capital, they will intentionally use it to help engage individuals they are connected to. The link for the spiritual leader is the recognition that spiritual capital helps establish connections that give them an advantage in situations which materialism cannot. The most important aspect of spiritual capital in relationship to spiritual leadership is that when utilized for the good of everyone, it is a resource to help the leader and their followers grasp the importance of their influence and relationship-building skills to create the needed climate for participation, trust, and harmony (Burgess, 2011).

The model summarizes the specific components for how spiritual leadership operates on a practical level. Once an individual has come to terms with connecting their inner spiritual life with their leadership style and integrating this intentionally in the workplace, they will more likely be able to connect and serve ideals that are more than just doing what is right for the sake of earning a living or gaining a promotion. The greater good serves as a goal to strive for where the lives of more people are impacted versus only focusing on the individual benefits of work. Thus, when adversity, challenges, or difficulties arise, the leader has a strong inner place from which to pull and to make decisions that are more altruistic and a source of strength for leading. Ultimately, the bottom line is that the greater good of all people matter more than using people for personal gain or solely focusing on just the bottom-line goal.

When Spiritual Leadership Works and When It Does Not

To gain perspective about spiritual leadership from leaders and non-leaders in terms of roles and responsibilities, we asked several individuals about spiritual leadership. We asked individuals to define spiritual leadership from their perspective and to provide an example of what spiritual leadership looks like when it is working and when it is not. Lastly, we asked the individuals to share three things that must be present for spiritual leadership to be effective.

What Is Your Definition of Spiritual Leadership? Provide an Example of What Spiritual Leadership Looks Like When It's Working and When It Is Not Working

Senior Pastor of a Megachurch—This pastor is a member of Generation X.

Along with all the other practical principles of leadership in general, Spiritual Leadership is leadership that is submitted to the will of God. First I'll give you a biblical example: Jesus in the Garden of Gethsemane, He had His own will and His own plan and since spiritual leadership is someone who is submitted to the will of God. God had a will and a plan and that was for Jesus to die and go to the cross, he submitted to God and said nevertheless not my will, but thy will be done. We saw what happened, salvation came into the world. When spiritual leadership works in a spiritual or a Christian organization there is productivity, there is fruit that comes as a result of it, when it's submitted to God's will you see results, outcomes or should I say the desired results and outcomes. Adam is an example of what it looks like when spiritual leadership is not working. Adam and Jesus were both in the Garden, but Adam was in the garden of Eden, and God had a will, he had a plan, He had specific instructions and Adam said unlike Jesus, nevertheless not thy will, but my will, my plans be done and we saw the result of that ... the Garden turned into patches of wheat and so when we look at a spiritual or Christian organization when it is not working then we are able to look at the fact that it is not productive, it is not producing and we are not receiving or seeing those desired results, so it's the opposite.

First Lady of a Megachurch—Generation X

My definition of spiritual leadership is the foundation on which we stand, but to add to that in a more practical way, is that you have to be a spiritual influencer, an encourager, an inspirer, able to guide other individuals not just through your teaching, but also through your life's examples through your journey and walk to help others to not only live their best life, but to locate their purpose in God. What spiritual leadership looks like when it's working you actually can see the visible fruit of it, you see the tangible fruit of it, you see the joy of it, you see the transformation, the change and the commitment to it. And when it's not working you do not see the results of it, but it's not based on what you have not done sometimes we can plant the seed, and God does supply the water to water it, but you have to be open to receive the water but you continue to sow the seeds and pray eventually that results will manifest.

Senior Engineering Manager—Generation X

Spiritual leadership is using GOD inspired guidance and direction towards a purpose, goal or vision.

When it's working your leadership lifts the team, gives them a sense of purpose and the vision is executed.

When it isn't working there's a lack of direction/organization and selfish goals manifest instead of each person striving to make each other better.

Corporate Grant Manager—Baby Boomer

When trying to define what spiritual leadership means, I am influenced by the work of Tim Barnett. In the article, "Spirituality in Leadership" (www.referenceforbusiness.com/management/Sc-Str/Spirituality-in-Leadership.html), Barnett suggested the starting point should be defining spirit and leader separately. According to Barnett, "One dictionary definition of spirit is 'that which is traditionally believed to be the *vital principle* or animating force within living beings.'" Thus, the spirit relates to the deeper sense, meaning, or significance of something. A dictionary definition of the leader is "one who shows the way by going in advance; one who causes others to follow some course of action or line of thought." Thus, the leader is one who influences followers to think or behave in some way. Based on the above I would define spiritual leadership as modeling self-reflection in order to influence others to look within themselves to discover what their purposes are.

An example of effective spiritual leadership in the workplace would be a leader using workplace issues and strategic development as tools to influence those they lead to discover their own identity and to overcome the challenges they are facing. When those we lead are functioning from a place of self-created identity and strength, they are going to be more productive than individuals who are operating from a place of just filling a job.

Daycare Teacher—Generation X

Spiritual leader is a person that has been called out and set aside by God to lead others deeper into the principles and in depth living with God. I do not agree that spiritual leaders must hold a title as pastors. God calls different people from different backgrounds and uses them as spiritual leaders. When spiritual leadership is working it creates a safe place for those following to be who they really are. It creates a strong sense of unity and belonging across the board for those who are following. It creates an environment where growth is encouraged and supported, even if it seems to surpass where they are as a leader. When spiritual leadership is not working it creates an unsafe environment where people feel they need to hide their weaknesses. It creates a hostile environment that does not foster growth. Leadership that is not working causes friction among the people. It causes them to feel afraid to connect on any level with each other for fear of being called out. An environment that feels unsafe creates stressors in those repeatedly exposed to it. This kind of environment causes those in it to feel controlled and often it causes them to become stagnant.

College Student—Generation Z

Spiritual leadership is the ability to serve others, the way Christ serves us through compassion and love. Spiritual leadership is not a position to use to be seen or praised, it is a selfless position which focuses on benefitting others instead of oneself. An example of what spiritual leadership looks like when it is working, would be seeing growth in those whom you serve; for a leader is only as great as the team they lead. If you notice that your team is not spiritually growing, then your spiritual leadership is not working. It does not mean that leading is not for you. However, it may mean that you are not meeting the needs of those you serve. For example, if you were struggling with suicide, you would need someone to show you love and compassion instead of yelling at you about your faults. The same goes for spiritual leadership, you must meet the needs of those you serve in order to see growth. When you meet the needs of those you serve, you are essentially strengthening them against the attack of the enemy. If those who you lead could not survive in their spiritual walk with Christ without you then you need to reassess the way you lead. Spiritual leadership should create disciples for Christ not followers for you. If those who you lead cannot turn around and lead others to Christ, then you need to reassess the way you lead. A great spiritual leader allows God to use them to produce more great spiritual leaders whom shall produce even more great spiritual leaders.

Regardless of the generation, there is a pretty common concept of what constitutes spiritual leadership. Each response involves working with others, being self-reflective, and caring about more than the basic bottom line. Based on these individuals, influencing spiritual leadership involves influencing and being in relationship with others. Lastly, it involves being in service to others. All the examples given represent people who are influencers and are willing to serve.

What Three Things Must Be Present for Spiritual Leadership to Be Effective?

Senior Pastor of a Megachurch—Generation X

We operate under four main principles. What we really believe and operate and produce in leaders are our CAFE Principals—C-Commitment, A-Accountability, F-Follow-up and E-Excellence. We believe it takes that in any arena for leadership.

First Lady of a Megachurch—Generation X

In addition to the CAFE principles you must have the Holy Spirit to lead and guide you, you must love, show empathy and compassion, and walk in humility as Jesus walked. These things embody you as a spiritual leader.

Senior Engineering Manager—Generation X

GOD centered principles are the foundation for effective leadership. A key value or principle would be expressed by true love for the people.

Accountability/Responsibility are tied together and drives a team towards great stewardship.

Leading by example is the final key to effective leadership which allows the team to not only see the vision but watch it in operation. Once experienced, this can be replicated by each team member and becomes standard practice.

Corporate Grant Manager—Baby Boomer

The leader and the organization will focus more on people than on formalized positions of power. There is a focus as well on transformation of people and the organization through diversity as opposed to focusing on the individuals conforming. Finally, the philosophy of the leader and the overall organization is about forming partnerships, collaborating with and inspiring those they lead as opposed to trying to control them.

Daycare Teacher—Generation X

The three things that must be present for spiritual leadership to be effective are integrity, passion, and a strong desire to hear God's heart for those they are leading.

College Student—Generation Z

Transparency must be present because no one wants to follow the person who seems like they have it all together. People cannot relate to perfection; people relate to what is real. Even Jesus struggled and he did not hide his struggles from those whom he led. Instead he allowed them to see him struggle so that he can show them how to cope spiritually with struggling.

The fruits of the spirit must be present because the fruits are what you should be feeding to those you lead when you serve them. When you feed the fruits of the spirit to those you serve, it tastes good to them. It instills a hunger for more of God inside of them. It is so important for spiritual leaders to be serving the fruits of the spirit because it is worth the cost and it tastes so much better than what the world has to offer.

Your own spiritual growth must be present because a leader can only lead their team as far as they can go themselves. When you are not growing spiritually, you cannot instruct those you lead and serve on how to grow spiritually. A great spiritual leader knows how to admit to their team when they are lost. It would be foolish of a leader to be lost and not speak up about it because they miss the opportunity to utilize the strength of their team. This opportunity is a chance for the team as individuals to practice their strengths and strengthen their weaknesses.

The individuals responding to what three things are needed for spiritual leadership to be effective noted primarily that accountability, God, love, compassion, and focus on people are most important. Of the many things noted, they all involve spiritual leadership by connecting to others in a positive way or leading by example, all of which can have implications for future leadership.

Implications for Future Leadership

As the dynamics of leadership continue to change, it will require that leaders adapt and build their resource pool for their leadership to be successful. One of these resources is spirituality. As leaders look for innovative and creative ways to move people to do what they need to do, they will need all available resources. Leaders must use natural resources, use spiritual resources, work as hard as their followers do, communicate even better, serve those they work with, stay positive, and be an influencer. Of all the requirements, most of them fit into the realm of spiritual leadership (influencer, positivity, service, hardworking).

This chapter has significant implications for the future of leadership. Most notably, leading while spiritual sets the stage for an organizational culture and climate shift that encourages and embraces the whole person, thus having implications for leaders in both religious and non-religious organizations. It creates the context for more dialogue to occur. Additionally, it allows the concept of leadership to be redefined. This redefinition is evident in the interviewee's responses. There was a consistent theme that resonated with the interviewees, which suggests that regardless of one's position, age, or title, spirituality equates to production, effectiveness, and purpose. The basic premise of spirituality is rooted in ethical and moral constructs around one's greater good and higher purpose beyond themselves. In effect, spiritual leadership empowers collaborative practices, supports inclusive authentic leadership, and influences a culture of intentionality undergirded by experiences that support equitable and fair organizational practices.

References

Aviolio, B., Gardner, W., Walumbwa, F., & May, D. (2004). Unlocking the mask: A look at the process by which authentic leaders impact follower attitudes and behaviors. *Leadership Quarterly*, *15*(6), 801–823.

Bates, S. (2017). *Great leadership style: The power of intentionality*. Retrieved from www.bates-communications.com/bates-blog/great-leadership-style-the-power-of-intentionality

Bilimoria, D. (2012). Inclusive leadership. *Leadership Excellence Essentials*, *29*(3).

Blackaby, H. T., & Blackaby, R. (2011). *Spiritual leadership: Revised and expanded*. Nashville, TN: Broadman & Homan Publishers.

Blackaby, H. T., & Blackaby, R. (2006). *Spiritual leadership: The interactive study*. Nashville, TN: Broadman & Holman Publishers.

Burgess, S. W. (2011). *Spiritual Capital: Relationship with civic engagement among faith-based leaders* (Doctoral dissertation, North Carolina Agricultural and Technical State University. Greensboro, NC).

Burgess, S. W., & Martin-Jones, K. (2019). Spirituality as a reflection of value-centeredness. In J. Marques (Ed.), *The Routledge companion to management and workplace spirituality*. New York, NY: Taylor & Francis.

Carmeli, A., Reiter-Palmon, R., & Ziv, E. (2010). Inclusive leadership and employee involvement in creative tasks in the workplace: The mediating role of psychological safety. *Creativity Research Journal*, *22*(3), 250–260.

Center for the Advancement of Christian Education—CACE. (2015). Effective Christian leadership: Prepare yourself to lead. *Cace.org*.

Conger, J. A. (1994). *Spirit at work*. San Francisco, CA: Jossey Bass Inc. Publishers.

Delbecq, A. (1999). Christian spirituality and contemporary business leadership. *Journal of Organizational Change Management*, *12*(4), 345–354. https://doi.org/10.1108/09534819910282180

Gotis, G., & Grimani, K. (2017). The role of spiritual leadership in fostering inclusive workplaces. *Personnel Review*, *46*(5), 908–935. https://doi.org/10.1108/PR-11-2015-0286

Lloyd, C. (2010). *University relations* (Doctoral Dissertation), North Carolina Agricultural and Technical State University, Greensboro.

Newman, L. L. (2004). Faith, spirituality, and religion: A model for understanding the differences. *The College of Student Affairs Journal*, 102–110.

Shore, L., Cleveland, J., & Sanchez, D. (2018). Inclusive workplaces: A review and model. *Human Resource Management Review*, *28*(2), 176–176.

Worthington, E., Hook, J., Davis, D., & McDaniel, M. (2011). Religion and spirituality. *Journal of Clinical Psychology*, *67*(2), 204.

21
INCLUSIVE SERVANT LEADERSHIP IN THE CONTEXT OF THE CHRISTIAN RELIGION

Peter Mutuku Lewa, Susan K. Lewa, and Paul S. Kioko

Introduction

There is general consensus that leadership is about influence. There is, however, no agreement on the best way to use to influence. It is commonly known that no one is born a leader; a leader is someone you become; it is the role you grow into; some people seek leadership but others have it thrust upon them. The question then becomes, what is leadership and what is the best way to influence followers and indeed other stakeholders in a leadership situation? There are many theories that attempt to explain the concept of leadership and the best way to influence. These theories are briefly outlined in this chapter. They include servant leadership that has a basis in spiritual leadership. Dhiman (2018, p. 31) observes that in recent years spirituality has been underscored as a critical element of leadership. He goes on to quote the observation by Astin and Astin (2000) that future leaders will need new skills and knowledge and will also be expected to display a high level of emotional and spiritual wisdom and maturity. We can add that such leaders will need a positive attitude different from the traditional predispositions about leadership. They will thus need new attitude, skills and knowledge (ASK) in order to operate successfully in today's business world, where the changeability and rapidity of change are humongous issues (Lewa et al, 2018).

Meaning and Scope of Leadership

The concept of leadership is nebulous and complex. The theory, practice and understanding of leadership is a complex phenomenon. This brings about a problem concerning the meaning, definition and scope of leadership. There is a consensus in many quarters that leadership is an interesting social phenomenon that occurs in all groups of people regardless of geographical region, religion, race, culture or nationality. Three critical elements are found in any leadership situation: leader, followers and situation. There is consensus that leadership is a process of influence, in which a leader influences followers in a given context to move towards a desired future state or vision through agreement with the followers in a given context. Selected definitions of leadership are provided later in this chapter to convey the meaning and scope of leadership.

Rost (1993a) defines leadership as an influence relationship among leaders and followers who intend real changes that reflect mutual purposes. This is a modern definition of leadership that takes cognizance of changing paradigms in today's world. Leadership can also be defined as a process used by an individual to influence group members toward the achievement of group goals, where the group members view the influence as legitimate. Kim and Mauborgne (1992, p. 123) define leadership as the ability to inspire confidence and support among the people who are needed to achieve organizational goals. Many well-known Christian leaders define leadership as the discipline of deliberately exerting special influence within a group to move it toward goals of beneficial permanence that fulfill the group's real needs.

These definitions and many other similar ones found in the leadership literature point out important elements of leadership: a leader (who influences), a group (followers), a goal, and a method to get to the goal (vision), generally speaking in a mutually beneficial way and all within a given context, because leadership happens within a given context or situation.

The definition by Rost (1991) fits today's context very well. Dhiman (2018, p. 31) observes that the definition by Rost has critical elements of leadership that should be applied to leadership today. That is, leadership is influence but must operate on mutual purposes. He goes on to observe that leadership is multidirectional in that the influence flows in all directions and is not coercive, meaning that it is not based on authority (right) and dictatorial actions (Cohen-Charash & Spector, 2001; Ehrhart, 2004). The definition implies that inclusivity is a critical element in leadership today. Inclusive leadership is about involving everyone as far as possible in leadership matters. Subsequent discussions in this chapter will elaborate more on this concept.

Theories of Leadership

Several leadership theories exist. They all attempt to explain the best way to achieve influence and hence intended outcomes (Bowman, 1997). Marques (2018, p. 5) observes that many leadership theories exist. They are tailored to different leaders in different situations. She goes on to observe that the biggest problem with most leadership theories of our times is that they do not adhere to today's most important requirement: *multi-applicability*. The world has changed in diverse ways. With globalization and its inherent challenges, today's leaders are forced to think outside the traditional box of leadership (Lewa, P.M., 2009). In the past leaders were placed in specific corners. A leader was either task oriented or people oriented or had superior qualities that gave him/her a upper hand in leading followers or used his/her charisma to get along; a leader was transactional or transformational. Leadership theories are of course very important in the discourse of leadership and have had their space. Today, there are unprecedented social, economic and political changes that demand flexibility on the part of leaders and managers if their organizations are to remain competitive. These challenges require what Marques and Dhiman (2018) describe as engaged leadership. This is a form of leadership in which leaders must apply design thinking, change or reform themselves as required and move on to engage with diverse groups of stakeholders in today's highly interconnected world. This, in essence, is inclusivity.

It suffices to outline briefly the key leadership theories in order to put inclusive servant leadership in the right context for the purposes of this chapter.

Trait Theory

The earliest leadership theory, in the late 19th to the mid-20th century, is trait, which focused on differing categories of traits or characteristics possessed by leaders believed to be causal in the performance of leaders (Lewa, P.M., 2015). These included physical characteristics—looks, size, ability to fight enemies, etc. This type of theory was traditionally very well received in many African countries where successful warriors in tribal wars held sway in their tribes. A good example is provided by the Zulus of South Africa and such famous warriors in Kenya as Nabongo Mumias (Luo Nyanza), Mwatu wa Ngoma (Kamba country) and Wang'u was Mang'eri (woman leader of the Kikuyu tribe in Kenya).

Behavioral Theory

Dissatisfaction with the trait theory led to behavioral theories that focused on what leaders did (behavior) to actuate results, as the causal agent in influencing followers, but the theories did not explicitly bring out the rejection or acceptance of a reciprocal relationship between leaders and followers.

Contingency Theories

While behavioral theories substantially improved explanation and prediction of leadership outcomes, situational elements were not adequately captured, particularly for identifying leader behaviors most effective in particular situations, hence the emergence of contingency theories. According to contingency theories, the contingency variables in a particular situation serve as moderators of leader behaviors to increase leader effectiveness.

Contemporary Theories

Contemporary theories of leadership primarily deal with organizational changes extending transactional theories beyond the leader-subordinate exchange process to incorporate change of the follower and hence change of organization. Such theories are seen in many quarters as an attempt to make leadership responsive to changes that we must contend with always. Change is a constant reality of life.

Strategic Leadership Theories

Strategic leadership theories have been categorized as *upper echelons theory, new leadership theories* (charismatic, transformational and visionary) and *the emergent theories* of leadership. The mid-1980s saw a shift away from the study of supervisory leadership towards the study of strategic leadership initially centering on the upper echelons theory. Strategic leadership theories focus on the creation of meaning and purpose for the organization. This implies that the creation of meaning and purpose must be shared by both the leaders and the followers as well as other interested stakeholders.

Supervisory Theories of Leadership

Supervision is a specialized function of management. Supervisory theories include the path-goal, contingency, leader-member exchange (LMX) focus on task and person-oriented behaviors of leaders in providing feedback, support and guidance to subordinates as they move towards the defined goal/s. They are widely discussed in human resources management (HRM) books.

New Leadership Theories

The new leadership theories include *charismatic, transformational* and *visionary leadership* aspects of leadership and tend to highlight the interpersonal processes and relationships between the leader and the follower. They have arisen to address the changing dynamics and paradigms in the management of human beings and organizations as well in today's dynamic world of business (Kark and Shamir, 2002, Rost, 1993b).

The theory of *charismatic leadership* emphasizes the personal identification of the followers with the charismatic leader. Some well-known modern charismatic leaders in Africa include the late Kwame Nkurumah of Ghana, the late Nelson Mandela of South Africa, the late Jomo Kenyatta of

Kenya, the late Oginga Odinga, the doyen of opposition politics in Kenya, the late Patrice Lumumba of Congo and the late Mwalimu Kabarage Nyerere of Tanzania, to name but a few. There are two forms of charisma: *visionary* and *crisis responsive*. Visionary charisma creates a world intrinsically valid for the followers, in which behaviors are linked to core values, purposes and meanings through articulation of vision and goals, while crisis responsive charisma creates a world that is extrinsically valid, in which outcomes are linked to behaviors.

Transformational leadership is viewed as a style of strategic leadership and is considered the most effective strategic leadership style. It entails motivating followers to exceed expectations, continuously enriching their capabilities and placing the organization's interest above their own (Kark and Shamir, 2002). Transformational leaders develop and communicate a vision and formulate strategies to achieve the vision by continuously encouraging followers to strive for higher levels of achievement. This is achieved mostly through what is described as the 4 I's, including intellectual stimulation, individualized consideration, inspirational motivation, and idealized influence.

Visionary leadership is about the mental picture, image or dream of the future desired state. It is concerned mostly with risk taking. Visionary leaders are not dependent on the organization for their sense of who they are. Visionary leaders maintain organizational control through socialization and the sharing of and compliance with a commonly held set of norms, values and shared belief. Lewa S.K. (2009) argues that leaders in public universities lack leadership skills in terms of talent management because there is a dearth of mentors in this area.

While House and Aditya (1997) treat charismatic, transformational and visionary theories of leadership virtually interchangeably, some other writers think that substantial differences exist between them in terms of level of analysis and the choice of dependent variables when carrying out studies on them.

The content of strategic leadership theories and transformational leadership theories are generally seen to be the same; they only differ in process and effect on followers. It is argued that transformational and charismatic leadership are subsets of strategic leadership and are delimited by the additional features that characterize the charisma building (e.g. impression management) and transformational (e.g. building of individual and collective interests) processes.

Managerial, Visionary and Strategic Leadership

Managerial leadership involves stability, order and the preservation of existing order (status quo) such that managerial leaders are more comfortable handling day-to-day activities while being short-term oriented. Managerial leaders thrive on order, not the chaos characteristic of human relations, they see their major responsibility as the conservation of the current state of organization's affairs and order, and they are sensitive to the past. Managerial leadership can be likened in some ways to transactional leadership.

Visionary leaders have attitudes towards goals that are opposite to those of managerial leaders, being more proactive in shaping ideas as opposed to being reactionary and usually exerting influence in a way that determines the direction the organization takes, working with high-risk positions, and seeking out risky ventures especially when the rewards are high. It is proposed that combining managerial leaders and visionaries to lead organizations is a good thing as they can complement each other from their points of strength.

Emergent Leadership Theories

The emergent theories of leadership explore behavioral and cognitive complexity as well as social intelligence and how they influence leadership efficacy and effectiveness. Many authors argue that the emergent leadership theories will extend the understanding of what they consider to be the three cornerstones of strategic leadership: the capacity to learn, the capacity to change and managerial wisdom (Rost, 1993b). Leadership effectiveness hinges on three factors: behavioral complexity/capacity, cognitive capacity and social intelligence. Behavioral complexity refers to the leader performing multiple leadership roles.

Cognitive complexity is premised on the assumption that cognitively complex individuals not only process information differently but perform certain tasks better than cognitively less complex individuals because they use more dimensions to distinguish between stimuli and hence identify more commonalities in these dimensions. Cognitive capacity implies the mental processes used to digest information, make conclusions and decisions, and take action. Leaders need important interpersonal skills such as empathy, motivation and communication in addition to the cognitive skills. The appropriate application of these skills is not easy and requires a thorough understanding of one's social setting, a phenomenon that has been referred to as social intelligence. A key component of social intelligence that contributes to effective leadership is the ability to differentiate emotions in self and others.

Servant Leadership in the Context Christian Leadership

The theories outlined previously all seem to suggest that followers have to move along with the leaders even when the leaders are autocratic and not necessarily democratic and where sometimes they may use dictatorship. Whatever leadership style is considered, followers must move along with the leader. That is, they have to be included in the process of leadership. Servant leadership is said to be the best demonstration of inclusive leadership and it is also argued that it elicits a high level of organizational commitment (Asag-gau & Van Dierendonck, 2011). According to Dhiman (2018, p. 35), it is regarded by many authors as "a valid, modern theory of leadership." Christian religion, the basis of servant leadership, provides what is seen to be a good example of inclusion if practiced well.

Christian leadership is part of religious leadership based on belief in and reverence for God or a deity. Religion involves teaching religion and practicing religious rites and ideals. Every religion attempts to practice religious leadership following the ideals of the religion in question.

There is no agreement on what Christian leadership encompasses, and therefore there as many definitions of Christian leadership as there are authors or books and other materials on the subject of leadership. However, there is consensus that Christian leadership has its basis in the person of Jesus Christ who practiced it and modeled the way to practice it. Many leaders claim to emulate Jesus, some fairly successfully and others miserably in terms of output. Christian leadership is ultimately expressed through the life, works and teachings (words) of Jesus as expressed in the New Testament of the Christian Bible. Christian leadership leaders influence followers to move towards a common goal or vision that is defined by God. Jesus is the embodiment of Christian leadership (Lewa et al., 2018). The Bible is very clear that one of the fundamental characteristics of God is to become a servant of God and His people. God, in Christ, demonstrates this aspect of His character in sending Jesus to be our Guide and Model, as well as our Savior. Jesus provides the model leadership that Christian leadership is based on. This is well captured in the words of Jesus in Matthew 20:26–28 and Matthew 23:11–12 (The Reformation Study BIBLE, 1995). Briefly, whoever wants to be the greatest must be a servant of the others and must not lord it over the followers. Lewa (2010) argues that there is dearth of leadership skills in managing public universities in Kenya. Dr. Susan Katinda Lewa is not the only one who holds this view. She seems to agree with Dr. Stanko John (2000) that there are so many leaders yet so little leadership. In our view, many Africans have not yet learned that good and practical leadership has a price.

The Bible teaching about the nature of Christian servant leadership is unique, valuable and worthy of investigation concerning its contribution to the aspect of inclusive leadership. In this kind of leadership, God selects, calls and equips His chosen leaders, who in turn are expected to live lives worthy of their calling. The Bible teaching about the nature of Christian leadership holds that Christian servant leaders are a special chosen people with a specific position and purpose. On this earth they are on a mission to do God's will, which is to serve others. In Christian leadership, the focus is therefore God and His love for human beings. Mathew 28:19–20 in the Christian Bible captures the essential elements of this kind of leadership by directing Christians to go into all the world to serve humanity and follow the things Jesus taught (including love, humility, and servanthood).

Servant leadership is a relatively new area in the leadership field, and the debate about whether it is or isn't a theory is still raging, especially in academic circles. Writers are still struggling to come up with consensus on an overall conceptual design of servant leadership. It is widely suggested that managers who merge their inspiration to lead with an immediate need to serve not only express but also practice servant leadership. Servant leadership is demonstrated by leaders attempting to move together to a defined vision through inclusion and consensus building. It is also expressed by offering a clear path at times of crises where there is no clarity on the way forward (Sendjaya and Sarros, 2002).

According to many studies and major works in leadership theory and practice, there are seven management concepts that expose the greatest overlap with servant leadership. These are transformational leadership, spiritual leadership, ethical leadership, empowering leadership, Level 5 leadership, authentic leadership and self-sacrificing leadership. Already one can see from the list that servant leadership is quite encompassing and can be critiqued based on unclear meaning that has consensus built around it by academics and practitioners (Luthans and Avolio, 2003; Spears, 1995).

Research in many quarters on the differences between two very close concepts—servant leadership and authentic leadership—says that the two leadership styles are root concepts underlying beneficial management approaches in today's business environments. Modern leaders need to be aware that authentic leadership works through an increased self-awareness, relational and internalized visibility, ethical viewpoint and balanced handling to encourage credibility in their supporters. Authenticity is carefully relevant to showing the True Self. It concentrates on owning one's personal experiences and full immersion in inclusive leadership efforts as a consequence. The leader's ideas, feelings, needs, wants, choices and principles must come into play (Luthans and Avolio, 2003). This, when practiced well, creates genuineness and especially in many African economies where leaders suffer from poor institutional frameworks, poor governance structures and systems, and lack of horizontal and vertical accountability (Plummer, 2000).

The two-way interaction described in ethical leadership significantly sounds identical to Greenleaf's emphasis on conviction and principles in servant leadership discussed in the next section.

The Theory of Inclusive Servant Leadership in the Context of the Christian Religion

Servant leadership is a term that was first used by Greenleaf (1904–1990) in one of his record-breaking and influential academic works: *Servant Is a Leader*. Greenleaf asserted that a *servant leader* must first be a servant. It starts with the natural sensation that one wants to lead, and to lead first. It is this awareness of the desire to offer service that leads one to want to serve and sets him or her to the course of leadership (Greenleaf, 2002). Be that as it may, there are some lingering questions concerning the definition: Do the people led by this leadership concept develop as persons? Do they become healthier, smarter, freer and more independent, and are they likely to become servants themselves? And, does the concept create some impacts on those believed less privileged among followers? How and what do they benefit from the concept, and are they cushioned from any further harm? We will not attempt to answer these questions, but students, professors and practitioners are encouraged to engage in dialogue about and take positions on these issues based on their experiences. Greenleaf placed "going beyond one's self-interest" as a primary attribute of servant leadership; a concept that despite being described in other management concepts has never been given meaningful consideration in any of the leadership theory literature (Carter & Baghurst, 2014). The servant leader is controlled by growing needs within an organization that put supporters' development before that of leaders (Greenleaf, 1977). In comparison to other management designs where the greatest objective is the well-being of the organization or company, a servant leader is truly involved with providing supporters with opportunities. This person-oriented mindset creates secure and strong connections between the employees (followers) and the company. As Greenleaf puts it, servants that are selected to be managers are significantly reinforced by their workers because they commit themselves and are efficient. In this way, an environment is designed that motivates followers to become the very best they can and to deliver as much quality as would be possible in ensuring customer satisfaction and loyalty and increased sustainable productivity (Spears, 1995).

It suffices to recognize that according to Greenleaf, the servant leader is the first among equals and does not use his or her energy to get his own thoughts in or done; instead, he/she tries to convince employees to see the point of view or argument through reinforcement of their morale. In other terms, a servant leader must play the part of a steward; must not only motivate followers, but also capture their attention through his/her determination and strong belief in the possibilities of the company that he/she serves. Such leaders, servant leaders, must be ready to go beyond self-interest. They are inspired by something more critical than the need for position and power. Greenleaf goes one step further and creates this need for reliable service to followers as a key to excellent leadership; it results in a dedication to the development of individual workers, the achievements of the company, and an asset to the group. This is quite contrary to what classical managers and researchers believed to be the foundation of organizational success—power and position. Being a servant before the eyes of subjects allows individuals to lead due to the established relational dependence (Greenleaf, 1977).

The characteristics of servant leadership have been well discussed in literature in spite of some disagreements on the meanings of some of the views and concepts. The deficiency of a precise meaning of servant leadership in existing literature as put forth by Greenleaf has given increase to many interpretations. At this time, the interpretations of this leadership are among the most significant. Ten significant features have come to be considered as the important elements of servant leadership: (1) *listening*, focusing on the significance of interaction and looking forward to recognizing the desires of followers; (2) *empathy*, understanding followers' problems and recognizing what they actually are; (3) *healing*, the capability to help make whole; (4) *attention (awareness)*, having the knowledge of what is happening; (5) *persuasion*, looking forward to influencing others based on justifications other than power and position; (6) *conceptualization*, considering beyond the present-day need and extending it into a possible future; (7) *foresight*, forecasting future conditions as well as working with instinct; (8) *stewardship*, having something in trust and satisfying the immediate needs of followers; and (9) *dedication to individual growth*, caring about the personal, expert and religious growth of others. Finally, (10) *community building*, which requires focusing, understanding and accepting that regional neighborhoods are important in the life and success of organizations.

Various writers have also offered modifications to the aforementioned features as explained by various writers and practitioners. Humility is a key attribute, though we posit that it should be the first and preeminent attribute. It represents the capability to put one's own achievements and abilities in an appropriate perspective. Servant leaders should explore and fortify the efforts of others as opposed to the traditional exploitation. Humility manifests itself where one places the interests of others first, helping sustain their efficiency and providing them with assistance and support efficiently and effectively. Authenticity, another significant element of servant leadership, is related to showing effectiveness with inner emotions and concepts. Credibility is also relevant to integrity, the sticking to a usually recognized ethical rule. Credibility is about being real to you, perfectly representing self—privately and publicly (Lewa, P.M., 2015). A servant leader's authenticity manifests itself in various aspects: doing what is guaranteed, exposure within the organization or company and honesty about one's weaknesses (Lewa, P.M., 2015). From a business viewpoint, it can be described as acting in such a way that one recognizes that expertise can be enhanced further by listening to others. Synergy is best achieved this way.

Developing Inclusive Servant Leadership

Developing inclusive servant leadership requires the use of the key aspects found in spiritual leadership. That is, intrinsically motivating and inspiring workers through hope/faith in a vision of service to key stakeholders and a corporate culture based on the values of altruistic love to produce a highly motivated, committed and productive workforce.

Inclusive servant leadership is synonymous with spiritual leadership. Spiritual leadership involves intrinsically motivating and inspiring workers through hope/faith in a vision of service to followers and other key stakeholders and a corporate culture based on the values of altruistic love to produce a highly motivated, committed and productive workforce and followership. The purpose of spiritual leadership is to tap into the fundamental needs of both leaders and followers for spiritual well-being through a calling that is based on one's gifts and passion, because life is to be lived with a purpose as God intended for every one of us.

Challenging Inclusive Servant Leadership Assumptions

- Servant leadership lacks a clear definition and consensus, and it straddles the provinces of other leadership styles. There is no total agreement and consensus on the meaning and scope. For example, there is no universal agreement on the traits of this leadership style, and now with inclusivity becoming a key part of servant leadership, more complications arise in regard to meaning.
- Being rated as an inclusive leader is not determined by *averaging* all members' scores but rather by the *distribution* of raters' scores. For example, it's not enough that, on average, raters agree that a leader "approaches diversity and inclusiveness wholeheartedly." Using a five-point scale (ranging from "strongly agree" to "strongly disagree"), an average rating could mean that some team members disagree while others agree. To be an inclusive leader, one must ensure that *everyone* agrees or strongly agrees that they are being treated fairly and respectfully, are valued, and have a sense of belonging and are psychologically safe.
- It is time consuming to train people on it and to let them practice it in order for their learning to be evaluated.
- Conversion in people's hearts is a personal matter and choice, and not everyone who is trained in inclusive servant leadership is able to practice all its principles. It is about leading from the heart (Lewa et al., 2018).
- It is hard to practice and implement. Companies increasingly rely on diverse, multidisciplinary teams that combine the collective capabilities of women and men, people of different cultural heritage, and younger and older workers. But simply throwing a mix of people together doesn't guarantee high performance; it requires *inclusive leadership*—leadership that assures that all team members feel they are treated respectfully and fairly, are valued and have the sense that they belong, and are confident and inspired.
- It is a tough concept to comprehend in a world where values are increasingly eroded due to changing paradigms in living. The personal development of supporters is seen within the viewpoint of what is excellent for the organization in order to enhance its performance. There is an obvious risk of conflict on whether to achieve business goals or to meet the leader's personal goals. Transformational leadership may lead to arrogance, whereby a concentration on short-term maximum profit may cause long-term negative repercussions. Given the ideals of

service in servant leadership, the principal difference between these two leadership concepts is that servant leadership focuses on humility, credibility and public approval, none of which are a particular aspect of transformational leadership. More explicitly, lifestyle-changing management concentrates on business objectives; they encourage their supporters to greater efficiency for the benefit of the organization. Servant leaders concentrate more on concern for their supporters by developing conditions that enhance followers' well-being and performance and thereby accomplish the understanding of a shared vision, namely enhanced firm performance and increased shareholder wealth; servant leaders trust supporters to do what is necessary for the organization.

Conclusion

Most theories on leadership styles focus mainly on the organization, for example in theories about transformational and transactional leadership (Bass, 1990; Burns, 1978; However, Robert Greenleaf (1904–1990) initiated a new approach to efficient leadership: servant leadership. This leadership style mainly focuses on the interests and needs of the followers (Graham, 1991, 1995; Spears, 1995). Greenleaf described a servant leader as a person who "is a servant first. . . . Then conscious choice brings one to aspire to Lead." Many writers in leadership theory hold similar views. The best test, which is difficult to administer, is this: Do those served grow as persons? The needs and wants of followers are central in this type of leadership. Servant leaders always try to find or create opportunities for their followers to grow within the organization. The Nairobi Chapel in Nairobi City in Kenya, through the leadership of Bishop Oscar Muriu, as discussed shortly, has demonstrated this very well. Most forms of leadership types especially in cultures where selfishness and corruption are prominent focus on the well-being of the organization, while for servant leadership, the well-being of followers is the most important concern (Greenleaf, 1977, 2002). This does not mean that followers overrule the leader; they are just encouraged and empowered to think for themselves (Bowie, 2000). When followers fail to exercise responsibility, as is common in almost all countries of Africa today where democracy is nascent, then problems can occur.

Featured Case

Nairobi Chapel (Rapid Church Planting Growth Through Inclusion)

The key lessons from the case study of Nairobi Chapel presented here and its viral growth in the world show what inclusive servant leadership is, and that inclusion must be looked at today in terms of what is happening in the current world of rapid change so that good results can be expected. The bishop of Nairobi Chapel churches in Kenya and globally, Rev. Oscar Muriu, always says that Africa has to take the gospel back from where it came and that this can only be achieved by raising leaders in an inclusive way. It will be recalled that Africans are highly religious, and all kinds of religions are found on the continent, with Christianity and Islam taking the largest percentages of religious followers. The Nairobi Chapel experience shows very clearly how inclusion can be achieved.

Various Nairobi Chapel brochures have summarized the history of the church very well (www.nairobichapel.org). What follows is an outline of the key dates in the growth of the chapel.

1952—A small group of British settlers, mostly from the Brethren tradition, had a vision to start a church that would be strong in evangelism and teaching and open to people from all denominations. They were the first non-denominational church in Kenya, even though earlier in 1944 the Africa Brotherhood Church (ABC) invited members of other churches to join it as associates in its African Christian Brotherhood Association (Rev. John Lewa Ndolo, 2019).

The small group of settlers soon began to be referred to as Nairobi Chapel. After just three years, they got a prime property next to the governor's mansion that is now the Mamlaka Hill Chapel building near the University of Nairobi student hostels in the city of Nairobi, Kenya.

1963—Independence came to Kenya, and most of the soldiers were recalled back home. One by one, many of the original members began to move back to England. At the same time, the University of Nairobi, formerly known as the Royal College, began buying up the land around the church and building up student housing, so that with time, the church building became surrounded by thousands of university students. But few of them were interested in coming through the church doors, as it was still seen as a church for foreigners.

Bishop Oscar Muriu worked relentlessly to change this attitude, and when students began to attend church, later on in life many became pastors of Nairobi Chapel. Bishop Oscar built the enviable DNA of Nairobi Chapel, and he is now called upon all over the world to share it and open churches in different cities of the world.

1988—The church dwindled, and with less than 20 adults left, it seemed inevitable that they would have to close the church down. They prayed desperately to God for help. After around six months of prayer and fasting, they felt led by God to make it an African-led church and asked for help. Humbling! But in 1989, Rev. Mutava Musyimi (former secretary general of the National Christian Church Council of Kenya, and a former member of parliament in Kenya), together with the elders of Nairobi Baptist Church, agreed to send over one of their pastoral interns to build the church. That's when Pastor Muriithi Wanjau, Nairobi Chapel's Mavuno church and the current senior pastor of Mavuno, then a first-year university student at the University of Nairobi, moved to pastor the small church. God began to do a new thing. The little church began to grow. From 20 adults in 1989, the church grew to 3,000 adults (and many children) by 2004.

1998—God began to speak to the elders of the church about the need to expand so that it could reach the needs of the society better. This was at the core of its calling. After prayer, the decision was made to buy 14 acres of land on Ngon'g Road that would cost 40 million KSh at the time.

In this insightful writeup and from conversations with Rev. Nick Korir (current senior pastor of Nairobi Chapel), Rev. Faith Mugera of the Justice Ministry of Nairobi Chapel and Bishop Oscar Muriu when writing the Chapel's strategic plan with Prof. Peter Mutuku Lewa and others, with Peter Mutuku Lewa as a key participant, it becomes possible to highlight some key aspects of inclusive servant leadership that Nairobi Chapel and its sister churches all over the world practice.

The bishop is an expert at multiplying churches, and he is a renowned international speaker on what it takes to plant churches aggressively. He shares the inspiring story of how the church he has led since 1991 began planting one church every three years followed by increases of 10, 20 and 40 per year. Fueled by five key inflection points, Nairobi Chapel in Kenya will plant 100 churches this year. Since dedicating his life to Christ in 1983, Bishop Muriu has worked to raise up a legacy of leaders, especially African leaders, for the church worldwide through carefully worked out inclusion principles of servant leadership. The key issues about inclusion are presented below in question format. Those training on inclusive leadership must keep reflecting on these and discussing them liberally to conviction in their hearts. By the time they finish their leadership training, they are able to literally sing about them (Dr. Paula Musuva, 2019). These questions are:

1. Do you have an emotional bond with your stakeholders?
2. Are you a fun place to work?
3. Are you built to change?
4. Do you embrace the value of values?
5. Are you as disciplined as you are creative?
6. Do you use technology to change expectations and reshape your business/church?
7. Have you built a company of leaders in your church?

8. Do you know when it is time to let others lead as you move to other areas of ministry?
9. Do you have a succession planning framework approved by your board?
10. Are you open and transparent in your dealings even when not being watched because God sees you anyway?
11. Do you love money too much to the point where you cannot trust God to provide?
12. Do you love your family as you love your neighbors?

Dr. Paula Musuva (2019) observes that at the core of these questions is the aspect of a personal relationship with Christ, the key qualification for being considered for deployment at Nairobi Chapel. Some people who have no relationship with Christ are allowed to be trained, since the church trains for humanity and wishes to be inclusive.

Kinara Leadership Development Program at Nairobi Chapel

Kinara is the Swahili word for "point man" or "captain" or can also mean "pinnacle," and its goal is to raise leaders who can speak to the issues of the day and bring kingdom-focused solutions to the problems facing the world. Kinara is a full-time leader development program designed to empower and instruct emerging leaders who are passionate about Jesus and intent on pursuing a life of ministry. The leadership development program began several years ago to provide an avenue for young people to discover and clarify their calling to full-time ministry. Kinara is a transformative experience that takes trainees into the "trenches" of ministry while developing personal character and spiritual growth. Kinara attracts trainees from all over the world: the United States, Germany, Australia, Africa, England, New Zealand and many other countries. Training in Kinara opens up many opportunities for growth and engagement, both locally and internationally. Partners all over the world are always looking for leaders trained at Nairobi Chapel because their DNA is purely inclusive servant leadership. They are guided and driven by five values: (1) dependence on God, (2) discipleship, (3) extending grace to others, (4) having work-life balance, and (5) fun.

The Kinara program serves the vision of Nairobi Chapel, which is to "Grow D.E.E.P. to reach W.I.D.E." "D" stands for Daily devotion, "E" is for Eccelesia or small group, "E" is for Engagement, and "P" is for Pulpit; while "W" stands for Witness to 1 million people, "I" is for Impact of society through social justice initiatives, "D" is for Discipleship or training of a target of 300,000 people, and "E" is for Establish an estimated 300 churches.

The inspiration and ministry philosophy is drawn from Mark 12:29–31, where Jesus in response to the Pharisees' question as to what is the greatest commandment said, "You shall love the Lord your God with all your heart and with all your strength. . . [and] Love your neighbor as yourself" (The Reformation Study BIBLE, 1995). The training objective is to develop well-rounded individuals in the following specific areas, which are called the *5Cs* (www.nairobichapel.org)

1. *Conviction*: Pursuing a call to ministry is a matter of deep conviction and faith and we believe that a deep and vibrant relationship with Jesus is vital for leadership and for ministry.
2. *Character*: It is vital for every leader to be above reproach in all matters. Through personal mentoring and group discipleship, every intern is encouraged to focus on personal character formation as part of their training for ministry and leadership.
3. *Comprehension*: Trainees are exposed to different fields of learning to widen their understanding of scripture, ministry and culture. This is done through weekly classes, training seminars and other leadership forums where trainees wrestle with different leadership concepts.
4. *Competence*: Avenues for trainees are created for them to acquire and develop the skills needed to serve competently in leadership and their areas of spiritual gifting. The interns are attached

to various departments and also serve high school and primary school ministries, where they develop practical skills such as teaching the Bible and leading prayer meetings and discipleship groups.
5. *Compassion*: Nairobi Chapel leadership recognizes that the commandment to love God can only be fulfilled as we love our neighbors. Our convictions, knowledge and skills must all be translated into love and compassion for others. Our ministry context in Nairobi, and indeed the world over, includes poverty and sickness and many ills of society. We seek to display Christ-likeness in these situations by showing love and acceptance. For this reason, our trainees are involved in different aspects of mission work through the year. They are observed keenly through a framework where those who cannot measure up will be allowed to get the training but cannot be utilized by the church. Any form of immorality and lewdness is never tolerated. Each of the trainees is assigned to one of the ministry departments where they serve during their first year of training. They are also involved in primary and high school ministry on a weekly basis where they teach and help develop the spiritual growth of children and youth. After the first year, the trainees go on church planting assignments for a year where they sharpen and grow their ministry and leadership skills even more.

For the duration of their time in Kinara, all the trainees will be part of a staff discipleship group. Disciple and Ecclesia groups provide an avenue for care and spiritual growth in the context of a community of peers.

The chapel recognizes that it has an international platform and extends the search to young people from beyond Africa to engage in this program. There are three options for international students joining the Kinara program:

1. One-month short-term internship—this is for the college student who desires a short term ministry experience for cross-cultural exposure or to fulfill academic training requirements. This internship runs from January-April, May-August and September-December.
2. Six-month short-term internship—this is aimed at those seeking an exploratory ministry experience and who may not be able to complete a full year.
3. One-year internship—this is a regular internship which runs in three intakes: January, May and September.

Bishop Oscar Muriu's anchor is his morality. Every time he stands to speak, he openly asks the congregation to raise issues for investigation, whether from rumor, experienced by a person or talked about in social media. Interns and covenant members must live beyond reproach in the church, the community and their own homes. They must remain active in home churches and communities and continually preach the gospel to all and especially the poor, the sick, widows and children, as per St. James 1:27. The argument in the Christin Bible is that true religion is helping the fatherless and widows (needy community members). There is definitely something for world leaders to learn from the story of Nairobi Chapel.

References

Asag-gau, L., & Van Dierendonck, D. (2011). The impact of servant leadership on organizational commitment among the highly talented: The role of challenging work conditions and psychological empowerment. *European Journal of International Management, 5*(5), 463–483.

Astin Alexander, W., & Astin Helen, S. (2000). *Leadership reconsidered: Engaging higher education in social change* (p. 1). Battle Creek, MI: W.K. Kellog Foundation.

Bass, B. M. (1990). From transactional to transformational leadership: Learning to share the vision. *Organizational Dynamics, 18*(4), 19–31.

Bowie, N. E. (2000). A Kantian theory of leadership. *Leadership and Organization Development: Journal, 21*(4), 185–193.

Bowman, M. A. (1997). *Popular approaches to leadership* (P. G. Northhouse, Ed.). Thousand Oaks, CA: Sage Publications.

Burns, J. M. (1978). *Leadership*. New York, NY: Harper & Row.

Carter, D., & Baghurst, T. (2014). The influence of servant leadership on restaurant employee engagement. *Journal of Business Ethics, 124*(3), 453–464.

Cohen-Charash, Y., & Spector, P. E. (2001). The role of justice in organizations: A meta-analysis. *Organizational Behavior and Human Decision Processes, 86*(2), 278–321.

Dhiman S. (2018). Self-leadership: Journey from position-power to self-power. In J. Marques & S. Dhiman (Eds.), *Engaged leadership*. Cham: Springer International Publishing AG.

Ehrhart, M. G. (2004). Leadership and procedural justice climate as antecedents of unit-level organizational citizenship behavior. *Personnel Psychology, 57*(1), 61–95.

Graham, J. W. (1991). Servant-leadership in organizations: Inspirational and moral. *The Leadership Quarterly, 2* (2), 105–119.

Graham, J. W. (1995). Leadership, moral development, and citizenship behavior. *Business Ethics Quarterly, 5*(1), 43–54.

Greenleaf, R. K. (1977). *Servant Leadership: A journey into the nature of legitimate power and greatness*. Mahwah, NJ: Paulist Press.

Greenleaf, R. K. (2002). Essentials of servant-leadership. In L. C. Spears & M. Lawrence (Eds.), *Focus of leadership: Servant leadership for the 21st century* (pp. 19–25). New York, NY: Wiley.

House, R., & Aditya, R. (1997). The social scientific study of leadership: Quo vadis? *Journal of Management, 23*, 409–473.

Kark, R., & Shamir, B. (2002). The dual effect of transformational leadership: Priming relational and collective selves and further effects on followers. In B. J. Avolio & F. J. Yammarino (Eds.), *Transformational and charismatic leadership: The road ahead* (pp. 75–102). Oxford: JAI/Elsevier.

Kim Chan W., & Mauborgne Reene, A. (1992). *Parables of leadership*. Brighton: Harvard Business Review, Harvard Business School, Harvard Business Publishing.

Lewa, P. M. (2009)*. Key Note Speech at the 1st KIM Annual Conference at the Kenyatta International Conference Centre (KICC) organized by the Kenya Institute of Management. (*Prof. Peter Lewa's talk was captured in videos by the Citizen TV and KTN TV arguing that the traditional box of leadership did not exist anymore. He was in a debate with a re-known Kenyan Rhetorician Mr. PLO Lumumba).

Lewa, P. M. (2015). Black board student notes for BUS 6030 graduate class on leadership at the United States International University (USIU). Africa.

Lewa, P. M. (2018). Discussion Notes on Transformational Leadership in the Public sector of Kenya presented during a workshop organized for some State Owned Enterprises (SOEs).

Lewa, P. M., Lewa, S. K., & Mutuku Sarah, M. (2018). Leading from the heart: Lessons from Christian leadership. In J. Marques & S. Dhiman (Eds.), *Engaged leadership*. Boston, MA: Springer.

Lewa, S. K. (2009, June). *Talent management and forecasting in Kenya's higher education sector: The case of public universities*. Paper presented at the 1st KIM Annual conference on Management at the Kenyatta International Conference (KICC), Nairobi, Kenya.

Lewa, S. K. (2010). Talent management and forecasting in Kenya's higher education sector: The case of public universities. *Journal of the KIM School of Management, II*, 150–155.

Luthans, F., & Avolio, B. (2003). Authentic leadership development. In K. S. Cameron & J. E. Dutton (Eds.), *Positive organizational scholarship* (pp. 241–254). San Francisco, CA: Berrett-Koehler.

Marques J., & Dhiman, S. (Eds.). (2018). *Engaged leadership: Transforming through future-oriented design thinking*. Cham: Springer Publications.

Marques, J. (2018). In J. Marques & S. Dhiman, (Eds.). *Engaged leadership*. Cham: Springer Publications.

Musuva, P. (2019). A Graduate of the Kinara Program and a Professor of ICT at the United States International University (USIU), Africa, Nairobi, Kenya.

Plummer, J. (2000). *Municipalities & community participation: A source book for capacity building*.

Research for DFID. Sterling, VA: Earthscan Publications Ltd. The Reformation Study BIBLE (The New King James Version). Nashville, 1995.

Rev. John Lewa Ndolo. (2019). Interview with the 91 Year Old Reverend of the Africa Brotherhood Church (ABC) on 10th August, 2019 at the Mua Hills home of his son during the Reverend's birth day celebrations.

Rev. Nick Korir. (2019). Interview, Nairobi Chapel.

Rev. Faith Mugera. (2019). Interview, Nairobi Chapel

Rost, J. C. (1991). *Leadership for the twenty-first century*. New York, NY: Praeger.

Rost, J. C. (1993a). *Leadership for the twenty-first century*. New York, NY: Praeger (reprint edition).

Rost, J. C. (1993b). Leadership development in the new millennium. *The Journal of Leadership Studies, 1*(1), 91–110.

Sendjaya, S., & Sarros, J. C. (2002). Servant leadership: Its origin, development, and application in organizations. *Journal of Leadership & Organizational Studies, 9*(2), 57–64.

Spears, L. C. (1995). *Reflections on leadership: How Robert K. Greenleaf's theory of servant-leadership influenced today's top management thinkers*. New York, NY: John Wiley.

Stanko John, W. (2000). *So many leaders – So little leadership: Beyond the Power of Position Lies the Price of Leadership*. Nairobi: Word Alive Publishers Limited, (Reprinted in 2012). Retrieved from www.nairobichapel.org

22
INCLUSIVE LEADERSHIP AND SOFT SKILLS

Birute Regine

The Landscape

Inclusive leadership has become a popular topic in the last few years, as we recognize the limits of a command/control style of leadership, which is not the most effective style. What is going on in the workplace that requires a reconsideration of what it means to be a leader?

Businesses have been wrestling to find best practices for a long time. It's what management theory is all about, going back to Henry Ford's mass production lines and Frederick Taylor's scientific management ideas. Until relatively recently, the focus was on ways to make the "machine" work more and more efficiently. Humans as people were not part of the business success equation, rather they were considered more like cogs in the machine.

In 1998 Jeffrey Pfeffer, a professor at the Stanford University School of Business, stepped into this conversation with a different focus. The title of his book, published that year, tells the whole story: *The Human Equation: Building Profits by Putting People First* (Pfeffer, 1998). The book was a compendium of organizational development data that showed that when managers treated their people as people, all traditional bottom-line numbers—profits, shareholder value, retention, and so on—improved significantly. Simply put, companies that employ human-centered management are consistently more successful than competitors in the same business sectors that adhere to the more traditional mechanistic concepts. The data were irrefutable.

If the data were indeed irrefutable, the obvious question was, why was human-centered management typically considered to be inferior as a business practice to the traditional, hard-driving "I alone can fix it" style of management favored at the time? Pfeffer, with John Sutton, addressed this question in their book, *The Knowing-Doing Gap*. Part of the answer, they suggested, was the prevailing "hard-driving, I alone can fix it" culture of top business schools that heavily influenced management practices and work cultures. It is a very macho, ego-driven, and apparently personally satisfying approach—and the antithesis of nurturing, democratic, and human-centered style of inclusive management (Pfeffer & Sutton, 2000).

It's no surprise, then, that for the past decades, surveys revealed a fairly disgruntled workforce, but not primarily over money or hours. A 2013 Gallup poll found that a stunning 70 percent of Americans hate their job, often because of a "boss from hell." And that finding has remained consistent since Gallup starting measuring job satisfaction in 2000. In 2018 a Gallup poll found the highest level of engagement ever with 34 percent engaged, 16.6 percent actively disengaged, and 53 percent not engaged, people who basically showed up but were not cognitively or emotionally connected to their work (Harter, 2018). That's the best engagement measure we've ever had, but that's really not that great, costing US companies upwards of $550 billion per year in lost productivity. The less engaged employees are with their work and their organization, the more likely they are to leave the organization. Turnover can be costly.

In another Gallup poll, more than 47,000 employed respondents in 116 countries, from Canada to Qatar, were asked to respond to 12 items on engagement, which are crucial predictors of positive workplace outcomes such as employee retention and productivity. In most global regions, two items were the most poorly rated among the 12: "In the last seven days, I have received recognition or praise for doing good work" and "In the last six months, someone at work has talked to me about my progress (Crabtree, 2011).

Employees who aren't engaged with their work also found praise was painfully absent from most companies. In fact, at any given company between one-fifth and one-third of its study participants reported they had not received any recent praise from their manager and also felt their best efforts were routinely ignored. Employees want to work for a manager who cares and with whom they have a connection (Wagner & Harter, 2007).

A poll in 2012 by TJinsite, a research division of TimeJobs.com, also found that "more than 35 percent of the employees consider lack of recognition of work as the biggest hindrance to their productivity." According to them, rewards and recognition for achievements at workplace act as a morale booster, which in turn increases their productivity (Irvine, 2012).

A 2017 survey by Globoforce WorkHuman Research Institute found that meaningful work is far more important to employees than salary and perks. Employees are looking for more social connection in their day-to-day work, recognition that what they do matters, and more opportunities to celebrate major life events with colleagues. Most people want to love their work and love who they work with, given the chance to do so. A majority would prefer to have a caring boss; and those that do are more productive and stay longer with their organizations, important measures of business success (*Bringing More Humanity* ..., 2017).

When leaders are preoccupied with and have a myopic focus on boosting the financial bottom line and meeting those quarterly numbers to the exclusion of everything else, an all-too-common condition in business, there is a price to be paid. The price is in the currency of a disgruntled and suboptimally effective workforce. In the wake of a moral crisis of greed, we see a morale crisis. This is a terrible indictment of business practices, practices that do not recognize people as human beings but rather as human doings.

It's no wonder we see those shocking statistics. When you dehumanize organizations, people suffer and organizations suffer. How long can a company keep revving up that engine without ever addressing whether they're providing enough gas or the right kind of gas? Leaders currently have an opportunity to turn this trend around, to find an alignment between cultural morals and workplace morale by embracing an inclusive style of leadership.

We hear clearly from these studies that there is a deep craving in people to be appreciated in the workplace, to feel recognized and included. Inclusive leadership is a way to meet that need. Strongly inclusive leaders show optimism, promote collaboration, are dependable, and are people oriented. It is a very democratic approach, where everyone has a say and everyone's voice is worth listening to. But these practices have largely been deemed not suitable to meet the exigencies of the business environment. They have also been disparaged as "soft," not sufficiently hard-nosed to lead to business success.

Now, these so-called soft behaviors come more naturally to women, because, collectively, these behaviors are nurturing behaviors, behaviors we tend to associate with women. But this is not simply a gender issue, because both men and women are capable of these behaviors, although women have more permission to employ them. Soft behaviors are *human* behaviors.

Cultural expectations also influence the differences in approaches to leadership in men and women. For instance, women are expected and even demanded by our society to be good listeners, be caring, and put other people first. This is what it means to be a good woman. At the same time, society has discouraged men from embracing their more nurturing side in its demands of being honorable and strong, which means to be autonomous, in charge, stoic, and going it alone. (Of course, no one really does it alone in business.)

I see the recognition that inclusive leadership is a highly effective management approach as an opportunity for men to develop this human aspect of themselves, just as women have lately been embracing their more assertive side, and thus find our shared humanity.

Two Simple Actions

Leaders who want to adopt the inclusive leadership can begin by taking two actions:

- Engage the power of appreciation.
- Create conditions for inclusive discussions that welcome diversity.

Inclusive Leaders Care and Strengthen Relationships by Engaging the Power of Appreciation

What does engaging the power of appreciation entail?

Truly engaging the power of appreciation requires genuine care. Care may not seem like a power *word*, but it is a power *action*. Caring is being able to empathize and put yourself in other people's shoes; it's that small "thank you," that small offering of "what can I do to help," that has an amazing impact on people. When our interactions are filled with genuine care, not only are our connections strengthened, but also our relationships are enriched. We all look for and long for security in our lives. Security, whether personal, professional, or global, resides in the strength of our positive connections to others. At some core level, we all know that we are interconnected, that we depend on each other. Caring about others can be a way of caring for ourselves, as I will discuss later in this chapter.

Companies spend a lot of money trying to motivate people. As we saw in the previously mentioned studies, appreciation is a great motivator and it doesn't cost a dime. But it does require that you care and care takes time: care enough to pay attention to what people are actually doing; care enough to take the time to acknowledge their hard work; care enough to notice people's efforts as well as their accomplishments; care enough to take the time out to appreciate and to do this on a regular basis.

Here's a simple, and I think rather surprising, example of the impact of appreciation on employees' self-esteem and efficacy. Not long ago I was in conversation with a recent college graduate who works at a big accounting company. She told me she had had one day off in the previous 50 days, and then worked 40 hours in two days to finish an important audit. Forget having a life. Personally, I think there is something wrong and inhumane with a system that requires that much out of their workers, exploits youthful energy, and doesn't consider burnout. But the amazing thing is that, although this young woman hates the hours, she likes working there. What keeps her motivated? She gets lots of appreciation and positive feedback. (Although, the last I heard she got a new job in a more humane work environment.)

As a speaker at a chief information officer conference some while ago, I was talking about the important role care plays in the workplace. These information technology (IT) guys looked back at me with an expression like "What did you have for breakfast?" Once I used the word "care," I felt I had lost my audience. And yet a poll of IT workers, who are not exactly known for their soft skills, showed nevertheless that the number one motivator for them was verbal thanks, number two written thanks, and number three public thanks. Money was number 12. This is a stark variation on what Pfeffer called the "knowing-doing gap":

- Survey numbers showed that caring through appreciation would be fulfilling and motivating for IT workers.
- And yet their managers saw care as an alien and irrelevant behavior.

Here's a story that illustrates the depth that work relationships can reach when people care for each other, told to me by Linda Rusch, former VP of Nursing at Hunterdon Medical Center in New Jersey. Like a crystal breaking reveals the lines of connection, this is a story of superficial disconnection that exposes the depth of the connection and care between coworkers.

The nursing staff at Hunterdon not only worked together, they played together. Every year they would go away on what they called the "girl's soul trip." Even though nurses cover for the vacationing nurses, Linda felt that the manager and the assistant manager of any one ward should not both be absent at the same time, as this puts too much responsibility on others if problems crop up.

It turned out that on this particular soul trip, the manager and assistant manager of one of the wards were both planning to go. "I was upset about it when I found out," Linda told me. When the ward manager saw that Linda wasn't too happy with her choice, she said, "OK, Linda. Help me. Tell me what to do." Linda refused and said she must make her own decision. "I was telling her she was a grown up," Linda explained. "I wasn't going to demand that she not go. But she knew how I felt." When Linda came to work the following Monday, she learned that the manager had decided to go on the trip, in spite of Linda's concerns.

The nurses' soul trip took place in Bermuda that year. The manager in question was splashing away in the water when suddenly she realized she wasn't having fun. She felt herself being propelled out of the water by a force beyond her, sobbing as she ran to her room. Everybody gaped. They had no idea why she was so upset. Once in her room, the manager called the hospital. Linda was pulled out of a meeting and was told the manager sounded horrible and to call her right back. "I thought that something terrible had happened." When Linda got on the phone, the manager was sobbing. "I can't believe I did this. I can't believe I disappointed you. I can't stand knowing you don't think highly of me."

"For me, that's all it took," Linda told me. "What mattered to me was that she felt bad enough to call me, and cared enough about how I felt. I said, 'It doesn't matter. What matters is our relationship. And you know, our relationship has just grown. It's on another level because your care for our relationship compelled you to act and you called me.'"

Pro-Social Behavior

Expressing appreciation to colleagues, and other social interactions that stem from genuine care, fall under the umbrella of what has been called "pro-social behavior," a topic that has attracted increasing research attention in recent years. It is producing some quite surprising insights into the fundamental nature of what it is to be human, particularly in the context of human social groups.

Simply put, pro-social behaviors are actions that are intended to help other people or society as a whole. They can range from helping an elderly person negotiate a tricky set of steps, for instance, to volunteering time and effort to rebuild a neighboring community after a natural disaster. Emotions such as empathy and a desire to do what is perceived to be the right thing underlie these actions, among many others.

Humans are quintessentially social creatures in the world of nature, so it is not surprising that individuals will from time to time make sacrifices (small and large) for the benefit of others. And it is also not surprising that the recipients of pro-social acts usually experience positive emotions, including happiness, through being helped. What is surprising, perhaps, is that research has demonstrated repeatedly that the benefactors of pro-social behaviors also experience positive emotions from their sacrifices, sometimes in greater measure than those who are being helped. Researchers see this, for instance, when they give participants in experiments $20, say, to spend either on themselves or on others, and find that the altruists in the experiment experience greater well-being than those who buy a treat for themselves. They also see it when they observe the brain's reward centers lighting up (in brain scans) just as much in givers of largesse as in recipients of largesse (Dunn et al., 2014).

The fact that both givers and recipients of pro-social actions experience positive emotions is central to the recognition of the power of the exercise of genuine care in organization: it leads to people having a stronger commitment to their work and to their colleagues, which creates highly effective teams and, as a result, the organization enjoys an edge over its competition.

The impact of simple pro-social behavior goes beyond the immediate positive response in the beneficiaries, as demonstrated by a 2018 NIH (National Institutes of Health) study (Chancellor, 2018). Practicing everyday prosociality, the report's authors found, is both emotionally reinforcing and contagious. Benefactors of pro-social behaviors experienced an increase in life satisfaction and job satisfaction and a decrease in depression, while beneficiaries felt happiness and motivated to look for ways to help their colleagues. The effects of the initial acts of pro-social behavior therefore rippled and multiplied through the organization. This study extended into many countries with similar results, demonstrating that care and kindness is our shared humanity. As Mother Teresa said, "Kind words can be short and easy to speak, but their echoes are truly endless."

The bottom line here is that care is a soft skill that many corporate and political worlds could usefully develop. Expressing appreciation is one small change that each one of us can make. One small change in the workplace equation that can make a big difference to people's well-being and efficacy and to organizations' success. But the care has to be sincere. If it's not sincere and managers see care as another "tool," a killer app with which to manipulate people and boost profits, workers will quickly understand what is going on. A heavy price will be paid in the loss of people's trust.

Inclusive Leaders Create Conditions for Discussions That Embrace Diversity

Creating conditions that invite openness and diversity requires really listening to people. Welcome their input, be open to ideas that may differ from yours. As Jim Kouzes and Barry Posner wrote in *The Leadership Challenge*, "Leadership is a dialogue, not a monologue. To enlist support, leaders must have intimate knowledge of people's dreams, hopes, aspirations, visions, and values" (Kouzes & Posner, 2002).

When leaders allow everyone a chance to be heard, they are likely to hear information they didn't know or consider viewpoints and perspectives that make them broaden their own views. This diversity in thinking encourages more creative and responsive solutions. Gaining input from others will improve decision-making.

How do you create those conditions that invite input? Inclusive leaders recognize they can't accomplish what they want by going it alone; they're not the only person who has great ideas and works hard. Inclusive leaders know the importance of recognizing the contributions of others. They understand the importance of the team *member* in doing team *work*. They care more about their team succeeding than their own ego needs. They acknowledge even the poorly conceived idea in an effort to encourage better ones. They are more likely to say "yes, and" rather than "yes, but." As a result, this democratic process stimulates better collaboration from their teams.

However, even with our best intentions, we may be preventing the openness we seek in discussions because of unconscious biases we may have. Here's an example which every woman I have talked to can relate to.

In the middle of the meeting on a controversial financial proposal, "Jane" has a flash of insight into a problem. She looks at the men and women around the table as she enthusiastically elaborates on what she believes to be an important point that can bridge the conversation.

After she finishes speaking, she waits to hear responses to her comments. No one responds. No one picks up on the idea. It was as if they didn't even hear what she had said.

"Jane" feels confused and frustrated. She thought she was bringing a lot to the table, but then why wasn't she getting any reinforcement? Maybe her observation wasn't really as worthwhile a contribution as she thought? Maybe she just doesn't have the leadership abilities needed?

Fifteen minutes later a male version of what Jane said, slightly reworded, is heard loud and clear. People think his idea is "brilliant!"

So what is going on? One way to explain it is "gender schemas."

In her book *Why So Slow? The Advancement of Women*, Virginia Valian, Professor of Psychology and Linguistics at Hunter College, New York, explored why women's advancement has crept at such a snail's pace (Valian, 1999). Along the way, she uncovered the world of what she called gender schemas: culturally bound assumptions about men and women that are unconscious.

The key insight here is that women are first assumed incompetent until proven otherwise. It's the opposite for men. If a woman is successful, it's assumed it is because she's a hard worker, or was lucky; if she fails, it's because she's incompetent. If a man succeeds, the assumption is that it's because he's competent; if he fails, it's because of bad luck. So right from the start women are not perceived as leaders.

Consequently, cultural biases consistently *overrate* men and *underrate* women. Self-assessment studies consistently show that men and women do the same to themselves. On a scale of 10, women tend to evaluate themselves two points lower than reality, while men will evaluate themselves two points higher (Zenger, 2018).

Assumed incompetence puts women on the defensive and can rattle their self-confidence. As a result, their struggle to prove themselves keeps them on a never-ending treadmill. So if you as a woman have felt held to a higher standard, it's not your imagination, you have been. It's the Fred Astaire/Ginger Rogers syndrome: Ginger has to do everything Fred does, except in high heels and backwards.

It's not just men assuming women are incompetent; women also fall prey to assuming incompetence in women. A woman may feel that she's competent but she likely won't assume that of other women. In one global experiment called the "Goldberg paradigm," researchers asked men and women in one group to evaluate a particular article or speech supposedly written by a man. Then they asked a similar group to judge the same material, this time supposedly authored by a woman. In countries all over the world, participants rated the very same words higher when putatively coming from a man than from a woman.

The fact that women often assume other women are incompetent may, in part, explain why women traditionally haven't been so great at helping each other up the ladder. That's changing, however, with the plethora of organizations and initiatives dedicated to women supporting women. A revolution is underway, a level of collaboration among women as we have never seen before.

When I talk with younger women about gender schemas, some say they don't experience this assumption. And may they never! It's a pretty level playing field when entering the workforce. After all, 46 percent of employees in Fortune 500 are women. The good news is the number of Fortune 500 companies with greater than 40 percent diversity has more than doubled from 69 to 145 since 2012, according to the "Missing Pieces Report: The 2018 Board Diversity Census of Women and Minorities on Fortune 500 Boards," a multiyear study published by the Alliance for Board Diversity (ABD), in collaboration with Deloitte. Women and minorities now comprise an all-time high of 34 percent of Fortune 500 board seats, up from 30.8 percent in 2016. We know more diverse boards lead to better business. The Fortune 100 is doing even better, outpacing the Fortune 500 with 38.6 percent of women and minorities holding board seats, compared with 34 percent in the Fortune 500.

The higher you go, however, the wider the gap. Caucasian white men still hold 66 percent of all Fortune 500 board seats and 91.1 percent of chairmanships.

Of the CEOs who lead the companies that make up the 2018 Fortune 500 list, just 24 are women. That number is down 25 percent from last year's record-breaking 32 female CEOs, the highest share of women since the Fortune's first 500 list in 1955. While women were at the helm of 6.4 percent of the companies on 2017's list, that number is now down to 4.8 percent.

Some women use the negative gender schemas against them to their advantage. These women play along as if they don't know what's going on when in reality they are five steps ahead of the guys. As Mae West put it, "Brains are an asset, if you hide them." Being underestimated can work to a woman's advantage when she is covertly outsmarting men, but that's a short-term benefit. In the end, feigning ignorance only helps perpetuate a misperception. What you permit, you promote.

It's important for inclusive leaders to be conscious of the assumptions of gender schemas. If you are a man heading a group, be more observant. If a woman is not being heard, go out of your way to ask her opinion and then value what you heard. If a woman says something that is out of your framework of thinking, don't jump to reject it but take time to understand that alternative. This is how you create conditions for an open and diverse discussion.

If you, as a woman, feel overlooked, don't assume you have nothing to contribute or are not a leader. Rather consider an unconscious assumption has kicked in. If you agree with what a woman coworker might be offering to the discussion, don't wait to tell her at the water cooler. Speak up and stand beside her in a project meeting and give her credit. If someone takes your idea and claims it as their own, do as one woman scientist researching cancer did. Tell that person, "Thanks, I'm so glad you love my idea!" As an inclusive leader, take stock of your own assumptions. Do you assume a woman isn't competent until proven otherwise? If so, it's a good way to keep good ideas out of the discussion.

Besides adding a diversity of opinions and ideas to the discussion, making sure women are included in the discussion has another benefit. Social scientists, such as Christopher Chabris at MIT's Center for Collective Intelligence, and Anita Williams Woolley at Carnegie Mellon University, have systematically examined the intelligence of groups. Although it is a complex issue, psychologists measure the intelligence of individuals by something called the "general intelligence factor," which integrates how an individual scores on a series of cognitive tests. Chabris and Woolley wondered whether an equivalent measure of intelligence might apply to the overall performance of groups.

What they discovered completely surprised them; it was not something they expected or were looking for. They learned that a group's performance is determined by what they called a "collective intelligence factor" that is not tied to either the smartest person on the team or to the average intelligence of the members of the team. *The one predictor for increasing collective intelligence is to have a good representation of women in the group.* Chabris and Woolley published their results in a paper, "Evidence for a Collective Intelligence Factor in the Performance of Human Groups," in *Science* in 2010 (Chabris & Woolley, 2010).

What do women bring to the table that catalyzes new thinking that generates a higher collective intelligence of the group? According to Chabris and Woolley, it is a superior social sensitivity in reading non-verbal cues and other people's emotion, and a fairness in turn taking. In a Q&A article in the June 2011 issue of *Harvard Business Review*, Woolley said the following about what characterizes great groups: "Not that the members are all really smart but that they listen to each other. They share criticism constructively. They have open minds. They're not autocratic." These are the democratic qualities that inclusive leaders strive to cultivate in their people. Woolley added the following comment: "And in our study we saw pretty clearly that groups that had smart people dominating the conversation were not very intelligent groups."

From my research on women in these situations, I would characterize women's "secret" as the possession and use of what may fairly be called soft skills: by this I mean relational intelligence, emotional intelligence, holistic perspective, inclusion, empathy, intuition. All those soft skills are pro-social skills and really powerful for true collaborations to succeed and for facilitating the emergence of collective intelligence. Of course such skills are not exclusively held by women. But on average they are more developed in women, and women are generally more willing to use them, as I mentioned earlier in this chapter.

Women not only bring diversity to the table, but they also bring the secret weapon of soft skills. So if leaders are serious about making progress, about finding new common ground, they will ensure that women occupy half the chairs at the table.

Complexity Science Explains Why Inclusive Leadership Works

The science of complexity is, well, complex, especially when it involves coding, algorithms, simulations, and other computer programming that address complicated issues, like timely train scheduling, supply/chain problems, and so on. However, the science of complexity also paradoxically holds a deep simplicity. It is this deep theoretical simplicity that I will translate into human terms for the purposes of this chapter.

Complexity science addresses the world of complex adaptive systems. Complex adaptive systems may be characterized as a collection of diverse "agents" that are free to "interact" with mutual effects, which generates adaptation and creativity of the system as a whole. Business organizations (indeed, all human organizations) are complex adaptive systems in this sense. A core property of complex adaptive systems is the emergence of shifting, often impossible-to-predict outcomes. It is the embodiment of that old, simple phrase, "the whole is greater than the sum of the parts." The late John Holland, a major player in the development of complexity science at the University of Michigan, preferred to describe the process as "Much coming from little." Nice.

The key word here is emergence. How does this happen?

In philosophy, systems theory, and art, emergence is the way patterns arise out of what appear to be relatively simple interactions. In complex adaptive systems, agents or entities interact, and when they have a mutual effect on one another something novel and unexpected emerges. Anything that enhances these interactions will also enhance what emerges, such as creativity and adaptability of the system.

In human organizations this translates into agents as *people*, and interactions as *relationships* that are grounded in a sense of mutuality: people share a mutual respect and interest, and have a mutual influence and impact on each other, even if not equal in power. From these relationships emerge genuine human connection, not simply "networking," and the potential for a higher self to emerge, what I call the soul at work.

When we have diversity in problem solving and discussions, this allows for something new to emerge, like a collective intelligence. Without that diversity, groups can fall into group think, as we saw in the financial crisis on Wall Street in 2008 and as we often see in politics.

Another principle of complex adaptive systems is that small actions can lead to big effects. It's counterintuitive; usually we think that small changes lead to small effects; big changes lead to big effects. As I said earlier, one of those small changes that can have a big effect on morale and motivation in organizations is the power of appreciation.

This deep simplicity in complexity is the importance of positive interaction as was so clearly evident in the experiments with being kind and appreciative in the workplace. In this way, relationships are the bottom line for business success in our complex environment, which is the conclusion Roger Lewin and I came to when we wrote our book, *The Soul at Work: Weaving Complexity Science for Business Success* (Simon & Schuster, 2000). How we interact with each other has everything to do with what emerges in our organizations. What can emerge from these interactions are the culture, the creativity, adaptability, and spirituality, that is, the soul at work. Depending on the quality of these interactions, a complex system can either evolve to higher levels of functioning or devolve into entropy and stasis.

★ ★ ★

The conclusion that relationships are the bottom line for success explains why inclusive leadership is so effective. People-oriented leadership improves bottom line numbers—in productivity, profitability, and retention, and so on, compared with command control leadership. A complexity science perspective therefore gives insight into why this should be so. It's a matter of perspective; what we value; where we put our energy.

The following Cherokee legend illustrates the importance of what you value in how we are in our world:

> A Cherokee elder is teaching his grandson about life. "A fight is going on inside me," he says to the boy.
>
> "It is a terrible fight and it is between two wolves. One is evil—he is anger, envy, sorrow, regret, greed, arrogance, self-pity, guilt, resentment, inferiority, lies, false pride, superiority, and ego." He continues, "The other is good—he is joy, peace, love, hope, serenity, humility, kindness, benevolence, empathy, generosity, truth, compassion, and faith. The same fight is going on inside you—and inside every other person, too."
>
> The grandson thinks about it for a minute and then asks his grandfather, "Which wolf will win?"
>
> The old Cherokee simply replies, "The one you feed."
>
> So as a leader or manager the question to ponder is: Which wolf are you feeding?

References

Bringing more humanity to recognition, performance, and life at work. (2017). Survey Report, WorkHuman Research Institute.
Chabris, C., & Woolley, A. (2010, October 29). Evidence for a collective intelligence factor in the performance of human groups. *Science, 330*, 686–688.
Chancellor, J., Margolis, S., Jacobs Baok, K., & Lyubomirsky, S. (2018). *Everyday prosociality in the workplace: The reinforcing benefits of giving, getting, and glimpsing.* Bethesda, MD: NIH.
Crabtree, S. (2011, April 13). What employees need to know. *Gallup Business Journal.*
Dunn, E., Aknin, L., & Norton, M. (2014). Prosocial behavior and happiness. *Current Directions in Psychological Science, 23*(1), 41–47.
Harter, J. (2018, August 26). Employment engagement on the rise in US. *Gallup News.*
Irvine, D. (2012, April 30). Recognitions impact on productivity: It's more than the Employee of the month. *TLNT, Talent Management and HR.*
Kouzes, J., & Posner, B. (2002). *The leadership challenge* (p. 15). San Francisco, CA: Jossey-Bass.
Pfeffer, J. (1998). *The human equation: Building profits by putting people first.* Boston, MA: Harvard Business School Press.
Pfeffer, J., & Sutton, R. (2000). *The knowing-doing gap.* Boston, MA: Harvard Business School Press.
Valian, V. (1999). *Why so slow? The advancement of women.* Cambridge, MA: MIT Press.
Wagner, R., & Harter, J. (2007, August 9). The fourth element of great managing. *Gallup Business Journal.*
Zenger, J. (2018, April 8). The confidence gap in men and women: Why it matters and how to overcome it. *Forbes.*

23
CREATING SPACE FOR TRANSFORMATION
Cultivating Containers for Inclusive Leadership Development

Trevor Cox

Introduction

Throughout this volume, we have seen the many applications and benefits of inclusive leadership. As the world continues to grow more complex, as well as more divided, inclusive leadership becomes more and more imperative to address the myriad concerns facing our world as leaders. As the field of inclusive leadership itself grows and as we dedicate ourselves to its practice, the next step logical step should be beginning to think about how to engage more people in the work. As research has shown, the experience of inclusion often creates the desire to be more inclusive, and can lead to further practice of inclusive leadership (Shore et al., 2011, p. 1279; Randel, Dean, Ehrhart, Chung, & Shore, 2016, p. 217). Pursuing inclusive leadership development gives people the skills and tools to enact more inclusion in the places where they lead. This chapter offers a framework for how to take this next step in inclusive leadership through leadership development practices.

Personally, the task of helping people grow and develop the capacity for inclusive leadership has always been an important pursuit in both practice and research. As a person who identifies with dominant American culture in almost all of my social identities, developing inclusive leadership has been and always will be a personal growth edge. I continue to try to push myself as a leader and as a person with privilege who wants to take those responsibilities seriously. Through mentoring and relationships with others, the ongoing experience of inclusive leadership development in my own life led to my doctoral research (Cox, 2017; which this chapter is developed upon) and has continually brought one fundamental question to the forefront: How do we continue to develop and grow the capacity for inclusive leadership in the people and places we lead?

In this chapter, I seek to engage this larger question by answering three more "on the ground" questions:

1. What does it mean to develop inclusive leadership?
2. What is necessary for inclusive leadership to be developed?
3. How do we create the kinds of environments where inclusive leadership is developed?

To answer the first question, I simply want to define my terms and assumptions about inclusive leadership and leadership development. The way these terms are defined and the assumptions made about them deeply affect the approach to development as well as what we hope to develop in others. I address the second question by talking about the fundamental task required for developing inclusive leaders: dialogue across difference on equal ground. We will explore this phrase in depth. Finally, the third and final question will be answered in a discussion about the "containers" we need to create to develop inclusive leadership as well as the leadership skills require to cultivate these containers.

Definitions and Assumptions

It is always helpful at the onset of a chapter of this nature to define terms well. Especially in the areas of diversity and inclusion, defining terms is a critical endeavor not only to provide sensitivity and inclusion in the writing, but also to distinguish between an ever growing list of terms within the literature and to acknowledge the power and politics of language (Hudgins, 2015; Smith, 2015; Williams, 2013).

Ironically, defining inclusion can be one of the most difficult steps. There is no standardized definition for inclusion (Ferdman, 2014; Shore et al., 2011), and how inclusion is defined determines how it is enacted. For the purposes of this chapter, inclusion is seen as a practice which acknowledges and honors all the various ways people are different and recognizes that each category of difference exists in unique, complex, and whole human beings (Ferdman, 2014, p. 11). It allows people to bring their full selves and make their full contribution to the workplace or environment "without losing sight of intergroup relations, intercultural dynamics, and systemic processes and structures" (Ferdman & Deane, 2014, pp. xxiv, xxii). Inclusion satisfies the needs for *belonging* as an esteemed member of a group while at the same time affirming a person's *uniqueness* (Shore et al., 2011, p. 1265) so that individuals do not have to "give up valuable identities or aspects of themselves" (Ferdman, 2014, p. 12).

Using this particular lens on inclusion sees diversity not as a problem to be solved, but resources from which organizations could both benefit and learn (Ferdman, 2014, p. 6). It takes it seriously both knowing what barriers are in place and seeks to identify and understand generative processes of inclusion that can help create paradigms and models for overcoming difficulties and facilitating individual and collective agency for diversity to been seen as a resource.

Beyond the definition, I am making a few assumptions about inclusion. First, diversity does not automatically result in inclusion. Diversity deals with the demographics and differences of those represented in a particular group. Inclusion, on the other hand, is the process designed to leverage differences and increase all members of the organization's ability to contribute fully and effectively (Roberson, 2006, pp. 215, 219,221). The analogy of the table is helpful here. Diversity is concerned with *who* is at the table, yet these efforts often stop short of being concerned with *what happens* at the table. Inclusion, on the other hand, is concerned with not only who is at the table, but ensuring uniqueness and belonging once they are there. As Miller and Katz (2002), in their seminal work in the area, pointed out, "Diversity without inclusion does not work" (p. 17).

The second assumption is that inclusion does not happen without leadership. Research continually shows the main difference between high-performing diverse teams and low-performing diverse teams is leadership (Maznevski & Chui, 2012, Loc 3256; Chrobot-Mason, Ruderman, & Nishii, 2014; Gotsis & Grimani, 2016). As Randel et al. (2018) point out, "simply placing individuals who differ from one another in a work group or promoting diverse individuals into leadership positions does not ensure positive outcomes" (p. 11). In order to fully leverage the diversity present in a group for the maximum benefit of everyone involved, leadership is required. Leadership is "the linchpin for inclusion," because it is not only a key part of inclusion for groups but it can help facilitate the expansion of inclusion to organizations and societies (Ferdman, 2014, p. 17). Inclusion is a concentrated effort and carefully managed group process that both addresses exclusion and leverages diversity (Gallegos, 2014, p. 190; Ferdman, 2014, p. 7). Leaders therefore need certain interpersonal skills, the ability to enact inclusion in groups, and have the responsibility of moving towards more inclusive organizations and societies by defining inclusion in context (Ferdman, 2014, p. 17).

Based on these understandings and assumptions, inclusive leadership is defined here as the collective capacity "for relational practice, collaboration, building inclusion for others, creating inclusive workplaces, and work cultures, partnerships and consensus building, and true engagement of all" (Wasserman, 2015, p. 335).

Inclusive leadership defined in this way is an adaptive, relational process. Working with diversity adds layers of ambiguity, uncertainty, and complexity on top of the already competitive, complex, and continually changing environments in today's workplace. There are no "blanket rules for inclusion" (Wasserman, Gallegos, & Ferdman, 2008), and working with diversity requires leaders to manage the complex relational dynamics of diverse groups and stakeholders (Wasserman & Blake-Beard, 2010, p. 198). Further, including people into a collective means inviting them into a well-defined system that enables continued inclusion (Ferdman, 2017, pp. 16–17). While rules and boundaries are necessary for organizations to function properly, those rules, boundaries, and norms are no longer clear and predictable (Gallegos, 2014, pp. 180, 184) and have the potential to produce automatic ways of interaction that prevent people from seeing the valuable ways other people are different (Wasserman & Blake-Beard, 2010, p. 200). Such complexity and ambiguity thus requires an adaptive approach (Heifetz & Laurie, 2001).

A relational approach to inclusive leadership means "being both *responsive* to differences and *responsible* for acting on them. This sense of responsibility—*to be responsive, responsible and accountable to others in our everyday interactions with them*—contrasts to individualized heroic models of leadership" (Cunliffe & Eriksen, 2011, p. 1439). Creating spaces for moments of dialogue that surface and address differences and being responsible to those differences (p. 1444) is an essential skill for the practice of inclusive leadership.

Finally, I want to say a word about leadership development. There is an important distinction between leader development and leadership development. Leader development is more concerned with the individual, while leadership development is concerned with the leadership capacities of a collective group. Inclusive leadership is not primarily for individual leaders; it is the development of a leadership capacity within a particular environment. Leadership in this case should be seen as a relational property more than an individual responsibility (Chrobot-Mason et al., 2014, p. 685). An individual leader's role is to moderate the relationship between team-member resources in order to enhance and build leadership capacity within the team (Day & Harrison, 2007, p. 365). While the individual leader is not ignored, it requires a more holistic approach to understand the dynamic and multilevel process of leadership (Avolio, Walumbwa, & Weber, 2009, p. 441).

The ability of an individual leader to shift their focus and approach from oneself to a more relational capacity requires a profound shift in identity (Day, Fleenor, Atwater, Sturm, & McKee, 2014; Ibarra, Wittman, Petriglieri, & Day, 2014). Such shifts are more than just behavioral and must engage the three facets of "knowing, doing, and being." As Booysen (2014) asserts, inclusive leadership development needs to pay attention to all three facets, and when any one of them is ignored, inclusive leadership is only partly being developed. As such, inclusive leadership development has to occur on a deeper, more transformative level.

In summary, inclusive leadership builds the collective capacity for inclusion across difference where people's whole selves are brought to the shared space. It must acknowledge the complexities of both the individuals and the multiple layers of the context that is occurring by working towards the common good of all and identifying the contextual, personal, and social barriers to inclusion (Booysen, 2014; Ferdman, 2014; Miller & Katz, 2002). Developing inclusive leadership requires a deep shift in knowing, doing, and being as people gain the "capacity to shift . . . attention from the individualistic cognitive perspective to the relational arena" (Wasserman, 2014, p. 150), as well as the ability to include more and more people across differences. Having established shared meaning around what it means to develop inclusive leadership, we now turn to the question of *how* to build this capacity.

Dialogue Across Difference on Equal Ground

The second question this chapter seeks to answer is: What is necessary for inclusive leadership to be developed? The primary process for the development of inclusive leadership is "dialogue across difference on equal ground" (Cox, 2017). As with anything in this area, such a sentence may sound simple but is actually complex in both its meaning and practice. Therefore, it is worth looking at the various components as a way to better understand how inclusive leadership is developed and also begin to point us to the next question of how to create environments where inclusive leadership is developed.

First, developing inclusive leadership assumes and requires a diverse group. The metaphor of "the table" is again helpful. Much of the rest of this chapter focuses on *what happens* at the table. But as we have seen, true inclusive leadership means we are concerned with both what happens at the table *and* who is at the table. While we could dedicate an entire chapter to creating more diverse spaces, suffice it to say here: If a leader is working in a homogenous environment, a majority of the work needs to be in creating a more diverse table.

Part of the reason diverse groups are so critical is because there is no substitute for actual contact and relationships with those who are different. This point cannot be overstated. Wasserman and Gallegos (2009) point out, "most people carry stereotypes about others that are more or less fixed depending on the extent of real life exposure one has to other groups.... Absent *real connection* across difference, we often base our assumptions on limited data or media depictions" (pp. 166–167, italics mine). In other words, there are no substitutes for real people in real places dialoging across and about differences to transform the way one thinks about members of other identity groups. Diverse groups are absolutely essential to the work of inclusive leadership development.

However, just having diverse groups is not enough. Just as diversity does not guarantee inclusion, a diverse group does not automatically mean inclusive leadership is being developed. One of the first steps towards development is making sure difference is engaged on *equal ground* (Leahy & Gilly, 2009, p. 31; Shore, Cleveland, & Sanchez, 2017; Nishii & Rich, 2014; Senge, 2006), especially for those unaccustomed to dialogue across difference. My own work has been primarily in higher education, and one of the most oft-cited examples is when faculty in primarily white institutions are dealing with white undergraduate students. Often these students' only experience with a person of color is in a service role, which is quite different from the experience where everyone's voice has equal value and weight. Such an experience is replicated in a variety of ways in any organization, and leaders must take care to ensure equal ground in the development space.

Miller and Katz (2002) talk about equal ground as "leveling" and "raising the playing field." Leveling the playing field first eliminates barriers that prevent equal participation, but then seeks to "raise the playing field" by elevating the elevating everyone's voice so *everyone* brings "all of their talents and energies to the workplace, working together to create something greater than any individual or monocultural group could do alone" (pp. 8, 13–15, 99–102). It is important to note that raising the playing field is the *second* of two steps. We must always begin by addressing the barriers and "isms" which prevent equal participation. If barriers are not first eliminated, we cannot seek to elevate everyone's voices.

We must also say at this point that no matter what kind of group you are leading to develop inclusive leadership—a work team, a leadership development group, an educational environment—the barriers and inequities that are present in the larger society and/or organization are present in the group. Leaders need to be aware of the sociohistorical bias and marginalization of certain social identities in order to counteract the problems in their environments, while respecting the unique identities of those in the group (Chrobot-Mason et al., 2014, p. 694). If, for example, a particular society or organization is racist, sexist, and/or homophobic, then those dynamics are somehow present in the group you are leading as well. Those realities do not stop because you are trying to lead an inclusive group. People in the group carry the resulting biases and trauma with them, so barriers and inequities need to be addressed early and steps need to be taken in order to ensure they are not replicated in the group.

Finally, the main activity of developing inclusive leadership is dialogue. For Isaacs (1999), one of the most influential dialogue scholars, dialogue is more than a technique or a tool. Dialogue is a way of being, a stance and way of looking at the world (p. 241). The self is continually in dialogue with its own multiple identities as well as others' identities (Ferdman, 2017, pp. 117–118), so all of our actions and decisions implicate others (Wasserman et al., 2008, p. 196). Hersted and Gergen (2013) further note that our organizations and institutions are also dialogically constructed, so dialogue is the primary process required to develop human beings and organizations.

In dialogue, individuals "try on" new perspectives in ways that are more inclusive and incorporate diverse points of view into the self. True dialogue requires people to suspend certainty so there is room for competing perspectives and everyone can hold their own position without the need to assimilate or oppose. As moments of dissonance occur and are reflected upon, new meaning is made in the context of relationship (Buber, 2003; Schapiro, Wasserman, & Gallegos, 2012; Wasserman et al., 2008). Dialogue across differences is thus the primary way assumptions are challenged, experiences are reexamined, and new ways of meaning making, relating, and being occur.

In terms of the kind of shifts required for developing inclusive leadership, these moments of dissonance, or "disorienting dilemmas" where "a person encounters something that does not fit with his or her expectations of how things should be" (Cranton, 2016, p. 15), often occur in the context of relationships. As Wasserman, Gallegos, and Taylor (2014) explain, "Stories of self and other are often so deeply embedded that for significant shifts to occur in the dynamics of relationships, transformative learning must occur *in relationships* and the culture of organizations rather than merely for individuals" (p. 456, italics in original). In order for these relational disorienting dilemmas (Wasserman & Gallegos, 2009, p. 165) to become transformative, difference must be engaged authentically through dialogue and leveraged in educative and generative ways. Transformative dialogic moments require the suspension of certainty, an exploration of differences through dialogue, and a willingness to work through the conflict inevitable across deep differences (Wasserman et al., 2008, p. 190).

Here again we must point to the importance of diversity within a group. Diverse groups in themselves have daily potential for relational disorienting dilemmas and transformative dialogic moments (Wasserman & Gallegos, 2009). Yet, much of the miscommunication across difference occurs because people are not willing to suspend their own certainty and make meaning across boundaries (Wasserman et al., 2008, p. 190). Inclusive leadership development requires leaders who pay attention to the ways diversity and difference is experienced and leverage inevitable relational disorienting dilemmas for transformation.

Additionally, true dialogue creates the conditions for equal ground. Dialogue pays attention to who is listening and what is being heard (hooks, 1988, p. 18). There is a willingness to speak when appropriate, name oppression, marginalization, and exclusion, but also know when to be silent and to listen (Booysen, 2014, p. 310). Dialogue helps inform whether to resist, transform, or move (hooks, 1988, p. 18). Just as leadership is a shared capacity, dialogue places responsibility on each member of the group to participate in creating equal ground. For people with marginalized identities, it is recognizing where they are silenced, then speaking up and using the voices which have been silenced, marginalized, or ignored (pp. 12–13). For people with privileged identities, this means owning their identities, using them responsibly, and examining how one's identity might silence others.

It is important to note that dialogue is not conversation for the sake of conversation. Dialogue in its purest sense is generative and transformative. Transformation can take various forms but for the purpose of this chapter, the goal is to transform one's knowing, doing, and being in ways that are more inclusive. Dialogue or development that does not have inclusion at the core of the experience is not developing inclusive leadership. Inclusive leadership development is an intentionally cultivated process of dialogue across differences on equal ground *in order to* develop greater capacity for inclusion.

Finally, dialogue is critical for the development of inclusive leadership in organizations. Cox (2017) found that the primary location for inclusive leadership development was at the group level, and this is supported in various other literature. Research indicates that especially when paying attention to issues of diversity and inclusion, a dialogic group environment is an essential requirement (Berkovich, 2014; Booysen, 2014). Critical dialogue enables those involved to reflect on themselves, their responsibilities, their cultural climate, and analyze their culturally conditioned levels of understanding (Freire, 2005, pp. 1–5, 13). Through critical dialogue, individuals and groups are able to reflect on the language and norms of the institutions, which can expose the hegemonic discourses taking place and the invisible factors oppressing specific groups, and renarrates the existing social setting (Berkovich, 2014, p. 253). As individual leaders are developed through dialogic space, these dialogic groups are often the primary catalysts for organizational change.

The discipline of organizational development (OD) further suggests that dialogic groups are an important source of change. Wasserman et al. (2014) argue that in order to address diversity and multicultural issues in OD, practitioners need to focus on creating inclusive cultures and systemic level changes through "relational transformative learning in groups" (pp. 456–460). Dialogic OD has also begun to emerge within the discipline, arguing that since organizations are dialogically constructed, the primary change events are the results of "the creation of a container: a time and space where normal, business as usual ways of interacting are suspended so that different, generative conversations can take place" (Bushe, 2013, p. 12). Creating inclusive, dialogic containers can lead to important changes and developments not only in individuals, but also in whole organizations.

Taken together, if we hope to develop the capacity for inclusive leadership in individuals, groups, organizations, and institutions, our efforts need to be concentrated on the group level. Just as leadership is the "linchpin" for inclusion, dialogue on the group level is the linchpin for inclusive leadership development. Further, the process and skills required for *practicing* inclusive leadership on the group level are the same process and skills needed to *develop* inclusive leadership in both individuals and organizations. As such, the rest of the chapter will concentrate on how to create environments for dialogue across difference on equal ground.

Cultivating Containers for Inclusive Leadership Development

Dialogue across difference on equal ground does not happen without intentional practice. One of the critical tasks, then, of developing inclusive leadership is cultivating well-defined "containers" for dialogue and development to happen (Ferdman, 2017, p. 17; Isaacs, 1999, p. 241). The development of inclusive leadership creates dialogue around identity, differences, privilege, and power, and thus the process is inherently paradoxical and filled with tension. The complexity of the process and uniqueness of each group means there can be no prescriptive rules. For Isaacs (1999), the quality of shared meaning and energy required for dialogue cannot be manufactured, but attention can be paid to the "container" where one creates the conditions for dialogue to occur (p. 241). We can point to common elements necessary within the containers as well as the leadership skills necessary to cultivate these environments. First, I will describe what needs to be present in an inclusive leadership development container, and then I will describe the necessary leadership tasks required to create and cultivate such environments.

The Container

Inclusive leadership development requires four main attributes in the container: brave space, co-authenticity, room for mistakes, and difficult conversations. We will look at each of these in turn.

Brave Space

One of the most critical elements of inclusive leadership development containers is "brave space." Often in conversations surrounding both dialogue and diversity, we see the notion of "safe space." There is an undeniable element of psychological safety that must be present to do the difficult work of developing inclusive leadership (Carmeli, Reiter-Palmon, & Ziv, 2010; Hirak, Peng, Carmeli, & Schaubroeck, 2012; Nembhard & Edmondson, 2006), but Arao and Clemens (2013) provide an important critique about the notion of safety. They believe that often safety and comfort are conflated to mean the same thing. When no one is willing to be uncomfortable, dialogue has to remain polite rather than the kind of provocative dialogue that creates space for transformation (p. 135). Authentic learning with regard to issues of identity, oppression, power, and privilege require "the qualities of risk, difficulty, and controversy that are defined as incompatible with safety" (p. 139).

Further, safety often encourages the "entrenchment of privilege" (p. 140). When safety is a condition for participation, people with dominant identities tend to define for others how confrontation and challenging assumptions should occur, which often means that people with marginalized identities must restrain their participation to conform to dominant resistance and denial (p. 140). People with marginalized identities may additionally see the experience of naming their exclusion as an unsafe act because it often results in "dismissal and condemnation as hyper sensitive or unduly aggressive" (p. 140). Rather than "safe space," Arao and Clemens suggest "brave spaces." Bravery is needed to share one's identities and experiences as well as be willing to be challenged to see things in new ways (p. 141). Creating brave spaces means creating an expectation for assumptions to be challenged and differing perspectives to be heard. Developing inclusive leadership is not intended to be polite, but to be inclusive, transformative, and developmental by creating relational disorienting dilemmas and engaging in dialogue.

One of the primary ways we can create relational disorienting dilemmas in brave space is the sharing of stories. Sharing stories in relationship helps people internalize these stories and become more empathetic towards others. Individuals make room inside themselves for others, and this creates a sense of responsibility to continue to create more inclusive spaces and, hopefully, more inclusive leaders. Both the voicing and the hearing of stories create the potential for change. People with dominant identities need to understand and admit their privilege, as well as the historical marginalization and oppression that have created that privilege. People with marginalized identities need to speak about the hurt, pain, and exclusion that they have experienced.

Stories need to be told not just for the sake of others, but for the individual's own freedom as well. As stories are told, groups can then begin to think about how to move forward. Stories do not simply make us aware of the marginalization and exclusion in the world but require us to be responsible agents in correcting those wrongs. Guilt, hurt, frustration, and anger are spoken so they can be transcended. Rather than stay in these emotions, these emotions spur one another to create a better world. Through sharing stories, people of privilege and those in marginalized communities develop their own capacity for inclusive leadership and can work together to create more inclusive environments, organizations, institutions, and societies.

Co-Authenticity

Isaacs (1999) argues that the "quality of authenticity is at the core of the dialogic state" (p. 240). Authenticity for Isaacs is about finding one's own voice and learning to tell the truth about one feels and knows (p. 63). Without authenticity, people are speaking at shallow, surface levels and cannot challenge deep-seated assumptions. Such authenticity across differences and diversity is even more difficult, and brave spaces become even more imperative. The authenticity and vulnerability needed for dialogue across difference requires an element of psychological safety to "express core aspects of their self-identities" (Nishii & Rich, 2014, p. 334), yet authentically encountering differences in others and allowing them to challenge one's assumptions also requires a great deal of discomfort (Ferdman, 2017, pp. 21–23).

Authenticity thus becomes not simply about one person or group, but something that is done for the common good. When a voice is overinflated, it crowds out others, and when a voice is underdeveloped, it is unable to create the desired change (Isaacs, 1999, p. 176). One participant in Cox's (2017) research described this care for the common good as "co-authenticity." She reflected that developing inclusive leadership is:

> all about you and it's not about you at all . . . I would really love to kind of replace [the word] authenticity with co-authenticity . . . how are we at being authentic in spaces that allows other people to be authentic in those spaces? . . . That's where it starts.
>
> *(p. 90)*

Authenticity needs be seen as something that moves beyond the individual. Becoming more authentic is not simply understanding your own voice and contribution, but also how it impacts and interacts with others (Ferdman & Roberts, 2014, pp. 114–115). True authenticity is not just simply being oneself fully, but allowing others to be fully themselves as well. Both dominant and non-dominant groups must mutually adapt while still retaining cultural identities (Nishii & Rich, 2014, pp. 333–334).

It is important to note that such adaptation is done for the sake of others and the development of the group. It is never forced or coerced. Co-authenticity is different than being evaluated by one's deviance from dominant norms (Nishii & Rich, 2014, p. 334) and subsequently punished for such difference. Co-authenticity is about being aware of the impact of one's authenticity and being willing to adapt to the other authentic selves in the space, without losing important parts of oneself. It is not losing a sense of one's own identities; it is adapting for the sake of another (Ferdman, 2017; Nishii & Rich, 2014). Much like a dance, each person retains their own unique self, while incorporating some of others into their selves.

Room for Mistakes

Mistakes should be assumed in both the practice and development of inclusive leadership. The very word "practice" implies there will be mistakes, so leaders must equip people with the skills for making mistakes, conflict, and engaging differences in ways previously unexplored. Even people who have engaged in meaningful dialogue may have never done so across differences, so there are bound to be mistakes as this capacity is developed. While leaders cannot be inclusive for others, they can equip them with tools, allow space for practice and mistakes, and provide important feedback in the process of development. Further, when mistakes are assumed, individuals are freer to bring their whole selves and spend less time and energy on impression management (Giscombe, 2015, pp. 86–87).

Admittedly, making room for mistakes is a difficult endeavor, especially since a "mistake" when it comes to diversity and inclusion is always at the expense of others. Exclusion cannot be tolerated, and leaders must create this as an expectation and have firm policies about how exclusion will be handled. When exclusion has to be specifically addressed, Cox (2017) noted that many inclusive leaders practice "calling in" rather than calling out. "Calling in" addresses the particular problem or exclusion, but in a way that creates dialogue and meaning making together. When leaders are willing to "call in" rather than "call out," inevitable mistakes can be turned into disorienting dilemmas that can be reflected on and learned from. Calling out builds more walls between people, but calling in addresses exclusion immediately with compassion and a willingness to listen. There needs to be space for mistakes, but the hurt these mistakes cause must be addressed and used as a tool for growth and development. Too often, even when mistakes are addressed, leaders do not take the time to help people learn from them, address the hurt they caused, or come back to the issue until it is resolved. Which leads to the next element of the container.

Difficult Conversations

Inclusive leadership development further assumes the presence of difficult conversations. Transformative dialogue does not occur through mere contact with those who are different or through polite conversation. As dialogue deepens across difference, there will always be discomfort, "damaging first impressions, unshared assumptions, awkward conversation, and perhaps conflict" (Menon & Chakravarti, 2015, p. 97). Just as transformation is spurred on by a disorienting dilemma, the capacity for inclusive leadership is developed in the crucible of difficult dialogues.

Yet talking about controversial subjects or difficult issues is not enough. For dialogue that leads to transformation, the difficult things that come up must be engaged, and conflict and discomfort have to be handled intentionally in order to produce generative results. Not only do the hard things have to be talked about, people have to remain with the tension and discomfort long enough for true change to take place. Our instinctual human response to difficulty is avoidance, so leaders have to help people persist in relationship and be more open to questioning and revising assumptions (Menon & Chakravarti, 2015, p. 98). Development groups must practice resilience in the face of social discomfort (p. 97) in order for creative alternatives and new ways of being and relating to emerge (Wasserman & Gallegos, 2009, p. 169). In this work, we cannot guarantee that hurtful words or exclusion will not happen. What we can guarantee is that when these things happen, they will be addressed. Adaptation and growth occur when groups remain resilient and engaged through difficult conversation (Ferdman, 2017, p. 25). By engaging the difficult conversations and remaining present to the conflict long enough, transformation becomes possible.

It should be noted here that privilege is one of the most needed areas for leaders to address (Cox, 2017). Booysen (2014) suggests that addressing "isms" was a primary task of the meso or group level (p. 310). However, Cox (2017) found inclusive leaders to actually be addressing privilege far more often. "Isms" were still discussed, but privilege was explored as the root of many of the "isms." While privilege is one of the most important assumptions to challenge, it also proves to be the most difficult, and leaders need to think strategically about how they address privilege. The ability to engage conversation on privilege (or any hard subjects) and stay with the discomfort requires leadership, which we will turn to next.

Leadership

Well-defined containers do not happen on their own. They require intentionality and leadership. Just as inclusion requires leadership, dialogue needs leadership in order to "create a climate in which it [is] possible to lay out seemingly opposing viewpoints and have enough perspective to see that there [is] room for both, and that by hearing both, everyone [is] able to learn" (Isaacs, 1999, p. 198). It is worth stating again that there are no prescriptive rules, but there are certain skills and tools that aid in cultivating the kinds of container described.

Modeling

Primarily, leaders must model inclusive leadership. There are several areas where modeling can be helpful. Perhaps the most important is the leader showing up authentically. Authenticity is once again for the sake of others. When a leader brings their full selves to the space, it invites others to do the same. Leaders can do this in a number of ways. Leaders should model a "growth mindset" as people who are continuing to develop and grow as inclusive leaders. Leaders do not come to the space having all the answers, but ask questions and are willing to make mistakes. Being willing to share, make, and admit mistakes, along with being willing to have mistakes pointed out, are critical in giving others permission to make mistakes and can instill bravery in those being developed. Leaders must see themselves on a journey of inquiry with the group, and their role to call attention to important issues not being addressed or being looked at problematically (Freire, 2005, p. 111).

Second, leaders should be vulnerable in sharing how their own identities affect the practice of leadership and how they approach the development process. It is important for the group not to think the leader speaks for all people of their identity, and leaders can be explicit about their own lenses and assumptions. Authenticity and vulnerability are not sharing every part of one's self, but strategically sharing real and deep parts of oneself for the sake of others. Wasserman et al. (2008) talk about how sharing experiences of ones' social identity can create affinity with those who share that identity but can potentially distance others. Leaders should be strategic in the way they share stories and experiences with the goal of helping everyone in the group be more authentic (p. 187).

Third, leaders need to attend to their own growth and development. The ability to attend to both the self and other is in itself a difficult task but "becomes exponentially more challenging when bridging across differences in race, gender, sexual orientation, or nationality" (Gallegos, 2014, p. 183). The practice of inclusive leadership requires leaders to continually expand, evolve, and transform (p. 197) by attending to their own growth and patterns of relating to others (Wasserman, 2015, pp. 336–337). Continual reflection on how one makes meaning keeps leaders from privileging certain perspectives over others and is essential to the work of inclusive leadership (Gallegos, 2014, p. 181). Critical reflection helps leaders to ask the important questions for inclusive leadership: "Whose voices or perspectives might we be missing?" or "What are the limitations to the current ways we are seeing the issue?" (p. 181).

Engaging Social Identity

Developing inclusive leadership requires a deep understanding of social identities in both leaders and those being developed. Strategic use of one's authenticity not only requires self-reflection and growth but reflection on the group's various social identities as well. Reflecting on the social identities of those involved in inclusive leadership development containers makes leaders more attuned to the way people may or may not be participating and allows leaders to identify the benefits of the identities present in order to encourage authenticity and voice. Leaders must create space where social identities are acknowledged and seen as valuable. Such space must be psychologically safe for those with marginalized identities to bring their whole selves and examine existing norms, boundaries, structures, and systems that potentially prevent certain identities showing up authentically. People in an inclusive environment need to feel that they are both unique and belong by knowing their voice matters and makes a difference in the environment.

Additionally, leaders need to help those being developed engage with social identity. Individuals must first be aware of the impact of their identities. Individuals with dominant identities may often be unaware of some, if not many, of their social identities. It is also helpful for people to understand that facets of one's identity are not static but grow and develop to support other identities, as well as how multiple identities are interconnected and influenced by certain contexts to produce "unequal power distribution and structural inequities" (Wasserman et al., 2014, p. 454). Leaders and participants need to become more aware of their social identity, how others are both similar to and different from oneself, how these differences are a benefit to the whole, and the reactions social identities may cause between people with different identities (Ferdman, 2017, p. 15).

Sharing Power

As modeling is such a huge piece of a leader's job in inclusive leadership development, another critical modeling element is co-authenticity. As a leader, co-authenticity takes the form of sharing power (Ferdman, 2017, p. 22). Addressing issues of power is a particularly salient issue for inclusive leadership development in education and organizations, as managers and educators are naturally in a position of power in the environment. Genuine relationships need to be built between those being developed and those with positional power. Individuals need to be empowered in their own practice and development of inclusive leadership, and there should be an emphasis on not having to have all the answers (Meyer, 2009, p. 54).

Ferdman (2017) describes how agency and sharing power contributes to both belonging and uniqueness. It is not enough for people to understand one's unique social identities or unique voice. One's voice has to matter in the environment. Individuals have to know that they are responsible and have the capability of influencing and making a difference in an environment. Further, environments are more inclusive when everyone has equal access to information and decision-making (Nishii & Rich, 2014), and dialogic environments are more transformative when learners have shared ownership and control over the space (Fisher-Yoshida, Geller, & Schapiro, 2009).

Sharing power means allowing those in the group to co-construct the container. Co-constructing the space helps the environment become more reflective of the unique individuals' concerns by giving agency to all members as full participants whose voice matters. Further, especially those who have been excluded or marginalized, it helps people become "agents of their own recuperation" (Freire, 2005, p. 12). Ultimately, it is up to the leader on the appropriate amount of co-construction, but examples include pursuing questions that are important to the individuals in the group, allowing the group to set their own goals, and establishing how to hold each other accountable.

One initial step that can be taken to co-construct brave developmental containers is creating ground rules (Arao & Clemens, 2013). Ground rules set expectations about what will and will not be allowed into the space. As the leader, this is an important task, but commitment to ground rules is much more likely to happen when the group co-constructs the rules themselves (Ferdman, 2017, pp. 18, 20). Allowing those being developed to set their own ground rules gives them agency and enables the rules to reflect the people actually in the room rather than an "imaginary other" (p. 21). Ground rules help leaders communicate up front what they consider to be exclusive and how exclusion will be handled. Guidelines must also be established for confrontation and conflict in order to prepare those involved in the container and shape their expectations for dialogue. Shaping expectations means preparing everyone for the inevitable conflict that will occur and helping them navigate both dissent and conflict.

Navigating Conflict

Leadership is especially important for the hard conversations. Leaders must have the skills and capabilities to manage emotions, predict faultlines, and navigate conflict. Not only is navigating conflict important for dialogue, a leader successfully navigating conflict gives those in the environment tools, skills, and agency to do so in the future. Two important general skills should be mentioned in engaging difficult conversations.

First, the leader needs to stay engaged at the "meta-level." If the leader is drawn into the conflict or not adept at dealing with conflict, difficult conversations will not be generative or educative. Leaders must be adaptive by seeing the conflict as object and being able to stand "on the balcony" (Heifetz & Laurie, 2001) to observe the conflict. Staying at the meta-level allows the leader to help manage the inevitable emotions in dealing with issues of identity and power, and helps individuals move from *being* the conflict to *looking at* the conflict (Wasserman & Gallegos, 2009, p. 158). It also helps leaders provide a broader narrative and perspective to the conflict (Wasserman et al., 2008). Remaining mindful in conflict allows the conversation to become generative, rather than unproductive.

Second, leaders should be able to predict certain conflict. Since engaging in inclusion and dialogue cannot be done without some sort of conflict or difficulty, leaders need to begin to predict where these conflicts will happen. Understanding where cultural faultlines exist (Wang, 2017), as well as reflecting on social identities, assists leaders in taking a relational and contextual approach that can predict where some of the deeper conflict will occur. As faultlines are predicted, leaders can better prepare for the accompanying emotions and be able to remain more mindful during intense dialogue.

Inclusive Leadership Development Cannot Be Forced

One final tension should be addressed for developing inclusive leadership. It should be heavily emphasized that inclusive leadership cannot be forced. Ferdman (2017) describes this as creating an inclusive environment where people are mutually adapting (co-authenticity) for the sake of the collective, but adaptation is *not a requirement for participation*. People are allowed to be who they are in the environment whether or not it leads to transformation or development (p. 9). Isaacs (1999) argues that while dialogue cannot be forced, what can be done is to create the conditions for dialogue across differences to occur. Leaders cannot coerce but can cultivate the space where people can be exposed to difference and new ways of thinking and invite individuals into dialogue. In fact, coercing people to engage in inclusion before they are developmentally ready can potential cause harm. Development depends on whether those involved are ready for change. What leaders can do is cultivate the kinds of containers discussed here and invite all people to engage in the dialogue.

Conclusion

The task of developing inclusive leadership is no small endeavor. While this chapter has looked at the important elements of development, it is important to note that each of these is a difficult task. Part of the reason inclusive leadership requires a shift in one's being is because the work is difficult. Beyond the business case for diversity, inclusive leadership must address the very real harm, injustice, inequity, and violence that exist in our world. While the workplace and higher education continue to grow more diverse and globalized, inequity and discrimination persist, and the result of exclusion fills news headlines daily. The willingness to do such difficult work often requires a shift in one's very being. This chapter is offered as a framework that can be used for developing more inclusive people, teams, organizations, and societies with the hope of a more just society and world. There are no easy answers, and the process requires hard work and sacrifice. Yet the hope for this chapter is that leaders will take inclusion seriously and begin to develop more and more people willing to practice inclusive leadership in their own environment. I hope in both this chapter and this volume that we have built the case that not only is inclusive leadership worth the effort, but it is the kind of hard work and sacrifice we need in the 21st century.

References

Arao, B., & Clemens, K. (2013). From safe spaces to brave spaces: A new way to dialogue around diversity and social justice. In L. M. Landreman (Ed.), *The art of effective facilitation: Reflections from social justice educators* (pp. 135–150). Sterling, VA and Washington, DC: Stylus Publishing.

Avolio, B. J., Walumbwa, F. O., & Weber, T. J. (2009). Leadership: Current theories, research, and future directions. *Annual Review of Psychology*, 60, 421–449. (2008-17628-016).

Berkovich, I. (2014). Between person and person: Dialogical pedagogy in authentic leadership development. *Academy of Management Learning & Education*, 13(2), 245–264.

Booysen, L. (2014). The development of inclusive leadership: Practice and processes. In B. M. Ferdman & B. R. Deane (Eds.), *Diversity at work: The practice of inclusion* (1st ed., pp. 296–329). San Francisco, CA: Jossey-Bass.

Buber, M. (2003). *Between man and man* (2nd ed.). New York, NY: Routledge.

Bushe, G. R. (2013). Theories of dialogic consultation. *OD Practitioner*, 45(1), 11–17.

Carmeli, A., Reiter-Palmon, R., & Ziv, E. (2010). Inclusive leadership and employee involvement in creative tasks in the workplace: The mediating role of psychological safety. *Creativity Research Journal*, 22(3), 250–260 (2010-17315-002).

Chrobot-Mason, D., Ruderman, M. N., & Nishii, L. H. (2014). Leadership in a diverse workplace. In D. Day (Ed.), *The Oxford handbook of leadership and organizations* (1st ed., pp. 683–708). New York, NY: Oxford University Press.

Cox, T. (2017). *Learning from and for "The Other": The development of inclusive leadership capacity by faculty members* (Ph.D. Dissertation), Trinity International University, Deerfield, IL.

Cranton, P. (2016). *Understanding and promoting transformative learning: A guide to theory and practice* (3rd ed.). Sterling, VA: Stylus Publishing.

Cunliffe, A. L., & Eriksen, M. (2011). Relational leadership. *Human Relations*, 64(11), 1425–1449.

Day, D. V., Fleenor, J. W., Atwater, L. E., Sturm, R. E., & McKee, R. A. (2014). Advances in leader and leadership development: A review of 25 years of research and theory. *Leadership Quarterly*, 25(1), 63–82.

Day, D. V., & Harrison, M. M. (2007). A multilevel, identity-based approach to leadership development. *Human Resource Management Review*, 17(4), 360–373 (2007-18074-003).

Ferdman, B. M. (2014). The practice of inclusion in diverse organizations: Toward a systemic and inclusive framework. In B. M. Ferdman & B. R. Deane (Eds.), *Diversity at work: The practice of inclusion* (1st ed., pp. 3–54). San Francisco, CA: Jossey-Bass.

Ferdman, B. M. (2017). Paradoxes of inclusion: Understanding and managing the tensions of diversity and multiculturalism. *The Journal of Applied Behavioral Science*, 53(2), 235–263.

Ferdman, B. M., & Deane, B. R. (Eds.). (2014). *Diversity at work: The practice of inclusion* (1st ed.). San Francisco, CA: Jossey-Bass.

Ferdman, B. M., & Roberts, L. M. (2014). Creating inclusion for oneself: Knowing, accepting, and expressing one's whole self at work. In B. M. Ferdman & B. R. Deane (Eds.), *Diversity at work: The practice of inclusion* (1st ed., pp. 3–54). San Francisco: Jossey-Bass.

Fisher-Yoshida, B., Geller, K. D., & Schapiro, S. A. (Eds.). (2009). *Innovations in transformative learning: Space, culture, and the arts*. New York, NY: Peter Lang Publishing.

Freire, P. (2005). *Education for critical consciousness*. London and New York, NY: Bloomsbury Academic.

Gallegos, P. V. (2014). The work of inclusive leadership: Fostering authentic relationships, modeling courage and humility. In B. M. Ferdman & B. R. Deane (Eds.), *Diversity at work: The practice of inclusion* (1st ed., pp. 177–202). San Francisco, CA: Jossey-Bass.

Giscombe, K. (2015). Resilience and failure. In L. M. Roberts, L. P. Wooten, & M. N. Davidson (Eds.), *Positive organizing in a global society: Understanding and engaging differences for capacity building and inclusion* (1st ed., pp. 85–89). New York, NY: Routledge.

Gotsis, G., & Grimani, K. (2016). Diversity as an aspect of effective leadership: Integrating and moving forward. *Leadership & Organization Development Journal*, 37(2), 241–264.

Heifetz, R. A., & Laurie, D. L. (2001). The work of leadership. *Harvard Business Review*, 79(11), 131–141.

Hersted, L., & Gergen, K. J. (2013). *Relational leading*. Chagrin Falls, OH: The Taos Institute Publications.

Hirak, R., Peng, A. C., Carmeli, A., & Schaubroeck, J. M. (2012). Linking leader inclusiveness to work unit performance: The importance of psychological safety and learning from failures. *The Leadership Quarterly*, 23(1), 107–117. https://doi.org/10.1016/j.leaqua.2011.11.009

hooks, bell. (1988). *Talking back: Thinking feminist, Thinking black 1st*. Cambridge, MA: South End Press.

Hudgins, C. A. (2015). *The impact of diversity courses on student attitudes toward sexual orientation and racial diversity*. Los Angeles: University of California.

Ibarra, H., Wittman, S., Petriglieri, G., & Day, D. V. (2014). Leadership and identity: An examination of three theories and new research directions. In D. V. Day & D. V. Day (Eds.), *The Oxford handbook of leadership and organizations* (pp. 285–301). New York, NY: Oxford University Press. (2014–16828–014).

Isaacs, W. (1999). *Dialogue: The art of thinking together* (1st ed.). New York, NY: Crown Business.

Leahy, M. J., & Gilly, M. S. (2009). Learning in the space between us. In B. Fisher-Yoshida, K. D. Geller, & S. A. Schapiro (Eds.), *Innovations in transformative learning: Space, culture, and the arts* (pp. 23–42). New York, NY: Peter Lang Publishing.

Maznevski, M. L., & Chui, C. (2012). Leading global teams. In M. E. Mendenhall, J. S. Osland, A. Bird, G. R. Oddou, M. L. Maznevski, M. J. Stevens, & G. K. Stahl (Eds.), *Global leadership 2e: Research, practice, and development* (2nd ed., pp. 3062–3506). New York, NY: Routledge.

Menon, T., & Chakravarti, A. (2015). Social resilience: Building persistence in interracial relationships. In L. M. Roberts, L. P. Wooten, & M. N. Davidson (Eds.), *Positive organizing in a global society: Understanding and engaging differences for capacity building and inclusion* (1st ed., pp. 96–100). New York, NY: Routledge.

Meyer, P. (2009). Learning space/work space: Can we make room for transformative learning in organizations? In B. Fisher-Yoshida, K. D. Geller, & S. A. Schapiro (Eds.), *Innovations in transformative learning: Space, culture, and the arts* (pp. 43–64). New York, NY: Peter Lang Publishing.

Miller, F. A., & Katz, J. H. (2002). *The inclusion breakthrough* (1st ed.). San Francisco, CA: Berrett-Koehler Publishers.

Nembhard, I. M., & Edmondson, A. C. (2006). Making it safe: The effects of leader inclusiveness and professional status on psychological safety and improvement efforts in health care teams. *Journal of Organizational Behavior, 27*(7), 941–966.

Nishii, L. H., & Rich, R. E. (2014). Creating inclusive climates in diverse organizations. In B. M. Ferdman & B. R. Deane (Eds.), *Diversity at work: The practice of inclusion* (1st ed., pp. 330–363). San Francisco, CA: Jossey-Bass.

Randel, A. E., Dean, M. A., Ehrhart, K. H., Chung, B., & Shore, L. (2016). Leader inclusiveness, psychological diversity climate, and helping behaviors. *Journal of Managerial Psychology, 31*(1), 216–234.

Randel, A. E., Galvin, B. M., Shore, L. M., Ehrhart, K. H., Chung, B. G., Dean, M. A., & Kedharnath, U. (2018). Inclusive leadership: Realizing positive outcomes through belongingness and being valued for uniqueness. *Human Resource Management Review, 28*(2), 190–203. https://doi.org/10.1016/j.hrmr.2017.07.002

Roberson, Q. M. (2006). Disentangling the meanings of diversity and inclusion in organizations. *Group & Organization Management, 31*(2), 212–236 (2006-02945-003).

Schapiro, S. A., Wasserman, I. L., & Gallegos, P. V. (2012). Group work and dialogue: Spaces and process for transformative learning relationships. In E. W. Taylor & P. Cranton (Eds.), *The handbook of transformative learning: Theory, research, and practice* (Kindle ed., pp. 8957–9372). San Francisco, CA: Jossey-Bass.

Senge, P. M. (2006). *The fifth discipline: The art & practice of the learning organization* (Revised & Updated ed.). New York, NY: Doubleday.

Shore, L. M., Cleveland, J. N., & Sanchez, D. (2018). Inclusive workplaces: A review and model. *Human Resource Management Review, 28*(2), 176–189. https://doi.org/10.1016/j.hrmr.2017.07.003

Shore, L. M., Randel, A. E., Chung, B. G., Dean, M. A., Holcombe Ehrhart, K., & Singh, G. (2011). Inclusion and diversity in work groups: A review and model for future research. *Journal of Management, 37*(4), 1262–1289.

Smith, D. G. (2015). *Diversity's promise for higher education: Making it work* (2nd ed.). Baltimore: Johns Hopkins University Press.

Wang, J. (2017). Strategies for managing cultural conflict: Models review and their applications in business and technical communication. *Journal of Technical Writing and Communication.* https://doi.org/10.1177/0047281617696985

Wasserman, I. C. (2014). Strengthening interpersonal awareness and fostering relational eloquence. In B. M. Ferdman & B. R. Deane (Eds.), *Diversity at work: The practice of inclusion* (1st ed., pp. 128–154). San Francisco, CA: Jossey-Bass.

Wasserman, I. C. (2015). Dialogic OD, diversity, and inclusion: Aligning mindsets, values, and practices. In D. A. Noumair & A. B. (Rami) Shani (Eds.), *Research in organizational change and development* (Vol. 24, pp. 329–356). Wagon Lane, Bingley, West Yorkshire: Emerald Group Publishing Limited.

Wasserman, I. C., & Blake-Beard, S. (2010). Leading inclusively: Mind-sets, skills and actions for a diverse, complex world. In K. Bunker, D. T. Hall, & K. E. Kram (Eds.), *Extraordinary leadership: Addressing the gaps in senior executive development* (1st ed., pp. 197–212). San Francisco, CA: Jossey-Bass.

Wasserman, I. C., & Gallegos, P. (2009). Engaging diversity: Disorienting dilemmas that transform relationships. In B. Fisher-Yoshida, K. D. Geller, & S. A. Schapiro (Eds.), *Innovations in transformative learning: Space, culture, and the arts* (pp. 155–176). New York, NY: Peter Lang Publishing.

Wasserman, I. C., Gallegos, P., & Taylor, E. (2014). Diversity and inclusion in organizational practice. In B. B. Jones & M. Brazzel (Eds.), *The NTL handbook of organization development and change* (pp. 445–465). San Francisco, CA: Wiley.

Wasserman, I. C., Gallegos, P. V., & Ferdman, B. M. (2008). Dancing with resistance: Leadership challenges in fostering a culture of inclusion. In K. M. Thomas (Ed.), *Diversity resistance in organizations* (pp. 175–200). New York, NY: Taylor & Francis Group/Lawrence Erlbaum Associates. (2008–06292–007).

Williams, D. A. (2013). *Strategic diversity leadership: Activating change and transformation in higher education.* Sterling, VA: Stylus Publishing.

24
FROM "I" TO "WE" THROUGH "FEMALE" LEADERSHIP
Bringing Inclusion and Inclusiveness to the Next Level

Eleftheria Egel

Introduction

The dramatic breakthroughs in technology we have witnessed at the end of the 20th century have not only created turbulence and uncertainty but also have changed the organizational landscape for good. During this relatively short period, the needs of the economy have shifted and so, accordingly, have the economic offerings. Today, disruption on both the supply and the demand side is the name of the game. In contrast to the past, when the production and distribution of material goods were the main sources of wealth, knowledge-based assets have become the principal source of value creation and sustainable competitive advantage (Nahapiet & Ghoshal, 1998; Nonaka & Takeuchi, 1995). Nowadays, organizations are called to constantly improve their ability to deliver intangible offerings to customers on demand. Improvement clearly depends on the organization's ability to learn and to exploit the capacity of individual employees to transform knowledge and experience, that is to say, intellectual capital into new or improved products and processes (Boisot, 1998; Drejer, Christensen, & Ulhoi, 2004; Nonaka & Von Krogh, 2009). In fact, companies today face more adaptive challenges—problems that require new learning, innovation, and new patterns of behavior—than technical problems in the way they design, market, and deliver products and services (Heifetz & Laurie, 2001; Parks, 2005).

This knowledge is embedded in and carried through multiple entities, including organizational culture and identity, routines, policies, systems, and documents, as well as individual employees (Grant, 1996; Nelson & Winter, 1982; Spender, 1996).

One implication of operating in the knowledge economy is that leaders rarely have the full expertise needed to solve organizational problems. Rather, individuals at all organizational levels must contribute information and ideas for their organizations to succeed (Bettis & Hitt, 1995). Answers handed down from above are less likely to generate the products, services, or solutions needed to succeed (Blackler, Reed & Whitaker, 1993). Another implication is the enhanced need for diverse talent to solve pressing business problems in the global economy. However, the more organizations become culturally diverse, the greater the tensions and conflicts that occur between people from different cultural backgrounds (Jehn & Mannix, 2001; Jehn, Northcraft, & Neale, 1999). When individuals from different cultures are unable to overcome their differences and manage their disagreements, they are inevitably led to ineffective communication which hampers—among other things—creative performance (Giambatista & Bhappu, 2010; Hackman, 1990; O'Reilly, 1998; Swann, Kwan, Polzer, & Milton, 2003).

In the following section, I will explore the literature reviews of the fields of leadership and inclusion in order to look into the challenges that both fields face and that hinder in reaching their full potential in the knowledge-based organization.

From Individual to Relational Leadership

Leadership models of the last century have been products of top-down, bureaucratic paradigms, suitable for an economy built on mass production and for a narrative that saw organizations as "brick" constructs. Taylor's principles of scientific management linked with Weber's bureaucratic hierarchy of authority and accountability generated the efficiencies consistent with views of the organization-as-machine (Lee & Edmondson, 2017; Pfeffer, 2013; Weber, 1946). Working meant compliance with supervisory directives, conformity to job descriptions, organizational rules, and imposed standards. Within this period of stable hierarchy, clear organizational boundaries, and well-defined roles, leadership was seen as solid (predictable, consistent across settings), detached (as if reality was "out there" and not "right here"), and singular (the influential act of an individual or individuals on their followers). At the beginning, it involved the application of proven solutions to known problems by a knowledgeable leader (an expert). With time, it raised to an elevated and romanticized position of the leader as a "hero"; a charismatic individual possessing a unique blend of traits, skills, and competencies that enable them to function at their highest potential independent of their psychological state or environmental conditions and complexities (Endres & Weibler, 2017; Meindl, Ehrlich, & Dukerich, 1985; Petriglieri, 2015).

Within this context, the (positional) leader has been given a central place in improving action processes, organizational performance, and adaptation through enforcing principles, motivating employees, and communicating future goals and visions to strive for (Day, 2000; Marion & Uhl-Bien, 2001). Part of this development was that the psychological contract between the organization and the employees shifted from inducement-contribution exchange to institutional values. Whereas in the past the inducements were mainly wages and benefits, now the inducements expanded to offer a sense of belonging. Assimilation to the organizational values and belief system led to membership to the "organizational family." Another point of interest in this traditional leadership approach was the implicit dependency between leader as a powerful subject and follower as a passive object. Followers were assumed to remain in a followership state to a leader who was assumed to know more than their followers and whose role was to provide continual motivation (Pearce & Conger, 2002). Accordingly, the quality of the relationship between the leader and the followers was functional and instrumental and not interactional.

In the knowledge economy, the sheer force of knowledge and knowledge creation in all its forms—know-how, know-where, know-what, know-when—has dominated all other means for creating value (Nonaka & Takeuchi, 1995). Information exchange and the quality of the social interaction between individuals and groups determine how knowledge will be shared in particular situations and shape the processes by which new knowledge is created, legitimized, and distributed in organizations (Stahl, Maznevski, Voigt, & Jonsen, 2010). Information flows more freely and faster throughout organizations and is accessible to everyone rather than being hoarded within the hierarchy. Also, organizations with more open and supportive features, such as those of trust, collaboration, and learning, are more likely to engage in effective knowledge creation and sharing practices, as well as to be more innovative and more flexible in responding rapidly to the needs of changing markets (Dirks & Ferrin, 2001; Edmondson, 1999).

The implications of this for management and leadership are significant, as they have led to numerous and varied efforts to re-envision the "who," "where," and "what" of leadership and to create an organizational environment that promotes value creation. The "who" is reimagined by focusing on the need to distribute the tasks and responsibilities of leadership up, down, and across the hierarchy (less hierarchy, less centralized decision-making). The "what" by articulating leadership as a social process that occurs in and through human interactions (more emphasis on collective achievement and social networks), and the "how" by focusing on the more mutual, less hierarchical leadership practices and skills needed to engage in collaborative, collective learning (the importance of teamwork and shared accountability) (Pearce & Conger, 2002).

Some of the most well-known theories that focus on one or more of the nonhierarchical, collective, and contextual aspects of leadership are shared leadership (Raelin, 2016), collaborative leadership (Collinson, 2011), dispersed/distributed leadership (Lindgre & Packendorff, 2009), relational leadership (Uhl-Bien, 2011), participatory leadership (Pearce, 2004), adaptive leadership (Heifetz, Grashow, & Linsky, 2009), discursive leadership (Fairhurst, 2008), systems leadership (Senge, Hamilton, & Kania, 2015), and quantum leadership (Wheatley, 2006).

Of significance in the aforementioned models is the blurring of the distinction between leader and follower, as leadership interactions are fluid, mutual, and two-directional. That is, while tasks and responsibilities differ dependent on organizational position, the notion of shared leadership practices suggests that leading and following are two sides of the same set of relational skills that everyone in an organization needs in order to work in a context of interdependence.

Their common denominator is a shift in the perception of self. Rather than the traditional image of self as an independent entity, these models recast the relationship between self and other, evoking a more relational concept of self as interdependent entity. This entity, something closer perhaps to the psychological concept of self-in-relation (Miller, 1994; Surrey, 1985), suggests a more welcoming, less competitive stand towards others.

From Management of Diversity to Inclusion

Merriam-Webster defines inclusion as "comprising as a part of whole or group." In the organizational literature, "inclusion" has mainly been examined with "diversity," as they both characterize different yet related approaches to the management of diversity (Mehta, 2000). More specifically, diversity focuses on organizational demography, whereas inclusion focuses on the degree to which individuals feel part of their organization and are able to contribute fully and effectively (Miller, 1998; Mor Barak, Cherin, & Berkman, 1998). The literature review on inclusive leadership originally defined inclusion "as the removal of obstacles to the full participation and contribution of employees" (Kelloway & Harvey, 1999)—the term "obstacles" referred to issues resulting from diversity. It referred to demographic differences or else observable dimensions of diversity (gender or sexual orientation) (McGrath, Berdahl, & Arrow, 1995) and to differences sourced in culture and identity as they are reflected in ethnicity, religion, generations, disabilities, and thought and skill diversity. These are also called non-observable dimensions of diversity (Milliken & Martins, 1996). The first ones are usually legally protected from discrimination. The second ones occupy a wider array of non-observable characteristics that include cultural, cognitive, and technical differences among employees (Kochan, 2003). For example, research has shown underlying attributes such as education, functional background, organizational tenure, socioeconomic background, and personality to influence patterns of interactions between group members (Jackson, May & Whitney, 1995; Tsui, Xin & Egan, 1995). The foregoing conceptualization led to two avenues of resolving issues of diversity and creating cohesion and inclusiveness: assimilation and multiculturalism. Organizations that follow assimilation policies exclude differences and concentrate on sameness. They emphasize a superordinate goal or identity (e.g. common affiliation with the broader organization, individual accomplishments and qualifications, fair treatment) (Chatman & Flynn, 2001). On the other hand, organizations that follow multiculturalism exclude sameness and base inclusion on differences. They emphasize the benefits of a diverse workforce and explicitly recognize employee differences as a source of strength (Cox, 1991). However, both strands have been critiqued over time, as organizations often do not manage to enable an inclusive culture with full participation of all employees and to leverage the diversity benefits of the organization (Baumeister & Leary, 1995; Ivancevich & Gilbert, 2000). On the contrary, each approach seems to be a paradox per se, as both strands are mutually exclusive: assimilation ignores different values and multiculturalism suppresses majority values. Exclusion of differences risks isolating individual employees of their creative nature and hindering them from making their unique contribution (Thomas & Gabarro, 1999). Exclusion of sameness can create skepticism and resentment on the part of some groups—in particular non-minorities (James, Brief, Dietz & Cohen, 2001).

Over time, "inclusion" has broadened its focus and concentrated on the importance the centrality of one's position has in order to realize organizational objectives (e.g. O'Hara, Beehr, & Colarelli, 1994; Schein, 1971). Pelled, Eisenhardt, and Xin (1999, p. 1014) defined inclusion as "the degree to which an employee is accepted and treated as an insider by others in a work system." More recently, Shore and colleagues (2011) came up with a comprehensive suggestion. They defined inclusion as "the degree to which an employee perceives they are esteemed members of a work group or organization as a result of treatment that satisfies belongingness and values uniqueness" (Shore et al., 2011, p. 1264).

This is a noble aim but is difficult to achieve, as people may risk fulfilling one need at the expense of the other: A one-sided focus on one's personal identity ("me") bears the risk of isolation; a one-sided focus on one's social identity ("we") bears the risk of depersonalization (Gebert, Bungeler, & Heinitz, 2017). The risk of depersonalization lies in the interpretation of the term "tolerance." According to the classical notion of tolerance, a person only had to put up with others' values to be regarded as tolerant. Nowadays, "tolerant" individuals are expected to value as positive the values they previously considered neutral or negative (Oberdiek, 2001). In that sense, there has been a transformation from the demand to bear to a demand to endorse (Von Bergen & Bandow, 2010). Accordingly, individuals are required to adjust, or if not possible, to deny their own values.

In an effort to solve this conundrum, Gebert et al. (2017) proposed that "tolerance" should be replaced by "acceptance" in the literature of "inclusion." The foundation of "acceptance" is sharing a relativist worldview that interprets one's own values as preliminary, socially constructed, and historically contingent rather than as definitive truth (Habermas, 2001; Hardy & Tolhurst, 2014; Toulmin, 1958). "Acceptance," then, would allow voicing of each person's real thoughts while counteracting dogmatic convictions about the rightness of values. That way, everyone would sustain and express their personal values even if these differ from others' values, and there would be a sincere and open dialogue-oriented practice of communication without superiority claims from the participants regarding their own values. In the opposite case, non-voicing can hinder the emergence of a zone of understanding, as it can seclude individuals into a perpetual spiral of silence. Dogmatic convictions and attitudes can lead to an exaggeration of differences and polarization.

In the same vein, Pless and Maak (2004) proposed going beyond assimilation or multiculturalism and establishing a culture that is built on ethical principles and honors the differences as well as the similarities of the individual self and the others. Specifically, they put forward a conceptual framework of inclusion based on a moral theory of recognition and introduced the founding principles of reciprocal understanding, standpoint plurality, and mutual enabling, trust, and integrity.

Leadership plays a vital role in creating inclusion. In the literature of inclusion, inclusive leadership is defined a set of positive leader behaviors that facilitate group members' perceiving belongingness in the work group while maintaining their uniqueness within the group (Nembhard & Edmondson, 2006; Randel et al., 2018).

To my understanding, there are two issues in the definition of inclusive leadership that need to be examined and acknowledged as they may—unintentionally—create obstacles to inclusion. First, the outdated leadership approach, and second, the implied power dynamics that shape the interaction between leader and follower. In the definition proposed earlier, the leader fits the profile of the traditional leader. This leader is seen as a charismatic individual, who possesses a unique blend of traits, skills, and competencies that enable them to function at their highest potential independent of their psychological state or of environmental conditions and complexities. Even in studies of leadership that examine the contribution of ethical leaders to inclusion—be it authentic (Boekhorst, 2015), transformational (Ng & Wyrick, 2011), servant (Gotsis & Grimani, 2016), or charismatic (Gebert, Heinitz, & Buengeler, 2016; Hollander, 2006)—the discourse is still about an exceptional, individual leader. Such a leader is seen as a guide to and motivator for their followers, as they are assumed to know more than their followers, and their role is to provide continual motivation (Pearce & Conger, 2002). However, having moved to the knowledge era, this kind of leader and their interventions—no matter how positive they may be—are not adapted to the new reality, which demands a collective leadership approach where the distinction between leader and follower is blurred.

Concerning the second issue, i.e. the implied power dynamics that play out in a leader's effort to facilitate belongingness and uniqueness of their employees, I believe we need to reflect on the term "facilitate" and determine whether "facilitate" encompasses "tolerance" or "acceptance" as the literature on inclusion explains the terms. One of the inducements that the psychological contract between the organization and the employees offers is a sense of "belongingness." Belonging to the organizational family—being an "insider"—implies assimilation to the organizational values and belief system. According to the literature of inclusion, assimilation (be it through promoting assimilation or multiculturalism) implies "tolerance" and not "acceptance." In that sense, an inclusive leader can only "facilitate" assimilation to the organizational values. In fact, the leader is seen as a powerful subject on whom the follower, as a passive object, is dependent. In this configuration, the leader's values are superior to the follower's values. How then can inclusive leadership satisfy "acceptance"? Isn't inclusive leadership itself an oxymoron?

In the previous sections, I demonstrated that both approaches of leadership and inclusion are divisive, as they take place in a polarized paradigm where the leader is considered the main initiator of organizational strategies and policies and the motivator of their followers—thus, superior both in power and knowledge to the followers. In this paradigm, belongingness is already predefined by the institutional values, leaving little space for a sincere and open dialogue-oriented practice of communication—indispensable to creating a culture of inclusiveness.

In the following section, I propose a conceptualization of a relational concept of self as interdependent entity through the philosopher Martin Buber's dialogical existentialism. I argue that this conceptualization encompasses the qualities required for the development of a relational leadership configuration that is suitable for an inclusive knowledge-based organization. Then, I look into the qualities needed to enable this sense of self-in-relation.

Martin Buber's Dialogic Existentialism

The philosopher Martin Buber distinguishes two different kinds of relationships: the "I-it" and the "I-Thou." He names the "I-it" relationship an egoic relationship and therefore secondary. It is an objectifying way of addressing another person: The other is an object, a thing among things. The "I-it" uses an externalized way of addressing the world and "experiencing." Therefore, the "I-it" is functional and instrumental, as in "what I can do for you in exchange for what you can do for me." It is also "experiencing" life and interaction based on past experience: "then and there."

In contrast, the "I-Thou" is a primary, non-egoistic relationship: The other is a presence whose deep humanity I acknowledge, fully engage, and reciprocate. The "I-Thou" implies interaction, as in "I am through interaction with You" (Buber, 1937). The "I-Thou" relationship is based on knowing myself as a subject seen through the other who is also a subject. The relationship is personal, egalitarian, and dialogic: one subject, I, confronts another subject, Thou. The other person, the Thou, is a reality that is. It is given to me by an experiencing subject, but it is not bounded by me and cannot be appropriated as an experienced object. We are meeting in the present moment of interaction—"here and now"—not in the past (we do not let our past disappointments dictate our present) and not in the future (we do not allow our fears to dictate our present). Our relationship is founded on a shared sense of caring, commitment, and mutual responsibility and is transformative for both.

Whereas the organization of the past has been a connection between things, "I-it," the organization of the future—if it is to realize its aspirations and succeed—should become a community of beings "I-Thou" (relation of persons).

It is interesting to reflect on how the "I-it" relationship has impacted the organizational landscape in which the traditional leadership has reigned. The organization of the past has been described as "mechanistic" in the literature (Roegen, 1971; Ims & Jakobsen, 2006). It is characterized by the idea that pieces of matter are isolated individuals (atoms) related to each other only externally (Ims & Jakobsen, 2006). In an ideal scenario, society runs like a well-oiled machine, where each of us plays a predetermined role and we reach our highest potential when we become highly efficient and effective. Capacity for creativity, spontaneity, self-movement, or novelty is conceptualized within the boundaries of our role. Coordination is regulated through external rules and connections. Within the "mechanistic" worldview, organizations exist to act autonomously in order to enhance their self-interest to the maximum. Connectedness among the various stakeholders—employees included—exists only when it cannot be avoided. Collaboration is then seen as an indispensable prerequisite for optimization of self-interest within the rationale of competitive behavior and remains limited in time and scope. As for communication, it serves the need to set the rules of the game clearly, to learn new information that may prove useful to maximize individual self-interest, and aims at solving problems while the transaction of collaboration takes place.

The organization of the future—wherein relational leadership of the type "I-Thou" should take place and where a sincere and open dialogue-oriented practice of communication should be established—is one that Whitehead (1967a), a prominent British philosopher and mathematician, calls "organic." In this worldview, connectedness becomes interconnectedness, in the sense that there is a spontaneous exchange that influences all parties involved and transforms them both individually and in their common exchange. The nature of this level of collaboration is holistic, and its foundation is the desire to act for the common good. Based on equality and mutuality among the involved actors, collaboration gives equal importance to the needs of all stakeholders and allows more integrated solutions, which will intrinsically be ethical. The relationship among the involved individuals is holistic; which means that polarization—the divisive belief of opposites (when one is right and/or good then the other is necessarily wrong and/or bad)—does not exist. Holism entails the acceptance of polarities as different expressions of the same, and coordination is not imposed from an outside authority but develops organically within the flow of the exchange. Communication, then, is much more than an exchange of information. It becomes sharing of the heart, based on a genuine desire to understand, to strengthen the interaction, and to reach the best solution for all parties involved.

In such a community, each person can express their uniqueness and belongingness at the same time, without suppressing one to the detriment of the other.

In order to establish a culture of relational "I-Thou" leadership, we need the cultivation of leadership qualities that are distinct from the ones we have been used to demanding from our leaders. In the following section, I look into how the cultivation of "female" leadership qualities is indispensable if we want the "I-Thou" conceptualization to take place and harvest the benefits of inclusiveness.

Creating the Future Organization Through "Female" Leadership

The traditional leadership approach has not only been individualistic and determined within the "I-it" framework, but also "masculine" or "male" (I will be using both terms interchangeably). Its culture, discourse, imaging, and practice have been construed as primarily a masculine enterprise, focusing on the desirability of stereotypically masculine qualities in leaders. Such "male" qualities are considered to be rationality, instrumentality, individualism, control, assertiveness, and skills of advocacy and domination (Acker, 2006; Blackmore, 2017; Cals & Smircich, 1993). This conflation of leadership with masculinity has also created the idea that feminine traits are of lesser value, subordinate, and suppressed with respect to masculine qualities (Miner, 1993; Rosaldo, 1974). Schein, for instance, conducted extensive research on the relationship between sex role stereotypes and requisite management characteristics. She found out that women, as well as men, promoted to senior management positions aspire to ways of managing that draw on styles widely perceived to be masculine rather than feminine. With specific reference to women, she found out that female senior managers were often more like men than men themselves (Schein, 2001/1975).

In contrast, the traits associated with relational leadership are feminine (Calvert & Ramsey, 1992; Fletcher, 2004; Fondas, 1997). Again, men or women can display them, but the traits themselves—such as empathy, helpfulness, caring, and nurturance; community, vulnerability, interpersonal sensitivity, attentiveness to and acceptance of others, responsiveness to their needs and motivations; orientation toward the collective interest and toward integrative goals such as group cohesiveness and stability; a preference for open, egalitarian, and cooperative relationships, rather than hierarchical ones; and an interest in actualizing values and relationships of great importance to community—are socially ascribed to women in our culture and generally understood as feminine. The knowledge of what it means to "grow" people and living systems is located in women and is conflated with displays of idealized femininity (Eisler & Skidmore, 1987; Fairbairn, 1954; Winnicott, 2018).

What we can deduce from this is that leadership is not a neutral concept but is gendered; it encompasses a power dynamic and has a sex. The existence of one gender excludes the other (i.e. those qualities belonging to masculine leadership are assumed to be inappropriate for feminine leadership and vice versa); that feminine leadership is of lower value (power) than the masculine one (i.e. labor in the work sphere is assumed to be skilled and dependent on training, whereas labor in the domestic sphere is assumed to be unskilled, innate, and dependent on personal characteristics); and that it is sex linked (i.e. men and images of idealized masculinity are associated with one and women and images of idealized femininity are associated with the other) (Fletcher, 1999; Williams, 2001).

To truly capture the transformational potential of relational leadership would require recognizing how these deeply embedded, emotional, and underexplored ideas on idealized masculinity and femininity influence leader and follower behavior, experience, and expectations. It would require acknowledging how they challenge current power dynamics, the myth of individual achievement, and related beliefs about what qualities are worth developing and rewarding. Whereas male power dynamics is associated with "power over" the subordinates, female power dynamics enacts a model of "power within" (Fletcher, 2004). In a system of unequal power, the one having the "power over" imposes the relational practices to be adopted and distorts the equal exchange required in the self-in-relation process (Jost, 1997). Coming to the myth of individual achievement, a "logic of effectiveness" has traditionally underlain business practice and has been founded on masculine-linked images about how "to produce things" in the work sphere, while the logic of effectiveness underlying relational leadership is deeply rooted in feminine-linked images and wisdom about how "to grow people" in the domestic sphere (Rapport, 2004). Similarly, research suggests that visible, individual work is recognized and rewarded, whereas equally vital, behind-the-scenes work (e.g. building a team, avoiding crises) more characteristic of women, tends to be overlooked.

It is obvious from the aforementioned that we will not be able to enact relational leadership as long as gender- and power-linked images exert implicitly potent influence on leader and follower behavior, experience, and expectations. As a first step, we need to change the mental model we function from; or as Lama Shenpen Drolma (2003, p. 4) eloquently expresses it,

> Trying to change the world without changing our mind is like trying to clean the dirty face we see in the mirror by rubbing the glass. However vigorously we clean it, our reflection will not improve. Only by washing our own face and combing our own unkempt hair can we alter the image.

Conclusion

In this chapter, I demonstrated the kind of leadership needed in the knowledge-based organizational environment. Different from the traditional leadership approach that concentrated on the achievements of the individual, "heroic" leader, current organizational needs demand a relational form of leadership where the distinction between leader and follower is blurred. Through an exploration of the literature review on inclusion, I argued that as long as the leadership paradigm remains the same, "inclusion" can be nothing more than assimilation to the organization's values. Then I proposed a conceptualization of relational leadership based on the philosopher Martin Buber's dialogical existentialism that has the potential to enable a knowledge-based organization. I finally proposed the cultivation of "female" leadership qualities as the means to realize the aspirations of relational leadership.

References

Acker, J. (2006). Gender and organizations. In *Handbook of the sociology of gender* (pp. 177–194). Boston, MA: Springer.
Baumeister, R. F., & Leary, M. R. (1995). The need to belong: Desire for interpersonal attachments as a fundamental human motivation. *Psychological Bulletin, 117*(3), 497.
Bettis, R. A., & Hitt, M. A. (1995). The new competitive landscape. *Strategic Management Journal, 16*(S1), 7–19.
Blackler, F., Reed, M., & Whitaker, A. (1993). Editorial introduction: Knowledge workers and contemporary organizations. *Journal of Management Studies, 30*(6), 851–862.
Blackmore, J. (2017). "In the shadow of men": The historical construction of educational administration as a 'masculinist' enterprise. In *Gender matters in educational administration and policy* (pp. 27–48). New York, NY: Routledge.
Boekhorst, J. A. (2015). The role of authentic leadership in fostering workplace inclusion: A social information processing perspective. *Human Resource Management, 54*(2), 241–264.
Boisot, M. H. (1998). *Knowledge assets: Securing competitive advantage in the information economy*. Oxford: Oxford University Press.
Buber, M. (1937). *Ich und Du. I and Thou...* (Ronald Gregor Smith, Trans.). Edinburgh: T. & T. Clark.
Cals, M. B., & Smircich, L. (1993). Dangerous liaisons': The "feminine in management meets globalisation". *Business Horizons, 36*(2), 73–83.
Calvert, L. M., & Ramsey, V. J. (1992). Bringing women's voice to research on women in management: A feminist perspective. *Journal of Management Inquiry, 1*(1), 79–88.
Chatman, J. A., & Flynn, F. J. (2001). The influence of demographic heterogeneity on the emergence and consequences of cooperative norms in work teams. *Academy of Management Journal, 44*(5), 956–974.
Collinson, D. (2011). Critical leadership studies. In Bryman, A., Collinson, D., Grint, K., et al. (Eds.), *The SAGE handbook of leadership* (pp. 181–194). London: Sage.
Cox, T. Jr. (1991). The multicultural organization. *Academy of Management Perspectives, 5*(2), 34–47.
Day, D. V. (2000). Leadership development: A review in context. *The Leadership Quarterly, 11*(4), 581–613.
Dirks, K. T., & Ferrin, D. L. (2001). The role of trust in organizational settings. *Organization Science, 12*(4), 450–467.
Drejer, A., Christensen, K. S., & Ulhoi, J. P. (2004). Understanding intrapreneurship by means of state-of-the-art knowledge management and organisational learning theory. *International Journal of Management and Enterprise Development, 1*(2), 102–119.
Edmondson, A. (1999). Psychological safety and learning behavior in work teams. *Administrative Science Quarterly, 44*(2), 350–383.

Eisler, R. M., & Skidmore, J. R. (1987). Masculine gender role stress: Scale development and component factors in the appraisal of stressful situations. *Behavior Modification*, *11*(2), 123–136.

Endres, S., & Weibler, J. (2017). Towards a three-component model of relational social constructionist leadership: A systematic review and critical interpretive synthesis. *International Journal of Management Reviews*, *19*(2), 214–236.

Fairbairn, W. R. D. (1952). An object-relations theory of the personality. In Fairbairn, W. R. (Ed.), *Psychoanalytic studies of the personality*. London: Routledge & Kegan Paul.

Fairhurst, G. T. (2008). Discursive leadership: A communication alternative to leadership psychology. *Management Communication Quarterly*, *21*(4), 510–521.

Fletcher, J. (1999). *Disappearing acts: Gender. power, and relational practice*. Boston, MA: MIT.

Fletcher, J. K. (2004). The paradox of postheroic leadership: An essay on gender, power, and transformational change. *The Leadership Quarterly*, *15*(5), 647–661.

Fondas, N. (1997). Feminization unveiled: Management qualities in contemporary writings. *Academy of Management Review*, *22*(1), 257–282.

Gebert, D., Buengeler, C., & Heinitz, K. (2017). Tolerance: A neglected dimension in diversity training? *Academy of Management Learning & Education*, *16*(3), 415–438.

Gebert, D., Heinitz, K., & Buengeler, C. (2016). Leaders' charismatic leadership and followers' commitment— The moderating dynamics of value erosion at the societal level. *The Leadership Quarterly*, *27*(1), 98–108.

Giambatista, R. C., & Bhappu, A. D. (2010). Diversity's harvest: Interactions of diversity sources and communication technology on creative group performance. *Organizational Behavior and Human Decision Processes*, *111*(2), 116–126.

Gotsis, G., & Grimani, K. (2016). The role of servant leadership in fostering inclusive organizations. *Journal of Management Development*, *35*(8), 985–1010.

Grant, R. M. (1996). Toward a knowledge-based theory of the firm. *Strategic Management Journal*, *17*(S2), 109–122.

Habermas, J. (2001). Constitutional democracy: A paradoxical union of contradictory principles? *Political Theory*, *29*(6), 766–781.

Hackman, J. R. (1990). *Groups that work and those that don't* (No. E10 H123). San Francisco: Jossey-Bass.

Hardy, C., & Tolhurst, D. (2014). Epistemological beliefs and cultural diversity matters in management education and learning: A critical review and future directions. *Academy of Management Learning & Education*, *13*(2), 265–289.

Heifetz, R. A., Grashow, A., & Linsky, M. (2009). *The practice of adaptive leadership: Tools and tactics for changing your organization and the world*. Boston, MA: Harvard Business Press.

Heifetz, R. A., & Laurie, D. L. (2001). The work of leadership. *Harvard Business Review*, *79*(11).

Hollander, E. P. (2006). Influence processes in leadership-followership: Inclusion and the idiosyncrasy credit model. In D. A. Hantula (Eds.), *Advances in social & organizational psychology: A tribute to Ralph Rosnow* (pp. 293–312). Mahwah, NJ: Lawrence Erlbaum & Associates.

Ims, K. J., & Jakobsen, O. D. (2006). Cooperation and competition in the context of organic and mechanic worldviews—a theoretical and case based discussion. *Journal of Business Ethics*, *66*(1), 19–32.

Ivancevich, J. M., & Gilbert, J. A. (2000). Diversity management: Time for a new approach. *Public Personnel Management*, *29*(1), 75–92.

Jackson, S. E., May, K. E., & Whitney, K. (1995). Understanding the dynamics of diversity in decision-making teams. In R. A. Guzzo, E. Salas, & Associates (Eds.), *Team effectiveness and decision making in organizations* (pp. 204, 261). San Francisco: Jossey-Bass.

James, E. H., Brief, A. P., Dietz, J., & Cohen, R. R. (2001). Prejudice matters: Understanding the reactions of Whites to affirmative action programs targeted to benefit Blacks. *Journal of Applied Psychology*, *86*(6), 1120–1128.

Jehn, K. A., & Mannix, E. A. (2001). The dynamic nature of conflict: A longitudinal study of intragroup conflict and group performance. *Academy of Management Journal*, *44*(2), 238–251.

Jehn, K. A., Northcraft, G. B., & Neale, M. A. (1999). Why differences make a difference: A field study of diversity, conflict and performance in workgroups. *Administrative Science Quarterly*, *44*(4), 741–763.

Jost, J. T. (1997). An experimental replication of the depressed-entitlement effect among women. *Psychology of Women Quarterly*, *21*(3), 387–393.

Kelloway, E. K., & Harvey, S. (1999). Learning to work: The development of work beliefs. In J. Barling & E. K. Kelloway (Eds.), *Young workers: Varieties of experience*. Washington, DC: American Psychological Society.

Kochan, T. A. (2003). Restoring trust in American corporations: Addressing the root cause. *Journal of Management and Governance*, *7*(3), 223–231.

Lama Shenpen Drolma (Compiler). (2003). *Change of heart: The Bodhisattva peace training of Chagdud Tulku*. Junction City, CA: Padma Publishing.

Lee, M. Y., & Edmondson, A. C. (2017). Self-managing organizations: Exploring the limits of less-hierarchical organizing. *Research in Organizational Behavior, 37*, 35–58.

Lindgren, M., & Packendorff, J. (2009). Project leadership revisited: Towards distributed leadership perspectives in project research. *International Journal of Project Organisation and Management, 1*(3), 285–308.

Marion, R., & Uhl-Bien, M. (2001). Leadership in complex organizations. *The Leadership Quarterly, 12*(4), 389–418.

McGrath, J. E., Berdahl, J. L., & Arrow, H. (1995). Traits, expectations, culture, and clout: The dynamics of diversity in work groups. In *Diversity in work teams: Research paradigms for a changing workplace* (pp. 17–45). Washington, DC: American Psychological Association.

Mehta, A. (2000). Advertising attitudes and advertising effectiveness. *Journal of Advertising Research, 40*(3), 67–72.

Meindl, J. R., Ehrlich, S. B., & Dukerich, J. M. (1985). The romance of leadership. *Administrative Science Quarterly*, 78–102.

Miller, C. R. (1994). The cultural basis of genre. In A. Freedman & P. Medway (Eds.), *Genre and the new rhetoric* (pp. 67–78). London: Taylor & Francis.

Miller, G. A. (1998). *WordNet: An electronic lexical database*. Cambridge, MA: MIT Press.

Milliken, F. J., & Martins, L. L. (1996). Searching for common threads: Understanding the multiple effects of diversity in organizational groups. *Academy of Management Review, 21*(2), 402–433.

Miner, J. B. (1993). *Role motivation theories*. New York, NY: Routledge.

Mor Barak, M. E., Cherin, D. A., & Berkman, S. (1998). Organizational and personal dimensions in diversity climate: Ethnic and gender differences in employee perceptions. *The Journal of Applied Behavioral Science, 34*(1), 82–104.

Nahapiet, J., & Ghoshal, S. (1998). Social capital, intellectual capital, and the organizational advantage. *Academy of Management Review, 23*(2), 242–266.

Nelson, R. R., & Winter, S. G. (1982). The Schumpeterian tradeoff revisited. *The American Economic Review, 72*(1), 114–132.

Nembhard, I. M., & Edmondson, A. C. (2006). Making it safe: The effects of leader inclusiveness and professional status on psychological safety and improvement efforts in health care teams. *Journal of Organizational Behavior: The International Journal of Industrial, Occupational and Organizational Psychology and Behavior, 27*(7), 941–966.

Ng, E. S., & Wyrick, C. R. (2011). Motivational bases for managing diversity: A model of leadership commitment. *Human Resource Management Review, 21*(4), 368–376.

Nonaka, I., & Von Krogh, G. (2009). Perspective—Tacit knowledge and knowledge conversion: Controversy and advancement in organizational knowledge creation theory. *Organization Science, 20*(3), 635–652.

Nonaka, I., & Takeuchi, H. (1995). *The knowledge-creating company: How Japanese companies create the dynamics of innovation*. Oxford: Oxford University Press.

Oberdiek, H. (2001). *Tolerance: Between forbearance and acceptance*. Lanham, MD: Rowman & Littlefield Publishers.

O'hara, K. B., Beehr, T. A., & Colarelli, S. M. (1994). Organizational centrality: A third dimension of intraorganizational career movement. *The Journal of Applied Behavioral Science, 30*(2), 198–216.

O'Reilly, R. C. (1998). Six principles for biologically based computational models of cortical cognition. *Trends in Cognitive Sciences, 2*(11), 455–462.

Parks, L. (2005). Cultures in orbit. *Satellites and the Televisual*, 37.

Pearce, C. L. (2004). The future of leadership: Combining vertical and shared leadership to transform knowledge work. *Academy of Management Perspectives, 18*(1), 47–57.

Pearce, C. L., & Conger, J. A. (2002). *Shared leadership: Reframing the hows and whys of leadership*. Thousand Oaks, CA: Sage Publications.

Pelled, L. H., Eisenhardt, K. M., & Xin, K. R. (1999). Exploring the black box: An analysis of work group diversity, conflict and performance. *Administrative Science Quarterly, 44*(1), 1–28.

Petriglieri, J. L. (2015). Co-creating relationship repair: Pathways to reconstructing destabilized organizational identification. *Administrative Science Quarterly, 60*(3), 518–557.

Pfeffer, J. (2013). You're still the same: Why theories of power hold over time and across contexts. *Academy of Management Perspectives, 27*(4), 269–280.

Pless, N., & Maak, T. (2004). Building an inclusive diversity culture: Principles, processes and practice. *Journal of Business Ethics, 54*(2), 129–147.

Raelin, J. A. (2016). Imagine there are no leaders: Reframing leadership as collaborative agency. *Leadership, 12*(2), 131–158.

Randel, A. E., Galvin, B. M., Shore, L. M., Ehrhart, K. H., Chung, B. G., Dean, M. A., & Kedharnath, U. (2018). Inclusive leadership: Realizing positive outcomes through belongingness and being valued for uniqueness. *Human Resource Management Review, 28*(2), 190–203.

Rapport, N. (2004). *I am dynamite: An alternative anthropology of power*. New York, NY: Routledge.

Roegen, N. G. (1971). *The entropy law and the economic process*. Cambridge, MA: Harvard University Press.

Rosaldo, M. Z. (1974). Woman, culture, and society: A theoretical overview. *Woman, Culture, and Society*, 21.

Schein, E. H. (1971). The individual, the organization, and the career: A conceptual scheme. *The Journal of Applied Behavioral Science*, 7(4), 401–426.

Schein, V. E. (1975). Relationships between sex role stereotypes and requisite management characteristics among female managers. *Journal of Applied Psychology*, 60(3), 340.

Schein, V. E. (2001). A global look at psychological barriers to women's progress in management. *Journal of Social issues*, 57(4), 675–688.

Senge, P., Hamilton, H., & Kania, J. (2015). The dawn of system leadership. *Stanford Social Innovation Review*, 13(1), 27–33.

Shore, L. M., Randel, A. E., Chung, B. G., Dean, M. A., Holcombe Ehrhart, K., & Singh, G. (2011). Inclusion and diversity in work groups: A review and model for future research. *Journal of Management*, 37(4), 1262–1289.

Spender, J. C. (1996). Making knowledge the basis of a dynamic theory of the firm. *Strategic Management Journal*, 17(S2), 45–62.

Stahl, G. K., Maznevski, M. L., Voigt, A., & Jonsen, K. (2010). Unraveling the effects of cultural diversity in teams: A meta-analysis of research on multicultural work groups. *Journal of International Business Studies*, 41, 690–709.

Surrey, J. (1985). *The self in relation*. Working Paper #13. Available from Centers for Women, Wellesley College, Wellesley, MA.

Swann, W. B. Jr., Kwan, V. S., Polzer, J. T., & Milton, L. P. (2003). Fostering group identification and creativity in diverse groups: The role of individuation and self-verification. *Personality and Social Psychology Bulletin*, 29(11), 1396–1406.

Thomas, D. A., & Gabarro, J. J. (1999). *Breaking through: The making of minority executives in corporate America*. Boston, MA: Harvard Business School Press.

Toulmin, S. E. (1958). *The philosophy of science* (Vol. 14). London: Genesis Publishing Pvt Ltd.

Tsui, A. S., Xin, K. R., & Egan, T. D. (1995). Relational demography: The missing link in vertical dyad linkage. In *Diversity in work teams: Research paradigms for a changing workplace* (pp. 97–129). Washington, DC: American Psychological Association.

Uhl-Bien, M. (2011). Relational leadership theory: Exploring the social processes of leadership and organizing. In *Leadership, gender, and organization* (pp. 75–108). Dordrecht: Springer.

Von Bergen, C. W., & Bandow, D. (2010). *Diversity and religion in the workplace*. Research Yearbook, 557.

Weber, M. (1946). Politics as a vocation" and "Bureaucracy." In H. H. Gerth & C. Wright Mills (Eds.), *Max weber: Essays in sociology*. New York, NY: Oxford University Press.

Wheatley, M. (2006). Leadership lessons from the real world. *Leader to Leader* (41), 16–20.

Whitehead, A. N. (1967a). *Science and the modern world*. New York, NY: The Free Press.

Williams, J. (2001). *Unbending gender: Why family and work conflict and what to do about it*. Oxford: Oxford University Press.

Winnicott, D. W. (2018). *The maturational processes and the facilitating environment: Studies in the theory of emotional development*. New York, NY: Routledge.

25
MAHATMA GANDHI'S LEGACY OF VALUES-BASED INCLUSIVE LEADERSHIP

Lessons to Transcend Religion, Caste, Gender, and Class in Today's Workplace

R. Ray Gehani and Anil K. Maheshwari

Introduction: Need for Values-Based Inclusive Leadership

Mahatma Mohandas Karamchand Gandhi (1869–1948), according to the millennial *Time Magazine* poll in 1999, was elected as one of the world's most inspirational and admired leaders of the 20th century. Without the use of any weapons, and with his key values-based inclusive leadership of a series of *Satyagraha* non-violent truthful protest actions, Gandhi helped 330 million Indians gain their independence from 190 years of British colonial influence and rule on August 15, 1947. Since his martyrdom on January 30, 1948, a number of leaders from different parts of the world, such as Dr. Martin Luther King Jr. of the US, Nelson Mandela of South Africa, Benigno and Corazon Aquino of the Philippines, Lech Walesa of Poland, Vaclav Havel of Czechoslovakia, Aung Sun Suu Qui of Myanmar, and many more, have followed Gandhi's example. They have used his practice of *Satyagraha* non-violent peaceful protest to liberate more than a billion people from their oppressive rulers.

Yet, the late 20th century and the dawn of the 21st century also saw a widespread use of violence and exploitation. A number of charismatic executive leaders at Enron, WorldCom, and Tyco became too self-centered and narcissistic, with their greed overriding the well-being of their stakeholders. Leaders at the heart of the recent mortgage financial crisis of 2007–2008 devastated the financial future of millions of households around the world with a deep recession. The transformational strategic leaders at General Motors and Eastman Kodak failed to transform their organizations with emerging technological innovations, and instead led their organizations to bankruptcies and expulsion from their privileged membership in the Dow Jones Index. These well-compensated leaders, driven by their materialistic performance outcomes, fell short on ethics and values.

The 21st-century world is facing wicked, unpredictable, and dynamic (WUD) problems such as political turmoil, frequent disruptive technological/social innovations, and accelerating climate change. Corporate scandals and flippant bankruptcies, at the expense of small-business suppliers and senior employees and their families, have created distrust and disgust for some executive business leaders and their business organizations. In the business organizations of the 21st century, some of the leadership theories developed in the 20th century fail to deliver on their promises. Values-driven leaders with character and ethical integrity are urgently needed in these troubled times in the 21st century.

From their interview of 300 leaders around the world, Crossan, Mazutis, Seijts, and Gandz (2012) reported in the *Academy of Management Learning and Education* the role of values and character in leadership. One participating leader shared,

> If you [as a leader] have a sense of what your vales are, it becomes a little bit easier for you to figure out what is right or wrong. It becomes a little bit easier for you to be courageous and say "I don't like it" or "I can't live with it," but it all comes from a sense of knowing what's important to you firstly.

In this regard, Mahatma Gandhi was many decades ahead of his times. Major leaders around the world have acknowledged that ethical values and integrity were the major drivers embodied in Gandhi's authentic and inclusive leadership. Gandhi's values inspired leaders and millions around the world for generations.

Albert Einstein noted, "in our age of moral decay, [Gandhi] was the only statesman who represented the highest conception of human relations in the political sphere to which we must aspire" (Nathan & Norden, 1981, p. 22).

Dr. Martin Luther King Jr. (1983, p. 206) shared, "If humanity is to progress, Gandhi is inescapable. He lived, thought, and acted inspired by the vision of humanity evolving toward a world of peace and harmony. We may ignore him at our own risk".

The Nobel Prize winner Aung Sun Suu Kyi (1991), who led a non-violent protest against military tyranny in Myanmar, shared that she had a lasting admiration for the principles of non-violence embodied in the life and philosophy of Mahatma Gandhi.

Jawaharlal Nehru was a close associate and keen observer of Mahatma Gandhi's inclusive leadership. He later emerged as Gandhi's successor and India's first prime minister after independence. In his *Discovery of India*, Nehru (1937, 1967) carefully presents and analyzes Gandhi's dynamic values-based inclusive leadership as follows,

> And then Gandhi came. He was like a powerful current of fresh air that made us stretch ourselves and take deep breaths, like a beam of light that pierced the darkness and removed the scales from our eyes; like a whirlwind that upset many things, but most of all the workings of people's minds.
>
> He did not descend from the top, he seemed to emerge from the millions of Indians, speaking their language and incessantly drawing attention to them and their appalling conditions. Get off the backs of these peasants and workers, he told us, all you who live by their exploitation; get rid of the system that produces this poverty and misery
>
> (p. 245).

Nehru further highlighted Gandhi's values-based leadership methodology as follows.

> the essence of his teaching was fearlessness and truth, and action allied to these, always keeping the welfare of the masses in view ... the dominant impulse in India under British rule was that of fear—pervasive, oppressing, strangling fear; fear of the army, the police, the widespread secret service; fear of the official class (bureaucracy); fear of laws meant to suppress and of prison; fear of landlord's agent; fear of the moneylender; fear of unemployment and starvation, which were always at the threshold. It was against this all-pervading fear that Gandhi's quiet and determined voice was raised: Be not afraid...
>
> So, suddenly, as it were, that black pall of fear was lifted from the people's shoulders, not wholly of course, but to an amazing degree. As fear is close companion to falsehood, so truth follows fearlessness
>
> (p.245).

Roadmap for This Research Study

In this research study, we use a phenomenological qualitative research method grounded in values-based leadership theory to longitudinally explore how Mahatma Gandhi relied extensively on his select ethical values. Gandhi's key values include (1) *Satya* (truthfulness), (2) *Ahimsa* (non-violence), (3) *Survodaya* (well-being of all), and (4) *Satyagraha* (truthful persuasion) non-violent civil disobedience. These were honed during his 21-year stay in South Africa from 1893 to 1914 and in India from 1915 until his martyrdom in January 1948.

We draw lessons from how Mahatma Gandhi used his values-based inclusion leadership to integrate, and frequently voice in his speeches and writings, inclusion of four major marginalized and minority groups by (1) integrating religious minorities, such as Muslims, (2) uplifting lower-caste *Harijans*, (3) empowering cloistered women, and (4) engaging rural poor with homespun *Khadi*.

We review how Gandhi used the lenses of his values and value-based inclusion to lead three innovative *Satyagraha* non-violent protests in a 1920–1921 national *hartal* strike, the 1930–1931 Dandi Salt March, and the 1942–1946 "Quit India" movement that led to India's independence on August 15, 1947, and freedom for 330 million Indians from 190 years of colonial rule and influence.

We then discuss how inclusive leaders can promote values-based inclusion in today's workplaces using our values into voice and actions (ViVA) inclusion model of values-based leadership. Finally, future implications are provided by discussing some barriers to using the ViVA model and the need for inclusion of three emerging marginalized groups: (1) individuals with disability and special abilities, (2) lesbian, gay, bisexual, and transsexual (LGBT) individuals with non-heterosexual sexual orientation, and (3) the fast-rising group of elders.

Values-Based Inclusion Leadership for the 21st Century

In the 20th century, we saw the rise of and praises for transformational and charismatic leaders replacing hierarchical transactional leaders (Bass, 1990; Yukl, 2008). The leaders' performance results continued to matter more than their ethics, often at the expense of their process and means. This became dysfunctional after some time. The dawn of the 21st century witnessed epic leadership failures at the Union Carbide plant in Bhopal, Exxon in Alaska, Dow Corning (for faulty silicone breast implants), Enron, Tyco International, and WorldCom (Avolio & Gardner, 2005). Furthermore, there were bankruptcies of pioneers like Eastman Kodak and General Motors (Gehani & Gamble, 2012). These seismic failures demanded a re-emphasis on ethics, integrity, and values to guide the charismatic and transformational leaders and organizations (see, for example, Brown & Trevino, 2006; May, Chan, Hodges, & Avolio, 2003; Yukl, 2008). Gandhi strongly believed that ethical values-based means matter as much, or even more, than the outcomes (Gehani & Spears, 2009).

Values-based leadership (VBL) is defined by Bass and Steidelmeier (1999), Brown and Trevino (2006), and Gardner and Schermerhorn (2004) as "leaders with an underlying moral and ethical foundation." They manifest behaviors seen in ethical, servant, spiritual, and authentic leadership styles. There is congruence between the values of the leaders and the values of their organizations and their stakeholders. In all the emerging ethical forms of leadership, organizational performance is postulated to increase in addition to a strengthening of the organizational culture.

The key differences between the 20th century workhorse transformational leadership and the 21st century's value-based leadership are (a) a higher reliance on ethics, and (b) more authenticity in the latter.

Whereas ethics have been considered at a philosophical level since the launch of commercial enterprises, the significance of ethical considerations enhanced as the failure of large enterprises severely hurt the pension funds and the millions of pensioners relying on them in the late years of their lives (Copeland, 2014). With the devastation caused by the moral depravity of a select few strategic leaders, the ethical values demanded deeper connections with leaders and their decision-making (Brown & Trevino, 2006; Yukl, 2008; Copeland, 2014). First, the Sarbanes-Oxley Act was passed into law, with enhanced oversight on accounting and fiduciary responsibilities of publicly traded organizations. With this came the revision of the US Federal Sentencing Guidelines for executive officers in corporations. The flagship Academy of Management organized a plenary session on ethics, and the business school accreditation agency Association to Advance Collegiate Schools of Business (AACSB) launched an independent task force to highlight the increased significance of ethics in leadership.

The various corporate failures resulted in losses of hundreds of billions of dollars to the US economy (May et al., 2003). This questioned the moral inner fiber of leaders in upper echelons of organizations (George, 2003) and demanded authentic leaders with "purpose, value, and integrity." Authenticity dates back thousands of years to Greek philosophers, defining authentic leaders as leaders with a deep sense of purpose and authentic values. They share their own and others' emotions, needs, wants, and beliefs (Gardner & Schemerhorn, 2004). As leaders seek to understand who they are and what they believe, they become more authentic.

Values Into Voice and Actions (ViVA) Model

In this study, we also extend the giving voice to values (GVV) ethical framework proposed by Gentile (2017) by including the additional step of values-based ethical actions. GVV was presented as an innovative approach to values-driven leadership development, by reframing "what is the right thing to do?" to "how can one get the right thing done effectively?" (Gentile, 2017, p. 471). The focus is on scripting, speaking your mind, and action planning. Using behavioral ethics provides "both intellectual rigor and integrity, without preaching, but also without abdicating any sort of moral perspective and commitment" (Gentile, 2017, p. 471).

Gandhi used a values-based inclusive leadership that voiced the values, such as *Ahimsa* non-violence and *Satya* truth, clearly and frequently through his extensive writing and speeches (Gandhi, 1968, 1999). Gandhi embodied these values and voices through well-planned and scripted *Satyagrahi* actions, such as the 1920–21 nationwide civil disobedience *hartal* strike and the 1930–1931 Dandi Salt March to protest against British colonists' unjust salt monopoly. Gandhi's values-based inclusive leadership and ViVA model thereby offers us a best practice for inclusive leadership for today's workplaces inclusion.

Gandhi's Inclusive Values-Based Leadership

We next briefly discuss Gandhi's four key values most closely related to his values-based inclusive leadership. (For details, see Gehani and Spears (2009) and Gehani (2018, 2019).

Satya Truthfulness

Gandhi saw his entire life primarily as a series of experiments in truth. He never asked anyone else, including his wife, to ever believe or do anything that he would not believe or do himself (Gehani, 2019). In Gandhi's *Autobiography or The Story of My Experiments*, he shared various experiments to extract truths and discard untruths.

During his youthful years of studying in London, Gandhi tried to align his identity with the English elite. He borrowed funds to buy an expensive suit, a chimney-pot hat, and a gold watch chain from fashionable Bond Street. When he returned to India and saw the impoverished conditions of Indian masses, he discarded the English clothing to empathize with the masses more truthfully.

Nehru noted in his autobiography, *Discovery of India*, the transformational influence of Mahatma Gandhi on millions of Indians as follows (1967, p. 385).

> The Indian people did not become much more truthful than they were, nor did they change their essential nature overnight; nevertheless a sea-change was visible as the need for falsehood and furtive behavior lessened. It was a psychological change, almost as if some expert in psychoanalytical methods had probed deep into the patient's past, found out the origins of his complexes, exposed them to his view, and thus rid him of that burden.

Ahimsa Non-Violence

Gandhi related his inward adherence to truth with an outward manifestation of *Ahimsa* or non-violence. This was rooted in his family's Jain background and a strict adherence to never take any life (Parekh, 1988). As vegetarians, Gandhi's family did not eat any meat or root vegetables such as onion and garlic (consuming which involves killing these plants). Gandhi elevated this day-to-day non-violence practice into his national political actions and civil disobedience protests that he had learned by studying American philosopher Henry Thoreau. Gandhi explained (Gehani, 2019),

> Non-violence is not a cloistered virtue to be practiced by the individual for his peace and final salvation, but a rule of conduct for society if it is to live consistently with human dignity.
> ...You do not become non-violent by merely saying "I shall not use force." It (non-violence) must be felt in the heart. There must be within you an up-swelling of love and piety towards the (oppressive) wrong-doer. When there is that feeling it will express itself through some action. It may be a sign, a glance, or even silence. But such as it is, it will melt the heart of the wrong-doer and check the wrong (at its source).

Gandhi was, therefore, shocked and devastated when thousands of Muslims responded to their Muslim League leader M.A. Jinnah's call to Muslims for violent action against Hindus just prior to India's rushed partition by the British colonists in August 1947. When Hindus responded to violence with violence, resulting in the senseless massacre of precious human lives, Gandhi was utterly disappointed.

Survodaya Awakening for All

Gandhi carefully examined how the Industrial Revolution in England, since the 1760s, created a huge economic disparity between a handful of capital and mill owners and the masses of mill workers, while destroying their home-based cottage industries. This created millions of poor masses. Gandhi shared with his English friend Henry Polak that the English machine-driven material civilization had invaded, overwhelmed, and colonized India's ancient spiritual civilization. Gandhi dreamed of an independent and free nation of self-sufficient and self-ruling people, that he called *Swaraj*. Gandhi (1999) elaborated,

> real Swaraj will come not by the acquisition of authority by a few but by the acquisition of the capacity by all to resist authority when it is abused.

Satyagraha Truthful Persuasion

Gandhi integrated *Satya* truthfulness and *Ahimsa* non-violence into *Satyagraha*, meaning truthful non-violent persuasion. Gandhi (1999) elaborates *Satyagraha* as follows,

> The world rests upon the bedrock of Satya or truth. A-Satya meaning untruth also means non-existent, and Satya means that which is (unchanging in past, present, and future). . . . Truth being that which can never be destroyed. This is the doctrine of Satyagraha in a nutshell.

How did Gandhi achieve inclusive transformation of millions of Indians using his four key ethical values? In Gandhi's (1967, in Dutton, 1996, pp. 14–15) manifesto *Hind Swaraj* or Indian self-rule, he underscores his key values by stating that,

> Real Swaraj (self-rule) is possible only where Satyagraha (truthful persuasion) is the guiding force of the people. This force may be described as love-force, soul-force. . . . The force of love is the same as the force of the soul or truth. We have evidence of it working at every step. The Universe would disappear without the existence of that force.
>
> The soul-force Satyagraha is contrasted with the brute-force. The force of arms is powerless when matched against the force of love or the soul, a force found in the moral universe comparable to the physical force of gravity. Non-violent action releases a natural power that when used correctly has fundamental political, social, and economic consequences.

Gandhi experimented, tested, and examined his key values repeatedly before he advocated these to others, including his own wife, sons, and close associates.

Gandhi's Values Into Voice of Inclusion

Next, we explore how Gandhi embedded his values into his voice of inclusion.

Transcending Inclusive Spirituality

Mohandas Gandhi was born in the port town of Porbander in the western state of Gujarat in a merchant-class family. They were devotees of the Vishnu Avatar, the Hindu god that sustains the world. In the pantheon of Indian gods and goddesses, who come in pairs, Vishnu's wife Laxmi is the goddess of money. Gujarati Vaishnavite Jain merchants consider material success as a sign of the grace of god Vishnu and goddess Laxmi. Their temple, Haveli, displays donations of the wealthy merchant class.

Over the years, religion to Gandhi evolved into "self-realization or knowledge of self," as derived from India's ancient Vedic philosophy. Sometimes he considered himself inclined towards atheism, which was more like spiritualism. Gandhi was also impressed by returning good for evil. Throughout his life, Gandhi admitted that he received "invaluable help in the moments of gloom" from reading *The Bhagavad Gita*. Gandhi tried to integrate the lessons of *Bhagavad Gita*, the Sermon on the Mount from the Bible, and the *Light of Asia* (by Sir Edwin Arnold, 2019). Thus, renunciation as the highest form of religion appealed to Gandhi greatly.

Inclusion of Minority Religions

Mahatma Gandhi believed that if different people in a country have a strong sense of nationality, then their religious differences would not matter. He was, however, well aware of the many basic foundational differences between India's Hindu majority and Muslim minority, though they had the same ancestors. Most Muslims in India were once Hindus who converted to Islam. For prayer, Muslims turn to the west to Mecca, whereas Hindus turn to the East to the rising sun. Hindus worship cows, value non-violence, and see the power of the universe in idols. Muslims do not believe in these. From the 1400s to 1757, successive generations of Muslim rulers controlled large parts of the Indian subcontinent, but some Hindus flourished. Gandhi believed that all religions have some truths, and all religions have some blind spots. Therefore, Gandhi strived hard throughout his 21-year stay in South Africa and for 33 years after his return to India in 1915 to unite Hindus and Muslims into one nation.

Gandhi was well aware that the English colonists wanted to divide Hindus and Muslims and make them fight with one another to rule them. But Gandhi also believed that if Hindus and Muslims were committed to stay united together, then no third party would be able to separate them. He believed that true liberty must be created within the hearts of Hindus and Muslims. Hindu-Muslim communal mistrust and fear must be shed through the strength of one's own spirit, and not by using an alien third party to outmaneuver the opponent.

Gandhi noted that the Muslim masses did not recognize a pressing necessity for *Swaraj* self-rule independence and that they did not take part in the independence movement as Hindus did. Gradually, with Gandhi's guidance, thousands of Muslims registered with the Indian National Congress party. Gandhi wanted every Hindu in every district to make special efforts to invite every Muslim they knew to join their efforts for India's freedom. Muslims must not feel their lack of education or numbers, which make them feel like a minority. To Gandhi, the character of a person mattered more than the sheer numbers or their religion. Gandhi wanted the minorities to not fear the stray actions of rare fanatical Hindus.

Gandhi urged repeatedly that Hindu-Muslim unity was the cornerstone of India's freedom, unity, and independence (Gandhi, 1999). Gandhi did not believe in converting Muslims to Hinduism. Instead, he urged Hindus to be better Hindus, Muslims to be better Muslims, and Christians to be better Christians (Gandhi, 1999, v35, p. 461). Gandhi shared,

> my innermost desire is not that the brotherhood of Hindus only may be achieved, but it essentially is that the brotherhood of [hu]man—be he Hindu, Mussalman, Christian, Parsi, or Jew—may be realized. For I believe in the fundamental truth of all great religions in the world. I believe that they are all God-given, and I believe that they were necessary for the people to whom these religions were revealed. And I believe that, if only we could all of us read the scriptures of the different faiths from the standpoint of the followers of those faiths we should find that they were at bottom all one and were all helpful to one another.

Inclusion of Individuals With Lower Caste

Gandhi had the courage to oppose an age-old pillar of traditional Hindu religious institution: caste and untouchability dating back to c. 1500 B.C. To achieve this goal, Gandhi urged purification and purging of Hinduism, calling it "the greatest reform of the Age." For organizational efficiency, the traditional Indian society was divided into four major *varnas* or caste groups: (1) Brahmin priests, (2) Kshatriya warriors, (3) Vaishya merchants, craftspeople, and farmers, and (4) Shudras, including butchers and cobblers, at the bottom of the society's hierarchy. In addition, there are untouchable sanitary workers, who fall below the caste hierarchy. They were considered unclean because they handle unclean garbage and sewage.

Initially, the castes and numerous sub-castes were just for the economic occupational stratification of the Indian society based on people's different talents. But over the generations, the individuals born in different families carried out the ancestral vocational heritage of their families' caste. A Brahmin priest's son could claim to be a Brahmin priest, irrespective of his talent. And, what is worst is that the children of a Shudra sanitary worker or a butcher are restricted to remain in Shudra caste and vocations, generation after generation, irrespective of their human talent. Their caste is determined by their birth. This has been ingrained into Indian society over multiple generations, with strict restrictions on inter-caste marriages and inter-caste dining together (Dalton, 1996, p. 117). In the past, Indian society denied the untouchables any access to public wells and stayed away even from their shadows, considered impure. The untouchables were denied the use of the roads they cleaned with the sweat of their brows.

To promote inclusion of the most excluded untouchables, Gandhi named them *Harijans*, or God's children, and called himself a *Harijan*. Gandhi also insisted that removal of the custom of untouchability was a prerequisite to India attaining its independence and freedom from oppressive alien rulers. He invited and included Harijans to live with him in his Sabarmati Ashram near Ahmedabad, an egalitarian spiritual community to be the role model for a free India. In 1933, Gandhi changed the name of his newspaper *Young India* to *Harijan*. In this regard, though Gandhi tried very hard to integrate Harijans with mainstream Indians, he failed to achieve this goal. Untouchability persisted, and even intensified in India long after Gandhi's martyrdom in January 1948.

In the Indian National Congress convention of 1920, just five years after his homecoming, Gandhi made a proposal to eradicate the "Sin of Untouchability" in India once for all. The National Congress passed the resolution acknowledging that the removal of untouchability was necessary for the self-rule of independence and freedom.

Inclusion of Women

The inclusion, empowerment, and emancipation of women was an important feature of Mahatma Gandhi's social reforms and values-based inclusive leadership. Gandhi strongly believed that at every level of national development, India must draw on the capabilities and energy of India's female population.

The centuries-old traditions of patriarchy cloistered many generations of Indian women behind a veiled *purdah* curtain (*burqa* for Muslim women). According to the ancient Indian scriptures, Manu assigned that a father's *Karma* was to protect his unmarried daughters until puberty. When she reached puberty, he was expected to arrange her marriage to the best groom he could find—often without her consent or against her wishes. Some of these traditions were customs borne out of women's illiteracy and total economic dependency on men during all the stages of her life as a daughter, a sister, a wife, or a mother. The smarter women accepted society's customs, but did a great job managing her household as a custodian of her father or her husband.

In 1907, when Gandhi was helping Indian settlers in South Africa, he noted the significance of women's education, and highlighted,

> Indian men have deliberately kept their women backward (veiled behind a purdah of inferiority and subservience), and if this state of affairs continues, India will remain in the present abominable condition even if she were to secure all her rights from the (colonial) British Government
>
> *(Dalton, 1996, p. 126).*

To transform masses of cloistered women into leaders, Gandhi included women in his nonviolent civil disobedience *Satyagraha* protests. Gandhi excluded women from the 1930 Dandi Salt *Satyagraha* march to avoid any inadvertent blackmail. Instead, he felt that women were best suited to lead the boycott of imported mill cloth and alcohol. He noted and leveraged the authentic attributes of self-sacrifice and silent suffering ingrained in the daily lives of Indian women. Their non-violent appeals to the merchants and buyers of foreign cloth melted the hearts of the merchants as well as some English colonists. As women participated actively in Gandhi's civil disobedience campaigns, the British colonists also saw the political advantage of engaging masses of women.

Within three decades of moving to India, Mahatma Gandhi had helped mobilize millions of Indian women as non-violent resisters in his successive *Satyagraha* non-violent protests. Gandhi addressed the All-India Women's Conference he had helped establish, and declared, "Swaraj [self-rule] and the progress of India in all directions [are] impossible without the advancement of women. When women whom we call Abla [without power weak] become Sabala [with power, strong], all those who are helpless will become powerful" (Dalton, 1996, pp. 126–127).

Gandhi saw prejudice against women as a matter of improving not only education of young girls but also the education of married women. He recommended bold action, that

> every patriotic husband should become his wife's own teacher, and prepare her for work among her less fortunate sisters. One implication [of this] is for husbands to cease to treat their wives as objects of their enjoyment, but to regard them as co-partners in their work of nation-building.

Inclusion of Rural Poor With Homespun Khadi

Mahatma Gandhi empathized with the poorest Indians, who lived mostly in thousands of remote villages. In 1915, when he landed in India with his family, he wore an elaborate Gujarati costume from his Saurashtra province. However, as he traveled to distant parts of India to familiarize himself with the worsening of living conditions for Indians since he had left more than two decades earlier, he realized that most poor Indians could not afford proper clothing. In order for the poorest rural Indian to trust and relate to him better, Gandhi decided to dress and live like the poorest rural Indian. He shed his Saurashtrian costume and switched to a simple cotton Dhoti garment.

Gandhi launched his social reforms for economic equality and welfare for all, or *Survodaya*, and connected it with his key values of *Satyagraha* or non-violent protest for *Swaraj* self-rule and *Swatantra* or national freedom. To him economic independence had to be an integral part of the social and political independence of all Indians. He campaigned that no one will be free until all attain freedom, and that liberty must come with social and economic equality. Gandhi urged capitalist landowners to allow some use of their idle land by the landless poor peasants. Gandhi wanted to transform gradually towards an egalitarian society where the prince and the pauper had the same rights (Dutton, 1996, p. 131).

Though Gandhi was often ridiculed for his eclectic economic ideas, he saw these as a non-violent alternative to an inevitable violent socialist war over widening economic power gulf between the rich and the poor, as in the French and Russian revolutions. Gandhi's *Survodaya* or welfare of all included economic equity and justice for all, and it did not imply the poor people's dependency on a welfare system as in the US. Gandhi's self-reliance was inspired from two American transcendentalists Ralph Waldo Emerson and Henry Thoreau.

To Gandhi, economic equality for all was "the master key to non-violent independence (*Swaraj*)." This meant non-violently resolving the eternal conflicts between the high-handed few imperial capital owners and the millions of semi-starved impoverished laborers. To Gandhi, non-violence *Ahimsa*, and *Survodaya* welfare for all, were gradual but permanent transformational processes of conversion. Economic exploitation had no place in a free and independent society and nation. If poor become poorer, and the rich wealthy class can continue to exploit the impoverished, then there is no *Swaraj* or *Survodaya* upliftment for all.

One of Gandhi's innovative reforms was for everyone, including elite doctors and lawyers, to do some manual labor in the form of hand-spinning and weaving cotton into homemade *Khadi* fabric.

Gandhi wanted them to switch to wearing clothes made from indigenously spun and woven *Khadi* instead of wearing textile mill-made and woven clothes imported from the mills of Manchester and Lancaster in England. This social reform was to help all to identify with the common masses of rural Indians who could not afford expensive imported goods made in England and to break India's economic dependence on England. Gandhi termed this as *Swadeshi*, or self-reliance, relying on using what is produced in one's own country.

Gandhi's Voice for Inclusion: In Summary

Mahatma Gandhi summarized the significance of inclusion in his leadership for the independence and freedom of 330 million Indians as follows,

> That freedom which is associated with the term Swaraj (self-rule) in the popular mind is no doubt unattainable without not only the removal of untouchability and the promotion of heart unity between the different sections but also without removing many other social evils that can be easily named. That inward growth, which must never stop, we have come to understand by the comprehensive term Swaraj. And the Swaraj cannot be held so long as walls of prejudice, passion, and superstition continue to stifle the growth of that stately oak
> *(Gandhi's Concept of Swaraj, 1999, p. 151).*

Gandhi's Values Into Voice and Actions (ViVA) Model

Gandhi noted that action was his main domain, and he repeatedly asserted throughout his life, "It's not what I say but what I do that matters" (McGeary, 1999). Gandhi transformed the Indian National Congress from a club-like gathering place for upper-class elite into an action-based mass crusade. Despite India's tendency of large gaps between ethnic and religious groups, Gandhi inspired legions of Indians to join his peaceful non-violent protests that made the colonial empire incapable of ruling Indians oppressively. In 1922, 30,000 Indians willingly followed Gandhi into jails in support of his call for nationwide civil disobedience (discussed later).

Gandhi's Means and Outcomes

Gandhi believed in a close logical connection between the means and the ends or outcomes of actions. He likened means to a seed and the end to a tree, with a similar inviolable connection between the two. And he stressed that we reap exactly as we sow. Therefore, he noted that the use of pure non-violent *Satyagraha* means as a method will result in pure *Swaraj* self-rule as the outcome, and the two are closely interconnected.

Such self-rule *Swaraj*, Gandhi believed, must be experienced individually by each person, and only such free self-ruling individuals will help create a self-ruling free nation. He believed that the British colonists were not to be blamed, as they came and stayed in India for 190 years because of the weaknesses of the Indian social fabric, and that they would leave only when the native people were ready to reform and self-rule.

The impact of Gandhi's new inclusive style of leadership therapeutically restored India's identity and authentic spirit. Gandhi achieved this transformation of Indian minds through three major non-violent civil disobedience campaigns after the Amritsar massacre of around 400 unarmed Indians celebrating their spring-harvesting festival in a park surrounded by homes in April 1919. Until then, Gandhi was mostly trying to improve and create a more harmonious and balanced relationship between colonial British rulers and the impoverished Indian masses. The ruthless Amritsar massacre, and its callous and unsympathetic response by British colonists and rulers, transformed Gandhi's mind against the British. Gandhi's three key non-violent civil disobedience campaigns were as follows:

In 1919–1920, Gandhi Led the First Non-Violent Nationwide Non-Cooperation Satyagraha Campaign

Gandhi first resorted to *Satyagraha* peaceful civil disobedience protests after the English colonists broke their promises made during World War I to give India more autonomy and freedom. Gandhi had helped recruit hundreds of thousands of Indian soldiers to help the democratic forces of Great Britain defeat the dictatorial forces of Germany. Instead, the colonist government passed the Rowlatt Act of 1919 to exercise more oppression on impoverished Indians, restricting their freedoms even further, without any trial. Gandhi responded by calling for a nationwide *Satyagraha* truthful *hartal* strike on April 6, 1919, when no Indian would do any work for the colonial foreign government (Gehani & Spears, 2009).

Gandhi's call received overwhelming nationwide support from millions of Indians, and everything came to a stop in most regions of India with no acts of violence as per the guidelines of *Satyagraha* (more on this in a later section). The innovative new peaceful protest process amazed the colonist government as well as the world. Gandhi took full responsibility for ensuring the peaceful actions of millions of participating Indian masses. Gandhi's persuasive and inclusive ethical command over most Indians made India practically ungovernable by the colonists.

Despite its effectiveness and almost perfect success, Gandhi suddenly discontinued this campaign in early 1922 the moment he saw early signs of violence by a handful of protesters in the remote rural province of Chauri Chaura. He took responsibility for their unethical failure. Gandhi noted that the *Swaraj* self-rule must be ruled from the discipline from within, and not merely freedom from an external oppressor. Violence had no place in Gandhi's *Swaraj*. Gandhi concluded that the Indian masses needed more training of their minds.

1930–1931 Dandi Salt March Satyagraha

The next major non-violent disobedience came almost a decade later on March 12, 1930. During the intervening decade-long period, Gandhi trained the minds of 78 close associates and volunteer *Satyagrahis* at his Sabarmati Satyagraha Ashram near the western city of Ahmedabad in his native Gujarat state. Gandhi announced that they would walk 240 miles in 25 days to the seacoast town of Dandi to make salt from seawater. By the time they reached Dandi, thousands of people joined Gandhi and his associates. There, in sets of 10, with Gandhi leading them, they symbolically broke the British colonist government's monopolistic ban on the manufacture and sale of salt.

Thousands of common Indians who joined Gandhi and his marchers broke the unjust salt law on the Dandi seacoast. They were brutally beaten with steel-tipped sticks and arrested. This time more than 60,000 Indians filled the jails (McGeary, 1999). A handful of reporters from around the world wrote about the merciless torturing of the unarmed non-violent protesters. Gandhi's influence spread as he vividly demonstrated his inclusion leadership and inspirational influence over millions of Indians. Britain was shamed by the small, unarmed old man and his unresisting supporters. The colonial viceroy acknowledged Gandhi as the true and effective inclusive leader of his millions of faithful Indian followers.

The 1942–1944 "Quit India" Civil Disobedience

As the whole world plunged into the violent World War II in 1942 between the Allied Forces led by the UK, the US, and France and the Axis Forces of Nazi Germany, Italy, and Japan, Gandhi opposed the participation of hundreds of thousands of Indians enlisting as soldiers supporting the British forces. Instead, Gandhi reluctantly endorsed the "Quit India" plan, asking the British colonists to leave India once and for all. Gandhi, Congress leaders, and many of their followers were arrested for indefinite periods. The colonist government struck hard and killed more than 1,000 Indians. A 74-year-old Gandhi was freed on May 5, 1944. By then, he had spent almost 78 months or six and a half years in jail for the altruistic sake of freeing impoverished others.

In 1946 and 1947, as the Muslim League party under the leadership of M.A. Jinnah provoked violent actions against Hindus, inter-religious riots broke out in the eastern provinces of Bengal, Bihar, and Delhi in the north. Gandhi boldly walked unarmed 116 miles through 47 riot-torn villages in Bengal and Bihar to pacify the angry rioters.

When India gained independence and freedom on August 15, 1947, after hurriedly partitioning off the Muslim states of West Pakistan and East Pakistan, Gandhi was devastated. He refused to join the Independence Day celebrations after 190 years of foreign rule and influence and fasted alone to pray for peace. Angry Indians seeking revenge forgot about tolerance and non-violence, reversing much of what Gandhi taught them for decades.

To protect Muslim minorities in Calcutta and Delhi, Gandhi "fasted until death" in September 1947 and January 1948. After weeks, thousands of rioters stopped their violence like a miracle.

Gandhi's selfless value-based inclusive leadership over multiple decades clearly demonstrated to the world the power of non-violence *Ahimsa* and non-violent truthful protest *Satyagraha* against colonial rulers.

Unfortunately, on January 30, 1948, a young zealot, Nathuram Godse, approached Mahatma Gandhi, rushing to his inter-religious evening prayer meeting in New Delhi. He knelt and touched Gandhi's feet and then shot three bullets into Gandhi's chest from close range. Gandhi whispered, "Hey Ram, Hey Ram, Hey Ram," and died instantly. Godse felt that Gandhi was yielding too many concessions to the new Muslim state Pakistan. The Hindu community was shocked. Gandhi's death stopped the violent mass killings and made Indians realize the fatal consequences of inter-religious hatred and the lasting value of non-violent conflict resolution of *Satyagraha*.

Gandhi's Values-Based Inclusive Leadership for Today's Workplaces

Inclusion in India After Gandhi

Inspired by Gandhi's inclusive leadership, the Indian government chartered a constitution in 1950 and developed and launched a wide variety of social schemes and programs for the protection of the marginalized minority groups in India (Ehmke, 2016).

For decades since independence in August 1947, Indian family-owned conglomerates such as Birlas, Tatas, Kirlloskars, Singhanias, and others were preoccupied with 4% economic development. Their strategic leaders often ignored the need for diversity or inclusion. With the opening of the Indian economy in the 1990s, globalization and glocalization made Indian leaders aware of the significance as well as the direct and indirect impact of diversity and inclusion in workplace on the organizations' performance. The dawn of the 21st century ushered in megatrends, such as

1. Expansion of knowledge and information technology sector,
2. Localization of operations of multinational enterprises (MNEs) such as Goodyear, Timken, Diebold, and Mars in India,
3. Indian enterprises moving their operations abroad or acquiring foreign operations such as Tetley and Land Rover, and
4. Facing the need to compete globally with fast-rising Korean and Chinese enterprises such as Samsung, Alibaba, and Huawei.

These megatrends demanded a higher need for inclusion.

A Deloitte (2011) report highlighted that diversity in organizations demands more than just having a sprinkling of women and people with different skin colors. It is inclusion and engagement of diverse individuals that results in improvement in business performance outcomes. Deloitte (2012) also discovered that a 10% increase in inclusion of employees results in one day/per employee/per year decrease in absenteeism.

Inclusive leaders like Mahatma Gandhi drive and significantly enhance workplace inclusion. The Deloitte (2012) report notes that inclusive leaders are collaborative, they visibly champion initiatives promoting diversity, and they seek out and value diverse employees' contributions and merit-based decision-making (Boland, Maheshwari, Te'eni, Schwartz, & Tenkasi, 1992). These inclusive leaders manage conflicts with cultural competence and create a collective sense of identity.

Whereas there is a consensus that high diversity and effective inclusion are needed for organizations, the research on what values, knowledge, and skills are needed is still in its nascent stage. Gandhi was multiple generations ahead in using values-based inclusive leadership to unify a highly diverse and ethically fragmented India in the first half of the 20th century.

Implications and Future Research

Obstacles to Workplace Inclusion

Finally, some of the biggest obstacles to workplace inclusion are related to some leaders' unethical practices such as corruption, nepotism, favoritism, fraud, corruption, and prejudicial biases (Venkatesan, 2014). As mentioned earlier, and unlike Gandhi's ethical leadership, some organizations around the world have undetected corrupt leaders who misappropriate their organizational resources, including their assigned and assumed power, for their private gains and self-glorification. In developing emerging economies like India, with a high real or perceived power distance between a supervisor and a subordinate, it is hard for a subordinate to voice opinions. On the other hand, in some capitalist Western countries, with rampant and frequent layoffs, any employee can be laid off on a short notice in the name of financial contingencies.

At the time of India's independence, Mahatma Gandhi suggested that the Congress Party members should disband (Heston & Kumar, 2008). Instead, many congressmen and -women took positions of power, became corrupt, and corrupted the civil servants to get themselves reelected again and again. The Indian government enacts anti-corruption laws but is lax in their implementation.

Mahatma Gandhi evolved into that rare great value-based inclusive leader and a moral icon who is held in universal esteem for decades after his martyrdom. His non-violent *Satyagraha* resistance has helped liberate more than a billion people around the world. Gandhi's transcendent inclusive message and guiding light inspires the imagination of millions of oppressed people everywhere seeking hope. Gandhi's values into voice and actions (ViVA) model is one of the best practices of values-based inclusive leadership to help us transcend our differences.

References

Arnold, E. (2019). *The light of Asia or the great renunciation*. Sydney, AU: Wentworth Press.
Aung Sun Suu Kyi. (1991). *Freedom from fear*. New York, NY: Penguin.
Avolio, B., & Gardner, W. (2005). Authentic leadership development: Getting to the roof of positive forms of leadership. *The Leadership Quarterly, 16*(3), 315–338.
Bass, B. M. (1990). From transactional to transformational leadership: Learning to share the vision. *Organizational Dynamics, 18*(3), 19–31.
Bass, B., & Steidelmeier, P. (1999). Ethics, character, and transformational leadership behavior. *The Leadership Quarterly, 10*(2), 81–117.

Boland, R. J. Jr., Maheshwari, A., Te'eni, D., Schwartz, D. G., & Tenkasi, R. V. (1992). Sharing perspectives in distributed decision making. In J. Turner & R. Kraut (Eds.), *Proceedings of CSCW'92, computer-supported cooperative work conference*. Toronto: ACM Press.

Brown, M., & Trevino, L. (2006). Ethical leadership: A review and future directions. *The Leadership Quarterly, 17*(3), 596–616.

Copeland, M. K. (2014). The emerging significance of values based leadership: A literature review. *International Journal of Leadership Studies, 8*(2), 105–135.

Crossan, M., Mazutis, D., Seijts, G., & Gandz, J. (2012). Developing leadership character in business programs. *Academy of Management Learning & Education, 12*(2), 285–305.

Dalton, D. (1996). *Gandhi: Selected political writings*. Indianapolis: Hackett Publishing Co.

Deloitte. (2011, September). Only skin deep? Re-examining the business case for diversity. *Human Capital Australia*.

Deloitte. (2012). Waiter, is that inclusion in my soup? A new recipe to improve business performance. *Deloitte Research Report*, Australia.

Dutton, D. (Ed.). (1996). *Mahatma Gandhi: Selected political writings*. Indianapolis: Hackett Publishing.

Ehmke, E. (2016). India's Mahatma Gandhi national rural employment act 2005: Assessing the quality of access and adequacy of benefits in MGNREGS public works. *International Social Security Review, 69*(2), 3–27.

Gandhi, M. K. (1968). *The selected works of Mahatma Gandhi (SWMG)*. New Delhi: Publications Division, Ministry of Information and Broadcasting, Government of India.

Gandhi, M. K. (1999). *The collected works of Mahatma Gandhi (CWMG)*. New Delhi: Ministry of Information and Broadcasting, Government of India.

Gandhi's Concept of Swaraj. (1999). Retrieved from https://shodhganga.inflibnet.ac.in/bitstream/10603/111059/9/09_chapter%204.pdf

Gardner, W., & Schermerhorn, J. (2004). Unleashing individual potential: Performance gains through positive organizational behavior and authentic leadership. *Organizational Dynamics, 33*(3), 270–279.

Gehani, R. R. (2018, November). Gandhi's dialectic struggle with interior—exterior integration: 6S lessons from paradoxical success of an integral leader. *Integral Leadership Review*, 15–33.

Gehani, R. R. (2019, June). Gandhi's integral leadership to greatness for all (Survodaya): With truth (Satya), Nonviolence (Ahimsa), and Self-rule (Swaraj). *Integral Leadership Review*, 24–36.

Gehani, R. R., & Gamble, J. E. (2012). Eastman Kodak's strategy and business model. In J. E. Gamble (Eds.), *Essentials of strategic management*. New York, NY: McGraw-Hill.

Gehani, R. R., & Spears, S. (2009). *Gandhi's relevance in today's times*. Cleveland: National Association of Asian-American Professionals (NAAP).

Gentile, M. C. (2017). Giving voice to values: A pedagogy for behavioral ethics. *Journal of Management Education, 41*(4), 469–479.

George, B. (2003). *Authentic leadership*. San Francisco, CA: Jossey-Bass.

Heston, A., & Kumar, V. (2008). Institutional flaws and corruption incentives in India. *Journal of Development Studies, 44*(9), 1243–1261.

Luther King, M. L. Jr. (1983). *The words of Martin Luther King Jr* (p. 71). New York, NY: New Market Press.

May, R., Chan, A., Hodges, T., & Avolio, B. (2003). Developing the moral component of authentic leadership. *Organizational Dynamics, 32*, 247–260.

McGeary, J. (1999, December 31). Mohandas Gandhi. *TIME Magazine, 154*(27).

Nathan, O., & Norden, H. (Eds.). (1981). *Einstein on peace*. New York, NY: Avenel Books.

Nehru, J. L. (1937/1967). *Discovery of India* (p. 385). Bombay: Asia Publishing House.

Pareikh, B. (1988). Gandhi's concept of Ahimsā. *Alternatives: Global, Local, Political, 13*(2), 195–217.

TIME Magazine. (1999, December 31). The children of Gandhi. *154*(27).

Venkatesan, R. (2014). Controlling corruption. *McKinsey Quarterly, 4*, 6–21.

Yukl, G. (2008). How leaders influence organizational effectiveness. *The Leadership Quarterly, 19*(6), 708–722.

26
ARE YOU JOKING? HUMOR AND INCLUSIVE LEADERSHIP

Laura E. Mercer Traavik

Introduction

Humor plays a vital role in human interaction and has strong evolutionary roots (Alexander, 1986; de Waal, 2019). Over the last 20 years, research on leader humor has shown a link between humor and leadership effectiveness (Kong, Cooper, & Sosik, 2019). Humor can unite social groups, increase subjective well-being, and relieve stress (Martin & Ford, 2018). Humor is a wonderful social glue, bonding people and leading to high-quality relationships, releasing tension, and creating positive affect. Humor is an essential organizational ingredient, leadership tool, and team resource (Cooper, Kong, & Crossley, 2018; Kong et al., 2019; Lehmann-Willenbrock & Allen, 2014). However, humor can also be used as a means to ostracize individuals and increase the proclivity for violence towards targeted groups (cf. Thomae & Viki, 2013). Jokes and humor can mask overt discrimination, reinforce status differences, change norms of acceptable behaviors, lead to reinforcing stereotypes, and lower performance (Hodson & MacInnis, 2016; Hodson, Rush, & MacInnis, 2010; Martin & Ford, 2018; Yam, Christian, Wei, Liao, & Nai, 2018).

For leaders who want to promote an inclusive environment, it is critical that they deeply reflect on and actively regulate the type of humor that takes place in their teams and in their organization. Although jokes are funny, they may not be a laughing matter. Jokes and humor often take the form of subtle discrimination (Jones, Peddie, Gilrane, King, & Gray, 2016), and there is evidence that this subtle discrimination can be more problematic and harmful than overt discrimination (Jones, Arena, Nittrouer, Alonso, & Lindsey, 2017).

In the wake of the "Me Too" movement and the increasing awareness and discussion of language and political correctness, there is substantial debate about what we say and how we act in the workplace. Research shows that prejudiced individuals look for ways to express bias that is socially acceptable (Jones et al., 2017) and that humor provides such a vehicle (Hodson & MacInnis, 2016). Putting prejudice in a humorous package gives it more weight than a disparaging comment alone (Ford & Ferguson, 2004). A diverse workplace will include both people who score high on prejudice and people from different social identity groups. People will have different ideas about what is funny and what is not, and there will be organizational members who are more vulnerable to the negative consequences of belittling humor. Recognizing the power of humor and its potential deleterious effects can give managers, leaders, and coworkers important knowledge to build work environments where everyone feels welcomed, whole, and included.

Creating an inclusive environment is about building a climate where everyone laughs together and no one is laughed at. Inclusive environments require leaders to use humor strategically and authentically and to manage the type of humor accepted in the workplace. A joke is funny until it is not. In this chapter, I briefly outline some of the theories of humor and why it is necessary to focus on humor in the workplace, and lastly I describe how to actively manage humor in order to achieve inclusive leadership.

Humor

Humor occurs in almost all interpersonal relationships, yet research interest has not always matched the subject area's importance (Martin & Ford, 2018). Although theories on humor extend back to Sigmund Freud, humor research has not been a heavily researched area in psychology. Research on humor had an upsurge in the 1970s, and by the turn of the century renewed attention was emerging. Within the leadership and management field, humor entered at the end of the last century (Avolio, Howell, & Sosik, 1999). Research interest remains modest (Yam et al., 2018), however, and construct clarity has not been achieved (Cooper et al., 2018). In this section, I introduce what humor is and theories about the why of humor.

Humor has evolutionary functionality in all social creatures, not just humans but other mammals as well (de Waal, 2019). Humor is playful and is comprised of stimuli, cognitive and perceptual processes, emotional responses, and behavior that we know as laughter (Martin & Ford, 2018). Humor is the experience of all these elements and is an emotional response that emerges when one assesses an event or situation as connected to some incongruity. In order to experience humor, a non-serious mindset needs to be activated where people suspend reason, rationality, and solemnity (Gray & Ford, 2013).

Humor serves several purposes—to strengthen and develop relationships, relieve tension, and assert dominance. Laughter plays a biosocial function as it creates social bonds and produces positive emotion (Martin & Ford, 2018). Humor has clear biological and neurological connections, with the different elements of humor activating diverse regions of the brain (Martin & Ford, 2018). But humor is more than biological, as it is directly embedded in culture. Culture dictates the norms of what is funny and what is acceptable, and humor for humans is very dependent on the social context.

So what constitutes humor? Over the centuries humor has been seen as a form of aggression and demonstration of superiority and intellect, but more recently humor has been seen as positive, kind, empathetic, and bonding.

Research and theories investigating humor have spanned from psychology to sociology to biology. Martin and Ford (2018) categorize the earlier theories on the causes of humor into three groups: relief, superiority, and incongruity theories of humor. Although all the theories in these groups contribute to our understanding of humor, each explanation alone is incomplete. Relief theories focus on how humor plays a cathartic role and relieves tension (for example, Freud's work arguing that humor releases sexual tension), whereas superiority theories emphasize how humor is used to gain or maintain a superior position by putting down others (Martin & Ford, 2018). This type of disparagement humor is mediated by self-esteem enhancement that is the consequence of social comparison (Martin & Ford, 2018). Both relief and superiority theory explain motivation as central for humor: either to relieve or to dominate. The third group of theories takes a cognitive approach, examining incongruity and humor arising from the discrepancy between sensory input and our understanding of the situation. With these theories, incongruences must be present, and in addition, there must be some sort of resolution to the apparent contradictions in the joke or humor situation. These three groups of theories emphasize different components of humor: relief, dominance, and cognitive inconsistencies. All of these approaches give us insight into the why of humor; however, alone they are not sufficient or complete to explain humor. Humor is multifaceted, and the reason we use humor is complex.

A recent psychological theory of humor that has tried to tap into this complexity, building on the tenets of incongruity is Benign violation theory (BVT). BVT adds a dimension of wrongness, an element that contradicts the "right" social norms (McGraw & Warren, 2010) to incongruity. BVT explains the occurrence of humor when moral, linguistic, or social norms are threatened (McGraw & Warren, 2010). Violations of norms can trigger fear, disgust, confusion, and other negative emotions; however, when violations are benign, they open up for humor (McGraw & Warren, 2010). These violations are seen as playful when they are interpreted as nonthreatening. Benign violation arises if there is a competing norm that would allow the violation, if the norm broken is not deemed important, or if the violation is distant either socially or temporally (McGraw & Warren, 2010). Humor arises from more than just incongruence; humor occurs because of the violation, an event that is both right and wrong at the same time. An example would be telling a humorous story about someone being hit by a bus—laughing at an accident violates a moral norm, but if the event is distant in time, this violation could be acceptable. BVT gives us direct insight into how we can understand derogatory humor, and it gives us clues about the role individuals and context has in determining whether humor is nonthreatening.

Humor can take on many forms. One typology used in the research on humor outlines four different types of humor reflected in the individual differences in humor styles: self-enhancing, self-defeating, aggressive, and affiliative (Martin, Puhlik-Doris, Larsen, Gray, & Weir, 2003). What is funny depends on the event/stimuli, the social context, and the individuals involved. Broadly speaking, we can divide humor into self, other, or event focused, and aggressive versus affiliative.

Humor can occur through intentional joke telling or unintentionally and spontaneously arise in conversations. Humor can convey messages that would not be allowed in a serious context and can serve as a facilitator or as an alienator in social relations.

Humor has a rich history in evolution, science, and literature. However, within psychology and the management fields, research and theories are only now gaining ground.

The Role of Humor in Organizational Life

Recently the role of humor in the workplace has received increased attention, and research findings have linked humor with leader skills (Cooper et al., 2018; Kong et al., 2019; Yam et al., 2018), employee health, job satisfaction, high-quality work performance, decreases in burnout and stress, increases in cohesion (Cooper & Sosik, 2012; Mesmer-Magnus, Glew, & Chockalingam, 2012), and work group effectiveness (Lehmann-Willenbrock & Allen, 2014).

The research on humor for leadership and within organizations has predominantly examined the positive effects of humor and affiliative humor (Kong et al., 2019). One of the first studies by Avolio et al. (1999) did note the mixed effect of humor, depending on the leadership style. Since that time, however, the majority of research has examined the positive effect of humor in the workplace (Mesmer-Magnus et al., 2012). The conclusion is that humor is critical for creating positive individual and team-level outcomes and increases leader effectiveness (Mesmer-Magnus et al., 2012). Although playfulness and humor can bring many benefits to the workplace and to relationships, the role of context for interpreting humor is critical to understand humor's impact (Gray & Ford, 2013). In Gray and Ford's research, for example, they found that in the workplace a more serious mindset exists as the starting point and therefore jokes can be found to be offensive. So those jokes that are denigrating can be seen as more aggressive at work than in other situations. Their experiment demonstrated that subjects who imagined hearing a sexist joke at the office rated it more offensive than hearing it at a comedy club (Gray & Ford, 2013).

There are some studies, especially recently, that have addressed the negative sides of humor in the workplace and called for more research into this dark side (Decker & Rotondo, 2001; Wijewardena, Härtel, & Samaratunge, 2017; Yam et al., 2018). For example, Wijewardena and colleagues showed that managerial humor was an affective event for employees. When employees perceived the humor as positive, it led to positive feelings, and when employees perceived the humor as negative, this led to negative experiences. This field experiment demonstrated that the employees' reactions were moderated by the type of relationships employees had with their manager. Another study by Huo, Lam, and Chen (2012) showed an increased level of strain, as well as alcohol-related problems, in employees whose leader used an aggressive form of humor—particularly, when this aggressive humor was directed towards specific employees rather than towards all the employees of a team (Huo et al., 2012).

Generally, the research on humor in the workplace has been quite limited, although there is more research taking place in this century and an increased recognition of the importance of humor at work. There is also movement towards understanding the potential negative effects of humor in the workplace and linking this to bullying and prejudice. This newer research is very important to understand if managers want to create an inclusive workplace. In the next section, I address in more detail the dark side of humor by examining humor and prejudice.

Humor and Prejudice/Domination

A negative attitude towards a social group or a person within that group is called prejudice (Allport, 1954), and discrimination is the behavioral correlate in which people are treated differently based on their membership to this group. "Discrimination refers to the differential or unfair treatment experienced by individuals or groups because of a devalued individual (i.e., stigmatized) attribute or group identity" (Potter, Brondolo, & Smyth, 2017: p. 1). Prejudice can be overt or subtle, and explicit or implicit (Gaertner & Dovidio, 2000). Some people can behave in a discriminatory fashion without being prejudiced (Carr, Dweck, & Pauker, 2012), and others do not discriminate but have prejudice (Son Hing, Chung-Yan, Hamilton, & Zanna, 2008; Umphress, Simmons, Boswell, & Triana, 2008). Prejudice and discrimination are a complex configuration of motivation, cognition, and behavior. Some people have an orientation, social dominance, which leads to active enforcement of social hierarchy, seeks to keep some groups down, and fuels both prejudice and discrimination (Hodson et al., 2010; Hodson & MacInnis, 2016). Often prejudice is directed towards groups in society who have low social status or who are stigmatized (Crandall, 1994; Goffman, 1963). Jones and colleagues' (2017) meta-analysis uncovered that overt and subtle discrimination had negative effects on mental and physical health, from substance abuse, to low cardiovascular health, to depression, to low self-esteem.

Humor can mask prejudice, reinforce discrimination and oppression, provide a vehicle for the expression of prejudice, and influence norms so that prejudiced individuals will demonstrate more discriminatory behavior. Humor can reflect prejudice or actively seek to assert hierarchy and delegitimize outgroups (Hodson & MacInnis, 2016). Disparaging humor allows people to make fun of other groups and target them for devaluation. So humor is very much linked to initiating, maintaining, and perpetuating prejudice.

Societal norms in many countries have moved towards egalitarian values and often do not sanction prejudice and discrimination. However, the societal movement towards egalitarian goals and human rights is not yet universal, nor is it a linear line, nor does it apply equally to all groups. For example, in some countries there have been reversals in basic human rights for LGBTQ+ people and an increase in criminalization (ILGA, 2019). Within most groups, countries, and cultures, there exists some groups towards which it is "ok" to harbor prejudice (West & Hewstone, 2012). When certain prejudices are "allowed" in the wider society, they can wreak destruction in an organization if these biases are imported into work relationships. "Allowable" prejudices can be imported through humor.

However, when norms are in place that do not condone prejudice, and direct prejudiced beliefs cannot be openly vocalized, then jokes and humor can be the perfect cover for expressing and encouraging negative attitudes towards targeted groups. For example, in the United States or the United Kingdom, to be openly racist is not only against social norms, but to discriminate based on race is also against the law. Even with egalitarian norms, prejudice does not disappear but instead reappears in other subtler forms. These subtler forms have been shown to be potentially even more damaging than overt displays of discrimination (Jones et al., 2016, 2017). Next are a few examples of research and theories that link prejudice and humor. These examples are not meant to be exhaustive, but to illustrate how humor can facilitate, transmit, or put forward a prejudiced agenda.

In organizations there are people who actually have a prejudice motivation, which goes beyond mere negative outgroup attitudes and is related to their social dominance orientation. Research by Hodson and colleagues found empirical evidence for cavalier humor beliefs (CHB), a playful, accepting, and relaxed approach to humor that discounts how humor can damage others. CHB is a "hierarchy enhancing legitimatizing myth" (Hodson et al., 2010, p. 660). They found that social dominance orientation predicted positive reactions to low-status outgroup jokes, and this was mediated through CHB. CHB mixes both positive and negative humor aspects and powerfully justifies derogatory humor. Intergroup humor can be simply playful or it can be a way to assert dominance or express bias against another group. This research shows that humor can allow prejudice to flower and strengthen unequal relations between groups. It also illustrates that people who are motivated to keep outgroups down use humor to do this. The CHB legitimizes those high on prejudice and can shape group norms about what is acceptable. Humor, often by its very nature, is ambiguous—and these situations can be fertile ground for expression of subtle bias or direct bias presented in an equivocal way. Humor can help to maintain the status quo of inequality. By making light of derogatory humor, people can become more accepting of prejudiced behavior.

People who have prejudice can also become more extreme in their behavior. Research has shown that sexist men exposed to sexist jokes or comedy, as opposed to just sexist statements or neutral jokes, reported greater rape proclivity (Thomae & Viki, 2013), and anti-Muslim jokes increased prejudice against Muslim people (Ford, Woodzicka, Triplett, Kochersberger, & Holden, 2014).

Jokes can prime stereotypes, but they do more than merely prime, they change norms and behavior (Ford, Woodzicka, Petit, Richardson, & Lappi, 2015). Behavior of the target of the jokes can also change. Experiments conducted by Ford and colleagues showed that sexist jokes affected women's self-objectification (seeing themselves as a social objects based on appearance), and these women reported more body surveillance (Ford et al., 2015). Basically, as women spend more time focused on "seeing and monitoring" themselves, they spend less time or have fewer cognitive resources to use for the tasks at hand. Jokes, beyond just sexist statements, increase these negative processes for women (Ford et al., 2015).

In 2004, Ford and Ferguson introduced the prejudiced norm theory, which addresses specifically the link between humor and prejudice. The theory outlines how derogatory humor directed at specific groups actually affects the tolerance of discrimination against members of these groups. They argue that a normative climate develops that increases tolerance for discrimination (Ford & Ferguson, 2004). Depending on the type of humor employed and by whom and to whom it is targeted, it can affect people's tolerance for prejudice and discrimination against these targeted groups (Ford et al., 2014). In work done by Ford and colleagues, they found the "prejudice releasing effect" of disparaging humor nurtures discrimination against some groups but not others and is not a release but actually produces more prejudice (Ford, Teeter, Richardson, & Woodzicka, 2017). Prejudice norm theory (Ford & Ferguson, 2004) postulates that a normative climate of tolerance of discrimination is created when people use denigrating humor. The norm established in a group affects those high in prejudice and leads to more acceptance of discrimination.

Disparagement humor is detrimental to intergroup relations (Hodson & MacInnis, 2016) and individuals (Ford et al., 2015). Humor not only reflects prejudice but also can lead to subtle and overt discrimination; it can negatively affect the target and leads to others becoming more tolerant of prejudice. The potentially damaging effects of humor are especially relevant for diverse organizations, in which people from different groups are represented and status differences abound.

What Is a Leader to Do?

A leader's role in a diverse organization is to create inclusion (Nembhard & Edmondson, 2006; Mitchell et al., 2015; Shore et al., 2011; Shore et al., 2018; Randel et al., 2018; Chung et al., 2019; Randel, Dean, Ehrhart, Chung, & Shore, 2016; Nishii & Mayer, 2009; Nishii, 2013; Chrobot-Mason, Ruderman, & Nishii, 2013). Inclusion entails ensuring that everyone is able to participate in decision-making, contribute fully to the work and organization, is treated fairly, is respected, and is seen (Mor Barak, 2014; Shore et al., 2018). Inclusive leadership is about making people feel they belong and that they are unique at the same time (Ely & Thomas, 2001; Randel et al., 2018; Shore et al., 2011). Shore et al. (2011, p. 1265) define inclusion as "the degree to which an employee perceives that he or she is an esteemed member of the work group through experiencing treatment that satisfies his or her needs for belongingness and uniqueness." In Nishii's (2013) research, she defines an inclusive environment as one that eliminates relational sources of bias.

With inclusive leadership, the deleterious effects of intergroup status differences can be overcome (Mitchell et al., 2015; Nembhard & Edmondson, 2006), and historical marginalization can be addressed and reduced (Chrobot-Mason et al., 2013; Ely & Thomas, 2001; Nishii, 2013). Shore and colleagues outline recommendations for inclusive organizations, based on Higgins's regulatory fit model (Higgins, 1998), in which managers and leaders need to have both a prevention and a promotion orientation (Shore et al., 2018). Prevention requires managing harassment and discrimination and the management of microinequities and subtle discrimination (Shore et al., 2018). I argue that humor is central here. For its promotion, orientation managers need to ensure psychological safety and use humor that creates belonging. I will use this broad framework to understand the role of humor for inclusive leaders.

First, in order to create workplaces where people feel they belong, leaders must prevent aggressive humor, which can damage individuals who are members of historically marginalized social identity groups (such as women, people of color, people with disabilities, etc.) and create group divisions. Humor can be harmful when it points to group differences in organization, reinforces status difference between groups, or promotes negative stereotypes. Intergroup theories address how intergroup differences can lead to ingroup favoritism, outgroup derogation, and stereotyping (Hewstone, Rubin, & Willis, 2002). Making jokes, no matter how innocuous, about for example, gender, age, or religion will make these group differences salient. This can inhibit people with these backgrounds from feeling a sense of belonging by bringing into question how supported they are by their group and whether justice and equity is being promoted. Ridgeway's status characteristics theory postulates that that social identity differences between groups and their members are only significant in organizational life when they are correlated with status rankings and access to resources commensurate with historical inequalities (Ridgeway, 1991, 2014). Leaders need to prevent humor that reinforces these status differences.

Directly dehumanizing and disparaging humor, or even humor that supports the current status quo of social structures which maintains marginalization and lower status for certain identity groups (Hodson & MacInnis, 2016), must be barred in organizations. This humor promotes exclusion and sends signals of devaluing different others for their uniqueness. Gallegos argues convincingly the need for leaders to go beyond simply the soft skills of caring and compassion; they need to have courage and call out incidents of structural inequity. This can be more challenging when discrimination is subtle and aggressive humor is presented as merely a joke. CHB must also not be allowed to take root within work groups, as this leads to the proliferation of disparaging humor. Gallegos emphasizes the negative impact of subtler versions of discrimination and microaggressions and asserts that leaders must explicitly outline the rules and limits for acceptable behavior (Gallegos, 2014). To create a culture of inclusion, leaders must not shy away from being politically correct (PC). In fact, being PC has been shown to lead to more creativity in mixed-sex groups (Goncalo et al., 2015). Goncalo and colleagues found that implementing a PC norm in mixed-sex groups promoted gender equality by enabling these groups to exchange information and share more freely (Goncalo et al., 2015). To move towards inclusive organization and leadership, it is essential that leaders prevent humor from being aggressive or divisive.

So how can humor promote inclusive leadership? Leaders and managers must also promote the appropriate norms by being a role model and demonstrating affiliative constructive humor. Affiliative humor has as its goal to enhance one's relationship with others and often includes witty banter and making jokes about everyday issues, not making jokes about different groups of people or putting others down. Using nonhostile humor and getting people to laugh together actively stimulates feelings of belonging. Affiliative humor is the opposite of aggressive humor, which uses sarcasm, teasing ridicule, and disparagement (Martin et al., 2003).

To promote inclusion, leaders need to ensure psychological safety (Nembhard & Edmondson, 2006; Shore et al., 2018). Psychological safety is "a shared belief that the team is safe for interpersonal risk taking" (Edmondson, 1999, p. 354). Psychological safety has been linked to team learning and inclusive leadership. Psychological safety reduces the advantages that people with more status have, such as more voice and influence. To ensure psychological safety, leaders must ensure that humor does not contribute to status differences that impede the free flow of information and allow all to contribute.

Humor for inclusion links most strongly to belonging. To create an inclusive environment, it is critical that the leader prevent hostile humor directed at groups and promote affiliative humor aimed at everyday life and witticisms. Using benign violation theory, it is important to remember that the violation of norms about prejudice is never benign. Kant and Norman recommend that BVT examine possible power asymmetries between two parties and how asymmetries might influence the social distance between the joke-teller and joke-listener (Kant & Norman, 2019). One rule of thumb here is to understand that intergroup humor is harmful, and in diverse organizations, it is particularly harmful.

Concluding Remarks

Leaders and managers act as role models, norm setters, and sanction givers. When implementing diversity practices and creating an inclusive environment, leaders are pivotal. They shape the meaning of and at work.

> Leaders verbally articulate the intended meanings and expectations, role model desired behaviors, reinforce preferred behaviors, and assess followers' interpretations of the provided meanings so that further adjustments can be made in the meaning-making process, that cohesive climate perceptions that drive a strong HR system will ensue.
> *(Nishii & Paluch, 2018, p. 319)*

As Hodson and MacInnis (2016, p. 63) state, "passing jokes off as 'just' jokes can have serious and negative intergroup consequences." As Wijewardena et al. (2017, p. 1316) state, "humor is an event that managers must responsibly manage in order to produce positive emotional experiences for employees." So leaders need to prevent the negative and aggressive type of humor through rules, guidelines, and examples.

The overall goal should be for leaders to create environments where people from different social groups feel a sense of belonging and uniqueness. It should be an environment that radiates safety and equality and be free from overt and subtle discrimination. This demands a strong leader to shape the norms and foster a playful, kind, and funny work environment. Are you joking? No, the path to inclusion is filled with laughter, kind laughter. A critical element for inclusive leadership in practice is to keep the laughter kind and not allow derogatory humor or jokes about groups.

References

Alexander, R. D. (1986). Ostracism and indirect reciprocity: The reproductive significance of humor. *Ethology & Sociobiology*, 7(3–4), 253–270. doi:10.1016/0162-3095(86)90052-X

Allport, G. (1954). *The nature of prejudice*. Reading, MA: Addison-Wesley Pub. Co.

Avolio, B. J., Howell, J. M., & Sosik, J. J. (1999). A funny thing happened on the way to the bottom line: Humor as a moderator of leadership style effects. *Academy of Management Journal*, 42, 219–227.

Carr, P. B., Dweck, C. S., & Pauker, K. (2012). "Prejudiced" behavior without prejudice? Beliefs about the malleability of prejudice affect interracial interactions. *Journal of Personality & Social Psychology*, 103, 452–471.

Chrobot-Mason, D., Ruderman, M. N., & Nishii, L. H. (2013). Leadership in a diverse workplace. In Q. M. Roberson (Ed.), *The Oxford handbook of diversity and work* (pp. 15–340). Oxford: Oxford University Press.

Chung, B. G., Ehrhart, K. H., Shore, L. M., Randel, A. E., Dean, M. A., & Kedharnath, U. (2019). Work group inclusion: Test of a scale and model. *Group & Organization Management*. doi:10.1177/1059601119839858

Cooper, C. D., Kong, D. T., & Crossley, C. D. (2018). Leader humor as an interpersonal resource: Integrating three theoretical perspectives. *Academy of Management Journal*, 61, 769–796.

Cooper, C. D., & Sosik, J. J. (2012). Humor. In K. S. Cameron & G. M. Spreitzer (Eds.), *The Oxford handbook of positive organizational scholarship* (pp. 474–489). New York, NY: Oxford University Press.

Crandall, C. S. (1994). Prejudice against fat people: Ideology and self-interest. *Journal of Personality and Social Psychology*, 66, 882–894.

Decker, W. H., & Rotondo, D. M. (2001). Relationships among gender, type of humor, and perceived leader effectiveness. *Journal of Managerial Issues*, 13, 450–465.

Edmondson, A. (1999). Psychological safety and learning behavior in work teams. *Administrative Science Quarterly*, 44, 350–383.

Ely, R. J., & Thomas, D. A. (2001). Cultural diversity perspectives on work group processes and outcomes. *Administrative Science Quarterly*, 46, 229–273.

Ford, T. E., & Ferguson, M. A. (2004). Social consequences of disparagement humor: A prejudiced norm theory. *Personality & Social Psychology Review (Lawrence Erlbaum Associates)*, 8, 79–94.

Ford, T. E., Teeter, S. R., Richardson, K., & Woodzicka, J. A. (2017). Putting the brakes on prejudice rebound effects: An ironic effect of disparagement humor. *Journal of Social Psychology*, 157, 458–473.

Ford, T. E., Woodzicka, J. A., Petit, W. E., Richardson, K., & Lappi, S. K. (2015). Sexist humor as a trigger of state self-objectification in women. *Humor: International Journal of Humor Research*, 28, 253–269.

Ford, T. E., Woodzicka, J. A., Triplett, S. R., Kochersberger, A. O., & Holden, C. J. (2014). Not all groups are equal: Differential vulnerability of social groups to the prejudice-releasing effects of disparagement humor. *Group Processes & Intergroup Relations*, 17, 178–199.

Gaertner, S. L., & Dovidio, J. F. (2000). The aversive form of racism. In *Stereotypes and prejudice: Essential readings* (pp. 289–304). New York, NY: Psychology Press.

Gallegos, P. V. (2014). The work of inclusive leadership. In B. Ferdman & B. Deane (Eds.), *Diversity at work: The practice of inclusion* (pp. 177–202). San Francisco, CA: Jossey-Bass.

Goffman, E. (1963). *Stigma: Notes on the management of spoiled identity*, New York, NY: Simon & Schuster Inc.

Goncalo, J. A., Chatman, J. A., Duguid, M. M., & Kennedy, J. A. (2015). Creativity from constraint? How the political correctness norm influences creativity in mixed-sex work groups. *Administrative Science Quarterly*, 60, 1–30.

Gray, J. A., & Ford, T. E. (2013). The role of social context in the interpretation of sexist humor. *Humor: International Journal of Humor Research*, 26, 277–293.

Hewstone, M., Rubin, M., & Willis, H. (2002). Intergroup bias. *Annual Review of Psychology*, 53, 575.

Higgins, E. T. (1998). Promotion and prevention: Regulatory focus as a motivational principle. In P. Z. Mark (Ed.), *Advances in experimental social psychology* (pp. 1–46). New York, NY: Academic Press.

Hodson, G., & MacInnis, C. C. (2016). Derogating humor as a delegitimization strategy in intergroup contexts. *Translational Issues in Psychological Science, 2*, 63–74.

Hodson, G., Rush, J., & MacInnis, C. C. (2010). A joke is just a joke (except when it isn't): Cavalier humor beliefs facilitate the expression of group dominance motives. *Journal of Personality and Social Psychology, 99*, 660–682.

Huo, Y., Lam, W., & Chen, Z. (2012). Am I the only one this supervisor is laughing at? Effects of aggressive humor on employee strain and addictive behaviors. *Personnel Psychology, 65*, 859–885.

ILGA. (2019). *International Lesbian, gay, bisexual, trans and intersex association*. Retrieved December 2019, from https://Ilga.Org/Ilga-Map-Sexual-Orientation-Laws-2019

Jones, K. P., Peddie, C. I., Gilrane, V. L., King, E. B., & Gray, A. L. (2016). Not so subtle: A meta-analytic investigation of the correlates of subtle and overt discrimination. *Journal of Management, 42*, 1588–1613.

Jones, K. P., Arena, D. F., Nittrouer, C. L., Alonso, N. M., & Lindsey, A. P. (2017). Subtle discrimination in the workplace: A vicious cycle. *Industrial and Organizational Psychology: Perspectives on Science and Practice, 10*, 51–76.

Kong, D. T., Cooper, C. D., & Sosik, J. J. (2019). The state of research on leader humor. *Organizational Psychology Review, 9*, 3–40.

Kant, L., & Norman, E. (2019). You must be joking! Benign violations, power asymmetry, and humor in a broader social context. *Frontiers in Psychology, 10*, 1380.

Lehmann-Willenbrock, N., & Allen, J. A. (2014). How fun are your meetings? Investigating the relationship between humor patterns in team interactions and team performance. *Journal of Applied Psychology, 99*, 1278–1287.

Martin, R. A., & Ford, T. (2018). *The psychology of humor: An integrative approach*. New York, NY: Academic Press.

Martin, R. A., Puhlik-Doris, P., Larsen, G., Gray, J., & Weir, K. (2003). Individual differences in uses of humor and their relation to psychological well-being: Development of the humor styles questionnaire. *Journal of Research in Personality, 37*, 48–75.

McGraw, A. P., & Warren, C. (2010). Benign violations: Making immoral behavior funny. *Psychological Science (0956-7976), 21*, 1141–1149.

Mesmer-Magnus, J., Glew, D. J., & Chockalingam, V. (2012). A meta-analysis of positive humor in the workplace. *Journal of Managerial Psychology, 27*, 155–190.

Mitchell, R., Boyle, B., Parker, V., Giles, M., Chiang, V., & Joyce, P. (2015). Managing inclusiveness and diversity in teams: How leader inclusiveness affects performance through status and team identity. *Human Resource Management, 54*, 217–239.

Mor Barak, M. E. (2014). *Managing diversity: Toward a globally inclusive workplace*. Thousand Oaks: Sage.

Nembhard, I. M., & Edmondson, A. C. (2006). Making it safe: The effects of leader inclusiveness and professional status on psychological safety and improvement efforts in health care teams. *Journal of Organizational Behavior, 27*, 941–966.

Nishii, L. H. (2013). The benefits of climate for inclusion for gender-diverse groups. *Academy of Management Journal, 56*, 1754–1774.

Nishii, L. H., & Mayer, D. M. (2009). Do inclusive leaders help to reduce turnover in diverse groups? The moderating role of leader-member exchange in the diversity to turnover relationship. *Journal of Applied Psychology, 94*, 1412–1426.

Nishii, L. H., & Paluch, R. M. (2018). Leaders as HR sensegivers: Four HR implementation behaviors that create strong HR systems. *Human Resource Management Review, 28*, 319–323.

Potter, L. N., Brondolo, E., & Smyth, J. M. (2017, September 14). Biopsychosocial correlates of discrimination in daily life: A review. *Stigma and Health*. Advance online publication. http://dx.doi.org/10.1037/sah0000012

Randel, A. E., Dean, M. A., Ehrhart, K. H., Chung, B., & Shore, L. (2016). Leader inclusiveness, psychological diversity climate, and helping behaviors. *Journal of Managerial Psychology, 31*, 216–234.

Randel, A. E., Galvin, B. M., Shore, L. M. Ehrhart, K. H., Chung, B. G., Dean, M. A., & Kedharnath, U. (2018). Inclusive leadership: Realizing positive outcomes through belongingness and being valued for uniqueness. *Human Resource Management Review, 28*, 190–203.

Ridgeway, C. (1991). The social construction of status value: Gender and other nominal characteristics. *Social Forces, 70*, 367–386.

Ridgeway, C. L. (2014). Why status matters for inequality. *American Sociological Review, 79*, 1–16.

Shore, L. M., Cleveland, J. N., & Sanchez, D. (2018). Inclusive workplaces: A review and model. *Human Resource Management Review, 28*, 176–189.

Shore, L. M., Randel, A. E., Chung, B. G., Dean, M. A., Holcombe Ehrhart, K., & Singh, G. (2011). Inclusion and diversity in work groups: A review and model for future research. *Journal of Management, 37*, 1262–1289.

Son Hing, L. S., Chung-Yan, G. A., Hamilton, L. K., & Zanna, M. P. (2008). A two-dimensional model that employs explicit and implicit attitudes to characterize prejudice. *Journal of Personality and Social Psychology, 94*, 971–987.

Thomae, M., & Viki, G. T. (2013). Why did the woman cross the road? The effect of sexist humor on men's rape proclivity. *Journal of Social, Evolutionary, and Cultural Psychology, 7*, 250–269.

Umphress, E. E., Simmons, A. L., Boswell, W. R., & Triana, M. (2008). Managing discrimination in selection: The influence of directives from an authority and social dominance orientation. *Journal of Applied Psychology, 93*, 982–993.

de Waal, F. (2019). *Mama's last hug: Animal emotions and what they tell us about ourselves*. New York: WW Norton & Company.

West, K., & Hewstone, M. (2012). Relatively socially acceptable prejudice within and between societies. *Journal of Community & Applied Social Psychology, 22*(3), 269–282. doi:10.1002/casp.1112

Wijewardena, N., Härtel, C. E. J., & Samaratunge, R. (2017). Using humor and boosting emotions: An affect-based study of managerial humor, employees' emotions and psychological capital. *Human Relations, 70*, 1316–1341.

Yam, K. C., Christian, M. S., Wei, W., Liao, Z., & Nai, J. (2018). The mixed blessing of leader sense of humor: Examining costs and benefits. *Academy of Management Journal, 61*, 348–369.

27
HUMILITY, COMPASSION, AND INCLUSIVE LEADERSHIP

Elliott Tyler Kruse

Introduction

Inclusion requires seeing the value of others, including those of different backgrounds. In turn, seeing the value of others is easier when you do not center the world on yourself. It is easier when you can see the strengths of others in terms of potential contributions rather than threats. It is easier when you recognize their experiences as part of a common human experience and any suffering caused by exclusion they experience as worthy of concern. Humility and compassion are two prosocial qualities marked by these perspectives and beliefs and, as such, may be primary antecedents of inclusive leadership (Randel et al., 2018).

In this chapter, I seek to develop the relationship between these three constructs. Notably, in it, I expand on the framework suggested by Randel et al. (2018) by elaborating on the relationship between humility and inclusive leadership and articulating how compassion may act as a key third factor in it. In particular, I propose that compassion can motivate inclusive leadership while humility can orient it, acting as the engine and the steering wheel of this leadership style. I argue that these two prosocial qualities are mutually dependent constructs in the sense that they solve problems specific to the other, and their joined functioning can guide inclusive leadership past pitfalls that could undermine its efficacy.

For the purposes of this chapter, I will follow the definition of inclusive leadership posed by Randel et al. (2018, p. 191), that it is "a set of leader behaviors that are focused on facilitating group members feeling part of the group (belongingness) and retaining their sense of individuality (uniqueness) while contributing to group processes and outcomes." Per this conception, the tension between belongingness and uniqueness is the conceptual heart of inclusive leadership and a core paradox that humility and compassion can help leaders navigate.

Defining Humility

Humility is a relatively new construct in the psychological literature, and yet research on it has grown rapidly recently (McElroy-Heltzel, Davis, DeBlaere, Jr, & Hook, 2019). Perhaps unsurprisingly, then, a single consensus definition of humility does not yet exist. Fully representing the scope of this conversation is beyond the limits of this chapter; for recent reviews on the topic, please consult Kruse (2019), McElroy-Heltzel et al. (2019), or Nielsen and Marrone (2018).

Lacking a single unified definition, humility is often then defined instead by the qualities that accompany it (Chancellor & Lyubomirsky, 2013). The most commonly cited framework posits that the humble are marked by (1) an accurate assessment of the self; (2) acknowledgment of one's own limitations and imperfections; (3) openness to new ideas and contradictory information; (4) keeping one's place in the world in perspective; (5) a lack of focus on the self; and (6) an appreciation of the value of all things (Tangney, 2000). Other researchers at times add other qualities, such as an egalitarian worldview (Chancellor & Lyubomirsky, 2013; Kruse, Chancellor, & Lyubomirsky, 2017), or condense the list to two components, such as low self-focus and high other-focus (Wright, Nadelhoffer, Ross, & Sinnott-Armstrong, 2018) or self-abasing and appreciative humility (Weidman, Cheng, & Tracy, 2018).

Notably, however, defining humility by its features may be an accurate approach. Normally, defining a psychological construct in this way would be unsatisfactory. In the case of humility, though, this approach may be uniquely appropriate, because one of its key functions may be to facilitate other virtues (Lavelock et al., 2017); it has even been called, perhaps ironically, a "master virtue." If true, then evidence of a broad array of other prosocial qualities would be essential to its identity and therefore definition.

We can also identify humility by that which it is not. In particular, humility is often confused with several closely related constructs. First, modesty is tightly intertwined and frequently co-occurs with it (Davis, McElroy, et al., 2016; Hilbig, Heydasch, & Zettler, 2014). However, the two constructs are separable in specific, theoretically relevant situations (Kruse et al., 2017; Shi, Sedikides, Cai, Liu, & Yang, 2017).

Second, humility is at times confused with low self-esteem. However, self-esteem rarely correlates either positively or negatively with humility (e.g., Kesebir, 2014; Kruse et al., 2017; Rowatt et al., 2006; Tong et al., 2016; cf. Weidman et al., 2018). Going further, experimentally inducing humility does not affect self-esteem (Tong et al., 2016).

Third, narcissism is often seen as the opposite pole of humility. Yet, at times, they may co-occur to influence leadership (Owens, Wallace, & Waldman, 2015), implying that they are not the same construct. In all three cases, the constructs are theoretically close to humility but empirically distinguishable.

For the purposes of this chapter, given the lack of a single consensus definition, I will adopt the view that humility is a self-conception that something greater than the self exists (Morris, Brotheridge, & Urbanski, 2005; Ou et al., 2014). This definition is relatively neutral and is echoed in several other definitions (Kruse et al., 2017; Weidman et al., 2018; Wright et al., 2018). It includes the elements of low self-focus and high other-focus, without necessarily implying a sense of self-denigration. As such, for the current purposes, this definition can guide theorizing in this chapter without inappropriately limiting it.

Humility and Inclusive Leadership

Although cultural beliefs differ (Exline & Geyer, 2004; Xu, Xu, Anderson, & Caldwell, 2019), humility is likely a strength for leaders (Vera & Rodriguez-Lopez, 2004), as it demonstrates a variety of relevant positive relationships and outcomes. For example, humility predicts relatively greater well-being (Kruse et al., 2017), which can buffer against stress. In particular, it appears to exist in an upward spiral with gratitude (Kruse, Chancellor, Ruberton, & Lyubomirsky, 2014), an other-directed emotion which can help build relationships (Bartlett, Condon, Cruz, Baumann, & Desteno, 2012). Experimentally inducing humility increases self-control and perseverance at difficult tasks (Tong et al., 2016). Humility even predicts greater creative problem solving, in contrast to narcissism, which predicts greater confidence in one's creativity but not actual performance (Kruse et al., 2017). Lastly, as mentioned, humility does not correlate with self-esteem, so contrary to some lay assumptions about humility, these potential benefits do not come at the cost of the leader's sense of confidence. To the degree that leaders must contend with stress, build bonds, endure at difficult tasks, and find creative solutions, humility is likely an asset for leaders.

Looking beyond leadership in general, humility may be a primary antecedent of inclusive leadership in particular. Randel et al. (2018) suggested that humility can facilitate inclusive leadership because it helps leaders see the needs of others, but also appreciate their unique strengths, not be threatened by differences, and therefore be better able to integrate member uniqueness in the group. In line with this framework, humility does predict empathy and altruism (e.g., Kruse et al., 2017), and so likely they are relatively more motivated to see others' needs. The intellectually humble are more open and less partisan in their assessments, without sacrificing their values, making it easier to see the value of ideologically different perspectives (Davis, Rice, et al., 2016; Krumrei-Mancuso, Haggard, LaBouff, & Rowatt, 2019; Leary et al., 2017). In line with Randel et al. (2018), tentative evidence suggests that humility is an antecedent of inclusive leadership.

However, from the current theory of humility, it is difficult to see how humility may be a *direct cause* of inclusive leadership. Revisiting the features that mark humility proposed by Tangney (2000), the verbs are comparatively passive or reflexive. The humble acknowledge limitations, are open to new ideas, keep their greatness in perspective, do not focus on themselves, and appreciate others' value. All of the features focus on perspective, feelings, and cognitive states. None of them are particularly invigorated behaviors; they are internal states, not motivated actions. Humility appears to often change the context for other behaviors but by itself does not drive much visible behavior. In contrast, inclusive leadership involves proactively seeking out opportunities for inclusion (Randel et al., 2018); it requires action. As such, a theoretical framework of these two constructs seems to need something to bridge the gap between perspective and behavior.

Compassion

Compassion is an other-oriented emotion marked by a concern for the needs and suffering of others (Goetz, Keltner, & Simon-Thomas, 2010). Compassion elicits prosocial motivation to address the pain that initiated it (Batson, 1987; Bierhoff, 2005). For example, empathic concern drives people to seek benefit of others without necessarily the expectation of reward in return (e.g., Omoto, Malsch, & Barraza, 2009). In particular, it can involve the expenditure of resources to manage the source of pain (Dutton, Worline, Frost, & Lilius, 2006). Failing to do so, to act to alleviate the witnessed pain, may even impose an "emotional tax" in the form of guilt (Elster, 1998).

Kanov et al. (2004) propose that compassion consists of three interlocking subprocesses, in which a person having a compassionate response first notices the suffering of another, experiences empathic concern for that person, and then is motivated to act to alleviate that pain. Strauss et al. (2016) echo this framework but add that a person might also recognize the others' suffering as part of the universal human experience and must be able to tolerate the uncomfortable feelings of empathic concern, rather than avoid them. In both frameworks, though, compassion leads to prosocial motivation.

In turn, this motivation is usually directed at a specific recipient. Notably, individual targets vary to the degree that they may be perceived as worthy of compassion. For example, people seen as altruistic and cooperative are more likely to be seen as worthy recipients (Atkins & Parker, 2012), and less so those that are seen to have brought the problem on themselves (Clark, 1987).

In particular, Dutton, Workman, and Hardin (2014) suggests three "features of the relational context" that influence compassion: similarity, closeness, and social power. For example, humans at times fail to perceive and attend to suffering experienced by people from different social groups from them (e.g., Batson & Ahmad, 2009). Those that people perceive to be similar to them, and to be socially close to them, are more likely to evoke compassion. Power, however, has a complex relationship with compassion that we will explore later.

Taken together, compassion is a prosocial emotion that motivates behavior. It is active, discrete, and targeted at specific recipients. It inspires people to help others even at their own cost and can even impose emotional punishments if people do not follow through on the motivation.

Compassion and Inclusive Leadership

Compassion may be an asset to leadership in general. Compassion reinforces connections between people (Frost, Dutton, Worline, & Wilson, 2000; Powley, 2009), likely because it builds trust (Dutton, Lilius, & Kanov, 2007). To the degree that a leader's legitimacy and social influence is partially based on the trust of their team members, compassion may serve to consolidate support for the leader. Witnessing compassionate acts may also induce feelings of elevation—an uplifted sense of moral inspiration (Haidt, 2003)—in team members and elicit other prosocial behaviors that benefit the organization and its culture.

Compassion may also be an asset to inclusive leadership in particular. Miller, Grimes, McMullen, and Vogus (2012) argue that compassion can increase integrative thinking and, in particular, greater cognitive flexibility (e.g., Grant & Berry, 2011) and attention to others' perspectives (e.g., De Dreu, Koole, & Steinel, 2000). It can enhance commitment to moral causes (Shamir, 1990; Thompson & Bunderson, 2003) and communities (Grant, 2007), as well as greater perseverance in the face of criticism (Meglino & Korsgaard, 2004). In other words, compassion may be an antecedent of inclusive leadership, because it helps leaders see team members' diverse strengths, understand their experiences, and find ways to integrate those factors into a coherent team. This effect may be especially potent when the leader has strong pro-diversity beliefs and perceives commitment to inclusion as a moral good (Randel et al., 2018).

However, compassion has drawbacks. One notable drawback is compassion fatigue (e.g., Figley, 2013), a form of burnout common in caregiving professions. If compassion motivates people to invest their personal resources to alleviate someone else's suffering, and a person is routinely called on to do this, they may eventually find their resources exhausted. Notably, some research suggests that it is not empathy itself that causes the fatigue, but the lack of resources and emotional support given to the empathizer (Coetzee & Laschinger, 2018). In other words, compassion itself may not be finite, but the resources it uses to act may be. To the degree that inclusive leadership is driven by compassion to alleviate the pain of exclusion, inclusive leaders may across time find themselves the victims of compassion fatigue.

Given this, one core problem of compassion is where to direct one's finite resources. Misapplying these resources may mean there is not enough to act on the suffering of those who most need it. For example, in the case of inclusive leadership, if a leader's resources go solely towards a person who was never at risk of being excluded, then marginalized team members may be bereft of needed support. In other words, mismanaged compassion may ultimately create more exclusion. For example, compassion going in only one direction can even create status differences and reinforce inequality (Clark, 1987). As such, while compassion may be a powerful antecedent of inclusive leadership, it also carries several pitfalls that may undermine inclusive leadership. In the next section, I will describe an affective phenomenon in which the misapplication of compassion can lead to greater exclusion and a failure of inclusive leadership.

Empathic Failures

Empathic failures occur when people experience no empathic concern in the face of another person's suffering, especially based on group membership (Cikara, Bruneau, & Saxe, 2011). In other words, empathic failures occur when a person has the opportunity to feel compassion but does not.

Some empathic failures are comparatively benign in origin, in the sense that they represent the difficulty of understanding experiences outside of those one has experienced. They are not the motivated rejection of others' pain, but rather the product of the intrinsically limited nature of cognition. Dutton et al. (2014, p. 290) notes that people

> vary in their familiarity with and knowledge about certain kinds of suffering. A focal actor's levels of knowledge and experience with the sufferer's situation are also likely to affect whether he/she notices the signs that someone is suffering, is able to take the sufferer's perspective (and impute meaning that prompts action), and acts compassionately.

For example, people tend to underestimate the intensity of social pain, the pain caused by exclusion, except for those who have experienced it (Nordgren, Banas, & MacDonald, 2011).

Although this lack of experience may not be intentionally malicious, it can still yield negative consequences. While people tend to respond empathetically to the emotional experiences of in-group members, they respond much less so to out-group members (Gutsell & Inzlicht, 2012). This disparity may be due to how we process the two kinds of information; the process by which we perceive the social pain of friends is more intimate and immediate, whereas that of strangers is more cognitive and 'mentalizing' (Meyer et al., 2013). In these intergroup empathy failures, people are not actively dismissing the pain of others; they are just less able to perceive and understand it, which ultimately impedes compassion.

However, other empathic failures are less benign. Cikara et al. (2011) identified the *intergroup empathy bias*, in which people not only feel less empathy towards individuals of other social groups (e.g., racial, religious, political), but even active enjoyment at their pain. Notably, this *'schadenfreude'* is not the result of a lack of empathy but rather by the presence of it. That is, empathic concern for the in-group can lead to endorsement of harm for the out-group (Bruneau, Cikara, & Saxe, 2017).

Other factors, such as a person's values, can shape this effect. People with antiegalitarian values, for example, are more likely to empathize with advantaged group members over disadvantaged ones (Lucas & Kteily, 2018). For people with these values, compassion does not lead them to aid the disempowered, but to actively support the empowered. However, inversely, for people with egalitarian values, the opposite pattern is true. They are more likely to respond to the suffering of the disadvantaged over the advantaged. Depending on one's values, compassion can be more or less susceptible to the intergroup empathy bias.

For individuals who belong to marginalized groups, who by definition are the out-group for an empowered in-group, the disparity caused by this bias can create a great deal of suffering. Even when people from marginalized groups are able to express their pain and have it be noticed, it is fully possible that a person from a different social group will witness it and find satisfaction in that pain, *because that person is being empathetic*. This response is not an example of clear sadism; it is compassion, but for someone else, that drives the cruelty.

Therefore, it is a tragic irony for inclusive leadership that empathic concern itself, one of the core subprocesses of compassion, can lead to suffering for marginalized groups. With this research in mind, indiscriminate calls for compassion in leadership may be inadvisable. In the next section, I will describe how humility may help guide compassion past empathic failures and, in particular, the intergroup empathy bias in inclusive leadership.

The Mutual Influence of Humility and Compassion

The effects of humility and compassion on inclusive leadership are likely intertwined. As discussed previously, compassion is an active emotion that motivates people to prosocial action and punishes them if they fail to take such action. Humility shapes the context in which other psychological phenomena function, to the point of being called a "master virtue" that regulates other prosocial qualities (Lavelock et al., 2017).

Furthermore, these two phenomena likely reinforce each other. For example, in one set of set studies, humility and gratitude, an other-directed positive emotion, existed in an upward spiral (Kruse et al., 2014). The experience of gratitude elicited humility, and this was mediated by the greater focus on others. In turn, people who were initially humble were more likely to experience gratitude after writing a heartfelt note of appreciation of someone else's influence in their life.

Compassion and humility may possess a similar relationship. In one direction, compassion is dependent on noticing the suffering of others (Kanov et al., 2004; Strauss et al., 2016), which may be even more difficult in workplaces where suffering may be comparatively faint and difficult to see (Dutton et al., 2014). Humility, with its relatively greater focus on others, sense of empathy, and altruism (e.g., Kruse et al., 2017), may predict greater facility at noticing others' suffering.

In turn, compassion directs one's attention outside of oneself, to the needs of others. As with gratitude, this effect of de-centering the self may itself be humbling. In addition, witnessing others' suffering may elicit a sense of shared humanity that makes the witness feel less alone in their own suffering, which in turn may be affirming (e.g., Neff, 2011). Taken together, humility and compassion are likely not just interrelated but mutually influencing, such that in general each may facilitate the other.

Humility and Compassion on Inclusive Leadership

In the context of inclusive leadership, each may depend on the other to accomplish their function. As previously described, humility is largely a passive or reflexive quality, marked more by different perspectives and beliefs rather than visible behavior. It can change the context for other psychological phenomena, but does not seem to directly act. To the degree that humble people have altruistic values, they need to experience prosocial emotions like compassion or gratitude to trigger behavior in order to act on those values. Compassion, on the other hand, can motivate behavior and yet at times may motivate behavior contrary to the goals of inclusive leaders. As described, compassion may fall victim to empathic failures and, in particular, the intergroup empathy bias. I propose that humility can help correct that bias.

Humility may serve to guide compassion past empathic failures via at least four pathways: other-focus, egalitarianism, open-mindedness, and power. First, the humble are identified by psychological characteristics that likely bolster compassionate responding. In particular, humility predicts relatively less focus on oneself and greater focus on others (Kruse et al., 2014; Wright et al., 2018). Additionally, humility positively predicts both altruistic values and empathic concern (Exline & Hill, 2012; Kruse et al., 2017). To the degree that compassion requires that one can notice others' pain and to care about that pain, then relatively greater attention to others and the value of their feelings should increase compassion. However, one notable caveat is that while this effect may help reduce empathic failures in general, it may not reduce the intergroup empathy bias. As previously outlined, this bias can be driven by in-group empathic concern. Indeed, from this perspective, the humble may be at *relatively greater* risk of the bias.

Looking directly at this bias, then, the humble are also marked by egalitarian beliefs. Humility correlates negatively with social dominance orientation, as strongly as it does with traditionally opposed constructs such as narcissism and pride (Kruse et al., 2017). The strength of this relationship may imply that egalitarian values are not incidental to humility but one of its core components. If egalitarian beliefs predict empathic support for the disadvantaged (Lucas & Kteily, 2018), and humility predicts these beliefs, then humility may help to direct compassion towards those who most need it—even when they are not in one's in-group. An additional follow-up study could also be informative, in which social advantage is contrasted with group status: will egalitarians prefer the disadvantaged even at the cost of their own in-group? What if their own in-group is the source of the disenfranchisement? The inverse of this relationship may also be true; if narcissists are more likely to be antiegalitarian, then they may be more likely to reserve their limited empathy only for the socially enfranchised.

Third, humility predicts relatively greater open-mindedness and willingness to understand other perspectives. In particular, intellectual humility predicts being more open, curious and tolerant of ambiguity and less dogmatic (Davis, Rice, et al., 2016; Krumrei-Mancuso et al., 2019; Leary et al., 2017). People who are comparatively more intellectually humble were less likely to claim knowledge they did not have (Krumrei-Mancuso et al., 2019). Otherwise stated, intellectual humility appears to predict a willingness to understand the limits of one's experience and perspective and a likelihood to listen to others.

Fourth, power is a particularly salient component here because the lack of it is a feature of being marginalized, and the presence of it is frequently a feature of being a leader. On one hand, power has been shown to reduce perspective taking and the ability to understand others' emotions (Galinsky, Magee, Inesi, & Gruenfeld, 2006). Power then may increase the likelihood of empathic failures. On the other, power has been shown to disinhibit goal-related behaviors, even prosocial goals (e.g., Grant & Mayer, 2009). Going further, the experience of power can actually increase empathic accuracy in people who are already motivated to be prosocial (Côté et al., 2011). To the degree that humility predicts other-focused, prosocial goals, then having power may have the surprising effect of making leaders more motivated and able to navigate the intergroup empathy bias.

Taken together, humility may be a novel intervention for the intergroup empathy bias. Interventions to reduce empathic failures are currently scarce, in part because empathy interventions often focus on general empathic concern, which may replicate this failure (Zaki & Cikara, 2015). Empathic failure interventions need to reduce the distance between in- and out-group focused empathy (Bruneau et al., 2017). Humility, as a "master virtue" that regulates other virtues, may be able to do just that.

Conclusion

Humility and compassion may be core antecedents of inclusive leadership. However, each has their limitation. Humility appears to work in the background, without directly motivating behavior. Compassion does seem to motivate prosocial behavior, but at the risk of directing one's resources away from people who need it. In a cruel irony, if inclusive leaders are motivated by empathic concern, they may find themselves victim to empathic failures that replicate historical inequality. Humility and compassion may then have mutually dependent influences on inclusive leadership, both driving it forward and guiding it past treacherous pitfalls.

References

Atkins, P.W., & Parker, S. K. (2012). Understanding individual compassion in organizations: The role of appraisals and psychological flexibility. *Academy of Management Review, 37*(4), 524–546.

Bartlett, M.Y., Condon, P., Cruz, J., Baumann, J., & Desteno, D. (2012). Gratitude: Prompting behaviours that build relationships. *Cognition & Emotion, 26*(1), 2–13.

Batson, C. D. (1987). Prosocial motivation: Is it ever truly altruistic? In *Advances in Experimental Social Psychology* (Vol. 20, pp. 65–122). Oxford: Elsevier.

Batson, C. D., & Ahmad, N.Y. (2009). Using empathy to improve intergroup attitudes and relations. *Social Issues and Policy Review, 3*(1), 141–177.

Bierhoff, H-W. (2005). *Prosocial behaviour*. New York, NY: Psychology Press.

Bruneau, E. G., Cikara, M., & Saxe, R. (2017). Parochial empathy predicts reduced altruism and the endorsement of passive harm. *Social Psychological and Personality Science, 8*(8), 934–942.

Chancellor, J., & Lyubomirsky, S. (2013). Humble beginnings: Current trends, state perspectives, and hallmarks of humility. *Social and Personality Psychology Compass, 7*(11), 819–833. https://doi.org/10.1111/spc3.12069

Cikara, M., Bruneau, E. G., & Saxe, R. R. (2011). Us and them: Intergroup failures of empathy. *Current Directions in Psychological Science, 20*(3), 149–153.
Clark, C. (1987). Sympathy biography and sympathy margin. *American Journal of Sociology, 93*(2), 290–321.
Coetzee, S. K., & Laschinger, H. K. (2018). Toward a comprehensive, theoretical model of compassion fatigue: An integrative literature review. *Nursing & Health Sciences, 20*(1), 4–15.
Côté, S., Kraus, M. W., Cheng, B. H., Oveis, C., Van der Löwe, I., Lian, H., & Keltner, D. (2011). Social power facilitates the effect of prosocial orientation on empathic accuracy. *Journal of Personality and Social Psychology, 101*(2), 217.
Davis, D. E., McElroy, S. E., Rice, K. G., Choe, E., Westbrook, C., Hook, J. N., . . . Worthington, L. W. (2016). Is modesty a subdomain of humility? *The Journal of Positive Psychology, 11*(4), 439–446. https://doi.org/10.1080/17439760.2015.1117130
Davis, D. E., Rice, K., McElroy, S., DeBlaere, C., Choe, E., Tongeren, D. R. V., & Hook, J. N. (2016). Distinguishing intellectual humility and general humility. *The Journal of Positive Psychology, 11*(3), 215–224. https://doi.org/10.1080/17439760.2015.1048818
De Dreu, C. K. W., Koole, S. L., & Steinel, W. (2000). Unfixing the fixed pie: A motivated information-processing approach to integrative negotiation. *Journal of Personality and Social Psychology, 79*(6), 975–987. https://doi.org/10.1037/0022-3514.79.6.975
Dutton, J. E., Lilius, J. M., & Kanov, J. M. (2007). The transformative potential of compassion at work. *Handbook of Transformative Cooperation: New Designs and Dynamics, 1*, 107–126.
Dutton, J. E., Workman, K. M., & Hardin, A. E. (2014). Compassion at work. *Annual Review of Organizational Psychology and Organizational Behavior, 1*(1), 277–304.
Dutton, J. E., Worline, M. C., Frost, P. J., & Lilius, J. (2006). Explaining compassion organizing. *Administrative Science Quarterly, 51*(1), 59–96.
Elster, J. (1998). Emotions and economic theory. *Journal of Economic Literature, 36*(1), 47–74.
Exline, J. J., & Geyer, A. L. (2004). Perceptions of humility: A preliminary study. *Self and Identity, 3*(2), 95–114. https://doi.org/10.1080/13576500342000077
Exline, J. J., & Hill, P. C. (2012). Humility: A consistent and robust predictor of generosity. *The Journal of Positive Psychology, 7*(3), 208–218. https://doi.org/10.1080/17439760.2012.671348
Figley, C. R. (2013). *Compassion fatigue: Coping with secondary traumatic stress disorder in those who treat the traumatized*. Abingdon-on-Thames, UK: Routledge.
Frost, P. J., Dutton, J. E., Worline, M. C., & Wilson, A. (2000). Narratives of compassion in organizations. *Emotion in Organizations, 2*, 25–45.
Galinsky, A. D., Magee, J. C., Inesi, M. E., & Gruenfeld, D. H. (2006). Power and perspectives not taken. *Psychological Science, 17*(12), 1068–1074.
Goetz, J. L., Keltner, D., & Simon-Thomas, E. (2010). Compassion: An evolutionary analysis and empirical review. *Psychological Bulletin, 136*(3), 351–374. https://doi.org/10.1037/a0018807
Grant, A. M. (2007). Relational job design and the motivation to make a prosocial difference. *Academy of Management Review, 32*(2), 393–417.
Grant, A. M., & Berry, J. W. (2011). The necessity of others is the mother of invention: Intrinsic and prosocial motivations, perspective taking, and creativity. *Academy of Management Journal, 54*(1), 73–96.
Grant, A. M., & Mayer, D. M. (2009). Good soldiers and good actors: Prosocial and impression management motives as interactive predictors of affiliative citizenship behaviors. *Journal of Applied Psychology, 94*(4), 900.
Gutsell, J. N., & Inzlicht, M. (2012). Intergroup differences in the sharing of emotive states: Neural evidence of an empathy gap. *Social Cognitive and Affective Neuroscience, 7*(5), 596–603. https://doi.org/10.1093/scan/nsr035
Haidt, J. (2003). The moral emotions. In R. J. Davidson, K. R. Scherer, & H. H. Goldsmith (Eds.), *Handbook of affective sciences* (pp. 852–870). Oxford: Oxford University Press.
Hilbig, B. E., Heydasch, T., & Zettler, I. (2014). To boast or not to boast: Testing the humility aspect of the honesty—Humility factor. *Personality and Individual Differences, 69*, 12–16. https://doi.org/10.1016/j.paid.2014.04.033
Kanov, J. M., Maitlis, S., Worline, M. C., Dutton, J. E., Frost, P. J., & Lilius, J. M. (2004). Compassion in organizational life. *American Behavioral Scientist, 47*(6), 808–827.
Kesebir, P. (2014). A quiet ego quiets death anxiety: Humility as an existential anxiety buffer. *Journal of Personality and Social Psychology, 106*(4), 610–623. https://doi.org/10.1037/a0035814
Krumrei-Mancuso, E. J., Haggard, M. C., LaBouff, J. P., & Rowatt, W. C. (2019). Links between intellectual humility and acquiring knowledge. *The Journal of Positive Psychology*, 1–16.
Kruse, E. (2019). Humility and social entrepreneurship. In J. Marques (Ed.), *Social entrepreneurship and corporate social responsibility*. New York, NY: Springer.

Kruse, E., Chancellor, J., & Lyubomirsky, S. (2017). State humility: Measurement, conceptual validation, and intrapersonal processes. *Self and Identity, 16*(4), 399–438. https://doi.org/10.1080/15298868.2016.1267662

Kruse, E., Chancellor, J., Ruberton, P. M., & Lyubomirsky, S. (2014). An upward spiral between gratitude and humility. *Social Psychological and Personality Science, 5*(7), 805–814. https://doi.org/10.1177/1948550614534700

Lavelock, C. R., Worthington, E. L., Griffin, B. J., Garthe, R. C., Elnasseh, A., Davis, D. E., & Hook, J. N. (2017). Still waters run deep: Humility as a master virtue. *Journal of Psychology and Theology, 45*(4), 286–303. https://doi.org/10.1177/009164711704500404

Leary, M. R., Diebels, K. J., Davisson, E. K., Jongman-Sereno, K. P., Isherwood, J. C., Raimi, K. T., ... Hoyle, R. H. (2017). Cognitive and interpersonal features of intellectual humility. *Personality and Social Psychology Bulletin, 43*(6), 793–813. https://doi.org/10.1177/0146167217697695

Lucas, B. J., & Kteily, N. S. (2018). (Anti-) egalitarianism differentially predicts empathy for members of advantaged versus disadvantaged groups. *Journal of Personality and Social Psychology, 114*(5), 665.

McElroy-Heltzel, S. E., Davis, D. E., DeBlaere, C. Jr., Worthington, L. W., & Hook, J. N. (2019). Embarrassment of riches in the measurement of humility: A critical review of 22 measures. *The Journal of Positive Psychology, 14*(3), 393–404. https://doi.org/10.1080/17439760.2018.1460686

Meglino, B. M., & Korsgaard, A. (2004). Considering rational self-interest as a disposition: Organizational implications of other orientation. *Journal of Applied Psychology, 89*(6), 946.

Meyer, M. L., Masten, C. L., Ma, Y., Wang, C., Shi, Z., Eisenberger, N. I., & Han, S. (2013). Empathy for the social suffering of friends and strangers recruits distinct patterns of brain activation. *Social Cognitive and Affective Neuroscience, 8*(4), 446–454. https://doi.org/10.1093/scan/nss019

Miller, T. L., Grimes, M. G., McMullen, J. S., & Vogus, T. J. (2012). Venturing for others with heart and head: How compassion encourages social entrepreneurship. *Academy of Management Review, 37*(4), 616–640.

Morris, J. A., Brotheridge, C. M., & Urbanski, J. C. (2005). Bringing humility to leadership: Antecedents and consequences of leader humility. *Human Relations, 58*(10), 1323–1350. https://doi.org/10.1177/0018726705059929

Neff, K. D. (2011). Self-compassion, self-esteem, and well-being. *Social and Personality Psychology Compass, 5*(1), 1–12.

Nielsen, R., & Marrone, J. A. (2018). Humility: Our current understanding of the construct and its role in organizations. *International Journal of Management Reviews, 20*(4), 805–824. https://doi.org/10.1111/ijmr.12160

Nordgren, L. F., Banas, K., & MacDonald, G. (2011). Empathy gaps for social pain: Why people underestimate the pain of social suffering. *Journal of Personality and Social Psychology, 100*(1), 120.

Omoto, A. M., Malsch, A. M., & Barraza, J. A. (2009). Compassionate acts: Motivations for and correlates of volunteerism among older adults. *The Science of Compassionate Love: Theory, Research, and Applications,* 257–282.

Ou, A. Y., Tsui, A. S., Kinicki, A. J., Waldman, D. A., Xiao, Z., & Song, L. J. (2014). Humble chief executive officers' connections to top management team integration and middle managers' responses. *Administrative Science Quarterly, 59*(1), 34–72. https://doi.org/10.1177/0001839213520131

Owens, B. P., Wallace, A. S., & Waldman, D. A. (2015). Leader narcissism and follower outcomes: The counterbalancing effect of leader humility. *Journal of Applied Psychology, 100*(4), 1203–1213. https://doi.org/10.1037/a0038698

Powley, E. H. (2009). Reclaiming resilience and safety: Resilience activation in the critical period of crisis. *Human Relations, 62*(9), 1289–1326.

Randel, A. E., Galvin, B. M., Shore, L. M., Ehrhart, K. H., Chung, B. G., Dean, M. A., & Kedharnath, U. (2018). Inclusive leadership: Realizing positive outcomes through belongingness and being valued for uniqueness. *Human Resource Management Review, 28*(2), 190–203.

Rowatt, W. C., Powers, C., Targhetta, V., Comer, J., Kennedy, S., & Labouff, J. (2006). Development and initial validation of an implicit measure of humility relative to arrogance. *The Journal of Positive Psychology, 1*(4), 198–211. https://doi.org/10.1080/17439760600885671

Shamir, B. (1990). Calculations, values, and identities: The sources of collectivistic work motivation. *Human Relations, 43*(4), 313–332.

Shi, Y., Sedikides, C., Cai, H., Liu, Y., & Yang, Z. (2017). Disowning the self: The cultural value of modesty can attenuate self-positivity. *The Quarterly Journal of Experimental Psychology, 70*(6), 1023–1032. https://doi.org/10.1080/17470218.2015.1099711

Strauss, C., Lever Taylor, B., Gu, J., Kuyken, W., Baer, R., Jones, F., & Cavanagh, K. (2016). What is compassion and how can we measure it? A review of definitions and measures. *Clinical Psychology Review, 47*, 15–27. https://doi.org/10.1016/j.cpr.2016.05.004

Tangney, J. P. (2000). Humility: Theoretical perspectives, empirical findings and directions for future research. *Journal of Social and Clinical Psychology, 19*(1), 70–82. https://doi.org/10.1521/jscp.2000.19.1.70

Thompson, J. A., & Bunderson, J. S. (2003). Violations of principle: Ideological currency in the psychological contract. *Academy of Management Review*, *28*(4), 571–586.

Tong, E. M. W., Tan, K. W. T., Chor, A. A. B., Koh, E. P. S., Lee, J. S. Y., & Tan, R. W. Y. (2016). Humility facilitates higher self-control. *Journal of Experimental Social Psychology*, *62*, 30–39. https://doi.org/10.1016/j.jesp.2015.09.008

Vera, D., & Rodriguez-Lopez, A. (2004). Strategic virtues: Humility as a source of competitive advantage. *Organizational Dynamics*, *33*(4), 393–408. https://doi.org/10.1016/j.orgdyn.2004.09.006

Weidman, A. C., Cheng, J. T., & Tracy, J. L. (2018). The psychological structure of humility. *Journal of Personality and Social Psychology*, *114*(1), 153–178. https://doi.org/10.1037/pspp0000112

Wright, J. C., Nadelhoffer, T., Ross, L. T., & Sinnott-Armstrong, W. (2018). Be it ever so humble: Proposing a dual-dimension account and measurement of humility. *Self and Identity*, *17*(1), 92–125. https://doi.org/10.1080/15298868.2017.1327454

Xu, F., Xu, B., Anderson, V., & Caldwell, C. (2019). Humility as enlightened leadership: A Chinese perspective. *Journal of Management Development*, *38*(3), 158–174.

Zaki, J., & Cikara, M. (2015). Addressing empathic failures. *Current Directions in Psychological Science*, *24*(6), 471–476.

28
AM I INCLUDED? LESSONS FROM LEADERSHIP RESEARCH IN AFRICA AND THE AFRICAN DIASPORA

Thomas Anyanje Senaji, Nicole S. Knight, Lemayon L. Melyoki, Bella L. Galperin, Terri R. Lituchy, and Betty Jane Punnett

Introduction

We start by exploring the inclusive leadership concept from the perspective of leadership effectiveness, which is the focus of the Leadership Effectiveness and Motivation in Africa and in the African Diaspora (LEAD) project. The LEAD project brings together researchers from Africa, the Caribbean, the US and Canada who are interested in generating Africa-specific leadership and management knowledge in response to various calls for Africa-specific leadership theory. In addition to developing an African measure of effective leadership conceptualization, this paper explores the relevance of the various LEAD project findings to inclusive leadership concept, where the *Ubuntu* philosophy and African culture's emphasis on inclusiveness though the practice of leadership appears to be largely in contest with *Ubuntu* philosophy.

Leadership effectiveness continues to preoccupy researchers, practitioners and scholars. The popular press and academia constantly lament the absence of effective leaders, which is particularly reflected in the mistrust of those in positions of authority. Further "recent surveys report that only one in four members of the general public trusts business leaders to correct issues, and only one in five trusts them to tell the truth and make ethical and moral decisions" (Hollensbe, Wookey, Hickey, George, & Nichols, 2014, p. 1227). Most emerging discourse on effective leadership dwells on two related notions: diversity and inclusivity. A discussion of diversity is important in the conversation of inclusive leadership because it involves appreciating and embracing people from all shades of life. In this regard, an understanding and practice of inclusion in addition to a clear understanding and appreciation of diversity are pertinent to leadership effectiveness. The objective this chapter is to present a review of studies on inclusive leadership and highlight implications for further studies to inform practice. It starts by examining diversity and inclusivity, which underpin inclusive leadership, and is followed by a review of studies on inclusive leadership and insights from the LEAD studies. This is then followed by implications for practice and research and a conclusion.

Diversity and Inclusivity

The concept of diversity encompasses acceptance, and respect and the understanding that each individual is unique, as well as recognizes our individual differences. Our differences can be along the dimensions of race, ethnicity, gender, socio-economic status, age, physical abilities, religious beliefs, political beliefs or other ideologies (Friedman & DiTomaso, 1996; Lorbiecki & Jack, 2000). Emphasis on diversity with accompanying implications and cultural sensitivity raises the important issue of inclusivity. While cultural sensitivity would imply the absence of a universal culture and the imperative to accept and respect the fact that as human beings we are different based on our socializations, inclusivity implies that every shade of opinion and cultural disposition, including beliefs, norms and preferences, must find expression in how we conduct affairs in business, the political arena, and education, to name just a few.

Though the definition or meaning of inclusion remains a subject of multiple interpretations has the possibility of misconceptions, Deloitte's research reveals that inclusion is expressed as feeling confident and inspired, and that a holistic definition comprises four related yet discrete elements (Deloitte, 2012). First, people feel included when they are treated "equitably and with respect". Participation without favouritism is the starting point for inclusion, and this requires attention to non-discrimination and basic courtesy. It should be noted here that the feeling of being excluded is the source of most protracted conflicts at country, business and even family unit levels. An example in Africa, where multiple nationalities strive and even clamour for space at the "national cake table", results not only in violent conflicts but also in civil wars. This has been witnessed the world over, such as with the US civil rights movement and Kenya's post-election violence (2007/8), where elections have been divisive because the winner more often than not "takes it all" and excludes "the losers". This is not unique to Kenya, Zimbabwe or Africa at large but is typical of anyone purporting to be a leader but lacking the temerity and magnanimity required of an effective leader anywhere in the world.

Second, "feeling valued and belonging" is an element of inclusion which is experienced "when people believe that their unique and authentic self is valued by others, while at the same time have a sense of connectedness or belonging to a group" (Bourke & Dillon, 2018). Third, inclusion is also expressed as feeling "safe" to speak up without fear of embarrassment or retaliation, and when people feel "empowered" to grow and do one's best work. In this regard, it is only when organizations are clear about the objective can they turn their attention to the drivers of inclusion, take action and measure results. The fourth element is that inclusion is expressed as feeling "confident and inspired". It is emphasized that being excluded or feeling this way can have serious psychological effects on an individual and has the potential to result in consequences such as individuals taking action to ensure inclusion, sometimes with devastating outcomes.

The examples of the effects of exclusion are many and diverse. In the 1930s, as a result of a rising cost of living from the worldwide depression coupled with the oppression of black people facing low wages across the region, spontaneous rioting erupted throughout the Caribbean commonwealth. In Barbados, 14 people were killed and 47 wounded in protests in 1937 ("Barbados Today", 2019). Again in Barbados on March 11, 2017, key stakeholders of the Social Partnership in Barbados, the private sector, trade unions and the main opposition political party led a nation-wide march protesting against several austere governmental initiatives which were implemented without proper consultation and inclusion of the said stakeholders ("March of Protest in the City", 2017). The Grenada revolution in the 1980s is also another example of the consequences of exclusion. The revolution was championed by Maurice Bishop and Bernard Coard and sought to adopt a more inclusive leadership approach by giving all citizens voice in the nation's social and political decision-making (Grenade, 2010).

Additional cases of the effects of exclusion include the Tamil Tigers of Sri Lanka; the conflict and civil war of Angola which led to the killing of Jonas Savimbi, the founding leader of *União Nacional para a Independência Total de Angola* (UNITA; in English, the National Union for the Total Independence of Angola); Umkhonto we Sizwe, the armed wing of the African National Congress (ANC) during apartheid in South Africa which was co-founded by Nelson Mandela in the wake of the Sharpeville massacre; and the Kenya Land and Freedom Army (KLFA), also known as the Mau Mau rebellion against the British colonial rule in Kenya. The war was between the Mau Mau and British colonists, who comprised the white European colonist-settlers in Kenya, the British Army and the local Kenya Regiment (British colonists, local auxiliary militia, and pro-British Kikuyu people).

Though it is unclear why extremists arise, it may be an expression of the feeling of being excluded or the motivation to exclude others. Exclusion has subtle expressions in the workplace as well. These may include aggression towards coworkers, sabotage of operations, pilferage and "go slow" at work; it may also lead to resignations. Even worse, the frustrations arising from being excluded usually spills over to the customers, yet these are the reasons for the existence of the organization. When this happens and is not addressed, it spells doom for the concerned organization.

Inclusive Leadership

Inclusive leadership is oriented significantly more towards the involvement rather than the manipulation of followers by those in power. Respect, recognition, responsiveness and responsibility are vital for the successful implementation of inclusive leadership (Hollander, 2008, p. 3). This approach to leadership appears to suggest empowerment of people in organizations where "Empowerment means that someone at the top must be wise or noble enough to give away some of his power" (Laloux, 2014, p. 62).

The importance of inclusivity continues to be reported in leadership studies. For example, Deloitte's research (Bourke & Dillon, 2018) shows that the behaviours of leaders (senior executives or managers) can drive up to 70 percentage points of the difference between the proportion of employees who feel highly included and the proportion of those who do not. This underscores the critical role that leadership plays in ensuring inclusivity, which draws heavily from the notion of diversity. It is therefore not surprising that "companies increasingly rely on diverse, multidisciplinary teams that combine the collective capabilities of women and men, people of different cultural heritage, and younger and older workers" (Burke & Espedido, 2019, p. 1). However, in order to achieve superior performance *inclusive leadership is required*—"leadership that assures that all team members feel they are treated respectfully and fairly, are valued and sense that they belong, and are confident and inspired" (Burke & Dillon, 2016). Further, in research involving 3,500 ratings by employees of 450 leaders, it was found that,

> Inclusive leaders share six behaviours—and that leaders often overestimate how inclusive they really are. The behaviours are: visible commitment, humility, awareness of bias, curiosity about others, cultural intelligence, and effective collaboration.
>
> *(Burke & Dillon, 2016, p. 8)*

As an example, leaders in Africa are motivated when they are involved with people, get respect of subordinates and are involved with the society in the development projects (Senaji et al., 2014). This finding suggests that the leaders should strive to earn their followers' respect, since it is a source of motivation. This appears to be conditional: they need to be effectively involved with the people and in the development of the people, which in itself should be an inclusive process. However, "while most business leaders now believe that having that a diverse and inclusive culture is critical to performance, they don't always know how to achieve that goal" (Bourke & Dillon, 2018, p. 1). Further, what constitutes effective leadership is still elusive, with inclusive leadership being even more ephemeral.

Effective leadership offers the opportunity to bend personal motivations, group norms and environmental opportunities toward organizational objectives (Senaji et al., 2016). Meanwhile, though the search for inclusive leadership remains pervasive, it may also find respite in the spiritual realm. This fact is aptly articulated by Cardinal Vincent Nichols in Hollensbe et al. (2014) by asserting,

> The deepest resources for the transformation of business, as for society as a whole, lie within the human heart. It is there we have to seek what it is we truly value and yearn for, and where we can harness the strongest motivation to change—ourselves, our organizations, and our world—for the better.
>
> (p. 1227)

Given the fact that inclusive leadership has become a critical leadership competence, it is necessary to explore who an inclusive leader is or should be. To the question, "what distinguishes highly inclusive leaders from their counterparts?" Deloitte's research identifies six signature traits (**Box 28.1**), all of which are interrelated and mutually reinforcing.

Part of inclusion is to ensure that people of different cultures are treated equally by the leaders. Culture, which is defined as "the collective programming of the mind that distinguishes the members of one group or category of people from others" (Hofstede, 2011, p. 3), plays an important role in what leadership effectiveness is. According to LEAD research in the African context, Senaji et al. (2014) found that the term culture may be used to mean the respect for the elderly/authority, modesty and moral behaviour that is expressed by people (Ghana), being accommodative, welcoming and showing happiness (Uganda), social behaviour, love of God/religious belief and being hardworking (Egypt, Nigeria) and ethnic group and language (Kenya).

Based on the foregoing finding of the study on leadership effectiveness in Africa, important cultural dispositions that have important implications for inclusive leadership come to the fore: first, there is modesty, the underlying implication is that a leader should listen and be open to a wide range of views from followers, and that someone who is pompous and "full of themselves" may not succeed in Ghana. There is also "love of God/religious belief", which has many linkages with spirituality and the related notion of altruism—a disposition to embrace others—hence inclusion.

Box 28.1 Inclusive Leaders' Six Signature Traits

1. *Commitment*: They are deeply committed to diversity and inclusion because it aligns with their personal values, and they believe in the business case for diversity and inclusion. They articulate their commitment authentically, bravely challenge the status quo, and take personal responsibility for change.
2. *Courage*: They are humble about their own capabilities and invite contributions by others.
3. *Cognizance of bias*: They are conscious of their own blind spots as well as flaws in the system, and work hard to ensure opportunities for others.
4. *Curiosity*: They have an open mind-set; they are deeply curious about others, listen without judgment, and seek to understand.
5. *Culturally intelligent*: They are attentive to others' cultures and adapt as required.
6. *Collaboration*: They empower others and create the conditions, such as team cohesion, for diversity of thinking to flourish.

Source: Bourke and Dillon (2018, January 2018). The diversity and inclusion revolution: Eight powerful truths. *Deloitte Review*, Issue 22, 2018, p. 87

Further, being "accommodative" as a cultural norm in Uganda implies inclusivity and sensitivity to diversity in terms of ensuring everybody, irrespective of their state or status, "are brought on board" in all aspects of an organization, whether a religious organization (church, mosque, synagogue, temple etc.), a firm, a local government or even national government and civil society. The "ethnic group and language" as a cultural descriptor has the implication that you cannot be perceived to be inclusive at the country level or even in business in Kenya unless you address tribal and ethnic diversities present in the country and strive to have a balance in key decisions, such as appointments to positions in organizations. This is not unique to Kenya; constitutions in some countries, such as Lebanon, prescribe who should be president or prime minister depending on their religious affiliations.

In an effort to ensure diversity and inclusion, governments and businesses alike have respectively enacted laws/constitutions and formulated business polices to address this important issue. However, leader disposition and commitment to these remain areas requiring empirical clarity to guide practice, since there appears to be a scarcity of appropriate leaders to deliver on this promise. Further, though recent studies have empirically determined preliminary descriptors of effective leadership, culture and what motivates leaders in the African and in the African diaspora context (e.g. Ford & Miller, 2014; Senaji et al., 2014), more needs to be done to establish what motivation, cultural disposition and effort are needed to realize inclusive leadership, which is increasingly being found to be the most appropriate approach in the present and unfolding environment. Further, the findings from the LEAD research project suggest that when leading people, it is important to consider the cultural dimensions on which they differ and ensure that any decisions take into account these cultural differences. In addition, Ncube (2010) asserts,

> Leadership is about knowledge, skills, and abilities for transformation. It is also increasingly about worldviews or visions of life—beliefs, values, and principles. But worldviews are also ways of life, for beliefs direct us, values guide us, and principles motivate us to certain kinds of action and behaviour.
>
> (p. 1)

This assertion complements these findings in an attempt to clarify what leadership is about, while at the same time pointing out aspects of differences that exist between people and which should form the approaches to inclusive leadership.

We next review empirical literature on inclusive leadership to highlight its conceptualization, related phenomena and practice.

Inclusive Leadership: A Review of Empirical Studies

Many views have been posited by researchers regarding the definition and purpose of leadership. For example, House et al. 1999, p. 184 (cited in Mughal & Kamal, 2019) describe leadership as "the ability of an individual to influence, motivate, and enable others to contribute toward the effectiveness and success of the organizations of which they are members" (p. 184). Resulting from this definition, many concepts and typologies have attempted to describe and explain leadership.

While many different definitions exist, there has been no agreement on a universal definition of leadership (Hollander, 2009). Yammarino and Dubinsky (1994) contend that apart from the lack of convergence on the definition, some confusion has been created due to the different levels of analysis presented on the subject. Despite the debate on leadership and lack of consensus regarding a universal definition, the topic of leadership continues to be a dominant concept that remains pervasive within the management, organizational and strategic literatures. As a result, this pervasiveness has influenced scholars to theorize on the nature and impact of leadership as a discipline.

Over the past 50 years, extensive empirical and theoretical research on types of leadership has been explored, utilizing various quantitative and qualitative approaches, in an effort to determine the best leadership style. Results from these studies highlighted a plethora of leadership styles that can be effectively used in organizations, teams and groups. However, with populations becoming more diverse and new problems arising, a new paradigm of leadership, known as inclusive leadership, has emerged.

Conceptualization of Inclusive Leadership

A number of theories have been posited on inclusive leadership. Many of these theories refer to the concept of inclusiveness in a broad and general manner. The overarching notion is that inclusiveness relates to the state of embracing everyone regardless of cultural background, age, sexual orientation, gender, disability, personality type, ways of working etc. Some of these theories are explored later.

Inclusive leadership is a two-way relationship between the leader and follower based upon respect, recognition, responsiveness and responsibility, and it entails a guiding principle of "doing things with people, not to people" (Hollander, 2009). Further, these leaders "appreciate everybody's contribution and inspire innovation by involving people at risk of being excluded from society" (Bortini, Paci, Rise, & Rojnik, 2016).

In 2016, Bourke and Dillon conducted a study on inclusive leadership, and from their findings developed six traits of an inclusive leader. The first trait "commitment" emphasizes attributes of fairness, a strong belief in personal values and business case for diversity and inclusion, which influence a sense of commitment to diversity and inclusion. Second, "courage" is having the tenacity to take risks and challenge the status quo. The third trait, "cognizance of bias", is the ability to identify and be aware of personal and group/company biases in making effective decisions. The fourth trait, "curiosity", relates to the leader being open-minded to other ideas and input from other individuals. The fifth trait, "cultural intelligence", refers to the capacity to correspond with individuals cross-culturally. The last trait, "collaboration", relates to empowering others to work together with the knowledge that a diverse team can produce better outcomes (Bourke & Dillon, 2016). Thus,

> inclusive leaders should be aware of their own biases and preferences, actively seek out and consider different views and perspectives in an effort to inform better decision-making; see diverse talent as a source of competitive advantage and inspire diverse people to drive organizational and individual performance towards a shared vision.
>
> *(Coppin, 2017)*

In addition to Bourke and Dillon's theory of inclusive leadership, some other researchers have posited their views on the concept. For example, Frederic Laloux suggested that the inclusive leader is one who is interested in assisting others in becoming leaders and in attaining autonomy themselves. "Empowerment means that someone at the top must be wise or noble enough to give away some of his power" (Laloux, 2014, p. 62).

Further, Laloux (2014) describes a scenario where an organization exists without differentiation between the powerful and the powerless. He adds that since the world has become more complex, the "predict and control system" should be replaced by a "sense and respond" approach. Laloux proposes that successful organizations are those that perceive themselves to be living with a sense of direction and individual genius. Laloux adds that to achieve this people should no longer wear a professional mask. Instead, individuals should seek wholeness and nurture their spiritual and rational aspects. He highlights that many organizations in today's world are devoid of life because very little life is injected into them. He suggests that soulful practices could assist in helping them to find their humanity.

In a similar vein, Otter Scharmer describes inclusive leaders as those "who engage in creating change and shaping their future, regardless of their formal positions". He suggests that there is a need to migrate from an ego-system-centric awareness of institutional decision makers to an eco-system reality.

> Decision makers must move from a place of only seeing their own viewpoint (ego-awareness) to experiencing the system through the lens of the other players, especially those who are most marginalized. The goal must be to co-sense, co-inspire and co-create an emerging future for their system that values the well-being of all rather than just a few.
> *(Scharmer & Kaufer, 2013, p. 12)*

Scharmer offers what he refers to as "Theory U", which is a process he introduced to support companies and institutions in collaboratively progressing towards future possibilities. It is important to underscore that all of these leadership theories incorporate the new dimension of diversity, which is a critical variable in today's organizations. Inclusive leadership has the potential to allow leaders to reach individuals who would otherwise be alienated within organizations. Once these individuals are empowered and included, the probability of them reaching their full potential within organizations and society as a whole is increased.

Similarly, Deloitte describes an inclusive leader as "a person who actively creates a workplace in which diverse talent is fostered, where diverse teams operate to their maximum potential". Further, they see a paradigm shift from "leading from the top to leading from the center" (Deloitte, 2012, p. 1).

Inclusive Leadership and Similar Leadership Styles

Scholars have alluded to the similarities of inclusive leadership to transformational leadership and servant leadership. Transformational leadership was first coined as such by James MacGregor Burns in 1978, until later in 1985 when Bernard M. Bass referred to the term as transformational leadership. Transformational leadership is described as a method whereby "leaders and followers help each other to advance to a higher level of morale and motivation" (Burns, 1978). Transformational leadership is characterized by intellectual stimulation, individual consideration, inspirational motivation and idealized influence. The transforming leader must be able stimulate ideas and challenge the status quo (intellectual stimulation), act as mentors and nurture the needs of their subordinates/followers (individual consideration), have a sense of charisma (inspirational motivation) and be an exemplar (idealized influence). Bono and Judge (2004) conducted a meta-analysis study to determine the relationship between personality and transformational and transactional leadership behaviours. Findings of that study revealed that transformational leaders have five major personality traits: neuroticism, extraversion, openness, agreeableness and conscientiousness.

Similarly, servant leadership, first coined by Robert Greenleaf in 1970, is described as a leadership style that seeks to enhance the lives of others whilst achieving organizational goals. Servant leaders exhibit characteristics such as "listening, empathy, healing, awareness, persuasion, conceptualization, foresight, stewardship, commitment to the growth of people, and building community" (Spears, 2010).

Like the inclusive leader, the transformational leader and servant leader "are people-oriented styles" (Parolini, 2007). Echols (2009) noted that these leadership perspectives do not disregard the importance of goal outcomes but are concerned with the human element. Emphasizing the importance of positive human relationships leads to a realization of individual and group potential that encourages growth and cohesiveness, resulting in goal attainment (Echols, 2009). Therefore, similar to studies on inclusive leadership, authors have reported positive outcomes from utilizing transformational or servant leadership approaches (Ng, 2017); (Lehmann-Willenbrock, Meinecke, Rowold, &

Kauffeld, 2015); (Bosch, Heras, Rofcanin, & Stollberger, 2019); (Czayka-Chełmińska, Daszkowska-Kamińska, Józefowicz, Makowska, & Szelągowska, n.d.); (Bentein & Chiniara, 2018).

Though these styles find the humanistic variable important in achieving goals, there is some difference. A transformational leader is focused on the organizational goals and exhibits characteristics that encourage followers' commitment to those goals, whilst the servant leader is primarily focused on the followers, and organizational goals become more of a secondary objective (Kantharia, 2012); (Patterson, Russell & Stone, 2002). However,

> inclusive leadership adds a new dimension to leadership concepts, by putting the focus on diverse groups and individuals; it addresses individuals at risk of exclusion by looking at their needs, aspirations and potential, and empowering them to participate fully in society.
> *(Czayka-Chełmińska et al., n.d., p. 5)*

Inclusive Leadership Outcomes

David, Dodds, Moss, and Sims (2016) conducted a study to explore organizations' understanding of inclusive leadership as well as the perception of its practice and its links to performance, productivity, satisfaction and well-being (David et al., 2016). From their study, three major findings were revealed. The first finding indicated that inclusive leaders embody 15 core competencies (consideration, idealized influence, inspirational motivation, intellectual stimulation, unqualified acceptance, empathy, listening, persuasion, confidence building, growth, foresight, conceptualization, awareness, stewardship and healing), all co-existing with equal importance. The second finding postulated that "people working with inclusive leaders are more productive, satisfied and engaged than those working with non-inclusive leaders" (David et al., 2016). Hence, the last finding unearthed several benefits of having inclusive leadership: enhanced performance and productivity, enhanced loyalty, the advance of underrepresented groups, enhanced creativity, better services to clients, customers and service users, better teamwork, motivation to go the extra mile, higher retention and a diverse talent pool. Participants within the study cited inclusive leadership as the major contributor to their overall productivity, satisfaction and engagement.

Similar results were found in a cross-cultural study conducted by Prime and Salib (2014), who sought to report on differences of opinions and effects of inclusive leadership among employees of 27 international companies in six countries (China, Australia, Germany, India, Mexico, and the United States). The findings revealed that regardless of culture, employees who were led by persons considered as inclusive felt more innovative and expressed higher team citizenship behaviours, which increased the company's overall productivity and product innovation (Prime & Salib, 2014).

Moreover, Carmeli, Hirak, Peng, and Schaubroeck (2012) also sought to understand how leadership inclusive behaviours impacted how groups and organizations learned from failures, affected their psychological safety and consequently influenced employee performance and company productivity. They found that there was a positive relationship between leader inclusiveness and performance. Specifically, individuals who performed at mediocre or unsuitable levels perceived inclusive leadership to be either non-existent or unfavourable. Consequently, they adopted a more negative view of psychological safety and responded to failures accordingly, resulting in low performance and productivity output. In contrast, those individuals who perceived and experienced leaders who were inclusive had more positive perceptions of their psychological safety, which affected their attitudes towards any occurring failures. These individuals were noted as having the highest levels of performance and productivity output.

Despite being a relatively new concept, inclusive leadership is also referred to as the 21st-century leadership style for competitive advantage showing multiple benefits (Nelson, 2016). As a result, more and more research is being conducted in this area, confirming the benefits of inclusive leadership (Choi, Kang, & Tran, 2017; Qi, Liu, Wei, & Hu, 2019).

LEAD and Inclusive Leadership

In this section, a synthesis of inclusive leadership elements, metaphors and insights from the LEAD findings from Africa and the Caribbean are presented.

Inclusive Leadership: The Caribbean Context

Culture, politics, religion and geography are some factors that influence leadership styles (Punnett, 2008). Hence, the current leadership atmosphere in the Caribbean has its eminence in the era of colonial power: a top-down decision-making style, where those in power make decisions with little to no input from subordinates (Greenidge & Punnett, 2009). These leaders generally believe that they are making the best-fit decisions. Instead, they are often perceived as individuals just seeking financial gain, not caring for the people they lead (Holder, Knight, Punnett, & Charles, 2014).

In the Caribbean, leadership is explored mostly within the context of politics and organizations. Typically, leadership roles over the years have been either democratic, autocratic or laissez-faire in nature (Hoebing, 1996). Inclusive leadership behaviours such as empowerment, commitment, accountability, courage and cultural intelligence can be recognized in some areas, but the term itself has not been considered as a typology of leadership.

Inclusive leadership is characterized by the ability to embrace and motivate individuals, especially those marginalized, to participate within a group and together achieve a common goal. Having a people-oriented focus makes it similar to the transformational leader and servant leader. However, it differs, as it focuses not only on individuals but also on issues of diversity. Though a relatively new concept of leadership, most international research examines inclusive leadership within the context of organizations reporting a plethora of benefits. These studies have shown that there is a positive relationship between inclusive leaders and an increase in individual health and overall productivity. Inclusive leadership, regardless of context, appears to assist in bringing about positive characteristics among members that aid in rectifying many challenges (see e.g. Bourke & Dillon, 2016, 2018).

Unfortunately, in the Caribbean, there is a dearth of literature regarding inclusive leadership, as expected. Research on inclusive leadership has its focus in education (still limited), but is unexplored in other settings such as organizations, politics, groups and teams, to name a few. Often, "inclusion" is discussed or studied as a mechanism for involving youth or future leaders into the activities of the region, to offer a better foundation for future economic growth and regional integration. These programmes' overarching goals are based on inclusivity, and participants learn some inclusive leadership behaviours. However, inclusive leadership as a style is yet to be acknowledged as an instrument that can be utilized for future growth.

It is important to highlight that the Caribbean as a region has a colonial past and as a direct result of this leadership style tends to be bureaucratic in nature and feature a top-down approach, which often runs contrary to the notions of inclusive leadership.

Inclusive Leadership: The African Context

Similar to the Caribbean, the literature on inclusive leadership in Africa is limited. This notwithstanding, at least two aspects about Africa provide clues as to how inclusive leadership in Africa may be understood: the concept of *Ubuntu* and the dominant culture in Africa. Both *Ubuntu* as a worldview and the African culture have received some attention in the literature. The *Ubuntu* philosophy is aptly presented in the words of Archbishop Desmond Tutu of South Africa:

> A person is a person through other persons. None of us comes into the world fully formed. We would not know how to think, or walk, or speak, or behave as human beings unless we learned it from other human beings. We need other human beings in order to be human.
> *(Tutu, 2004, p. 25)*

Ubuntu has attracted the attention of researchers (e.g. Ncube, 2010) and appears to resonate well with the notion of inclusive leadership as discussed in the previous sections. For example, it has been argued that *Ubuntu* represents the African worldview and it encompasses value systems, beliefs and practices that are common among the African people (Mnyaka & Motlhabi, 2005). This world is founded on the core values of humaneness, caring, sharing, respect and compassion (see Dandala, 1996; Mthembu, 1996 in Mnyaka & Motlhabi, 2005). Tutu (2011 in Buqa, 2015) posits that *Ubuntu* speaks of spiritual attributes such as generosity, hospitality, compassion, caring and sharing, which means that one could be affluent in material possessions but still be without *Ubuntu*. Other authors have described *Ubuntu* as a set of institutionalized ideals, which guide and direct the patterns of life of Africans with the hallmark of *Ubuntu* being its concern with harmony and continuity (Ncube, 2010). These descriptions suggest that *Ubuntu* philosophy and way of doing things are by default inclusive. Thus, leaders who operate from the vantage point of *Ubuntu* would be disposed to be inclusive in their leadership style in an attempt to ensure that harmony and continuity are preserved.

Though *Ubuntu* clearly implies humanity and inclusivity, the reality is that Africa still faces leadership problems, as most of the current styles of leadership are either not consistent with inclusivity or at best narrowly embrace inclusivity from an ethnic or tribal inclination, which is in itself exclusion. This always spills over from the national to organizational levels. The implication is that leadership practices are largely inconsistent with the African worldview and need to be more inclusive. As also noted, the African culture provides a way of understanding inclusive leadership in Africa. The research by Hofstede (2006) shows that Africans have a collectivist culture. As described by Punnett et al. (2019, p. 74),

> In collectivist cultures, people are members of a few groups and loyalty to the group is critically important.... Where collectivism is high, organizational plans are formulated on the basis of the larger group and societal good, with input from a variety of organizational members. The overall direction of the organization may be widely discussed throughout the organization. Decisions are made collectively, with affected parties participating in the process. Disagreements are dealt with throughout the process and consensus from all members is sought. Tasks and assignments are carried out by groups. There is pressure from the group for conformance to acceptable standards. When decisions need to be made, they are made by the group as a whole. The quality circle approach is popular, because it incorporates the idea of bottom-up decision making, consensus among members, and group involvement, both in the process and implementation of decisions.

The implication of collectivist culture in most of Africa is that leadership should be exercised from a collectivist follower perspective. This means that groups of people rather than an individual should be consulted by the leader before making decisions that affect the people in organizations, otherwise a feeling of being excluded can quickly set in and impair the prospects of an organization.

Implications for Practice and Future Research

A review of theoretical and empirical literature on leadership and practices from an inclusive leadership lens provides insights on how inclusive leadership is important but needs further conceptualization and operationalization in Africa, the Caribbean and African diaspora. We next present implications for practice and future research.

Implications for Practice

Absence of inclusive leadership has been shown to have serious consequences in organization—be they firms or even nation states, as already pointed out in this chapter. As seen from previous studies that have been reviewed and from the findings from the LEAD research, it is apparent that leaders should discern diversity in their followers and use this diversity as a means of enacting a leadership that is inclusive—one that celebrates diversity and unlocks the potential that is embedded therein though inclusive approaches to leadership. Further, it is noted that *Ubuntu*—humanness, collectivist tendencies and spirituality—are prominent in the African context. In this regard, a leadership style that reflects these aspects is encouraged among leaders of organizations of all types.

Implications for Future Research

Though inclusive leadership is reported in extant literature as having positive influence on performance of organizations, its conceptualization still needs more refinement and clarity. For example, the relationship between *Ubuntu* philosophy and inclusive leadership is an interesting area of further research. Another area of potential research is on predictors of inclusive leadership. In addition, the relationship between inclusive leadership descriptors and performance require further research to ascertain which among them are more significantly related to performance. Findings of such studies will guide practice and training on effective leadership in order to improve performance of organizations. It is also noted that from the LEAD project-developed leadership measure, spirituality appears not to be equally perceived as important for leadership effectiveness in Africa and in the Caribbean (Michaud et al., 2019). This implies that there could be some differences in the conceptualization of inclusive leadership between the Caribbean and Africa with important implications for practice; hence, a need exists to empirically inquire into this possible phenomenon, because spirituality is closely linked to *Ubuntu*. Lastly, it is also important to empirically ascertain the conceptual distinctions between inclusive leadership and other styles, such as servant leadership and transformational leadership.

Conclusions and Reflections

Since inclusive leadership is an intentional and effortful process, leaders need to adjust their behaviours and that of the workplace to be in line with the requirements of diverse talent, ideas, customers and markets. This is because the old "hero" style of leadership has fallen by the wayside as the context within which organizations are led continues to become much more diverse. Inclusive leadership has become critical to success, yet little is known about it. The situation regarding inclusive leadership at the organizational level is a reflection of the situation at the country level, hence the need to approach this phenomenon at all levels in order to realize the benefits that inclusive leadership promises.

References

Barbados Today. (2010). March of Protest in the City. (2017, March 12). *Nation News*. Retrieved May 30, 2019, from www.nationnews.com/nationnews/news/94484/march-protest-city; http://countrystudies.us/caribbean-islands/83.htm May 30, 2019

Bentein, K., & Chiniara, M. (2018). The servant leadership advantage: When perceiving low differentiation in leader-member relationship quality influences team cohesion, team task performance and service OCB. *The Leadership Quarterly*, 29(2), 333–345. https://doi.org/10.1016/j.leaqua.2017.05.002

Bortini, P., Paci, A., Rise, A., & Rojnik, I. (2016). *Inclusive leadership: Theoretical framework*. European Union. Retrieved December 21, 2019, from http://inclusiveleadership.eu/il_theoreticalframework_en.pdf

Bosch, M. J., Heras, M. L., Rofcanin, Y., & Stollberger, J. (2019). Serving followers and family? A trickle-down model of how servant leadership shapes employee work performance. *Journal of Vocational Behaviour*, 158–171. https://doi.org/10.1016/j.jvb.2019.02.003

Bourke, J., & Dillon, B. (2016, April 14). *The six signature traits of inclusive leadership: Thriving in a diverse new world*. Retrieved May 25, 2019, from https://www2.deloitte.com/insights/us/en/topics/talent/six-signature-traits-of-inclusive-leadership.html

Burke, J., & Dillon, B. (2018, January 22). The diversity and inclusion revolution: Eight powerful truths. *Deloitte Review* (22). Retrieved December 21, 2019, from https://www2.deloitte.com/us/en/insights/deloitte-review/issue-22/diversity-and-inclusion-at-work-eight-powerful-truths.html

Burke, J., & Espedido, A. (2019, March). Why inclusive leaders are good for organizations, and how to become one. *Harvard Business Review*. Retrieved December 21, 2019, from https://hbr.org/2019/03/why-inclusive-leaders-are-good-for-organizations-and-how-to-become-one

Buqa, W. (2015). Storying Ubuntu as a rainbow nation. *Verbum et Ecclesia*, *36*(2), Art. #1434, 8 pages. http://dx.doi.org/10.4102/ve.v36i2.1434. Retrieved June 15, 2019, from www.scielo.org.za/pdf/vee/v36n2/01.pdf

Burns, M. J. (1978). *Leadership*. New York, NY: Harper & Row.

Carmeli, A., Hirak, R., Peng, A. C., & Schaubroeck, J. M. (2012). Linking leader inclusiveness to work unit performance: The importance of psychological safety and learning from failures. *The Leadership Quarterly*, 107–117. http://dx.doi.org/10.1016/j.leaqua.2011.11.009

Coppin, A. (2017). *The human capital imperative: Valuing your talent*. Springer International Publishing.

Czayka-Chełmińska, K., Daszkowska-Kamińska, A., Józefowicz, J., Makowska, M., & Szelągowska, A. (2016). *Inclusive leadership: Manual for trainers*, 5. David, A., Dodds, A., Moss, G., & Sims, C. (2016). *Inclusive leadership . . . driving performance through diversity*. Bucks New University and Employers Network For Equality and Inclusion. Retrieved from www.dca.org.au/sites/default/files/enei-inclusive-leadership-research-report-march-2016.pdf

Dillon, B., & Burke, J. (2016). *The six signature traits of inclusive leadership: Thriving in a diverse new world* (pp. 1–26). Westlake: Deloitte University Press.

Deloitte. (2012). *Inclusive leadership will a hug do?* Human Capital, Deloitte Australia Point of View, March 2012.

Echols, S. (2009). Transformational/servant leadership: A potential synergism for an inclusive leadership style. *Journal of Religious Leadership*, *8*(2). Retrieved from http://bishopperryinstitute.org.au/uploads/EcholsSteve-TransformationalLeadership.pdf

Ford, D. L. Jr., & Miller, C. D. (2014). Leadership and motivation in Africa and the African Diaspora (LEAD): Summary and epilogue. *Canadian Journal of Administrative Sciences*, *31*(4), 270–279, doi:10.1002/cjas.1294

Friedman, J., & DiTomaso, N. (1996). Myths about diversity: What managers need to know about changes in the US labor force. *California Management Review*, *38*, 54–77.

Greenidge, D., & Punnett, B. J. (2009). Cultural mythology and global leadership in the Caribbean Islands. In E. Kessley & J. Wong-MingJi Diana (Eds.), *Cultural mythology and global leadership* (pp. 65–78). Cheltenham. Retrieved from www.researchgate.net/publication/301567704_Cultural_Mythology_and_Global_Leadership_in_the_Caribbean_Islands

Grenade, W. (2010, September–December). Grenada revolution: (30) Years after: An introduction. *Journal of Eastern Caribbean Studies*, *35*(3/4), 1–3; ProQuest Central.

Hoebing, J. (1996, September). *Leadership in the Caribbean: Working papers* (Vol.V11). Retrieved from https://csis-prod.s3.amazonaws.com/s3fs-public/legacy_files/files/media/csis/pubs/ppcaribb%5B1%5D.pdf

Hofstede, G. (2006). What did GLOBE really measure? Researchers' minds versus respondents' minds. *Journal of International Business Studies*, *37*, 882–96.

Hofstede, G. (2011). Dimensionalizing cultures: The Hofstede model in context. *Online Readings in Psychology and Culture*, *2*(1). http://dx.doi.org/10.9707/2307-0919.1014

Holder, K., Knight, N., Punnett, B. J., & Charles, R. (2014). Culture, leadership and motivation in wo Commonwealth Caribbean countries: One look at the African Diaspora. *Canadian Journal of Administrative Sciences*, *31*(4), 245–256. doi:https://doi.org/10.1002/cjas.1297

Hollander, E. P. (2008). *Inclusive leadership. The essential leader-follower-relationship*. New York: Routledge/Psychology Press.

Hollander, E. P. (2009). *Inclusive leadership: The essential leader—follower relationship*. New York, NY: Routledge/Taylor & Francis Group.

Hollensbe, E., Wookey, C., Hickey, L., George, G., & Nichols, C.V. (2014). Organizations with a purpose. *Academy of Management Journal*, *57*(5), 1227–1234. http://dx.doi.org/10.5465/amj.2014.4005

Joyce, B., & Judge, T. A. (2004). Personality and transformational and transactional leadership: A meta-analysis. *Journal of Applied Psychology*, *89*(5), 901–910. doi:CiteSeerX 10.1.1.692.7909

Kantharia, B. (2012). Servant leadership: An imperative leadership style for leader managers. *SSRN Electronic Journal, 7*. doi:10.2139/ssrn.1980625

Laloux, F. (2014). *Reinventing organizations: A guide to creating organizations.* Brussels: Nelson Parker.

Lehmann-Willenbrock, N., Meinecke, A. L., Rowold, J., & Kauffeld, S. (2015). How transformational leadership works during team interactions: A behavioral process analysis. *The Leadership Quarterly, 26*(6), 1017–1033. https://doi.org/10.1016/j.leaqua.2015.07.003

Lorbiecki, A., & Jack, G. (2000). Critical turns in the evolution of diversity management. *British Journal of Management, 11*, S17–S31.

Makowska, M., Szelągowska, A., Daszkowska-Kamińska, A., Józefowicz, J., & Czayka-Chełmińska, K. (2016). *Inclusive leadership: Manual for trainers. European Union.* Retrieved December 22, 2019, from https://inclusive-leadership.eu/inclusive-leadership-manual-for-trainers/

March of Protest in the City. (2017, March 12). *Nation News.* Retrieved May 30, 2019, from www.nationnews.com/nationnews/news/94484/march-protest-city

Michaud, J., Lvina, E., Lituchy, T. R., Galperin, B. L., Punnett, B. J., Taleb, A., Mukanzi, C., Senaji, T. A., Bagire, V., Asiedu-Appiah, F., Agyapong, A., Metwally, E., Melyoki, L., Woodham, O., Knight, N., Corbin, A., Charles, R., Singh, R., Ballwant, P., Stephanson, J., & Williams, L., Alleyne, A. (2019). Development and validation of the leadership effectiveness in Africa and the Diaspora (Lead) Scale. *IAABD Proceedings*, Dar es Salaam, Tanzania.

Mnyaka, M., & Motlhabi, M. (2005). The African concept of Ubuntu/Botho and its socio-moral significance. *Black Theology, 3*(2), 215–237. doi:10.1558/blth.3.2.215.65725

Mughal, Y. H., & Kamal, S. (Eds.) (2019). *Servant leadership styles and strategic decision making.* Hershey, PA: Information Science Reference, IGI Global

Ncube, L. B. (2010). Ubuntu: A transformative leadership philosophy. *Symposium: Journal of Leadership Studies.* https://doi.org/10.1002/jls.20182. Retrieved June 15, 2019, from https://onlinelibrary.wiley.com/doi/abs/10.1002/jls.20182

Nelson, T. (2016, July 16). *Inclusive leadership Is a 21st century competitive advantage.* Retrieved from www.theceomagazine.com/business/finance/inclusive-leadership-is-a-21st-century-competitive-advantage/

Ng, T. W. H. (2017). Transformational leadership and performance outcomes: Analyses of multiple mediation pathways. *The Leadership Quarterly*, 385–417. https://doi.org/10.1016/j.leaqua.2016.11.008

Parolini, J. L. (2007). Investigating the distinctions between transformational and servant leadership. (Ph.D. diss. Regent University). Retrieved from www.jeanineparolini.com/Jeanine%20Parolini%20Dissertation.pdf

Patterson, K., Russell, R. F., & Stone, G. A. (2002). Transformational versus servant leadership: A difference in leader focus. *Leadership & Organization Development Journal*, 145–157. https://pdfs.semanticscholar.org/34b

Prime, J., & Salib, E. R. (2014). *Inclusive leadership: The view from six countries.* Retrieved from www.catalyst.org/wp-content/uploads/2019/01/inclusive_leadership_the_view_from_six_countries_0.pdf

Punnett, B. A. (2008). *International perspectives on organizational behaviour and human resource management.* New York, NY: M.E. Sharpe Inc.

Punnett, B. J., Galperin, B., Lituchy, T., Melyoki, L., Michaud, J., & Mukanzi, C. (2019). Cultural values and management in African countries. In C. Sims & B. Hall (Eds.), *Cultures of the world – Past, present and future* (pp. 39–100). New York: Nova Science Publishers.

Qi, L., Liu, B., Wei, X., & Hu, Y. (2019). Impact of inclusive leadership on employee innovative behavior: Perceived organizational support as a mediator. *PLoS One*, 1–14. doi:10.1371/journal.pone.0212091

Senaji, T. A., Terri R. Lituchy, T. R., Metwally, E., Acquaah, M., Corbin, A., Michaud, J., Galperin, B. L., Melyoki, L., Ngunjiri, F., Muthuri, J., Adedoyin-Rassaq, H., Mukanzi, C., & Bagire, V. (2016). Leadership in Africa: Insider and outsider perspectives. *Symposium IAABD Proceedings.* Strathmore University, Nairobi, Kenya.

Senaji, T. A., Metwally, E., Puplampu, B. B., Sejjaaka, S., Michaud, J., & Adedoyin-Rasaq, H. (2014). LEAD—Leadership effectiveness, motivation, and culture in Africa: Lessons from Egypt, Ghana, Kenya, Nigeria, and Uganda. *Canadian Journal of Administrative Sciences, 31*(4), 228–244. doi:10.1002/CJAS.1298

Scharmer, O., & Kaufer, K. (2013). *Leading from the emerging future: From ego-system to eco-system economies.* San Francisco: Berrett-Koehler Publishers, Inc.

Spears, L. (2010). Character and servant leadership: Ten characteristics of effective, caring leaders. *The Journal of Virtues & Leadership, 1*(1), 25. Retrieved from www.regent.edu/acad/global/publications/jvl/vol1_iss1/Spears_Final.pdf

Tutu, D. M. (2004). *God has a dream: A vision of hope for our time.* London: Rider.

Yammarino, F. J., & Dubinsky, A. J. (1994). Transformational leadership theory: Using levels of analysis to determine boundary conditions. *Personnel Psychology, 47*, 787–811. http://dx.doi.org/10.1111/j.1744-6570.1994.tb01576.x

29
PATHWAYS TO INCLUSIVE LEADERSHIP AND FLOURISHING ORGANIZATIONS

Creating Shared Ventures That Nurture Individual and Team Excellence

Satinder Dhiman

Introduction

Leadership plays a central role in creating effective, empowering, and inclusive organizations. This chapter seeks to explore the pathways to developing inclusive organizations and leaders that harness workplace engagement, belonging, contribution, flourishing, and well-being. This subject is especially important given the ongoing widespread disengagement at work among current employees in the United States and around the world. The overall aim is to examine how we can harness organizational excellence through inclusiveness, as well as work with the inherent paradoxes and competing values at both the individual and the organizational level.

Additionally, this chapter will also explore the construct of inclusive organizations and leadership in the context of the Indian wisdom text, the Bhagavad Gītā—"the most translated text after the Bible"—which, although by some accounts more than 5,000 years old, still inspires and guides the personal and work lives of more than a billion people in the world. It will briefly present the ethical and spiritual philosophy of the Gītā pertaining to empowering work cultures, various psychological types, and universally cherished values that foster workplace inclusiveness and belonging.

The central goal of this chapter is to explore ways in which leadership plays a key role in designing effective and inclusive organizations—*organizations founded on the liberating tenet of shared individual and collective responsibility*. For, only such organizations provide the felicitous space for creative work that is mind enriching, heart fulfilling, soul satisfying, and financially rewarding.

While this chapter recognizes the importance of the role of inclusive leadership in nurturing inclusive organizations, it places such responsibility on the shoulders of every member of the organization. It garners the unique view that inclusive organizations are fundamentally shared ventures, individually and collectively. Only by fostering shared responsibility, individually and collectively, can we hope to bring about happy individuals and harmonious communities and improve the overall human condition.

Organizations Are Shared Ventures: Nexus of Individual and Group Responsibilities

In *12 Rules for Life: Antidote to Chaos*, Peterson (2018), a Canadian clinical psychologist, cultural critic, and professor of psychology at the University of Toronto, underscores the fact that we are all part of something great and are vitally interconnected. We are complicated pieces in an even more complex puzzle. What is the dialectic between the individual pieces and the puzzle—between the search for order at the individual level and the inevitable logic of the chaos at the organizational level? What solution does Peterson offer by way of an antidote to the inevitable chaos?

Peterson's operating thesis in the book hinges on self-responsibility as a precursor to social harmony: When we take steps to sort ourselves out, we also trigger a symbiotic process of bringing order to the world around us. This is no new theme; writers from Plato (*Republic*) to Rousseau (*Candide*) to Bertrand Russell (*Political Ideals*) to J. Krishnamurti (*Education and the Significance of Life*) have opined that social harmony is as much a personal mandate as it is a state responsibility and that individual ethics is politics writ large. *Community well-being starts and ends with engaged personal responsibility.* This has far-reaching implications for leaders and followers.

Two most important rules of Peterson's *12 Rules*, in their scope and implications, related to the theme of inclusive organizations and leadership, are:

1. Treat yourself like someone you are responsible for helping (Rule 2).
2. Set your house in perfect order before you criticize the world (Rule 6).

Rule one furnishes the guidepost for leaders; rule two, for individuals. Together, they can guide an organization's journey toward greater inclusiveness and empowerment. In essence, both of these rules highlight the importance of Kant's two categorical imperatives (see Beck, 1997).

First Formulation of Categorical Imperative:

There is only one categorical imperative and it is this: act only according to that maxim [principle] whereby you can at the same time will that it should become a universal law.
—*Immanuel Kant*

Golden Rule and the Reverse Clause

The first formulation of categorical imperative may be described as a restatement of the Golden Rule, *with a reverse clause*:

1. It has to be universalizable, without restriction.
2. It has to be reversible ("what-if-someone-does-that-to-you" test).
   It is "imperative" in the sense that it "must be done," and it is "categorical" in the sense that the moral laws admit "no exceptions"—they have to be good for everyone or they are not good for anyone! And for Kant, "doing one's duty, no matter what" is the essence of duty ethics. And this following of one's moral sense is unconditionally good, an unconditional value. Kant says that all other things that we conventionally desire and value—happiness, courage etc.—are good but only with qualification. Goodwill or good motive is good, and you do not need to qualify it; it is just good. What is goodwill or good motive, according to Kant? When you act for the sake of your duty alone, not for the sake of happiness or gain or inclination. You do right because it the right thing to do; for no other reason. In his seminal work *Foundations of the Metaphysics of Morals and, What Is Enlightenment?*, Kant goes so far to suggest that if you get a kick out of doing good, it doesn't count—*in the moral sense*. It is like flossing your teeth—good thing to do, but you get no medals or little prizes for doing it! For Kant, morality is about good motive (goodwill), not good consequences.

> Therefore, acting solely for the sake of duty (out of pure motive or goodwill) is the essence of Kant's duty ethics. This begs a further question: What is my duty? Duty is when one acts

out of reverence for the moral law. It is here that Kant provides us with his first categorical imperative, a single moral rule, general enough to cover all moral commandments (like the Ten Commandments or the Golden Rule).

The first formulation of Kant's categorical imperative boils down to this: Any action you do, ask if you could make a universal rule/law of it. For example, you have promised your friend to have dinner. But on that day, you feel very tired. You do not want to go with your friend and you lie. Now ask yourself, could you write a law, about lying/breaking promises, that would be universally applicable? That would mean there wouldn't be any promises. Kant would say you have broken the first categorical imperative. The second reason you have acted in an unbecoming manner is because it is not reversible: Would I want anyone to do that to me? Obviously not. So, Kant would say, do not do it. It is not the morally right thing to lie, to break promises. This is the long and short of Kant's duty ethics. Kant adds the second categorical imperative to embellish the first imperative and draws further important principles from it, as follows:

Second Formulation of Categorical Imperative:

The practical imperative therefore will be the following: Act in such a way that you treat humanity, whether in our own person or in the person of another, always at the same time as an end, and never simply as a means.

—*Immanuel Kant*

The first principle Kant draws from the first categorical imperative is called "Ends Principle": Always treat others and yourself as though they/you were an end and never a mere means. You treat others and your activities as an end in themselves and not as means. If we all do so, we will be able to create what Kant calls the "Kingdom of Ends." Imagine living in a community where no one is used as a means to anyone's end but always as an end in themselves. That will be a culture of complete trust and goodwill toward each other, which is the essence of inclusive, flourishing organizations and societies.

In addition to the "Ends Principle," Kant draws the following three more postulates from the first categorical imperative:

1. *Principle of Freedom*: This is a practical postulate. You may not be free (for example, someone may be in a prison and still act freely), but always act on the principle that your moral decisions make the difference. Note the similarity between this principle and what Professor Jordan Peterson says; that is, act as if your life matters, as if what you do matters.
2. *Principle of Autonomy*: Always act as though you can regard your will as making universal moral law. Kant believed that moral decisions come from within you (from a moral sense "within") and not out of decisions that are *made for you*. You are autonomous to choose right for right's sake and are not under the will of another. Kant went so far to say that even if God were to descend and tell you to do this or that, and you did so, it wouldn't be wrong—but it would not be moral. Moral decisions come from within you.
3. *Principle of Human Dignity*: The human capacity to be a moral agent gives each human a strong sense of dignity. And this dignity, for Kant, is unconditional.

Kant postulated that if all of us acted out of a profound sense of duty, according to the moral sense within, we would be in a Kingdom of Ends—treating each other as ends, not as means—a kingdom in which no one uses anyone and no one gets used! If we could live as if in a Kingdom of

Ends, it would lead to a kingdom of Perpetual Peace.[1] To bring peace and harmony in the present war-ravaged world, no more urgent message than this can be conceived!

Creating Inclusive Organizations Through Workplace Flourishing and Personal Well-Being

Series of recent flourishing polls show that the majority of US workers are not engaged at work. A 2014 flourishing survey found that almost 90% of workers were either "not engaged" with, or "actively disengaged" from, their jobs. (Recent flourishing polls have indicated that 71% of US workers were "not engaged," or "actively disengaged" from their jobs.[2] This state of disengagement is not limited to workers alone. Craig and Snook (2014, pp. 105, 111) offer research that "fewer than 20% of leaders have a strong sense of their own individual purpose" and that "articulating purpose and finding the courage to live it is the single most important developmental task" a leader can undertake. These findings show that the engagement crisis is germane to both leaders and followers and have far-reaching implications for workplace engagement, wellness, and contribution (Dhiman, 2017).

It an issue concerning organizations at their most fundamental level. These findings have far-reaching implications for organizational inclusiveness, workplace engagement, wellness, and success. Organizational well-being is a multifaceted construct, consisting of physical, psychological, emotional, and spiritual components.

The VUCA (volatile, uncertain, complex, and ambiguous) world of the 21st century is calling for a new type of leadership that can create inclusive workplaces and organizations where people and organizations can thrive simultaneously. Humans are hungry for engagement in the workplace that emanates from a sense of belonging and desired sense of purpose (Craig & Snook, 2014; Grant, 2017; Hollander, 2009). As society evolves, there is an ever-increasing demand for a new type of leadership, one that is inclusive and focuses not on just individual fulfillment, but also on how the entire organization can find meaning and purpose. This calls for a "hallowing of work and workplaces" that can nurture the spiritual dimension of human existence—the need to create organizations that are at once whole and holy (Dhiman, 2015, 2017, 2019; Dhiman & Amar, 2019).

To attain and sustain workplace flourishing, one must first be personally fulfilled, which requires alignment with one's true self in the form of spiritual clarity, conviction, and psychological freedom. Well-being is a multifaceted construct, consisting of physical, psychological, emotional, and spiritual components. Considering the prominent disconnect with spirituality in the workplace, as well as the chasm between personal and professional life, most individuals are imperatively in need of such awareness and guidance. Cultivating personal fulfillment requires humility, compassion, and patience, which this chapter discusses in further detail.

Moreover, spiritual practices and self-knowledge pointers are underlined as integral parts of the aforementioned self-growth and transformation; such notions include, but are not limited to, mindfulness, meditation and yoga, self-understanding and self-compassion, humility, gratitude, emotional intelligence, personal values and ethics, intrinsic motivation, goal aspiration, and total self-sincerity and honesty. By harnessing spirituality in the workplace, leaders can improve the culture of the workplace, as well as the productivity and self-fulfillment of employees. The next section outlines the facets of an intolerant leader and how the existence of this toxicity in the workplace stumps productivity and threatens personal and organizational well-being.

Belonging and Individuality in Inclusive Organizations

The secret to creating and empowering high-performing inclusive organizations is to first create *inclusion* and *belonging*. This requires engaged humility. A humble leader recognizes their place in the universe of their organization and is not afraid to show their shortcomings, because they understand the power of self-acceptance. The humble leader accepts his/her own strengths and, in turn, empowers others to develop their own unique strengths.

According to a study by *Catalyst* (2015, p. 2), the humble leader that creates belonging and uniqueness will create inclusion, which ultimately creates a workplace where employees feel "connected to and supportive of one another, and where everyone can advance and thrive." Belonging and uniqueness may be misinterpreted as opposites; the feeling of belonging to a group with similar mindsets may be seen as opposed to a group with unique personalities. However, in this case, belonging refers to the connectedness that employees feel because of their unique personalities; a feeling only created by a leader who understands that self-acceptance and uniqueness are valuable to a well-rounded team.

The study by *Catalyst* revealed that only 34% of individuals in the US feel a sense of belonging in their workplace and are part of a working group in which they feel they add value. A dismal 19% of US employees feel they are unique and that this distinctiveness is valued by others in the group: almost 5% lower than their Chinese and Australian counterparts. Humble leaders understand the value of promoting inclusiveness by suspending judgments and allow the free flow of ideas from employees. The more an employee feels that their uniqueness is valued, the more likely they will contribute their ideas and think innovatively, since they do not fear their out-of-the-box ideas will be criticized.

The Bhagavad Gītā: Old Text, New Leadership Context

The *Bhagavad Gītā*, the classic Hindu scripture, holds a special place in the world's sacred literature. Count Hermann Keyserling, a German philosopher, hailed it as "perhaps the most beautiful work of the literature of the world" (Durant, 1930, p. 6). Noting its widespread appeal and popularity, Minor (1982, p. 5), a modern exegetical commentator, states that the Bhagavad Gītā has become "the most translated text after the *Bible*." Its universal message speaks endearingly to people from all walks of life who are in search of abiding answers to the fundamental questions of life. According to Aldous Huxley, "The *Bhagavad Gītā* is perhaps the most systematic scriptural statement of the Perennial Philosophy" (Prabhavananda & Isherwood, 1951/2002, p. 22).

Mahatmā Gandhī regarded the Bhagavad Gītā as "a spiritual reference book" (cited in Gandhi & Strohmeier, 2009, p. 15). According to the great Indian commentator, Ādi Śaṅkarācārya, "From a clear knowledge of the *Bhagavad Gītā* all the goals of human existence become fulfilled. Bhagavad Gītā is the manifest quintessence of all the teachings of the Vedic scriptures." In his authoritative commentary on the Gītā, Śaṅkarācārya extols it as "the compendium of the quintessence of all the teachings of the *Vedas*" (*samasta-vedārtha-sārasaṅgraha-bhūtaṁ*).

This section shows that the Bhagavad Gītā can be approached as a powerful tool for change management and as a catalyst for organizational transformation. The Bhagavad Gītā teaches us how to harmonize the needs of the individual with the needs of society and, by extension, how to harmonize the needs of employees and the organization. It employs an inside-out leadership development approach based on self-knowledge and self-mastery, two highly important areas for practicing true inclusive leadership in contemporary organizations ruled by a knowledge factor.

The Bhagavad Gītā contains timeless inclusive leadership lessons for contemporary organizations. Modern leadership concepts such as vision, motivation and empowerment, self-awareness, self-mastery, excellence in work, importance of ethical means in achieving righteous ends, attaining meaning and fulfillment at work, service before self, and well-being of all beings are all lucidly discussed in the Gītā. Likewise, many contemporary leadership constructs, such as authentic leadership, servant leadership, and values-based leadership, were already discussed, albeit notionally, in the Bhagavad Gītā thousands of years ago.

Building Inclusive, Empowering Organizations, According to the Bhagavad Gītā

When faced with the importance of an organization's health, the main focus becomes how effectively that organization can succeed in ensuring a workplace to flourish. Workplace flourishing is different from flourishing in the workplace in that it focuses on the organization's health as a whole from upper management to lower management and beyond. Workplace flourishing means ensuring that the many moving parts in the organization can work harmoniously together to create an effective, sustainable working environment.

Leaders have been told repeatedly what the ingredients are for a healthy organization, but they either believe that they have already achieved it or find that there are other more important issues that they need to invest their time in.

In Chapter 16 of the Bhagavad Gītā, the Indian wisdom text, we find very practical guidance on building an empowering work culture—characterized by fearlessness, purity, self-restraint, sacrifice, straightforwardness, nonviolence, truthfulness, tranquility, gentleness, modesty, forgiveness, and the absence of fault-finding, greed, ostentatiousness, envy, and pride (B.G. 16.1–3; Dhiman, 2015, 2019). Leaders should strive to embody these qualities and to foster an environment where these qualities can be nurtured. A strong work ethic marked by these empowering qualities goes a long way in achieving workplace excellence and harmony and, in turn, an inclusive organization.

Similarly, the Gītā goes on to describe what may be called a disempowering work culture—characterized by hypocrisy, arrogance, self-conceit, anger, harshness, and lack of discrimination between the real and unreal, duty, and nonduty (B.G. 16.4). The Gītā also teaches us that excessive desire, anger, and greed are subtle forms of violence against oneself, others, and the universe. They thwart the spirit of inclusiveness and rob the sanctity of the workplace. It is to be noted that a strong work ethic is not enough to build an empowering work culture; after all, a hard-core criminal also has a very strong work ethic. What is needed is a work ethic guided by ethics in work (Dhiman, 2015, 2019).

The deeper message here is that we should not focus on the faults of others; rather, we should tackle our own shortcomings. A too-critical, carping attitude toward our fellow beings is a source of much unhappiness. "If you want peace of mind," says Sri Sarada Devi (Satprakashananda, 1977, p. 93), "do not find fault with others." (We are told that this is the last recorded message of Sri Sarada Devi, the worthy consort of Sri Ramakrishna Paramahamsa, the greatest Indian sage-saint of the 19th century.) Swami Dayananda, a modern Advaita teacher, says that the purpose of knowing about these values is not self-judgment or judgment of others.

> All kinds of people make up this world. You want to change others so that you can be free, but it never works that way.... People are what they are because they have their own backgrounds, and they cannot be otherwise.
>
> *(cited in Prasad, 1999, p. 246)*

Understanding this fosters tolerance, empathy, and consideration that lead to all-around wellness.

The Bhagavad Gītā: Key Leadership Lessons

Leadership, according to the Gītā, is an "inside-the-mind" affair. All dilemmas are first fought within the mind (Chatterjee, 2012, p. 3). Mind matters most in leadership. The Gītā's conception of personal mastery in the form of an ideal sage mostly centers on emotional maturity—*the ability to manage emotional disturbances and reactions calmly*. Right thinking and right conduct serve as the two unshakable pillars of leadership. Thus, the Gītā emphasizes the training of the mind. It starts with self-awareness, which ultimately depends upon self-knowledge (B.G. 2.52–72; 13.7–11). Self-knowledge means the knowledge of one's true self at the *soul level*, beyond senses, mind, and intellect.

It is only when a leader is able to relinquish self-interest and egotism that he/she is able to attain true contentment—rejoice and repose of the true self. Such a person then has nothing left here to do for himself (B.G. 3.17), but for others. According to the Gītā (6.32), that person "is considered best who judges happiness and sorrow in all beings by the same standard as he would apply to himself." Selfless leaders do their duty for duty's sake (cf. Kant's duty ethics), to set an example for others, to bring communities together, for the well-being of all, and above all, for the purification of the mind and the heart. This is the essence of what we know as servant leadership.

The greatest practical lesson that the Gītā teaches leaders to follow is the *Karma Yoga*—the highest discipline to live by, i.e., use the right means for a just cause and leave the results in hands of the higher power (God).

Inclusive Organizations Through Wise Leadership

>Where is the Life we have lost in living?
>Where is the Wisdom
>Where is the knowledge we have lost in information?
>—*T.S. Eliot, from* The Rock
>(The Collected Poems of T. S. Eliot, *1909–1962*)

In relatively stable times, formal organizational power may be sufficient to execute an effective strategy and to realize the organization's mission. However, during turbulent times, organizations need to draw upon the collective wisdom of all of its members to be truly effective. Wise leadership is an alternative to top-down autocratic, heroic leadership. The integrative function of leadership calls for developing wisdom at all levels of a firm (i.e., inclusive) to be able effectively to address inflection points. Such an inclusive approach to leadership is well suited for the multifaceted issues faced by contemporary organizations. In this section, we will approach leadership as a matter of holistic awareness of issues and solutions rather than as dependent on the formal position, power, or title of the leader. We will describe *inclusive* strategies for serving organizations, their stakeholders, and associated relevant communities.

Wise leaders are *engaged* leaders. They are *inclusive* leaders. We find that this conception of an *engaged* sage/leader lies at the heart of all wisdom traditions of the world as well. In the first chapter of his masterly work *A Short History of Chinese Philosophy*, Dr. Yu-Lan Fang (1997, p. 3) describes the character of Chinese Sage as that of "sageliness *within* and kingliness *without*" (emphasis added). Similarly, we find the same theme in Plato's conception of the philosopher-kings, who, having cultivated wisdom, is *fit* to rule. Why did the great Greek philosopher insist on philosophers being kings and kings becoming philosophers to save the world from all evil? Plato provides the classic answer to the classic question, why should philosophers rule?, in what is perhaps the most famous passage in all of Plato (Cooper, 1997; see also Hamilton & Cairns, 1961) as follows:

>Unless . . . philosophers become kings in the cities or those whom we now call kings and rulers philosophize truly and adequately and there is a conjunction of political power and philosophy . . . there can be no cessation of evils . . . for cities nor, I think, for the human race.
>(*Republic, V.473c11–d6*)

This is the final verdict of Plato, perhaps the greatest philosopher of the entire Western world: *Only the wise can truly sustain the world*. In all his dialogues, Plato brings out this inherent conflict between power and knowledge. Those who have power seldom have wisdom and those have wisdom seldom have power. Unless power and wisdom meet in one leader, humankind will not be saved from misery. The history has vindicated Plato time and again, from world wars, to political fiascos, to outrageous failures of organizations such as Enron and Lehman Brothers.

Another perspective of wise leadership that fosters inclusive cultures and communities comes from the Bhagavad Gītā, the wisdom text of India. In the Gītā's view, only those who know themselves are truly wise (*paṇḍitāḥ*). Hence, only those who have self-knowledge should lead. Only then, humanity may have happy individuals and harmonious society. Self-knowledge (wisdom) brings a certain measure of "integration" in human personality. Only a well-integrated (*yoga-yukta*) person can be an effective leader.

An unexamined life, said Socrates, is not worth living (*Apology*, 38a). It is only through the sincere examination of our lives that we realize the true meaning and understanding of our life's full potential. For leaders who strive to live "examined lives," journey is more important than destination. This self-examination is called discernment, the art of living attentively. The Buddha's last words (cited in Calasso, 1999, p. 396) were, "Act without inattention" [*Digha Nikāya* II. 156].

The essence of wise leadership consists of

1. discovering and knowing the truth about ourselves as individuals;
2. helping others to uncover and embody this truth in action;
3. living this truth moment by moment in a life marked by guiding purpose, integrity, humility, compassion, courage, and organizational contribution; and
4. achieving deep insight into the art and science of effective leadership.

Core Premises of Wise, Inclusive Leadership

1. Wisdom, anchored in ethical action that takes into account whole systems, needs to be inclusive and should be made accessible to leaders and managers at all levels, as well as those aspiring to leadership positions.
2. The deepest roots of wisdom lie in the great spiritual and religious traditions of humankind.
3. Wise leadership is about what wisdom is and how it can be applied at all levels of scale—from the individual to the organizational to the societal—moment by moment, decision by decision.
4. Without the presence of guiding wisdom, a group, an organization, a country, a society will become like a ship adrift without a rudder in a sea of turbulence.
5. An overriding and pervasive need to deal with the dynamic tension between the deterministic forces of the internal and external environments forces on one hand, and the free will of individual leaders to create new avenues for creativity and action on the other.

Life, said Aristotle, is a gift of nature. Beautiful living is a gift of wisdom. In his book, *Nicomachean Ethics*, Aristotle asks a question, what is the essence of life? And answers, The essence of life is *to serve others and do good*.[3] Thus we see that wisdom has its natural flowering in compassion—selfless benevolence for all beings. In fact, wisdom and compassion are two sides of the same coin. *Sageliness within; kingliness without.*

No higher ideal for authentic leadership can be conceived!

How Can Inclusive Leaders Increase Workplace Flourishing and Well-Being?

Engaged leaders model behavior and inspire others through actions, not just words or slogans. To achieve this, they approach employees in a holistic manner, acknowledging and appreciating the gifts they bring to the organization. More often than not, we find that organizations fail to effectively harness all the talent available to them.

Jack Welsh notes that a middle-aged appliance worker at a GE Work-Out session once said, "For 25 years, you paid for my hands when you could have had my brain as well—for nothing" (p. 56). In his magnum opus on management, titled *Winning*, Welch offers the following pointers for employee engagement: Include all voices in the decision-making process, spread energy and enthusiasm, establish trust by being candid, transparent, and giving credit where it is due, and, above all, celebrate. Whenever he would ask groups if they celebrate enough, surprisingly, "almost no one raises a hand," he notes (p. 78). Empowering leaders constantly strive to create a culture of celebration and appreciation. Instead of looking for people doing something wrong, they catch people doing something right.

Concluding Thoughts: Workplace Wellness, Individual Fulfillment, and Organizational Excellence

Workplace contentment, fulfillment, or wellness may seem intangible, but it can tangibly affect the growth and success of an organization. There are obvious, unmistakable signs by which it can be recognized. Organizations have less absenteeism, turnover, and stress when employees have a sense of purpose and belonging, enhanced contribution, and more engagement and trust. On the other hand, people merely going through the motions are more likely to be absent and eventually leave the company. Organizations are not just numbers, and you do not want to pursue profits in an unbridled manner. Leaders need to remember that organizations are about people. Being highly fulfilled takes a conscious decision and intentional effort; it is not something that just comes on its own accord. Leaders are responsible for creating an environment where human beings can flourish and realize their dreams.

We need more good work and respectable workplaces: work that is mind enriching, heart fulfilling, soul satisfying, and financially rewarding and workplaces where joy of creation and contribution reign supreme, where everyone acts out of benevolence and empathy for the good of others, where people go out of their way to help each other, and where employees realize their dreams of higher purpose and meaning. We close with a quote from Lewis Munford (1895–1990, p. 354), renowned American historian, architectural critic, and sociologist: "Rome fell not because of political or economic ineptitude, not even because of barbarian invasions; Rome collapsed through a leaching away of meaning and a loss of faith. Rome fell because of a barbarization from within (cited in Robertson, 2017, p. 5)." It is leaders' prime job to prevent this decadence of human spirit through moral rejuvenation and inclusiveness. Only then can we expect to have "organizations worthy of human habitation," to use a felicitous phrase coined by Margaret J. Wheately (1999, p. xi). This would also be the advent of Kant's Kingdom of Ends *leading to* a Kingdom of Peace in the world!

Notes

1 This section is largely based on Professor Rick Roderick's fine lecture "Kant and the Path to Enlightenment" [full length], available on YouTube. Retrieved September 6, 2019, from www.youtube.com/watch?v=m-JW4X6QpPk&t=1125s
2 See Flourishing Report: "70% of US workers not engaged at work." State of the American Workplace. The report highlights findings from flourishing's ongoing study of the American workplace from 2010 through 2012. Retrieved from December 9, 2018, from www.gallup.com/services/178514/state-americanworkplace.aspx?g_source=position1&g_medium=related&g_campaign=tiles
3 Retrieved June 10, 2017, from www.quora.com/What-are-some-great-quotes-of-Aristotle

References

Beck, L. W. (Trans.). (1997). *Kant: Foundations of the metaphysics of morals and, What is enlightenment?* Upper Saddle River, NJ: Prentice Hall.
Calasso, R. (1999). *Kā: Stories of the mind and Gods of India* (p. 396). New York, NY: Alfred A. Knopf.

Catalyst. (2015). Inclusion matters. *Catalyst.* New York, NY. Retrieved December 7, 2018, from www.catalyst.org/knowledge/inclusion-matters

Chatterjee, D. (2012). *Timeless leadership: 18 leadership sutras from the Bhagavad Gita.* Hoboken, NJ: Wiley.

Cooper, J. (Ed.). (1997). *Plato: Complete works.* Indianapolis: Hackett.

Craig, N., & Snook, S. A. (2014, May). From purpose to impact: Figure out your passion and put it to work. *Harvard Business Review, 92*(5), 105–111.

Dhiman, S. (2015). *Gandhi and leadership: New horizons in exemplary leadership.* New York, NY: Palgrave Macmillan.

Dhiman, S. (2017). *Holistic leadership: A new paradigm for today's leaders.* New York, NY: Palgrave Macmillan.

Dhiman, S. (2019). *Bhagavad Gītā and leadership: A catalyst for organizational transformation.* Basel: Palgrave Macmillan/Springer Nature.

Dhiman, S., & Amar, A. D. (2019). *Managing by the Bhagavad Gītā: Timeless lessons for today's managers.* Basel: Springer Nature.

Durant, W. (1930). *The case for India.* New York: Simon and Schuster.

Eliot, T. S. (2002). *The collected poems of T.S. Eliot (1909–1962).* New York: Faber and Faber.

Fang, Y. L. (1997). *A short history of Chinese philosophy: A systematic account of Chinese thought from its origins to present day* (Reissue ed.). New York, NY: Free Press.

Gandhi, M., & Strohmeier (Eds.). (2009). *The Bhagavad Gita according to Gandhi.* Berkeley, CA: North Atlantic Books.

Grant, G. B. (2017). Exploring the possibility of peak individualism, humanity's existential crisis, and an emerging age of purpose. *Frontiers in Psychology, 8,* 1478.

Hamilton, E., & Cairns, H. (Eds.). (1961). *The collected dialogues of Plato.* Princeton, NJ: Princeton University Press. Bollingen Series (General).

Hollander, E. (2009). *Inclusive leadership: The essential leader-follower relationship.* New York, NY: Routledge.

Minor, R. N. (1982). *Bhagavad-Gītā: An exegetical commentary.* New Delhi: Heritage Publishers.

Peterson, J. (2018). *12 rules for life: An antidote to chaos.* New York: Random House.

Prabhavananda, S., & Isherwood, C. (1951/2002). *Bhagavad-Gita: The song of god.* New York: Signet.

Prasad, R. (1999). *The Bhagavad Gita: The song of God.* Freemont, CA: American Gita Society.

Robertson, S. (2017, June 7). Herding cattle into the seductive depravity of Hollywood's great karmic corral. *The Blog.* Retrieved December 22, 2019, from https://www.huffpost.com/entry/herding-cattle-into-the-s_b_10315170

Satprakashananda, S. (1977). *The goal and the way: The vedantic approach to life's problems.* St. Louis, MO: The Vedanta Society of St. Louis.

Welsh, J. (2006). *Winning: How to win in business and in life!* New York, NY: Harper.

Wheately, M. J. (1999). *Leadership and the new science: Discovering order in a chaotic world.* San Francisco, CA: Berrett Koehler Publishers.

30
INCLUSIVE LEADERSHIP DEVELOPMENT THROUGH PARTICIPATORY INQUIRY
Cultivating Cultural Humility

Ester R. Shapiro and Tariana V. Little

In Memoriam: Sherry Penney Livingston (1937–2019), Chancellor, UMass Boston (1988–2000), Interim President, UMass 5 College System (1995), Founding Director and faculty, UMass Boston Center for Collaborative Leadership and Emerging Leaders Program (2000–2012).

Each person has a special gift—her/his voice. Use it to share your vision and to help people understand who you are and what motivates you (Penney & Nielson, 2010, p. 37).

Ester remembers: Invited to write this chapter based on the Emerging Leaders Program (ELP), I was preparing to reach out to Founder Sherry Penney, who remained active in retirement, when I learned of her tragic accidental death. In her many impactful roles at our urban public university, in Boston, and nationally, she transformed others' lives through her vision and actions as a committed inclusive leader and mentor. When I arrived at UMass Boston (1989), and learned Chancellor Penney was a historian with a faculty appointment in American Studies, I was told by an amused feminist colleague that our History Department had refused to appoint her among their faculty, reportedly saying, "We already have a woman in the department." In her Author's Note (Penney & Nielson, 2010, xi–xii), Penney recounts her sources of inspiration, rooted in intergenerational family experiences. She describes both supports she received and the gender barriers she overcame as a young girl, graduate student, faculty member and leader in higher education. Focused on mentoring in "modeling the way" for emerging leaders, she cultivated a collaborative approach to nurturing the next generation. Chancellor Penney was consistently vigilant to ensure individuals from underrepresented groups experiencing educational and workplace discrimination received the personal support, mentorship and orientation to how work was conducted, valued and evaluated, the code to advancement. Stepping down as chancellor, she chose a position in our College of Management and had visionary role as founding director of the Center for Collaborative Leadership and its ELP, which leveraged her power, knowledge and extensive social networks to open executive and leadership roles for those historically excluded. To create its annual class of 35–40 diverse emerging leaders, she persistently reached out to her leadership network from business, government and nonprofit organizations, inviting them to nominate a promising emerging leader from an underrepresented group in their organization. We could see, as she urged the city's powerful men (and some women) to identify a promising rising leader outside the typical configuration of power and commit to their continuing mentorship, that her request already changed their appreciation of organizational culture and customary choreographies of relationship toward greater inclusion. The intensive year-long program became a community-building opportunity for mentors and skill-building experience for participants. Senior leaders took responsibility for ongoing inclusive mentoring, while program participants learned skills in collaborative problem solving, networking and listening/learning across differences. Building on our urban public university's commitment to community-engaged policy research, which she fully supported, the ELP's heart was the creation of small teams identifying a meaningful Boston-centered policy research project. I was grateful that when Jennifer Leigh, a PhD student in clinical health psychology, wanted to conduct her research in organizational psychology, Sherry opened the program's curriculum development and first cohort experience to us for a collaborative process and outcome evaluation (Leigh, Shapiro, & Penney, 2010). The 800+ alumni of the continuing ELP, now an engaged community of inclusive leaders and mentors, have transformed the face of Boston's leadership. Unitarian Universalist by religious practice, expansive in her family, kinship and community ties, Sherry was a practicing evangelist for the beautiful diversity and impact we could bring into being through the generative power of inclusion. We dedicate this chapter in gratitude for all we learned from/with her and carry forward in her name.

Introductions

The coauthors are both Latinx-identified women educators and professionals, with educational and organizational roles in public health, educational equity, leadership development, communications for social change and transdisciplinary social justice research supporting emancipatory learning generating social inclusion. Ester, a Cuban Eastern European Jewish American who at age 8 immigrated to South Florida with her twice-refugee family, is most often "read/categorized" due to name and appearance as "white, North American, Jewish." In Boston's environment of ethnic enclaves, she is often asked to explain how she is "also" Cuban. She has dedicated her work to better understanding how immigrant families like her own seek ways to survive and thrive, and how services and social policies can best assist family thriving and supporting culturally sensitive gender equity. Tariana is proudly and unapologetically a queer, multicultural, first-generation college student from a working-class Dominican-German-Mexican immigrant family in Boston. Her work, driven by science, storytelling and social justice, embodies what she terms "intentional creativity for social change." A research scientist-turned-social entrepreneur, Tariana leads and cofounded EmVision, a media boutique that helps progressive organizations harness social impact storytelling™ to achieve their goals. Together in community, we are committed to democratizing approaches to inclusive inquiry applying trans/disciplinary methods to co-create knowledge supporting innovative, equitable solutions. In this chapter, we explore how collaborative, practice-oriented policy research incorporating cultural humility advances inclusive leadership.

Transdisciplinarity is a holistic approach to social justice oriented, problem-solving research incorporating critical perspectives on societal power, collaborative creation of knowledge and accountability to using results to advance equity (Espina Prieto, 2007; Leavy, 2016). Our transdisciplinary practice-based approach has co-evolved through years of shared learning as mentor and mentee, co-researchers and colleagues at the Mauricio Gastón Institute for Latino Public Policy and Community Development (Gastón Institute) and in development of the Critical Ethnic and Community Studies (CECS) master's program, a critical multiethnic studies program emphasizing transdisciplinary, community-engaged social justice research benefitting local communities. We draw on our ongoing trans/generational dialogues and transdisciplinary readings on creating culturally diverse collaborative teams supporting inclusive innovation. We use examples from UMass Boston's Emerging Leaders Program (ELP) and Latino Leadership Opportunity Program (LLOP). Continuing since its founding in 2002, the ELP (Leigh et al., 2010; Leigh, 2003; Penney & Nielson, 2010; DeAngelis, Penney & Scully, 2015) recruits mid-level professionals from underrepresented groups for a year-long program for leadership growth. The LLOP selects undergraduate Latinx and other historically excluded students to use their lived experiences alongside transdisciplinary policy research to advance their work in/with professional organizations. Both ELP and LLOP offer examples of inclusive leadership development programs grounded in community-engaged public policy research, through teamwork incorporating diverse perspectives to achieve organizational and community change towards valued goals. We review and apply systemic approaches to equity grounded in cultural, developmental, health, participatory public health and organizational studies, identifying organizational processes and leadership skills that can multiply/amplify positive social change towards increased inclusion. We identify leadership skills grounded in participatory inquiry mobilizing these processes, focusing on cultural humility, a term used in public health, which reaches beyond the widely used cultural competence approach. Cultural humility emphasizes lifelong learning from personal reflexivity, honest, empathic critical dialogues appreciating power differences emerging from intersectional social locations, and institutional accountability in using knowledge for greater equity (Tervalon & Murray-Garcia, 1998; Chavez & Minkler, 2010; Minkler, 2012).

Participatory Inquiry as Inclusive Leadership Practice: Recognizing Social Complexity, Learning From Differences and Taking Action

Writers and practitioners in inclusive leadership recognize the value of leadership development training to promote organizational diversity, yet appreciate that institutional change has been limited (Chin, Trimble, & Garcia, 2018; Combs, Milosevic, & Bilimoria, 2019; George, Baker, Tracey, & Joshi, 2019). Increasing organizational inclusion towards effective, equitable decision-making is widely regarded as an ethical and economic imperative. Cross-disciplinary research demonstrates that inclusion generates financial successes and nurtures innovation, supporting organizational change responsive to increased social and economic complexity (Galinsky et al., 2015; George et al., 2019; Page, 2017). In management and organizational studies, scholars, policymakers and advocates argue that engaging diverse perspectives towards authentic social inclusion, while simultaneously addressing systemic/structural barriers impeding full access to opportunities, is critical in developing innovations promoting societal-level change (Boitano, Dutra, & Schockman, 2017; George et al., 2019; Zanoni, Janssens, Benschop, & Nkomo, 2010). However, doing so requires tools for learning from differences and managing conflicts constructively to advance shared goals.

Learning from diverse life and work experiences allows us to contextualize knowledge towards more creative, effective solutions, because conversations in mixed company consider roadblocks or opportunities potentially overlooked by homogeneous groups. Yet we also appreciate that learning from differences is constrained by segregation of residence, schooling and affiliations such as redlining neighborhoods to preserve racial segregation (Rothstein, 2017), and through social pressures and preferences in who we work with or share bread with, limiting what we learn from/with others. Social capital, the networks of relationships supporting our sense of belonging and instrumental problem solving, differs greatly depending on histories of educational or economic access and social location, impacting our ability to reach out to others in solving problems both personally and organizationally (Booysen, 2014). Power and privilege protect us from knowing worlds of societally imposed hardship or having to look beneath celebrated public histories for erased stories continuing to haunt us. Salter and Adams (2016) found that Black History Month displays of Black enslavement rather than only cultural celebrations were more likely to lead college students to recognize current-day racism, especially for students at predominantly white institutions.

When first learning from others' perspectives, we may be surprised by our own ignorance or find cherished beliefs challenged. Yet, as US-based Nigerian writer Chimamanda Ngozi Adichie (2009) persuasively relates in her TED talk, "The Danger of a Single Story," all of us have to battle stereotypes handed to us through family and culture, to imagine the reality of lives different from our own. As she proposes, doing so offers us a kind of paradise—a hard-won ethical perspective cultivated by many of our religions and social justice communities. Power, operating at entangled levels in our institutions and communities, willfully and/or inadvertently permits us to overlook or censor voices who might teach us something new (and uncomfortable). We obscure knowledge about how we benefit from racialized, gendered histories and current conditions producing and protecting inequality. Yet navigating power asymmetries towards constructive learning is foundational to our culturally grounded, co-evolving social/neurodevelopment. From a culturally informed developmental systems perspective, we establish our views of self, others and the world through engagement with family and culture, creating stable schemas to navigate the world (Juster et al., 2016; Shapiro, 2013, 2018). Breaking through to new learning requires what developmental psychologist Piaget called accommodation (creating new categories/schemas) rather than assimilation (incorporating new information into established categories/schemas). Spiritually informed and social justice ethical perspectives addressing these challenges of learning across power inequalities include philosopher Martin Buber's theory of I/it versus I/Thou relations, Latinx mujerista and African American womanist theologies, and Paulo Freire's emancipatory education. These writers offer the empathic intersubjectivity of dialogue as a radicalizing equalizer, transforming ourselves and our worlds by envisioning the subjective world of others with the compassion we afford ourselves (Bryant-Davis & Comas Diaz, 2016; Shapiro, 2018). Yet even when we cherish these values, learning from differences requires recognizing our multisystemic barriers to this knowledge, particularly when they expose power inequalities from which we benefit.

Complexity and Systems-Minded Leadership: Identifying Skills Contributing to Learning From Differences

Increasingly, those committed to organizational inclusion suggest that leadership development that recognizes the complexity of organizations, alongside the systemic processes protecting exclusion, requires critical, intersectional, ecosystemic/complexity sciences approaches applying practice-based frameworks cultivating mindsets and skills that promote collaborations attuned to equity (George et al., 2019; Mendes, Gomes, Marques-Quinteiro, Lind, & Curral, 2016; Schneider & Somers, 2006; Wandersman, 2003). Collaborations instigate continuous learning in establishing knowledge for shared policy planning, contextualized by the inclusion of diverse voices and stakeholder positions, agreeing to accountability in evaluating outcomes and revising based on mutually recognized sources of evidence. Many disciplines have turned to complex adaptive systems to better understand how to promote innovation and adaptive success of organizations and communities in a rapidly changing world. Complexity sciences view any system—cell, organism, organization, community, city, planet—holistically as interdependent. These approaches seek to identify potential stressors, available resources and barriers to access that increase vulnerability or promote success at dynamically interrelated levels. Frameworks exploring the dynamic relationships of parts to whole in producing emergent and valued or unintended and undesired outcomes have helped to map specific interdependent processes and identify leverage points and linkages.

Complexity sciences, originating in studies of self-organizing living systems, have been valued and applied in organizational change and leadership development studies, (Capra & Luisi, 2016; Dawkins & Barker, 2018; Page, 2017, Wheatley, 1992, 2017), human development (Juster et al., 2016) and public health (Rutter et al., 2017). The field of organizational change has focused on identifying systems processes supporting flexibility and innovation, while remaining accountable to efficiency and effectiveness. These adaptive management processes include experimentation and reflection, communication and feedback, future visioning, and cultivating constructive diversity and tension by attending to domains that provide stability under new conditions (Palmberg, 2009). Complexity sciences illuminate the contributions of diverse perspectives, much like the role of species and habitat diversity in environmental sciences, to protecting possibilities for creative adaptation to both ordinary and unexpected changes (Ungar, 2018; Page, 2017; Rockefeller Foundation, 2019). The Rockefeller Foundation's 100 Resilient Cities Project (Rockefeller Foundation, 2019) developed a City Resilience Framework through collaborative inquiry that emphasizes inclusive leadership, collaborations and community participation, transparent communication and societal equity as resilience. In developmental systems and public health, we identify "vicious circles," in which family poverty co-occurs with other damaging factors, such as unsafe neighborhoods or underfunded/underperforming schools, and "virtuous circles" in which well-off neighborhoods with housing stability co-occur with better schools and public safety. Knowledge towards inclusive, effective solution-oriented change requires adjustments in scale and perspective, moving from big picture/macro to the specificity of a micro-perspective, mindful of how parts relate to whole.

Senge, Hamilton, and Kania (2015) suggest that a systems mindset requires collaborative leadership skills. These skills include seeing systems from multiple perspectives, encouraging trust-based generative conversations about divergent views and seeing past current crises towards future possibilities. Yet when we live and work in segregation or homogeneity, we lack opportunities to learn these skills or to overcome societal barriers communicating, explicitly and implicitly, who holds valued knowledge and who can be dismissed/excluded. These skills are best developed when individuals are exposed to complex perspectives generated by differences—cross-cultural encounters, immigration and multiculturalism, the open listening to differences that allows for personal insights and new learning. Bringing together complexity sciences and intersectional social justice perspectives allows us to appreciate the multifaceted dimensions of unique individuals, their relationships and organizations/settings, called forth by specific tasks and challenges. Inclusive leadership requires mobilizing our power while appreciating our impacts on others, recognizing the shifting landscape of positionality and intersecting identities depending on group composition and tasks, managing self-protective impulses and cherishing the surprises of new learning.

Across disciplines, writers using holistic, multicultural and social innovation approaches and applying complexity sciences to identify skills that promote inclusive social change recognize the importance of questioning assumptions regarding groups experiencing discrimination, identifying ideologies and practices preserving inequalities, and appreciating cultural resources/cultural wealth and ingenuity needed to survive adversity. Jones (2000) identifies "levels of racism" co-occurring and entangled multi-systemically, impacting individuals and their internalized beliefs, relationships and their choreographies, and institutional beliefs and practices. Scanning the literature, we identify skills and strategies that speak to inclusion and empowerment of disadvantaged groups, development of cross-cultural sensitivity or cultural competence by groups in positions of power, and collaboration towards inclusion in mixed company. Complexity sciences help document the multidimensional ways that inequalities operate in altering possibilities for positive adaptation over the course of development when confronting inevitable challenges of change, while identifying potential leverage points destabilizing the status quo or delivering high-yield positive impacts, whether for individuals, organizations, communities or cities. These approaches can then lead to more realistic, evidence-informed practice or policy change. Lichtenstein et al. (2006) argue that in complex adaptive systems, leadership is a quality of relationships in context (rather than specific to individuals), and conflicts can catalyze new perspectives and actions. Coleman et al. (2017) use a dynamical systems model of multicultural organizational change, focused on constructive conflict management to disrupt the interwoven mechanisms for systems stability termed "attractors." These authors outline how leveraging conflicts grounded in experiences of interpersonal or organizational discrimination can help break down destructive multicultural attractors, or change-resistant patterns of intergroup bias and discrimination, and promote more constructive attractors through increased institutional accountability for enacting fair and just workplace reforms. Community organizer and organizational consultant adrienne maree brown (2017) uses critical/intersectional and complexity perspectives to identify "emergent strategies" that correct unequal power relations towards greater inclusion in organizations historically centered on White male leadership. She argues that in complex adaptive systems, small acts can transform relations and outcomes towards justice. Trittin and Schoeneborn (2017) suggest that an intercultural communications approach can advance how inclusive teams communicate across differences. Experiences in connection through inclusion expand the social networks, or access to social capital, that we can use towards innovative solutions.

Leaders from historically excluded groups draw on personal and cultural resources emerging from their culturally informed life experiences overcoming adversities, what Yosso and Burciaga term "cultural wealth" (2016). Focusing on leaders from underrepresented groups, Chin, Desormeaux, and Sawyer (2016) convened underrepresented psychologists working in inclusive organizational leadership practice and consulting for a dialogue identifying a competency framework for diversity leadership. They identified four multidimensional competencies:

1. *Leveraging personal and social identities*: leading authentically, balancing self-promotion with humility, projecting confidence amidst identity backlash, and building trust and demonstrating integrity across diverse groups;
2. *Utilizing a global and diverse mindset*: being culturally competent, demonstrating cross-cultural flexibility and promoting diverse and inclusive leadership styles;
3. *Leveraging community and organizational contexts*: drawing from lived experiences, developing affinity networks, engaging with diverse communities, and protecting oneself; and
4. *Promoting a diversity-supportive and inclusive climate*: communicating across diverse groups, advancing a shared vision of diversity, mentoring diverse employees and maintaining accountability for promoting organizational diversity.

Inclusive leadership development requires commitment from senior leadership and other organization members who benefit from dominant White and male status. In their review of inclusive organizational practices, Galinsky et al. (2015) argue that a multicultural approach to inclusion, fostering both individual and collective learning from diverse personal experiences, needs to persuade individuals holding dominant or privileged organizational roles of the value of de-centering power to amplify voices of and benefit from multiple perspectives. In a special issue critiquing the state of organizational inclusion, Combs et al. (2019) argue that advancing organizational diversity and inclusion requires focusing on three domains: (1) multifaceted expressions of diversity; (2) work relationships in diversity and inclusion; and (3) diversity and inclusion in the highest organizational leadership. Their review highlights the complexity and interrelatedness of individual identities, organizational processes, public policies and social contexts, especially beliefs and practices such as intersectional gender/ethnic/racial stereotyping designed to protect the privileges of those holding the most organizational and societal power (Combs et al., 2019).

From Cultural Competence to Cultural Humility

We find that cultural humility (Chavez & Minkler, 2010; Tervalon & Murray-Garcia, 1998) offers an approach to learning cross-culturally that recognizes how power inequities create barriers to learning. Cultural humility, a term used primarily in training for equitable healthcare services for diverse individuals and communities, helps bring together central processes proposed in the varied literatures addressing knowledge and action promoting inclusive leadership and holding different levels of societal and institutional power in multiple domains. Although the term "cultural competence" is widely used in healthcare, and increasingly in other fields including organizational studies and cross-cultural communication, it can be misused as offering a formula for training. Training in cultural competence without a systems-minded, critical perspective puts too much weight on individual practitioners, when what we need is an organizational, multisystemic perspective that promotes culturally sensitive practices in organizational spheres (Betancourt, Green, Carrillo, & Owusu Ananeh-Firempong, 2003). As an individual training strategy, cultural competence that does not cultivate a systemic mindset and critical consideration of power inequalities can inadvertently slip into supporting societal preconceptions and stereotyping "other" marginalized or cultural groups while ignoring impactful contextual factors. Clinicians who have been taught that Latinx individuals overstate pain may overlook a stoic single working mother's moment of succumbing to unbearable distress.

Cultural humility is a principles-based, process-oriented position on inquiry supporting the knowledge needed to work with or serve others in various roles towards shared goals. Chavez and Minkler (2010) define "cultural humility" as a lifelong learning process that incorporates openness, power-balancing, and critical self-reflection when interacting with people for mutually beneficial partnerships and institutional change. In a training video on practicing cultural humility (Chavez, 2012), speakers emphasize four dimensions:

1. Lifelong learning and critical self-reflection;
2. Recognizing and changing power imbalances;
3. Developing mutually beneficial partnerships; and
4. Insisting on institutional accountability.

Rather than seeing cultural knowledge as knowledge towards which we acquire "competence," cultural humility appreciates that, like learning a language alongside its implicit cultural codes, we undertake a lifelong, in-depth understanding that expands our power to communicate with and learn from others. Cultural humility allows us to learn from others whose cultural, racial, gender, spiritual beliefs or religious practices, national origin and immigration status, educational and economic status, or other characteristics and life experiences differ from ours, as we create and pursue commonly held goals. Addressing community organizers working in health and social services, Minkler (2012) encourages "cultural humility" to highlight the conscious intention and self-awareness, whether operating as "insiders" or "outsiders," when working with communities to establish shared goals. Cultural humility appreciates the multiple domains—social class and level of education, gender identities/sexualities, immigration and documentation status—that may be relevant to a specific work group and setting.

Consistent with perspectives on learning from differences through dialogue and empathy, cultural humility requires respect and commitment to ethical equity perspectives even when, especially when, they cause us to question our assumptions or privileges. Lifelong learning with/from others includes continuous self-questioning of personal and professional assumptions through personal reflexivity, open dialogues in listening to/learning from differences, particularly in situations where privilege makes the workings of inequality invisible. Even in groups seemingly homogeneous by gender, race, ethnicity or other visible statuses, our complex backgrounds and lived experiences are likely to generate non-visible, unexpected sources of difference from which we can all learn. This attitude of shared learning in community is supported by participatory inquiry.

Participatory Inquiry as Inclusive Leadership Development Practice

Complexity and systems-minded approaches to inclusive leadership recognize the importance of teamwork to acquiring knowledge. Historically, Kurt Lewin's work in group-centered action research that builds knowledge through inclusion and constructive conflict management has influenced both management practices (Burnes, 2004) and community-based participatory research (Wallerstein, Duran, Oetzel, & Minkler, 2017). Participatory inquiry can illuminate wide-ranging lived experiences, including of those historically oppressed, and harness new knowledge to solve urgent problems. Our obliviousness to the complexity of lives constrained by challenges we have not directly experienced limits our knowledge of our world and of ourselves. Narrowing our relationships and knowledge of a complex world, we miss out on learning how others, enriched by cultural resources and strivings for success, survive and flourish in spite of obstacles, suggesting lessons for us all.

Methods for inclusive knowledge creation require focus on how power inequalities are designed to silence certain voices and privilege others. Participatory Action Research (PAR) emerged from Kurt Lewin's work on group processes required for constructive action and from emancipatory/empowerment education or critical pedagogy associated with the work of Brazilian educator Paulo Freire (Wallerstein et al., 2017). These PAR methods emphasize stakeholder collaboration across social positions and the need for methods for equalizing knowledge exchange and honoring the experiences of individuals and communities most excluded from power. Their highest priority is accountability in using excluded knowledge towards equity. The UMass Boston research institutes, including both the Gastón Institute (LLOP) and the Center for Collaborative Leadership (ELP), have historically supported community-engaged research addressing urgent social problems specific to Boston's histories of inequalities. Research in organizational and cultural psychology suggest that the challenges faced by excluded individuals who live in multiple worlds require that they creatively discern and negotiate multifaceted social identities and deploy them differentially, leading to greater creativity in their lives (Gocłowska & Crisp, 2014) and in their contributions to organizations and capacity for entrepreneurship (Sanchez-Burks et al., 2015). These forms of everyday inquiry, designed for survival, expand personal understanding of the world and team capabilities.

Participatory inquiry offers an approach to research-supported assessment of organizational goals, practices and outcomes that encourages democratization of "inquiry" as a constant process of coproduced knowledge to achieve common goals (Wandersman, 2003; Wallerstein et al., 2017). Wandersman emphasizes that in real-world and community settings, only community collaborations can generate the knowledge of real-world contexts as they impinge on stakeholders holding different levels of knowledge and power, while holding teams accountable to applying the knowledge to achieve equity with effectiveness. This requires continuous learning through collaborations, sharing sources of knowledge, agreement about fair measurement of outcomes of a shared enterprise, and respect for different stakeholders and assessment methods. This approach combines personal reflexivity and dialogues that teach comparative readings of power alongside empathy so that we illuminate the inevitable "blind spots," where holding power or privilege keeps us from seeing how others are placed in subordinate positions. Participatory inquiry cultivates knowledge promoting both inclusion and effectiveness in establishing and evaluating shared goals through collaboration. PAR redefines "research" democratically, using Appadurai's concept of research as a human right (2006) generating knowledge needed for living. Participatory methods encourage the emergence of new thinking enriched by the dynamics of exchange, with collaborations helping to establish, implement and evaluate shared goals relevant to a specific organization or community.

Participatory policy research is not characterized by specific methods, but rather by a philosophy of inclusion and accountability (Wallerstein et al., 2018). A useful method is the storytelling/counter-storytelling narrative approach (Solórzano & Yosso, 2002; Yosso & Burciaga, 2016), which encourages incorporation of critical perspectives into personal narratives to illuminate how the same environment can create different lived experiences, while valuing these differences. Counter-storytelling affirms the strengths mobilized to succeed under challenging circumstances, countering societal discrimination with elevation of cultural resources as "cultural wealth" and a valuable form of social capital. Storytelling/counter-storytelling cultivates knowledge through emotionally evocative sharing foundational to dialogue, affirming and empowering participants experiencing inequity, while making those experiences visible, inspiring empathy and increased commitment for participants protected by privilege. Participatory policy research also addresses macro-level factors illuminated by these more experiential methods. For example, in a policy working group comprising diverse members, we can establish the realities of "segmented assimilation" documenting how population-level outcomes such as education, income or wealth in the same city operate differently in access to opportunities depending on one's social characteristics. Working from systems-minded developmental psychology (Juster et al., 2016), counter-storytelling allows a diverse work group to appreciate the different developmental pathways, some rich with opportunities, others strewn with obstacles yet innovating to promote resilience, bringing each individual to the shared organizational space. These dialogues and resulting learning help inclusive leaders analyze systematically and strategically how environments are structured, so that depending on how we are viewed by others we experience the seemingly "same" work space differently.

The Emerging Leaders Program (ELP): Project-Based Collaboration as Foundational to Leadership Promoting Inclusion

The ELP, founded by Center for Collaborative Leadership Director Sherry Penney in 2002 and continuing since with 800+ fellows, recruits mid-career individuals working in a wide range of organizations in Greater Boston for a nine-month leadership program. Participants, themselves from diverse backgrounds, are committed to increasing their collaboration with other diverse individuals. The ELP began with the intergenerational, collaborative practice-based and inclusive leadership approach Sherry Penney brought to the Center, beautifully captured through both experiential storytelling and analysis in *Next Generation Leadership* (Penney & Nielson, 2010). From the start, they applied Kouzes and Posner's (1987) leadership development model as offering an inquiry-based identification of skills involved in practicing effective leadership, including a leadership practices assessment. These leadership skills include:

1. *Challenging the process*—searching for opportunities to improve the organization, being willing to take risks and view disappointments as learning opportunities;
2. *Inspiring a shared vision*—believing that one can make a difference and enlisting others in your dreams;
3. *Enabling others to act*—showing mutual respect and fostering collaboration, and striving to make each person feel capable and powerful;
4. *Modeling the way*—setting an example for others and establishing interim goals for small wins along the way; and
5. *Encouraging the heart*—recognizing others' contributions and celebrating accomplishments.

When the program was developed, Director Penney and the faculty and staff invited Jennifer Leigh, a clinical psychology PhD student interested in studying organizational change, to interview faculty as they developed the framework and curriculum, and then participate in and evaluate the experiences of the first cohort (Leigh, 2003; Leigh et al., 2010). The quantitative study component had a quasi-experimental design, with pre/post participation testing while also identifying a matched comparison group of participant nominees and attendees at an ELP recruitment information session. The study found significant differences in four of five leadership practices after program participation: challenging the process; inspiring a shared vision; modeling the way; and encouraging the heart. Other significant areas of growth documented in the first-year quantitative evaluation included expansion of networks and enhanced access to mentorship. The evolving ELP has used for continuous assessment and shared learning both the leadership practices survey and shared reflection. Consistent with their value of voice and storytelling for organizational leaders who have experienced exclusion, the ELP built its continuing exploration of leadership development experiences grounded in experiential storytelling. These assessments culminated in two books: *Voices of the Future: Emerging Leaders*, which captured an array of personal narratives and *Next*

Generation Leadership: Insights From Emerging Leaders, synthesizing a broad assessment of participant experiences and shared reflections on skill development (Penney & Nielson, 2010).

Over time, the ELP has applied and further developed a collaborative leadership model built on teamwork, trust and respect for diversity of thought (DeAngelis, Penney, & Scully, 2014; DeAngelis & Penney, 2015). It continues to be centered on collaboration through teamwork and specific skills development as foundational to learning from diverse perspectives, supporting the communication that helps reduce isolation and break down silos, achieving better business and other organizational results. Recognizing the institutional challenges limiting collaboration, the program views this as a leadership skill to be learned and practiced. In the fall, the ELP brings 40–50 rising leaders (ELP fellows), nominated by mentors and other community members, selected for inclusion and cultivation of leaders with diverse backgrounds and perspectives. These fellows also bring diversity due to their organizational setting, including corporate, nonprofit and government sectors, a unique domain of inclusion that the ELP features as necessary in working together to support organizations to solve complex urban problems.

DeAngelis et al. (2014) reflected on the ELP approach to teaching leadership development through teamwork and collaboration, reporting on their insights from 90+ project teams during the 12 years of conducting and evaluating the program at that time. The heart of the program promotes hands-on collaboration practice through collectively selected team projects. The Center connects project teams (participants working across sectors) with nonprofit organizations to conduct research and propose solutions aligned with the organization's strategic initiatives, concentrating on possibilities and fostering civic engagement. Projects have addressed pressing economic and societal issues, including retaining talented professionals in Greater Boston; ensuring affordable housing, which supports workers whose contributions are vital, for example, retail clerks and childcare providers; building toolkits to educate organizations and decision makers on gun violence; engaging the community in race and place dialogues centered on inclusion; and developing strategic plans to help college students secure employment post-graduation. Recent project sponsors include educational entities both within and outside UMass Boston (UMass Boston Institute for Community Inclusion; UMass Boston Office of Community Partnerships; Massasoit Community College); business groups (Massachusetts Business Roundtable); nonprofit organizations and advocacy groups (Boston Athletic Association; Stop Handgun Violence); and government organizations (Boston Municipal Research Bureau; Boston Public Library). Teams decide on their own working procedures, refining their project through shared continuous learning, establishing constructive relationships with stakeholders, and presenting a report within the program's nine-month span. The team experience emphasizes complexity and ongoing reflection. Reflecting on the impact of the collaborative, teamwork approach, the authors identify seven leadership skills developed by emerging leaders: (1) coping with ambiguity; (2) working cross-functionally beyond their usual expertise; (3) knowing when to get outside help; (4) understanding different stakeholders; (5) working effectively across dimensions of diversity; (6) dividing labor in a leaderless team; and (7) identifying an end-point advancing, without finalizing, a complex problem. This collaborative inquiry and problem-solving approach cultivates "the crucible of teamwork": participants shift toward the leadership challenges of defining project scale and significance, listening to multiple voices, pivoting accordingly and learning from challenges. Through evaluation, they find that ELP fellows emerge with broadened awareness of local issues, enhanced civic engagement and expanded networks.

One incident during the inaugural cohort's process of work group selection illustrated the power of listening across differences in establishing the trust required for cultural humility that could cultivate inclusive leadership development. The deliberative structuring of the group to cultivate explicit racial gender and class differences, alongside the open dialogue, led to a critical, transformative incident for the group (described in detail in Leigh et al., 2010, p. 376). During a first week of intensive meetings, facilitators devised a voting system for identifying first choices for group topics. As group selection was completed, an African American woman said to the group:

> I'm the only person that didn't get to work on my topic of choice—the only one who didn't get to have her vote count is a Black woman and that bothers me. When I brought it up to [the group facilitators] I was told I should go to a team that needed an underrepresented group member. . . . When the people in power pull an underrepresented group member to the side and say "How can we fit you in?" . . . I feel passionate about bringing transparency to that . . . I thought it was supposed to be different here.

Responding to her expressed concern, which was "coded/categorized" in the published article as "anger" (but which in retrospect may have been overly emphasized due to gendered racialized stereotyping of Black women's self-assertion), a White male in the group asked her, "How can I get you through this so you feel good?" The woman replied, "Don't patronize me. I'm not here to teach you how to do your job better. . . . There's a whole system going on you don't know about." At this point other participants joined in, sharing their perceptions of each person's comments and their own reactions to the process, addressing with intensity and immediacy the dynamics of diversity-related challenges they faced at work. The facilitators asked for a time-out to convene and consult, returning with an acknowledgment that they had intentionally, and mistakenly, chosen not to speak about group diversity issues at the start to wait until the group was more cohesive. They also recognized how this avoidance, combined with the topic selection voting process, inadvertently replicated exclusion. Based on this difficult dialogue, facilitators and fellows agreed to revise their agenda and procedures, beginning with a discussion of their own experiences of diversity, to which the facilitators were invited. Forming a circle, participants shared personal, often painful, experiences, accompanied by deep emotions and tears, relating discrimination based on race, gender, sexual orientation and socioeconomic status. White male participants shared fears that they would be presumed prejudiced because of their status. The fact that a participant experiencing exclusion felt safe enough to raise her voice, and that both faculty and participants responded to her concerns by changing the group topic selection process, hugely impacted the collective experience of inclusion. Tyler (2019) suggests that for organizational inclusion to be emancipatory, rather than an instrumental appearance of equality, organizations have to consider a relational, ethical approach that challenges normativity.

Latino Leadership Opportunity Program: Pan-Latinx Leadership and Applied, Community-Based Research for Latinx Public Policy

In contrast to the ELP, which recruits mid-career professionals, LLOP recruits promising Latinx undergraduate students. Nominated by faculty, staff and other students, LLOP fellows are recruited to a semester-long academic enrichment and leadership development program offered by UMass Boston's Gastón Institute, where students engage in applied research and public policy analysis. The Gastón Institute is part of the national Inter-University Program of Latinx Research (IUPLR) Centers, whose 33 members are at a university center that partners with local Latinx communities to conduct impactful action research. LLOP was initiated in the 1980s as a multi-center initiative to prepare Latinx students to excel academically and strive for leadership positions. Initially using a regional meeting model, by the 1990s LLOP evolved into a university-based program, many with an onsite IUPLR center (like Gastón Institute). Common framework and goals included a selective program for academically accomplished Latinx students (and others interested in working with Latinx communities), emphasizing policy research and leadership development training, mentoring and end-of-year presentations at a public policy conference.

The Participatory Research Model for Latino Social Policy (Diaz & Mora, 2004) used by many centers emerged from the struggle by growing Latinx communities to conduct systematic inquiry on the concerns of local communities, engage those most impacted in a co-creative process of mutual education and systematic exploration of the question, and take action. Many IUPLR centers emerged from and worked with a specific Latinx community, for example the UCLA Center for Chicano Studies, Hunter College Center for Puerto Rican Studies, and Florida International University Center for Cuban Studies. When the Gastón Institute was created in 1989 with the state legislature to identify Latino demographics in Massachusetts, the state's communities had grown from predominantly Puerto Rican to Central American, Dominican and other Caribbean, and Latin American nations (e.g. Colombia, Brazil), with migrations/immigration instigated by civil wars, US-backed dictatorships, economic crises and educational strivings.

In their semester-long seminar, LLOP fellows work with a faculty member to learn about Latinx policy issues locally and nationally and identify a working group and topic. The seminar incorporates presentations by Latinx faculty, graduate students, program alumni and community leaders about their life journey, educational and career inspirations, and insights on pursuing leadership positions. As in the ELP, LLOP combines mentorship with collaborative, group-based policy research. Representing Latinx diversities, each cohort encounters and incorporates into their research projects different realities of Boston's Latinx migration experiences. Ester led LLOP 2019 and recruited a class representing students from indigenous, Afro-diasporic and/or European backgrounds from Puerto Rico, Dominican Republic and other Caribbean islands, Brazil and Cape Verde, Colombia, El Salvador and Mexico. Early on, we identified complex racial/cultural identities as a shared interest. Together with Ashley Torres, an Afro-Boricua student in CECS and working at the Gastón Institute as a research and LLOP teaching assistant, we created team policy research projects.

We began by learning from Ed Morales's book *Latinx* (2019), which asserted that the only way US Latinx communities can bypass racialization based on hypodescent/the one drop rule is to "embrace the collective black" as proposed by sociologist Bonilla-Silva (2012). The alternative is whether, deliberately or inadvertently, to accept the "honorary whiteness" of groups that can "pass for White" because of light skin, facial features and other racialized social characteristics (like wealth or education). Starting with discussions of Morales's text, in a cohort of Latinx communities across national origin, racial backgrounds, immigration and documentation status, gender and sexuality, students explored these questions in honest, sometimes conflictual dialogue and engagement with Latinx community leaders and faculty who spoke of their rise to leadership as a process of collective cultural empowerment. They also completed group policy research projects and university or community outreach and identified next steps for their work. Through collaborative learning and mobilization of social capital/cultural wealth, students who were leaders of campus or community-based organizations joined with policy research project teams in planning, financially supporting, conducting outreach and implementing events based on our projects.

Our collaborative projects included two well-attended and well-received arts-based PAR projects: in one, LLOP students conducted an arts-based evaluation documenting impacts of a reading of Ntozake Shange's 1974 choreopoem "For Colored Girls Who Have Considered Suicide, When the Rainbow Is Enuf," updated by and for Afro-descendant millennial women to explore enduring racialized gender inequalities. The evaluation showed that both participants and audience felt that the choreopoem spoke to Black young women today, countering constraining/stereotyping social scripts through greater freedom to proclaim authentic self-hood. In another project, two graduate students in CECS, Dominican Jeannette Mejia and Haitian/Dominican Mirlande Thermidor, conducted co-research projects exploring the development of Dominican consciousness regarding anti-Haitian racism and recognizing and appreciating Black heritage. Another LLOP project conducted primarily by Brazilian students focused on culturally sensitive outreach to youth and communities regarding the Special Immigrant Juvenile Status Petition, a pathway to legal status for youth under

21 who have experienced parental abuse or neglect. The team included two Deferred Action for Childhood Arrival students, one of whom could have qualified for special status had she known prior to turning 21, and students from mixed-status families who felt passionate about educating communities regarding their rights.

Bringing community voices into the classroom, two leaders spoke about complex cultural and racial identities. Betty Francisco, lawyer, business leader and co-creator of Amplify Latinx (a nonprofit organization developing Latinx leadership in Massachusetts), shared on her background as Chinese and Puerto Rican and the importance of embracing her cultural heritage as an asset in promoting equity of opportunity in Boston and ensuring that organizations come together to collaborate and multiply their impacts. Yvette Modestin, Founder/Director of Encuentro Diaspora Afro (to promote knowledge and pride of Afro-Latinx heritage locally and globally), challenged the class to examine stereotypes among the Latinx community about Blackness, including assumptions about social class and education which pit Black immigrants against African Americans. Student differences regarding their standing within the complex backgrounds and realities we term "Latinx" enhance fellows' self-knowledge and leadership across communities and settings.

For Tariana, an alum (2011) and teaching assistant (2012), LLOP holds a special place in her heart; it represents a community of Latinx leaders, scholars and students that inspired to keep growing and keep going. Reflecting on her experience, Tariana notes that the bonds created within and across cohorts (250 alumni and counting) have cultivated social capital consistent with cultural values facilitating personal, professional and leadership growth well after the program ends. Modeled after her cohort's weekend trip to Springfield, MA, for the class's community research project, since 2013 she has hosted yearly LLOP getaways, which connect older cohorts with new alumni and adjacent peers (e.g. young Latinxs connected to the Gastón Institute, UMass Boston students and graduates who did not get the chance to be in LLOP)—all affectionately called "LLOPrimix," referring to primos/primas who become like cousins and extended family/familia. This growing community provides emotional support, peer mentorship, career guidance and access to networks and gives back. For example, inspired by John Arroyo, an LLOPrimix who donated funds from the Massachusetts Institute of Technology's People Help People Award to benefit the 2018 cohort, Tariana donated her McKinsey Advanced Professional Degree Diversity Impact Award funds to support the 2019 cohort and co-chaired the Gastón Institute's Community Advisory Board (with an LLOPrimix who previously served with her as Boston Peer Leader interns for the Obama Foundation) to further contribute to the organization's efforts in advancing young leaders. This is but one of many ways that LLOPrimxs are exercising their cultural wealth (Yasso & Burciaga, 2016). LLOP paves a legacy of leadership, positioning students, alumni and allies to promote their communities' development and influence.

Conclusion

Inclusive leadership requires strategic mobilization of personal, relational and collective knowledge, social capital and cultural wealth to better achieve both immediate and long-term goals in specific, highly complex contexts. Multisystemic approaches linking personal, organizational and sociocultural dimensions of power and distribution of resources contributing to inclusion or creating barriers require a collaborative learning, mutual empowerment approach to leadership development connecting individual, institutional and collective processes of change. Cultural humility contributing to inclusive leadership requires intersectionally informed personal reflexivity and capacity for open-minded and open-hearted communication with others, seeking in our differences the affirmation of our shared ethical and practical commitments to the value added by dialogues across differences. We learn to conduct participatory inquiry incorporating strategic readings of power in context in order to leverage resources, recognize barriers, communicate in ways that build connection rather than intensify conflicts, and adapt innovative strategies to achieve desired results in unpredictable new environments. Inclusive leadership becomes a collaborative practice of discovery, designed to learn from diversity of perspectives, identify and leverage system resources supporting achievement of mutually agreed-upon goals.

Cultivating cultural humility can help develop critical, collaborative and strategic reflexivity and skills promoting inclusive leadership, including:

1. Making contextual readings of power specific to a setting;
2. Understanding how our own social characteristics and personal history (both visible and non-visible statuses) impact how we are seen and how we see ourselves in the setting;
3. Deciding based on strategic goals personal, team, organizational; and
4. Developing capabilities for work across differences in complex environments as a stance of openness, valuing differences, interest in relating to others from diverse backgrounds, and desire to make a contribution, as characteristics that promote collective success and thriving.

Both the Emerging Leaders Program and the Latino Leadership Opportunity Program, cultivating inclusive leadership development through participatory inquiry, enhance personal reflection and appreciation of the different landscapes of opportunity we each encounter. Becoming inclusive leaders, in the spirit of Chancellor Sherry Penney's life and work, we dedicate ourselves to democratizing inquiry towards appreciating differences and elevating the next generation of diverse and inclusive leaders.

References

Adichie, C. (2009). *The danger of a single story*. Video and transcript retrieved from www.ted.com/talks/chimamanda_adichie_the_danger_of_a_single_story

Appadurai, A. (2006). The right to research. *Globalisation, Societies and Education*, 4(2), 167–177.

Betancourt, J. R., Green, A. R., Carrillo, J. E., & Owusu Ananeh-Firempong, I. I. (2003). Defining cultural competence: A practical framework for addressing racial/ethnic disparities in health and health care. *Public Health Reports*, 118, 293–302.

Boitano, A., Dutra, R. L., & Schockman, H. E. (Eds.). (2017). *Breaking the zero-sum game: Transforming societies through inclusive leadership*. Bingley, UK: Emerald Group Publishing.

Booysen, L. (2014). The development of inclusive leadership practice and processes. In B. Ferdman & B. Deane (Eds.), *Diversity at work: The practice of inclusion* (pp. 296–330). San Francisco, CA: Jossey Bass.

Brown, A. M. (2017). *Emergent strategy: Shaping change, changing worlds*. Chico, CA: AK Press.

Bryant-Davis, T., & Comas Diaz, L. (Eds.). (2016). *Womanist and mujerista Psychologies: Voices of fire, acts of courage*. Washington, DC: American Psychological Association Press.

Burnes, B. (2004). Kurt Lewin and complexity theories: Back to the future? *Journal of Change Management*, 4(4), 309–325.

Capra, F., & Luisi, P. (2016). *The systems way of life: A unifying vision*. Cambridge: Cambridge University Press.

Chavez, V. (2012). *Cultural humility: People, principles and practices*. Training video retrieved from www.youtube.com/watch?v=SaSHLbS1V4w

Chavez, V., & Minkler, M. (2010). Cultural humility. In L. Cohen, V. Chavez, & S. Chehimi (Eds.), *Prevention is primary: Strategies for community well-being*. New York, NY: John Wiley & Sons.

Chin, J. L., Desormeaux, L., & Sawyer, K. (2016). Making way for paradigms of diversity leadership. *Consulting Psychology Journal: Practice and Research*, 68(1), 49.

Chin, J. L., Trimble, J. E., & Garcia, J. E. (Eds.). (2018). *Global and culturally diverse leaders and leadership: New dimensions and challenges for business, education and society*. Bingley, UK: Emerald Group Publishing.

Coleman, P. T., Coon, D., Kim, R., Chung, C., Bass, R., Regan, B., & Anderson, R. (2017). Promoting constructive multicultural attractors: Fostering unity and fairness from diversity and conflict. *The Journal of Applied Behavioral Science*, 53(2), 180–211.

Combs, G. M., Milosevic, I., & Bilimoria, D. (2019). Introduction to the special topic forum: Critical discourse: Envisioning the place and future of diversity and inclusion in organizations. *Journal of Leadership & Organizational Studies*, 277–286.

Dawkins, C. E., & Barker, J. R. (2018). A complexity theory framework of issue movement. *Business & Society*, 1–41.
DeAngelis, L., & Penney, S. H. (2015). Teaching leaders. *Journal of Leadership Education, 14*, 126–137.
DeAngelis, L., Penney, S., & Scully, M. (2014). Leadership lessons from teamwork. *Leader to Leader* (73), 19–25.
Espina Prieto, M. P. (2007). Complejidad, transdisciplina y metodología de la investigación social/Complexity, transdisciplinarity and social research methods. *Utopía y praxis latinoamericana, 12*(38), 29–43.
Galinsky, A. D., Todd, A. R., Homan, A. C., Phillips, K. W., Apfelbaum, E. P., Sasaki, S. J., . . . Maddux, W. W. (2015). Maximizing the gains and minimizing the pains of diversity: A policy perspective. *Perspectives on Psychological Science, 10*(6), 742–748.
George, G., Baker, T., Tracey, P., & Joshi, H. (2019). Inclusion and innovation: A call to action. In *Handbook of Inclusive Innovation*. Cheltenham, United Kingdom: Edward Elgar Publishing.
Gocłowska, M. A., & Crisp, R. J. (2014). How dual-identity processes foster creativity. *Review of General Psychology, 18*(3), 216–236.
Jones, C. P. (2000). Levels of racism: A theoretic framework and a gardener's tale. *American Journal of Public Health, 90*(8), 1212–1217.
Juster, R. P., Seeman, T., McEwen, B. S., Picard, M., Mahar, I., Mechawar, N., . . . Lanoix, D. (2016). Social inequalities and the road to allostatic load: From vulnerability to resilience. *Developmental Psychopathology*, 1–54.
Kouzes, J. M., & Posner, B. Z. (1987). *The leadership challenge: How to get extraordinary things done in organizations (1st ed.)*. San Francisco: Jossey-Bass.
Leavy, P. (2016). *Essentials of transdisciplinary research: Using problem-centered methodologies*. Routledge Press.
Leigh, J. (2003). Outcome assessment of Boston's emerging leaders program: Evaluating effectiveness of training in collaboration and diversity (Doctoral Dissertation), University of Massachusetts, Boston.
Leigh, J. M., Shapiro, E. R., & Penney, S. H. (2010). Developing diverse, collaborative leaders: An empirical program evaluation. *Journal of Leadership & Organizational Studies, 17*(4), 370–379.
Lichtenstein, B. B., Uhl-Bien, M., Marion, R., Seers, A., Orton, J. D., & Schreiber, C. (2006). Complexity leadership theory: An interactive perspective on leading in complex adaptive systems. Management Department Faculty Publications.
Mendes, M., Gomes, C., Marques-Quinteiro, P., Lind, P., & Curral, L. (2016). Promoting learning and innovation in organizations through complexity leadership theory. *Team Performance Management, 22*(5/6), 301–309.
Minkler, M. (2012). *Community organizing and community building for health and welfare*. New Brunswick: Rutgers University Press.
Page, S. (2017). *The diversity bonus: How great teams pay off in the knowledge economy*. Princeton, NJ: Princeton University Press.
Mora, J. M., & Diaz, D. R. (2004). *Latino social policy: A participatory research model*. Haworth Press.
Morales, E. (2019). *Latinx: The new force in American politics and culture*. Verso Book.
Palmberg, K. (2009). Complex adaptive systems as metaphors for organizational management. *The Learning Organization*, 483–498.
Penney, S., & Nielson, P. (2010). *Next generation leadership*. New York, NY: Palgrave Macmillan.
Rockefeller Foundation. (2019). *Resilient cities, resilient lives: Learning from the 100 resilient cities network*. Final Report. Retrieved from http://100resilientcities.org/capstone-report/
Rothstein, R. (2017). *The color of law: A forgotten history of how our government segregated America*. New York; London: Liveright Publishing Corporation.
Rutter, H., Savona, N., Glonti, K., Bibby, J., Cummins, S., Finegood, D. T., . . . Petticrew, M. (2017). The need for a complex systems model of evidence for public health. *The Lancet, 390*(10112), 2602–2604.
Salter, P. S., & Adams, G. (2016). On the intentionality of cultural products: Representations of Black history as psychological affordances. *Frontiers in Psychology, 7*, 1166.
Sanchez-Burks, J., Karlesky, M. J., & Lee, F. (2015). Psychological bricolage: Integrating social identities to produce creative solutions. In *The Oxford handbook of creativity, innovation, and entrepreneurship* (pp. 93–102). New York, NY: Oxford University Press.
Schneider, M., & Somers, M. (2006). Organizations as complex adaptive systems: Implications of complexity theory for leadership research. *The Leadership Quarterly, 17*(4), 351–365.
Senge, P., Hamilton, H., & Kania, J. (2015). The dawn of system leadership. *Stanford Social Innovation Review, 13*(1), 27–33.
Shapiro, E. (2013). Chronic illness and family resilience. In D. Becvar (Ed.), *Handbook of family resilience*. New York, NY: Palgrave Macmillan/Springer.
Shapiro, E. (2018). Transforming development through just communities: A life-long journey of inquiry. In L. Comas-Diaz & C. Vasquez (Eds.), *Latina psychologists: Thriving in the cultural borderlands*. New York: Routledge.

Bonilla-Silva, E. (2012). The invisible weight of whiteness: The racial grammar of everyday life in America. *Michigan Sociological Review*, *26*, 1–15.

Solórzano, D. G., & Yosso, T. J. (2002). Critical race methodology: Counter-storytelling as an analytical framework for education research. *Qualitative Inquiry*, *8*(1), 23–44.

Tervalon, M., & Murray-Garcia, J. (1998). Cultural humility versus cultural competence: A critical distinction in defining physician training outcomes in multicultural education. *Journal of Health Care for the Poor and Underserved*, *9*(2), 117–125.

Trittin, H., & Schoeneborn, D. (2017). Diversity as polyphony: Reconceptualizing diversity management from a communication-centered perspective. *Journal of Business Ethics*, *144*(2), 305–322.

Tyler, M. (2019). Reassembling difference? Rethinking inclusion through/as embodied ethics. *Human Relations*, *72*(1), 48–68.

Ungar, M. (2018). Systemic resilience. *Ecology and Society*, *23*(4), 1–17.

Wallerstein, N., Duran, B., Oetzel, J., & Minkler, M. (Eds.). (2017). *Community-based participatory research for health: Advancing social and health equity* (3rd ed.). San Francisco, CA: Jossey Bass.

Wandersman, A. (2003). Community science: Bridging the gap between science and practice with community-centered models. *American Journal of Community Psychology*, *31*, 227–242.

Wheatley, M. J. (1992). *Leadership and the new science: Learning about organizations from an orderly universe*. San Francisco, CA: Berrett-Koehler.

Wheatley, M. J. (2017). *Who do we choose to be? Facing reality, claiming leadership, restoring sanity*. Oakland, CA: Berrett-Koehler Publishers.

Yosso, T. J., & Burciaga, R. (2016). Reclaiming our histories, Recovering community cultural wealth. *Center for Critical Race Studies at UCLA Research Brief*, 1–4.

Zanoni, P., Janssens, M., Benschop, Y., & Nkomo, S. (2010). Guest editorial: Unpacking diversity, grasping inequality: Rethinking difference through critical perspectives. *Organization*, *17*(1), 9–29.

INDEX

Note: Page numbers in *italic* indicate a figure and page numbers in **bold** indicate a table on the corresponding page.

action: and participatory inquiry 358–359; and responsible innovation 115
ADKAR model (Awareness, Desire, Knowledge, Ability, Reinforcement) 71–72, 76
affinity relationships 193–196, *194*
Africa 143, 150, 182, 219, 333–337, 341–343; and inclusive servant leadership 251–255, 258–261; South Africa 45, 124, 184, 251–252, 299, 301, 305–306, 334–335, 342
African diaspora 333, 337, 343
Ahimsa non-violence 149, 301–304, 307, 310
Amish leadership 131–139, 141
appreciation 266–267
appreciative inquiry 37–38
approach 151; intentional approach to spiritual leadership 241–242; wakeful approach 231–234
assignments 146
Asumah, Seth N. 37
authenticity 230–231
automation 16–18
awakened leadership 225–228; characteristics of awakened leaders 234–235; dimensions of the wakeful approach 231–234; foundational structures of 228–231; roadmap to inclusion and morality 235–236, *236*
awakening for all: *Sarvodaya* 303, 307
awareness 30

balance 229; *see also* work-life balance
Beckhard and Harris: change formula of 67
behavior *see* behavioral theory; leadership behavior; pro-social behavior; *and under* oneness
behavioral theory 144, 252
being-centered leadership 35–36, 39

belonging 349–350
Bhagavad Gītā 18, 154, 156–158, 162, 304, 346, 350–353
body 31–33, 154–155, 179
bonding 147
brave space 279
Brazil 215–216, 219–220, 363–367
Bridges, William: model of 68–69
Bullock and Batten: planned change 66
Buber, Martin 292–293, 295, 359
Burgess, Sylvia W. 243–244
business growth: limit of 134–136

Canada 14–15, 45–47, 138, 215–217, 265, 333
care 266–267
Caribbean, the 333–334, 341, 343, 367
Carnall, C.A.: change management model of 69
caste 301, 305–306
categorical imperative 347–349
celebration 139, 147, 354, 358
change 63–77; being mindful of 72–73; resistance to 73–75; *see also* change management
change management: case study on 75–76; meaning and scope of 63–64; models of 65–72; theories of 64–72
Christian leadership: servant leadership in the context of 254–255
Christian religion 251; developing inclusive servant leadership 257–258; inclusive servant leadership in the context of 255–257; Nairobi Chapel 258–261; servant leadership in the context of 254–255
church leadership 138–139
civil disobedience 302–303, 306–310
class 304, 307–308

Index

co-authenticity 279–280 283–284
collaboration 14–17, 45–46, 185–187, 335–336, 338–339; and emotional intelligence 106–107; and oneness 37–38; and participatory inquiry 356–357, 359–360, 363–369; and responsible innovation 109–110; and soft skills 268–269; and spiritual leadership 240–241, 248–249
community aid 133–134
compassion 160–161, 323, 325–327; and inclusive leadership 326, 328–329; mutual influence of humility and compassion 327–329
competencies 14–16, *15*; *see also* cultural competence
complexity 359–364; *see also* complexity science; social complexity
complexity science 271–272
conceptual distinctiveness 79, **80–89**, 89–91
conflict 283–284
consciousness: and leadership behavior 27–30, *29–30*; *see also* consciousness gap; interpersonal consciousness; relational consciousness; unity consciousness
consciousness gap 28–30; end results of 29–30, *29–30*
Consultancy, Research and Training Associates (CORETRA) Limited 150–152
containers 274, 278–284
contemporary theories 252
contingency perspective 109–117
contingency theories 144, 252
conversations 146; difficult 281
CORETRA Limited *see* Consultancy, Research and Training Associates (CORETRA) Limited
Cox, Trevor 278, 280–281
creativity *see* radical creativity
cross-cultural differences 215–221
cultural competence 361–363
cultural differences 121–129; *see also* cross-cultural differences
cultural humility 357–358, 361–363, 365, 368
culture 42–48, 51–52, 55–58, 89–92, 333–337, 340–342; and cross-cultural differences 217–218; and everyday leadership 140–147; and "female" leadership 290–294; and India 198–200, 204–207, 210–212; and participatory inquiry 356–359; and respectful pluralism 123–124; and shared ventures 348–349; and spiritual leadership 248–249; and work-life balance 172–174

Dandi Salt March 301–302, 306, 309
Dean, Debra J. 121–124
demographics 44–45, 177–178
Dhiman, Satinder 251
dialogic existentialism 292–293
dialogue 276–278
diaspora *see* African diaspora
difference 276–278; and participatory inquiry 358–359; and systems-minded leadership 359–364; *see also* cross-cultural differences; cultural differences
dignity *see* human dignity

discussion 268–271
disequilibrium 114, 116
diversity 177–180, 182, 184–188, 333–335; categories to be considered during diversity and inclusion programs 209–210; conceptualizing 204–205; and discussion 268–271; diversity effects 192; diversity types and theories 191–192; and inclusion 92, 210–211; in Indian context 205, 207, 207–210, *208*, **208**; issues leading towards 211–212; and leadership across the world 215–221; management of 290–295; and problems that companies face 210–211; transition from diversity to inclusion 203–204, 206, 213–214; unity in 162–163; and wakefulness 3, 5–7, 10–11, *11*; and well-being 191–193, **195**, **197**, 198–199, *198–199*, 200–201; what we know about diversity 191–192; workplace diversity and inclusion 91–94; *see also* diversity management
diversity management 37, 78, 92, 187; and India 191–192, 200–201, 203, 207, 211
domination 294, 316–318

Egel, Eleftheria 35
emergent leadership theories 144, 253–254
emerging economy 74–76, 311
Emerging Leaders Program (ELP) 356–358, 363–369
emotional intelligence (EI) 99–108, 230; characteristics of 104–107; enhancing the effect of 107–108
empathic failures 326–327
employees: role of 50
ending 68
engagement 43–45, 47–50, 52; engagement agreement 49; principles of 48–49
equity 93–94, 146, 177–186, 318–319, 357–363
ethics 18–19, 233–234, 299–302, 347–353
everyday leadership 131–132, 141; development in a classroom 140–141; teaching and development of 139–140; what it looks like 132–139
everyday skills 139
excellence 346–354
existentialism *see* dialogic existentialism

failure *see* empathic failures
fairness 146
"female" leadership 288–295; creating the future organization through 293–294
financial advisor group 133–134
financial breakeven 114
flux: organizations as in flux 65, 68–72
followership 123–125; *see also* leader-follower dynamics
forgiveness 136–138
fulfillment 354
future: automated future of work 16–18; and "female" leadership 293–294

Gandhi, Mahatma 299–301; means and outcomes 308–309; *Satyagraha* campaign 309; values-based inclusive leadership of 302–304, 310–311; values and voice of inclusion 304–310; Values into Voice and Action (ViVA) model 308
Gehani, R. Ray 302
gender 177, 185–186, 306–307, 311; mapping 178–184; stereotypes **179**; *see also* women
generations 46–47; Baby Boomers 246–247; Generation X 245–247; Generation Z 246–248
global mindset 35–36
Golden Rule 162, 347–349
Gotsis, George 243–244
Great Man Theory 177–178, 184
Grimani, Aikaterini 243–244
growth *see* business growth
Guillory, William A. 233–234
Guman, E.C.: systemic model 69–71

human dignity 127–129
humility 164–166, 323–329; defining 323–325; and inclusive leadership 324–325, 328–329; mutual influence of humility and compassion 327–329; *see also* cultural humility
humor 313–315; and prejudice/domination 316–318; role in organizational life 315–316

identity *see* social identity
immigration 126–127
implementation phase 152
inception report 152
inclusion 205–206, 225–226, 288–295; categories to be considered during diversity and inclusion programs 209–210; conceptualizing 204–205; and diversity 92, 210–211; framework of 206, *206*; in Indian context 207, 310–311; of individuals with lower caste 305–306; issues leading towards 211–212; leader inclusion 111–112; and management of diversity 290–295; of minority religions 304–305; organizational inclusion practice and climate 113; perceived organizational inclusion 112; and problems that companies face 210–211; roadmap to 235–236, *236*; of rural poor 307–308; and spirituality 238–239; style inclusions 229; trait inclusions 229; transition from diversity to inclusion 203–212; voice of 304–310; and the wakeful approach 231, 234; of women 306–307; work group inclusion 111; in the workplace 91–94
inclusive leaders 57–59; and appreciation 266–267; and diversity 268–271; six signature traits 336
inclusive leadership 42–43, 52, 177–184, 187–188, 335–341; African context 341–342; in Brazil 219–220; in Canada 216–217; Caribbean context 341; common traits in 145; and compassion 323–329; and complexity science 271–272; conceptualization of 338–339; and consciousness 27–30; core premises of 353–354; cross-cultural differences in perception and application of 215–221; definitions and contingency factors 109–110; and emotional intelligence 99–108; and engagement 47–50; and failure in diversity management 187; and humility 323–329; and humor 313–320; importance of 56–57; in India 218–219; and LEAD 341–342; and leadership models for the disadvantaged 184–185; and limited access 30–39; in Mexico 217–218; and oneness 36–37; outcomes 340–341; pathways to 346–354; and people 44–47; and performance 50–51; principles of 145–147; and religion 143–152; and responsible innovation 109–117; and soft skills 264–272; and other styles of leadership 93–94; in Poland 220–221; and religion 144–145; review of empirical studies 337–341; and similar leadership styles 339–340; and stakeholder engagement 54–56; through unity consciousness and the act of oneness 26–40; and transactional and transformational paradigms 185–187, **186**; and virtuous leadership 92–93; and wakefulness 3–5, 10–11, *11*; what and why 99–104; WISE case of 114–117; at WISEs 110–113; and work-life balance 168–175; *see also* inclusive leader; inclusive leadership development; inclusive servant leadership; values-based inclusive leadership
inclusive leadership development 273–275, 284; and complexity and systems-minded leadership 359–364; cultivating containers for 278–284; and dialogue across difference 276–278; and the Emerging Leaders Program (ELP) 364–368; through participatory inquiry 356–371
inclusive meetings 146
inclusiveness 288–295, 333–335; and leading work-life balance 171–174; and metaphysical perspective 156, 157–158, 160–162, 165; path to 39; performance-oriented inclusion survey analysis 47; and Sākṣī 158–160; and spiritual maturity 154–157; transcending inclusive spirituality 304; and vedantic leadership 157–158
inclusive organizations 37–38, 94–95; belonging and individuality in 349–350; and the *Bhagavad Gītā* 351; and virtuous leadership 78–91, **80–89**; through wise leadership 352–353; and workplace diversity 91–94
inclusive practice: and stakeholder engagement 53–62
inclusive servant leadership 250–251, 250–261; case study 258–261; challenging assumptions 257–258; in the context of the Christian religion 255–257; development of 257–258; and theories of leadership 251–255
inclusive values-based leadership; *see* values-based inclusive leadership
India 190–198, *194*, **195**, *196*, **197**, *198*, 203–212; categories to be considered during diversity and inclusion programs 209–210; and diversity dimensions and organizational challenges 207–208, *208*, **208**; and diversity effects 192; and diversity types and theories 191–192; emerging perspectives

198–200, *199*; inclusion after Gandhi 310–311; inclusive leadership in 218–219; and relevance of diversity and inclusion 207; the road ahead 200–201; *see also* Gandhi, Mahatma
India Inc. 204, 209–210
Indian Constitution 192–193, 209
individual, the 30–31
individual contributors: role of 50
individuality 349–350
individual leadership 289–290
information technology 46–47
innovation *see* responsible innovation
inquiry *see* appreciative inquiry; participatory inquiry
integral approach: and leading work-life balance 171–174
interdependency 10–11, *11*, 33–34
interpersonal consciousness 29, *29*

Japan *see under* leadership training

Kant, Immanuel 347–349
Khadi fabric 301, 307–308
Kleiner, A.: systemic model 69–71
Kotter, J.P.: eight-step model 66–67, 76
Kruse, Elliott Tyler 323–325

Latino Leadership Opportunity Program (LLOP) 357–358, 363, 366–368
LEAD *see* Leadership and motivation in Africa and the African Diaspora (LEAD)
leader-follower dynamics 109–117
leaders: characteristics of awakened leaders 234–235; and emotional intelligence 104–107; and humor 318–319; leader inclusion 111–112; *see also* inclusive leaders; leader-follower dynamics
leadership 225–228, 281–284; and the *Bhagavad Gītā* 350, 351, 352–353; and diversity across the world 215–221; leading as one 34–39; leading work-life balance 171–174; mapping 178–184; meaning of 143–144, 250–251; quality of 226–229; and relationships 28; role of 50; scope of 250–251; theories of 251–255; visible/high profile/leadership opportunities 47–48; *see also* Amish leadership; awakened leadership; being-centered leadership; Christian leadership; church leadership; everyday leadership; "female" leadership; inclusive leadership; inclusive servant leadership; individual leadership; leadership behavior; leadership development; leadership models; leadership research; leadership styles; leadership training; relational leadership; servant leadership; spiritual leadership; systems-minded leadership; values-based inclusive leadership; vedantic leadership; virtuous leadership; whole-soul leadership; wise leadership
Leadership and motivation in Africa and the African Diaspora (LEAD) 341–342
leadership behavior 90, 166, 225; and consciousness 27–30, *29–30*

leadership development 132, 139–140; in a classroom 140–141; transactional and transformational paradigms in 185–187; *see also* inclusive leadership development; leadership training
leadership models 177–178, 186–187, 217, 242, 289, 365; for the disadvantaged 184–185
leadership research 333, 342–343; and diversity and inclusivity 333–335; and inclusive leadership 335–340; LEAD findings 341–343
leadership styles 93–94, 229, 339–340; values-laden 90–91; *see also* inclusive leadership
leadership training **82**, 259; Japanese corporate training 139–140
Lewa, Peter Mutuku 259
Lewa, Susan Katinda 253–254
Lewin, Kurt 362–363; three-step model 65–66, 76

machines: organizations as 64, 68–69
management: diversity management 187, 290–295; managing performance 48; role of 50
managerial leadership 253
Marques, Joan 251
Martin-Jones, Karen 243
means 308–309
megachurch 245, 247
meetings *see* inclusive meetings
metaphysical perspective: and compassion 160–161; and humility 164–166; and the ideal vedantic leader 157–158; and Sākṣī 158–160; and spiritual maturity 154–157; and unity in diversity 162–163
Mexico 215–219, 340, 367
mindset *see* global mindset
mistakes 280–281
modeling 282
monitoring and evaluation (M&E) 152
morality 225–227, 231–232, 234; roadmap to 235–236, *236*
Mutuku, Sarah M. 63–64

Nadler and Tushman: congruence model 67–68
Nagel, Mechthild 37
Nairobi Chapel 258–261; Kinara leadership development program at 260–261
neutral zone 68–69
new beginning 69
new leadership theories 144, 252–253
Noble Eightfold Path 3, 8–10, *9*
non-cooperation 309
non-violence 299–302, 304–308, 310–311; *Ahimsa* 303; *Satyagraha* campaign 309

oneness 26–27, 39–40; and consciousness 27–30; and inclusive leadership 36–37; and limited access 30–39; oneness behaviors 38–39; path to 39
organism: organizations as 64, 67–71
organizations: creating inclusive organizations 349–250; and "female" leadership 293–294; as in flux and transformation 65; how organizations

really work 64–65; as machines 64; as organisms 64; organizational challenges in Indian context 207–209, *208*, **208**; organizational excellence 354; organizational inclusion practice and climate 113; pathways to flourishing organizations 346–354; perceived organizational inclusion 112; as political systems 64–65; role of humor 315–316; *see also* inclusive organizations; shared ventures

other, the: moving from one-self to the other 33–34

outcomes 308–309; inclusive leadership outcomes 340–341

participatory inquiry 356–359, 368–369; and complexity and systems-minded leadership 359–364; and the Emerging Leaders Program 364–368

people 43–47, 48, 51–52

performance 42–43, 45–46, 48–52; managing performance 48; performance-oriented inclusion survey analysis 47

phronesis 20–21, 23

pluralism *see* respectful pluralism

Poland 215–216, 220–221, 299

political systems: organizations as 64–65, 67–71

power 21–23, 177–180, 184–186, 278–279, 283–284, 328–329; and being mindful of change 64–66, 73–75; and cross-cultural differences 216–220; and "female" leadership 291–292; and Gandhi 311; and oneness 34–35, 38–39; and participatory inquiry 356–363, 368–369; and respectful pluralism 121–122; and virtuous leadership 93–94

practice 342–343

prejudice 316–318

project leader: role of 151

project steering committee: role of 151

project team: role of 151

promotions 146

proposals: jointly developing technical and financial proposals 151–152

pro-social behavior 267–268

public policy 366–368

Punnett, Betty Jane 342

race 91–92, 177, 206–207, 365–366; mapping 178–184

radical creativity 21–23

relational consciousness 28

relational leadership 37, 289–290, 292–295

relationships: affinity relationships *194*; and appreciation 266–267; and leadership 28; *see also* relational consciousness; relational leadership

religion 143–144, 301, 308, 310; inclusion of minority religions 304–305; inclusive leadership and 147–150; and spirituality 239; *see also* Christian religion

research 366–368; *see also* leadership research

resources 115

respectful pluralism 121–130

responsibilities 346–349

responsible innovation (RI) 109–118; and action 115; sustained 116–117; WISE case of 114–117

Roberts, C.: systemic model 69–71

Ross, R.: systemic model 69–71

Roth, G.: systemic model 69–71

Sākṣī 158–160, 166

Satyagraha truthful persuasion 299, 301, 304, 306–311; Dandi Salt March 309

Satya truthfulness 301–304

scope 150–151

self: contracted self *30*; expanded self *29*, 38–39; moving from one-self to the other 33–34

Senaji, Thomas Anyanje 335–337

Senge, P.: systemic model 69–71, 360

servant leadership: in the context of Christian leadership 254–255; *see also* inclusive servant leadership

shared ventures 346–354; and the nexus of individual and group responsibilities 346–349

sharing 133–134; sharing power 283; *see also* shared ventures

skills 359–364; *see also* everyday skills; soft skills

Smith, B.: systemic model 69–71

social complexity 359–364

social identity 282–283

soft skills 264–272

soul 31–33; *see also* whole-soul leadership

space: brave space 279; *see also* containers

spirituality: and inclusion 238–239; and religion 239; transcending inclusive spirituality 304

spiritual leadership 238–242; effectiveness 247–248; future leadership 248–249; intentional approach to 241–242; model of 242–248, *243*; preparation for 239–241

spiritual maturity: defining 154–156; effects of 156–157

stabilization 116–117

Stacey and Shaw: complex responsive processes 71

stakeholder engagement 53–62; engaging stakeholders through inclusive leadership 61–62; why stakeholder engagement matters 59

stakeholders: addressing stakeholder expectations 61; engaging stakeholders through inclusive leadership 61–62; understanding stakeholder expectations 59–60; *see also* stakeholder engagement

states of being 35

strategic leadership theories 252–253

strengths 115

style *see* leadership styles

supervisory theories of leadership 252

Survodaya awakening for all 301, 303, 307

systems-minded leadership 359–364

Telkom Kenya Limited 75–76

traits 229; signature traits of inclusive leaders 336

trait theory 27, 144, 251–252

transactional paradigms 185–187, **186**

Index

transformation 275–279, 281–284; organizations as in transformation 65, 68–71; *see also* transformational paradigms
transformational paradigms 185–187, **186**
trust 18–20, 48–50, 78–79, 172–174, 181–182, 191–192; and awakened leadership 234–235; and cross-cultural differences 220–221; and participatory inquiry 360–361; and spiritual leadership 240–241, 243–244
truthfulness: *Satya* 302–303
truthful persuasion: *Satyagraha* 304

unity: in diversity 162–163; *see also* unity consciousness
unity consciousness 26–30, 39–40; and limited access 30–39

values *see also* values-based inclusive leadership
values-based inclusive leadership 299–311, 166; and future research 311; of Gandhi 302–311; and humility 164–166; need for 299–300; for the 21st century 301–302, 310–311; and unity in diversity 162–163; and voice of inclusion 304–310
Values into Voice and Action (ViVA) model 302, 308
vedantic leadership (VL) 154; and compassion 160–161; perfectly inclusive 157–158; and Sākṣī 158–160; and spiritual maturity 154–157
ventures *see* shared ventures
virtuous leadership 78–79, 94–95; and conceptual distinctiveness 79–80, 89–91; ideal 157–158; main varieties of **80–89**; and values-laden leadership styles 90–91; and workplace diversity and inclusion 91–94
visionary leadership **82**, 252–253
voice of inclusion: of Gandhi 304–310

wakeful approach 231–235
wakefulness 3, 7–11, *9*, *11*; dimensions of 231–234; external 233; integrated 233–234; internal 232–233; *see also* wakeful approach
well-being 191–193, **195, 197**, 198–201, *198–199*, 349–350, 353–354
wellness 173, 349, 351, 354
whole-soul leadership 36
wise leadership 352–353; core premises of 353–354
women 18–19, 177–187, 204–206, 265–266, 269–272, 294; and humor 317–318; inclusion of 306–307; and participatory inquiry 356–357, 366–367; *see also* "female" leadership
work 136; automated future of 16–18; work group inclusion 111; *see also* work-life balance; workplace
work integration social enterprises (WISEs) 109–117
work-life balance 168–175; leading inclusively and integrally 171–174
workplace: diversity and inclusion in 91–94; effect of EI in 107–108; and flourishing 349–350, 353–354; inclusion framework *206*; and inclusive leadership 99–104; obstacles to workplace inclusion 311; and values-based inclusive leadership 301–302, 310–311; wellness 354

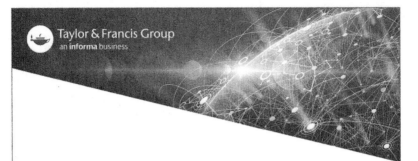